Contents

A note about copyright

Dear Customer

What does the little © mean and why does it matter?

Your market-leading BPP books, course materials and e-learning materials do not write and update themselves. People write them: on their own behalf or as employees of an organisation that invests in this activity. Copyright law protects their livelihoods. It does so by creating rights over the use of the content.

Breach of copyright is a form of theft – as well as being a criminal offence in some jurisdictions, it is potentially a serious breach of professional ethics.

With current technology, things might seem a bit hazy but, basically, without the express permission of BPP Learning Media:

- Photocopying our materials is a breach of copyright

- Scanning, ripcasting or conversion of our digital materials into different file formats, uploading them to Facebook or emailing them to your friends is a breach of copyright

You can, of course, sell your books, in the form in which you have bought them – once you have finished with them. (Is this fair to your fellow students? We update for a reason.) Please note the e-products are sold on a single user licence basis: we do not supply 'unlock' codes to people who have bought them second-hand.

And what about outside the UK? BPP Learning Media strives to make our materials available at prices students can afford by local printing arrangements, pricing policies and partnerships which are clearly listed on our website. A tiny minority ignore this and indulge in criminal activity by illegally photocopying our material or supporting organisations that do. If they act illegally and unethically in one area, can you really trust them?

ACCA

PAPER P7

ADVANCED AUDIT AND ASSURANCE

(UNITED KINGDOM)

BPP Learning Media is an **ACCA Approved Learning Partner – content** for the ACCA qualification. This means we work closely with ACCA to ensure our products fully prepare you for your ACCA exams.

In this Practice and Revision Kit, which has been reviewed by the **ACCA examination team,** we:

- Discuss the **best strategies** for revising and taking your ACCA exams

- Ensure you are well **prepared** for your exam

- Provide you with **lots of great guidance** on tackling questions

- Provide you with **three** mock exams

- Provide **ACCA exam answers** as well as our own for selected questions

Our **Passcard** and **i-pass** products also support this paper.

FOR EXAMS UP TO JUNE 2015

BPP
LEARNING MEDIA

First edition 2007
Eight edition June 2014

ISBN 9781 4727 1112 0
(previous ISBN 9781 4453 8006 3)

e-ISBN 9781 4727 1176 2

British Library Cataloguing-in-Publication Data
A catalogue record for this book
is available from the British Library

Published by

BPP Learning Media Ltd
BPP House, Aldine Place
London W12 8AA

www.bpp.com/learningmedia

Printed in the United Kingdom by

RICOH UK Limited
Unit 2
Wells Place
Merstham
RH1 3LG

We are grateful to the Association of Chartered Certified
Accountants for permission to reproduce past
examination questions. The suggested solutions in the
practice answer bank have been prepared by BPP
Learning Media Ltd, except where otherwise stated.

Your learning materials, published by BPP Learning
Media Ltd, are printed on paper obtained from
traceable, sustainable sources.

ii

Question index

The headings in this checklist/index indicate the main topics of questions, but questions are expected to cover several different topics.

Questions set under the old syllabus paper *Audit and Assurance Services* (AAS) are included because their style and content are very similar to that of the current P7 exam. The questions have been amended to reflect the current exam format.

BPP
LEARNING MEDIA

Mock exam 1

Mock exam 2

Mock exam 3 (December 2013 paper)

Topic index

Listed below are the key Paper P7 syllabus topics and the numbers of the questions in this Kit covering those topics.

If you need to concentrate your practice and revision on certain topics or if you want to attempt all available questions that refer to a particular subject, you will find this index useful.

Syllabus topic		Question numbers
A	**REGULATORY ENVIRONMENT**	
1	International regulatory frameworks for audit and assurance services	20(d)
2	Money laundering	1, 8(a), 11(c), 13(a)
3	Laws and regulations	39, 56(b)(ii), 69(a)
B	**PROFESSIONAL AND ETHICAL CONSIDERATIONS**	
1	Code of Ethics for professional accountants	1(b), 2(b), 3–9, 13, 14(a), 15(a), 16, 22(b), 25(b), 56(a), 70(b), 72(a)
2	Fraud and error	15(b)–(c), 20(d), 68(a)
3	Professional liability	15(d), 42(d), 68(b), 70(c)
C	**PRACTICE MANAGEMENT**	
1	Quality control	2, 11, 12, 18(c), 35(c), 43(b), 68(c)
2	Advertising, publicity, obtaining professional work and fees	4, 10
3	Tendering	9(b), 17(b)
4	Professional appointments	7, 14(a), 17(a), 33(a), 56(a), 72(a)
D	**AUDIT OF HISTORICAL FINANCIAL INFORMATION**	
1(i)	Planning, materiality and assessing the risk of material misstatement	14(b), 22(b), 25(a), 29–30, 32(a)–(b), 35–40, 43(a), 44, 47–51, 52(c)–(d), 53(a), 54, 56(b)–(d)
1(ii)	Evidence	18(a), 24, 47(c)
1(iii)	Evaluation and review	11(a), 18(b), 19, 26–28, 35(c), 36(b), 38(b)–(c), 39(c), 40(c), 44(b), 46, 47(d), 52(c)–(d), 54(b)–(c), 55(b), 60(a), 63(a), 64(a), 65(a), 66(a)
2	Group audits	25(a), 40, 49–50, 55(c), 59(b), 69(b)
E	**OTHER ASSIGNMENTS**	
1	Audit-related services	41, 55(a)
2	Assurance services	31(a)–(b), 34, 73(b)–(c)
3	Prospective financial information	21, 23, 33(a), 37(a), 42(a)–(c)
4	Forensic audits	20(c), 31(c), 45(a)–(b), 52(a)–(b)
5	Internal audit	20(a)–(b)
6	Outsourcing	20(a)–(b), 54(a)
7	Auditing aspects of insolvency (and similar procedures)	33(b), 37(b), 59, 60
F	**REPORTING**	
1	Auditor's reports	59, 60(b), 61–62, 63(b), 64(b)–(c), 65(b), 66(b), 67(a), 68(b), 69(b), 70(c), 71, 71(b), 73(a)
2	Reports to those charged with governance and management	70(a)
3	Other reports	70(a)
G	**CURRENT ISSUES AND DEVELOPMENTS**	
1	Professional and ethical	22(a), 45(c)
2	IFAC developments	4
3	Transnational audits	17(c)
4	Social and environmental auditing	32(c), 50(c)
5	Other current issues	22(a), 24(a)

Helping you with your revision

BPP Learning Media – Approved Learning Partner – content

As ACCA's **Approved Learning Partner – content**, BPP Learning Media gives you the **opportunity** to use **exam team reviewed** revision materials. By incorporating the examiner's comments and suggestions regarding syllabus coverage, the BPP Learning Media Practice and Revision Kit provides excellent, **ACCA-approved** support for your revision.

Tackling revision and the exam

Using feedback obtained from the ACCA exam team review:

- We look at the dos and don'ts of revising for, and taking, ACCA exams
- We focus on Paper P7; we discuss revising the syllabus, what to do (and what not to do) in the exam, how to approach different types of question and ways of obtaining easy marks

Selecting questions

We provide signposts to help you plan your revision.

- A full **question index**
- A **topic index** listing all the questions that cover key topics, so that you can locate the questions that provide practice on these topics, and see the different ways in which they might be examined

Making the most of question practice

At BPP Learning Media we realise that you need more than just questions and model answers to get the most from your question practice.

- Our **Top tips** included for certain questions provide essential advice on tackling questions, presenting answers and the key points that answers need to include.
- We show you how you can pick up **Easy marks** on some questions, as we know that picking up all readily available marks often can make the difference between passing and failing.
- We include **marking guides** to show you what the examiner rewards.
- We include **comments from the examiners** to show you where students struggled or performed well in the actual exam.
- We refer to the **2014 BPP Study Text** (for exams up to June 2015) for detailed coverage of the topics covered in questions.
- In a bank at the end of this Kit we include the **official ACCA answers** to the June and December 2013 papers. Used in conjunction with our answers they provide an indication of all possible points that could be made, issues that could be covered and approaches to adopt.

Attempting mock exams

There are three mock exams that provide practice at coping with the pressures of the exam day. We strongly recommend that you attempt them under exam conditions. **Mock exams 1 and 2** reflect the question styles and syllabus coverage of the exam; **Mock exam 3** is the December 2013 paper.

Revising P7

Paper P7 is a challenging higher level paper consisting of two compulsory case-study style questions in Section A (worth a total of 60 marks) and two out of three short scenario questions in Section B.

The P7 examiner, has stated that planning and risk assessment are key areas which are likely to form part of a compulsory question. Evidence is also likely to feature in Section A. Reporting could come up in either a compulsory or optional question (although it has tended to be optional), similarly ethical and professional issues. Current issues could come up anywhere on the paper so it is important that students do not ignore this area and make sure they keep up to date by reading *Student Accountant* and reviewing the accountancy and financial press. It has been a feature of P7 in recent years for questions to mix together several different syllabus areas. One consequence of this is to make it more difficult for candidates to avoid areas of the syllabus that they do not like, because exam questions would include this area along with others that the student might be strong on,

One of the general features of Professional level papers is the availability of professional marks. These will generally be awarded in Section A and comprise four marks. They will be awarded for the degree of professionalism with which answers are presented. For example, if you are asked to set out your answer as a letter or a report, marks will be awarded for presentation – using the correct heading at the start, and including an appropriate introduction and conclusion. Other professional marks could be awarded for the form of your answer such as the structure or logical flow of arguments, as well as your appropriate use of language.

To summarise, although this paper does contain an optional element, we **strongly advise** that you do not selectively revise certain topics – any topic from the syllabus could be examined anywhere on the paper. Selective revision will limit the number of questions you can answer and hence reduce your chances of passing.

Question practice

You should use the Passcards and any brief notes you have to revise the syllabus, but you mustn't spend all your revision time passively reading. **Question practice is vital;** doing as many questions as you can in full will help develop your ability to analyse scenarios and produce relevant discussion and recommendations.

Make sure you leave enough time in your revision schedule to practise Section A questions, as such questions are compulsory in the exam. The requirements of Section A questions are more complex and will integrate several parts of the syllabus, therefore practice is essential. Also ensure that you attempt all three mock exams under exam conditions.

Passing the P7 exam

Displaying the right qualities and avoiding weaknesses

(a)   Reading time

You have 15 minutes of reading time – make sure you use it wisely. Given that Section A will consist of two compulsory questions, worth 60 marks in total, you could spend the time analysing and planning these questions and doing them first, and then choose and tackle the optional questions from Section B.

(b)   The following are examples of things to avoid – and note our comments about action to take in each case.

Failure to complete the paper	This problem can be avoided by ensuring that you have a very disciplined exam technique and that you set times in which to answer questions and, when that time is over, you move on to the next question. Lots of practice at answering questions in timed conditions will help you to discipline yourself in this way. Remember, it is easier to get marks at the outset of answering a question (when all the marks are still available) than to get the last few remaining marks for a question (when you have made all the easy points and are struggling with the most difficult aspects of the question).
Not reading the question	We recommend that you read each question more than once. Try to force yourself to read slowly as well. Although the exam is time-limited, reading the question properly is a good investment.
Lack of comprehension and analytical skills	These are higher level skills which you have to learn at this level and the best way to enhance them is to practise as many questions as you can. In addition, once you have completed your own answer, you should always work through the suggested answer referring back to the question so that you can see the links that have been made.
Lack of lower level assumed knowledge	You should endeavour not to commence your P7 studies until you have completed your F8/2.6 studies. It is not possible to pass P7 unless you have a very firm understanding of basic auditing theory.
Lack of awareness of current issues	You should ensure that you keep up to date with current issues in the auditing and business world, by reading examiner articles as a minimum, but preferably by keeping an eye on the accountancy press throughout your studies.
Failure to respond in a practical/commercial way	The answer to this problem is to practice lots of questions, read other people's answers to questions in this Kit and on the ACCA website and to try and think about how you would respond in practice if it were one of your clients.
Lack of relevant practical experience	You may not be able to do anything about this if you are not employed in a relevant field. However, if you can, do. For example, if you can discuss with your managers the necessity of getting relevant experience and they are able to meet that need, try and obtain as much relevant experience as you can. If not, the best you can do is follow the advice for the previous point, which should stand you in good stead.
Inability to reach a conclusion/make a decision	You must get into the habit of drawing conclusions where the requirement is to do so. Again, practise questions where this is required, and, when reading questions note whether you are required to draw a conclusion or make a decision.
Poor exam technique/time allocation	This point links to the first point made above. There is a great deal of guidance concerning exam technique in this kit. Read it and put it into practice.

Using the reading time

We recommend that you spend the first part of the 15 minutes reading time choosing the Section B questions you will do, on the basis of your knowledge of the syllabus areas being tested and whether you can fulfil all the question requirements. Remember that Section B questions can cover different parts of the syllabus, and you should be happy with all the areas that the questions you choose cover. We suggest that you should note on the paper any ideas that come to you about these questions.

However don't spend all the reading time going through and analysing the Section B question requirements in detail; leave that until the three hours' writing time. Instead you should be looking to spend as much of the reading time as possible looking at the Section A scenario, as this will be longer and more complex than the Section B scenarios and cover more of the syllabus. You should highlight and annotate the key points of the scenario on the question paper.

Choosing which questions to answer first

Spending most of your reading time on the compulsory Section A questions will mean that you can get underway with planning and writing your answer to the Section A questions as soon as the three hours start. It will give you more actual writing time during the one and a half hours you should allocate to it, and it's writing time that you'll need. Comments from examiners of other syllabuses that have similar exam formats suggest that students appear less time-pressured if they do the big compulsory questions first.

During the second half of the exam, you can put Section A aside and concentrate on the two Section B questions you've chosen.

However our recommendations are not inflexible. If you really think the Section A questions looks a lot harder than the Section B questions you've chosen, then do those first, but **DON'T run over time on them.** You must leave yourself almost one hour and 50 minutes (108 minutes to be exact) to tackle the Section A questions. When you come back to it, having had initial thoughts during the reading time, you should be able to generate more ideas and find the question is not as bad as it looks.

Remember also that small overruns of time during the first half of the exam can add up to your being very short of time towards the end.

Tackling questions

You'll improve your chances by following a step-by-step approach to Section A scenarios along the following lines.

Step 1   **Read the background**

Usually the first couple of paragraphs will give some background on the company and what it is aiming to achieve. By reading this carefully you will be better equipped to relate your answers to the company as much as possible.

Step 2   **Read the requirements**

There is no point reading the detailed information in the question until you know what it is going to be used for. Don't panic if some of the requirements look challenging – identify the elements you are able to do and look for links between requirements, as well as possible indications of the syllabus areas the question is covering.

Step 3   **Identify the action verbs**

These convey the level of skill you need to exhibit and also the structure your answer should have. A lower level verb such as define will require a more descriptive answer; a higher level verb such as evaluate will require a more applied, critical answer. It should be stressed that **higher level requirements and verbs** are likely to be most significant in this paper.

Action verbs that are likely to be frequently used in this exam are listed below, together with their intellectual levels and guidance on their meaning.

Intellectual level		
1	Define	Give the meaning of
1	Explain	Make clear
1	Identify	Recognise or select
1	Describe	Give the key features
2	Distinguish	Define two different terms, viewpoints or concepts on the basis of the differences between them
2	Compare and contrast	Explain the similarities and differences between two different terms, viewpoints or concepts
2	Contrast	Explain the differences between two different terms, viewpoints or concepts
2	Analyse	Give reasons for the current situation or what has happened
3	Assess	Determine the strengths/weaknesses/ importance/ significance/ability to contribute
3	Examine	Critically review in detail
3	Discuss	Examine by using arguments for and against
3	Explore	Examine or discuss in a wide-ranging manner
3	Criticise	Present the weaknesses of/problems with the actions taken or viewpoint expressed, supported by evidence

Intellectual level		
3	Evaluate/critically evaluate	Determine the value of in the light of the arguments for and against (critically evaluate means weighting the answer towards criticisms/arguments against)
3	Construct the case	Present the arguments in favour or against, supported by evidence
3	Recommend	Advise the appropriate actions to pursue in terms the recipient will understand

Also make sure you identify all the action verbs; some question parts may have more than one.

Step 4   Identify what each part of the question requires

Think about what frameworks or theories you could choose if the question doesn't specify which one to use.

When planning, you will need to make sure that you aren't reproducing the same material in more than one part of the question.

Also you're likely to come across part questions with two requirements that may be at different levels; a part question may for example ask you to explain X and discuss Y. You must ensure that you **fulfill both requirements** and that your discussion of Y shows greater depth than your explanation of X (for example by identifying problems with Y or putting the case for and against Y).

Step 5   Check the mark allocation to each part

This shows you the depth anticipated and helps allocate time.

Step 6   Read the whole scenario through, highlighting key data

Put points under headings related to requirements (eg by noting in the margin to what part of the question the scenario detail relates).

Step 7   Consider the consequences of the points you've identified

Remember that you will often have to provide recommendations based on the information you've been given. Consider that you may have to criticise the code, framework or model that you've been told to use. You may also have to bring in wider issues or viewpoints, for example the views of different stakeholders.

Step 8   Write a brief plan

You may be able to do this on the question paper as often there will be at least one blank page in the question booklet. However any plan you make should be reproduced in the answer booklet when writing time begins.

Make sure you identify all the requirements of the question in your plan – each requirement may have sub-requirements that must also be addressed. If there are professional marks available, highlight in your plan where these may be gained (such as preparing a report).

Step 9   Write the answer

Make every effort to present your answer clearly. The pilot paper and exam papers so far indicate that the examiner will be looking for you to make a number of clear points. The best way to demonstrate what you're doing is to put points into separate paragraphs with clear headers.

Remember that **depth of discussion** will be important. Discussions will often consist of paragraphs containing 2-3 sentences. Each paragraph should:

- **Make a point**

- **Explain the point** (you must demonstrate why the point is important)

- **Illustrate the point** (with material or analysis from the scenario, perhaps an example from real-life)

In this exam a number of requirement verbs will expect you to express a viewpoint or opinion, for example construct an argument, criticise, evaluate. When expressing an opinion, you need to provide:

- **What the question wants**. For instance, if you are asked to criticise something, don't spend time discussing its advantages. In addition if a scenario provides a lot of information about a situation, and you are (say) asked to assess that situation in the light of good practice, your assessment is unlikely to be favourable.

- **Evidence** from theory or the scenario – again we stress that the majority of marks in most questions will be given for applying your knowledge to the scenario.

BPP
LEARNING MEDIA

Gaining the easy marks

Knowledge of the core topics that we list under topics to revise should present you with some easy marks. The pilot paper suggests that there will be some marks available on certain part questions for definitions, explanations or descriptions that don't have to be related to the scenario. However don't assume that you can ignore all the scenarios and still pass!

As P7 is a Professional level paper, 4 **professional level marks** will be awarded. Some of these should be easy to obtain. The examiner has stated that some marks may be available for presenting your answer in the form of a letter, presentation, memo, report or briefing notes. You may also be able to obtain marks for the style and layout of your answer.

Reports should always have an appropriate title. They should be **formally written**, with an **introductory paragraph** setting out the aims of the report. You should use **short paragraphs** and **appropriate headings**, with a summary of findings as a **conclusion**.

Memoranda and **Briefing notes** should have the following four things at the beginning:

> **Subject; name of recipient; name of author; date**

The language can be **less formal** than a report but the content should still have an **introduction and conclusion**, and be divided into small paragraphs with appropriate headings.

Letters should be addressed appropriately to the correct person and be dated. They should have a short introductory paragraph, a conclusion and should be in a formally writing style. Letters beginning with 'Dear Sir/Madam' should end with 'Yours faithfully'.

Exam information

The exam paper

The exam is a three-hour paper consisting of two sections.

Section A will consist of two compulsory 'case study' style questions. These will include detailed information including, for example, extracts from financial statements and audit working papers. The questions will include a range of requirements covering different syllabus areas.

Section B questions will tend to be more focused towards specific topic areas, such as ethical issues and auditor's reports. Short scenarios will be provided as a basis for these questions.

		Number of marks
Section A:	Two compulsory questions:	
	Question one	35
	Question two	25
Section B:	Choice of two from three questions (20 marks each)	40
		100

Accounting standards – IFRS for P7 UK

For exams from 2011 onwards, **UK stream papers have been based on International Financial Reporting Standards (IFRS)**, rather than on UK GAAP as in the past. It is very important that you are familiar with the requirements of IFRS. If you did not previously study IFRS, you will need to spend some time doing so before your P7 UK-stream exam.

The most obvious difference between IFRSs and UK GAAP is that the terminology is different. The following are some of the more obvious changes.

UK GAAP term	IFRS equivalent term
Balance sheet	Statement of financial position*
Profit and loss account	Statement of profit or loss and other comprehensive income*
Statement of recognised gains and losses	Statement of changes in equity*
Cash flow statement	Statement of cash flows*
Fixed asset	Non-current asset
Stock	Inventory
Debtor	Receivable
Creditor	Payable
Turnover	Revenue

*The differences between the primary financial statements are substantial, and are in no way only differences in terminology. You should refer to the BPP P2 *Corporate Reporting* Study Text for further information.

The accounting standards also have different names. Although there are not always exact one-to-one equivalences between international and UK standards, the following is a very quick summary.

UK GAAP	IFRS equivalent
Companies Act 2006	IAS 1 *Presentation of Financial Statements*
SSAP 9 *Stocks and long-term contracts*	IAS 2 *Inventories*
FRS 1 *Cash flow statements*	IAS 7 *Statement of Cash Flows*
FRS 3 *Reporting financial performance*	IAS 8 *Accounting Policies, Changes in Accounting Estimates and Errors*
FRS 21 *Events after the balance sheet date*	IAS 10 *Events After the Reporting Period*
SSAP 9 *Stocks and long-term contracts*	IAS 11 *Construction Contracts*
FRS 19 *Deferred taxation*	IAS 12 *Income Taxes*
FRS 15 *Tangible fixed assets*	IAS 16 *Property, Plant and Equipment*
SSAP 21 *Accounting for leases and hire purchase contract*	IAS 17 *Leases*
FRS 5 *Application Note G, Revenue recognition*	IAS 18 *Revenue*
FRS 17 *Retirement benefits*	IAS 19 *Employee Benefits*
SSAP 4 *Accounting for government grants*	IAS 20 *Accounting for Government Grants and Disclosure of Government Assistance*
FRS 23 *The effects of changes in foreign exchange rates*	IAS 21 *The Effects of Changes in Foreign Exchange Rates*
FRS 15 *Tangible fixed assets*	IAS 23 *Borrowing Costs*
FRS 8 *Related Party Disclosures*	IAS 24 *Related Party Disclosures*
FRS 2 *Accounting for subsidiary undertakings*	IFRS 10 *Consolidated Financial Statements*
	IFRS 12 *Disclosure of Interests in Other Entities*
FRS 9 *Associates and joint ventures*	IAS 28 *Investments in Associates and Joint Ventures*
FRS 24 *Financial Reporting in Hyperinflationary Economies*	IAS 29 *Financial Reporting in Hyperinflationary Economies*
FRS 9 *Associates and joint ventures*	IFRS 11 *Joint arrangements*
FRS 22 *Earnings Per Share*	IAS 33 *Earnings Per Share*
ASB Statement – *Interim reporting*	IAS 33 *Interim financial reporting*
FRS 11 *Impairment of fixed assets and goodwill*	IAS 36 *Impairment of Assets*
FRS 12 *Provisions, Contingent Liabilities and Contingent Assets*	IAS 37 *Provisions, Contingent Liabilities and Contingent Assets*
FRS 10 *Goodwill and intangible assets*	IAS 38 *Intangible Assets*
SSAP 13 *Accounting for research and development*	
FRS 26 *Financial Instruments: Recognition and Measurement*	IAS 39 *Financial Instruments: Recognition and Measurement*
SSAP 19 *Accounting for investment properties*	IAS 40 *Investment Property*
[No equivalent UK standard]	IFRS 1 *First-time Adoption of International Financial Reporting Standards*
FRS 20 *Share-based Payment*	IFRS 2 *Share-based Payment*

UK GAAP	IFRS equivalent
FRS 6 *Acquisitions and mergers* FRS 7 *Fair values in acquisition accounting* FRS 10 *Goodwill and intangible asset*	IFRS 3 *Business Combinations*
FRS 3 *Reporting financial performance*	IFRS 5 *Non-current Assets Held for Sale and Discontinued Operations*
FRS 29 *Financial Instruments: Disclosures*	IFRS 7 *Financial Instruments: Disclosures*
FRS 25 *Segmental reporting*	IFRS 8 *Operating Segments*
[No equivalent UK standard]	IFRS 9 *Financial Instruments*
[No equivalent UK standard]	IFRS 13 *Fair value measurement*

The differences between IFRSs and UK GAAP are **much more than just skin deep** though, and **you will need to know much more than just the new terminology and the names of the standards**. The best way of familiarising yourself with IFRSs would be to quickly work through the BPP P2 *Corporate Reporting* Study Text. You should pay particular attention to the formats of the financial statements, which are radically different, and to the chapters on group accounting.

Examinable documents

Knowledge of new examinable regulations issued by 31st August will be examinable in examination sessions being held in the following calendar year. Documents may be examinable even if the effective date is in the future. This means that all regulations issued by 31st August 2013 will be examinable in the June and December 2014 and June 2015 examinations.

The study guide offers more detailed guidance on the depth and level at which the examinable documents should be examined. The study guide should therefore be read in conjunction with the examinable documents list.

Accounting Standards

The accounting knowledge that is assumed for Paper P7 is the same as that examined in Paper P2. Therefore, candidates studying for Paper P7 should refer to the Accounting Standards listed under Paper P2.

Note. P7 will only expect knowledge of accounting standards and financial reporting standards from Paper P2. Knowledge of exposure drafts and discussion papers will not be expected.

	Title	F8	P7
	International Standards on Auditing (ISAs) (UK and Ireland)		
	Summary of changes to the new ISAs (UK and Ireland)		✓
	Glossary of terms 2009	✓	✓
ISA 200	*Overall objectives of the independent auditor and the conduct of an audit in accordance with ISAs (UK and Ireland)*	✓	✓
ISA 210	*Agreeing the terms of audit engagements*	✓	✓
ISA 220	*Quality control for an audit of financial statements*	✓	✓
ISA 230	*Audit documentation*	✓	✓
ISA 240	*The Auditor's responsibilities relating to fraud in an audit of financial statements*	✓	✓
ISA 250A	*Consideration of laws and regulations in an audit of financial statements*	✓	✓
ISA 260	*Communication with those charged with governance*	✓	✓
ISA 265	*Communicating deficiencies in internal control to those charged with governance and management*	✓	✓
ISA 300	*Planning an audit of financial statements*	✓	✓
ISA 315	*Identifying and Assessing the Risks of Material Misstatement through Understanding the Entity and Its Environment*	✓	✓
ISA 320	*Materiality in Planning and Performing an Audit*	✓	✓
ISA 330	*The Auditor's Responses to Assessed Risks*	✓	✓
ISA 402	*Audit Considerations Relating to an Entity Using a Service Organisation*	✓	✓
ISA 450	*Evaluation of Misstatements Identified During the Audit*	✓	✓
ISA 500	*Audit Evidence*	✓	✓
ISA 501	*Audit Evidence – Specific Considerations for Selected Items*	✓	✓
ISA 505	*External Confirmations*	✓	✓
ISA 510	*Initial Audit Engagements – Opening Balances*	✓	✓
ISA 520	*Analytical Procedures*	✓	✓
ISA 530	*Audit Sampling*	✓	✓
ISA 540	*Auditing Accounting Estimates, Including Fair Value Accounting Estimates and Related Disclosures*	✓	✓
ISA 550	*Related Parties*		✓
ISA 560	*Subsequent Events*	✓	✓

	Title	F8	P7
ISA 570	*Going Concern*	✓	✓
ISA 580	*Written Representations*	✓	✓
ISA 600	*Special Considerations – Audits of Group Financial Statements (Including the Work of Component Auditors)*		✓
ISA 610	*Using the Work of Internal Auditors*	✓	✓
ISA 620	*Using the Work of an Auditor's Expert*	✓	✓
ISA 700	*(Revised – September 2012) The auditor's report on financial statements*	✓	✓
ISA 705	*(Revised – September 2012) Modifications to the Opinion in the Independent Auditor's Report*	✓	✓
ISA 706	*(Revised – September 2012) Emphasis of Matter Paragraphs and Other Matter Paragraphs in the Independent Auditor's Report*	✓	✓
ISA 710	*Comparative Information – Corresponding Figures and Comparative Financial Statements*	✓	✓
ISA 720A	*(Revised – September 2012) The auditor's responsibilities relating to other information in documents containing audited financial statements*	✓	✓
ISA 720B	*The auditor's statutory reporting responsibility in relation to directors' reports*	✓	✓
	International Standards on Quality Control (ISQC)		
ISQC 1	*Quality control for firms that perform audits and reviews of financial statements and other assurance and related services engagements*		✓
	Practice Notes (PNs)		
PN 16	*Bank reports for audit purposes in the United Kingdom (Revised)*	✓	✓
PN 25	*Attendance at stocktaking*	✓	✓
PN 26	*Guidance for smaller entity documentation*	✓	✓
	Ethical Standards (ESs)		
ES	*(Revised – December 2010) Provisions available for small entities*	✓	✓
ES1	*(Revised – December 2011) Integrity, objectivity and independence*	✓	✓
ES2	*(Revised – December 2010) Financial, business, employment and personal relationships*	✓	✓
ES3	*(Revised – December 2009) Long association with the audit engagement*	✓	✓
ES4	*(Revised – December 2010) Fees, remuneration and evaluation policies, litigation, gifts and hospitality*	✓	✓
ES5	*(Revised – December 2011) Non-audit services provided to audit clients*	✓	✓
	Glossary (Revised December 2010)	✓	✓
	Bulletins		
2008/01	Audit issues when financial market conditions are difficult and credit facilities may be restricted		✓
2008/06	The 'senior statutory auditor' under the United Kingdom Companies Act 2006		✓
2008/10	Going Concern Issues During the Current Economic Conditions	✓	✓
2009/4	Developments in corporate governance affecting the responsibilities of auditors of UK companies	✓	
2010/1	XBRL tagging of information in audited financial statements – guidance for auditors		✓

	Title	F8	P7
2010/2	(Revised) Compendium of illustrative reports on United Kingdom private sector financial statements for periods ended on or after 15 December 2010	✓	✓
	Statement of Standards for Reporting Accountants (SSRAs)		
ISRE (UK and Ireland) 2410	*Review of Interim Financial Information Performed by the Independent Auditor of the Entity*		✓
	Exposure Drafts (EDs) (UK and Ireland)		
	FRC Invitation to Comment on IAASB Exposure Draft (July 2013) Reporting on Audited Financial Statements: Proposed new and Revised International Standards on Auditing (ISAs)		✓
	Other Documents		
	ACCA's 'Code of Ethics and Conduct'	✓	✓
	ESBA's 'Code of Ethics for Professional Accountants'		✓
	The UK Corporate Governance Code (Revised September 2012)	✓	
	The UK Corporate Governance Code (Revised September 2012) in relation to audit committees		✓
	FRC Going Concern and Liquidity Risk : Guidance for Directors of UK Companies 2009		✓
	Scope and Authority of Audit and Assurance Pronouncements March 2013	✓	✓
	ACCA's Technical Factsheet 145 – Anti-Money Laundering (Proceeds of Crime and Terrorism) Guidance for the Accountancy Sector		✓
	IAASB Practice Alert Challenges in Auditing Fair Value Accounting Estimates in the Current Market Environment (October 2008)		✓
	IAASB Applying ISAs Proportionately with the Size and Complexity of an Entity (August 2009)		✓
	IAASB Auditor Considerations Regarding Significant Unusual or Highly Complex Transactions (September 2010)		✓
	FRC Briefing Paper : Professional Scepticism (March 2012)		✓

Note. Topics of exposure drafts are examinable to the extent that relevant articles about them are published in *Student Accountant.*

Useful websites

The websites below provide additional sources of information of relevance to your studies for *Advanced Audit and Assurance*.

- www.accaglobal.com

  ACCA's website. The students' section of the website is invaluable for detailed information about the qualification, past issues of *Student Accountant* (including technical articles) and a free downloadable Student Planner App.

- www.bpp.com

  Our website provides information about BPP products and services, with a link to the ACCA website.

- www.ft.com

  This website provides information about current international business. You can search for information and articles on specific industry groups as well as individual companies.

- www.ifac.org

  This site has links to the International Auditing and Assurance Standards Board for up-to-date information on auditing issues.

Analysis of past papers

The table below provides details of when each element of the syllabus has been examined and the question number and section in which each element appeared.

Covered in Text chapter		D 13	J 13	D 12	J 12	D 11	J 11	D 10	J 10	D 09	J 09	D 08	J 08	D 07	PP
	Regulatory environment														
1	International regulatory frameworks for audit and assurance services								2(d)					5(b)	
1	Money laundering				3(a)						2(c)			4(a)	5(a), 5(b)
1	Laws and regulations	3 (b)									4(b)				
	Professional and ethical considerations														
2	Code of ethics for professional accountants	1 (c) 4	1 (b) 2 (a)	1(a), 3(b)	1(b), 3(b), 4	2(b)	3(a)	2(a), 4(b)	3(b), 4	4(b)	4	4	4, 5(b)	4(b), 4(c)	5(b)
3	Fraud and error		4 (a)						2(d)		5(a)				
3	Professional liability									5(b)			5(c)		
	Practice Management														
4	Quality control		2 (a)				1(b)				2(b) 5(c)		3(c)	1(c)	3, 5(b)
5	Advertising, publicity, obtaining professional work and fees						1(b)	4(a)			4(b)				
5	Tendering				3 (a)						2(b), 2(c)				
5	Professional appointments						3(a)	4(a)			2(a), 2(c)		1(c)		
	Assignments														
6,7,8, 9,10	The audit of historical financial information including: • Planning, materiality and assessing the risk of misstatement • Evidence • Evaluation and review	1, 3 5	1 (a) 3 4 (b) 5(b-c)	1, 2, 3(a) – (b), 5(a)	1(a), 3(a)–(b), 5(a)	1(a), 2(a)–(b), 3(a)-(c), 5(a)–(b)	1, 2(a), 3(b), 5(b)	1(a), 2(c), 3(a)–(c),	1, 3(b), 5(a)	1, 2(a)–(b), 5	1(a), 1(b), 1(c), 3(a), 3(b)	1(a), 1(b), 3, 5	1(a), 1(b), 3(a), 3(b)	1(a), 1(b), 2(b), 2(c), 2(d)	
11	Group audits	1 (b)	5 (a)		1(a)						2(d)		2(b), 2(c)		1(a), 1(b), 1(c), 1(d)
	Other assignments														
12	Audit-related services	2					4				3(b)			5(c)	
12	Assurance services							2(a), 2(b)			3(b)		2(a)	3(a), 3(b)	
13	Prospective financial information					2(a)	2(a)			3					
13	Insolvency					2(b)	2(b)								

Covered in Text chapter		D 13	J 13	D 12	J 12	D 11	J 11	D 10	J 10	D 09	J 09	D 08	J 08	D 07	PP
14	Forensic audits		2 (b)	3(c)		4(a)–(b)			2(c)			2		3(c)	2(a), 2(b), 2(c), 2(d)
15	Social and environmental auditing							2(a), 2(b)				1(c)			
16	Internal audit and outsourcing						4(a)		2(b), (b)					2(a)	
	Reports														
17	Auditor's reports	5 (b)	5	5	5(b)	5(a)–(b)	5(a)	5(a)	5(a)		5(b)			5(a)	4
17	Reports to management							5(b)					5(a)		
17	Other reports										3(b)				
	Current issues and developments														
1,2,3	Professional, ethical and corporate governance			3(b)		4(c)		4(b)			4				
6	Information technology														
11	Transnational audits										2(d)				
15	Social and environmental auditing														
18	Other current issues			4(a)					3(a)	4(a)	5(a)				

IMPORTANT!

The table above gives a broad idea of how frequently major topics in the syllabus are examined. It should not be used to question spot and predict for example that Topic X will not be examined because it came up two sittings ago. The examiner's reports indicate that the examiner is well aware some students try to question spot. You can assume that she will therefore take care to ensure that the exams avoid falling into a predictable pattern, and may examine the same topic two sittings in a row for example.

Questions

REGULATORY ENVIRONMENT AND PROFESSIONAL AND ETHICAL CONSIDERATIONS

Questions 1 to 9 cover Regulatory Environment and Professional and Ethical considerations, the subjects of Parts A and B of the BPP Study Text for Paper P7.

1 Lark (6/12)   27 mins

(a)   You are a manager in Lark & Co, responsible for the audit of Heron Ltd, an owner-managed business which operates a chain of bars and restaurants. This is your firm's first year auditing the client and the audit for the year ended 31 March 20X2 is underway. The audit senior sends a note for your attention:

'When I was auditing revenue I noticed something strange. Heron Ltd's revenue, which is almost entirely cash-based, is recognised at £5.5 million in the draft financial statements. However, the accounting system shows that till receipts for cash paid by customers amount to only £3.5 million. This seemed odd, so I questioned Ava Gull, the financial controller about this. She said that Jack Heron, the company's owner, deals with cash receipts and posts through journals dealing with cash and revenue. Ava asked Jack the reason for these journals but he refused to give an explanation.

'While auditing cash, I noticed a payment of £2 million made by electronic transfer from the company's bank account to an overseas financial institution. The bank statement showed that the transfer was authorised by Jack Heron, but no other documentation regarding the transfer was available.

'Alarmed by the size of this transaction, and the lack of evidence to support it, I questioned Jack Heron, asking him about the source of cash receipts and the reason for electronic transfer. He would not give any answers and became quite aggressive.'

Required

(i)   Discuss the implications of the circumstances described in the audit senior's note; and   **(6 marks)**

(ii)   Explain the nature of any reporting that should take place by the audit senior.   **(3 marks)**

(b)   You are also responsible for the audit of Coot Ltd, and you are currently reviewing the working papers of the audit for the year ended 28 February 20X2. In the working papers dealing with payroll, the audit junior has commented as follows.

'Several new employees have been added to the company's payroll during the year, with combined payments of £125,000 being made to them. There does not appear to be any authorisation for these additions. When I questioned the payroll supervisor who made the amendments, she said that no authorisation was needed because the new employees are only working for the company on a temporary basis. However, when discussing staffing levels with management, it was stated that no new employees have been taken on this year. Other than the tests of controls planned, no other audit work has been performed.'

Required

In relation to the audit of Coot Ltd's payroll, explain the meaning of the term 'professional skepticism', and recommend any further actions that should be taken by the auditor.   **(6 marks)**

(Total = 15 marks)

2   Plant (12/12)   29 mins

(a)   You are an audit manager in Weller & Co, an audit firm which operates as part of an international network of firms. This morning you received a note from a partner regarding a potential new audit client:

'I have been approached by the audit committee of the Plant Group, which operates in the mobile telecommunications sector. Our firm has been invited to tender for the audit of the individual and group financial statements for the year ending 31 March 20X3, and I would like your help in preparing the tender document.

This would be a major new client for our firm's telecoms audit department.

The Plant Group comprises a parent company and six subsidiaries, one of which is located overseas. The audit committee is looking for a cost effective audit, and hopes that the strength of the Plant Group's governance and internal control mean that the audit can be conducted quickly, with a proposed deadline of 31 May 20X3. The Plant Group has expanded rapidly in the last few years and significant finance was raised in July 20X2 through a stock exchange listing.'

Required

Identify and explain the specific matters to be included in the tender document for the audit of the Plant Group. **(8 marks)**

(b) Weller & Co is facing competition from other audit firms, and the partners have been considering how the firm's revenue could be increased. A proposal has been made that all audit managers should suggest to their audit clients that, as well as providing the external audit service, Weller & Co can provide the internal audit service as part of an 'extended audit' service.

Required

Comment on the ethical and professional issues raised by the proposal to increase the firm's revenue, and explain how the Auditing Practices Board responded to the ethical issues raised by audit firms offering an 'extended audit' service. **(8 marks)**

(Total = 16 marks)

3 Becker (12/08)   36 mins

You are a senior manager in Becker & Co, a firm of Chartered Certified Accountants offering audit and assurance services mainly to large, privately owned companies. The firm has suffered from increased competition, due to two new firms of accountants setting up in the same town. Several audit clients have moved to the new firms, leading to loss of revenue, and an over staffed audit department. Bob McEnroe, one of the partners of Becker & Co, has asked you to consider how the firm could react to this situation. Several possibilities have been raised for your consideration:

1   Murray Ltd, a manufacturer of electronic equipment, is one of Becker & Co's audit clients. You are aware that the company has recently designed a new product, which market research indicates is likely to be very successful. The development of the product has been a huge drain on cash resources. The managing director of Murray Ltd has written to the audit engagement partner to see if Becker & Co would be interested in making an investment in the new product. It has been suggested that Becker & Co could provide finance for the completion of the development and the marketing of the product. The finance would be in the form of convertible debentures. Alternatively, a joint venture company in which control is shared between Murray Ltd and Becker & Co could be established to manufacture, market and distribute the new product.

2   Becker & Co is considering expanding the provision of non-audit services. Ingrid Sharapova, a senior manager in Becker & Co, has suggested that the firm could offer a recruitment advisory service to clients, specialising in the recruitment of finance professionals. Becker & Co would charge a fee for this service based on the salary of the employee recruited. Ingrid Sharapova worked as a recruitment consultant for a year before deciding to train as an accountant.

3   Several audit clients are experiencing staff shortages, and it has been suggested that temporary staff assignments could be offered. It is envisaged that a number of audit managers or seniors could be seconded to clients for periods not exceeding six months, after which time they would return to Becker & Co.

Required

Identify and explain the ethical and practice management implications in respect of:

(a)   A business arrangement with Murray Ltd.   **(7 marks)**
(b)   A recruitment service offered to clients.   **(7 marks)**
(c)   Temporary staff assignments   **(6 marks)**

(Total = 20 marks)

4 Peaches (12/09) (amended)

29 mins

(a) Following the International Audit and Assurance Standards Board's Clarity Project, many revised and redrafted ISAs (UK and Ireland) were effective for audits of financial statements for periods ending on or after 15 December 2010. One of the objectives of the Clarity Project was to clarify mandatory requirements. This was done by changing the wording used in the ISAs to indicate requirements which are expected to be applied in all audits. Some argue that this will introduce a more prescriptive (rules-based) approach to auditing, and that a principles-based approach is more desirable.

Required

    (i) Contrast the prescriptive and the principles-based approaches to auditing; and **(2 marks)**

    (ii) Outline the arguments for and against a prescriptive (rules-based) approach to auditing. **(5 marks)**

(b) You are a manager in the audit department of Peaches & Co, a firm of Chartered Certified Accountants. One of your responsibilities is to act as a mentor to new recruits into the department. A new junior auditor, Glen Rambaran, has asked you to answer some questions which relate to issues encountered in his first few weeks working at Peaches & Co. The questions are shown below.

    (i) When I was on my initial training course, there was a session on ethics in which the presenter talked about being intimidated by a client. I assume this does not mean physical intimidation, so what is an intimidation threat? **(3 marks)**

    (ii) I know that Peaches & Co is facing competition from a new audit firm, and that our firm is advertising its services in a national newspaper. What are the rules on advertising for new clients? **(3 marks)**

    (iii) I heard one of the audit managers say that our firm had lost an audit client to a competitor because of lowballing. What is lowballing and is it allowed? **(3 marks)**

Required

For each of the three questions raised, provide a response to the audit junior, in which you identify and explain the ethical or professional issue raised.

(Total = 16 marks)

5 Retriever (6/13)

45 mins

Kennel & Co, a firm of Chartered Certified Accountants, is the external audit provider for the Retriever Group (the Group), a manufacturer of mobile phones and laptop computers. The Group obtained a stock exchange listing in July 20X2. The audit of the consolidated financial statements for the year ended 28 February 20X3 is nearing completion.

You are a manager in the audit department of Kennel & Co, and you have just received a note from Barry Bark, one of the audit partners:

'I need your help with a couple of matters relating to the Retriever Group. The audit engagement partner has fallen ill and I have taken on responsibility for this client.

'First, one of the audit juniors has made some comments about how the audit was planned and carried out. To help me to understand the implications of these comments can you evaluate the quality control, ethical and other professional matters arising in relation to the planning and performance of the Group audit.

'Second, the audit committee of the Group has contacted Kennel & Co to discuss a theft that took place in the warehouse on 1 June 20X3. Details of the incident are provided below. In short, our firm has been asked to perform a forensic investigation into the amount that can be claimed from the insurance provider. In relation to this, I need you to identify and explain the matters to be considered and the steps to be taken in planning the forensic accounting service. You should also recommend the procedures to be performed in determining the amount of the claim. It is thought that the amount of the claim will be immaterial to the Group's financial statements, and there is no ethical threat in Kennel & Co's forensic accounting department providing the forensic accounting service.

'As this is the first involvement that you have had with the Group, I have also provided you with some background information.'

Retriever Group – Business background and extract from draft financial statements

The Group was formed six years ago and has grown rapidly to become a well-known manufacturer of high-tech mobile phones and laptop computers. It uses the very latest technology in its products and brings new designs to market every six months. To keep up with competition, a lot is invested in research and development, and expensive advertising campaigns are continually used to promote the latest innovations to its products.

The Group comprises a parent company and three subsidiaries, and there are plans to acquire a new subsidiary in the Far East in order to begin product development in that market. The Group is structured such that one of the subsidiaries conducts most of the research and development but generates little revenue.

The draft consolidated financial statements recognises revenue of £250 million (£210 million – 20X2), profit before tax of £23 million (£20 million – 20X2) and total assets of £180 million (£170 million – 20X2).

Audit junior's comments

'The audit has been quite time-pressured. The audit manager told the juniors not to perform some of the planned audit procedures on items such as directors' emoluments and share capital as they are considered to be low risk. He also instructed us not to use the firm's statistical sampling methods in selecting trade receivables balances for testing, as it would be quicker to pick the sample based on our own judgement.

'Two of the juniors were given the tasks of auditing trade payables and going concern. The audit manager asked us to review each other's work as it would be good training for us, and he didn't have time to review everything.

'I was discussing the Group's tax position with the financial controller, when she said that she was struggling to calculate the deferred tax asset that should be recognised. The deferred tax asset has arisen because one of the Group's subsidiaries has been loss-making this year, creating unutilised tax losses. As I had just studied deferred tax at college I did the calculation of the Group's deferred tax position for her – I worked it out to be £20 million. The audit manager said this saved time as we now would not have to audit the deferred tax figure.

'The financial controller also asked for my advice as to how the tax losses could be utilised by the Group in the future. I provided her with some tax planning recommendations, for which she was very grateful.'

Note from Group audit committee

On 1 June 20X3, there was a burglary at the Group's warehouse where inventory is stored prior to despatch to customers. CCTV filmed the thieves loading a lorry belonging to the Group with boxes containing finished goods. The last inventory count took place on 30 April 20X3.

The Group has insurance cover in place which covers the cost of assets lost as a result of theft. The Group's internal audit department, which would normally carry out this kind of work, is very short staffed at the moment, so we would like to engage Kennel & Co to provide a forensic investigation into the amount that can be claimed under our insurance cover. The provision of this non-audit service by your firm's forensic accounting department would adhere to the Group's corporate governance policy as long as the service is conducted by non-audit personnel.

Required

Respond to the instructions from the audit partner. **(25 marks)**

6 Smith & Co (6/08)   31 mins

You are an audit manager in Smith & Co, a firm of Chartered Certified Accountants. You have recently been made responsible for reviewing invoices raised to clients and for monitoring your firm's credit control procedures. Several matters came to light during your most recent review of client invoice files:

Norman Ltd, a large company, has not paid an invoice from Smith & Co dated 5 June 20X7 for work in respect of the financial statement audit for the year ended 28 February 20X7. A file note dated 30 November 20X7 states that Norman Ltd is suffering poor cash flows and is unable to pay the balance. This is the only piece of information in the file you are reviewing relating to the invoice. You are aware that the final audit work for the year ended 28 February 20X8, which has not yet been invoiced, is nearly complete and the auditor's report is due to be issued imminently.

Wallace Ltd, whose business is the manufacture of industrial machinery, has paid all invoices relating to the recently completed audit planning for the year ended 31 May 20X8. However, in the invoice file you notice an invoice received by your firm from Wallace Ltd. The invoice is addressed to Valerie Hobson, the manager responsible for the audit of Wallace Ltd. The invoice relates to the rental of an area in Wallace Ltd's empty warehouse, with the following comment handwritten on the invoice: 'rental space being used for storage of Ms Hobson's speedboat for six months – she is our auditor, so only charge a nominal sum of £100'. When asked about the invoice, Valerie Hobson said that the invoice should have been sent to her private address. You are aware that Wallace Ltd sometimes uses the empty warehouse for rental income, though this is not the main trading income of the company.

In the 'miscellaneous invoices raised' file, an invoice dated last week has been raised to Software Supply Ltd, not a client of your firm. The comment box on the invoice contains the note: 'referral fee for recommending Software Supply Ltd to several audit clients regarding the supply of bespoke accounting software'.

Required

Identify and discuss the ethical and other professional issues raised by the invoice file review, and recommend what action, if any, Smith & Co should now take in respect of:

(a)	Norman Ltd	**(8 marks)**
(b)	Wallace Ltd	**(5 marks)**
(c)	Software Supply Ltd	**(4 marks)**

(Total = 17 marks)

7 Carter (6/10)   36 mins

You are a manager in the audit department of Carter & Co, and you are dealing with several ethical and professional matters raised at recent management meetings, all of which relate to audit clients of your firm:

1   Fernwood Ltd has a year ending 30 June 20Y0. During this year, the company established a pension plan for its employees, and this year end the company will be recognising for the first time a pension deficit on the statement of financial position, in accordance with IAS 19 *Employee benefits*. The finance director of Fernwood Ltd has contacted the audit engagement partner, asking if your firm can provide a valuation service in respect of the amount recognised.

2   The finance director of Hall Ltd has requested that a certain audit senior, Kia Nelson, be assigned to the audit team. This senior has not previously been assigned to the audit of Hall Ltd. On further investigation it transpired that Kia Nelson is the sister of Hall Ltd's financial controller.

3   Collier Ltd has until recently kept important documents such as title deeds and insurance certificates in a safe at its head office. However, following a number of thefts from the head office the directors have asked if the documents could be held securely at Carter & Co's premises. The partners of Carter & Co are considering offering a custodial service to all clients, some of whom may want to deposit tangible assets such as paintings purchased as investments for safekeeping. The fee charged for this service would depend on the value of item deposited as well as the length of the safekeeping arrangement.

4   Several audit clients have requested that Carter & Co provide technical training on financial reporting and tax issues. This is not a service that the firm wishes to provide, and it has referred the audit clients to a training firm, Gates Ltd, which is paying a referral fee to Carter & Co for each audit client which is referred.

Required

Identify and evaluate the ethical and other professional issues raised, in respect of:

(a)	Fernwood Ltd	**(6 marks)**
(b)	Hall Ltd	**(6 marks)**
(c)	Collier Ltd	**(5 marks)**
(d)	Gates Ltd	**(3 marks)**

(Total = 20 marks)

8 Dedza (Pilot paper)

36 mins

(a)   Comment on the need for ethical guidance for accountants on money laundering.   **(5 marks)**

(b)   You are senior manager in Dedza & Co, a firm of Chartered Certified Accountants. Recently, you have been assigned specific responsibility for undertaking annual reviews of existing clients. The following situations have arisen in connection with three clients.

   (i)   Dedza was appointed auditor to Kora Ltd last year and has recently issued an unmodified opinion on the financial statements for the year ended 31 March 20X8. To your surprise, the tax authority has just launched an investigation into the affairs of Kora on suspicion of underdeclaring income.

   (7 marks)

   (ii)   The chief executive of Xalam Ltd, an exporter of specialist equipment, has asked for advice on the accounting treatment and disclosure of payments being made for security consultancy services. The payments, which aim to ensure that consignments are not impounded in the destination country of a major customer, may be material to the financial statements for the year ending 31 December 20X8. Xalam does not treat these payments as tax deductible.   **(4 marks)**

   (iii)   Your firm has provided financial advice to the Pholey family for many years and this has sometimes involved your firm in carrying out transactions on their behalf. The eldest son, Esau, is to take up a position as a senior government official to a foreign country next month.   **(4 marks)**

Required

Identify and comment on the ethical and other professional issues raised by each of these matters and state what action, if any, Dedza & Co should now take.

Note. The mark allocation is shown against each of the three situations.

(Total = 20 marks)

9 Clifden (6/09)

31 mins

(a)   The IESBA's *Code of Ethics for Professional Accountants* states that a professional accountant is required to comply with five fundamental principles, one of which is the principle of 'professional competence and due care'.

Required

Explain what is meant by the term 'professional competence and due care', and outline how firms of Chartered Certified Accountants can ensure that the principle is complied with.   **(4 marks)**

(b)   You are a senior manager in Clifden & Co, and you are responsible for the audit of Headford Ltd, a manufacturer of plastic toys which are exported all over the world. The following matter has been brought to your attention by the audit senior, who has just completed the planning of the forthcoming audit for the year ending 30 June 20X9.

During a discussion with the production manager, it was revealed that there have been some quality control problems with the toys manufactured between March and May 20X9. It was discovered that some of the plastic used in the manufacture of the company's products had been contaminated with a dangerous chemical which has the potential to explode if it is exposed to high temperatures. Headford Ltd did not recall any of the products which had been manufactured during that time from customers, as management felt that the risk of any injury being caused was remote.

Your firm has been invited to tender for the provision of the external audit service to Cong Ltd. You are aware that Cong Ltd operates in the same industry as Headford Ltd, and that the two companies often enter into highly publicised, aggressive advertising campaigns featuring very similar products. Cong Ltd is a much larger company than Headford Ltd, and there would be the opportunity to offer some non-audit services as well as the external audit.

Required

Assess the ethical and professional issues raised, and recommend any actions necessary in respect of the:

(i)	Contaminated plastic used by Headford Ltd; and	**(8 marks)**
(ii)	Invitation to audit Cong Ltd.	**(5 marks)**

(Total = 17 marks)

PRACTICE MANAGEMENT

Questions 10 to 17 cover Practice management, the subject of Part C of the BPP Study Text for Paper P7.

10 Hawk Associates (AAS 6/04)   27 mins

You are a training manager in Hawk Associates, a firm of Chartered Certified Accountants. The firm has suffered a reduction in fee income due to increasing restrictions on the provision of non-audit services to audit clients. The following proposals for obtaining professional work are to be discussed at a forthcoming in-house seminar.

(a)   'Cold calling' (ie approaching directly to seek new business) the chief executive officers of local businesses and offering them free second opinions.   **(5 marks)**

(b)   Placing an advertisement in a national accountancy magazine that includes the following.

'If you have an asset on which a large chargeable gain is expected to arise when you dispose of it, you should be interested in the best tax planning advice. However your gains might arise, there are techniques you can apply. Hawk Associates can ensure that you consider all the alternative fact presentations so that you minimise the amount of tax you might have to pay. No tax saving – no fee!'   **(6 marks)**

(c)   Displaying business cards alongside those of local tradesman and service providers in supermarkets and libraries. The cards would read:

'Hawk ACCA Associates
For PROFESSIONAL Accountancy, Audit,
Business Consultancy and Taxation Services
Competitive rates. Money back guarantees'

(4 marks)

Required

Comment on the suitability of each of the above proposals in terms of the ethical and other professional issues that they raise.

Note. The mark allocation is shown against each of the three issues.   **(Total = 15 marks)**

11 Grape (12/09)   65 mins

You are a manager in Grape & Co, a firm of Chartered Certified Accountants. You have been temporarily assigned as audit manager to the audit of Banana Ltd, because the engagement manager has been taken ill. The final audit of Banana Ltd for the year ended 30 September 20X9 is nearing completion, and you are now reviewing the audit files and discussing the audit with the junior members of the audit team. Banana Ltd designs and manufactures equipment such as cranes and scaffolding, which are used in the construction industry. The equipment usually follows a standard design, but sometimes Banana Ltd designs specific items for customers according to contractually agreed specifications. The draft financial statements show revenue of £12.5 million, net profit of £400,000, and total assets of £78 million.

The following information has come to your attention during your review of the audit files.

During the year, a new range of manufacturing plant was introduced to the factories operated by Banana Ltd. All factory employees received training from an external training firm on how to safely operate the machinery, at a total cost of £500,000. The training costs have been capitalised into the cost of the new machinery, as the finance director argues that the training is necessary in order for the machinery to generate an economic benefit. After the year end, Cherry Ltd, a major customer with whom Banana Ltd has several significant contracts, announced its insolvency, and that procedures to shut down the company had commenced. The administrators of Cherry Ltd have suggested that the company may be able to pay approximately 25% of the amounts owed to its trade payables. A trade receivable of £300,000 is recognised on Banana Ltd's statement of financial position in respect of this customer.

In addition, one of the junior members of the audit team voiced concerns over how the audit had been managed. The junior said the following:

'I have only worked on two audits prior to being assigned the audit team of Banana Ltd. I was expecting to attend a meeting at the start of the audit, where the partner and other senior members of the audit team discussed the audit, but no meeting was held. In addition, the audit manager has been away on holiday for three weeks, and left a senior in charge. However, the senior was busy with other assignments, so was not always available.

'I was given the task of auditing the goodwill which arose on an acquisition made during the year. I also worked on the audit of inventory, and attended the inventory count, which was quite complicated, as Banana Ltd has a lot of work-in-progress. I tried to be as useful as possible during the count, and helped the client's staff count some of the raw materials. As I had been to the inventory count, I was asked by the audit senior to challenge the finance director regarding the adequacy of the provision against inventory, which the senior felt was significantly understated.

'Lastly, we found that we were running out of time to complete our audit procedures. The audit senior advised that we should reduce the sample sizes used in our tests as a way of saving time. He also suggested that if we picked an item as part of our sample for which it would be time consuming to find the relevant evidence, then we should pick a different item which would be quicker to audit.'

Required

In respect of the specific information provided:

(a)   Comment on the matters to be considered, and explain the audit evidence you should expect to find during your file review in respect of:

    (i)   The training costs that have been capitalised into the cost of the new machinery; and

    (ii)   The trade receivable recognised in relation to Cherry Ltd.   **(12 marks)**

(b)   Evaluate the audit junior's concerns regarding the management of the audit of Banana Ltd.   **(10 marks)**

(c)   There are specific regulatory obligations imposed on accountants and auditors in relation to detecting and reporting money laundering activities. You have been asked to provide a training session to the new audit juniors on auditors' responsibilities in relation to money laundering.

    Required

    Prepare briefing notes to be used at your training session in which you:

    (i)   Explain the term 'money laundering'. Illustrate your explanation with examples of money laundering offences, including those which could be committed by the accountant

    (ii)   Explain the policies and procedures that a firm of Chartered Certified Accountants should establish in order to meet its responsibilities in relation to money laundering   **(10 marks)**

    Professional marks will be awarded in part (c) for the format of the answer, and the quality of the explanations provided.   **(4 marks)**

(Total = 36 marks)

12 Ingot & Co (Pilot paper)   36 mins

You are a manager in Ingot & Co, a firm of Chartered Certified Accountants, with specific responsibility for the quality of audits. Ingot was appointed auditor of Argenta Co, a provider of waste management services, in July 20X8. You have just visited the audit team at Argenta's head office. The audit team is comprised of an accountant in charge (AIC), an audit senior and two trainees.

Argenta's draft financial statements for the year ended 30 June 20X8 show revenue of £11.6 million (20X7 – £8.1 million) and total assets of £3.6 million (20X7 – £2.5 million). During your visit, a review of the audit working papers revealed the following.

(a)   On the audit planning checklist, the audit senior has crossed through the analytical procedures section and written 'not applicable – new client'. The audit planning checklist has not been signed off as having been reviewed.   **(4 marks)**

(b) The AIC last visited Argenta's office when the final audit commenced two weeks ago on 1 August. The senior has since completed the audit of tangible non-current assets (including property and service equipment) which amount to £0.6 million as at 30 June 20X8 (20X7 – £0.6 million). The AIC spends most of his time working from Ingot's office and is currently allocated to three other assignments as well as Argenta's audit.

(4 marks)

(c) At 30 June 20X8 trade receivables amounted to £2.1 million (20X7 – £0.9 million). One of the trainees has just finished sending out first requests for direct confirmation of customers' balances as at the end of the reporting period.

(4 marks)

(d) The other trainee has been assigned to the audit of the consumable supplies that comprise inventory amounting to £45,000 (20X7 – £37,000). The trainee has carried out tests of controls over the perpetual inventory records and confirmed the 'roll-back' of a sample of current quantities to book quantities as at the year end.

(3 marks)

(e) The AIC has noted the following matter for your attention. The financial statements to 30 June 20X7 disclosed, as unquantifiable, a contingent liability for pending litigation. However, the AIC has seen a letter confirming that the matter was settled out of court for £0.45 million on 14 September 20X7. The auditor's report on the financial statements for the year ended 30 June 20X7 was unmodified and signed on 19 September 20X7. The AIC believes that Argenta's management is not aware of the error and has not brought it to their attention.

(5 marks)

Required

Identify and comment on the implications of these findings for Ingot & Co's quality control policies and procedures.

Note. The mark allocation is shown against each of the five issues.

(Total = 20 marks)

13 Nate & Co (12/07)   36 mins

You are an audit manager in Nate & Co, a firm of Chartered Certified Accountants. You are reviewing three situations, which were recently discussed at the monthly audit managers' meeting:

1   Nate & Co has recently been approached by a potential new audit client, Fisher Ltd. Your firm is keen to take the appointment and is currently carrying out client acceptance procedures. Fisher Ltd was recently incorporated by Marcellus Fisher, with its main trade being the retailing of wooden storage boxes.

2   Nate & Co provides the audit service to CF Ltd, a national financial services organisation. Due to a number of errors in the recording of cash deposits from new customers that have been discovered by CF Ltd's internal audit team, the directors of CF Ltd have requested that your firm carry out a review of the financial information technology systems. It has come to your attention that while working on the audit planning of CF Ltd, Jin Sayed, one of the juniors on the audit team, who is a recent information technology graduate, spent three hours providing advice to the internal audit team about how to improve the system. As far as you know, this advice has not been used by the internal audit team.

3   LA Shots Ltd is a manufacturer of bottled drinks, and has been an audit client of Nate & Co for five years. Two audit juniors attended the annual inventory count last Monday. They reported that Brenda Mangle, the new production manager of LA Shots Ltd, wanted the inventory count and audit procedures performed as quickly as possible. As an incentive she offered the two juniors ten free bottles of 'Super Juice' from the end of the production line. Brenda also invited them to join the LA Shots Ltd office party, which commenced at the end of the inventory count. The inventory count and audit procedures were completed within two hours (the previous year's procedures lasted a full day), and the juniors then spent four hours at the office party.

Required

(a) Define 'money laundering' and state the procedures specific to money laundering that should be considered before, and on the acceptance of, the audit appointment of Fisher Ltd. **(5 marks)**

(b) With reference to CF Ltd, explain the ethical and other professional issues raised. **(9 marks)**

(c) Identify and discuss the ethical and professional matters raised at the inventory count of LA Shots Ltd. **(6 marks)**

(Total = 20 marks)

14 Wexford (6/11)   32 mins

(a) Your firm has been approached by Wexford Ltd to provide the annual audit. Wexford Ltd operates a chain of bookshops across the country. The shops sell stationery such as diaries and calendars, as well as new books. The financial year will end on 31 July 20X1, and this will be the first year that an audit is required, as previously the company was exempt from audit due to its small size.

The potential audit engagement partner, Wendy Kwan, recently attended a meeting with Ravi Shah, managing director of Wexford Ltd regarding the audit appointment. In this meeting, Ravi made the following comments.

'Wexford Ltd is a small, owner-managed business. I run the company, along with my sister, Rita, and we employ a part-qualified accountant to do the bookkeeping and prepare the annual accounts. The accountant prepares management accounts at the end of every quarter, but Rita and I rarely do more than quickly review the sales figures. We understand that due to the company's size, we now need to have the accounts audited. It would make sense if your firm could prepare the accounts and do the audit at the same time. We don't want a cash flow statement prepared, as it is not required for tax purposes, and would not be used by us.

'Next year we are planning to acquire another company, one of our competitors, which I believe is an existing audit client of your firm. For this reason, we require that your audit procedures do not include reading the minutes of board meetings, as we have been discussing some confidential matters regarding this potential acquisition.'

Required

Identify and explain the professional and ethical matters that should be considered in deciding whether to accept the appointment as auditor of Wexford Ltd. **(10 marks)**

(b) Wexford Ltd's financial statements for the year ended 31 July 20X0 included the following balances.

Profit before tax	£50,000
Inventory	£25,000
Total assets	£350,000

The inventory comprised stocks of books, diaries, calendars and greetings cards.

Required

In relation to opening balances where the financial statements for the prior period were not audited:

Explain the audit procedures required by ISA 510 (UK and Ireland) *Initial audit engagements – opening balances*, and recommend the specific audit procedures to be applied to Wexford Ltd's opening balance of inventory. **(8 marks)**

Note. Assume it is 7 June 20X1. **(Total = 18 marks)**

15 Spaniel & Bulldog (6/13)

36 mins

You are a manager in Groom & Co, a firm of Chartered Certified Accountants. You have just attended a monthly meeting of audit partners and managers at which client-related matters were discussed. Information in relation to two clients, which were discussed at the meeting, is given below:

(a) **Spaniel Ltd**

The audit report on the financial statements of Spaniel Ltd, a long-standing audit client, for the year ended 31 December 20X2 was issued in April 20X3, and was unmodified. In May 20X3, Spaniel Ltd's audit committee contacted the audit engagement partner to discuss a fraud that had been discovered. The company's internal auditors estimate that £4.5 million has been stolen in a payroll fraud, which has been operating since May 20X2.

The audit engagement partner commented that neither tests of controls nor substantive audit procedures were conducted on payroll in the audit of the latest financial statements as in previous years' audits there were no deficiencies found in controls over payroll. The total assets recognised in Spaniel Ltd's financial statements at 31 December 20X2 were £80 million. Spaniel Ltd is considering suing Groom & Co for the total amount of cash stolen from the company, claiming that the audit firm was negligent in conducting the audit.

Required

Explain the matters that should be considered in determining whether Groom & Co is liable to Spaniel Ltd in respect of the fraud. **(12 marks)**

(b) **Bulldog Ltd**

Bulldog Ltd is a clothing manufacturer, which has recently expanded its operations overseas. To manage exposure to cash flows denominated in foreign currencies, the company has set up a treasury management function, which is responsible for entering into hedge transactions such as forward exchange contracts. These transactions are likely to be material to the financial statements. The audit partner is about to commence planning the audit for the year ending 31 July 20X3.

Required

Discuss why the audit of financial instruments is particularly challenging, and explain the matters to be considered in planning the audit of Bulldog Ltd's forward exchange contracts. **(8 marks)**

(20 marks)

16 Raven (6/12)

27 mins

You are a senior manager in the audit department of Raven & Co. You are reviewing two situations which have arisen in respect of audit clients, which were recently discussed at the monthly audit managers' meeting:

1   Grouse Ltd is a significant audit client which develops software packages. Its managing director, Max Partridge, has contacted one of your firm's partners regarding a potential business opportunity. The proposal is that Grouse Ltd and Raven & Co could jointly develop accounting and tax calculation software, and that revenue from sales of the software would be equally split between the two firms. Max thinks that Raven & Co's audit clients would be a good customer base for the product.

2   Plover Ltd is a private hospital which provides elective medical services, such as laser eye surgery to improve eyesight. The audit of its financial statements for the year ended 31 March 20X2 is currently taking place. The audit senior overheard one of the surgeons who performs laser surgery saying to his colleague that he is hoping to finish his medical qualification soon, and that he was glad that Plover Ltd did not check his references before employing him. While completing the subsequent events audit procedures, the audit senior found a letter from a patient's solicitor claiming compensation from Plover Ltd in relation to alleged medical negligence resulting in injury to the patient.

Required

Identify and discuss the ethical, commercial and other professional issues raised, and recommend any actions that should be taken in respect of:

(a)   Grouse Ltd   (8 marks)
(b)   Plover Ltd   (7 marks)

(Total = 15 marks)

17 Dragon Group (6/09)   58 mins

(a)   Explain **four** reasons why a firm of auditors may decide **not** to seek re-election as auditor.   (6 marks)

You are Jennifer Meadows, a newly-qualified audit supervisor in Unicorn & Co, a global firm of Chartered Certified Accountants, with offices in over 150 countries across the world. Unicorn & Co has been invited to tender for the Dragon Group audit (including the audit of all subsidiaries). You work in a department within the firm which specialises in the audit of retail companies, and have just received the following email from Cameron Wells, a senior partner in the department.

To:	Jennifer Meadows
From:	Cameron Wells
Date:	June 20X9
Subject:	The Dragon Group

Jennifer

We are currently considering tendering for the audit of a new client called the Dragon Group.

The Dragon Group is a large group of companies operating in the furniture retail trade. The group has expanded rapidly in the last three years, by acquiring several subsidiaries each year. The management of the parent company, Dragon plc, has decided to put the audit of the group and all subsidiaries out to tender, as the current audit firm is not seeking re-election. The financial year end of the Dragon Group is 30 September 20X9.

I recently held a meeting with Edmund Jalousie, the group finance director, in which we discussed the current group structure, recent acquisitions, and the group's plans for future expansion. I made some notes from the meeting, on the basis of which I would like you to prepare some briefing notes for me which recommend and describe the principal matters to be included in the firm's tender document to provide the audit service to the Dragon Group, and which evaluate the matters that should be considered before accepting the audit engagement, in the event of us being successful in the tender.

You'll need to collect my meeting notes from my secretary.

Thanks

Cameron Wells

Meeting notes – Dragon Group

Group structure

The parent company owns 20 subsidiaries, all of which are wholly owned. Half of the subsidiaries are located in this country, and half overseas. Most of the foreign subsidiaries report under the same financial reporting framework as Dragon plc, but several prepare financial statements using local accounting rules.

Acquisitions during the year

Two companies were purchased in March 20X9, both located in this country:

- Mermaid Ltd, a company which operates 20 furniture retail outlets. The audit opinion expressed by the incumbent auditors on the financial statements for the year ended 30 September 20X8 was modified by a material misstatement in relation to the non-disclosure of a contingent liability. The contingent liability relates to a court case which is still on-going.

- Minotaur Ltd, a large company, whose operations are distribution and warehousing. This represents a diversification away from retail, and it is hoped that the Dragon Group will benefit from significant economies of scale as a result of the acquisition.

Other matters

The acquisitive strategy of the group over the last few years has led to significant growth. Group revenue has increased by 25% in the last three years, and is predicted to increase by a further 35% in the next four years as the acquisition of more subsidiaries is planned. The Dragon Group has raised finance for the acquisitions in the past by becoming listed on the stock exchanges of three different countries. A new listing on a foreign stock exchange is planned for January 20Y0. For this reason, management would like the group audit completed by 31 December 20X9.

Required

(b)   Respond to Cameron Wells' email.   **(17 marks)**

Professional marks will be awarded in part (b) for the clarity and presentation of the evaluation.   **(4 marks)**

(c)   (i)   Define 'transnational audit', and explain the relevance of the term to the audit of the Dragon Group.
                                                                                                                                                                (3 marks)

(ii)   Discuss **two** features of a transnational audit that may contribute to a high level of audit risk in such an engagement.   **(4 marks)**

(Total = 34 marks)

AUDIT OF HISTORICAL FINANCIAL INFORMATION AND OTHER ASSIGNMENTS

Questions 18 to 58 cover Audit of historical financial information and other assignments, the subject of Parts D and E of the BPP Study Text for Paper P7.

18 Pulp (6/08)   31 mins

(a)   Discuss why the identification of related parties, and material related party transactions, can be difficult for auditors.   **(5 marks)**

(b)   You are an audit manager responsible for providing hot reviews on selected audit clients within your firm of Chartered Certified Accountants. You are currently reviewing the audit working papers for Pulp Ltd, a long standing audit client, for the year ended 31 January 20X8. The draft statement of financial position of Pulp Ltd shows total assets of £12 million (20X7 – £11.5 million). The audit senior has made the following comment in a summary of issues for your review:

'Pulp Ltd's statement of financial position shows a receivable classified as a current asset with a value of £25,000. The only audit evidence we have requested and obtained is a written representation from management stating that:

1   The amount is owed to Pulp Ltd from Jarvis Ltd
2   Jarvis Ltd is controlled by Pulp Ltd's chairman, Peter Sheffield
3   The balance is likely to be received six months after Pulp Ltd's year end

'The receivable was also outstanding at the last year end when an identical written representation from management was provided, and our working papers noted that because the balance was immaterial no further work was considered necessary. No disclosure has been made in the financial statements regarding the balance. Jarvis Ltd is not audited by our firm and we have verified that Pulp Ltd does not own any shares in Jarvis Ltd.'

Required

In relation to the receivable recognised on the statement of financial position of Pulp Ltd as at 31 January 20X8:

(i)   Comment on the matters you should consider   **(5 marks)**
(ii)   Recommend further audit procedures that should be carried out   **(4 marks)**

(c)   Discuss the quality control issues raised by the audit senior's comments.   **(3 marks)**

(Total = 17 marks)

19 Aspersion (AAS 12/01)   36 mins

You are the manager responsible for the audit of Aspersion, a limited liability company, which mainly provides national cargo services with a small fleet of aircraft. The draft financial statements for the year ended 30 September 20X8 show profit before taxation of £2.7 million (20X6 – £2.2 million) and total assets of £10.4 million (20X6 – £9.8 million).

The following issues are outstanding and have been left for your attention.

(a)   The sale of a cargo carrier to Abra, a private limited company, during the year resulted in a loss on disposal of £400,000. The aircraft cost £1.2 million when it was purchased in September 1999 and was being depreciated on a straight-line basis over 20 years. The minutes of the board meeting at which the sale was approved record that Aspersion's finance director, Iain Jolteon, has a 30% equity interest in Abra.
                                                                            (7 marks)

(b)   As well as cargo carriers, Aspersion owns two light aircraft which were purchased in 20X5 to provide business passenger flights to a small island under a three year service contract. It is now known that the contract will not be renewed when it expires at the end of March 20X9. The aircraft, which cost £450,000 each, are being depreciated over fifteen years.   **(7 marks)**

(c)   Deferred tax amounting to £570,000 as at 30 September 20X8 has been calculated relating to accelerated capital allowances at a tax rate of 30% under the full provision method (IAS 12 *Income taxes*). In a budget statement in October 20X8, the government announced an increase in the corporation tax rate to 34%. The directors are proposing to adjust the draft financial statements for the further liability arising.   **(6 marks)**

Required

For each of the above points:

(i)   Comment on the matters that you should consider

(ii)   State the audit evidence that you should expect to find in undertaking your review of the audit working papers and financial statements of Aspersion.

(Total = 20 marks)

Note. The mark allocation is shown against each of the three issues. Assume that it is 11 December 20X8.

20 Mac (6/10)   47 mins

Mac Ltd is a large, private company, whose business activity is events management, involving the organisation of conferences, meetings and celebratory events for companies. Mac Ltd was founded ten years ago by Danny Hudson and his sister, Stella, who still own the majority of the company's shares. The company has grown rapidly and now employs more than 150 staff in 20 offices.

You are a manager in the business advisory department of Flack & Co. Your firm has just been engaged to provide the internal audit service to Mac Ltd. In your initial conversation with Danny and Stella, you discovered that currently there is a small internal audit team, under the supervision of Lindsay Montana, a recently qualified accountant. Before heading up the internal audit department, Lindsay was a junior finance manager of the company. The members of the internal audit team will be reassigned to roles in the finance department once your firm has commenced the provision of the internal audit service.

Mac Ltd is not an existing client of your firm, and to gain further understanding of the company, you held a meeting with Lindsay Montana. Notes from this meeting are shown below.

Notes of meeting held with Lindsay Montana on 1 June 20Y0

The internal audit team has three employees, including Lindsay, who reports to the finance director. The other two internal auditors are currently studying for their professional examinations. The team was set up two years ago, and initially focused on introducing financial controls across all of Mac Ltd's offices. Nine months ago the finance director instructed the team to focus their attention on introducing operational controls in order to achieve cost savings due to a cash flow problem being suffered by the company. The team does not have time to perform much testing of financial or operational controls.

In the course of her work, Lindsay finds many instances of management policies not being adhered to, and the managers of each location are generally reluctant to introduce controls as they want to avoid bureaucracy and paperwork. As a result, Lindsay's recommendations are often ignored.

Three weeks ago, Lindsay discovered a fraud operating at one of the offices while reviewing the procedures relating to the approval of new suppliers and payments made to suppliers. The fraud involved an account manager authorising the payment of invoices received from fictitious suppliers, with payment actually being made into the account manager's personal bank account. Lindsay reported the account manager to the finance director, and the manager was immediately removed from office. This situation has highlighted to Danny and Stella that something needs to be done to improve controls within their organisation.

Danny and Stella are considering taking legal action against Mac Ltd's external audit provider, Manhattan & Co, because their audit procedures did not reveal the fraud.

Danny and Stella are deciding whether to set up an audit committee. Mac Ltd is not required to have an audit committee, but the external auditors recommend that a disclosure note explaining whether an audit committee has been established, is included in the annual report.

Required

(a) Evaluate the benefits to Mac Ltd of outsourcing its internal audit function. **(6 marks)**

(b) Explain the potential impacts on the external audit of Mac Ltd if the decision is taken to outsource its internal audit function. **(4 marks)**

(c) Recommend procedures that could be used by your firm to quantify the financial loss suffered by Mac Ltd as a result of the fraud. **(4 marks)**

(d) Prepare a report to be presented to Danny and Stella in which you:

    (i) Compare the responsibilities of the external auditor and of management in relation to the prevention and detection of fraud **(4 marks)**

    (ii) Assess the benefits and drawbacks for Mac Ltd in establishing an audit committee **(4 marks)**

Professional marks will be awarded in respect of requirement (d) for the presentation of your answer, and the clarity of your discussion. **(4 marks)**

(Total = 26 marks)

21 Falcon
58 mins

Imperiol Ltd manufactures and distributes electrical and telecommunications accessories, household durables (eg sink and shower units) and building systems (eg air-conditioning, solar heating, security systems). The company has undergone several business restructurings in recent years. Finance is to be sought from both a bank and a venture capitalist in order to implement the board's latest restructuring proposals.

You are a Helen Heller, a manager in Hal Falcon, a firm of Chartered Certified Accountants. Jennifer Jones, a partner in Hal Falcon, has just sent you the following email.

To:	Helen Heller <Hel@halfalcon.com>
From:	Jennifer Jones <Jennie@halfalcon.com>
Date:	December
Subject:	Imperiol Ltd

Helen

We have been approached by Paulo Gandalf, the chief finance officer of Imperiol, to provide a report on the company's business plan for the year to 31 December 20Y0. From a brief telephone conversation with Paulo Gandalf, I have ascertained that the proposed restructuring will involve discontinuing all operations except for building systems, where the greatest opportunity for increasing product innovation is believed to lie. Imperiol's strategy is to become the market leader in providing 'total building system solutions' using new fibre optic technology to link building systems. A major benefit of the restructuring is expected to be a lower on-going cost base. As part of the restructuring it is likely that certain of the accounting functions, including internal audit, will be outsourced.

We have obtained a copy of Imperiol's Interim Report for the six months to 30 June 20X9 on which the company's auditors, Discorpio, provide a conclusion giving negative assurance. I have attached to this email an extract of information from the Interim Financial Report.

I am going to be meeting with Paulo next week, and would like you to prepare some briefing notes for me to use at the meeting, in which you:

(a) Explain what is meant by prospective financial information, distinguishing between forecasts and projections. Comment briefly on the level of assurance provided on engagements to review prospective financial information.

(b) Explain the matters Hal Falcon should consider before accepting the engagement to report on Imperiol Ltd's prospective financial information

(c) Describe the procedures that a professional accountant should undertake in order to provide a report on a profit forecast and forecast Statement of financial position for Imperiol Ltd for the year to 31 December 20X9

Regards,

Jennifer Jones

1 Chairman's statement

The economic climate is less certain than it was a few months ago and performance has been affected by a severe decline in the electrical accessories market. Management's response will be to gain market share and reduce the cost base.

2 Statement of financial position

	30 June 20X9 (unaudited) £m	31 December 20X8 £m
Intangible assets	83.5	72.6
Tangible non-current assets	69.6	63.8
Inventory	25.2	20.8
Receivables	59.9	50.2
Cash	8.3	23.8
Total assets	246.5	231.2
Issued capital	30.4	30.4
Reserves	6.0	9.1
Retained earnings	89.1	89.0
Interest bearing borrowings	65.4	45.7
Current liabilities	55.6	57.0
Total equity and borrowings	246.5	231.2

3 Continuing and discontinued operations

	Six months to 30 June 20X9 (unaudited) £m	Year to 31 December 20X8 £m
Revenue		
Continuing operations		
Electrical and telecommunication accessories	55.3	118.9
Household durables	37.9	77.0
Building systems	53.7	94.9
Total continuing	146.9	290.8
Discontinued	–	65.3
Total revenue	146.9	356.1
Operating profit before interest and taxation –		
Continuing operations	13.4	32.2

Required

Respond to the partner's email. **(28 marks)**

Professional marks are available for the format and clarity of answers. **(4 marks)**

Note. Assume it is 11 December 20X9. **(Total = 32 marks)**

22 Juliet (6/10)

36 mins

(a) Auditors should accept some of the blame when a company on which they have expressed an unmodified audit opinion subsequently fails, and they should also do more to highlight going concern problems being faced by a company.

Required

Discuss this statement.   **(8 marks)**

(b) You are the manager responsible for the audit of Juliet Ltd, and you are planning the final audit of the financial statements for the year ending 30 June 20X0. Juliet Ltd is a supplier of components used in the manufacture of vehicle engines. Due to a downturn in the economy, and in the automotive industry particularly, the company has suffered a decline in sales and profitability over the last two years, mainly due to the loss of several key customer contracts. Many of Juliet Ltd's non-current assets are impaired in value, and a significant number of receivables balances have been written off in the last six months.

In response to the deteriorating market conditions, the management of Juliet Ltd decided to restructure the business. The main manufacturing facility will be reduced in size by two-thirds, and investment will be made in new technology to make the remaining operations more efficient, and to enable the manufacture of a wider variety of components for use in different types of engines and machinery. In order to fund this restructuring, the management of Juliet Ltd approached the company's bank with a request for a significant loan. You are aware that without the loan, Juliet Ltd is unlikely to be able to restructure successfully, which will raise significant doubt over its ability to continue as a going concern.

Your firm has been asked to advise on the necessary forecasts and projections that the bank will need to see in order to make a decision regarding the finance requested. Management has also requested that your firm attend a meeting with the bank at which the forecasts will be discussed.

Required

(i) Identify and explain the matters that should be considered, and the principal audit procedures to be performed in respect of the additional funding being sought.   **(6 marks)**

(ii) Comment on the ethical and other implications of the request for your firm to provide advice on the forecasts and projections, and to attend the meeting with the bank.   **(6 marks)**

(Total = 20 marks)

23 Apricot (12/09)

29 mins

Your audit client, Apricot Ltd, is intending to purchase a new warehouse at a cost of £500,000. One of the directors of the company, Pik Choi, has agreed to make the necessary finance available through a director's loan to the company. This arrangement has been approved by the other directors, and the cash will be provided on 30 March 20X0, one day before the purchase is due to be completed. Pik's financial advisor has asked to see a cash flow projection of Apricot Ltd for the next three months. Your firm has been asked to provide an assurance report to Pik's financial advisor on this prospective financial information.

The cash flow forecast is shown below.

	January 20X0 £'000	February 20X0 £'000	March 20X0 £'000
Operating cash receipts:			
Cash sales	125	135	140
Receipts from credit sales	580	600	625
Operating cash payments:			
Purchases of inventory	(410)	(425)	(425)
Salaries	(100)	(100)	(100)
Overheads	(175)	(175)	(175)
Other cash flows:			
Dividend payment		(80)	
Purchase of new licence	(35)		
Fixtures for new warehouse			(60)
Loan receipt			500
Payment for warehouse			(500)
Cash flow for the month	(15)	(45)	5
Opening cash	100	85	40
Closing cash	85	40	45

The following information is relevant:

1. Apricot Ltd is a wholesaler of catering equipment and frozen food. Its customers are mostly restaurant chains and fast food outlets.

2. Customers who pay in cash receive a 10% discount. Analysis has been provided showing that for sales made on credit, 20% of customers pay in the month of the sale, 60% pay after 45 days, 10% after 65 days, 5% after 90 days, and the remainder are bad debts.

3. Apricot Ltd pays for all purchases within 30 days in order to take advantage of a 12% discount from suppliers.

4. Overheads are mainly property rentals, utility bills, insurance premiums and general office expenses.

5. Apricot Ltd needs to have a health and safety licence as it sells food. Each licence is valid for one year and is issued once an inspection has taken place.

6. A profit forecast has also been prepared for the year ending 31 December 20X0 to help with internal planning and budgeting.

This is the first time that Apricot Ltd has requested an assurance report, and the directors are unsure about the contents of the report that your firm will issue. They understand that it is similar in format to an audit report, but that the specific contents are not the same.

Required

(a) Recommend the procedures that should be performed on the cash flow forecast for the three months ending 31 March 20X0 in order to provide an assurance report as requested by Apricot Ltd.   **(11 marks)**

(b) Explain the main contents of the report that will be issued on the prospective financial information.
          (5 marks)

          (Total = 16 marks)

24 Poppy (12/08)

36 mins

(a) Financial statements often contain material balances recognised at fair value. For auditors, this leads to additional audit risk.

Required

Discuss this statement. **(7 marks)**

(b) You are the manager responsible for the audit of Poppy Ltd, a manufacturing company with a year ended 31 October 20X8. In the last year, several investment properties have been purchased to utilise surplus funds and to provide rental income. The properties have been revalued at the year end in accordance with IAS 40 *Investment Property* they are recognised on the statement of financial position at a fair value of £8 million, and the total assets of Poppy Ltd are £160 million at 31 October 20X8. An external valuer has been used by management to provide the fair value for each property.

Required

(i) Recommend the enquiries to be made in respect of the external valuer, before placing any reliance on their work, and explain the reason for the enquiries. **(7 marks)**

(ii) Identify and explain the principal audit procedures to be performed on the valuation of the investment properties. **(6 marks)**

(Total = 20 marks)

25 Magpie (6/12)

67 mins

You are a manager in Magpie & Co, responsible for the audit of the CS Group. An extract from the permanent audit file describing the CS Group's history and operations is shown below:

Permanent file (extract)

Crow Ltd was incorporated 100 years ago. It was founded by Joseph Crow, who established a small pottery making tableware such as dishes, plates and cups. The products quickly grew popular, with one range of products becoming highly sought after when it was used at a royal wedding. The company's products have retained their popularity over the decades, and the Crow brand enjoys a strong identity and good market share.

Ten years ago, Crow Ltd made its first acquisition by purchasing 100% of the share capital of Starling Ltd. Both companies benefited from the newly formed CS Group, as Starling Ltd itself had a strong brand name in the pottery market. The CS Group has a history of steady profitability and stable management.

Crow Ltd and Starling Ltd have a financial year ending 31 July 20X2, and your firm has audited both companies for several years.

(a) You have received an email from Jo Daw, the audit engagement partner:

To:	Audit manager
From:	Jo Daw
Regarding:	CS Group audit planning

Hello

I have just been to a meeting with Steve Eagle, the finance director of the CS Group. We were discussing recent events which will have a bearing on our forthcoming audit, and my notes from the meeting are attached to this email. One of the issues discussed is the change in group structure due to the acquisition of Canary Ltd earlier this year. Our firm has been appointed as auditor of Canary Ltd, which has a year ending 30 June 20X2, and the terms of the engagement have been agreed with the client. We need to start planning the audits of the three components of the Group, and of the consolidated financial statements.

Using the attached information, you are required to:

(i) Identify and explain the implications of the acquisition of Canary Ltd for the audit planning of the individual and consolidated financial statements of the CS Group

(ii) Evaluate the risks of material misstatement to be considered in the audit planning of the individual and consolidated financial statements of the CS Group, identifying any matters that are not relevant to the audit planning

(iii) Recommend the principal audit procedures to be performed in respect of the goodwill initially recognised on the acquisition of Canary Ltd.

Thank you.

Attachment: Notes from meeting with Steve Eagle, finance director of the CS Group

Acquisition of Canary Ltd

The most significant event for the CS Group this year was the acquisition of Canary Ltd, which took place on 1 February 20X2. Crow Ltd purchased all of Canary Ltd's equity shares for cash consideration of £125 million, and further contingent consideration of £30 million will be paid on the third anniversary of the acquisition, if the Group's revenue grows by at least 8% per annum. Crow Ltd engaged an external provider to perform due diligence on Canary Ltd, whose report indicated that the fair value of Canary Ltd's net assets was estimated to be £110 million at the date of acquisition. Goodwill arising on the acquisition has been calculated as follows.

	£m
Fair value of consideration:	
Cash consideration	125
Contingent consideration	30
	155
Less fair value of identifiable net assets acquired	(110)
Goodwill	45

To help finance the acquisition, Crow Ltd issued loan stock at par on 31 January 20X2, raising cash of £100 million. The loan has a five-year term, and will be repaid at a premium of £20 million. 5% interest is payable annually in arrears. It is Group accounting policy to recognise financial liabilities at amortised cost.

Canary Ltd manufactures pottery figurines and ornaments. The company is considered a good strategic fit to the Group, as its products are luxury items like those of Crow Ltd and Starling Ltd, and its acquisition will enable the Group to diversify into a different market. Approximately 30% of its sales are made online, and it is hoped that online sales can soon be introduced for the rest of the Group's products. Canary Ltd has only ever operated as a single company, so this is the first year that it is part of a group of companies.

Financial performance and position

The Group has performed well this year, with forecast consolidated revenue for the year to 31 July 20X2 of £135 million (20X1 – £125 million), and profit before tax of £8.5 million (20X1 – £8.4 million). A breakdown of the Group's forecast revenue and profit is shown below.

	Crow Ltd	Starling Ltd	Canary Ltd	CS Group
	£m	£m	£m	£m
Revenue	69	50	16	135
Profit before tax	3.5	3	2	8.5

Note. Canary Ltd's results have been included from 1 February 20X2 (date of acquisition), and forecast up to 31 July 20X2, the CS Group's financial year end.

The forecast consolidated statement of financial position at 31 July 20X2 recognises total assets of £550 million.

Other matters

Starling Ltd received a grant of £35 million on 1 March 20X2 in relation to redevelopment of its main manufacturing site. The government is providing grants to companies for capital expenditure on environmentally friendly assets. Starling Ltd has spent £25 million of the amount received on solar panels which generate electricity, and intends to spend the remaining £10 million on upgrading its production and packaging lines.

During the year to 31 July 20X2 it was discovered that an error had been made by a member of Crow Co's finance department which had resulted in the overstatement of deferred revenue by £10,000 in the prior period. A thorough investigation of the causes of the error was conducted, which concluded that the error was isolated.

On 1 January 20X2, a new IT system was introduced to Crow Ltd and Starling Ltd, with the aim of improving financial reporting controls and to standardise processes across the two companies. Unfortunately, Starling Ltd's finance director left the company last week.

Required

Respond to the email from the partner. **(31 marks)**

(b) Magpie & Co's ethics partner, Robin Finch, leaves a note on your desk:

'I have just had a conversation with Steve Eagle concerning the CS Group. He would like the audit engagement partner to attend the CS Group's board meetings on a monthly basis so that our firm can be made aware of any issues relating to the audit as soon as possible. Also, Steve asked if one of our audit managers could be seconded to Starling Ltd in temporary replacement of its finance director who recently left, and asked for our help in recruiting a permanent replacement. Please provide me with a response to Steve which evaluates the ethical implications of his requests.'

Required

Respond to the note from the partner. **(6 marks)**
(Total = 37 marks)

26 Beech (12/11)   32 mins

You are a manager in the audit department of Beech & Co, responsible for the audits of Fir Ltd, Spruce Ltd and Pine Ltd. Each company has a financial year ended 31 July 20X1, and the audits of all companies are nearing completion. The following issues have arisen in relation to the audit of accounting estimates and fair values.

(a) **Fir Ltd**

Fir Ltd is a company involved in energy production. It owns several nuclear power stations, which have a remaining estimated useful life of 20 years. Fir Ltd intends to decommission the power stations at the end of their useful life and the statement of financial position at 31 July 20X1 recognises a material provision in respect of decommissioning costs of £97 million (20X0 – £110 million). A brief note to the financial statements discloses the opening and closing value of the provision but no other information is provided.

Required

Comment on the matters that should be considered, and explain the audit evidence you should expect to find in your file review in respect of the decommissioning provision. **(8 marks)**

(b) **Spruce Ltd**

Spruce Ltd is also involved in energy production. It has a trading division which manages a portfolio of complex financial instruments such as derivatives. The portfolio is material to the financial statements. Due to the specialist nature of these financial instruments, an auditor's expert was engaged to assist in obtaining sufficient appropriate audit evidence relating to the fair value of the financial instruments. The objectivity, capabilities and competence of the expert were confirmed prior to their engagement.

Required

Explain the procedures that should be performed in evaluating the adequacy of the auditor's expert's work. **(5 marks)**

(c)   **Pine Ltd**

Pine Ltd operates a warehousing and distribution service, and owns 120 properties. During the year ended 31 July 20X1, management changed its estimate of the useful life of all properties, extending the life on average by ten years. The financial statements contain a retrospective adjustment, which increases opening non-current assets and equity by a material amount. Information in respect of the change in estimate has not been disclosed in the notes to the financial statements.

Required

Identify and explain the potential implications for the auditor's report of the accounting treatment of the change in accounting estimates. **(5 marks)**

(Total = 18 marks)

27 Setter (6/13) 36 mins

You are the manager responsible for the audit of Setter Stores Ltd, a company which operates supermarkets across the country. The final audit for the year ended 31 January 20X3 is nearing completion and you are reviewing the audit working papers. The draft financial statements recognise total assets of £300 million, revenue of £620 million and profit before tax of £47.5 million.

Three issues from the audit working papers are summarised below.

(a)   **Assets held for sale**

Setter Stores Ltd owns a number of properties which have been classified as assets held for sale in the statement of financial position. The notes to the financial statements state that the properties are all due to be sold within one year. On classification as held for sale, in October 20X2, the properties were re-measured from carrying value of £26 million to fair value less cost to sell of £24 million, which is the amount recognised in the statement of financial position at the year end. **(8 marks)**

(b)   **Sale and leaseback arrangement**

A sale and leaseback arrangement involving a large property complex was entered into on 31 January 20X3. The property complex is a large warehousing facility, which was sold for £37 million, its fair value at the date of the disposal. The facility had a carrying value at that date of £27 million. The only accounting entry recognised in respect of the proceeds raised was to record the cash received and recognise a non-current liability classified as 'Obligations under finance lease'. The lease term is for 20 years, the same as the remaining useful life of the property complex, and Setter Stores Ltd retains the risks and rewards associated with the asset. **(7 marks)**

(c)   **Distribution licence**

The statement of financial position includes an intangible asset of £15 million, which is the cost of a distribution licence acquired on 1 September 20X2. The licence gives Setter Stores Ltd the exclusive right to distribute a popular branded soft drink in its stores for a period of five years. **(5 marks)**

Required

Comment on the matters to be considered, and explain the audit evidence you should expect to find during your file review in respect of each of the issues described above.

Note. The split of the mark allocation is shown against each of the issues above.

(Total = 20 marks)

28 Lamont (AAS 6/07) 36 mins

You are the manager responsible for the audit of Lamont Co. The company's principal activity is wholesaling frozen fish. The draft consolidated financial statements for the year ended 31 March 20X8 show revenue of £67.0 million (20X7 – £62.3 million), profit before taxation of £11.9 million (20X7 – £14.2 million) and total assets of £48.0 million (20X7 – £36.4 million).

The following issues arising during the final audit have been noted on a schedule of points for your attention.

(a)   In early 20X8 a chemical leakage from refrigeration units owned by Lamont caused contamination of some of its property. Lamont has incurred £0.3 million in clean up costs, £0.6 million in modernisation of the units to prevent future leakage and a £30,000 fine to a regulatory agency. Apart from the fine, which has been expensed, these costs have been capitalised as improvements.   **(7 marks)**

(b)   While the refrigeration units were undergoing modernisation Lamont outsourced all its cold storage requirements to Hogg Warehousing Services. At 31 March 20X8 it was not possible to physically inspect Lamont's inventory held by Hogg due to health and safety requirements preventing unauthorised access to cold storage areas. Lamont's management has provided written representation that inventory held at 31 March 20X8 was £10.1 million (20X7 – £6.7 million). This amount has been agreed to a costing of Hogg's monthly return of quantities held at 31 March 20X8.   **(7 marks)**

(c)   Lamont owns a residential apartment above its head office. Until 31 December 20X7 it was let for £3,000 a month. Since 1 January 20X8 it has been occupied rent-free by the senior sales executive.   **(6 marks)**

Required

In undertaking your review of the audit working papers and financial statements of Lamont Co for the year ended 31 March 20X8, for each of the above issues:

(i)   Comment on the matters that you should consider; and

(ii)   State the audit evidence that you should expect to find.

Note. The mark allocation is shown against each of the three issues.   **(Total = 20 marks)**

29 Papaya (12/09)   65 mins

(a)   ISA 520 (UK and Ireland) *Analytical procedures* requires that the auditor performs analytical procedures during the initial risk assessment stage of the audit. These procedures, also known as preliminary analytical review, are usually performed before the year end, as part of the planning of the final audit.

Required

(i)   Explain, using examples, the reasons for performing analytical procedures as part of risk assessment.

(ii)   Discuss the limitations of performing analytical procedures at the planning stage of the final audit.
     (6 marks)

(b)   Explain and differentiate between the terms 'overall audit strategy' and 'audit plan'.   **(4 marks)**

You are the manager responsible for the audit of Papaya plc, a listed company, which operates a chain of supermarkets, with a year ending 31 December 20X9. There are three business segments operated by the company – two segments are supermarket chains which operate under internally generated brand names, and the third segment is a new financial services division.

The first business segment comprises stores branded as 'Papaya Mart'. This segment makes up three quarters of the supermarkets of the company, and are large 'out of town' stores, located on retail parks on the edge of towns and cities. These stores sell a wide variety of items, including food and drink, clothing, household goods, and electrical appliances. In September 20X9, the first overseas Papaya Mart opened in Farland. This expansion was a huge drain on cash resources, as it involved significant capital expenditure, as well as an expensive advertising campaign to introduce the Papaya Mart brand in Farland.

The second business segment comprises the rest of the supermarkets, which are much smaller stores, located in city centres, and branded as 'Papaya Express'. The Express stores offer a reduced range of products, focusing on food and drink, especially ready meals and other convenience items.

The company also established a financial services division on 1 January 20X9, which offers loans, insurance services and credit cards to customers.

The following information was provided during a recent meeting held with the finance director of Papaya plc. All of the matters outlined in the notes below are potentially material to the financial statements.

Notes from meeting held 29 November 20X9

On 31 August 20X9, Papaya plc received notice from a government body that it is under investigation, along with three other companies operating supermarket chains, for alleged collusion and price fixing activities. If it is found guilty, significant financial penalties will be imposed on Papaya plc. The company is vigorously defending its case.

To help cash flows in a year of expansion, the company raised finance by issuing debentures which are potentially convertible into equity on maturity in 20Y5.

To manage the risk associated with overseas expansion, in October 20X9, the company entered for the first time into several forward exchange contracts which end in February 20Y0. The contracts were acquired at no cost to Papaya plc and are categorised as financial assets at fair value.

The property market has slumped this year, and significant losses were made on the sale of some plots of land which were originally acquired for development potential. The decision to sell the land was made as it is becoming increasingly difficult for the company to receive planning permission to build supermarkets on the land. Land is recognised at cost in the statement of financial position.

Papaya plc has 35 warehouses which store non-perishable items of inventory. Due to new regulation, each warehouse is required to undergo a major health and safety inspection every three years. All warehouses were inspected in January 20X9, at a cost of £25,000 for each inspection.

Required

Using the specific information provided in respect of Papaya plc:

(c)   Explain the information that you would require in order to perform analytical procedures during the planning of the audit. **(6 marks)**

(d)   Assess the financial statements risks to be addressed when planning the final audit for the year ending 31 December 20X9, producing your answer in the form of briefing notes to be used at the audit planning meeting. **(16 marks)**

Professional marks will be awarded in part (d) for the format of the answer, and for the clarity of assessment provided. **(4 marks)**

(Total = 36 marks)

30 Bill (6/11) (amended)   71 mins

(a)   You are a senior audit manager in Suki & Co, a firm of Chartered Certified Accountants. This morning you have been re-assigned to the audit of Bill Ltd, a long-standing audit client of your firm, as the manager previously assigned to the client has been taken ill. Bill Ltd has a year ending 30 June 20X1, and the audit planning has been largely completed by the previously assigned audit manager, Tara Lafayette, who had been recruited by your firm four months ago.

Bill Ltd is a property development company, specialising in the regeneration and refurbishment of old industrial buildings, which are sold for commercial or residential use. All property developments are performed under specifically negotiated fixed-price contracts. The company was founded 35 years ago by two brothers, Alex and Ben Bradley, who own the majority of the company's share capital. Alex and Ben are nearing retirement age, and are planning to sell the company within the next two years. The forecast revenue for the year ending 30 June 20X1 is £10.8 million, and the forecast profit before tax is £2.5 million. The forecast statement of financial position recognises total assets of £95 million.

You have just received the following email from the audit engagement partner.

Hello,

Thanks for taking on the role of audit manager for the forthcoming audit of Bill Ltd.

(i) I have just received some information on two significant issues that have arisen over the last week, from Sam Compton, the company's finance director. This information is provided in Attachment 1.

I am asking you to prepare briefing notes, for my use, in which you explain the matters that should be considered in relation to the treatment of these two issues in the financial statements, and also explain the risks of material misstatement relating to them. I also want you to recommend the planned audit procedures that should be performed in order to address those risks.

(ii) In addition, please critically evaluate the planning that has been completed by the previously assigned audit manager. Relevant details are provided in Attachment 2, which contains notes made by her, and placed on the current year audit file. Make sure you include discussion of any ethical matters arising from the notes, and recommend any actions you think necessary.

Thanks.

Attachment 1: Information from Sam Compton, finance director of Bill Ltd

In the last week, two significant issues have arisen at Bill Ltd. The first issue concerns a major contract involving the development of an old riverside warehouse into a conference centre in Bridgetown. An architect working on the development has discovered that the property will need significant additional structural improvements, the extra cost of which is estimated to be £350,000. The contract was originally forecast to make a profit of £200,000. The development is currently about one third complete, and will take a further 15 months to finish, including this additional construction work. The customer has been told that the completion of the contract will be delayed by around two months. However, the contract price is fixed, and so the additional costs must be covered by Bill Ltd.

The second issue concerns a property held under a ten-year operating lease. The property is a large warehousing facility, where Bill Ltd until recently stored equipment and inventory such as bricks and cement. Bill Ltd has purchased a new warehouse to store these items, so the leased facility is currently unused. A board minute dated 1 June 20X1 states 'the operating lease has eight years left to run and it cannot be cancelled without incurring a significant penalty. We are considering sub-letting the leased facility, but have been advised that the market rent that we could charge is considerably less than the rental payments that we are making under the lease.'

Attachment 2: Planning Summary – Bill Ltd, year ending 30 June 20X1, prepared by Tara Lafayette, manager previously assigned to the audit

The planning for the forthcoming audit is almost complete. Time has been saved by not carrying out procedures considered unnecessary for this long-standing audit client. Forecast accounts have been obtained and placed on file, and discussions held with management concerning business developments during the year. Analytical procedures have been performed on the statement of profit or loss and other comprehensive income, but not on the statement of financial position, as there did not appear to be any significant movements in assets or liabilities since last year.

Management confirmed that there have been no changes to accounting systems and controls in the financial year. For this reason we do not need to carry out walk-through tests or review our documentation of the systems and controls.

Management also confirmed that there have been no changes to business operations. All divisions are operating normally, generating sufficient profit and cash. For this reason, the business risk of Bill Ltd is assessed as low, and no further comments or discussions about business operations have been placed on file.

The matter that will demand the most audit work is the valuation of properties currently under development, especially the determination of the percentage completion of each development at the reporting date. Historically, we have engaged a property valuation expert to provide a report on this area. However, Bill Ltd has recently employed a newly qualified architect, who will be happy to provide us with evidence concerning the stage of completion of each property development contract at the year end. Using this person to produce a report on all properties being developed will save time and costs.

Bill Ltd has recently completed the development of a luxury new office building in Newtown. Several of the office units are empty, and the management of Bill Ltd has offered the office space to our firm for a nominal rent of £100 per year.

Required

Respond to the partner's email. **(27 marks)**

Note. The split of the mark allocation is shown within the partner's email.

Professional marks will be awarded for the format and clarity of your response. **(4 marks)**

(b) Ben and Alex Bradley have a sister, Jo, who runs an interior design company, Lantern Ltd. During a review of board minutes, performed as part of the planning of Bill Ltd's audit, it was discovered that Bill Ltd has paid £225,000 to Lantern Ltd during the year, in respect of refurbishment of development properties. On further enquiry, it was also found that Lantern Ltd leases an office space from Bill Ltd, under an informal arrangement between the two companies.

Required

(i) Explain the inherent limitations which mean that auditors may not identify related parties and related party transactions. **(4 marks)**

(ii) Recommend the audit procedures to be performed in relation to Bill Ltd's transactions with Lantern Ltd. **(4 marks)**

Note. Assume it is 7 June 20X1. **(Total = 39 marks)**

31 Mulligan (12/07) 36 mins

You are an audit manager in Webb & Co, a firm of Chartered Certified Accountants. Your audit client, Mulligan Ltd, designs and manufactures wooden tables and chairs. The business has expanded rapidly in the last two years, since the arrival of Patrick Tiler, an experienced sales and marketing manager.

The directors want to secure a loan of £3 million in order to expand operations, following the design of a completely new range of wooden garden furniture. The directors have approached LCT Bank for the loan. The bank's lending criteria stipulate the following.

'Loan applications must be accompanied by a detailed business plan, including an analysis of how the finance will be used. LCT Bank need to see that the finance requested is adequate for the proposed business purpose. The business plan must be supported by an assurance opinion on the adequacy of the requested finance.'

The £3 million finance raised will be used as follows.

	£'000
Construction of new factory	1,250
Purchase of new machinery	1,000
Initial supply of timber raw material	250
Advertising and marketing of new product	500

Your firm has agreed to review the business plan and to provide an assurance opinion on the completeness of the finance request. A meeting will be held tomorrow to discuss this assignment.

(a) Identify and explain the matters relating to the assurance assignment that should be discussed at the meeting with Mulligan Ltd. **(8 marks)**

(b) State the enquiries you would make of the directors of Mulligan Ltd to ascertain the adequacy of the £3 million finance requested for the new production facility. **(7 marks)**

(c) During the year the internal auditor of Mulligan Ltd discovered several discrepancies in the inventory records. In a statement made to the board of directors, the internal auditor said:

'I think that someone is taking items from the warehouse. A physical inventory count is performed every three months, and it has become apparent that about 200 boxes of flat-packed chairs and tables are disappearing from the warehouse every month. We should get someone to investigate what has happened and quantify the value of the loss.'

Required

Define 'forensic accounting' and explain its relevance to the statement made by the internal auditor.

(5 marks)

(Total = 20 marks)

32 Parker (6/13)　　　　　　　　　　　　　　　　　　　　　　63 mins

You are an audit manager in Hound & Co, responsible for the audit of Parker Ltd, a new audit client of your firm. You are planning the audit of Parker Ltd's financial statements for the year ending 30 June 20X3, and you have just attended a meeting with Ruth Collie, the finance director of Parker Ltd, where she gave you the projected results for the year. Parker Ltd designs and manufactures health and beauty products including cosmetics.

Parker Ltd was incorporated 20 years ago and was founded by Peter Parker and his sister Polly, who retain a controlling interest in the company. The company's manufacturing base is in the Midlands and it employs 4,000 people, approximately half of these at the main factory and distribution centre. Parker Ltd sells its products to supermarkets and high street retailers and aims to establish an internet-based revenue stream within the next two years.

The previous audit firm, Muzzle & Co, resigned last year. The resignation was prompted by the closure of Muzzle & Co's office in the Midlands and the retirement of the partner responsible for the audit of Parker Ltd. Peter and Polly did not want to liaise with a new partner in a distant location, and approached Hound & Co to tender for the audit due to the proximity of its large audit department to Parker Ltd's head office in the Midlands.

You have just received an email from Harry Shepherd, the audit engagement partner:

To:	Audit manager
From:	Harry Shepherd, Partner
Subject:	Parker Ltd

Hello,

I understand you met with Ruth Collie at Parker Ltd recently and that you are planning the forthcoming audit. To bring me up to date on this new client, I would like you to use the information obtained in your meeting to prepare briefing notes for my use in which you evaluate the audit risks to be considered in planning the audit of the financial statements. You should also identify further information that would help to perform the assessment of audit risk. In your briefing notes you should also discuss any ethical or professional issues raised, and recommend the relevant actions to be taken by our firm.

Thank you.

Parker Ltd – Statement of profit or loss and other comprehensive income

	Notes	30 June 20X3 Projected	30 June 20X2 Actual
		£'000	£'000
Revenue		7,800	8,500
Cost of sales	1	(5,680)	(5,800)
Gross profit		2,120	2,700
Operating expenses		(1,230)	(1,378)
Operating profit		890	1,322
Finance costs		(155)	(125)
Profit before tax		735	1,197
Taxation		(70)	(300)
Profit for the year		665	897

Note 1. Cost of sales includes £250,000 relating to a provision for a potential fine payable. The advertising regulatory authority has issued a notice of a £450,000 fine payable by Parker Ltd due to alleged inappropriate claims made in an advertising campaign. The fine is being disputed and the matter should be resolved in August 20X3.

Parker Ltd – Statement of financial position

	Notes	30 June 20X3 Projected £'000	30 June 20X2 Actual £'000
Non-current assets			
Property, plant and equipment		21,500	19,400
Intangible asset – development costs	2	2,250	–
		23,750	19,400
Current assets			
Inventory		2,600	2,165
Trade receivables		900	800
Cash		–	1,000
		3,500	3,965
Total assets		27,250	23,365
Equity		8,000	8,000
Share capital		2,500	2,000
Revaluation reserve	3	1,275	1,455
Retained earnings		11,775	11,455
Non-current liabilities			
2% preference shares		3,125	3,125
Bank loan		3,800	2,600
Obligations under finance leases		4,900	4,000
		11,825	9,725
Current liabilities			
Trade payables		1,340	1,000
Taxation		50	300
Obligations under finance leases		860	685
Provisions		500	200
Overdraft		900	–
		3,650	2,185
		27,250	23,365

Notes

2   The development costs relate to a new range of organic cosmetics.

3   All of the company's properties were revalued on 1 January 20X3 by an independent, professionally qualified expert.

Notes from your meeting with Ruth Collie

Business review

Parker Ltd is facing difficult trading conditions. Consumer spending is depressed due to recession in the economy. The health and beauty market remains very competitive and a major competitor launched a very successful new cosmetics range during the year, which led to a significant decline in sales of one of Parker Ltd's most successful brands. It has been necessary to cut prices on some of the company's product ranges in an attempt to maintain market share. However, a new brand using organic ingredients is being developed and is due to launch in September 20X3.

Financial matters

Cash flow has been a problem this year, largely due to the cash spent on developing the new product range. Cash was also needed to pay dividends to both equity and preference shareholders. To help to reduce cash outflows, some new assets were acquired under finance leases and an extension to the company's bank loan was negotiated in December 20X2.

Human resources

In December 20X2 Parker Ltd's internal audit team performed a review of the operation of controls over the processing of overtime payments in the human resources department. The review found that the company's specified internal controls procedures in relation to the processing of overtime payments and associated tax payments were not always being followed. Until December 20X2 this processing was split between the human resources and finance departments. Since then, the processing has been entirely carried out by the finance department.

Expansion plans

Management is planning to expand Parker Ltd's operations into a new market relating to beauty salons. This is a growing market, and there is synergy because Parker Ltd's products can be sold and used in the salons. Expansion would be through the acquisition of an existing company which operates beauty salons. A potential target, Beauty Boost Ltd, has been identified and preliminary discussions have taken place between the management of the two companies. Parker Ltd's managing director has asked for our firm's advice about the potential acquisition, and specifically regarding the financing of the transaction. Beauty Boost Ltd is an audit client of our firm, so we have considerable knowledge of its business.

New plant and equipment

Management is considering installing new plant and equipment into the factory in 2014, depending on the success of the new organic cosmetics range, at a potential cost of £200,000. There is potential for the assets to be leased if cash is not available for the capital expenditure.

Required

Respond to the email from the audit partner.   **(31 marks)**

Professional marks will be awarded for the presentation, logical flow and clarity of explanation of the briefing notes.
(4 marks)

(Total = 35 marks)

33 Lapwing (6/12)

59 mins

(a) You are a manager in Lapwing & Co. One of your audit clients is Hawk Ltd which operates commercial real estate properties typically comprising several floors of retail units and leisure facilities such as cinemas and health clubs, which are rented out to provide rental income.

Your firm has just been approached to provide an additional engagement for Hawk Ltd, to review and provide a report on the company's business plan, including forecast financial statements for the 12-month period to 31 May 20X3. Hawk Ltd is in the process of negotiating a new bank loan of £30 million and the report on the business plan is at the request of the bank. It is anticipated that the loan would be advanced in August 20X2 and would carry an interest rate of 4%. The report would be provided by your firm's business advisory department and a second partner review will be conducted which will reduce any threat to objectivity to an acceptable level.

Extracts from the forecast financial statements included in the business plan are given below:

Statement of profit or loss (extract)

	Notes	FORECAST 12 months to 31 May 20X3 £'000	UNAUDITED 12 months to 31 May 20X2 £'000
Revenue		25,000	20,600
Operating expenses		(16,550)	(14,420)
Operating profit		8,450	6,180
Profit on disposal of Beak Retail	1	4,720	–
Finance costs		(2,650)	(1,690)
Profit before tax		10,520	4,490

Statement of financial position

	Notes	FORECAST 31 May 20X3 £'000	UNAUDITED 31 May 20X2 £'000
Assets			
Non-current assets			
Property, plant and equipment	2	330,150	293,000
Current assets			
Inventory		500	450
Receivables		3,600	3,300
Cash and cash equivalents		2,250	3,750
		6,350	7,500
Total assets		336,500	300,500
Equity and liabilities			
Equity			
Share capital		105,000	100,000
Retained earnings		93,400	92,600
Total equity		198,400	192,600
Non-current liabilities			
Long-term borrowings	2	82,500	52,500
Deferred tax		50,000	50,000
Current liabilities			
Trade payables		5,600	5,400
Total liabilities		138,100	107,900
Total equity and liabilities		336,500	300,500

Notes

1   Beak Retail is a retail park which is underperforming. Its sale is currently being negotiated, and is expected to take place in September 20X2.

2   Hawk Ltd is planning to invest the cash raised from the bank loan in a new retail and leisure park which is being developed jointly with another company, Kestrel Ltd.

Required

In respect of the engagement to provide a report on Hawk Ltd's business plan:

(i)   Identify and explain the matters that should be considered in agreeing the terms of the engagement

        Note. You are **not** required to consider ethical threats to objectivity.   **(6 marks)**

(ii)   Recommend the procedures that should be performed in order to examine and report on the forecast financial statements of Hawk Ltd for the year to 31 May 20X3   **(10 marks)**

(b)   You are also responsible for the audit of Jay Ltd, a company with a year ended 30 September 20X1, in relation to which an unmodified audit report was issued in December 20X1. Jay Ltd operates two separate divisions both of which manufacture food supplements – 'Jay Sport' manufactures food supplements targeted at athletes, and 'Jay Plus' is targeted at the general public. The audit engagement partner, Bill Kingfisher, sent you the following email this morning.

To: Audit manager
From: Bill Kingfisher, audit engagement partner, Jay Ltd
Regarding: Jay Ltd – financial results

Hello,

I have just received some worrying news from the finance director of Jay Ltd. The company's latest results are not looking good – I have attached an extract from the latest management accounts for your information.

It seems that one of the key ingredients used in the 'Jay Sport' range has been found to have harmful side effects, so very few sales from that range have been made in the current financial year. The company is struggling to manage its working capital and meet interest payments on loans.

In light of all this, the directors are anxious about the future of the company, and I have been asked to attend a meeting with them tomorrow to discuss their concerns over the financial performance and position of Jay Ltd.

I am asking you to prepare briefing notes for my use in the meeting with the directors, in which you:

(i)   Examine the financial position of Jay Ltd and determine whether the company is insolvent; and
                                                                                                          (4 marks)

(ii)   Evaluate, reaching a recommendation, the options available to the directors in terms of the future of the company.   **(9 marks)**

Thank you.

Attachment: Extract from Jay Ltd's management accounts at 31 May 20X2 (unaudited)

Statement of financial position

	£'000
Property, plant and equipment	12,800
Inventory	500
Trade receivables	400
Cash	0
Total assets	**13,700**
Share capital	100
Retained earnings	(1,050)
Long-term borrowings (secured with a fixed charge over property, plant and equipment)	12,000
Trade payables (including employees wages of £300,000)	1,250
Bank overdraft	1,400
Total equity and liabilities	**13,700**

Statement of profit or loss (extract)

	Figures for the eight months to 31 May 20X2		
	'Jay Sport'	'Jay Plus'	Jay Ltd
	£'000	£'000	£'000
Revenue	50	1,450	1,500
Operating costs	(800)	(1,200)	(2,000)
Operating loss/profit	(750)	250	(500)
Finance costs			(800)
Loss before tax			**(1,300)**

Required

Respond to the partner's email.   **(13 marks)**

Note. The split of the mark allocation is shown within the partner's email.

Professional marks will be awarded in part (b) for the presentation and clarity of your answer.   **(4 marks)**

(Total = 33 marks)

34 Azure Airline (AAS 12/04)   63 mins

Azure Ltd was incorporated in Sepiana on 1 March 20X8. In April, the company exercised an exclusive right granted by the government of Pewta to provide twice weekly direct flights between Lyme, the capital of Pewta, and Darke, the capital of Sepiana.

The introduction of this service has been well advertised as 'efficient and timely' in national newspapers. The journey time between Sepiana and Pewta is expected to be significantly reduced, so encouraging tourism and business development opportunities in Sepiana.

Azure operates a refurbished 35-year old aircraft which is leased from an international airline and registered with the Pewtan Aviation Administration (the PAA). The PAA requires that engines be overhauled every two years. Engine overhauls are expected to put the aircraft out of commission for several weeks.

The aircraft is configured to carry 15 First Class, 50 Business Class and 76 Economy Class passengers. The aircraft has a generous hold capacity for Sepiana's numerous horticultural growers (eg of cocoa, tea and fruit) and general cargo.

The six hour journey offers an in-flight movie, a meal, hot and cold drinks and tax-free shopping. All meals are prepared in Lyme under a contract with an airport catering company. Passengers are invited to complete a 'satisfaction' questionnaire which is included with the in-flight entertainment and shopping guide. Responses received show that passengers are generally least satisfied with the quality of the food – especially on the Darke to Lyme flight.

Azure employs ten full-time cabin crew attendants who are trained in air-stewardship including passenger safety in the event of accident and illness. Flight personnel (the captain and co-pilots) are provided under a contract with the international airline from which the aircraft is leased. At the end of each flight the captain completes a timesheet detailing the crew and actual flight time.

Ticket sales are made by Azure and travel agents in Sepiana and Pewta. On a number of occasions Economy seating has been over-booked. Customers who have been affected by this have been accommodated in Business Class as there is much less demand for this, and even less for First Class. Ticket prices for each class depend on many factors, for example, whether the tickets are refundable/non-refundable, exchangeable/non-exchangeable, single or return, mid-week or weekend, and the time of booking.

Azure's insurance cover includes passenger liability, freight/baggage and compensation insurance. Premiums for passenger liability insurance are determined on the basis of passenger miles flown.

Required

(a)   Identify and explain the business risks facing Azure Ltd.   **(9 marks)**

(b)   Describe how the risks identified in (a) could be managed and maintained at an acceptable level by Azure.
                                                                                                               (9 marks)

(c)   Suggest four measures of operational performance and the evidence that should be available to provide assurance on their accuracy.   **(6 marks)**

Note. Assume it is 11 December 20X8.

The management of Azure is considering producing an integrated report on the company which would include a range of financial and non-financial information. A particular focus would be the company's attempts to contribute positively to its social and natural environment.

In order to add credence to the proposed report, management would like to engage a firm of professional accountants to provide an assurance report on its contents. It is worried, however, that such a report would be of little benefit to its users, and would like some clarification about the level of assurance that would be provided, and the types of conclusion that might be given.

Required

(d)   Identify and explain the assurance that might be provided by an assurance engagement on an integrated report.   **(5 marks)**

(e)   Identify the types of possible conclusion which such a report might give.   **(6 marks)**

Note. You should base your answer on the most recently available technical guidance in this area.

                                                                                                 (Total = 35 marks)

35 Island (12/07) (amended)   58 mins

You are Sanjay Patel, an audit manager at Pond & Co, a firm of Chartered Certified Accountants. Your client, Island Ltd, is a manufacturer of machinery used in the coal extraction industry. You are currently planning the audit of the financial statements for the year ended 30 November 20X8. The draft financial statements show revenue of £125 million (20X7 – £103 million), profit before tax of £5.6 million (20X7 – £5.1 million) and total assets of £95 million (20X7 – £90 million). Your firm was appointed as auditor to Island Ltd for the first time in June 20X8.

Island Ltd designs, constructs and installs machinery for five key customers. Payment is due in three installments: 50% is due when the order is confirmed (stage one), 25% on delivery of the machinery (stage two), and 25% on successful installation in the customer's coal mine (stage three). Generally it takes six months from the order being finalised until the final installation.

At 30 November, there is an amount outstanding of £2.85 million from Jacks Mine Ltd. The amount is a disputed stage three payment. Jacks Mine Ltd is refusing to pay until the machinery, which was installed in August 20X8, is running at 100% efficiency.

One customer, Sawyer Ltd, communicated in November 20X8, via its legal counsel with Island Ltd, claiming damages for injuries suffered by a drilling machine operator whose arm was severely injured when a machine malfunctioned. Kate Shannon, the chief executive officer of Island Ltd, has told you that the claim is being ignored as it is generally known that Sawyer Ltd has a poor health and safety record, and thus the accident was their fault. Two orders which were placed by Sawyer Ltd in October 20X8 have been cancelled.

Work in progress is valued at £8.5 million at 30 November 20X8. A physical inventory count was held on 17 November 20X8. The chief engineer estimated the stage of completion of each machine at that date. One of the major components included in the coal extracting machinery is now being sourced from overseas. The new supplier, Locke Ltd, is located in Spain and invoices Island Ltd in euros. There is a trade payable of £1.5 million owing to Locke Ltd recorded within current liabilities.

All machines are supplied carrying a one year warranty. A warranty provision is recognised on the statement of financial position at £2.5 million (20X7 – £2.4 million). Kate Shannon estimates the cost of repairing defective machinery reported by customers, and this estimate forms the basis of the provision.

Kate Shannon owns 60% of the shares in Island Ltd. She also owns 55% of Pacific Ltd, which leases a head office to Island Ltd. Kate is considering selling some of her shares in Island Ltd in late January 20X9, and would like the audit to be finished by that time.

You have just received the following email from Marcus Fish, the engagement partner for the Island Ltd audit.

To:	Sanjay Patel
From:	Marcus Fish
Re:	Island Ltd planning meeting

Sanjay,

Can you draft some briefing notes for me in advance of tomorrow's planning meeting for the Island audit, in which you outline and explain what you consider to be the principal audit risks, along with any other matters that we will need to consider when planning the audit.

Thanks,

Marcus

Required

(a)   Respond to the partner's email.

Requirement (a) includes four professional marks.   **(15 marks)**

(b)   Explain the principal audit procedures to be performed during the final audit in respect of the estimated warranty provision in the statement of financial position of Island Ltd as at 30 November 20X8.   **(5 marks)**

(c)   (i)   Identify and describe **four** quality control procedures that are applicable to the individual audit engagement.   **(8 marks)**

        (ii)   Discuss **two** problems that may be faced in implementing quality control procedures in a small firm of Chartered Certified Accountants, and recommend how these problems may be overcome.
                                                                                          (4 marks)

Note. You should assume that it is 4 December 20X8.   **(Total = 32 marks)**

36 Meadow (AAS 12/02)

52 mins

You are Minim Sladky, an audit manager in Robert Bracco, a firm of Chartered Certified Accountants. One of your audit clients, Meadow, is a company listed on a stock exchange with a 30 September accounting year end. The principal activity of Meadow is retailing under the Vazandt brand name. The retail industry has recently suffered from a reduction in consumer spending.

Meadow has two operating divisions: Domestic and International. Each retail division is sub-divided into four business units: Ladieswear, Menswear, Home Furnishings and Foods. The International retail business consists of three broad geographic areas: Africa, South America and the Far East. Robert Bracco is represented by affiliated offices in all relevant countries.

You have just received the following email from Maxim Gorky, the audit engagement partner.

To: Minim Sladky
From: Maxim Gorky
Regarding: Meadow audit

Hello,

I need you to start working on the planning for the Meadow audit.

Please prepare for me some briefing notes in which you identify and explain the principal audit risks and other matters to be considered when planning the approach to the final audit of Meadow for the year ended 30 September 20X8.

(17 marks)

You will need to use the information attached to this email.

Thanks,

Maxim

Email attachments

1   **Financial extracts**

	For the year ended 30 September	
	20X8 £m	20X7 £m
STATEMENT OF PROFIT OR LOSS		
Revenue	2,585.00	2,638.80
Total operating profit	129.10	120.00
Provision for loss on operations to be discontinued (Note 1)	(83.80)	–
Finance cost (net)	(4.70)	(4.80)
Profit before tax	40.60	115.20

	As at 30 September	
	20X8 £m	20X7 £m
STATEMENT OF FINANCIAL POSITION		
Tangible non-current assets		
Land and buildings	950.50	964.00
Store fit out, fixtures and equipment	448.90	481.80
Inventory (Note 2)	164.20	165.90
Trade and other receivables	22.50	36.90
Cash and cash equivalents	53.70	104.60

Notes

1   The company has announced its intention to close loss-making businesses in Africa, subject to the full consultation that the Board recognises will need to take place. The decision to close would be taken only after consultation with employee representative bodies and if no other solution is found during the consultation. Net closure costs of £83.8 million have been provided, covered future trading losses, losses on disposal of assets and redundancy costs.

2   Inventory is valued at the lower of cost and net realisable value. Cost is ascertained using the retail method (ie current selling price less normal gross profit margin).

2   **Segmental information**

	Revenue		Operating profit	
	20X8 £m	20X7 £m	20X8 £m	20X7 £m
International				
Africa	99.00	96.70	(11.80)	(9.00)
South America	264.00	250.50	11.10	5.30
Far East	38.30	38.90	2.80	(1.20)
Total International	401.30	386.10	2.10	(4.90)
Domestic	2,183.70	2,252.70	127.00	124.90
Total operating activities	2,585.00	2,638.80	129.10	120.00

	Number of stores	
	20X8	20X7
International		
Africa	14	13
South America	86	87
Far East	4	4
Total International	104	104
Domestic	107	106
Total	211	210

3   International restructure

On 29 September 20X8, the company announced the intention to:

*   Close all African operations (representing 14 stores)
*   Sell the South American businesses

Required

(a)   Respond to the partner's email.   **(17 marks)**

Professional marks will be awarded for the format and clarity of your response   **(4 marks)**

(b)   Describe the audit work that you would undertake to determine whether the accounting treatment and disclosure for the:

(i)   Segmental information
(ii)   International restructuring

are appropriate.   **(8 marks)**

Note. Assume it is 11 December 20X8.   **(Total = 29 marks)**

37 Butler (6/11) (amended)   58 mins

(a)   Butler Ltd is a new audit client of your firm. You are the manager responsible for the audit of the financial statements for the year ended 31 May 20X1. Butler Ltd designs and manufactures aircraft engines and spare parts, and is a subsidiary of a multi-national group. Extracts from the draft financial statements are shown below.

Statement of financial position

	31 May 20X1 Draft £m	31 May 20X0 Actual £m
Assets		
Non-current assets		
Intangible assets (Note 1)	200	180
Property, plant and equipment (Note 2)	1,300	1,200
Deferred tax asset (Note 3)	235	20
Financial assets	25	35
	1,760	1,435
Current assets		
Inventory	1,300	800
Trade receivables	2,100	1,860
	3,400	2,660
Total assets	5,160	4,095
Equity and liabilities		
Equity		
Share capital	300	300
Retained earnings	(525)	95
	(225)	395
Non-current liabilities		
Long-term borrowings (Note 4)	1,900	1,350
Provisions	185	150
	2,085	1,500
Current liabilities		
Short-term borrowings (Note 6)	800	400
Trade payables	2,500	1,800
	3,300	2,200
Total equity and liabilities	5,160	4,095

Notes to the statement of financial position:

1   Intangible assets comprise goodwill on the acquisition of subsidiaries (£80 million), and development costs capitalised on engine development projects (£120 million)

2   Property, plant and equipment includes land and buildings valued at £25 million, over which a fixed charge exists.

3   The deferred tax asset has arisen following several loss-making years suffered by the company. The asset represents the tax benefit of unutilised tax losses carried forward.

4   Long-term borrowings include a debenture due for repayment in July 20X2, and a loan from Butler Ltd's parent company due for repayment in December 20X2.

5   Provisions relate to warranties provided to customers.

6   Short-term borrowings comprise an overdraft (£25 million), a short term loan (£60 million) due for repayment in August 20X1, and a bank loan (£715 million) repayable in September 20X1.

You have received an email from the audit partner responsible for the audit of Butler Ltd:

To: Audit manager
From: Audit partner
Regarding: Butler Ltd – going concern issues

Hello,

I understand that the audit work on Butler Ltd commences this week. I am concerned about the future of the company, as against a background of economic recession, sales have been declining, several significant customer contracts have been cancelled unexpectedly, and competition from overseas has damaged the market share previously enjoyed by Butler Ltd.

(i) Please prepare briefing notes, for my use, in which you identify and explain any matters arising from your review of the draft statement of financial position, and the cash flow forecast, which may cast significant doubt on the company's ability to continue as a going concern. The cash flow forecast has just been sent to me from the client, and is attached. It covers only the first three months of the next financial year, the client is currently preparing the forecasts for the whole 12-month period. Please be sceptical when reviewing the forecast, as the assumptions may be optimistic.

(ii) In addition, please recommend the principal audit procedures to be carried out on the cash flow forecast, and identify any additional information that would be needed in order to carry out these procedures. Your recommendations can be included in a separate section of the briefing notes.

Thanks.

Attachment: Cash flow forecast for the three months to 31 August 20X1

	31 June 20X1 £m	31 July 20X1 £m	August 20X1 £m
Cash inflows			
Cash receipts from customers (Note 1)	175	195	220
Loan receipt (Note 2)		150	
Government subsidy (Note 3)			50
Sales of financial assets	50		
Total cash inflows	225	345	270
Cash outflows			
Operating cash outflows	200	200	290
Interest payments	40	40	40
Loan repayment			60
Total cash outflows	240	240	390
Net cash flow for the month	(15)	105	(120)
Opening cash	(25)	(40)	65
Closing cash	(40)	65	(55)

Notes to the cash flow forecast:

This cash flow forecast has been prepared by the management of Butler Ltd, and is based on the following assumptions.

1 Cash receipts from customers should accelerate given the anticipated improvement in economic conditions. In addition, the company has committed extra resources to the credit control function, in order to speed up collection of overdue debts.

2 The loan expected to be received in July 20X1 is currently being negotiated with our parent company, Rubery Ltd.

3 The government subsidy will be received once our application has been approved. The subsidy is awarded to companies which operate in areas of high unemployment and it subsidises the wages and salaries paid to staff.

Required

Respond to the email from the audit partner. **(21 marks)**

Professional marks will be awarded for presentation, and for the clarity of explanations provided. **(4 marks)**

(b) The management of Butler Ltd is concerned that given the company's poor liquidity position, the company could be placed into compulsory liquidation.

Required

(i) Explain the procedures involved in placing a company into compulsory liquidation. **(4 marks)**

(ii) Explain the consequences of a compulsory liquidation for Butler Ltd's payables (creditors), employees and shareholders. **(3 marks)**

Note. Assume it is 7 June 20X1. **(Total = 32 marks)**

38 Grohl (12/12) 72 mins

(a) You are a manager in Foo & Co, responsible for the audit of Grohl Ltd, a company which produces circuit boards which are sold to manufacturers of electrical equipment such as computers and mobile phones. It is the first time that you have managed this audit client, taking over from the previous audit manager, Bob Halen, last month.

The audit planning for the year ended 30 November 20X2 is about to commence, and you have just received an email from Mia Vai, the audit engagement partner:

To: Audit manager
From: Mia Vai, Audit partner, Foo & Co
Subject: Grohl Ltd – audit planning

Hello,

I am meeting with the other audit partners tomorrow to discuss forthcoming audits and related issues. I understand that you recently had a meeting with Mo Satriani, the finance director of Grohl Ltd. Using the information from your meeting, I would like you to prepare briefing notes for my use in which you:

(i) Evaluate the business risks faced by Grohl Ltd, and identify and explain the risks of material misstatement to be considered in planning the audit; and **(20 marks)**

(ii) Discuss any ethical issues raised and recommend the relevant actions to be taken by our firm.

(8 marks)

Thank you.

Comments made by Mo Satriani in your meeting

Business overview

Grohl Ltd's principal business activity remains the production of circuit boards. One of the key materials used in production is copper wiring, all of which is imported. As a cost cutting measure, in April 20X2 a contract with a new overseas supplier was signed, and all of the company's copper wiring is now supplied under this contract. Purchases are denominated in a foreign currency, but the company does not use forward exchange contracts in relation to its imports of copper wiring.

Grohl Ltd has two production facilities, one of which produces goods for the export market, and the other produces goods for the domestic market. About half of its goods are exported, but the export market is suffering due to competition from cheaper producers overseas. Most domestic sales are made under contract with approximately 20 customers.

Recent developments

In early November 20X2, production was halted for a week at the production facility that supplies the domestic market. A number of customers had returned goods, claiming faults in the circuit boards supplied. On inspection, it was found that the copper used in the circuit boards was corroded and therefore unsuitable for use. The corrosion is difficult to spot as it cannot be identified by eye, and relies on electrical testing. All customers were contacted immediately and, where necessary, products recalled and replaced. The corroded copper remaining in inventory has been identified and separated from the rest of the copper.

Work has recently started on a new production line which will ensure that Grohl Ltd meets new regulatory requirements prohibiting the use of certain chemicals, which come into force in March 20X3. In July 20X2, a loan of £30 million with an interest rate of 4% was negotiated with Grohl Ltd's bank, the main purpose of the loan being to fund the capital expenditure necessary for the new production line. £2.5 million of the loan represents an overdraft which was converted into long-term finance.

Other matters

Several of Grohl Ltd's executive directors and the financial controller left in October 20X2, to set up a company specialising in the recycling of old electronic equipment. This new company is not considered to be in competition with Grohl Ltd's operations. The directors left on good terms and replacements for the directors have been recruited. One of Foo & Co's audit managers, Bob Halen, is being interviewed for the role of financial controller at Grohl Ltd. Bob is a good candidate for the position, as he developed good knowledge of Grohl Ltd's business when he was managing the audit.

At Grohl Ltd's most recent board meeting, the audit fee was discussed. The board members expressed concern over the size of the audit fee, given the company's loss for the year. The board members would like to know whether the audit can be performed on a contingent fee basis.

Financial Information provided by Mo Satriani

Extract from draft statement of profit or loss and other comprehensive income for the year ended 30 November 20X2

	20X2 Draft £'000	20X1 Actual £'000
Revenue	12,500	13,800
Operating costs	(12,000)	(12,800)
Operating profit	500	1,000
Finance costs	(800)	(800)
Profit/(loss) before tax	(300)	200

The draft statement of financial position has not yet been prepared, but Mo states that the total assets of Grohl Ltd at 30 November 20X2 are £180 million, and cash at bank is £130,000. Based on draft figures, the company's current ratio is 1.1, and the quick ratio is 0.8.

Required

Respond to the email from the audit partner.   **(28 marks)**

Note. The split of the mark allocation is shown within the partner's email.

Professional marks will be awarded for the presentation, structure, logical flow and clarity of your answer.
                                                                                                                              (4 marks)

(b)   You have just received a phone call from Mo Satriani, Grohl Ltd's finance director, in which he made the following comments.

'There is something I forgot to mention in our meeting. Our business insurance covers us for specific occasions when business is interrupted. I put in a claim on 28 November 20X2 for £5 million which I have estimated to cover the period when our production was halted due to the problem with the corroded copper. This is not yet recognised in the financial statements, but I want to make an adjustment to recognise the £5 million as a receivable as at 30 November.'

Required

Comment on the matters that should be considered, and recommend the audit procedures to be performed, in respect of the insurance claim.   **(8 marks)**

                                                                                                         (Total = 40 marks)

39 Champers (6/09)

65 mins

You are an audit senior in Carter & Co, working on the audit of Champers Ltd, and you have received the following email from Geoff Forest, the engagement partner responsible for the Champers audit.

To: Audit Senior
From: Geoff Forest
Date: 2 June 20X9
Subject: Audit of Champers Ltd

Hi,

I need you to draft some briefing notes for me to use at the Champers audit planning meeting, which evaluate the business risks facing Champers Ltd. **(13 marks)**

There will be junior staff at the meeting, so you need to explain everything you say clearly, avoiding using any technical terms that they might not be familiar with. The permanent file contains a report on Champers that was produced recently by an external business consultant. You may find this useful.

Please have the notes ready for me to review as soon as you can. I look forward to reading them.

Regards,

Geoff Forest

The following is an extract from the permanent file.

Champers Ltd operates a large number of restaurants throughout the country, which are operated under four well known brand names. The company's strategy is to offer a variety of different dining experiences in restaurants situated in city centres and residential areas, with the objective of maximising market share in a competitive business environment.

Key financial information

	31 May	
	20X9 Draft £m	20X8 Draft £m
Company revenue	1,500	1,350
Revenue is derived from four restaurant chains, each having a distinctive brand name:		
Happy Monkeys family bistros	800	660
Quick-bite outlets	375	400
City Sizzler grills	300	290
Green George cafés	25	–
Company profit before tax	135	155
Company total assets	4,200	3,350
Company cash at bank	116	350

Business segments

The Happy Monkeys chain of restaurants provides family-friendly dining in an informal setting. Most of the restaurants are located in residential areas. Each restaurant has a large children's play area containing climbing frames and slides, and offers a crèche facility, where parents may leave their children for up to two hours. Recently there has been some media criticism of the quality of the child care offered in one crèche, because a child had fallen from a climbing frame and was slightly injured. One of the Happy Monkeys restaurants was closed in December 20X8 for three weeks following a health and safety inspection which revealed some significant breaches in hygiene standards in the kitchen.

The Quick-bite chain offers fast-food. The restaurants are located next to busy roads, in shopping centres, and at railway stations and airports. Champers Ltd has launched a significant marketing campaign to support the Quick-bite brand name. The draft statement of profit or loss for the year ended 31 May 20X9 includes an expense of £150 million in relation to the advertising and marketing of this brand. In January 20X9 the company started to provide nutritional information on its menus in the Quick-bite restaurants, following pressure from the government for all restaurants to disclose more about the ingredients of their food. 50% of the revenue for this business segment is derived from the sale of 'chuckle boxes' – self-contained children's meals which contain a small toy.

The City Sizzler grills offer a more sophisticated dining experience. The emphasis is on high quality food served in luxurious surroundings. There are currently 250 City Sizzler grills, and Champers Ltd is planning to expand this to 500 by May 20Y0. The grills are all situated in prime city centre locations and are completely refurbished every two years.

The Green George café chain is a recent addition to the range of restaurants. There are only 30 restaurants in the chain, mostly located in affluent residential areas. The restaurants offer eco-friendly food, guaranteed to be free from artificial flavourings and colourings, and to have been produced in an environmentally sustainable manner. All of the 30 restaurants have been newly constructed by Champers Ltd, and are capitalised at £210 million. This includes all directly attributable costs, and borrowing costs capitalised relating to loans taken out to finance the acquisition of the sites and construction of the restaurants. Champers Ltd is planning to double the number of Green George cafés operating within the next twelve months.

Laws and regulations

Two new regulations were issued by the government recently which will impact on Champers Ltd. The regulations come into effect from September 20X9:

(a)   Minimum wage regulation has increased the minimum wage by 15%. One third of Champers Ltd's employees earn the minimum wage.

(b)   Advertising regulations now forbid the advertising of food in a manner specifically aimed at children.

Three audit juniors are joining your team for the forthcoming audit of Champers Ltd, and you have asked them to read through the permanent file to familiarise themselves with the client. One of the juniors has told you that he appreciates that auditors need to have a thorough understanding of the business of their client, but he does not know what aspects of the client's business this relates to, or how the understanding is developed.

Required

(a)   (i)   Identify and explain the aspects of a client's business which should be considered in order to gain an understanding of the company and its operating environment.   **(6 marks)**

        (ii)   Recommend the procedures an auditor should perform in order to gain business understanding.
                                                                                                (4 marks)

(b)   Respond to the partner's email.   **(13 marks)**

        Note. Professional marks will be awarded in part (b) for the clarity, format and presentation of the briefing notes.   **(4 marks)**

(c)   Describe the principal audit procedures to be performed in respect of the amount:

        (i)   Capitalised in relation to the construction of the new Green George cafés   **(5 marks)**
        (ii)   Recognised as an expense for the advertising of the Quick-bite brand   **(4 marks)**

                                                                                        (Total = 36 marks)

40 Grissom (6/10)   **68 mins**

You are a senior audit manager in Vegas & Co, responsible for the audit of the Grissom Group, which has been an audit client for several years. The group companies all have a financial year ending 30 June 20Y0, and you are currently planning the final audit of the consolidated financial statements. The group's operations focus on the manufacture and marketing of confectionery and savoury snacks. Information about several matters relevant to the group audit is given below. These matters are all potentially material to the consolidated financial statements. None of the companies in the group are listed.

Grissom Ltd

This is a non-trading parent company, which wholly owns three subsidiaries – Willows Ltd, Hodges Ltd and Brass Co, all of which are involved with the core manufacturing and marketing operations of the group. This year, the directors decided to diversify the group's activities in order to reduce risk exposure. Non-controlling interests representing long-term investments have been made in two companies – an internet-based travel agent, and a chain of pet shops. In the consolidated statement of financial position, these investments are accounted for as associates, as Grissom Ltd is able to exert significant influence over the companies.

As part of their remuneration, the directors of Grissom Ltd receive a bonus based on the profit before tax of the group. In April 20Y0, the group finance director resigned from office after a disagreement with the chief executive officer over changes to accounting estimates. A new group finance director is yet to be appointed.

Willows Ltd

This company manufactures and distributes chocolate bars and cakes. In July 20X9, production was relocated to a new, very large factory. One of the conditions of the planning permission for the new factory is that Willows Ltd must, at the end of the useful life of the factory, dismantle the premises and repair any environmental damage caused to the land on which it is situated.

Hodges Ltd

This company's operations involve the manufacture and distribution of packaged nuts and dried fruit. The government paid a grant in November 20X9 to Hodges Ltd, to assist with costs associated with installing new, environmentally friendly, packing lines in its factories. The packing lines must reduce energy use by 25% as part of the conditions of the grant, and they began operating in February 20Y0.

Brass Co

This company is a new and significant acquisition, purchased in January 20Y0. It is located overseas, in Chocland, a developing country, and has been purchased to supply cocoa beans, a major ingredient for the goods produced by Willows Ltd. It is now supplying approximately half of the ingredients used in Willows Ltd's manufacturing. Brass Co's financial statements are prepared using the local accounting rules of Chocland. The company uses local currency to measure and present its financial statements.

Further information

Your firm audits all components of the group with the exception of Brass Co, which is audited by a small local firm, Sidle & Co, based in Chocland. Audit regulations in Chocland are not based on International Standards on Auditing.

You have just received the following email from Warwick Stokes, the audit engagement partner.

To:	Audit manager
From:	Warwick Stokes
Regarding:	Grissom Group audit planning

Hello,

I need you to get started on the planning for the audit of the consolidated financial statements of the Grissom Group. We will be holding an audit planning meeting next week, so can you put together some briefing notes to be used at that meeting? I want you to evaluate the principal audit risks, but do not consider issues to do with reliance on another auditor, as that will be dealt with separately. The briefing notes will be the basis of a discussion with the audit team.

Thanks,

Warwick

Required

(a)   Respond to the email from the engagement partner.   **(18 marks)**

Professional marks will be awarded in part (a), for the format of the answer, and for the clarity of the evaluation.   **(4 marks)**

(b)   Explain the factors that should be considered, and the procedures that should be performed, in deciding the extent of reliance to be placed on the work of Sidle & Co.   **(8 marks)**

(c)   Recommend the principal audit procedures that should be performed on:

   (i)   The classification of non-controlling investments made by Grissom Ltd   **(4 marks)**
   (ii)   The condition attached to the grant received by Hodges Ltd   **(4 marks)**

                                                                                                                                (Total = 38 marks)

41 Jacob (6/11)

32 mins

Jacob Ltd, an audit client of your firm, is a large privately owned company whose operations involve a repair and maintenance service for domestic customers. The company offers a range of services, such as plumbing and electrical repairs and maintenance, and the repair of domestic appliances such as washing machines and cookers, as well as dealing with emergencies such as damage caused by flooding. All work is covered by a two-year warranty.

The directors of Jacob Ltd have been seeking to acquire expertise in the repair and maintenance of swimming pools and hot-tubs as this is a service increasingly requested, but not offered by the company. They have recently identified Locke Ltd as a potential acquisition. Preliminary discussions have been held between the directors of the two companies with a view to the acquisition of Locke Ltd by Jacob Ltd. This will be the first acquisition performed by the current management team of Jacob Ltd. Your firm has been asked to perform a due diligence review on Locke Ltd prior to further discussions taking place. You have been provided with the following information regarding Locke Ltd.

1   Locke Ltd is owner-managed, with three of the five board members being the original founders of the company, which was incorporated 30 years ago. The head office is located in a prestigious building, which is owned by the founders' family estate. The company recently acquired a separate piece of land on which a new head office is to be built.

2   The company has grown rapidly in the last three years as more affluent customers can afford the cost of installing and maintaining swimming pools and hot-tubs. The expansion was funded by a significant bank loan. The company relies on an overdraft facility in the winter months when less operating cash inflows arise from maintenance work.

3   Locke Ltd enjoys a good reputation, though this was tarnished last year by a complaint by a famous actor who claimed that, following maintenance of his swimming pool by Locke Ltd's employees, the water contained a chemical which damaged his skin. A court case is on-going and is attracting media attention.

4   The company's financial year end is 31 August 20X1. Its accounting function is outsourced to Austin Ltd, a local provider of accounting and tax services.

Required

(a)   Explain **three** potential benefits of an externally provided due diligence review to Jacob Ltd.   **(6 marks)**

(b)   Recommend additional information which should be made available for your firm's due diligence review, and explain the need for the information.   **(12 marks)**

Note. Assume it is 7 June 20X1.   **(Total = 18 marks)**

42 Cusiter (AAS 6/07)

52 mins

You are Trevor Ennui, an audit manager in a firm of Chartered Certified Accountants. You have just received this email from Douglas Groan, the audit partner for Cusiter Co:

To:	Trevor Ennui
From:	Douglas Groan
Regarding:	Custer Co – review assignment

Hello Trevor,

Our audit client Cusiter Co has engaged us to review and report on the following prospective financial information, which it has produced. The information has been produced to support an application for a £250,000 long-term loan from a bank. The funds from the loan will be invested, on 1 January 20X9, in new plant and equipment that will be used to manufacture a new product range following a recent purchase of a patented technology.

Please produce a memorandum for me in which you:

(a)   Explain the term 'prospective financial information' ('PFI');

	Actual year to 31 December 20X7	Actual quarter to 31 March 20X8	Forecast year to 31 December 20X8	Forecast year to 31 December 20X9
	£'000	£'000	£'000	£'000
Non-current assets				
Intangible asset – Patent	0	0	10	10
Property, plant and equipment	257	262	289	569
Accumulated deprecation	(123)	(128)	(139)	(191)
Net book value	134	134	150	378
Investments	7	6	7	7
Current assets				
Accounts receivable	71	65	84	100
Inventory	50	59	59	69
Cash and cash equivalents	6	7	7	0
	127	131	150	169
Total assets	268	271	317	564
Equity				
Share capital	1	1	1	1
Retained earnings	26	30	67	109
	27	31	68	110
Non-current liabilities				
Term borrowings	174	174	151	343
Current liabilities				
Accounts payable	23	21	27	32
Accrued expenses	21	22	25	28
Short-term borrowings	23	23	46	51
	67	66	98	111
Total equity and liabilities	268	271	317	564
Statement of profit or loss	£'000	£'000	£'000	£'000
Revenue	394	86	466	556
Cost of good sold	(278)	(61)	(329)	(390)
Gross profit	116	25	137	166
Gross profit %	29.4%	29.1%	29.4%	29.9%
Operating expenses	(47)	(12)	(55)	(80)
Earnings before interest and tax (EBIT)	69	13	82	86
EBIT %	17.5%	15.1%	17.6%	15.5%
Interest expense	(21)	(4)	(18)	(44)
Earnings before tax	48	9	64	42

Required

Respond to the partner's email.   **(25 marks)**

Professional marks will be awarded for the format and clarity of the answer.   **(4 marks)**

(Total = 29 marks)

43 Oak (12/11) (amended)   74 mins

(a)   You are a manager in Maple & Co, responsible for the audit of Oak Plc, a listed company. Oak Plc manufactures electrical appliances such as televisions and radios, which are then sold to retail outlets. You are aware that during the last year, Oak Plc lost several customer contracts to overseas competitors. However, a new division has been created to sell its products directly to individual customers via a new website, which was launched on 1 November 20X1.

You are about to commence planning the audit for the year ending 31 December 20X1, and you have received an email from Holly Elm, the audit engagement partner:

To:	Audit manager
From:	Holly Elm, Audit partner
Subject:	Oak Plc – audit planning

Hello,

(i)   I would like you to start planning the audit of Oak Plc. You need to perform a preliminary analytical review on the financial information and accompanying notes provided by Rowan Birch, the finance director of Oak Plc. Using this information and the results of your analytical review, please prepare notes for inclusion in the planning section of the working papers, which identify and explain the principal audit risks to be considered in planning the final audit. Your notes should include any calculations performed.   **(23 marks)**

(ii)   Please also recommend the principal audit procedures which should be performed in respect of:

(1)   The recognition and measurement of the share-based payment plan, and
(2)   The classification of the new lease.   **(8 marks)**

Thank you,

Holly

Financial information provided by Rowan Birch:

STATEMENT OF PROFIT OR LOSS (extract from management accounts)

	Notes	11 months to 30 November 20X1 £'000	11 months to 30 November 20X0 £'000
Revenue		25,700	29,300
Cost of sales		(15,420)	(15,900)
Gross profit		10,280	13,400
Operating expenses	1	(6,200)	(7,750)
Operating profit		4,080	5,650
Finance costs		(1,500)	(1,500)
Profit before tax		2,580	4,150

STATEMENT OF FINANCIAL POSITION

	Notes	11 months to 30 November 20X1 £'000	11 months to 30 November 20X0 £'000
ASSETS			
Non-current assets			
Property plant and equipment	2, 3	90,000	75,750
Intangible assets	4	1,250	–
		91,250	75,750
Current assets			
Inventory		1,800	1,715
Trade receivables		4,928	4,815
Cash and cash equivalents		100	2,350
		6,828	8,880
Total assets		98,078	84,630
EQUITY AND LIABILITIES			
Equity			
Share capital		20,000	20,000
Revaluation reserve	3	10,000	–
Retained earnings		32,278	34,895
Total equity		62,278	54,895
Non-current liabilities			
Long-term borrowings	5	25,000	25,000
Provisions	6	1,000	1,250
Finance lease payable	2	5,000	–
		31,000	26,250
Current liabilities			
Bank overdraft	7	1,300	–
Trade and other payables		3,500	3,485
		4,800	3,485
Total liabilities		35,800	29,735
Total equity and liabilities		98,078	84,630

Notes

1   Oak Plc established an equity-settled share-based payment plan for its executives on 1 January 20X1. 250 executives and senior managers have received 100 share options each, which vest on 31 December 20X3 if the executive remains in employment at that date, and if Oak Plc's share price increases by 10% per annum. No expense has been recognised this year as Oak Plc's share price has fallen by 5% in the last six months, and so it is felt that the condition relating to the share price will not be met this year end.

2   On 1 July 20X1, Oak Plc entered into a lease which has been accounted for as a finance lease and capitalised at £5 million. The leased property is used as the head office for Oak Plc's new website development and sales division. The lease term is for five years and the fair value of the property at the inception of the lease was £20 million.

3   On 30 June 20X1 Oak Plc's properties were revalued by an independent expert.

4   A significant amount has been invested in the new website, which is seen as a major strategic development for the company. The website has generated minimal sales since its launch last month, and advertising campaigns are currently being conducted to promote the site.

5   The long-term borrowings are due to be repaid in two equal instalments on 30 September 20X2 and 20X3. Oak Plc is in the process of renegotiating the loan, to extend the repayment dates, and to increase the amount of the loan.

6   The provision relates to product warranties offered by the company.

7   The overdraft limit agreed with Oak Plc's bank is £1.5 million.

Required

Respond to the email from the audit partner. **(31 marks)**

Note. The split of the mark allocation is shown within the partner's email.

Professional marks will be awarded for the presentation and clarity of your answer. **(4 marks)**

(b)   Maple & Co is suffering from declining revenue, and as a result of this, another audit manager has been asked to consider how to improve the firm's profitability. In a conversation with you this morning he mentioned the following.

'We really need to make our audits more efficient. I think we should fix materiality at the planning stage at the maximum possible materiality level for all audits, as this would reduce the work we need to do.

'I also think we can cut the firm's overheads by reducing our spending on training. We spend a lot on expensive training courses for junior members of the audit team, and on Continuing Professional Development for our qualified members of staff.

'We could also guarantee our clients that all audits will be completed quicker than last year. Reducing the time spent on each assignment will improve the firm's efficiency and enable us to take on more audit clients.'

Required

Comment on the practice management and quality control issues raised by the audit manager's suggestions to improve the audit firm's profitability. **(6 marks)**

(Total = 41 marks)

44 Geno Vesa Farm (AAS 6/05)   47 mins

Geno Vesa Farm Ltd (GVF) is a cheese manufacturer. Its principal activity is the production of a traditional 'Farmhouse' cheese that is retailed around the world to exclusive shops, through mail order and web sales. Other activities include the sale of locally produced foods through a farm shop and cheese-making demonstrations and tours.

The farm's herd of 700 goats is used primarily for the production of milk. Kids (ie goat offspring), which are a secondary product, are selected for herd replacement or otherwise sold. Animals held for sale are not usually retained beyond the time they reach optimal size or weight because their value usually does not increase thereafter.

There are two main variations of the traditional farmhouse cheese; 'Rabida Red' and 'Bachas Blue'. The red cheese is coloured using Innittu, which is extracted from berries found only in South American rain forests. The cost of Innittu has risen sharply over the last year as the collection of berries by local village workers has come under the scrutiny of an international action group. The group is lobbying the South American government to ban the export of Innittu, claiming that the workers are being exploited and that sustaining the forest is seriously under threat.

Demand for Bachas Blue, which is made from unpasteurised milk, fell considerably in 20X7 following the publication of a research report that suggested a link between unpasteurised milk products and a skin disorder. The financial statements for the year ended 31 March 20X8 recognised a material impairment loss attributable to the equipment used exclusively for the manufacture of Bachas Blue. However, as the adverse publicity is gradually being forgotten, sales of Bachas Blue are now showing a steady increase and are currently expected to return to their former level by the end of March 20X9.

Cheese is matured to three strengths – mild, medium and strong – depending on the period of time it is left to ripen which is 6, 12 and 18 months respectively. When produced the cheese is sold to a financial institution, Abingdon Bank, at cost. Under the terms of sale, GVF has the option to buy the cheese on its maturity at cost plus 7% for every six months which has elapsed.

All cheese is stored to maturity on wooden boards in GVF's cool and airy sheds. However, recently enacted health and safety legislation requires that the wooden boards be replaced with stainless steel shelves with effect from 1 January 20X9. The management of GVF has petitioned the government health department that to comply with the legislation would interfere with the maturing process and the production of medium and strong cheeses would have to cease.

In 20X7, GVF applied for and received a substantial regional development grant for the promotion of tourism in the area. GVF's management has deferred its plan to convert a disused barn into holiday accommodation from 20X8 until at least 20Y0.

Required

(a) Identify and explain the principal audit risks to be considered when planning the final audit of GVF for the year ending 31 March 20X9. **(14 marks)**

(b) Describe the audit procedures to be performed in respect of the carrying amount of the following items in the statement of financial position of GVF Ltd as at 31 March 20X9.

    (i)   Goat herd **(4 marks)**
    (ii)   Equipment used in the manufacture of Bachas Blue **(4 marks)**
    (iii) Cheese **(4 marks)**

(Total = 26 marks)

Note. You are not required to apply the principles of IAS 41 *Agriculture* in answering this question. Assume it is 11 December 20X8.

45 Cedar (12/11)   32 mins

You are an audit manager in Cedar & Co, responsible for the audit of Chestnut Ltd, a large company which provides information technology services to business customers. The finance director of Chestnut Ltd, Jack Privet, contacted you this morning, saying:

'I was alerted yesterday to a fraud being conducted by members of our sales team. It appears that several sales representatives have been claiming reimbursement for fictitious travel and client entertaining expenses and inflating actual expenses incurred. Specifically, it has been alleged that the sales representatives have claimed on expenses for items such as gifts for clients and office supplies which were never actually purchased, claimed for business-class airline tickets but in reality had purchased economy tickets, claimed for non-existent business mileage and used the company credit card to purchase items for personal use.

'I am very worried about the scale of this fraud, as travel and client entertainment is one of our biggest expenses. All of the alleged fraudsters have been suspended pending an investigation, which I would like your firm to conduct. We will prosecute these employees to attempt to recoup our losses if evidence shows that a fraud has indeed occurred, so your firm would need to provide an expert witness in the event of a court case. Can we meet tomorrow to discuss this potential assignment?'

Chestnut Ltd has a small internal audit department and in previous years the evidence obtained by Cedar & Co as part of the external audit has indicated that the control environment of the company is generally good. The audit opinion on the financial statements for the year ended 31 March 20X1 was unmodified.

Required

(a) Assess the ethical and professional issues raised by the request for your firm to investigate the alleged fraudulent activity. **(6 marks)**

(b) Explain the matters that should be discussed in the meeting with Jack Privet in respect of planning the investigation into the alleged fraudulent activity. **(6 marks)**

(c) The Auditing Practices Board's Ltd consultation paper The provision of non-audit services by auditors summarises differing views as to whether there should be an outright prohibition on the provision of non-audit services to audit clients.

Required

Evaluate the arguments for and against the prohibition of auditors providing non-audit services to audit clients. **(6 marks)**

(Total = 18 marks)

46 Willow (12/11) (amended)   49 mins

Willow Ltd is a print supplier to businesses, printing catalogues, leaflets, training manuals and stationery to order. It specialises in using 100% recycled paper in its printing, a fact which is promoted heavily in its advertising.

You are a senior audit manager in Bark & Co, and you have just been placed in charge of the audit of Willow Ltd. The audit for the year ended 31 August 20X1 is nearing completion, and the audit engagement partner, Jasmine Berry, has sent you an email:

To:	Audit manager
From:	Jasmine Berry, Audit partner
Subject:	Audit completion and other issues – Willow Ltd

Hello,

The manager previously assigned to the audit of Willow Ltd has been moved to another urgent assignment, so thank you for stepping in to take on the manager's role this late in the audit. The audit report is due to be issued in two weeks' time, and the audit senior has prepared a summary of matters for your consideration.

I have been asked to attend a meeting with the audit committee of Willow Ltd tomorrow, so I need you to update me on how the audit has progressed. I am asking you to prepare briefing notes for my use in which you:

(a) Assess the audit implications of the **three** issues related to audit work raised by the audit senior. Your assessment should consider the sufficiency of evidence obtained, explain any adjustments that may be necessary to the financial statements, and describe the impact on the audit report if these adjustments are not made. You should also recommend any further audit procedures necessary.   **(15 marks)**

(b) Explain the matters, other than the three issues related to audit work raised by the audit senior, which should be brought to the attention of the audit committee of Willow Ltd.   **(8 marks)**

Thanks

Summary of issues for manager's attention, prepared by audit senior

Materiality has been determined as follows.

- £800,000 for assets and liabilities
- £250,000 for income and expenses

Issues related to audit work performed:

(i) **Audit work on inventory**

Audit procedures performed at the inventory count indicated that printed inventory items with a value of £130,000 were potentially obsolete. These items were mainly out of date training manuals. The finance director, Cherry Laurel, has not written off this inventory as she argues that the paper on which the items are printed can be recycled and used again in future printing orders. However, the items appear not to be recyclable as they are coated in plastic. The junior who performed the audit work on inventory has requested a written representation from management to confirm that the items can be recycled and no further procedures relevant to these items have been performed.

(ii) **Audit work on provisions**

Willow Ltd is involved in a court case with a competitor, Aspen Ltd, which alleges that a design used in Willow Ltd's printed material copies one of Aspen Ltd's designs which are protected under copyright. Our evidence obtained is a verbal confirmation from Willow Ltd's lawyers that a claim of £125,000 has been made against Willow Ltd, which is probable to be paid. Cherry Laurel has not made a provision, arguing that it is immaterial. Cherry refused our request to ask the lawyers to confirm their opinion on the matter in writing, saying it is not worth bothering the lawyers again on such a trivial matter.

(iii) **Audit work on current assets**

Willow Ltd made a loan of £6,000 to Cherry Laurel, the finance director, on 30 June 20X1. The amount is recognised as a current asset. The loan carries an interest rate of 4% which we have confirmed to be the market rate for short-term loans and we have concluded that the loan is an arm's length transaction. Cherry has provided written confirmation that she intends to repay the loan by 31 March 20X2. The only other audit work performed was to agree the cash payment to the cash book. Details of the loan made to Cherry have not been separately disclosed in the financial statements.

Other issues for your attention:

Property revaluations

Willow Ltd currently adopts an accounting policy of recognising properties at cost. During the audit of non-current assets Willow Ltd's property manager said that the company is considering a change of accounting policy so that properties would be recognised at fair value from 1 January 20X2.

Non-current asset register

The audit of non-current assets was delayed by a week. We had asked for the non-current asset register reconciliation to be completed by the client prior to commencement of our audit procedures on non-current assets, but it seems that the person responsible for the reconciliation went on holiday having forgotten to prepare the reconciliation. This happened on last year's audit as well, and the issue was discussed with the audit committee at that time.

Procurement procedures

We found during our testing of trade payables that an approved supplier list is not maintained, and invoices received are not always matched back to goods received notes. This was mentioned to the procurement manager, who said that suppliers are switched fairly often, depending on which supplier is the cheapest, so it would be difficult to maintain an up-to-date approved supplier list.

Financial controller

Mia Fern, Willow Co's financial controller, owns a holiday home overseas. It appears that she offered the audit team free use of the holiday home for three weeks after the audit, as a reward for the team's hard work. She also bought lunch for the audit team on most days.

Required

Respond to the partner's email. **(23 marks)**

Professional marks will be awarded for the format and clarity of your answer. **(4 marks)**

(Total = 27 marks)

47 Jovi (12/12) 50 mins

(a) You are a manager in Sambora & Co, responsible for the audit of the Jovi Group (the Group), which is listed. The Group's main activity is steel manufacturing and it comprises a parent company and five subsidiaries. Sambora & Co currently audits all components of the Group.

You are working on the audit of the Group's financial statements for the year ended 30 June 20X2. This morning the audit engagement partner left a note for you:

'Hello,

The audit senior has provided you with the draft consolidated financial statements and accompanying notes which summarise the key audit findings and some background information.

At the planning stage, materiality was initially determined to be £900,000 and was calculated based on the assumption that the Jovi Group is a high risk client due to its listed status. During the audit, a number of issues arose which meant that we needed to revise the materiality level for the financial statements as a whole. The revised level of materiality is now determined to be £700,000. One of the audit juniors was unsure as to why the materiality level had been revised. There are two matters you need to deal with:

(i) Explain why auditors may need to reassess materiality as the audit progresses. **(4 marks)**

(ii) Assess the implications of the key audit findings for the completion of the audit. Your assessment must consider whether the key audit findings indicate a risk of material misstatement. Where the key audit findings refer to audit evidence, you must also consider the adequacy of the audit evidence obtained, but you do not need to recommend further specific procedures. **(18 marks)**

Thank you'

The Group's draft consolidated financial statements, with notes referenced to key audit findings, are shown below:

Draft consolidated statement of profit or loss and other comprehensive income

	Notes	30 June 20X2 Draft £'000	30 June 20X1 Actual £'000
Revenue	1	98,795	103,100
Cost of sales		(75,250)	(74,560)
Gross profit		23,545	28,540
Operating expenses	2	(14,900)	(17,500)
Operating profit		8,645	11,040
Share of profit of associate		1,010	900
Finance costs		(380)	(340)
Profit before tax		9,275	11,600
Taxation		(3,200)	(3,500)
Profit for the year		6,075	8,100
Other comprehensive income/expense for the year, net of tax:			
Gains on property revaluation	3	800	–
Actuarial losses on defined benefit plan	4	(1,100)	(200)
Other comprehensive income/expense		(300)	(200)
Total comprehensive income for the year		5,775	7,900

Notes. Key audit findings – statement of profit or loss and other comprehensive income

1 Revenue has been stable for all components of the Group with the exception of one subsidiary, Copeland Ltd, which has recognised a 25% decrease in revenue.

2 Operating expenses for the year to June 20X2 is shown net of a profit on a property disposal of £2 million.

Our evidence includes agreeing the cash receipts to bank statement and sale documentation, and we have confirmed that the property has been removed from the non-current asset register. The audit junior noted, when reviewing the sale document, that there is an option to repurchase the property in five years time, but did not discuss the matter with the management.

3 The property revaluation relates to the Group's head office. The audit team have not obtained evidence on the revaluation, as the gain was immaterial based on the initial calculation of materiality.

4 The actuarial loss is attributed to an unexpected stock market crash. The Group's pension plan is managed by Axle Ltd – a firm of independent fund managers who maintain the necessary accounting records relating to the plan. Axle Ltd has supplied written representation as to the value of the defined benefit plan's assets and liabilities at 30 June 20X2. No audit work has been performed other than to agree the figure from the financial statements to supporting documentation supplied by Axle Ltd.

Draft consolidated statement of financial position

	Notes	30 June 20X2 Draft £'000	30 June 20X1 Actual £'000
ASSETS			
Non-current assets			
Property, plant and equipment		81,800	76,300
Goodwill	5	5,350	5,350
Investment in associate	6	4,230	4,230
Assets classified as held for sale	7	7,800	–
		99,180	85,880
Current assets			
Inventory		8,600	8,000
Receivables		8,540	7,800
Cash and cash equivalents		2,100	2,420
		19,240	18,220
Total assets		118,420	104,100
EQUITY AND LIABILITIES			
Equity			
Share capital		12,500	12,500
Revaluation reserve		3,300	2,500
Retained earnings		33,600	29,400
Non-controlling interest		4,350	4,000
Total equity		53,750	48,400
Non-current liabilities			
Defined benefit pension plan		10,820	9,250
Long-term borrowings	9	43,000	35,000
Deferred tax		1,950	1,350
Total non-current liabilities		55,770	45,600
Current liabilities			
Trade and other payables		6,200	7,300
Provisions		2,700	2,800
Total current liabilities		8,900	10,100
Total liabilities		64,670	55,700
Total equity and liabilities		118,420	104,100

Notes. Key audit findings – statement of financial position

5 The goodwill relates to each of the subsidiaries in the Group. The management has confirmed in writing that the goodwill is stated correctly, and our other audit procedure was to arithmetically check the impairment review conducted by the management.

6 The associate is a 30% holding in James Ltd, purchased to provide investment income. The audit team have not obtained evidence regarding the associate as there is no movement in the amount recognised in the statement of financial position.

7 The assets held for sale relate to a trading division of one of the subsidiaries, which represents one third of that subsidiary's net assets. The sale of the division was announced in May 20X2, and is expected to be complete by 31 December 20X2. Audit evidence obtained includes a review of the sales agreement and confirmation from the buyer, obtained in July 20X2, that the sale will take place.

8 Two of the Group's subsidiaries are partly owned by shareholders external to the Group.

9 A loan of £8 million was taken out in October 20X1, carrying an interest rate of 2%, payable annually in arrears. The terms of the loan have been confirmed to documentation provided by the bank.

Required

Respond to the note from the audit engagement partner.   **(22 marks)**

Note. The split of the mark allocation is shown within the partner's note.

(b)   The audit engagement partner now sends a further note regarding the Jovi Group:

'The Group finance director has just informed me that last week the Group purchased 100% of the share capital of May Co, a company located overseas in Farland. The Group audit committee has suggested that due to the distant location of May Co, a joint audit could be performed, starting with the next financial statements for the year ending 30 June 20X3. May Co's current auditors are a small local firm called Moore & Co who operate only in Farland.'

Required

Discuss the advantages and disadvantages of a joint audit being performed on the financial statements of May Co.   **(6 marks)**

(Total = 28 marks)

48 Kobain (12/12)   29 mins

(a)   'Revenue recognition should always be approached as a high risk area of the audit.'

Required

Discuss this statement.   **(6 marks)**

(b)   You are a manager in Beck & Co, responsible for the audit of Kobain Ltd, a new audit client of your firm, with a financial year that ended 31 July 20X2. Kobain Ltd's draft financial statements recognise total assets of £55 million and profit before tax of £15 million. The audit is nearing completion and you are reviewing the audit files. Kobain Ltd designs and creates high-value items of jewellery. Approximately half of the jewellery is sold in Kobain Ltd's own retail outlets. The other half is sold by external vendors under a consignment stock arrangement, the terms of which specify that Kobain Ltd retains the ability to change the selling price of the jewellery, and that the vendor is required to return any unsold jewellery after a period of nine months. When the vendor sells an item of jewellery to a customer, legal title passes from Kobain Ltd to the customer.

On delivery of the jewellery to the external vendors, Kobain Ltd recognises revenue and derecognises inventory. At 31 July 20X2, jewellery at cost price of £3 million is held at external vendors. Revenue of £4 million has been recognised in respect of this jewellery.

Required

Comment on the matters that should be considered, and explain the audit evidence you should expect to find in your file review in respect of the consignment stock arrangement.   **(6 marks)**

(c)   Your firm also performs the audit of Jarvis Ltd, a company which installs windows. Jarvis Ltd uses sales representatives to make direct sales to customers. The sales representatives earn a small salary, and also earn a sales commission of 20% of the sales they generate.

Jarvis Ltd's sales manager has discovered that one of the sales representatives has been operating a fraud, in which he was submitting false claims for sales commission based on non-existent sales. The sales representative started to work at Jarvis Ltd in January 20X2. The forensic investigation department of your firm has been engaged to quantify the amount of the fraud.

Required

Recommend the procedures that should be used in the forensic investigation to quantify the amount of the fraud.   **(4 marks)**

(Total = 16 marks)

49 Cuckoo Group

You are currently at the planning stage of the audit of the Cuckoo Group, and have just received the following email from the audit engagement partner.

To:	Audit manager
From:	Audit partner
Regarding:	Cuckoo Group audit

Hello,

I understand that the audit work on the Cuckoo Group is due to start shortly. We are currently auditing the consolidated financial statements of the Cuckoo Group. I'd like you to start scrutinising the accounting policies being used by the group for the valuation of inventory. The group has three principal subsidiaries; Loopy, Snoopy and Drake Retail. We are not currently the auditors of Loopy as Cuckoo only recently acquired this subsidiary company. Cuckoo, the holding company, carries on business as a dealer in gold bullion and other precious metals. It purchased the three subsidiaries in order to diversify its activities. It felt that dealing in commodities was quite risky and wished to spread the operating risk. I've attached to this email a schedule of the accounting policies proposed by Cuckoo Group regarding the valuation of inventory.

I'd like you to prepare some briefing notes for me, in which you:

(i)   Describe the matters to consider and the audit procedures to carry out as part of the planning and evaluation of the work of the auditors of Loopy, and

(ii)   Discuss whether you feel that the current accounting policies adopted by Cuckoo and its three subsidiaries regarding inventory are acceptable to us as principle auditor.

Thanks.

Email attachment

Cuckoo plc proposes to include the bullion and other precious metals in the statement of financial position at the year-end market values. It does not enter into any contracts for the forward purchase or sale of precious metals. Cuckoo does not manufacture products from the precious metals but simply buys and sells the metals on the bullion markets.

Loopy plc manufactures domestic products such as cutlery, small electrical appliances and crockery. The inventory is valued at the lower of cost or market value applied to the total of the inventory. Cost is determined by using the last in, first out (LIFO) method of valuation. Overhead costs are allocated on the basis of normal activity and are those incurred in bringing the inventory to its present location and condition.

Snoopy plc manufactures similar domestic products to Loopy. The inventory is valued at the lower of cost and net realisable value for the purpose of the group statement of financial position. However, inventory is further reduced to its base value for the purpose of the group statement of profit or loss and other comprehensive income. This reduction is not material in the context of the group financial statements. Overheads are allocated on the basis of normal activity levels and the costs incurred in bringing the inventory to its present location and condition.

Drake Retail plc acts as the retail outlet for approximately 60% of the combined output of Loopy plc and Snoopy plc. It values its inventory at the lower of cost and net realisable value. Inventories mainly consist of goods held for resale. Cost is computed by deducting the gross profit margin from the selling value of inventory. When computing net realisable value, an allowance is made for any future markdowns to be made on inventory.

The directors of Cuckoo Group plc wish the following accounting policy note to be included in the group financial statements regarding inventory. 'Inventory is stated at the lower of cost and net realisable value and comprises raw material inventory (including bullion), work in progress and finished goods.'

Required

(a)   Respond to the partner's email.   **(24 marks)**

      Note. Professional marks will be available for the format and clarity of your response.   **(4 marks)**

(b)   Comment on the extent to which ISA 600 *Special considerations – Audits of Group Financial Statements (including the work of component auditors)* provides guidance on the following issues in the context of a group audit.

     (i)   Co-operation between auditors
     (ii)   Multi-location auditors
     (iii)   Joint audits   **(6 marks)**

                                                            (Total = 34 marks)

50 Bluebell   65 mins

Bluebell Ltd operates a chain of 95 luxury hotels. This year's results show a return to profitability for the company, following several years of losses. Hotel trade journals show that on average, revenue in the industry has increased by around 20% this year. Despite improved profitability, Bluebell Ltd has poor liquidity, and is currently trying to secure further long-term finance.

You have been the manager responsible for the audit of Bluebell Ltd for the last four years, Extracts from the draft financial statements for the year ended 30 November 20X8 are shown below.

Extracts from the statement of profit or loss

	20X8	20X7
	£m	£m
Revenue (Note 1)	890	713
Operating expenses (Note 2)	(835)	(690)
Other operating income (Note 3)	135	10
Operating profit	190	33
Finance charges	(45)	(43)
Profit/(loss) before tax	145	(10)

Notes

1   *Revenue recognition*

     Revenue comprises sales of hotel rooms, conference and meeting rooms. Revenue is recognised when a room is occupied. A 20% deposit is taken when the room is booked.

2   *Significant items included in operating expenses*

	20X8	20X7
	£m	£m
Share-based payment expense (i)	138	–
Damaged property repair expenses (ii)	100	–

3   *Other operating income includes*

	20X8	20X7
	£m	£m
Profit on property disposal (iii)	125	10

(i)   In June 20X8 Bluebell Ltd granted 50 million share options to executives and employees of the company. The cost of the share option scheme is being recognised over the three year vesting period of the scheme. It is currently assumed that all of the options will vest and the expense is calculated on that basis.

(ii)   In September 20X8, three hotels situated near a major river were severely damaged by a flood. All of the hotels, which were constructed by Bluebell Ltd only two years ago, need extensive repairs and refurbishment at an estimated cost of £100 million, which has been provided in full. All of the buildings are insured for damage caused by flooding.

(iii)   Eight properties were sold in March 20X8 to Daffodil Fund Enterprises (DFE). Bluebell Ltd entered into a management contract with DFE and is continuing to operate the eight hotels under a 15-year agreement. Under the terms of the management contract, Bluebell Ltd receives an annual financial return based on the profit made by the eight hotels. At the end of the contract, Bluebell Ltd has the option to repurchase the hotels, and it is likely that the option will be exercised.

Extracts from the statement of financial position

	20X8	20X7
	£m	£m
Tangible non-current assets (Note 4)	1,265	1,135
Deferred tax asset (Note 5)	285	335
Deferred tax liability (Note 6)	(735)	(638)
Total assets	2,870	2,230

4   *Tangible Non-current assets (extract)*

On 31 October 20X8 all of Bluebell Ltd's owned hotels were revalued. A revaluation gain of £250 million has been recognised in the statement of changes in equity, and in the statement of financial position.

5   *Deferred Tax Asset (extract)*

The deferred tax asset represents unutilised tax losses which accumulated in the loss making periods 20X4–20X7 inclusive. Bluebell Ltd is confident that future taxable trading profits will be generated in order for the tax losses to be utlilised.

6   *Deferred Tax Liability (extract)*

	Timing differences relating to Tangible Non-current assets
	£m
1 December 20X7	638
Charged to equity	88
Charged to tax expense	9
30 November 20X8	735

Required

(a)   Using the specific information provided, identify and explain the risk of material misstatement to be addressed when planning the final audit of Bluebell Ltd for the year ended 30 November 20X8.   **(14 marks)**

Note. Ignore any deferred tax implications in respect of the share-based payment scheme.

(b)   Describe the principal audit procedures to be carried out in respect of the following.

(i)   The measurement of the share-based payment expense   **(6 marks)**
(ii)   The recoverability of the deferred tax asset   **(4 marks)**

(c)   You have just received the following email from the audit engagement partner on the Bluebell audit.

To: Audit manager
From: Audit partner
Regarding: Bluebell Ltd

Hello,

I have a meeting with Daisy Roseptal tomorrow for which I need you to prepare some briefing notes. Please prepare notes that recommend EIGHT KPIs which could be used to monitor Bluebell Ltd's social and environmental performance, and outline the nature of evidence that should be available to provide assurance on the accuracy of the KPIs recommended.

Required

Respond to the partner's email above.   **(12 marks)**

Note. Requirement (c) includes four professional marks.

51 Robster (6/09)

31 mins

Robster Ltd is a company which manufactures tractors and other machinery to be used in the agricultural industry. You are Jo Russell, the manager responsible for the audit of Robster Ltd, and you are reviewing the audit working papers for the year ended 28 February 20X9. The draft financial statements show revenue of £10.5 million, profit before tax of £3.2 million, and total assets of £45 million.

The audit senior has left you the following note on the audit file, relating to assets recognised in the statement of financial position for the first time this year.

Leases

In July 20X8, Robster Ltd entered into five new finance leases of land and buildings. The leases have been capitalised and the statement of financial position includes leased assets presented as tangible non-current assets at a value of £3.6 million, and a total finance lease payable of £3.2 million presented as a payable falling due after more than one year.

Financial assets

Non-current assets include financial assets recognised at £1.26 million. A note to the financial statements describes these financial assets as investments classified as at fair value, and the investments are described in the note as 'held for trading'. The investments are all shares in listed companies. A gain of £350,000 has been recognised in net profit in respect of the revaluation of these investments.

Required

(a) In your review of the audit working papers, comment on the matters you should consider, and state the audit evidence you should expect to find in respect of:

    (i) The leases **(8 marks)**

    (ii) the financial assets **(5 marks)**

(b) You are aware that Robster Ltd is seeking a listing in September 20X9. The listing rules in this jurisdiction require that interim financial information is published half-way through the accounting period, and that the information should be accompanied by a review report issued by the company's independent auditor.

    Required

    Explain the principal analytical procedures that should be used to gather evidence in a review of interim financial information. **(4 marks)**

(Total = 17 marks)

52 Efex Engineering (Pilot paper) (amended)

61 mins

You are Reginald Perrin, an audit manager in Sunshine Audit Co, a firm of Chartered Certified Accountants. You have just taken a phone call from CJ, a senior partner at the firm, in which he told you:

'We have been asked to carry out an investigation by the management of Xzibit Co. One of the company's subsidiaries, Efex Engineering Ltd, has been making losses for the past year. Xzibit's management is concerned about the accuracy of Efex Engineering's most recent quarter's management accounts.'

CJ talked you through Xzibit's concerns. He then asked you to prepare some briefing notes for him which identify and describe the matters that you should consider and the procedures you should carry out in order to plan an investigation of Efex Engineering Co's losses.

Your notes from the conversation with CJ include the following information.

The summarised statements of profit or loss for the last three quarters are as follows.

	Quarter to		
	30 June 20X8	31 March 20X8	31 December 20X7
	£'000	£'000	£'000
Revenue	429	334	343
Opening inventory	180	163	203
Materials	318	251	200
Direct wages	62	54	74
	560	468	477
Less closing inventory	(162)	(180)	(163)
Cost of goods sold	398	288	314
Gross profit	31	46	29
Less overheads	(63)	(75)	(82)
Net loss	(32)	(29)	(53)
Gross profit (%)	7.2%	13.8%	8.5%
Materials (% of revenue)	78.3%	70.0%	70.0%
Labour (% of revenue)	14.5%	16.2%	21.6%

Xzibit's management board believes that the high material consumption as a percentage of revenue for the quarter to 30 June 20X8 is due to one or more of the following factors.

1   Under-counting or under-valuation of closing inventory
2   Excessive consumption or wastage of materials
3   Material being stolen by employees or other individuals

Efex Engineering has a small number of large customers and manufactures its products to each customer's specification.

The selling price of the product is determined by:

1   Estimating the cost of materials
2   Estimating the labour cost
3   Adding a mark-up to cover overheads and provide a normal profit

The estimated costs are not compared with actual costs. Although it is possible to analyse purchase invoices for materials between customers' orders this analysis has not been done.

A physical inventory count is carried out at the end of each quarter. Items of inventory are entered on inventory sheets and valued manually. The company does not maintain perpetual inventory records and a full physical count is to be carried out at the financial year end, 30 September 20X8.

The direct labour cost included in the inventory valuation is small and should be assumed to be constant at the end of each quarter. Historically, the cost of materials consumed has been about 70% of revenue.

The management accounts to 31 March 20X8 are to be assumed to be correct.

Required

(a)   Define 'forensic auditing' and describe its application to fraud investigations.   **(5 marks)**

(b)   Respond to CJ's request.   **(10 marks)**

   Note. Professional marks will be available for the format and clarity of answers to part (b) above.   **(4 marks)**

(c)   (i)   Explain the matters you should consider to determine whether closing inventory at 30 June 20X8 is undervalued.

   (ii)   Describe the tests you should plan to perform to quantify the amount of any undervaluation.   **(8 marks)**

(d)   (i)   Identify and explain the possible reasons for the apparent high materials consumption in the quarter ended 30 June 20X8.

   (ii)   Describe the tests you should plan to perform to determine whether materials consumption, as shown in the management accounts, is correct.   **(7 marks)**

   (Total = 34 marks)

53 Bateleur Zoo Gardens

61 mins

Your name is Laura Liver, and you are an audit manager in a firm of Chartered Certified Accountants. You are responsible for the audit of Bateleur Zoo Gardens (BZG), the principal activity of which is the conservation of animals. Approximately 80% of the zoo's income comes from admission fees, money spent in the food and retail outlets and animal sponsorship. The remainder comprises donations and investment income.

Admission fees include day visitor entrance fees ('gate') and annual membership fees. Day tickets may be pre-booked by credit card using a telephone booking 'hotline' and via the zoo's website. Reduced fees are available (eg to students, senior citizens and families).

Animal sponsorships, which last for one year, make a significant contribution to the cost of specialist diets, enclosure maintenance and veterinary care. Animal sponsors benefit from the advertisement of their names at the sponsored animal's enclosure.

You have just received an email from Charlotte Brain, who is a senior partner in your firm:

To:	Laura Liver <lauraliver@organco.com>
From:	Charlotte Brain <charlottebrain@organco.com>
Date:	December
Subject:	Bateleur Zoo Gardens

Dear Laura,

It's that time of the year again, and it falls upon us to get started on the planning for the BZG audit. The new management team has so far shown itself to be very diligent, and has identified a number of risks that are in need of further consideration so that they can be managed actively. I'd like you to review the list and then prepare a memorandum for me, letting me know what sort of internal controls we'd expect to be in place to help manage each of the risks, as well as what risks of material misstatement arise from each applicable risk. Please also comment on the factors to consider when planning the extent of substantive analytical procedures to be performed on BZG's income.

Here is the list of applicable risks that management has identified:

(i)   Reduction in admission income through failure to invest in new exhibits and breeding programmes to attract visitors

(ii)   Animal sponsorships may not be invoiced due to incomplete data transfer between the sponsoring and invoicing departments.

(iii)   Corporate sponsorships may not be charged for at approved rates – either in error or due to arrangements with the companies. In particular, the sponsoring department may not notify the invoicing department of reciprocal arrangements, whereby sponsoring companies provide BZG with advertising (eg in company magazines and annual reports).

(iv)   Cash received at the entrance gate ticket offices ('kiosks') may not be passed to cashiers in the accounts department (eg through theft).

(v)   The ticket booking and issuing system may not be available.

(vi)   Donations of animals to the collection (eg from taxation authority seizures and rare breeds enthusiasts) may not be recorded.

Thanks for this. I look forward to reading your thoughts!

Charlotte

Required

(a)   Respond to Charlotte's email.   **(25 marks)**

       Note. Professional marks will be available for the format and clarity of answers to part (a) above. **(4 marks)**

(b)   Comment on the responsibilities of management and auditors for internal controls. Discuss auditing and other current guidance in this area.   **(5 marks)**

(Total = 34 marks)

54 Sci-Tech (12/07) (amended)

You are James Cotter. You were recently promoted to the level of audit manager at Rab & Co, a large firm of Chartered Certified Accountants, and are now responsible for the audit of Sci-Tech Ltd, a pharmaceutical research company. You are planning the substantive audit procedures to be used in the forthcoming audit of intangible assets and operating expenses. Relevant extracts from the financial statements are as follows.

	30 November	
	20X8 (draft)	20X7
	£'000	£'000
Statement of financial position		
Intangible assets: development costs		
Cost	2,750	2,000
Accumulated amortisation	(1,450)	(850)
	1,300	1,150
Total assets	18,500	15,000
Statement of profit or loss		
Revenue	4,500	3,800
Operating expenses include:		
Research costs	160	200
Amortisation of development costs	600	450
Salary expenses	380	400
Profit before tax	1,800	1,530

The following is an extract from the notes to the draft financial statements:

'Expenditure on product development is capitalised as an intangible asset from the point at which it is probable that future economic benefits will result from the product once completed. Any product development costs which do not meet the above criteria are expensed as incurred as research costs. Two products are currently in the development phase: Medex, an antiseptic cream; and Flortex, a medicine to reduce the symptoms of fever.

'Amortisation of development costs commences with commercial production, the amortisation period being the estimated life span of the product. Currently two products are being amortised over the following periods:

1   Plummet Cold Cure: five years
2   Blingo Cough Cure: three years

During the initial planning of the audit, the audit senior made the following note on the working papers:

'Bio-Cert Ltd is the main competitor of our client. It appears that Bio-Cert Ltd is developing a rival product to Flortex. This rival product is expected to be launched in June 20X9, six months prior to the expected launch of Flortex.'

Sci-Tech Ltd decided to outsource its payroll function, commencing in June 20X8. The service is being provided by ProPay Ltd, a small local company. All of the accounting records relating to payroll are maintained and kept by ProPay Ltd. In previous years the audit of salary expenses was performed using a systems based approach with limited substantive procedures.

Sci-Tech Ltd receives funding from governmental health departments, as well as several large charitable donations. This funding represents on average 25% of the company's research and development annual expenditure. The amount of funding received is dependent on three key performance indicator (KPI) targets being met annually. All three of the targets must be met in order to secure the government funding.

Extracts from Sci-Tech Ltd's operating and financial review are as follows.

KPI target	Draft KPI 20X8	Actual KPI 20X7
Pharmaceutical products donated free of charge to health care charities: 1% revenue	0.8% revenue	1.2% revenue
Donations to, and cost of involvement with, local community charities: 0.5% revenue	0.6% revenue	0.8% revenue
Accidents in the work place: Fewer than 5 serious accidents per year	4 serious accidents	2 serious accidents

In addition to performing the financial statement audit, your firm is engaged to provide an assurance opinion on the KPIs disclosed in the operating and financial review.

You have just received an email from Robert Nesbitt, the engagement partner responsible for Sci-Tech:

To: James Cotter <jamesie@rabandco.co.uk>
From: Robert Nesbitt <rabc@rabandco.co.uk>
Date: December 20X8
Subject: Sci-Tech planning

James,

As this is your first job in your new role, I'd like you to prepare a memorandum for me outlining what your approach will be to a few of the key issues in the Sci-Tech audit and review engagements. In particular, please ensure that you cover the following.

(a)   Define outsourcing is explain and the matters to be in considered in planning the audit of salary expense.
(9 marks)

(b)   Matters to consider in relation to the capitalised development costs (5 marks), and evidence that should be sought regarding the assertion that development costs are technically feasible (3 marks).   **(8 marks)**

(c)   Procedures to perform on the amortisation rate of five years being applied to development costs in relation to Plummet.   **(5 marks)**

(d)   (i)   Discuss why it may not be possible to provide a high level of assurance over the stated key performance indicators.   **(4 marks)**

        (ii)   Describe the procedures to verify the number of serious accidents in the year ended 30 November 20X8.   **(4 marks)**

I'd like you to get to work on this straight away so that we can get the planning itself done in time.

Regards,

Robert

Required

Respond to Robert's email.   **(30 marks)**

Note. Four professional marks will be available for the format and clarity of answers.   **(4 marks)**

(Total = 34 marks)

55 Rosie (6/08) (amended)

Rosie Ltd is the parent company of an expanding group of companies. The group's main business activity is the manufacture of engine parts. In January 20X8 the acquisition of Dylan Ltd was completed, and the group is currently considering the acquisition of Maxwell Ltd, a large company which would increase the group's operating facilities by around 40%. All subsidiaries are wholly owned. The group structure is summarised below.

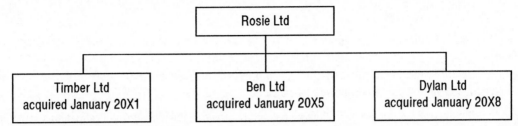

You are John Hayes, a senior audit manager in Chien & Co, a firm of Chartered Certified Accountants. Today you received the following email from Stephen Ferris, who has recently been promoted to the role of audit supervisor, and who is currently working on the Rosie Group audit.

To:	John Hayes, senior manager <john.hayes@chienco.com>
From:	Stephen Ferris, audit supervisor <stephen.ferris@chienco.com>
Date:	June 20X8
Subject:	Rosie Group audit

Hello John,

I am about to start reviewing the working papers completed on the final audit of Rosie Ltd and the Rosie Group for the year ended 31 January 20X8. I was hoping you would be able to help me get a few things clear in my mind before I do the review.

Goodwill on the acquisition of Dylan Ltd is recognised in the consolidated statement of financial position at £750,000. The client has given us this calculation:

	£'000
Cost of investment:	
Cash consideration	2,500
Deferred consideration payable 31 January 20X9	1,500
Contingent consideration payable 31 January 20Y2 if Dylan Co's revenue grows 5% per annum	1,000
	5,000
Net assets acquired	(4,250)
Goodwill on acquisition	750

Can you tell me what matters I need to consider, and what sort of evidence I should expect to find in respect of the carrying value of the cost of the investment in Dylan Ltd in the financial statements of Rosie Ltd?

Also, what procedures should I expect to have been done on the consolidation schedule of the Rosie Group?

Thanks for your help with this. I can't wait to get started – this is my first piece of review work and I think it will be interesting to see things 'from the other side'!

Regards,

Stephen Ferris

Note. All of the figures in Stephen's email are material to the financial statements of Rosie Ltd and the Rosie Group.

Your firm has audited all current components of the group for several years, but the target company Maxwell Ltd is audited by a different firm. The management of Rosie Ltd has provided the audit team with some information about Maxwell Ltd to aid business understanding, but little audit work is considered necessary as the acquisition, if it goes ahead, will be after the auditor's report has been issued.

You have just received an email from Leo Sabat, the finance director of the Rosie Group:

To:	John Hayes, <john.hayes@chienco.com>
From:	Leo Sabat, Group Finance Director, <lsabat@rosierose.com>
Date:	June 20X8
Subject:	Maxwell Ltd

John,

It was good to see to you the other day. As promised, please find attached the information you requested on the Maxwell Ltd acquisition. I have included audited financial statements for the year ended 31 January 20X8, an organisational structure, several customer contracts, and prospective financial information for the next two years. We don't have much available so I'm giving you all we've got!

I'm hoping that the other directors will agree that an externally provided due diligence investigation should be carried out urgently, before any investment decision is made. The other directors, though, feel this is not needed as the financial statements of Maxwell Ltd have already been audited.

I need you to prepare a report to the other directors in which you:

• Describe the purpose, and evaluate the benefits of a due diligence investigation to the potential purchaser of a company, and

• Compare the scope of a due diligence investigation with that of an audit of financial statements.

Thanks John. I look forward to hearing from you soon.

Best regards,

Leo

Required

(a) Respond to Leo Sabat's email. **(14 marks)**

Note. Four professional marks are available in part (a) for the format and clarity of the answer. **(4 marks)**

(b) Respond to Stephen Ferris' email. **(11 marks)**

(c) Maxwell Ltd is audited by Lead & Co, a firm of Chartered Certified Accountants. Leo Sabat has enquired as to whether your firm would be prepared to conduct a joint audit in cooperation with Lead & Co, on the future financial statements of Maxwell Ltd if the acquisition goes ahead. Leo Sabat thinks that this would enable your firm to improve group audit efficiency, without losing the cumulative experience that Lead & Co has built up while acting as auditor to Maxwell Ltd.

Required

Define 'joint audit', and assess the advantages and disadvantages of the audit of Maxwell Ltd being conducted on a 'joint basis'. **(7 marks)**

(Total = 36 marks)

56 Medix (6/08) (amended)

65 mins

You are Charles Banks, an audit senior in Mitchell & Co, a firm of Chartered Certified Accountants. Gavin Jones is an audit manager in your firm who has recently returned to practice after working for some years in industry. You have just received the following email from him.

To: Charles Banks, audit senior
From: Gavin Jones, audit manager
Subject: Potential new client – Medix Ltd

Charles,

I would like you to prepare some briefing notes for me to use to help me decide whether or not to proceed with the appointment as auditor to a new client, Medix Ltd. There are a number of pieces of information that you'll need to take into account when preparing them.

I recently held a meeting with the finance director of Medix Ltd, Ricardo Feller, and I've attached my notes from it to this email (Attachment 1).

I have also held a discussion with the current audit partner of Medix Ltd, Mick Evans, who runs a small accounting and audit practice in which he is one of two partners. I have attached an extract from an email that I recently received from him (Attachment 2).

Finally, I have come across an article in a local newspaper that mentions Medix Ltd, but I haven't had a chance to read through it yet. I've attached some extracts from it (Attachment 3).

Be sure that your notes include the following.

(a) An assessment of the professional, ethical and other issues to be considered in deciding whether to proceed with the appointment as auditor of Medix Ltd **(10 marks)**

(b) (i) A discussion of the relationship between the concepts of 'business risk' and 'risk of material misstatement' **(4 marks)**

     (ii) Identify and explain the potential risks of material misstatement caused by the breach of planning regulations discussed in the press cutting. **(6 marks)**

(c) Identify and explain the principal business risks facing Medix Ltd. **(12 marks)**

Thanks for your help with this.

Regards,

Gavin

Attachment 1

Meeting notes – meeting held 1 June 20X8 with Ricardo Feller

Medix Ltd is a provider of specialised surgical instruments used in medical procedures. The company is owner managed, has a financial year ending 30 June 20X8, and has invited our firm to be appointed as auditor for the forthcoming year-end. The audit is not going out to tender. Ricardo Feller has been with the company since January 20X8, following the departure of the previous finance director, who is currently taking legal action against Medix Ltd for unfair dismissal.

Company background

Medix Ltd manufactures surgical instruments which are sold to hospitals and clinics. Due to the increased use of laser surgery in the last four years, demand for traditional metal surgical instruments, which provided 75% of revenue in the year ended 30 June 20X7, has declined rapidly. Medix Ltd is expanding into the provision of laser surgery equipment, but research and development is at an early stage. The directors feel confident that the laser instruments currently being designed will eventually receive the necessary licence for commercial production, and that the laser product will replace surgical instruments as a leading source of revenue. There is currently one scientist working on the laser equipment, subcontracted by Medix Ltd on a freelance basis. The building in which the research is being carried out has recently been significantly extended by the construction of a large laboratory.

A considerable revenue stream is derived from agents who are not employed by Medix Ltd. The agents earn a commission based on the value of sales they have secured for Medix Ltd during the year. There are many suppliers into the market and agents are used by all manufacturers as a means of marketing and distributing their products.

The company's manufacturing facility is located in another country, where operating costs are significantly lower. The facility is under the control of a local manager who visits the head office of Medix Ltd annually for a meeting with senior management. Products are imported via aeroplane. The overseas plant and equipment is owned by the company and was constructed 12 years ago specifically for the manufacture of metal surgical instruments.

The company has a bank overdraft facility and makes use of the facility most months. A significant bank loan, which will carry a variable interest rate, is currently being negotiated. The terms of the loan will be finalised once the audited financial statements have been viewed by the bank.

Attachment 2

Extract from email from Mick Evans

'Medix Ltd has been an audit client for three years. We took over from the previous auditors following a disagreement between them and the directors of Medix Ltd over fees. As we are a small practice with low overheads we could offer lower fees than our predecessors. We could also do the audit very quickly, which pleased the client, as they like to keep costs as low as possible.

'During our audits we have found the internal systems and controls to be quite weak. Despite our recommendations, there always seemed to be a lack of interest in making improvements to the accounting systems, as this was seen to be a "waste of money". There have been two investigations by the tax authorities, which we did not deal with, as we are not tax experts. In the end the directors sorted it all out, and I believe that the tax matter is now resolved. We never had a problem getting access to accounting books and records. However, the managing director, Jon Tate, once gave us what he described as "the wrong cash book" by mistake, and replaced it with the "proper version" later in the day. We never found out why he was keeping two cash books, but cash was an immaterial asset so we didn't worry about it too much.

'We are resigning as auditors because the work load is too much for our small practice, and as Medix Ltd is our only audit client we have decided to focus on providing non-audit services in the future.'

Attachment 3

Extract from local newspaper – business section, 2 June 20X8

It appears that local company Medix Ltd has breached local planning regulations by building an extension to its research and development building for which no local authority approval has been given. The land on which the premises is situated has protected status as a 'greenfield' site which means approval by the local authority is necessary for any modification to commercial buildings.

A representative of the local planning office stated today: 'We feel that this is a serious breach of regulations and it is not the first time that Medix Ltd has deliberately ignored planning rules. The company was successfully sued in 20X3 for constructing an access road without receiving planning permission, and we are considering taking legal action in respect of this further breach of planning regulations. We are taking steps to ensure that these premises are shut down within a month. A similar breach of regulations by a different company last year resulted in the demolition of the building.'

Required

Respond to Gavin's email. **(32 marks)**

Professional marks will be awarded for the appropriateness of the format and presentation of the notes and the effectiveness with which the information is communicated. **(4 marks)**

(Total = 36 marks)

57 Prosperitas   32 mins

You are Khalid Huq, an audit senior at Veritas & Co, a medium-sized audit firm based in the UK.

You have just received the following email from Sue Dixon, a partner at Veritas.

To:	Khalid Huq
From:	Sue Dixon
Date:	15 June 20X1
Subject:	New audit client – Prosperitas Ltd

Khalid,

As you know, the auditor's report for Prosperitas Ltd contained an Emphasis of Matter paragraph in relation to the doubts that existed over going concern. Well, since then Prosperitas' situation has gotten worse, and the directors have asked me to meet with them to discuss insolvency proceedings with them. I'd like you to prepare some briefing notes for me, in which you (a) identify and explain the two main grounds under which a company may be wound up by the court under Section 122 of the Insolvency Act 1986; (b) identify and explain the distinguishing characteristics of a creditors' voluntary winding up; and (c) explain the immediate legal effect of an order of the court for the compulsory winding up of a company.

Regards,

Sue

Required

Respond to Sue's email. **(14 marks)**

Professional marks will be awarded for the appropriateness of the format and presentation of the notes and the effectiveness with which the information is communicated. **(4 marks)**

(Total = 18 marks)

58 Peter

You are currently a senior working at the audit firm Cameron Clarke Co. You have just received an e-mail from Trevor McDouglas, an audit partner at the firm:

To:	A Senior
From:	Trevor McDouglas
Date:	21 July 20X0
Subject:	Peter plc

I have just received a call from Pierre Petit, the group finance director of Peter plc. Peter plc has a number of subsidiaries and two of them, Sebastian Ltd and Simon Ltd, have been experiencing financial difficulties. Mr. Petit wants our advice on whether liquidation is the best course of action.

Peter Plc does not think that things are likely to improve, and is therefore considering their liquidation. Mr. Petit has calculated that Sebastian Ltd has a negative net present value of around £1m, and that Simon Ltd has a positive net present value of around £1m.

Firstly, please produce some notes for me on the additional risks associated with the audit of Sebastian Ltd and Simon Ltd for the year to 30 June 20X0.

I then want you to draft a brief report for me to use as the basis for our advice to Peter Plc on whether liquidation is the best course of action. I have pasted at the bottom of this email some information that Mr. Petit has given me on the subsidiaries. In addition to this, the two subsidiaries' bankers are worried that they may not be repaid what they are owed; I need your report to give an assessment of this.

Please have the report and the notes on my desk as soon as possible.

Regards,

Trevor McDouglas

Peter group – information from Mr. Petit

	Sebastian Ltd		Simon Ltd	
	Carrying amount	Net realisable value (NRV)	Carrying amount	Net realisable value (NRV)
	£'000	£'000	£'000	£'000
Freehold land	3,000	3,800	2,500	4,500
Other non-current assets	2,000	600	2,700	700
Current assets	1,100	400	1,300	800
Debenture holders	1,600		1,500	
Bank overdraft	2,900		1,000	
Preferential creditors	100		200	
Unsecured creditors	700		700	

Both Sebastian Ltd and Simon Ltd have significant retained losses. Both subsidiaries' debentures are secured by a fixed charge against the freehold land of each company. Each company's bank loans are secured by a floating charge against the other net assets of the individual company. There are no cross-guarantees within the group. The liquidator's costs are estimated at £250,000 for each company.

Required

Respond to the partner's email. **(14 marks)**

Professional marks will be awarded for the appropriateness of the format and presentation of the notes and the effectiveness with which the information is communicated. **(4 marks)**

(Total = 18 marks)

REPORTING

Questions 59 to 73 cover Reporting, the subject of Part F of the BPP Study Text for Paper P7.

59 Yew (12/11)

32 mins

(a) You are the manager responsible for the audit of Yew Ltd, a company which designs and develops aircraft engines. The audit for the year ended 31 July 20X1 is nearing completion and the audit senior has left the following file note for your attention:

'I have just returned from a meeting with the management of Yew Ltd, and there is a matter I want to bring to your attention. Yew Ltd's statement of financial position recognises an intangible asset of £12.5 million in respect of capitalised research and development costs relating to new aircraft engine designs. However, market research conducted by Yew Ltd in relation to these new designs indicated that there would be little demand in the near future for such designs. Management has provided written representation that they agree with the results of the market research.

'Currently, Yew Ltd has a cash balance of only £125,000 and members of the management team have expressed concerns that the company is finding it difficult to raise additional finance.

'The new aircraft designs have been discussed in the chairman's statement which is to be published with the financial statements. The discussion states that 'developments of new engine designs are underway, and we believe that these new designs will become a significant source of income for Yew Co in the next 12 months.

'Yew Ltd's draft financial statements include profit before tax of £23 million, and total assets of £210 million.

'Yew Ltd is due to publish its annual report next week, so we need to consider the impact of this matter urgently.'

Required

Discuss the implications of the audit senior's file note on the completion of the audit and on the auditor's report, recommending any further actions that should be taken by the auditor. **(12 marks)**

(b) You are responsible for answering technical queries from other managers and partners of your firm. An audit partner left the following note on your desk this morning.

    (i)   'I am about to draft the audit report for my client, Sycamore Ltd. I am going on holiday tomorrow and want to have the audit report signed and dated before I leave. The only thing outstanding is the written representation from management – I have verbally confirmed the contents with the finance director who agreed to send the representations to the audit manager within the next few days. I presume this is acceptable?' **(3 marks)**

    (ii)   'We are auditing Sycamore Ltd for the first time. The prior period financial statements were audited by another firm. We are aware that the auditor's report on the prior period was qualified due to a material misstatement of trade receivables. We have obtained sufficient appropriate evidence that the matter giving rise to the misstatement has been resolved and I am happy to issue an unmodified opinion. But should I refer to the prior year modification in this year's auditor's report?' **(3 marks)**

Required

Respond to the audit partner's comments.

Note. The split of the mark allocation is shown within the question.

(Total = 18 marks)

60 Snipe (6/12)

You are the partner responsible for performing an engagement quality control review on the audit of Snipe Ltd. You are currently reviewing the audit working papers and draft audit report on the financial statements of Snipe Ltd for the year ended 31 January 20X2. The draft financial statements recognise revenue of £8.5 million, profit before tax of £1 million, and total assets of £175 million.

(a) During the year Snipe Ltd's factory was extended by the self-construction of a new processing area, at a total cost of £5 million. Included in the costs capitalised are borrowing costs of £100,000, incurred during the six-month period of construction. A loan of £4 million carrying an interest rate of 5% was taken out in respect of the construction on 1 March 20X1, when construction started. The new processing area was ready for use on 1 September 20X1, and began to be used on 1 December 20X1. Its estimated useful life is 15 years.

Required

In respect of your file review of non-current assets, comment on the matters that should be considered, and the evidence you would expect to find regarding the new processing area. **(8 marks)**

(b) Snipe Ltd has in place a defined benefit pension plan for its employees. An actuarial valuation on 31 January 20X2 indicated that the plan is in deficit by £10.5 million. The deficit is not recognised in the statement of financial position. An extract from the draft audit report is given below.

Auditor's opinion

In our opinion, because of the significance of the matter discussed below, the financial statements do not give a true and fair view of the financial position of Snipe Ltd as at 31 January 20X2, and of its financial performance and cash flows for the year then ended in accordance with International Financial Reporting Standards.

Explanation of adverse opinion in relation to pension

The financial statements do not include the company's pension plan. This deliberate omission contravenes accepted accounting practice and means that the accounts are not properly prepared.

Required

Critically appraise the extract from the proposed audit report of Snipe Ltd for the year ended 31 January 20X2.

Note. You are **not** required to re-draft the extract of the audit report. **(7 marks)**

(Total = 15 marks)

61 Nassau Group (6/11)

(a) You are the manager responsible for the audit of the Nassau Group, which comprises a parent company and six subsidiaries. The audit of all individual companies' financial statements is almost complete, and you are currently carrying out the audit of the consolidated financial statements. One of the subsidiaries, Exuma Ltd, is audited by another firm, Jalousie & Ltd. Your firm has fulfilled the necessary requirements of ISA 600 *Special Considerations – Audits of Group Financial Statements (Including the Work of Component Auditors)* and is satisfied as to the competence and independence of Jalousie & Ltd.

You have received from Jalousie & Co the draft audit report on Exuma Ltd's financial statements, an extract from which is shown below.

'Basis for Qualified Opinion (extract)

'The company is facing financial damages of £2 million in respect of an on-going court case, more fully explained in Note 12 to the financial statements. Management has not recognised a provision but has disclosed the situation as a contingent liability. Under International Financial Reporting Standards, a provision should be made if there is an obligation as a result of a past event, a probable outflow of economic benefit, and a reliable estimate can be made. Audit evidence concludes that these criteria have been met, and it is our opinion that a provision of £2 million should be recognised. Accordingly, net profit and shareholders' equity would have been reduced by £2 million if the provision had been recognised.

'Qualified Opinion (extract)

'In our opinion, except for effects of the matter described in the Basis for Qualified Opinion paragraph, the financial statements give a true and fair view of the financial position of Exuma Ltd as at 31 March 20X1...'

An extract of Note 12 to Exuma Ltd's financial statements is shown below.

Note 12 (extract)

The company is the subject of a court case concerning an alleged breach of planning regulations. The plaintiff is claiming compensation of £2 million. The management of Exuma Ltd, after seeking legal advice, believe that there is only a 20% chance of a successful claim being made against the company.

Figures extracted from the draft financial statements for the year ending 31 March 20X1 are as follows.

	Nassau Group	Exuma Ltd
	£m	£m
Profit before tax	20	4
Total assets	85	20

Required

Identify and explain the matters that should be considered, and actions that should be taken by the group audit engagement team, in forming an opinion on the consolidated financial statements of the Nassau Group. **(8 marks)**

(b) In February 20X1, the entire share capital of Andros Ltd, a wholly owned subsidiary of the Nassau Group, was disposed of. The consolidated statement of profit or loss includes profit on disposal of £5 million.

Required

Comment on the matters that you should consider and the evidence that you expect to find, in your review of the audit working papers in respect of the disposal of Andros Ltd. **(10 marks)**

(Total = 18 marks)

62 Cinnabar Group (AAS 6/02)   27 mins

(a) Explain the auditor's responsibilities for the appropriateness of the going concern assumption as a basis for the preparation of financial statements. **(5 marks)**

(b) You are a manager in the quality control review department of Scheel, a firm of Chartered Certified Accountants. You are currently responsible for reviewing the appropriateness of your firm's proposed auditor's reports on financial statements.

The draft financial statements of Cinnabar group for the year to 30 June 20X8 disclose the following notes.

Notes

1 *Significant event*

During the year, Cinnabar sold a significant amount of its business and certain assets (plant and equipment and inventory) and commenced a systematic winding down of its operations. The group's remaining assets (including property, trade receivables and cash) were sufficient to meet the group's liabilities, as at 30 June 20X8.

2 *Accounting policies*

The consolidated financial statements have been prepared under the historical cost convention and in accordance with applicable accounting standards. As described in Note 1, the group has commenced the winding down of its operations and remaining assets have been restated to their net realisable values.

There are no other disclosures relating to the going concern basis although the 'significant event' is referred to in the directors' report under the heading 'principal activities and business review'.

Cinnabar ceased to trade in October 20X8. The auditor's report on Cinnabar's financial statements for the year ended 30 June 20X7 was unmodified.

Required

Comment on the suitability or otherwise of an unmodified auditor's report for Cinnabar for the year ended 30 June 20X8. Your answer should discuss the appropriateness of alternative audit opinions. **(10 marks)**

Note. Assume it is 11 December 20X8. **(Total = 15 marks)**

63 Poodle (6/13) 36 mins

You are the manager responsible for the audit of the Poodle Group (the Group) and you are completing the audit of the consolidated financial statements for the year ended 31 March 20X3. The draft consolidated financial statements recognise revenue of £18 million (20X2 – £17 million), profit before tax of £2 million (20X2 – £3 million) and total assets of £58 million (20X2 – £59 million). Your firm audits all of the components of the Group, apart from an overseas subsidiary, Toy Ltd, which is audited by a small local firm of accountants and auditors.

The audit senior has left a file note for your attention. You are aware that the Group's annual report and financial statements are due to be released next week, and the Group is very reluctant to make any adjustments in respect of the matters described.

Toy Ltd

The component auditors of Toy Ltd, the overseas subsidiary, have been instructed to provide the Group audit team with details of a court case which is ongoing. An ex-employee is suing Toy Ltd for unfair dismissal and has claimed £500,000 damages against the company. To comply with local legislation, Toy Ltd's individual financial statements are prepared using a local financial reporting framework. Under that local financial reporting framework, a provision is only recognised if a cash outflow is virtually certain to arise. The component auditors obtained verbal confirmation from Toy Ltd's legal advisors that the damages are probable, but not virtually certain to be paid, and no provision has been recognised in either the individual or consolidated financial statements. No other audit evidence has been obtained by the component auditors.

Trade receivable

On 1 June 20X3, a notice was received from administrators dealing with the winding up of Terrier Ltd, following its insolvency. The notice stated that the company should be in a position to pay approximately 10% of the amounts owed to its trade payables. Poodle Ltd, the parent company of the Group, includes a balance of £1.6 million owed by Terrier Ltd in its trade receivables.

Chairman's statement

The draft chairman's statement, to be included in the Group's annual report, was received yesterday. The chairman comments on the performance of the Group, stating that he is pleased that revenue has increased by 20% in the year.

Required

Assess the implications of the matters described above for the completion of the Group audit, and describe the impact on the Group audit report if any adjustments considered necessary are not made.

(Total = 20 marks)

64 Dexter (12/08) 36 mins

(a) Compare and contrast the responsibilities of management, and of auditors, in relation to the assessment of going concern. You should include a description of the procedures used in this assessment where relevant.
(7 marks)

(b) You are the manager responsible for performing hot reviews on audit files where there is a potential disagreement between your firm and the client regarding a material issue. You are reviewing the going concern section of the audit file of Dexter Ltd, a client with considerable cash flow difficulties, and other, less significant operational indicators of going concern problems. The working papers indicate that Dexter Ltd is currently trying to raise finance to fund operating cash flows, and state that if the finance is not received, there is significant doubt over the going concern status of the company. The working papers conclude that the going concern assumption is appropriate, but it is recommended that the financial statements should contain a note explaining the cash flow problems faced by the company, along with a description of the finance being sought, and an evaluation of the going concern status of the company. The directors do not wish to include the note in the financial statements.

Required

Consider and comment on the possible reasons why the directors of Dexter Ltd are reluctant to provide the note to the financial statements. **(5 marks)**

(c)   Identify and discuss the implications for the auditor's report if:

(i)   The directors refuse to include the disclosure note   **(4 marks)**
(ii)   The directors agree to include the disclosure note.   **(4 marks)**

(Total = 20 marks)

65 Johnston and Tiltman (AAS 6/06) (amended)   27 mins

(a)   The purpose of ISA 510 *Initial audit engagements – opening balances* is to establish standards and provide guidance regarding opening balances when the financial statements are audited for the first time or when the financial statements for the prior period were audited by another auditor.

Required

Explain the auditor's reporting responsibilities that are specific to initial engagements. **(5 marks)**

(b)   You are the audit manager of Johnston Ltd, a private company. The draft consolidated financial statements for the year ended 30 September 20X8 show profit before taxation of £10.5 million (20X7 – £9.4 million) and total assets of £55.2 million (20X7 – £50.7 million).

Your firm was appointed auditor of Tiltman Ltd when Johnston Ltd acquired all the shares of Tiltman Ltd in September 20X8. Tiltman's draft financial statements for the year ended 30 September 20X8 show profit before taxation of £0.7 million (20X7 – £1.7 million) and total assets of £16.1 million (20X7 – £16.6 million). The auditor's report on the financial statements for the year ended 30 September 20X7 was unmodified.

You are currently reviewing two matters that have been left for your attention on the audit working paper files for the year ended 30 September 20X8:

(i)   In June 20X7 Tiltman installed a new computer system that properly quantified an overvaluation of inventory amounting to £2.7 million. This is being written off over three years.

(ii)   In November 20X8, Tiltman's head office was relocated to Johnston's premises as part of a restructuring. Provisions for the resulting redundancies and non-cancellable lease payments amounting to £2.3 million have been made in the financial statements of Tiltman for the year ended 30 September 20X8.

Required

Identify and comment on the implications of these two matters for your auditor's reports on the financial statements of Johnston Ltd and Tiltman Ltd for the year ended 30 September 20X8.   **(10 marks)**

Note. Assume it is 11 December 20X8.   **(Total = 15 marks)**

66 Lychee (12/09)   29 mins

(a)   Guidance on subsequent events is given in ISA 560 (UK and Ireland) *Subsequent events*.

Required

Explain the auditor's responsibility in relation to subsequent events.   **(6 marks)**

(b)   You are the manager responsible for the audit of Lychee Ltd, a manufacturing company with a year ended 30 September 20X9. The audit work has been completed and reviewed and you are due to issue the auditor's report in three days. The draft audit opinion is unmodified. The financial statements show revenue for the year ended 30 September 20X9 of £15 million, net profit of £3 million, and total assets at the year end are £80 million.

The finance director of Lychee Ltd telephoned you this morning to tell you about the announcement yesterday, of a significant restructuring of Lychee Ltd, which will take place over the next six months. The restructuring will involve the closure of a factory, and its relocation to another part of the country. There will be some redundancies and the estimated cost of closure is £250,000. The financial statements have not been amended in respect of this matter.

Required

In respect of the announcement of the restructuring:

(i)   Comment on the financial reporting implications, and advise the further audit procedures to be performed   **(6 marks)**

(ii)   Recommend the actions to be taken by the auditor if the financial statements are not amended
                                                                                                                                                          (4 marks)

                                                                                                                                       (Total = 16 marks)

67 Grimes (6/10)   36 mins

(a)   You are the partner responsible for the audit of Grimes Ltd, for the year ended 30 April 20X0. Grimes Ltd's main operating activity is property development. The management of Grimes Ltd have asked that the audit report be issued by no later than 25 June 20X0, and you are aware that Grimes Ltd is hoping to secure finance based on the audited financial statements. The audit manager has been reviewing the audit files and has noted several points for your review, both relating to material balances or transactions, which are described below.

A stated accounting policy of Grimes Ltd is to recognise revenue on the legal completion of a property sale. However, revenue on the sale of five properties, which were legally completed on 8 May 20X0, has been recognised in the financial statements for the year ended 30 April 20X0.

Properties being developed are recognised at cost, including directly attributable development costs, such as labour costs, materials and a proportion of overheads. For several large development projects, the project manager was unable to provide evidence to verify the costs included, saying that his computer files had been corrupted by a virus, and that no other records had been kept regarding the costs allocated to the properties. The audit team has therefore not been able to conclude on the audit work performed on the valuation of these properties at the year end.

Required

For each of the two matters above:

(i)   Explain and recommend the further actions to be taken by the audit partner in respect of the matters outlined above, and   **(6 marks)**

(ii)   Evaluate the potential impact on the auditor's report of these matters.   **(4 marks)**

Note. Marks will be allocated equally between the two matters.

(b)   You are also responsible for providing guidance to more junior members of the audit department of your firm on technical matters. Several recent recruits have asked for guidance in the area of auditor's liability. They are keen to understand how an audit firm can reduce its exposure to claims of negligence. They have also heard that in the UK, following the introduction of the Companies Act 2006, it is possible to restrict liability by making a liability limitation agreement with an audit client.

Required

(i) Explain **four** methods that may be used by an audit firm to reduce exposure to litigation claims.

(4 marks)

(ii) Assess the potential implications for the profession, of audit firms signing a liability limitation agreement with their audit clients.

(6 marks)

(Total = 20 marks)

68 Pluto (6/09)　　　　　　　　　　　　　　　　　　　31 mins

(a) Explain the term 'fraudulent financial reporting', illustrating your explanation with examples. **(4 marks)**

(b) You are the partner responsible for performing an engagement quality control review on the audit of Pluto plc, a listed company. You are currently reviewing the engagement partner's proposed auditor's report on the financial statements of Pluto plc for the year ended 31 March 20X9. During the year the company has undergone significant reorganisation, involving the discontinuance of two major business segments. Extracts of the proposed auditor's report are shown below.

Basis for adverse opinion

The directors have not recognised a provision in relation to redundancy costs associated with the reorganisation during the year. The reason is that they do not feel that a reliable estimate of the amount can be made, and so the recognition criteria of IAS 37 have not been met. We disagree with the directors as we feel that an estimate can be made. This matter is more fully explained in a note to the financial statements. We feel that this is a material misstatement as the profit for the year is overstated.

In our opinion, the financial statements do not give a true and fair view of the financial position of the company as of 31 March 20X9, and of its financial performance and its cash flows for the year then ended in accordance with International Financial Reporting Standards as adopted by the European Union.

Emphasis of matter – Earnings per Share

The directors have decided not to disclose the Earnings per Share for 20X9, as they feel that the figure is materially distorted by significant discontinued operations in the year. Our opinion is not qualified in respect of this matter.

Required

Critically appraise the proposed auditor's report of Pluto plc for the year ended 31 March 20X9.

Note. You are **not** required to re-draft the extracts from the auditor's report. **(9 marks)**

(c) Explain the matters to be considered in deciding who is eligible to perform an engagement quality control review for a listed client.

(4 marks)

(Total = 17 marks)

69 Cleeves (AAS 12/06)　　　　　　　　　　　　　　　　27 mins

(a) The purpose of ISA 250A *Consideration of laws and regulations in an audit of financial statements* is to establish standards and provide guidance on the auditor's responsibility to consider laws and regulations in an audit of financial statements.

Explain the auditor's responsibilities for reporting non-compliance that comes to the auditor's attention during the conduct of an audit. **(5 marks)**

(b) You are an audit manager in a firm of Chartered Certified Accountants currently assigned to the audit of Cleeves Ltd for the year ended 30 September 20X8. During the year Cleeves acquired a 100% interest in Howard Ltd. Howard is material to Cleeves and audited by another firm, Parr & Co. You have just received Parr's draft auditor's report for the year ended 30 September 20X8. The wording is that of an unmodified report except for the opinion paragraph which is as follows:

Audit opinion

As more fully explained in Notes 11 and 15 impairment losses on non-current assets have not been recognised in profit or loss as the directors are unable to quantify the amounts.

In our opinion, provision should be made for these as required IAS 36 *Impairment of assets.* If the provision had been so recognised the effect would have been to increase the loss before and after tax for the year and to reduce the value of tangible and intangible non-current assets. However, as the directors are unable to quantify the amounts we are unable to indicate the financial effect of such omissions.

In our opinion, because of the effects of the matter referred to above, the financial statements do not give a true and fair view of the state of the company's affairs at 30 September 20X8 and of its loss and its cash flows for the year then ended in accordance with International Financial Reporting Standards.

Your review of the prior year auditor's report shows that the 20X7 audit opinion was worded identically.

Required

(i)   Critically appraise the appropriateness of the audit opinion given by Parr & Co on the financial statements of Howard Ltd, for the years ended 30 September 20X8 and 20X7.   **(7 marks)**

(ii)   Briefly explain the implications of Parr & Co's auditor's opinion for your auditor's opinion on the consolidated financial statements of Cleeves Ltd for the year ended 30 September 20X8.   **(3 marks)**

(Total = 15 marks)

70 Blod (6/08)   31 mins

You are the manager responsible for the audit of Blod plc, a listed company, for the year ended 31 March 20X8. Your firm was appointed as auditors of Blod plc in September 20X7. The audit work has been completed, and you are reviewing the working papers in order to draft a report to those charged with governance. The statement of financial position shows total assets of £78 million (20X7 – £66 million). The main business activity of Blod plc is the manufacture of farm machinery.

During the audit of tangible non-current assets it was discovered that controls over capital expenditure transactions had deteriorated during the year. Authorisation had not been gained for the purchase of office equipment with a cost of £225,000. No material misstatements of the financial statements were revealed by audit procedures performed on tangible non-current assets.

An internally generated brand name has been included in the statement of financial position at a fair value of £10 million. Audit working papers show that the matter was discussed with the financial controller, who stated that the £10 million represents the present value of future cash flows estimated to be generated by the brand name. The member of the audit team who completed the work programme on intangible assets has noted that this treatment appears to be in breach of IAS 38 *Intangible assets* and that the management refuses to derecognise the asset.

Problems were experienced in the audit of inventory. Due to an oversight by the internal auditors of Blod plc, the external audit team did not receive a copy of inventory counting procedures prior to attending the count. This caused a delay at the beginning of the inventory count, when the audit team had to quickly familiarise themselves with the procedures. In addition, on the final audit, when the audit senior requested documentation to support the final inventory valuation, it took two weeks for the information to be received because the accountant who had prepared the schedules had mislaid them.

Required

(a)   (i)   Identify the main purpose of including 'findings from the audit' (management letter points) in a report to those charged with governance.   **(2 marks)**

(ii)   From the information provided above, recommend the matters which should be included as 'findings from the audit' in your report to those charged with governance, and explain the reason for their inclusion.   **(7 marks)**

(b)   The finance director of Blod plc, Uma Thorton, has requested that your firm type the financial statements in the form to be presented to shareholders at the forthcoming company general meeting. Uma has also commented that the previous auditors did not use a liability disclaimer in their auditor's report, and would like more information about the use of liability disclaimer paragraphs.

Required

Discuss the ethical issues raised by the request for your firm to type the financial statements of Blod plc.

(3 marks)

(c)   In the context of a standard unmodified auditor's report, describe the content of a liability disclaimer paragraph, and discuss the main arguments for and against the use of a liability disclaimer paragraph.

(5 marks)

(Total = 17 marks)

71 Axis & Co (Pilot paper) (amended)   27 mins

You are the manager responsible for four audit clients of Axis & Co, a firm of Chartered Certified Accountants. The year end in each case is 30 June 20X8.

You are currently reviewing the audit working paper files and the audit seniors' recommendations for the auditor's reports. Details are as follows.

(a)   During the year Lorenze Ltd has changed its accounting policy for purchased brands from amortisation over their useful lives to annual impairment review. No disclosure of this change has been given in the financial statements. The carrying amount of goodwill in the statement of financial position as at 30 June 20X8 is the same as at 30 June 20X7 as management's impairment review shows that it is not impaired.

The audit senior has concluded that a qualification is not required but suggests that attention can be drawn to the change by way of an emphasis of matter paragraph. **(6 marks)**

(b)   The directors' report of Abrupt Ltd states that investment property rental forms a major part of revenue. However, a note to the financial statements shows that property rental represents only 1.6% of total revenue for the year. The audit senior is satisfied that the revenue figures are correct.

The audit senior has noted that an unqualified opinion should be given as the audit opinion does not extend to the directors' report. **(4 marks)**

(c)   Audit work on the after-date bank transactions of Jingle Ltd has identified a transfer of cash from Bell Ltd. The audit senior assigned to the audit of Jingle has documented that Jingle's finance director explained that Bell commenced trading on 7 July 20X8, after being set up as a wholly-owned foreign subsidiary of Jingle.

The audit senior has noted that although no other evidence has been obtained an unmodified opinion is appropriate because the matter does not impact on the current year's financial statements. **(5 marks)**

Required

For each situation, comment on the suitability or otherwise of the audit senior's proposals for the auditor's reports. Where you disagree, indicate what audit modification (if any) should be given instead.

Note. The mark allocation is shown against each of the three issues.   **(Total = 15 marks)**

72 Dylan (12/12)   29 mins

(a)   You are the manager responsible for the audit of Dylan plc and you are reviewing the working papers of the audit file for the year ended 30 September 20X2. The audit senior has left a note for your attention:

'Dylan plc outsources its entire payroll, invoicing and credit control functions to Hendrix Ltd. In August 20X2, Hendrix Ltd suffered a computer virus attack on its operating system, resulting in the destruction of its accounting records, including those relating to Dylan plc. We have therefore been unable to perform the planned audit procedures on payroll, revenue and receivables, all of which are material to the financial statements. Hendrix Ltd has manually reconstructed the relevant figures as far as possible and has supplied a written statement to confirm that they are as accurate as possible, given the loss of accounting records.'

Required

(i) Comment on the actions that should be taken by the auditor and the implications for the auditor's report. **(7 marks)**

(ii) Discuss the quality control procedures that should be carried out by the audit firm prior to the audit report being issued. **(3 marks)**

(b) You are also responsible for the audit of Squire plc and you are completing the review of its interim financial statements for the six months ended 31 October 20X2. Squire plc is a car manufacturer and historically has offered a three-year warranty on cars sold. The financial statements for the year ended 30 April 20X2 included a warranty provision of £1.5 million and recognised total assets of £27.5 million. You are aware that on 1 July 20X2, due to cost cutting measures, Squire plc stopped offering warranties on cars sold. The interim financial statements for the six months ended 31 October 20X2 do not recognise any warranty provision. Total assets are £30 million at 31 October 20X2.

Required

Assess the matters that should be considered in forming a conclusion on Squire plc's interim financial statements, and the implications for the review report. **(6 marks)**

(Total = 16 marks)

73 Bertie & Co (12/07)   36 mins

You are the audit manager for three clients of Bertie & Co, a firm of Chartered Certified Accountants. The financial year-end for each client is 30 September 20X8.

You are reviewing the audit senior's proposed auditor's reports for two clients, Alpha plc and Deema Ltd.

Alpha plc, a listed company, permanently closed several factories in May 20X7, with all costs of closure finalised and paid in August 20X8. The factories all produced the same item, which contributed 10% of Alpha Co's total revenue for the year ended 30 September 20X8 (20X7 – 23%). The closure has been discussed accurately and fully in the chairman's statement and Directors' Report. However, the closure is not mentioned in the notes to the financial statements, nor separately disclosed on the financial statements.

The audit senior has proposed an unmodified audit opinion for Alpha plc as the matter has been fully addressed in the chairman's statement and Directors' Report.

In October 20X8 a legal claim was filed against Deema Ltd, a retailer of toys. The claim is from a customer who slipped on a greasy step outside one of the retail outlets. The matter has been fully disclosed as a material contingent liability in the notes to the financial statements, and audit working papers provide sufficient evidence that no provision is necessary as Deema Ltd's legal counsel has stated in writing that the likelihood of the claim succeeding is only possible. The amount of the claim is fixed and is adequately covered by cash resources.

The audit senior proposes that the audit opinion for Deema Ltd should not be modified, but that an emphasis of matter paragraph should be included after the audit opinion to highlight the situation.

Hugh Ltd was incorporated in October 20X7, using a bank loan for finance. Revenue for the first year of trading is £750,000, and there are hopes of rapid growth in the next few years. The business retails luxury hand made wooden toys, currently in a single retail outlet. The two directors (who also own all of the shares in Hugh Ltd) are aware that due to the small size of the company, the financial statements do not have to be subject to annual external audit, but they are unsure whether there would be any benefit in a voluntary audit of the first year financial statements. The directors are also aware that a review of the financial statements could be performed as an alternative to a full audit. Hugh Co currently employs a part-time, part-qualified accountant, Monty Parkes, who has prepared a year-end statement of financial position and statement of profit or loss, and who produces summary management accounts every three months.

Required

(a)   Evaluate whether the audit senior's proposed auditor's report is appropriate, and where you disagree with the proposed report, recommend the amendment necessary to the auditor's report of:

(i)   Alpha plc   **(6 marks)**

(ii) Deema Ltd   **(4 marks)**

(b)   Describe the potential benefits for Hugh Ltd in choosing to have a financial statement audit.   **(4 marks)**

(c)   With specific reference to Hugh Ltd, discuss the objective of a review engagement and contrast the level of assurance provided with that provided in an audit of financial statements.   **(6 marks)**

(Total = 20 marks)

Answers

1 Lark

Marking scheme

			Marks

(a)   (i)   **Implications of the audit senior's note**

Generally 1 mark for each matter discussed relevant to money laundering:
- Definition of money laundering
- Placement – cash-based business
- Owner posting transactions
- Layering – electronic transfer to overseas
- Secrecy and aggressive attitude
- Audit to be considered very high risk
- Senior may have tipped off the client
- Firm may consider withdrawal from audit
- But this may have tipping off consequences

Maximum marks   **6**

     (ii)   **Reporting that should take place**

Generally 1 mark for each comment:
- Report suspicions immediately to MLRO
- Failure to report is itself an offence
- Examples of matters to be reported (identity of suspect, etc)
- Audit senior may discuss matters with audit manager but senior responsible for the report

Maximum marks   **3**

(b) **Professional scepticism**
Generally 1 mark for each comment:
–   Definition of professional skepticism
–   Explain – alert to contradictory evidence/unusual events/fraud indicator
     (up to 2 marks)
–   Part of ethical codes
–   Reference to FRC discussion paper on auditor scepticism
–   Coot Ltd – evidence is unreliable and contradictory
–   Absence of authorisation is fraud indicator
–   Additional substantive procedures needed
–   Management's comments should be corroborated
–   Control deficiency to be reported to management/those charged with governance
–   Audit junior needs better supervision/training on how to deal with deficiencies
     identified

Maximum marks   6

Total   15

(a) (i)   The implication of the circumstances described is that there may be money laundering going on at
           Heron Ltd, involving its owner-manager Jack Heron.

           Money laundering is a process by which criminals may attempt to conceal the origins of the proceeds
           of criminal activity. The aim is to transform 'dirty' money, which can be tied to its criminal origin, into
           'clean' money which can be spent.

           The fact that Heron Ltd's revenue is almost entirely cash makes it an ideal 'front' business for a
           money laundering regime. The aim here would be to transform the 'dirty' money into revenue from
           the legitimate business. What appears to be happening here is that the legitimate cash receipts of
           £3.5m are being topped up with £2m 'dirty' money. This is the placement stage of the money
           laundering regime. The idea is that the £5.5m revenue will eventually appear legitimate if it can be
           said to all come from a legitimate business (Heron Ltd).

           The £2m electronic transfer is then part of the layering process, which aims to maximise the distance
           between the placement of the 'dirty' money and its eventual 'integration' into the financial system as
           'clean' money. The fact that this is an overseas transfer only heightens its suspiciousness, as money
           launderers often move money across national boundaries to make it harder to trace.

           The fact that Jack Heron has sole responsibility for cash receipts and postings gives him the
           opportunity to launder money in this way. The fact that no documentation was available to support
           the transfer means it is possible that it was done to launder money. The fact that Jack did not answer
           the senior's questions and became aggressive seems to confirm his desire for secrecy here.

           There is a risk that the senior has 'tipped off' Jack Heron by questioning him about the transfer. This
           is itself an offence, although it may be argued here that the senior was not aware that the disclosure
           could prejudice any future money laundering investigation.

           From the point of view of the audit, the amount is clearly highly material. It is possible that Lark & Co
           may seek to withdraw from the engagement; however, there is a risk that this could be construed as
           'tipping off' if Jack Heron thinks it is because the audit firm has suspicions over money laundering.
           The firm should obtain advice from its legal counsel.

     (ii) The audit senior should report the situation to Lark & Co's Money Laundering Reporting Officer
           (MLRO). The MLRO is the internal person responsible for receiving and evaluating reports of
           suspected money laundering, and for making any reports to external bodies.

           The report would typically include the name of the suspect, the amounts involved, the reasons for
           suspicion and the whereabouts of any laundered cash.

           The report must be made as soon as possible, as it is an offence to not report suspicions as soon as
           practicable.

The senior would be allowed to discuss his suspicions with the audit manager – in order to assure herself that her suspicions were reasonable – but should alert the MLRO herself.

(b) **Professional skepticism**

Professional skepticism is an attitude that includes a questioning mind, being alert to conditions which may indicate possible misstatement due to error or fraud, and a critical assessment of audit evidence.

This means being alert to the actual circumstances of the engagement and the work being done, and to the possibility that things may not be as they appear to be on first sight, eg that evidence obtained is unreliable, or may point to fraud. If an auditor is not skeptical in this way then they may not realise that something is unusual; they may not tailor audit procedures to the actual risk at hand; or they may jump to hasty conclusions.

Professional skepticism lies at the heart of auditing, both in the sense that it is part of being a competent auditor, and that it is an important part of being ethically independent.

Further actions

The evidence obtained already may not be reliable.

The payroll supervisor's assertion that no authorisation is needed for temporary workers must be corroborated. Evidence should also be gathered about the claim that the employees are temporary.

If the supervisor is correct that no authorisation is required for new employees, then this is a major deficiency of internal controls that should have been identified as part of controls testing. It may be a management letter point.

There is a contradiction between the supervisor's claim that there were new temporary staff, and management's claim that there are no new staff. It should be clarified that when management said there were no new employees, this included temporary staff.

It is possible that there is a fraud taking place here, possibly by the payroll supervisor. The new employees could be 'ghost employees' to whom money is paid via payroll but who do not exist. The money is then taken criminally, eg by the payroll supervisor or an associate of his.

The audit junior should be made aware that when he comes across issues like this, she must raise them with her supervisor.

2   Plant

Chapter references. Chapter 5.

Top tips. Part (a) should not have posed you many difficulties. The contents of the audit tender document are basic knowledge at this level. This question is fairly typical of the way this area is examined in P7: here, you really need to apply your knowledge to the situation of the Plant Group. You can use the basic contents of the tender as a starting point, and then bring in points from the scenario where they are relevant. For example, the tender must assess 'the needs of the prospective client'; here, the tender must clarify that all of the subsidiaries will require audits.

There are also points that come out of the scenario itself. These are likely to be practical points; here, the proposed deadline was very close to the year end, and should be discussed in the tender document as a practical issue.

In part (b), the first suggestion might have been trickier than the second, which was clear-cut. With the first suggestion (on the bonus for cross-selling to audit clients) you should be able to work out that there is a self-interest threat here. You then needed to know that the crucial issue was whether the person was a key audit partner or not.

With suggestion two, you should be well aware of the ethical issues surrounding the provision of internal audit services, and this part of the question was pretty much just knowledge recall. You should have scored well on this part of the question, and if you didn't then you need to make sure that you are happy with this area in the future.

Easy marks. There were easy marks in part (a) for noting that the tight deadline would cause problems – this came straight from the scenario and should stand out prominently.

Marks

(a)   **Matters to be included in tender document**
Up to 1½ marks for each matter identified and explained with relevance to the Plant Group
(up to a maximum of 2 marks in total for matters identified only):
- Outline of the audit firm including international network
- Audit firm specialism in telecoms
- Client audit requirements
- Outline of audit firm's audit methodology
- Deadlines
- Discuss provision of audit-related services
- Quality control and ethics
- Fees
- Discuss provision of non-audit services

Maximum marks   8

(b)   **Ethical matters**
Up to 1 mark for each relevant comment:
- Outline of the audit firm including international network
- Identify APB's revision to Ethical Standard 5 as a response to emerging practice of 'extended audits'
- Identify impact on professional skepticism
- Explain self-review threat arising on internal audit service
  (max 2 marks if made relevant to listed companies)
- Explain management threat arising in internal audit service
  (max 2 marks if made relevant to listed companies)
- Safeguards (1 mark each), eg separate team, review by second partner
- Generally not allowed for listed companies
- Separate engagement letter/billing arrangements
- Approval of those charged with governance

Maximum marks   8

Total   16

(a)   **Matters to include in tender**

Overview of Weller & Co

A brief overview of the firm's structure. This should state that the firm is part of an international network of firms, and that it therefore has access to a considerable depth of audit expertise.

This could be particularly relevant to the audit of the Plant Group's overseas subsidiary.

Areas of expertise

The firm has a telecoms audit department, and therefore already has staff with expertise in the Plant Group's specific industry. This may make it particularly well placed to audit the Plant Group.

Assessment of Plant Group's needs

The Plant Group is composed of a parent and six subsidiaries, and it should be clarified that the tender includes the audit of each of the subsidiaries as single companies, together with the parent company and the group as a whole.

Audit approach

A brief description of Weller & Co's audit approach. In the case of the Plant Group, this is likely to include reliance on the internal controls, which are described as strong. The tender document should point out that controls would be tested before they were relied upon, but that if they did prove reliable then the audit should indeed be cost-effective.

Deadline

The proposed deadline is just two months after the year end. It would be very difficult to meet such a deadline while still maintaining audit quality. It might make it difficult to obtain evidence in specific areas, such as receivables recoverability or going concern. There is also a risk of putting significant pressure on the audit team to do work quickly rather than thoroughly, which could result in things being missed.

The tender should therefore propose a later deadline for audit completion.

Fees

The tender should state the proposed audit fee, together with a breakdown of the fee. The fee proposed should be sufficient to ensure that a high quality audit could be conducted.

Non-audit services

The firm may wish to outline any relevant non-audit services that it could provide to the Plant Group. These will be curtailed by the fact that the Plant Group is now listed and thus a public interest entity, but there may still be some areas in which Weller & Co could provide help.

(b) **Internal audit**

There are two potential issues here: a self-review threat, and the threat from taking on a management responsibility.

Self-review threat

If Weller & Co seeks to rely on work performed by internal audit as part of its external audit, then there will be a self-review threat if it has itself performed the internal audit. The risk is that the internal audit work relied upon is not treated with enough professional skepticism. It may be possible to surmount this problem by using a team or department that is separate from the external audit team, to perform the internal audit.

Management responsibility

If firm personnel assume a management responsibility as part of the internal audit, then this threat would be so significant that either the internal audit service must not be provided, or the firm must withdraw from the external audit.

A management responsibility would be assumed where, for example, the auditor performs internal control procedures, or takes responsibility for designing, implementing and maintaining internal controls.

Public interest entities

If the audit client is a public interest entity (eg a listed company), then internal audit services relating to the following areas cannot be provided:

- A significant part of controls over financial reporting
- Accounting systems that generate information significant to the client's accounting records or financial statements
- Amounts or disclosures that are material to the financial statements

FRC response on 'extended audit'

The 2009 case of KPMG and Rentokil triggered debate in this area when KPMG provided an 'extended audit serivce' to Rentokil, which included services which had previously been done by internal audit.

The FRC (then the Auditing Practices Board) responded by revising its Ethical Standard for Auditors 5 *Non-audit services provided to audit clients* to state that if extended work is authorised by those charged with governance, and the work is integrated with that done by the external audit team, then it can be considered an 'audit-related service' rather than a non-audit service. This means that these services are not caught by ES 5's provisions on internal audit.

ES 5 states that the main threats with internal audit services are the self-review and management threats. Generally, these services may be undertaken, provided adequate safeguards are in place. These could include:

- Using different staff for internal and external audits
- Review of the external audit work by a partner who was not involved with it

However, the internal audit services may not be provided along with the audit if the auditor would place significant reliance on the work done by internal audit, or where the audit firm would take on a management role.

3 Becker

Text reference. Chapter 2.

Top tips. Ethical questions where you are asked to consider a number of scenarios come up frequently in this exam. The best way to be prepared is to practise as many of this type of question as you can. Always try to explain the risks fully rather that just stating what they are and try to come up with relevant safeguards.

Easy marks. All three areas were roughly similar in difficulty. If you are well-prepared, this type of question should not be difficult.

Examiner's comments. This question focused on ethics and practice management. Answers tended to be inadequate overall. This is disappointing, given that ethics is regularly tested, and that many candidates seem to think that the ethics question is the 'easy question'. The scenario relevant to requirement (a) described a business opportunity for which an audit client required funding. Most candidates spotted the obvious ethical problems of making loans to clients, and of having a mutual financial interest. However few candidates really explained why this is a problem. Many candidates would simply state a type of threat – 'self- interest' and 'intimidation' being the most common, with little attempt to explain how the threat arose and if anything could be done to mitigate the threat. Stronger candidates responded well to the practice management issues, discussing whether the audit firm has the relevant skills for such a business venture and whether attention would be better focussed on attracting new audit and assurance clients.

Requirement (b)'s scenario discussed the audit firm potentially setting up a recruitment advisory service. Similar problems appeared here, with many candidates stating threats but not explaining them. Some candidates devoted much of their answer to the fee based on salary, maintaining that it was a contingent fee, banned under ethical guidelines.

Requirement (c) tended to be unsatisfactorily answered. Many candidates simply repeated the same comments they had made for requirement (b), seeming not to realise that the two were entirely different proposals. This shows the importance of explaining the threats, as similar threats may indeed arise from the possibilities described in (b) and in (c), but why they arise and the implication for the audit firm is completely different.

Marking scheme

Marks

(a) **Joint business arrangement**

Generally 1 – 1½ marks per comment:
(i)   Self-interest independence threats
  – Loans to clients generally prohibited
  – Convertible loan stock would lead to equity stake in client – prohibited
  – Joint venture arrangement is significant business interest
  – Audit firm would share control of JV with audit client
  – Finance involved likely to be significant

(ii) Can only proceed with business venture if resign as auditors

(iii) Potentially lucrative business opportunity BUT

(iv) Auditors lack commercial experience in this type of venture

(v)   Should spend time on client retention and attraction

Maximum   7

(b) **Recruitment service**

Generally 1–1$\frac{1}{2}$ marks per comment

(i)   Explanation of self-interest threat
(ii)   Explanation of familiarity threat
(iii) Explanation of management involvement threat
(iv)   Threats increase with seniority of recruitee
(v)   Can look at CVs and draw up shortlist but management to take final decision
(vi)   Ingrid lacks specific, recent experience
(vii) May not be much demand for the service
(viii) Need to train second person – cost implication
(ix)   Consider setting up as separate business

Maximum   7

(c) **Temporary staff assignment**

Generally 1–1$\frac{1}{2}$ marks per comment:

(i)   Explanation of self-review threat
(ii)   Explanation of management involvement threat
(iii) Explanation of familiarity threat
(iv)   Description of safeguards
(v)   Problem when secondee returns to audit firm – reassign to other client
(vi)   Individual benefits from different work experience…
(vii) But may be offered permanent employment by the client
(viii) Issues with competence of people seconded
(ix)   Eases audit firms over-staffing problem

Maximum $\underline{6}$

Total $\underline{\underline{20}}$

(a) **Murray Ltd**

Threat to independence and objectivity

If the investment in Murray Ltd was to go ahead, Becker & Co would create self-interest and intimidation threats to their objectivity and independence. ACCA's Code of ethics and conduct states that the audit firm must be seen to be independent of the client. If Becker & Co and Murray Ltd are working together on the new product, the audit firm will not be seen to be independent. Additionally, ES 2 Financial, business, employment and personal relationships states that an audit firm should not hold any direct financial interest in an audit client.

Loan to audit client

Under the first option, Becker & Co would provide finance in the form of convertible debentures. This is a loan between the audit firm and its client and creates a self-interest threat to independence. Both ES2 and the Code specifically state that audit firms should not enter into any loan arrangement with a client that is not a bank or similar institution and no safeguard would reduce the self-interest threat to an acceptable level. Becker & Co should therefore not provide finance to Murray Ltd unless they resign as auditors.

Equity shares in audit client

The convertible debentures will eventually be converted to equity resulting in Becker & Co holding shares in Murray. This presents a self-interest threat to independence as Becker & Co will hold a financial interest in an audit client. The Code and ES2 both state that an audit firm is not allowed to own a direct financial interest in a client. Disposing of the equity or resigning from the audit will be the only applicable safeguards in this instance.

Joint venture

Under the second option, Becker & Co would form a joint venture with Murray Ltd. This would create a self-interest threat to independence as the audit firm and audit client would have an inappropriately close business relationship. Under the Code, an assurance provider should not participate in such a venture with an assurance client unless the interest is clearly insignificant. In this case the interest would be significant. Becker & Co should therefore not enter into the joint venture unless they resign as auditors of Murray Ltd.

Diversification

Entering into a business arrangement with Murray Ltd would be a new area of business for Becker & Co. The firm should consider whether it wants to diversify into an area in which it has little expertise or knowledge. It would be necessary to carry out a full commercial evaluation and business risk analysis before deciding if this is a growth strategy the firm would like to pursue.

Additionally, the firm needs to consider whether it has the time and resources to devote to this new area without the audit business suffering. Time may be better spent attracting and retaining audit clients, rather than pursuing new areas of business.

Business opportunity

If the firm does decide (after research and careful consideration) that this is a business opportunity it would be lucrative to pursue, then they should immediately resign as auditors of Murray Ltd.

(b) **Recruitment service**

Providing a recruitment service to a client is not specifically prohibited by the ACCA *Code of ethics and conduct*. However, the Code does say certain threats to independence could be created. Additionally, ES 5 *Non-audit services provided to audit clients* states that:

(i) The audit firm should not undertake recruitment services for an audited entity if this involves taking responsibility for appointing directors or other employees at that entity

(ii) For an audit client that is a listed entity, the audit firm shall not provide recruitment services for key management positions at that entity

(iii) The audit firm should not provide advice to audit clients on remuneration of directors or key management positions

Self-interest threat

Becker & Co are considering the provision of recruitment services to audit clients, earning fees based on a percentage of the salary of the person recruited. This creates a financial self-interest threat to independence. The firm may be tempted to recommend an individual to a client in order to earn a fee, and not consider whether that individual is suited to the role.

Familiarity threat

The provision of recruitment services will create a familiarity threat. During audits, Becker & Co will have to assess the work of individuals they helped recruit. The firm may be or may be perceived to be less likely to criticise or challenge such individuals because this could discredit their recruitment services.

Self-review threat

A self-review threat occurs where an audit firm makes management decisions for an audit client. Becker & Co could be seen to be making such decisions by providing recruitment services to audit clients. The firm could review candidates' CVs and recommend individuals to interview but the final decision of who to recruit should always rest with the client.

This threat is increased with the seniority of the individual being recruited, for example if Becker & Co were to advise on a new finance director. The threat could be reduced by only providing services for the recruitment of junior staff members.

Demand for services

Becker & Co would need to carry out market research to ensure that there is a demand for recruitment services before embarking on any new business venture.

Training costs

The firm should also consider whether it has the time and resources to enter into a new area of business. Ingrid Sharapova only worked in recruitment for a year and seems to be the only employee with any experience. She may require further training in order to recruit finance professionals and update her skills.

An additional member of staff at Becker & Co will also require some training so the recruitment business can be kept running whilst Ingrid is away or on sick leave.

If successful, the recruitment business may prove too much for Ingrid to handle alone and the firm will have to either train or hire additional staff to assist her.

Damage to reputation

Becker & Co's reputation could be damaged if the quality of recruitment services is low. This risk can be reduced by setting up the recruitment services as a separate company.

(c) **Temporary staff assignments**

Self-review threat

Becker & Co are proposing audit managers and seniors to be seconded to audit clients. This creates a self-review threat as there is the risk that the manager or senior will be auditing their own work on return to the audit firm. Even if the seconded individual is not on the audit team, there is a risk that the audit firm over relies on work carried out by their own employee.

Safeguards would need to be in place to ensure that staff are not assigned to audit teams for clients where they have completed a secondment. This safeguard is described in ES 2. It could cause some internal difficulties at Becker & Co as clients are likely to request staff who are familiar with their business and have been part of the audit team. Becker & Co may find that they can no longer allocate the staff with the most experience to clients where there has been a secondment. This difficulty could be overcome somewhat if staff are seconded to areas outside of the finance department.

Management involvement

By seconding an audit manager or senior, Becker & Co could be or could be perceived to be making management decisions for audit clients. This poses a problem as it creates a self-review threat to independence. The threat is greater when a more senior staff member is seconded as there is an increased likelihood the individual will be making important decisions.

The firm would need to apply safeguards to ensure that Becker & Co employees are not involved in any management decisions, responsible for approving or signing agreements or given the authority to enter into commitments whilst on secondment at the client. These safeguards are detailed in ES 2.

Familiarity threat

An individual from Becker & Co could be seconded to a client for a time period covering the audit. A familiarity threat to independence arises as the audit team may be over familiar with the seconded individual and not apply professional scepticism.

Reputation risk

Becker & Co's reputation could be adversely affected if seconded staff do not have the correct level of expertise for the role in question. The firm should make sure that any seconded employees are suitably competent and qualified for the seconded role.

Loss of staff

There is a risk that key staff may leave Becker & Co if clients offer them a permanent position. The situation could be exacerbated by staff being concerned about redundancy as the audit department is over staffed. Signed agreements where clients agree not to offer seconded staff permanent roles would reduce this risk.

Benefits

The main benefit of this suggestion is that it will ease the problems with over staffing in the audit department in the short term. In the long term, Becker & Co will still need to find new business or consider where they could reassign excess staff.

Individuals seconded to clients may learn and gain new perspectives from working in a finance department rather than in an accountancy firm. These new skills will benefit Becker & Co on their return.

4 Peaches

Marks

(a) (i) **Prescriptive and principles-based approach to auditing**
- Up to 2 marks for contrast

(ii) **Arguments for and against prescriptive approach**
- 1 mark for each advantage – clarity, increase in quality, uniformity, easy to monitor
- 1 mark for each disadvantage – lack of tailoring, over-auditing, no use of skill/judgement, process becomes mundane/routine, issues for staff retention
- Additional marks may be given for relevant comments on practical issues related to adoption of clarified ISAs, eg additional costs, increase in audit fee, training needs

Maximum 7

(b) (i) **Intimidation threat**
1 mark per comment explained:
- Independence/objectivity threat
- Example – aggressive individual
- Example – fear of dismissal/legal action
- Link to familiarity (or other) threat
- Safeguards needed

Maximum 3

(ii) **Advertising**
1 mark per comment explained:
- Must abide by professional
- Must not make false/exaggerated claims
- Must not make disparaging remarks about other firms
- Must abide by local rules on advertising generally

Maximum 3

(iii) **Lowballing**
1 mark per comment explained:
- Definition
- Why is problem – low quality audit, not acting with due care/competence
- Not prohibited but not encouraged
- $\frac{1}{2}$ mark ref ES 4

Maximum 3

Total 16

(a) (i) Rules-based (prescriptive) auditing is where the auditor follows prescribed rules on how to audit a particular area, but does not use any judgement about how to apply the rules.

Principles-based auditing is where no detailed rules are prescribed, but where the auditor must apply more general, guiding principles to the particular area being audited.

(ii) **Advantages**

Improved clarity and understandability. Prescriptive auditing standards leave the auditor in no doubt as to what he needs to do to audit a particular area. He just needs to follow the rules precisely and to the letter. As long as he has done this, he will be able to say that he has auditing in accordance with the standards.

It can be argued that prescriptive standards lead to an improvement in the quality of audits because they leave less scope for the auditor to choose how to audit each area, which reduces the risk that the auditor might make the wrong choice or might make a poor judgement. This also makes it much easier for the regulatory authorities to monitor audit quality, as it is much clearer what the auditor needs to do in accordance with the standards.

Disadvantages

The key disadvantage is that it reduces the auditor's ability to take into account the individual circumstances of the entity that is actually being audited. There is a danger of just applying the rules irrespective of whether the audit procedures are appropriate in this particular case. Worse than this, there may not even be a rule for the particular situation being audited, leaving the auditor in a very difficult position. This would lead to audit procedures being done that may not be adequate to gather sufficient appropriate audit evidence.

Prescriptive approaches diminish the extent to which auditors need to use their own judgement. This may not be too much of a problem in the case of a simple entity that is straightforward to audit, but it can be problematic in the case of a complex entity that is difficult to audit.

There is therefore a danger that a prescriptive approach might actually reduce the quality of audits.

(b)   (i)   An intimidation threat is a threat to compliance with the fundamental principle of an auditor's objectivity, which is a crucial part of his independence.

An example of an intimidation threat would be a client threatening to replace the auditor if the auditor intends to modify the audit opinion.

When an auditor identifies that there is a threat to his independence, he should apply safeguards to reduce the threat to an acceptably low level. There may, for instance, be a specific mode of recourse available through the individual regulatory framework that the auditor is operating in.

(ii)   The ACCA's general rule on advertising is that the medium used should not reflect adversely on the member, ACCA or the accountancy profession.

In particular, adverts should not discredit the services offered by others, whether by claiming superiority for the member's or firm's own services or otherwise. They should also not be misleading, either directly or by implication – they must not make false claims.

It is important that short adverts do not include information about fees. It is possible to mention fees in longer adverts, but these must include information about the basis on which fees would be calculated, such as hourly rates, etc.

(iii)   Lowballing is tendering for an audit for a very low fee, with the hope of under-cutting competitors and winning the audit tender. It is associated with audit firms recovering any losses they incur from the low fee, by just raising the fees significantly in future years.

The short answer is that lowballing is allowed, but that the fact that a firm is charging a low fee does not mean that it can cut costs by doing less audit work. It must do the same amount of work as on any other audit, ie the amount required to provide reasonable assurance that the financial statements are not materially misstated. The danger is that the firm tries to cut back on the audit work done in order to lessen any loss it is making on the audit – which is a serious risk to its independence.

The ACCA's *Code of Ethics and Conduct* emphasises that where a firm obtains an appointment with a significantly lower fee than competitors, it must be able to demonstrate that the audit has been conducted in accordance with auditing standards.

5 Retriever

Quality control, ethical and other professional matters

Up to 2 marks for each matter evaluated
(up to a maximum 3 marks for identification only)

- Time pressure
- Planned procedures ignored on potentially material item
- Sampling method changed – increases sampling risk
- Inappropriate review by juniors
- Inappropriate delegation of tasks
- Deferred tax – management not competent
- Deferred tax – self-review/management responsibility threat
- Deferred tax – materiality
- Tax planning – non-audit service with advocacy threat
- Junior lacks experience for this work regardless of ethical issues
- Junior not supervised/directed appropriately
- Overall conclusion

Planning the forensic investigation

Up to 1½ marks for each planning matter identified and explained
(up to a maximum 2 marks for identification only)

- Develop understanding of the events surrounding the theft
- Meeting with client to discuss the investigation
- Confirm insurance policy details (period covered, what is covered)
- Agree output of investigation
- Confirm access to necessary information
- Discuss confidentiality and ability to discuss with police/insurance company
- Consider resources for the investigation team
- Deadlines/fees

Procedures to be performed

1 mark for each specific procedure recommended:

- Watch the CCTV to form an impression of the quantity of goods stolen
- If possible, from the CCTV, determine the type of goods stolen
- Determine how many items of finished goods are in each box
- Agree the cost of an individual item to accounting records such as cost cards
- Perform an inventory count on the boxes of goods remaining in the warehouse and reconcile to the latest inventory movement records
- Discuss the case with the police to establish if any of the goods have been recovered and if, in the opinion of the police, this is likely to happen
- Obtain details of the stolen lorry and agree to the non-current asset register

Total   **25**

Quality control, ethical and other professional matters

The Group obtained a listing during the year which means that its financial statements will be the subject of particular scrutiny. This raises the overall risk level of this assignment, which means it should be subject to especially stringent quality control. This does not appear to have been the case.

Engagement quality control review

The fact that there is an engagement quality control review taking place is an encouraging sign, as it summons the prospect of some of the more egregious failings of quality control being made good before the auditor's report is signed.

Time pressure

The existence of time pressure points to poor planning. The purpose of the audit plan is not only to direct audit work to appropriate areas of the financial statements, but also to decide on the resources and deadlines necessary to complete the audit satisfactorily.

Time pressure increases detection risk. Procedures are likely to be rushed, resulting in a lack of professional scepticism and misstatements going undetected. This seems to be what has happened here.

Directors' emoluments

The audit manager described these as low risk, but they are material by nature. Not only are they related party transactions, they carry a high risk of manipulation as directors may attempt to conceal their remuneration from shareholders and other users of the financial statements.

There will also be additional reporting requirements as this is a listed group, which only increases the risk to the auditor.

Even if they were low risk, planned audit procedures would still need to be performed. The fact they are high risk only heightens this necessity.

Share capital

If the group were not listed, then share capital might be low risk. However, the fact it obtained a listing during the year means that share capital could have changed significantly. This is a highly visible area, and is therefore high risk.

Sampling method

ISA 530 *Audit Sampling* does allow samples to be selected haphazardly, which is effectively the exercise of judgement which the manager appears to be advocating. However, several points can be made against the manager's advocacy of judgmental sampling.

Firstly, the audit plan prescribes statistical sampling. It is possible to deviate from the audit plan, but only if this would provide better evidence. Yet this is not the manager's stated argument, so the suggestion should not have been made.

Secondly, haphazard sampling requires the exercise of judgement which juniors are unlikely to possess in view of the fact that their firm usually samples statistically. There is a risk that juniors will not understand how to select samples in this way, and will simply select eg large balances.

Thirdly, the manager's claim that haphazard sampling is quicker is manifestly false. When done properly, haphazard sampling requires the exercise of judgement and this takes time. Statistical sampling is much quicker to implement as it is relatively mechanical.

In fact the manager's suggestion that this would save time amounts to an incitement to the juniors to select the samples without due care, perhaps only picking the items that are close to hand. This is a serious breach of the IESBA *Code of Ethics*.

Trade payables

It is acceptable for juniors to be involved in the audit of trade payables, however the suggestion appears to be that one junior has been made responsible for the whole of trade payables on a listed company audit. This is clearly unacceptable, as the junior would possess neither the skills nor the time to perform the work to a satisfactory standard.

Going concern

Going concern is a difficult area to audit as it usually involves making judgements about a business's future prospects, which requires substantial experience. Juniors are very unlikely be able to do this and so should not have been assigned going concern.

A more senior member of the audit team should have been assigned going concern, such as the audit manager or partner.

Taken together with trade payables, this reveals a disturbing failure of direction on the audit, which is a key quality control.

Review

It may well be good training for juniors to review each other's work, but this is no substitute for proper supervision and monitoring by more senior members of the audit team. Being at the same level, juniors are unlikely to be able to spot any errors or invalid conclusions drawn, so the reviews are likely to be of little use. Moreover, the juniors are likely to be very familiar with each other and may be unwilling to criticise each other's work. The work should have been reviewed by the audit manager.

Financial controller

The financial controller of a listed company should be able to calculate deferred tax, so the fact that she could not raises issues about the Group's internal controls. The audit team should therefore revisit the risk assessment done at the audit planning, as deficient internal controls may mean that more substantive testing will be required.

The junior should not have been discussing the tax position with the financial controller in the first place. Given that the time on the audit is so short, what time there is would be better allocated to performing audit procedures. This points to a lack of supervision, and also to a need for further training for the audit junior.

Deferred tax asset

This is a good example of the principle of professional competence and due care, which the junior appears to have breached. Although the junior has studied deferred tax in college, they lack the experience to know than in practice the recognition of deferred tax assets is rare. Given that the Group's subsidiaries have been suffering losses it is not certain that any such asset will be recoverable; making the judgement over the asset's recoverability requires experience that the junior does not yet possess.

The self-review threat created by providing an accounting service to this client – whereby the firm would then be auditing accounts that it has itself prepared – would be deemed by the *Code* to be insurmountable in this instance.

In line with ES 5 *Non-audit services provided to audited entities*, a management threat could be said to be present here. The amount in question here is material to the financial statements at 11% of total assets. Given that the client is a listed company, this accounting service should not have been provided.

The audit manager said that this would save time and that the figure would not need to be audited. This is wrong. Now that the junior has calculated the figure it will need to be carefully reviewed and re-performed, and discussed with the management of the Group. The audit manager's suggestion is indicative of a lack of due care.

Tax planning

The audit junior should not be providing tax planning recommendations. This is a non-audit service, which the junior is providing free of charge and without the required professional skills. There is a self-review threat here because the tax balances calculated on the basis of the junior's advice would be included in the audited financial statements. There is a danger that the junior has been taking management decisions. It would usually be possible for a tax planning service to be provided to a listed client, but the auditor would have to put in place safeguards such as separate engagement teams which clearly do not exist here.

There is a risk that the firm may be the subject of litigation as well as reputational damage if the client relies on wrong advice given by the junior. Steps should therefore be taken to inform the Group of the situation and to prevent it from relying on this advice.

ES 5 states that the auditor must not provide tax services where doing so would involve taking on a management role.

Planning the forensic investigation

It would be helpful to arrange a meeting with Group management in order to help obtain an understanding of the theft and the circumstances around it, and to clarify matter in relation to the engagement.

The objective should be specified precisely, and clarification may be needed regarding whether quantification is to be made of the amount to be claimed from the insurer, or of the amount of the loss.

It should be clarified whether the Group wants us to investigate the crime itself and to identify the perpetrator, as this would be a radically different type of investigation which may be outside the scope of Kennel & Co's professional competence.

Clarification should be sought on whether the Group has already made any calculations of the amount to be claimed, in which case it may simply want us to audit its calculation. Alternatively it may want us to calculate the loss ourselves from scratch. This would have an effect on fees, which should also be discussed at the meeting.

Kennel & Co appears likely to have sufficient resources to conduct the investigation as it has a forensic accounting department. It should, however, be determined whether the firm has the requisite staff available for this assignment.

It will be necessary to discuss timings with the Group, and in particular any planned deadlines for submission of the insurance claim. Any such deadlines should allow enough time for the work to be completed without sacrificing quality. This will in turn affect the consideration of whether sufficient staffing resources are available at the right times.

It must be confirmed that the assurance team will have full access to any information required to conduct the investigation.

The Group should have reported the theft to the police, and it may be helpful to obtain a copy of any police reports available. It should be established whether the perpetrator(s) have been caught, and if so whether they are likely to be prosecuted. Kennel & Co should be alive to the possibility that the Group might ask it to act as an expert witness if there were a court case, in which case there may be an advocacy threat to the firm's independence.

It is possible that the perpetrator(s) have been caught and that some of the assets have been recovered. This should be ascertained, and any recovered assets excluded from the calculation of the loss. It is also possible that these assets may have been damaged, in which case this should be taken into account.

From the circumstances described it is possible that the thieves may have been Group employees. This information should be obtained from management.

The insurance policy should be scrutinised. It is stated that assets lost as a result of thefts are covered, and this should be confirmed. It should also be determined whether there are any restrictions in the case of thefts perpetrated by Group employees, as this may affect the amount that can be claimed. Finally, it should be confirmed that the date of the theft falls within the period insured.

Finally, the output of the investigation should be confirmed. The Group may require eg a report to the insurance company, or alternatively a report addressed to itself but which it can use for the purposes of the insurance claim. It should be clarified that the report would not be distributable to any other parties.

Procedures to be performed

- Watch the CCTV to determine the quantity of goods stolen, eg how many boxes loaded onto lorry
- If possible determine if the boxes contain mobile phones or laptops
- Inspect boxes of goods in the warehouse to determine how many finished goods are in each
- Agree cost of an individual phone and laptop to accounting records, eg cost cards
- Perform inventory count on boxes of goods in the warehouse and reconcile to latest inventory movements
- Discuss the case with police to establish if any goods have been recovered and if this is likely to happen
- Obtain details of stolen lorry, eg licence plate, and agree the lorry to non-current asset register

6 Smith & Co

Marking scheme

Marks

(a) **Norman Ltd**

Generally 1 mark each per comment and action point

(i)   Poor credit control
(ii)   ES 4 – Independence threat – free audit/loan
(iii) ES 4 – Independence threat – self-interest in 20X8 report
(iv)   Financial distress leads to going concern threat for the company
(v)   Non payment due to financial distress does not necessitate resignation
(vi)   Discuss with client – ethical problem/payment arrangements
(vii) Ethics partner notification
(viii) Assess significance of amount outstanding
(ix)   Policy to check prior invoices paid
(x)   Continue to improve credit control
(xi)   Second partner review
(xii) Review of audit work performed on going concern

Maximum   8

(b) **Wallace Ltd**

Generally 1 mark each per comment and action point

(i)   ES 2 – Non arm's length commercial transaction
(ii)   Material to audit manager
(iii) Self-interest/intimidation threat
(iv)   Question audit manager's integrity
(v)   Potential disciplinary action
(vi)   Remove Valerie from audit team
(vii) Review all work performed on Wallace Ltd
(viii) Consider Valerie's relationship with and likelihood of bias towards her other clients
(ix)   Disclosure of ethical threat to those charged with governance
(x)   Provide clear communication to all staff regarding transactions with clients

Maximum   5

(c)   **Software Supply Ltd**
       Generally 1 mark each per comment and action point
       (i)   Self review threat
       (ii)   Self-interest threat
       (ii)   Independence check
       (iv)   Client disclosure and acknowledgement
       (v)   QC monitoring
       Maximum   4
Total   **17**

(a)   **Norman Ltd**

       Credit control

       The fees for the 20X7 audit have been outstanding for over twelve months and it seems that little has been done to collect them. Since the file note states that Norman Ltd is suffering poor cash flows, the balance may no longer be recoverable. Credit control has been poorly managed at Smith & Co with regards this client and the debt should not have remained outstanding for so long.

       Action

       Credit control procedures at the firm need to be reviewed to prevent this situation reoccurring. It appears that some improvements have already been made with the audit manager now being responsible for reviewing client invoices raised and monitoring credit control procedures.

       Independence

       The overdue fees for the 20X7 audit may make it appear the audit has been performed for free or could effectively be seen as a loan from Smith & Co to Norman Ltd. The ACCA *Code of Ethics and Conduct* specifically states that an audit firm should not enter into a loan arrangement with a client that is not a bank or similar institution. It highlights overdue fees as an area where a self-interest threat could arise and independence is threatened. Smith & Co should not have allowed outstanding fees to build up as their independence is now compromised.

       Action

       Smith and Co should discuss the recoverability of the 20X7 audit fee with the audit committee (if one exists) or those charged with governance. A payment plan should be put into place.

       If the overdue fees are not paid, the firm should consider resigning as auditors per ES 4 *Fees, remuneration and evaluation policies, litigation, gifts and hospitality.* In this case a valid commercial reason appears to exist as to why the fees remain unpaid. Smith & Co can remain as auditors provided that adequate safeguards are in place and the amount outstanding is not significant. If the overdue fees are significant, it may be that no safeguards could eliminate the threat to objectivity or independence or reduce them to an acceptable level.

       The ethics partner at Smith & Co should be informed of the situation. The ethics partner should evaluate the ethical threat and document the conclusions including the significance of the overdue fees.

       ES4

       Under ES4, the 20X7 audit fee and arrangements for payment should have been agreed before Smith & Co formally accepted appointment as auditor for the 20X8 audit. Since the 20X8 audit has now almost been completed, it appears this could not have happened.

       Action

       The ethics partner at Smith & Co should take steps to ensure that there are no outstanding audit fees before commencing new client work. This could involve a new firm-wide policy that audit managers check payment of previous invoices.

Self-interest in 20X8 report

The 20X8 audit report has not yet been signed. This creates a self-interest threat to Smith & Co's objectivity and independence because the issue of an unqualified audit report may enhance their prospects of securing payment of the overdue 20X7 audit fees.

Action

The working papers for the 20X8 audit of Norman Ltd should undergo an independent review by the engagement quality control reviewer.

Going concern

Norman Ltd is known to be having cash flow problems and so there is an issue of whether the company is a going concern for the 20X8 audit report.

Action

Smith & Co should carry out a review of the 20X8 audit working papers on going concern. It may be necessary to carry out further audit procedures to ensure that sufficient evidence has been gathered to support the audit opinion.

(b) **Wallace Ltd**

Terms of ES2

Under ES2 *Financial, business, employment and personal relationships,* persons in a position to influence the conduct and outcome of the audit should not enter into business relationships with a client except where they involve the purchase of goods and services from the client in the ordinary course of business, are on an arm's length basis and are clearly inconsequential to each party.

As audit manager of Wallace Ltd, Valerie Hobson has influence over the audit outcome and should only rent the warehouse space if the conditions prescribed by ES2 are met. Since the warehouse space is already known to be used for rental income, this transaction is in the ordinary course of business. However, the note on the invoice about only charging a nominal sum indicates that the transaction is not on an arm's length basis. The criteria in ES2 have therefore been breached. It is also worth noting that the transaction may represent a material discount for Valerie Hobson.

Action

Valerie Hobson should not retain the position of audit manager at Wallace Ltd and a new manager should be assigned. All planning work for the 20X8 audit should be independently reviewed as planning decisions may have been influenced by the transaction. The situation should be disclosed to those charged with governance at Wallace Ltd and the audit committee, if one exists.

Self-interest threat

Valerie Hobson has created a self-interest threat, by renting the warehouse space at a reduced rate. Valerie's objectivity could be biased by her desire to please Wallace Ltd so that she can benefit financially.

Action

Valerie Hobson may need to be disciplined for her actions by Smith & Co who could also send her for ethics training. Smith & Co should investigate for evidence of bias in other audits where Valerie Hobson has had influence.

(c) **Software Supply Ltd**

Self-interest threat

Smith & Co may have entered into an inappropriate close business relationship by accepting a fee for recommending Software Supply Ltd to audit clients. This could be seen as a self-interest threat and compromise the independence and objectivity of Smith & Co. The business relationship can be allowed to continue provided that Smith & Co put safeguards in place.

Action

Smith & Co should ensure that where Software Supply Ltd has been used by a client the following safeguards exist.

- Audit staff have no financial or personal interest in Software Supply Ltd
- The arrangement between Smith & Co and Software Supply Ltd has been fully disclosed
- Smith & Co should obtain written confirmation that the client is aware of the referral fee

Additionally, Smith & Co should monitor the quality of the products supplied to ensure they are not associated with inferior goods.

7 Carter

Text reference. Chapter 2.

Top tips. This question looks at a number of ethical dilemmas. Care must be taken when reading the information to ensure that the key issues are identified. It can be easy to become sidetracked by minor details or basic misunderstandings and end up missing the point of the question.

Easy marks. Parts (a) and (d) were probably the easiest, but the easiest marks were the first few in each part of the question – and to get these, it was crucial that you kept to your timings for each part.

Examiner's comments. As usual, the 'ethics question' was the most popular of the optional questions. This question contained four brief ethical situations, from which candidates were required to identify and evaluate the ethical and other professional issues raised. Answers were mixed in quality – some were sound, but many did little more than identify threats but provided no discussion or evaluation of those threats identified.

Requirement (a) was well answered, with almost all candidates able to identify and explain the self-review threat and to suggest appropriate safeguards. Few candidates however considered the key issues of the materiality of the pension deficit to the financial statements, and the highly subjective nature of the valuation.

In requirement (b), most candidates could identify the familiarity threat to objectivity, though this was often not well explained, and most suggested that the best safeguard would be to exclude Kia from the audit team. Inevitably, many candidates wanted to see Kia disciplined for her 'gross misconduct' and reported immediately to ACCA.

In requirement (c), most candidates identified the potential self-interest threat created but few could go further to evaluate the potential risk exposure to the firm or additional costs that may be incurred if such a service were offered.

In requirement (d), the situation was dealt with well, with most candidates able to identify and explain the threats and to suggest that full disclosure would be the best course of action.

On the whole this ethics question produced better answers than ethics questions in previous examinations. However, candidates' performance is hampered by the fact that often only one ethical issue or threat per requirement is dealt with in their answers, which tend to be too brief for the marks available. Many candidates wrote the same amount for each requirement, despite the fact that requirements (a) and (b) were worth twice the marks of requirement (d).

Marks

(a) **Fernwood Ltd**

Up to 1 mark each point explained:

- Self-review threat (restrict to ½ mark if not explained)
- Provision of non-audit service
- Threat depends on materiality of balance
- Threat depends on degree of subjectivity
- Can only perform if low threat and safeguards used
- Pension very subjective so unlikely to be able to reduce threat to acceptable level
- If service provided assess skills and competence

Maximum   6

(b) **Hall Ltd**

Up to 1 mark each point explained:

- Client should not influence selection of audit team members
- Kia has no experience of the client
- Family relationship creates three objectivity threats (1 mark each explained)
- Degree of threat depends on level of influence
- Do not assign Kia to the team
- Explain to client why Kia has not been assigned

Maximum   6

(c) **Collier Ltd**

Up to 1 mark each point explained:

- Custodial service creates self-interest threat (½ mark if not explained)
- Safeguards to be applied (1 mark each)
- Money laundering consideration
- Consider security of offices/availability of space
- Extra costs eg insurance, more security measures
- Reputational risk in event of theft/loss of documents
- Confidentiality issues

Maximum   5

(d) **Gates Ltd**

Up to 1 mark each point explained:

- Referral fee creates self-interest threat
- Allowed if safeguards in place (1 mark for each safeguard)
- Consider quality of service provided

Maximum   3

Total   20

(a) The issue is whether there is a self-review threat, as the valuation of the amount recognised would be included in the financial statements. The IESBA *Code of Ethics for Professional Accountants* states that where the valuation service relates to a material amount in the financial statements, and the valuation involves a significant degree of subjectivity, even with the application of safeguards the self-review threat created could not be reduced to an acceptable level. If this is the case, the firm must choose between providing the audit and providing the valuation service.

Carter & Co therefore needs to assess the materiality of the figure, and the degree of subjectivity involved. If it considers that safeguards could reduce the threat to an acceptable level, then it can go ahead with both the audit and the valuation service. Safeguards may include:

- Using separate personnel for the valuation service and the audit
- Performing a second partner review
- Confirming that the client understands the valuation method and the assumptions used

There is a further question over whether an audit firm would be likely to possess the requisite competence to provide such a valuation service. Professional competence and due care is a fundamental ACCA ethical principle, which in this context would mean that the firm should only do work which it is professionally qualified to do. The firm would therefore have to ensure that it could perform the work competently.

(b) There are a number of possible threats to Carter & Co's independence here:

- Familiarity: Kia may fail to exercise professional scepticism.

- Intimidation: the financial controller may be able to intimidate and influence Kia's work.

- Self-interest: Kia may have an interesting in not causing problems for her relative, and may be unwilling to challenge them if required to do so.

To assess the severity of the threat, the degree of influence held by the family member and by Kia must be considered. As financial controller and audit senior respectively, both would have some influence over the financial statements. It would therefore be unlikely that Kia would be able to be assigned to this audit engagement.

Furthermore, allocation of staff to audit teams should be the decision of Carter & Co alone. Staff should be allocated on the basis of their experience and skills. There is a risk of the audit team possessing an inappropriate mix of experience and skills for this audit if Carter & Co were not able to select the audit team, which may impair audit quality. The fact that Kia has not worked on this client before suggests that this may be the case. It is therefore crucial that Carter & Co exercise a free choice over the composition of the audit team.

(c) Usually documents such as title deeds are held by the audit client, but sometimes the service is provided by the accountant.

Appropriate safeguards to be used in the provision of a custodial service could include:

- Keeping the assets physically separate from the firm's assets

- Keeping orderly documentation regarding the assets and be ready to account for them to the client when requested

- Establishing strict controls over physical access to the assets

- Complying with all relevant laws and regulations in respect of holding the assets

Confidentiality is also a key issue – the firm must ensure that documentation is only ever given to the client and to no-one else.

In addition Carter & Co should be vigilant in respect of money laundering regulations. The tangible assets could be purchased using the proceeds of crime, and as such the firm would be deemed to be involved with money laundering. The firm would have to be careful to ascertain the true origin of the assets.

A further issue is whether Carter & Co has sufficient security to offer such a service. Employment of extra security methods such as alarm systems and CCTV could be costly. This could be compounded if, in order to maximise the revenue from this source of income, Carter & Co were tempted to concentrate on holding high value assets, as these would attract the highest fees.

If there were ever a problem such as documents being lost, then Carter & Co would face major reputational risk. This risk, along with the extra costs discussed above, may outweigh the relatively small revenue stream that the service would provide.

(d) Referral fees are not prohibited by IESBA's *Code of Ethics*, but a self-interest threat can arise, as the audit firm receives financial benefit for each audit client referred. The referrals and payments to Carter & Co can continue, provided that safeguards are put in place, such as:

- Disclosing to audit clients that a referral fee arrangement exists, and the details of it
- Receiving confirmation that audit clients are aware of the referral arrangement
- Receiving confirmation from all employees of Carter & Co that they have no interest in Gates Ltd

Carter & Co may also wish to consider the quality of the training provided by Gates Ltd. Any problems with it could cause damage to Carter & Co 's reputation.

8 Dedza

Marking scheme

Marks

(a) **Need for ethical guidance for accountants**

Generally 1 mark a point up to
Ideas (illustrative)

(i) Legal responsibilities
(ii) Risk of offence
(iii) Confidentiality
(iv) Other reporting responsibilities
(v) Professional etiquette
(vi) Accountants working in other jurisdictions
Maximum

5

(b) **Ethical and other professional issues**

Generally ½ mark each issue identified + 1 mark each comment/action
Ideas

(i) Tax investigation

– New client (relatively) – CDD
– 'Professional etiquette' – change in professional appointment
– Quality control eg second review
– Criminal property includes proceeds of tax evasion
– Money laundering offence?
– Suspicion of fraud (intent) vs error in incorrect tax returns
– Disclosure by Dedza vs voluntary (confidentiality)
– Need for STR

(ii) Advice on payments

– Not a tax issue
– Corruption and bribery/extortion – designated categories of offence
– Clear intent
– Seriousness in context of domestic laws
– Need to report to FIU?

(iii) Financial advisor

– Designated non-financial profession
– Customer due diligence/record keeping
– Politically exposed person (PEP)
– Reputational risk
– Additional measures
– Refusal to act

15

Total

20

(a) **Need for ethical guidance**

Accountants are in a position where they deal with other people's money and financial matters. Therefore they may unwittingly, or worse, intentionally, be drawn into other people's criminal activity in relation to money laundering.

For example, there are a number of regulations relevant to professionals such as accountants which accountants must therefore comply with relating to appointing money laundering officers and making reports of suspicions of money laundering. It is also a criminal offence to continue to act if there is a suspicion that a transaction relates to criminal proceeds.

It is also a criminal offence to prejudice a money laundering investigation by letting the person being investigated know something is happening. This offence is called 'tipping off'.

There are substantial criminal penalties for these offences and accountants are at rise in incurring these penalties.

Although there is some legal protection given, some of these requirements appear to be at odds with the accountant's duty of confidentiality to a client (particularly the requirement to report knowledge or suspicion of criminal activity).

The ACCA produced a Factsheet for members (Technical Factsheet 94) summarising the responsibilities of members. Principles that ensure compliance with the OECD's Financial Action Task Force on Money Laundering recommendations are included in the ACCA's Professional Conduct Regulations. This includes guidance on:

- Internal controls and policies relating to staff training
- Client identification procedures
- Record keeping (minimum five years)
- Recognition of what constitutes suspicion
- Reporting of suspicious transactions
- Not tipping-off potential suspects

(b) (i) **Kora Co**

Client acceptance procedures

As Kora, a relatively new client, is being investigated for tax fraud, it is possible that Dedza's quality control and other procedures on acceptance of a client may not be as robust as would be ideal, and that they have accepted a client without obtaining sufficient knowledge and understanding.

In accepting a new client, Dedza should have completed the following:

–   Obtained references about key personnel in the company and the company

–   Obtained professional clearance from the previous auditors

–   Carried out procedures in line with Dedza's anti-money laundering policies which should include detailed client identification procedures and customer due diligence

It is possible that Dedza did not obtain appropriate references or obtain professional clearance. There is no reason why the client identification procedures would necessarily have raised any issues if Kora has previously had a clean record.

Concealed, previously undiscovered fraud?

Alternatively, given that under-declaring income is a fraud, it is possible that staff at Kora were under-declaring income and concealing the fact, and that both the old and the new auditors were unaware that it was going on. There is not necessarily any suggestion that negligent audits were carried out.

Confidentiality

Dedza has a duty of confidentiality to its client, and the partners and staff of Dedza must ensure that they do not breach their duty of confidentiality if asked questions by the tax authority during the course of their investigation.

This may be complicated by the fact that if Kora has been underdeclaring income, this may become an investigation into the crime of money laundering, in which case, Dedza may have legal duties of disclosure that are not subject to the duty of confidentiality.

Members are entitled to make disclosures to defend themselves and their professional reputation, and if the investigation includes members of the tax department of Dedza personally, they may need to make disclosures in their own interests.

Actions to take

Dedza should take legal advice on disclosures that they are required to make and disclosures that they are not permitted to make before they make any disclosures to the tax authorities in the course of this investigation.

Tutor's note. It is assumed in this answer that the investigation is a public investigation into tax irregularities which Kora Co is fully aware of. If it were a secret money laundering investigation, Dedza would also need to be wary of committing the offence of 'tipping off' and letting staff of Kora Co know that the company was under investigation.

(ii)   **Xalam Co**

Ethical matters

In terms of carrying out future audits of Xalam Co, there are two ethical issues which are relevant here.

(1)   The auditors must ensure that they do not find themselves in a position where they are to be auditing their own work (a self-review threat).

(2)   The auditors must not breach ACCA's general rule that they should not make management decisions on behalf of the company.

Preparation of the financial statements

Given that management is responsible for the preparation and presentation of financial statements, then it is the responsibility of management to determine how items are presented in financial statements. The auditors must therefore ensure that they do not take management responsibility in determining how the items are accounted for.

However it is reasonable for a company to ask advice from its auditors on how to account for a difficult item, so it is important for the audit firm to get the balance right. In this instance, the item involved is substantial and likely to be material to the financial statements. Given that the company has a tax policy in relation to them, it appears that this is not a new expense to the company, hence the provisions of IAS 8 *Accounting policies, changes in accounting estimates and errors* become relevant. This states that a company should only change its accounting policy towards an item if required to do so by an accounting standard, or if the change in policy would give a more reliable and relevant reflection of the substance of the transaction.

Tax deductible

Whether the matters are tax deductible or not depends on the tax legislation of the jurisdiction in which Xalam operates. If there is any doubt as to whether these expenses should be tax deductible or not, Dedza should recommend that Xalam obtains tax advice. Given that the matter is material, it may or may not have a material effect on the tax charge reported in the statement of profit or loss. If Dedza disagrees with the tax treatment of this matter, and the matter is material to the reported tax charge, then Xalam would have to modify its audit report over this issue.

It is possible that these 'payments' are more like bribes to various parties to ensure that business runs smoothly. Bribery is illegal and the auditor should clearly advise against such payments.

Actions to take

The audit manager should clarify the nature of the chief executive's request.

If the company has requested advice as a separate engagement and intends to pay separately from the audit for this service, then it would be inappropriate to accept an engagement on those terms.

However, if this matter has been raised in the context of the audit service and it is clearly the giving of advice (for example, clarifying that under IAS 8 the accounting policy should not change unless fairer presentation would result) rather than the provision of a management service, then it may be acceptable for Dedza to give advice about the accounting issue.

If the payments amount to a bribe, then this casts serious doubts on the integrity of the directors of Xalam. The auditors should resign from their position. Xalam benefits from these payments in receiving income from the related customer. This could constitute money laundering. Dedza must therefore make an appropriate money laundering report.

(iii)   **Pholey family**

Carrying out transactions on behalf of a client

Particularly in the light of the money laundering requirements incumbent on accountants and auditors, it is extremely ill-advised for auditors to carry out transactions on behalf of their clients, in case they inadvertently carry out the crime of money laundering.

In addition, being asked to carry out a transaction on behalf of a client might give rise to a suspicion of money laundering that the accountant was required to report to the appropriate authority.

Actions to take

Dedza should stop carrying out transactions for clients, however innocent they may have been in the past, so as to avoid any suspicion or any problem arising.

Politically exposed persons (PEPs)

Esau's new position as a senior foreign government official makes him a politically exposed person (PEP). This increases the reputational risk for Dedza as there will be more publicity if something goes wrong.

Actions to take

The senior partner at Dedza should be alerted of the change in circumstances and judge whether the firm should continue to act as advisors for Esau and the Pholey family given the increased risk. If the relationship continues, the firm should take reasonable measures to establish the source of Esau's wealth and conduct ongoing monitoring of Dedza's relationship with Esau.

Dedza should also ensure that it has a risk management system in place to determine whether individuals are PEPs on acceptance or if circumstances change.

9 Clifden

Text reference. Chapter 2.

Top Tips. Part (a) was straightforward, requiring you only to explain some book knowledge in an area of the syllabus that you should be very familiar with by this stage in your studies. Note that only two marks are available for each part of the requirement. Part (b)(i) was a difficult requirement, and you would probably have run out of ideas before getting to eight marks. Try to generate as many ideas as you can, and don't be tempted to move on before you've used up your time allocation. Part (b)(ii) was probably easier than (b)(i). The important thing for both of these parts was not to overlook the professional issues. The examiner likes candidates to think about the audit from a commercial point of view as well as just a technical one.

Easy marks. Part (a) contained marks just for showing your knowledge, so make sure you got these.

Examiner's comments. As noted in previous Examiners' Reports, candidates seem to think that the 'ethics question' is an easy option, but the performance of candidates in this question continues to be disappointing. Some answers to part (a) were sound, including a clear definition, and a number of practical suggestions. However, some candidates could not provide a definition other than 'professional competence is when you are competent to take on a professional engagement,' which does not add anything to what is given in the question.

Answers to (b)(i) were often limited to brief comments relating to the client's lack of integrity, and the need to recall the products. Many candidates missed the main point of the requirement, which was the auditor's duty to maintain confidentiality, and whether that duty should be breached in this case in the public interest. A significant proportion of candidates focussed entirely on what the client should do in this situation, (better quality control, sack the production manager, put a notice in newspapers, etc), and hardly mentioned the ethical and professional issues relating to the audit firm at all. Although the mark allocation for (b)(ii) was lower than that of (b)(i), most candidates wrote the same, or more, for (b)(ii). Answers here tended to be adequate.

Marking scheme

		Marks

(a) **Competence and due care**

Generally 1 mark per comment from ideas list:

(i)   Definition competence, including for example:
(ii)   Competence – attain knowledge/skills
(iii)   Competence – maintain knowledge/skills
(iv)   Definition due care
(v)   To ensure compliance: training, study support, QC, appraisals, etc

Max 2 marks for definition/explanation of term and 2 marks for compliance comments

Maximum   4

(b)   (i)   **Plastic ingredients**

Generally 1 mark per comment/specific action to be taken:

- Management lack integrity
- Encourage management to disclose
- Auditor's duty of confidentiality
- Consider law and regs
- Consider disclosure in public interest
- Legal advice
- Consider resignation
- Seek evidence/information re matter
- Impact on financial statements and planned audit procedures
- Safety of staff attending inventory count

Maximum   8

(ii)   **Audit of Cong Ltd**

Generally 1 mark per comment/specific action to be taken:

- Conflict of interest – explain why
- Disclosure to both parties
- Other safeguards (1 mark each max 3)
- Commercial considerations

Maximum   5

Total   17

(a)   **Professional competence and due care**

An accountant must have the knowledge and skill to offer a service based on current developments in the profession. Having once attained the requisite level, he must then make sure that he maintains it, for example by keeping up to date with changes in legislation, practices and techniques.

The accountant must then actually act in line with this level of knowledge and skill, making sure that he does in fact apply current practises and techniques, for instance. This would include practical considerations, such as making sure there is enough time to do the work with due care, or ensuring that any staff being used act with professional competence and due care themselves.

Compliance by firms

Firms should only use staff who are competent to do the work assigned to them, as shown by a combination of professional qualifications and experience. This can be achieved by recruiting staff with the requisite competence, or by providing training where it is needed.

The second element is quality control. Firms must ensure that all engagements are actually performed with due care. This would entail the use of review procedures, with more senior staff reviewing the work of junior staff, as well as the use of hot and cold review.

(b) (i) **Ethical issues**

The fact that management has decided not to recall any of the contaminated products casts doubt over its integrity. Its assertion that the risk of injury being caused is remote should be treated with scepticism. Even in spite of there being a low level of risk, it would still be right for management to announce the problem, so that customers could return any defective products. There is a risk that management's assessment of risk may have been determined by commercial rather than ethical concerns.

The failure of Headford Ltd's quality controls in this regard, when taken together with these doubts over management's integrity, puts into question the quality of the control environment. This would affect Clifden's assessment of control risk at the planning stage of the audit.

Clifden & Co should seek to persuade management to announce the problem to the public. If management refuse to disclose it, then Clifden needs to weigh up its duty of confidentiality against the need to disclose in order to protect Headford's customers. The ACCA Code of Ethics states that auditors should not disclose information to the public unless there is a legal right or duty to do so.

ISA (UK & Ireland) 250A *Consideration of Laws and Regulations in an Audit of Financial Statements* provides guidance here. There may be industry-specific regulations in the case of children's toys, under which Clifden & Co may have a duty to report to a relevant statutory authority.

Even if this is not the case, there may be a duty to disclose in the public interest. This is a difficult area, as it is not clear whether in this circumstance there would be sufficient public interest in disclosure to override the auditor's duty of confidentiality. Clifden & Co would need to obtain more information about the contamination, and about the basis for management's assessment of the risk of injury being 'remote'.

If it becomes clear that the issue is of sufficient severity and management still refuses to disclose it, then Clifden & Co should consider resigning from the audit as a last resort.

Professional issues

There is a possibility that a contingent liability already exists here. This will need to be considered as part of the audit planning process, taking into account the need to ensure that the requirements of IAS 37 have been complied with.

There is a possibility that there will be some sales returns of faulty items, in respect of which Clifden needs to consider whether a provision might be required.

Since the items were produced up to a month from the year end, there is a chance that some of them remain in inventory. It may therefore be necessary to write off a significant proportion of inventory, so Clifden needs to ensure that the correct adjustments have been made.

There may also be a risk to the safety of audit staff attending a year-end inventory count. Careful consideration needs to be given to this matter, perhaps with Headford making special provisions in order to keep any affected items safe. It may be that audit staff cannot attend the inventory count, in which case there may be a difficulty in obtaining sufficient audit evidence in respect of inventory.

(ii) **Ethical issues**

The principle issue raised is the possibility of a conflict of interests between the audit client, Headford Ltd, and the potential client, Cong Ltd. There is likely to be a difference here between clients' perceptions of a conflict of interests, and the reality for the audit firm.

The way to tackle any perceived conflict is to use disclosure so that the clients can see that it has been dealt with. Clifden & Co should tell each company about the services being offered to the other in respect of which they might perceive there to be a conflict. The audit of Cong Ltd should only be accepted once both companies have given their consent.

It would also be wise from a commercial point of view to provide the firms with information about how any potential conflict of interest would be prevented from arising. This would include informing them of the following safeguards, which should be implemented if both audits do go ahead.

- Each audit should have separate engagement teams
- Engagement teams briefed clearly on the need to ensure confidentiality
- Review of safeguards by an independent partner

Professional issues

In the event that the firms do not consent to Clifden & Co auditing both of them, the decision as to which firm to audit needs to be made on commercial grounds. On this basis, Cong Ltd is a much larger company to which some non-audit services could be sold, so higher fee income could probably be generated than from the Headford audit. However, since the overall profitability of the job would depend on the costs involved, the decision could only be taken once more detail is known about exactly what would be involved. Given the professional and ethical doubts that exist over the audit of Headford Ltd, it is likely that the Cong Ltd audit would be the more attractive.

Clifden & Co also needs to consider whether it has sufficient resources to audit a company as large as Cong Ltd, particularly if both companies were to be audited together as the strain on resources would be greater as a result of having two separate engagement teams.

10 Hawk Associates

Text references. Chapters 2 and 5.

Top tips. Break each section of this question into discrete parts. As noted below, some parts are easier than others and there are easy marks to be had. If you break each part down, you can ensure that you gain the one or two marks available for each little section and gain good answer coverage. For example in part (a), focus on cold calling, then on second opinions, then on free services. There are three areas for five marks, so if you comment on each, you should pass this section of the question. The answer below has been broken down into sections indicated by the subheaders. If you indicate your answer has been so broken down, then it is easier for a marker to give you marks in each section.

Easy marks. Each of these segments contains an item which has basic ACCA or IESBA guidance connected with it which you should be able to outline. For example, in (a), if you are not sure about cold calling, you should have learnt the rules about second opinions. In part (b), you might be unsure about contingent fees, but you should know the rules concerning an advert. You will gain easy marks outlining the guidance relating to each of these items.

Examiner's comments. The question called for an extension of lower level auditing knowledge on obtaining professional work in the areas of advertising, fees and firms' names. Easy marks were thrown away if candidates did not state one way or the other whether each of the proposals was suitable.

In part (a), most candidates knew little about 'cold calling'. Many homed in on second opinions, but incorrectly supposed that a free audit was being offered. Candidates should not drop jargon into their answers which they do not properly understand.

In part (b), although most candidates had some idea of the basic rules on advertising, few were able to relate them to the suggested advertisement and thereby explain why it was inappropriate. However, candidates who took time to sift through the wording for ideas earned good marks.

Few candidates observed in part (c) that offering such a wide range of services conflicted with the increasing restrictions on the provision of non-audit services set out in the opening paragraph of the scenario.

Marks

Generally 1 mark each comment

Ideas

- Whether prohibited
- Permitted (ACCA)
- Commercial/competitive practice
- Fundamental principles apply
- 'Free' – when permitted
- Second opinions – discouraged

Tax planning advertisement

- Advertising restrictions
- The 'best'?
- How ensure?
- Assertion of 'all'
- Exposure to litigation
- Contingency fees

Business cards

- Where advertised
- Size of advertisement
- Use of ACCA name
- PROFESSIONAL
- Range of non-audit services
- Basis of asserting 'competitive rates'
- 'Money back'
- Cannot guarantee opinions

(a)	Maximum	5
(b)	Maximum	6
(c)	Maximum	4
Total		**15**

(a)   **Cold calling and second opinions**

Cold calling

ACCA's general rule about advertising is that 'the medium used should not reflect adversely on the accountancy profession'. Cold calling is generally unpopular, but this does not necessarily make it unprofessional. However, advertisements must be in line with ACCA guidance that it should not discredit other members of the profession by claiming superiority for the member's own services, it should not be misleading and it should be legal, honest, decent, clear and truthful.

Cold calling itself is legal and there is no reason why it should not be honest and truthful. However, it may present a problem in terms of clarity, as it is oral and therefore there is scope for misunderstanding on the part of the companies being rung, and the customer being misled. In addition, any advertising technique that results in harassment is inappropriate.

Specifically, as we shall see below, cold calling about second opinions may discredit other members of the profession.

Second opinions

A second opinion is where a company is unhappy with the audit opinion that the auditor has proposed and therefore seeks an opinion from a different firm of auditors as to whether another audit opinion might be possible.

If a client requests a second opinion from an auditor, it is generally considered acceptable to give one if certain conditions are met. These are that the second firm of auditors communicates with the first set to ensure that they have access to all the information (to ensure that the second opinion is not formed negligently) and the two firms of auditors communicate frequently during the process to ensure that the first firm are not pressurised into giving a second opinion.

However, an audit firm offering to give second opinions does not appear to be so acceptable. This immediately gives the impression that all audit opinions are negotiable, and automatically puts pressure on the first firm of auditors. If the second firm is under pressure to give a different opinion (otherwise the service they have offered is negligible) then different opinions might be formed negligently.

In addition, the service they are providing discredits other auditors as it makes the suggestion that such a service is necessary, that is, that other auditors may have drawn incorrect or inappropriate audit conclusions.

Free service

Offering a free service is not prohibited so long as the client is not misled about the potential fees for future services.

Conclusion

In general terms, cold calling potential customers is not inappropriate for an audit firm. However, if it is used, it should be done so with great care so as not to mislead potential customers. It would probably be appropriate for small services other than audit-related services. Specifically, auditors should not offer services to give second opinions as this discredits the profession.

(b) **Tax planning advert**

Tax planning

Tax planning is an important part of many accountancy firms' portfolios. People in business want to operate tax efficiently and it is a perfectly legitimate service.

Advertising

ACCA's guidance on advertising was outlined above. It must not discredit the services of other accountants, it must not be misleading and it must not fall short of the British Code of Advertising Practice, meaning that it must be legal, decent, clear, honest and truthful.

In this advert, Hawk Associates claim to give 'the best' tax planning advice, which both implies the services of others are not as good (in other words it discredits them) and also may not be a claim they can live up to, opening the firm up to liability. In addition, the advert promises to consider 'all' the tax planning options available, which is an exaggerated claim and may also open them up to liability if they do not achieve this promise. In other words, the advert exaggerates the extent of Hawk Associates' service and is therefore potentially misleading.

In addition, the advert could imply to a potential client lacking in integrity that legitimate taxes might be avoided, and while the advert does not make any illegal suggestions, it could be read to mean that taxes can be avoided by any means (ie, potentially illegally). The firm should ensure that it is seen to uphold the professional standard of integrity.

Contingent fees

The advert offers a contingent fee (that is, a charge will only be made if a tax saving is made). Contingent fees on assurance work are prohibited because the risks to independence are too great to be safeguarded against. Tax consultancy is not assurance work and there are circumstances in which the IESBA would allow contingent fees for non assurance work. The firm should consider issues such as the range of fee amounts (which could be a substantial range), the degree of variability, the basis on which the fee is to be determined, whether the outcome of the work is to be reviewed by a third party (it is likely to be reviewed by tax authorities) and the effect of the transaction on any assurance engagement performed.

Given that audit clients might want to take up such an offer and that the work is likely to be scrutinised by the tax authorities, it is unlikely to be appropriate to offer contingent fees for work of this nature. If contingent fees were offered, then safeguards would need to be put into place by the firm, and the extent of these safeguards could not be explained in an advert of this size, making the advertising of the fees (or lack of them) potentially misleading.

Conclusion

The advert breaches the ACCA's guidance as it discredits other members. It is misleading as it implies a level of service which the firm cannot guarantee and therefore exposes the firm to liability. In addition, contingent fees are likely to be inappropriate as audit clients might accept this offer.

(c) **Business cards**

Use of ACCA designation

Hawk Associates are unlikely to be entitled to refer to themselves as Hawk ACCA Associates without permission from the ACCA, which is unlikely to be given. The firm is entitled to refer to itself as Hawk Associates, Chartered Certified Accountants, if 51% or more of the partners are ACCA members.

Use of the word professional

The highlighted use of the word professional appears inappropriate. Firstly it implies that other accountants are not professional, which is discrediting to the profession. In addition, the fact that Chartered Certified Accountants are professional is implied, it is not an additional selling point.

Competitive rates

There appears to be little basis for advertising that rates are competitive – with whom? for what? and it would be better to advertise that fees are reasonable and can be discussed in detail with the firm.

Money back guarantees

It is unclear in what circumstances a client would receive money back but it appears to be a claim that a firm of accountants should not make. A guarantee to give money back is akin to receiving a loan or dealing in contingent fees and it is inappropriate for a firm providing assurance services.

Location of advertisement

In principle, there is no issue in advertising in the local supermarkets and libraries where local businesses and tradesmen advertise. However, the brevity of the advert could lead to it being misleading due to the complexity of some of the services being offered, and it might be more advisable to run expanded adverts in different media.

Conclusion

The advertisements are inappropriate as they imply a discredit to the profession, they are potentially misleading and they should not offer money back guarantees.

11 Grape

Study text reference. Chapters 9, 6 and 2.

Top Tips. The scenario gives you the figures to calculate materiality in a fairly obvious way (by stating that the 'draft financial statements show revenue of £12.5m, net profit of £400,000, and total assets of £78m'). This is almost always a hint that you're going to have to calculate materiality at some point in your answer, and the opportunity to do so comes up straight away in part (a)(i)'s requirement for 'matters to consider' in relation to audit evidence. These are easy marks, so to make sure you get them, calculate materiality, and then apply it to the scenario by stating whether or not the matter in question is actually material.

Part (a)(i) was a tricky requirement. If you read the question carefully, you could have noticed that it is asking for the 'audit evidence you should expect to find **during your file review**' in relation to the 'training costs **that have been capitalised**'. In other words, you're being asked for the evidence that you would find for the training costs as non-current asset additions in the year, **given that the audit team have not yet realised that the accounting treatment is wrong.** This is tricky, but these questions do come up. When they do, it's important not to panic. Read the requirement very carefully – as long as you answer the requirement, you should get marks for every (correct) thing that you say. Once you've understood the requirement correctly, it's actually a very straightforward question on audit evidence.

Part (b) should have been straightforward, as there were plenty of points in the scenario that you should have picked up on. You should have been looking to pass this part of question well – but without exceeding the time allocation for it!

Part (c) did require you to go into quite a lot of detail about money laundering. If you have trouble remembering the policies and procedures (part (ii)), then you could try just thinking of the sorts of procedures that firms could implement in order not to get caught money laundering, as many of them are fairly common-sense.

Easy marks. There is one mark for just writing a conclusion to your answer to part (b), indicated by the word 'evaluate' in the requirement. As a general point, this examiner does like candidates to write introductions and conclusions to their answers, so get into the habit of writing something, no matter how short.

As usual, make sure you get at least two of the four professional marks available in part (c).

Examiner's comments. This question was the best answered on the paper. It was pleasing to see that many candidates appeared to have read and understood the examiner's article on audit evidence and matters to be considered, as the quality of answers was undoubtedly better than previous sittings. Most candidates could discuss the relevant accounting treatments with a degree of confidence, most determined materiality, and most could come up with several specific pieces of audit evidence.

Approximately 10% of answers agreed with the accounting treatment for the capitalised training costs, which is not allowed. A further disappointment was how few candidates considered any inventory held by Banana Co in relation to its insolvent customer, which would need to be considered in terms of obsolescence.

For requirement (b), the vast majority of answers were sound, with almost all candidates able to identify some, if not all, of the quality control issues in the scenario. The lack of a planning meeting, inappropriate delegation of work, poor direction and supervision were identified by most. Some candidates considered not only the most obvious issues from the scenario, but also the overall impact on the audit, and went beyond simply repeating points from the scenario. However, some candidates failed to really evaluate the quality control issues, and did little more than copy out sentences from the question, providing little explanation and development of the issue identified.

Requirement (c) was on money laundering. This topic seemed to polarise candidates. Well prepared candidates performed very well here, and while most candidates could at least define money laundering, a significant minority of candidates attempted this requirement inadequately, if at all. Some candidates did not attempt this requirement. Candidates are reminded that money laundering is a crucial issue that auditors must consider with every client engagement, and the anti-money laundering rules are an important part of the syllabus.

Marking scheme

Marks

(a) (i) **Training Costs**
Generally 1 mark per matter/evidence point:
Matters
- Correct calculation and assessment of materiality
- Cannot capitalise training costs
- Expenditure does not create an asset which the entity controls
- Potential qualification re material misstatement
Evidence
- Schedule of costs ($\frac{1}{2}$ only)
- Agree costs to supporting documentation
- Agree costs to cash book/bank statement ($\frac{1}{2}$ mark only)
- Cut-off procedure
- Compare to budgeted cost
- Confirm cost to approved plan/budget
Maximum   6

(ii) **Trade receivable**

Generally 1 mark per matter/evidence point:

Matters

- Correct calculation and assessment of materiality (max 1 ½ marks)
- Receivable impaired
- Consider any inventory in relation to Cherry Ltd
- Potential qualification re material misstatement
- Impact of the two issues together on the audit opinion

Evidence

- Initial correspondence with administrators of Cherry Ltd
- Confirmation with the administrators
- Agreement to receivables ledger
- Recalculations of impairment losses
- Review of inventory schedules

Maximum 6

(b) **Quality control matters**

Up to 1 ½ marks for each point evaluated from ideas list, plus 1 mark for overall conclusion

- No audit planning meeting – lack of direction
- Absence of manager and senior – lack of supervision
- Junior assigned difficult audit work (goodwill and WIP)
- Junior helped out with inventory count – lack of understanding/supervision
- Junior asked to challenge FD – inappropriate delegation
- Audit running out of time – poor planning?
- Changed sample size – inappropriate response to time pressure
- Changed item selected in sample – inappropriate response to time pressure

Maximum 10

(c) **Money laundering briefing notes**

Professional marks to be awarded for format (heading, introduction, conclusion) – 1 mark, and clarity of explanation – 1 mark

Generally up to 1 ½ marks for each explanation from list below:

- Definition of money laundering (1 mark)
- Examples of money laundering activities (½ mark each up to 3 marks)
- Procedures – appoint MLRO
- Procedures – enhanced record keeping systems
- Procedures – know your client
- Procedures – staff training
- Procedures – internal controls, monitoring and management of compliance

Maximum – technical 10

Professional marks 4

Total 36

(a) (i) **Matters to consider**

Materiality

Materiality on revenue: $\frac{£500,000}{£12.5m} = 4\%$

Materiality on net profit: $\frac{£500,000}{£400,000} = 125\%$

Materiality on total assets: $\frac{£500,000}{£78m} = <1\%$

The training costs are not material to the statement of financial position. They would, however, be material to revenue and profit if they were reclassified as expenses, turning a profit into a loss.

Accounting treatment

The training costs are currently recognised as non-current assets. This is not in accordance with IAS 16 *Property, Plant and Equipment*, which states that the costs of training staff should always be treated as an expense, as they do not meet the definition of an asset, which requires that the entity has control of the asset. This is very unlikely to be the case with training costs, as the staff will probably have the right to leave the company, meaning that Banana Ltd would not receive any subsequent economic benefit from having trained them.

The training costs should be treated as an expense in the statement of profit or loss.

Audit opinion

If Banana Ltd does not amend its financial statements, the audit opinion will be modified due to a material misstatement. This would probably be an 'except for' modification as the misstatement is material but not pervasive.

Evidence

The file should contain:

- A review of the nature of the expenses themselves to verify that they are classified correctly and that they are in fact training costs

- Testing of entries selected according to sampling procedures detailed in the audit plan to supporting documentation, such as purchase invoices, and agreement of payment of related payables to the cashbook and to bank statements

- Evidence that a sample (selected according to audit plan) of entries are included in the accounts in the correct period

Testing for completeness and that all invoices that should have been accrued for were in fact accrued for.

(ii) **Matters to consider**

Materiality for whole receivable

Materiality on revenue: $\dfrac{£30,000}{£12.5m} = 2.4\%$

Materiality on net profit: $\dfrac{£300,000}{£400,000} = 75\%$

Materiality on total assets: $\dfrac{£300,000}{£78m} = <1\%$

The receivable is not material to the statement of financial position. It would, however, be material to the statement of profit or loss and other comprehensive income if an impairment loss were recognised in relation to it.

Accounting treatment

IFRS 9 *Financial Instruments* requires receivables to be recognised at fair value. The fair value of the Cherry Ltd receivable is the 25% that the administrators suggest it may be able to pay, ie £75,000. £225,000 should therefore be recognised as an impairment loss in the statement of profit or loss.

Calculating materiality for the impairment loss:

Materiality on revenue: $\dfrac{£225,000}{£12.5m} = 1.8\%$

Materiality on net profit: $\dfrac{£225,000}{£400,000} = 56\%$

This is clearly material to profit for the year.

Inventory

As Cherry Ltd is a customer, it is possible that Banana Ltd is holding inventory or work in progress that was ordered by Cherry Ltd. Grape & Co needs to ascertain whether this is the case, and if so whether the inventory can in fact be sold. If it cannot be, then it may be impaired and should be written down, recognising the loss in profit for the year.

Audit opinion

If Banana Ltd does not amend its financial statements, the audit opinion will be modified due to a material misstatement. This would probably be an 'except for' qualification as the misstatement is material but not pervasive.

If the misstatement in respect of the receivable is taken together with the misstatement in respect of the training costs, the overall result may be that Grape & Co judges the statement of profit or loss and other comprehensive income to be rendered meaningless. In this case it would issue an adverse audit opinion.

Audit evidence

- External documentation confirming the insolvency of Cherry Ltd and the possible repayment of only 25% of the receivable
- Confirmation from the administrator of the 25% to be paid, including an indication of when this is likely to happen
- Agreement of the amount owed from the receivables listing to the ledger
- Review of inventory documentation, and evidence of enquiries made of management, regarding the value and the potential recoverability of any inventory relating to contracts with Cherry Ltd
- Calculations regarding the amount to be recognised as an impairment loss

(b) **Selection of engagement staff**

The fact that the junior had only worked on two audits before this is not a problem. However, it is important that they be given work appropriate to their level of skill and experience. This does not appear to have happened here, as detailed below.

No audit planning meeting

The audit planning meeting, led by the partner, is a crucial part of the audit. It is the best way of giving the team an understanding of the client, and should discuss both the overall strategy and the detailed audit plan, perhaps going into difficulties that have been experienced in previous years and which could come up again. The discussion should focus on what individual members of the team need to do. This is particularly important for less experienced and junior members of the team.

Audit manager away

The manager should not have given the senior responsibility for the audit while they were away on holiday for three weeks. It is important that an audit is properly supervised, and it may have been more appropriate for another manager to take responsibility for the audit.

Senior busy

Not only is there a question mark over whether they have the experience to manage the audit, but the senior is also busy with other assignments and thus unable to devote sufficient time to this one. It is very important that someone is available to supervise junior members of the audit team. This is not happening here.

It is also possible that the lack of attention paid by both the manager and the senior has led to the misstatements in respect of the trading costs and trade receivables not being picked up by the audit team.

Junior auditing goodwill and inventory

Goodwill is a complex accounting area to audit, and should not be given to a junior to do. The same can be said of inventory and in particular work-in-progress. A junior is very unlikely to have developed the judgement needed to audit these areas. This seems to be the case here, as shown by the junior's error at the inventory count (see below).

Inventory count

The junior helped the client's staff to count raw materials at the inventory count, when they should instead have been observing that the client's staff were counting them correctly and in accordance with the count procedures. This would seem to imply that the junior had not been properly briefed on their responsibilities at the inventory count, as this is a relatively basic error.

It is likely that more audit evidence will be needed to be done on inventory as a result of this error.

Junior asked to challenge FD

It is not appropriate for a junior to be asked to challenge a client's finance director regarding an accounting issue that they are unlikely to understand fully. This should have been done by either the audit manager or the partner, as they would be in a position to understand the technical issues involved, and would carry sufficient authority with the client to make the challenge effective.

Running out of time to complete procedures

Pressure of time is an important contributor to audit risk. Audit time budgets should allow staff enough time to complete the audit to the required quality. It is also possible that the lack of supervision of the audit team's work has led to the audit being conducted inefficiently, with inadequate monitoring of progress and discussion of issues as they arise.

Reduction of sample sizes

It is clearly unacceptable to reduce sample sizes as a way of saving time. The sample sizes detailed in the audit plan should have been designed to gather sufficient appropriate audit evidence. Reducing the sample size beneath this point increases detection risk, and the risk of the auditor giving the wrong opinion.

Basis of sample selection

Selecting a sample on the basis of the ease of finding evidence for an item, is not an appropriate basis. Indeed, this might actively increase detection risk as it means by definition that those items for which evidence is not readily available, or might not even exist, are not tested.

Conclusion

The litany of failures above suggests that this engagement has not been adequately supervised, and that the audit work performed is inadequate in some areas. A detailed review should be performed so that any other shortcomings can be addressed.

Doubt is also cast over the sufficiency of the firm's quality control procedures. This matter should be referred to the relevant partner for consideration.

(c)   (i)   **Briefing notes for training session**

            By: Audit manager
            Subject: Money laundering

            Introduction

            These notes explain what money laundering is, using examples of offences including those that could be committed by an accountant. They also explain the policies and procedures that a firm of Chartered Certified Accounts should establish in order to meet its responsibilities in relation to money laundering.

Definition

Money laundering is the process by which criminals attempt to conceal the true origin and ownership of the proceeds of their criminal activity, allowing them to maintain control over the proceeds and, ultimately, providing a legitimate cover for their sources of income.

Explanation

The money laundering process has three stages:

(1) Placement: getting money (usually cash) into the system in the first place. This could be by making bank deposits, making investments (eg in a unit trust), or through a 'front' business, which is a legitimate business that is used to launder money (eg a betting shop, which legitimately receives high levels of cash, could be used to deposit stolen cash).

(2) Layering: using lots of different transactions to create so many 'layers' of transactions between the initial placement of 'dirty' money and the money that is taken out at the end, that it is difficult to trace.

(3) Integration: extracting funds from the laundering system, and 'integrating' them back into the world of legitimate and use-able money.

Examples of offences

− Handling the proceeds of criminal activities

− Arranging the acquisition or use of criminal property. This may include becoming involved with tax evasion.

− Tipping off – when the MLRO or any individual discloses something that might prejudice any investigations

(ii) **Appoint a 'Money Laundering Reporting Officer' (MLRO) and implement internal reporting procedures**

The MLRO should have a suitable level of seniority and experience. Individuals should make internal reports of money laundering to the MLRO. The MLRO must then consider whether to report to SOCA, and document this process.

Train individuals

Train individuals to ensure that they are aware of the relevant legislation, know how to recognise and deal with potential money laundering, how to report suspicions to the MLRO, and how to identify clients.

Internal procedures

Establish internal procedures appropriate to forestall and prevent money laundering, and make relevant individuals aware of the procedures. Procedures should cover:

− Client acceptance
− Gathering 'know your client' (KYC) information
− Controls over client money and transactions through the client account
− Advice and services to clients that could be of use to a money launderer

Verify client identities

The firm must be able to establish that new clients are who they claim to be. They should verify the identity of new and existing clients, and keep the evidence of this on file – typically, copies of evidence such as passports, driving licences and utility bills. For a company this will include identities of directors and certificates of incorporation.

Record keeping

Maintain records of client identification, and any transactions undertaken for or with the client. Special care needs to be taken when handling clients' money to avoid participating in a transaction involving money laundering.

Conclusion

There are a number of ways that the accountant could become involved in money laundering. It is important that a firm has adequate procedures in place to ensure that it does not fall foul of anti-money laundering legislation, and that it ensures that these procedures are adhered to.

12 Ingot & Co

> **Text references.** Chapters 4, 9 and 10.
>
> **Top tips.** This question for 20 marks on quality control is split further into five mini scenarios. You need to consider each of the scenarios carefully and their impact on the firm's quality control policies and procedures. Remember to consider materiality where possible – you are given draft figures for revenue and total assets in the introductory information so are expected to use them where relevant. Make sure that the points you make are succinct and well explained and can be related to quality control. Use a separate sub-heading for each mini scenario and consider the mark allocation against each one.
>
> **Easy marks.** This is a tough question and there are no easy marks as such. Make sure your answers are coherent and logical for each mini scenario and this will help you to score marks.

Marking scheme

		Marks
Implications of findings		
Generally up to 1½ marks each (good) implication		
Specific finding ideas		
– Relevant ISAs		
(a) APs mandatory at planning stage (520)	Maximum	4
(e) Subsequent events (560)		
– Materiality (ISA (UK & Ireland) 320)		
(b) Non-current assets 17%	Maximum	4
(c) Receivables 58%	Maximum	4
(d) Inventory 1.25%	Maximum	3
(e) Prior period error 12.5%	Maximum	5
– Inappropriate procedures?		
Inventory 'roll back' (immaterial)		
– Inappropriate timing		
External confirmations (ISA (UK & Ireland) 505) – too late?		
QC at audit firm level ideas/Conclusions		
– professional behaviour		
– skills and competence		
– assignment/delegation		
– consultation		
– acceptance of clients		
– monitoring		
Total		__20__

(a) **Analytical procedures**

Analytical procedures can be used at all stages of the audit but ISA (UK & Ireland) 520 *Analytical Procedures* states that they must be used at the planning and review stages. At the planning stage, analytical procedures are a very useful tool as they assist in identifying areas of potential audit risk and therefore help direct the approach that the audit will take.

The audit plan should have been prepared by the audit supervisor and reviewed by the audit manager and partner. It should have been finalised before the commencement of the audit. The fact that the AIC has not signed off the planning checklists indicates that the memo might not have been finalised. This may mean the audit plan is not sufficient to ensure the audit is completed adequately and competently.

(b) **AIC's review**

The audit senior appears to have been assigned to low risk tangible non-current assets which comprise 17% of total assets. Audit work on **receivables** on the other hand has been assigned to a trainee – this is a more risky area of the financial statements as it comprises 58% of total assets and has doubled from the previous year.

The plan appears to be significantly flawed which is likely to result in a poor quality and perhaps even negligent audit. It is implied that the partner has not reviewed the plan which it is her duty under auditing standards to do.

It is also doubtful whether the audit is being suitably supervised since the AIC is working on three other assignments at the same time and it is unclear whether sufficient time has been spent on the audit of Argenta.

(c) **Trade receivables**

A **receivables** confirmation is a common method used to obtain audit evidence of the amount outstanding at the year end of a sample of **receivables**. However, given that it is now several weeks after the year end and it may take a while to obtain all the responses from the confirmation requests, the team should have considered whether other audit procedures to provide evidence of this material balance would have been more suitable in the circumstances, eg after-date cash.

There is also an indication that the trainees are not being adequately supervised and their work reviewed. This should have been done on a continuing basis throughout the final audit.

(d) **Inventory**

Inventory comprises an immaterial balance in the financial statements of Argenta (1.25% of total assets). The audit approach used – tests of controls and roll-back – is therefore unsuitable for such an immaterial and low risk balance.

Adequate planning, including preliminary analytical procedures, would have identified a far more suitable audit approach for this account balance. Also adequate review of trainees' audit work by the senior and AIC on a continuous basis would have identified areas of concern.

(e) **Events after the end of the reporting period**

This is a material subsequent event (the settling of litigation) which occurred before the signing of the prior year's audit report and was not picked up. This is a quality issue as it suggests that somebody did not properly complete the subsequent events procedures as required by ISA (UK & Ireland) 560 *Subsequent Events* before the audit report was signed. Alternatively it could be that the procedures were carried out and management deliberately or in error gave audit staff the wrong information about the litigation, or that the matter was not referred to in the management representation letter (which would be a different quality control problem, as under ISA (UK & Ireland) 580 *Written Representations*, this matter should have been referred to in a written representation from management).

As this matter is material to the financial statements, this error does require adjustment in the current financial statements in accordance with IAS 8 *Accounting Policies, Changes in Accounting Estimates and Errors*. The AIC should therefore appraise the client of the situation so that the financial statements can be adjusted.

If management fail to adjust the financial statements and the matter is material, this would result in Argenta having to modify the 20X8 audit report, because the provision should have been recognised last year, so the current year statement of profit or loss and other comprehensive income is incorrect.

If this matter was included in the written representation last year and was incorrect, the auditors must consider the effect this has on the quality of representations made by management in the current year's audit and must also consider whether it means that there was a lack of sufficient evidence about the prior year figures that would lead either to more work being required to substantiate the comparatives, or a modified audit opinion in respect of the comparatives. It might also lead to the need to report by exception on the fact that the auditors were not given all the information and explanations they required for their audit in respect of the comparatives.

This situation is likely to result in additional audit work being carried out (as discussed above) and therefore it is possible that the audit engagement partner will have to allocate additional staff to the audit for 20X8.

Lastly, the audit partner should ensure that the year-end 20X8 audit is carried out more effectively. Attention should be paid in particular to the written representation from management and to the subsequent events review.

13 Nate & Co

Text references. Chapters 1 and 2.

Top tips. In part (a) it is important to make your answer specific to the scenario, it is not just a straight 'textbook knowledge' requirement. In parts (b) you need to focus on **explaining** and **discussing** the issues, it is not enough to state facts from the question or to quote from the *Code of Ethics and Conduct*. You need to apply your knowledge to the facts given and show that you understand **why** they may be seen as problematic. In part (c) it is important to notice that you are not merely being asked for a definition but you must also link this with the quotation given in the question.

Easy marks. There are not many easy marks to be found in this question – each requirement demands professional judgement and application of knowledge. The basic definition in part (a) and the broad issues relating to the acceptance of the appointment are probably the easiest elements.

Examiner's comments. Requirement (a) asked candidates to define money laundering and to state procedures relevant to money laundering that should take place on the acceptance of a new audit client. Candidates appeared to have prepared for the topic of money laundering, as the definitions were usually sound. Unfortunately, few candidates could provide many, if any, specific procedures. A significant minority of answers suggested that Fisher Co should appoint an MLRO, totally misunderstanding the facts of the scenario, ie that Fisher Co is a potential audit client, not a firm of auditors. Only the best answers discussed 'know your client' procedures, and the need for clarification in the engagement letter of matters to do with money laundering.

Candidates should remember to allocate their time carefully between question requirements. Most scripts contained answers to requirements (a), (b) and (c) of a similar length, when it is clear that the mark allocation differs significantly for requirement (b).

Marks

(a) **Money laundering**

Definition – 1 mark

Procedures – generally 1 mark each

Ideas list:

(i)   Client identity

(ii)   Client business activity

(iii)   Client address

(iv)   Client principal shareholders and directors

(v)   Engagement letter clarification

Maximum   5

(b) **Ethical and professional issues**

Generally 1–1$^1/_2$ marks per issue explained

(i)   Extra work on control deficiencies

(ii)   Review work of internal audit

(iii)   Expand audit testing

(iv)   Cost/budget implication

(v)   2 partner review

(vi)   Lack of supervision and direction

(vii)   Lack of understanding of extent of responsibilities

(viii)   Inappropriate advice

(ix)   Provision of non-audit service

(x)   Safeguards

Maximum   9

(c) **Ethical and professional issues**

Generally 1–1$^1/_2$ marks per issue explained

–   Perception of bribe

–   Modesty of gift

–   Interference with count procedures

–   Review of work performed

–   Possible reperformance/alternative procedures

–   Lack of professional behaviour

–   QC issues

Maximum   6

Total   20

(a) **Money laundering**

Money laundering is the process by which criminals attempt to conceal the true origin and ownership of the proceeds of their criminal activity, allowing them to maintain control over the proceeds and, ultimately, providing a legitimate cover for their sources of income.

Money laundering procedures – before acceptance

The firm should carry out client identification procedures, such as:

- Obtaining evidence that the client exists, such as looking at the certificate of incorporation and establishing the identities of all directors (Mr Fisher and any others) by taking copies of passports or driving licenses

- Conducting a Companies House search on Fisher Ltd

- Confirming the registered address (by obtaining headed paper)

- Obtaining a list of shareholders and directors

Money laundering procedures – after acceptance

The firm should obtain 'know your client' information, such as:

- The expected patterns of Fisher Ltd's business, are there peak seasons for selling wooden storage boxes, are there any major clients or suppliers?

- The business model of the client (in this instance Marcellus Fisher appears to be acting individually through a company – does he own any other companies and what activities do they have?)

- The source of the client's funds (is Mr Fisher the only investor, or are there others, does the company also have debt finance and, if so, from whom?)

The firm should include a paragraph about money laundering responsibilities in the engagement letter.

(b)   **CF Ltd**

Ethical and professional considerations in connection with audit

There seems to have been a failure in quality control over the planning of the audit if an audit junior found time to spend three hours offering informal advice on the systems rather than carrying out planning work. As an audit junior, he should have been supervised, and the senior member of staff should have prevented him giving this informal advice.

It would have been appropriate for the audit team to make formal advice on systems in a management letter that was therefore reviewed by the audit partner and documented between the parties. The informal advice given was inappropriate and does create the possibility that the firm will be liable if the advice was found to be inappropriate.

The audit junior appears to misunderstand his role on the audit team and therefore should be given additional training in what is expected of an audit junior. The firm's initial training procedures should be reviewed to see if this is a general failing of that training.

The errors in the system will also have an impact on the audit which the firm should consider and take steps about. The increased control risk over cash deposits from customers should lead to extended testing in this area, which is likely to be significant to CF Ltd. Due to the problems in controls, additional substantive testing should be carried out.

The extent of the problems in controls should be determined, to discover if the problem is more widespread than cash deposits and whether it continued throughout the year. The auditors should review internal audit's work to assess this and the materiality of the errors should be documented. Then the approach to any other areas affected should be documented.

The industry is highly regulated and such breaches might result in the need for the firm to report the client to the Financial Services Authority. This would also lead to the need to qualify the audit report for non-compliance with laws and regulations.

The failure to record client monies correctly is also an indication that money laundering might have occurred, and this suspicion should be raised in a report to the firm's money laundering reporting officer, who must review the evidence and determine whether to make a report to SOCA.

Ethical and professional considerations in connection with proposed review

When considering whether to accept an additional service at an audit client, the firm must consider whether it will adversely impact on the independence of the audit. Two key things to consider are:

(i)   The nature of the work
(ii)   The fee level

In this instance, the firm have been asked to carry out a review of the financial information technology system as a result of errors found in it by the internal audit department, with a view to improving it. The firm must make sure that it follows the guidance of the Code of Ethics and conduct in relation to non-audit services provided to audit clients.

The auditors are likely to review the IT systems and possibly rely on them as part of their audit, so carrying out an engagement to improve the systems represents a self-review threat. The firm should assess whether the risk is too great for the firm to take on the engagement, or whether appropriate safeguards might be applied.

In this instance, appropriate safeguards might include using staff not involved with the audit to carry out this engagement. The firm would have to ensure that the staff members used are suitably qualified. The audit junior, who is a recent IT graduate, appears to be qualified to be involved in such an engagement. If he were, he should not be involved with the audit again.

If the firm decides it can reduce the self-review threat to a reasonable level to accept the engagement, then it must consider whether a self-interest threat is raised by taking on additional work for the same client.

As the review would be a one-off exercise, the fees would also be a one-off amount and would not affect the recurring fee income from the client. As a result, it is unlikely to threaten the independence of the audit sufficiently to decline the engagement.

(c) **LA Shots Ltd**

Control problems

It is a problem in the control over the inventory count that the office party was scheduled to start 'at the end of the inventory count', because it meant that the staff involved in the count were motivated to complete the count quickly rather than well. It would have been better if the party did not start until a specified later time.

The control environment for the count appears to have been poor, as the person in charge of the count seems keen to get it finished fast, with the implication being that this was rather than well. She may also have been unaware that it is inappropriate to offer gifts and hospitality to auditors, but this should be communicated to her.

Giving inventory away during the inventory count is also a sign of poor controls, as ideally there would be no unnecessary movements of inventory during the count.

Due to these problems with controls, it might have been appropriate for the auditors to have extended samples and taken longer over their procedures due to the higher control risk, but in the event, they did the opposite.

Ethical problems

The *Code of Ethics* states that a gift or hospitality from a client affects independence unless it is clearly insignificant. Similar guidance is provided in the FRC Ethical Standard 4 *Fees, remuneration and evaluation policies, litigation, gifts and hospitality*. In this case, while bottles of juice and attendance at an office party may seem insignificant, whether they were or not should have been determined by a more senior member of the audit team than the juniors, probably their manager. Given that the juniors accepted the incentives and then appeared to be motivated by them, their independence does appear to have been compromised.

These matters should be discussed with the juniors and disciplinary action taken, particularly if they attended the party in work hours without permission from their manager.

Quality control

The fact that two audit juniors with so little understanding of what they should have done on being offered incentives were sent out on this inventory count may be a sign that it was not planned or reviewed properly.

Possible action to take

As the inventory count was carried out so recently, it is probable that the firm could carry out other procedures now in order to ensure that they can rely on the figure for inventory in the financial statements if the manager determines that it is not possible to rely on the work carried out by the juniors. The work should be reviewed and concluded on as a point of priority to determine this.

14 Wexford

Text reference. Chapter 2.

Top tips. Part (a) contained a lot of matters for you to consider, both audit risks and ethical issues. The mark scheme offers up to two marks per matter that is identified and explained, and restricts the number of identification marks to three out of ten. You should therefore be looking to get at least 3 identification marks, but it is crucial here that you explain your points fully and clearly.

Part (b) was more difficult. ISA 510 is not examined very often, so you may have struggled to recall its specific requirements. Here the number of marks available for general points on ISA 510 is capped at two, and you needed to concentrate on applying your knowledge to the audit of inventory in this situation. Although you aren't told in the question that there is this cap on marks, in paper P7 you should always be looking to apply your knowledge to the scenario. If you did this, you should have been able to score well.

Easy marks. There were some fairly easy marks in part (a) for things that almost come straight out of the scenario, such as the issue of unaudited opening balances, or the potential limitation on the scope of the audit.

Examiner's comments. This was the most popular of the optional Section B questions. Unfortunately candidates' obvious lack of knowledge of the requirements of ISA 510 on opening balances meant that for many this was actually an inadequate choice of question.

Requirement (a) involved a new potential new audit client, and candidates were asked to identify and explain the matters that should be considered in deciding whether to accept the audit appointment. Candidates who had practised previous similar exam questions would have been well prepared, and there were many sound answers. Candidates were comfortable in discussing the specific ethical issues relevant to the scenario including self-review, confidentiality and conflicts of interest, and it was good to see a good number of answers refer to the requirements of ISA 210 on audit preconditions, which had been the subject of a recent Examiner's article.

Some answers were not made specific to the scenario, and discussed general matters such as resourcing, fees and engagement letters. It was interesting to see so many candidates being overly critical of the client's part-qualified accountant, who was often accused of incompetence, lack of integrity, and even fraudulent activities.

Requirement (b) dealt with opening balances and was inadequately answered by the majority. Some candidates could explain the audit procedures required by ISA 510, but few could recommend more than a couple of specific procedures in relation to the opening balance of inventory as specified in the requirement. Many answers gave procedures for non-current assets, receivables and cash which were not asked for, and many forgot that the company in the question had not been audited before, leading to irrelevant discussion of "previous auditor's working papers". Many suggested impossible procedures, eg "reperform last year's inventory count" and very few picked up on the major issue of obsolescence given the company's inventory comprise calendars and diaries.

Marks

(a) **Acceptance issues**

Up to 2 marks per matter identified and explained (max 3 marks for identification):

- Initial engagement – higher risk
- Lack of internal control – higher risk
- Non-audit service – ethical issue
- Cashflow statement – management lack understanding of responsibility
- Conflict of interest – ethical issue
- Limitation on scope – precondition not met

Maximum   10

(b) **ISA 510 requirements**

1 mark per principal audit procedure (to max 2):

- Read prior year financial statements
- Determine whether brought forward correctly
- Determine whether appropriate accounting policies applied to opening balances
- Specific procedures on certain items eg if risk of material misstatement
- Review for consistency of accounting policies in current period

1 mark per procedure specific to opening inventory (to max 6):

- Review records of prior year inventory count
- Reconcile results of current year inventory count back to opening balances
- Analytical procedures on gross profit
- Sales value confirmation for items in opening inventory
- Discussion with management re any inventory write offs relevant to opening balances
- Review of management accounts for any inventory write offs relevant to opening balances
- Analytical procedures such as inventory turnover periods

Maximum   8

Total   18

(a) **First year audit**

The fact that this is a first year audit means that the opening balances on Wexford Ltd's statement of financial position have not been audited. Sufficient appropriate evidence must be obtained about these balances. If this cannot be obtained, then this is likely to lead to a modified auditor's opinion.

Internal controls

Wexford is a small owner-managed business, with only one part-qualified accountant. Internal controls are therefore likely to be weak, with limited scope for segregation of duties, for example. There is a high risk of management override of controls, with only one part-qualified accountant and owner(s).

The effectiveness of internal controls should be assessed in line with ISA (UK and Ireland) 315 *Identifying and Assessing the Risks of Material Misstatement through Understanding the Entity and Its Environment*. If control risk is high, then more audit evidence will need to be obtained.

Accounts preparation

The IESBA *Code of Ethics* states that there may be a self-review threat to independence and objectivity where a firm prepares and audits financial statements for the same entity.

The FRC's Ethical Standard 5 *Non-audit services provided to audit clients* emphasises the possible management threat arising here. It states that an audit firm should not provide non-audit services if this involves the auditor taking on a management role.

As Wexford Ltd is not a public interest entity, both services could be provided if safeguards are put in place to reduce this threat to an acceptable level. This might include the financial statements being prepared by a separate team from that which conducts the audit. The firm must consider whether it has the resources to do this.

A further risk is that the firm becomes involved in making managerial judgements for the client. As long as the work undertaken is of a technical nature, this should not be the case. The auditor should be careful that any adjustments to the amounts included in the financial statements are approved in advance by management.

Statement of cash flows

IAS 7 *Statement of cash flows* requires entities to prepare a statement of cash flows if they are to comply with IFRS. If one is not prepared, then the financial statements will not have been prepared in accordance with IFRS. The auditor's opinion would therefore be modified – probably an adverse opinion.

The fact that Ravi has made this comment calls into question his knowledge of financial reporting, as well as the strength of the control environment in place at Wexford. This may affect the assessment of control risk.

Conflict of interest

If the firm takes on the audit of Wexford, it will be auditing two direct competitors. This is a potential threat to objectivity, and the *Code of Ethics* requires that the threat be reduced to an acceptable level by applying safeguards. If the threat cannot be reduced, then the firm should either resign from its existing audit assignment, or not take on the audit of Wexford.

Safeguards would include disclosure of the conflict to both companies, and the use of separate engagement teams for each audit. The firm would again need to evaluate whether it has the resources to do this.

Potential limitation on scope

If board minutes cannot be accessed, there may be an inability to obtain sufficient appropriate audit evidence.

The auditor has the right of access to all information that is relevant to the preparation of the financial statements, and ISA 210 (UK and Ireland) *Agreeing the Terms of Audit Engagements* requires the auditor to obtain the agreement of management to provide such information as one of the preconditions of accepting the audit engagement. If management does not agree to this, then the engagement should not be undertaken.

(b)   **ISA 510 procedures**

ISA 510 (UK and Ireland) *Initial audit engagements – opening balances* requires that the auditor read the financial statements for information relevant to opening balances, including disclosures.

The auditor then obtains evidence about whether the opening balances contain misstatements that are material to the current year's financial statements. The first thing to do here is to verify that he prior period's closing balances have been brought forward correctly.

The auditor then determines whether the opening balances reflect accounting policies in line with IFRS.

Specific audit procedures may then be performed in specific areas of the financial statements. This would be required if there is a risk that the opening balances contain misstatements that could materially affect the current period's financial statements.

Finally, the auditor determines whether accounting policies are consistent between the opening balances and the current period. Any changes must be accounted for and disclosed in accordance with IAS 8 *Accounting Policies, Changes in Accounting Estimates and Errors*.

Specific procedures for inventory

- Inspect records of inventory counts held at the prior period end (31 July 20Y0), to confirm that opening inventory agrees to accounting records

- Observe an inventory count at the current period year end (31 July 20Y1) and reconcile closing inventory quantities back to opening inventory quantities

- Perform analytical procedures on gross profit margins, comparing the opening and closing gross profit margins year on year for the various types of items held in inventory

- Verify that inventory is held at the lower of cost and net realisable value. Test a sample of the values of items sold in the current financial year of items held in opening inventory, and compare this with cost

- Inspect management accounts for evidence of inventory items written off in the current period. This is important for inventory of calendars and diaries which are likely to be obsolete

- Discuss with management whether there are any slow moving items of inventory within opening inventory

- Perform analytical procedures such as inventory turnover calculations to highlight slow moving inventory from the opening balance

15 Spaniel & Bulldog

Text references. Chapters 3 and 9.

Top tips. Part (a) represented a little bit of a twist on this issue. Usually one might expect questions on auditors and fraud to require candidates to state that the auditor is not responsible for preventing and detecting fraud. While you should have done this here, there was also the twist that the auditor appears to have been negligent in performing the audit.

Part (b) was difficult, and was actually a good reason for not choosing this question as one of your options. The choice of optional questions is very important to whether or not you pass, and choosing this question is likely have meant gambling that you would score enough on part (a) to offset your relative losses on part (b).

That being said, it was possible to pass this part of the question with some fairly generic remarks on the audit of financial instruments, mentioning things like the complexity of the accounting standards in this area and the difficulty in determining the correct treatment.

Easy marks. Calculating materiality in part (a) was easy, as was listing out the three things to prove in order to prove negligence.

Marking scheme

	Marks

(a) **Fraud and auditor's liability**

Generally up to 2 marks for each point explained:

- Not auditor's primary responsibility to detect fraud unless it is material in impact on FS
- Determine that the payroll fraud would have been material (include calculation)
- Reasons why fraud is hard to detect
- Audit firm may not have been sufficiently skeptical
- Non-adherence to ISAs on controls assessment and evidence obtained
- Discuss whether duty of care owed to client
- Discuss breach of duty of care
- Identify financial loss suffered and firm likely to have been negligent

Maximum   12

(b) **Audit of financial instruments**

Generally up to 1½ marks for each point explained:

Why is audit of financial instruments challenging?
- Financial reporting requirements complex
- Transactions themselves difficult to understand
- Lack of evidence and need to rely on management judgement
- Auditor may need to rely on expert
- May be hard to maintain attitude of skepticism
- Internal controls may be deficient

Planning implications
- Obtain understanding of accounting and disclosure requirements
- Obtain understanding of client's financial instruments
- Determine resources, ie skills needed and need for an auditor's expert
- Consider internal controls including internal audit
- Determine materiality of financial instruments
- Understand management's method for valuing financial instruments

Maximum

Total

8

20

(a) **Responsibilities**

Detecting fraud is the primary responsibility of management, not the auditor. However, the matter is complicated because the auditor is required to give reasonable assurance that the financial statements are not materially misstated as a result of fraud (or error). Moreover, auditors are required by ISA 240 *The auditor's responsibilities relating to fraud in an audit of financial statements* to identify and assess the risks of material misstatement due to fraud. This means that an audit conducted in line with ISAs should obtain evidence specifically in relation to fraud.

The audit process is, however, subject to inherent limitations which are particularly pertinent to the problem of fraud. Fraud may involve sophisticated attempts at concealment, which can make it difficult to detect. Furthermore, there may be collusion by management which makes the auditor's task even more difficult. It is therefore quite possible for the auditor to have conducted an audit in accordance with ISAs, but still have failed to detect a material misstatement resulting from fraud.

Materiality

The total amount stolen is 5.6% of total assets. If it was stolen at a constant rate, then 8/12 months fall within the year in question, which is £3m or 3.8% of total assets. This is material, and appears to have result in an incorrect auditor's opinion having been expressed.

Conduct of audit

Professional scepticism is a key weapon in the auditor's attempt to detect misstatements resulting from fraud. The audit of Spaniel does not appear to have been conducted with an attitude of professional scepticism, possibly as a result of it being a long-standing audit client.

However, irrespective of the auditor's specific duties in relation to fraud, sufficient appropriate evidence does not in any case seem to have been obtained in relation to payroll. ISAs require the auditor to design and perform tests of controls in each period under audit. Substantive evidence should have been obtained in relation to payroll. This is particularly important given that payroll is likely to be a material area.

On this basis it is apparent that the audit was not conducted in accordance with ISAs. The audit partner may therefore find it very difficult to defend the conduct of the audit.

Negligence?

Three things must be proved for the auditor to be found to have been negligent:

- A duty of care existed
- The duty of care was breached
- A financial loss resulted from the negligence

As there is a contract between Groom & Co and Spaniel, a duty of care can be shown to have existed (in this case, to the shareholders as a body).

The financial loss here would be the value of the theft, although it is not clear whether the auditor could be held responsible for the full amount of the theft.

It is likely that Groom & Co were negligent, and that Spaniel would be able to prove this in court.

(b) Audit of financial instruments

Financial instruments themselves may be difficult to understand. Management themselves may fail to understand the risks involved with them, which may expose the entity to substantial risks.

Financial reporting requirements in this area can be complex, which increases the risk of misstatement. It is possible that neither management nor the auditor will properly understand how the instruments should be accounted for.

Accounting for financial instruments may also involve an element of subjectivity, eg in determining fair values. Fair values may be estimated with the use of models which will involve making assumptions. Therefore is therefore a risk that the assumptions made by management are not reasonable.

Given the presence of subjectivity, it is all the more important that the auditor is professionally sceptical in this area, although this is likely to be difficult.

Alternatively, some financial instruments may be fairly simple to audit, eg where there is an active market, it may be possible to agree fair values to a broker's report. This would of course be subject to the requirements of ISA 500 *Audit evidence* in relation to the use of a management's expert.

It may be necessary to make use of an auditor's expert, in which case the auditor must ensure that the expert is independent and competent, and must evaluate the suitability of the expert's work as audit evidence. This may not be straightforward to do, given the complexity of the subject matter. Using an auditor's expert may also have the effect of increasing the audit fee, which should be explained to and discussed with the client.

Matters to consider

The company's treasury management function has only been set up recently, so it is possible that there will be problems in an area such as this. Internal controls may not be well established, so the auditor will need to spend time obtaining an understanding of them. This increases audit risk in this area.

Consideration should be given to the level of competence of staff in the new department. If they are skilled in this area then they may be new to the company, in which case there may be difficulties integrating the department with the rest of Bulldog's finance function. Alternatively, there is a risk that staff do not have adequate knowledge or experience in this area.

It will be necessary to obtain an understanding of the kinds of financial instruments Bulldog uses to hedge transactions, including Bulldog's reasons for entering into them and the kinds of risks it may be exposed to thereby.

The materiality of the instruments should be considered, bearing in mind especially the possibility that transactions with either no, or very little, initial value may turn out to have effects on the financial statements that are material. Some types of derivative financial instruments may fall into this category.

Management's method for valuing financial instruments should be considered, and the auditor must choose whether to audit management's valuation model, or whether to construct a model of its own. This would depend on the assessed reliability of internal controls in this area.

16 Raven

Marking scheme

	Marks

(a) Grouse Ltd
- Situation is a close business arrangement giving rise to threat to objectivity
- Explain self-interest threat
- Explain intimidation threat
- Only acceptable if financial interest immaterial and relationship insignificant
- Sale of software to audit clients would require full disclosure of financial benefit
- Sale of software to audit clients creates self-review threat
- Sale of software perceive as providing non-audit service
- Risks heightened for listed/public interest entities
- If enter business arrangement must withdraw from audit of Grouse Ltd
- Commercial consideration – demand for product
- Commercial consideration – experience of partners

Maximum   **8**

(b) Plover Ltd
- Potential breach of law and regulations
- Further understanding to be obtained
- Consider potential impact on financial statements
- Discuss with those charged with governance
- Management should disclose to relevant regulatory body
- Auditor could disclose in public interest
- Issues with confidentiality
- Take legal advice
- Extend audit work in relation to the legal claim
- Risk of material misstatement
- Consider integrity of audit client

Maximum   <u>7</u>

Total   <u>15</u>

(a) **Close business relationship**

Grouse Ltd's proposal would create very significant threats to Raven's independence.

This would be a 'close business relationship' per the IESBA *Code of Ethics*, and may give rise to self-interest and intimidation threats. The *Code* states that unless the financial interest is immaterial, and the business relationship insignificant, then no safeguards can reduce the threat to an acceptable level. Therefore Raven should not enter into this relationship if it still wants to be Grouse's auditor.

It should be remembered that independence includes independence in appearance. A joint venture with an audit client would probably have a severe affect on how Raven appeared, so even if it had been acceptable on ethical grounds, the fact that it looks so bad may well have ruled it out anyway.

Selling to clients

In addition to the close business relationship, Grouse is also proposing that the software be sold to Raven's audit clients. There are several issues here.

Firstly, there is a self-interest threat to Raven's independence if its joint venture is selling to its clients. It may be possible to reduce this to an acceptable level by using the safeguard of disclosing the relationship to clients, along with the benefit that Raven would receive from any sales.

Secondly, there would be a self-review threat if any of the audit clients used the accounting and tax software to prepare its financial statements. It may be possible to use an auditor's expert here; however, accounting software is usually pervasive to the internal controls over financial reporting, so it may be that the expert would have to be used to conduct most of the audit. This would be extremely expensive and impracticable.

Thirdly, the use of the firm's accounting and tax software could be seen as a non-audit service. This could create a perception of taking on management's responsibilities. The risk would be greater still for clients that are public interest entities, and the firm should not be involved in any tax calculations for these clients.

Taking into account these factors, Raven must choose between selling the software to its clients, and continuing to act as their auditor. It would not be possible to sell this software to clients and continue to audit them. Raven must therefore make a business decision to choose between the potential income from the software, and the loss of audit fees from every client to whom the software is sold. Raven should also take into account the loss of the audit fee from Grouse itself.

The software joint venture therefore represents a major diversification from audit to the preparation of accounting and tax software. This is a major decision that must be considered very carefully, taking into account the firm's long-term interests, where its expertise really lies, and the potential risks from diversifying into such an unknown area.

(b) **Unqualified surgeon?**

The audit senior has heard that one of the surgeons has not finished his medical qualification. This appears to be connected to the solicitor's letter that was later found which alleged medical negligence. As an auditor, we need to deal with each issue separately.

ISA 250 *Consideration of laws and regulations in an audit of financial statements* states that compliance with laws and regulations is management's responsibility, and that it is not the auditor's responsibility to either prevent or detect it. However, if – as here – we become aware of possible non-compliance then we must consider its effect on the financial statements.

As auditors we have no expert knowledge of medicine, and it is possible that we may be jumping to conclusions about whether the surgeon is qualified to do his work. It may be, for example, that he is a qualified doctor, and the 'medical qualification' he is hoping to finish is merely a further qualification that is not a requirement for his work as a surgeon. Although he was glad that Plover did not check his references, this could be a separate issue from whether or not he is qualified.

We must therefore obtain further evidence about this surgeon's qualifications, and whether they meet the requirements for his job. This could entail simply reviewing the personnel file, which may contain evidence about his qualifications.

Effect of unqualified surgeon

If we find that the surgeon is not qualified to do his job, then we must consider the effect on the financial statements. There are two main risks:

(i)   Risk of litigation resulting from errors made by the surgeon
(ii) Risk of action by regulatory bodies

In relation to (i), this is potentially a very serious problem. If the surgeon has made many errors then this could result in multiple patients suing the company. The potential cost of these actions is not know, but could be very considerable indeed. It is even possible that Plover's ability to continue as a going concern could be affected. Further evidence must be obtained about the extent of further errors and possible legal actions. It may be necessary to obtain advice from our legal counsel.

In relation to (ii), the medical profession is highly regulated and it is possible that Plover will be fined by any relevant regulatory authorities. There is a legal question about whether Plover's management could be found guilty of possible negligence as a result of breaking its duty of care to patients. It may be necessary to obtain legal advice here.

It is even possible that any licences which Plover requires to operate will be removed, and that its ability to continue as a going concern will be in doubt. It may be necessary to use an auditor's expert here to advise of the possible regulatory consequences, and/or to obtain legal advice.

Control failure?

The surgeon's comment that his references were not checked raises questions about the effectiveness of Plover's internal controls over recruitment. It will be necessary to obtain evidence about whether or not there are other employees in this position – the main issue being that there could be other employees (eg surgeons) who are not qualified to do their work. Uncovering these could lead to the discovery of further liabilities.

Public interest?

If the surgeon is not qualified, then it is possible that management will not disclose this to the relevant authorities. In this case, it may be necessary to make this disclosure in the public interest. This is a difficult issue to decide, as the auditor must balance the duty of confidentiality that is owed to Plover, with the duty to the public. Matters to consider here include the gravity of the situation, whether members of the public may be affected, and the likelihood of further non-compliance. This will all depend on whether the surgeon was in fact unqualified, and on what impact this may have had on patients.

Disclosure in the public interest would require careful consideration, and it may be necessary to obtain legal advice before doing so.

Legal claim

The letter that was found in the subsequent events review may be evidence of a liability under IAS 37 *Provisions, contingent liabilities and contingent assets*. The key question is whether the event in question took place before or after the year end. The crucial date here is likely to be the date on which the medical service was provided.

If the surgery was after the year end, then this is a non-adjusting event and no provision is necessary. If the surgery was before the year end, then a provision may be required. This will depend on how probable it is that Plover will have to pay to settle the claim, with a provision being necessary if it is probable that a payment will be made. If the matter is material and Plover's management refuse to make any necessary provisions or disclosures, then it may be necessary to express a qualified auditor's opinion.

17 Dragon Group

Marking scheme

                                                                                         Marks

(a) **Identify and explain using examples why an audit firm may not seek re-election**

Generally $\frac{1}{2}$ mark for identification and 1 mark for explanation/example, any **four**:
- (i) Disagreement
- (ii) Lack of integrity
- (iii) Fee level
- (iv) Late payment of fees
- (v) Resources
- (vi) Overseas expansion
- (vii) Competence
- (viii) Independence
- (ix) Conflict of interest

Maximum   6

(b) **Contents of tender document**

Up to $1\frac{1}{2}$ marks per matter described:
- (i) Outline of firm
- (ii) Specialisms
- (iii) Audit requirement of Dragon Group
- (iv) Outline audit approach (max 3 marks if detailed description)
- (v) QC
- (vi) Communication with management
- (vii) Timing
- (viii) Key staff/resources
- (ix) Fees
- (x) Extra services

Maximum   10

Matters to consider re acceptance

Professional marks to be awarded for clarity of evaluation, use of headings, and conclusion based on points discussed.   4

Generally $^1/_2$ mark for identification – cap at max 3, 1 further mark for explanation, from ideas list.

(i)	Large and expanding group – availability of staff now and in the future
(ii)	Use of overseas offices
(iii)	Visits to overseas audit teams
(iv)	Skills/experience in retail/foreign subsidiaries consolidation
(v)	Timing – tight deadline
(vi)	Mermaid Ltd – implication of prior year qualification
(vii)	Minotaur Ltd – implication of different business activity
(viii)	Highly regulated – risk/additional reporting requirements
(ix)	Reason for previous auditors leaving office

Maximum   7

(c) (i) **Define transnational audit and relevance to Dragon Group**

1 mark for definition
2 marks for relevance to Dragon Group
Maximum   3

(ii) **Audit risk factors in a transnational audit**

2 marks per difference explained:
- Auditing standards
- Regulation of auditors
- Financial reporting standards
- Corporate governance/control risk

Maximum   4

Total   **34**

(a) **Reasons for not seeking re-election**

Disagreement with client

The auditor may have disagreed with the client in past, for instance over accounting treatments. There is a possibility that the relationship between auditor and client could break down, which would make it very difficult to carry out the audit effectively.

Resources

An auditor may find that it lacks the resources to carry out an audit, perhaps because the client has grown rapidly so that the firm lacks the staff to provide a big enough audit team.

Competence

An auditor might believe itself not to be competent enough to carry out the audit, perhaps because the client operates in an industry with highly specialised accounting requirements, in respect of which the firm lacks the necessary expertise.

Ethics – management's integrity

The auditor might feel that it has reason to doubt the integrity of management, for instance because of a breakdown in relationship, or an unproven suspected fraud. This would lead to a breakdown in the relationship between auditor and management.

Ethics – fee level

The fees necessary to make a profit may have reached an inappropriate level, for instance 15% of total practice income in line with ACCA guidance. If the fees are too high, there is considered to be an independence problem because the audit opinion might be influenced by a fear of losing the client.

(b)   **Briefing Notes**

To: Cameron Wells
From: Jennifer Meadows
Date: June 20X9
Subject: The Dragon Group

These briefing notes outline the matters to include in our tender document for the Dragon Group audit.

Fees

The proposed fee should be included, along with an explanation of how it is calculated. This would include details of the charge-out rates of the staff likely to be used on the audit, along with estimates of the amount of time the audit would be likely to take.

Dragon Group's needs and how Unicorn & Co could meet them

(i)   An explanation of the need for each subsidiary (as well as Dragon Co) to have its own individual audit, and for the consolidated financial statements then to be audited too.

(ii)   That Unicorn & Co is a large firm and would be capable of auditing a large group such as this.

(iii)   The Dragon Group may also need some non-audit services (see below).

(iv)   That Unicorn & Co can provide a variety of non-audit services, should they be required.

(v)   Several subsidiaries prepare accounts under local accounting rules, so the auditor of these

(vi)   That Unicorn & Co is a global firm with offices in over 150 countries. It would well placed to audit under local accounting rules, and to audit their consolidation into the group accounts.

(vii)   The Dragon Group operates in the furniture retail trade.

(viii) That Unicorn & Co has a specialist retail department and therefore has the experience to audit the group efficiently.

Proposed audit approach

This section should include a description of the methodology to be used in the audit. For instance:

(i)   How the firm would acquire knowledge of the business
(ii)   Methods used in planning and risk assessment
(iii)   Procedures used to gather audit evidence

Brief outline of Unicorn & Co

A short history of the firm, including a description of its organisational structure, the services it can offer and the locations in which it operates.

Other services

A description of any other services Unicorn & Co can offer, such as offering advice in relation to the proposed stock exchange listing. Careful consideration should be given to ethical requirements relating to independence when offering other services to a potential audit client.

Key staff

Details of the proposed engagement partner and of his experience that is relevant to this audit. Details should also be given of the approximate size and composition of the audit team, together with a description of the relevant experience of key members of that team.

Communication with management

An outline of the various communications will be made to management over the course of the audit. This may include information on the way in which these reports could add value to the Dragon Group's business, for instance the production of a written report on the effectiveness of internal control procedures.

Timing

Details should be provided of the timeframe envisaged for the various aspects of the audit. This might include details of when the subsidiaries would be audited, when the consolidation process would be audited, and an estimate of by when the group audit opinion could be completed.

Conclusion

This is a large, transnational group, carrying a high level of risk. Unicorn & Co should take on the audit only once it is sure that it is able to do so, and is assured of a fee that adequately compensates it for the level of risk involved in undertaking the audit.

Matters to consider if tender is successful

Size of Dragon Group

The Dragon Group is large and expanding group of companies, and would therefore require a high level of resources to audit. Unicorn & Co must consider whether it has sufficient staff available to audit a growing group of this size.

Overseas subsidiaries

Half of the subsidiaries are located overseas. Unicorn & Co has a large number of overseas offices which could perform some or all of the overseas audits. However, these offices may not all have specialist retail audit departments, so consideration needs to be given to whether there is enough experienced staff to carry out the audit.

If some of the overseas audit work needs to be done by auditors outside of Unicorn & Co, then this work would need to be evaluated in order to express an opinion on the group financial statements.

Relevant expertise

As Unicorn & Co has a department specialising in retail audits, it is likely that it will have sufficient expertise in this country.

As a large auditing firm, it is also likely that Unicorn & Co will have staff sufficiently experienced in auditing the consolidation process to audit the consolidation of the Dragon Group's results.

Time pressure

The group's year end is 30 September 20X9, and management wants the audit completed by 31 December 20X9. This represents a tight deadline, given that the audit involves a large number of subsidiaries located in several different countries and reporting under a number of different accounting rules. The fact that this would be the first year that Unicorn & Co would have audited the group also makes the deadline tight. There is also a possibility that management do not fully understand what is required for an audit.

Planned listing

Management are planning a new listing on a foreign stock exchange. This will increase the risk of management manipulation of the accounts, as management may under pressure to report favourable results. Audit risk is also increased by the fact that as a result of the listing, the financial statements will be subject to heavy scrutiny by regulators.

Previous auditor

Unicorn & Co should consider the reason for the group seeking to change its auditor, as this might affect the decision to accept the engagement. On the face of it, it appears likely that the quickly-growing group has outgrown its previous auditors, but Unicorn & Co should still seek to obtain the reason for the change from the previous auditors.

Mermaid Ltd

Mermaid Ltd's previous auditors expressed a qualified audit opinion. Unicorn & Co should gather information about the related contingent liability, part of which would involve contacting the previous auditors. Management's refusal to disclose the contingent liability may indicate a lack of integrity on their part, which would increase audit risk. Consideration then needs to be given to whether any future non-disclosure would be material to the group financial statements.

Minotaur Ltd

Minotaur Ltd operates in a different business area from the rest of the group, so Unicorn & Co must consider whether it has staff available with the appropriate level of expertise. This difficulty should be straightforward for a firm of Unicorn & Co's size to overcome.

(c) **Transnational audits**

(i)   A transnational audit means an audit of financial statements which are or may be relied upon outside the audited entity's home jurisdiction for purposes of significant lending, investment or regulatory decisions.

This will include the Dragon Group because it is listed on the stock exchange, and also because it is listed on the stock exchanges of several different countries, and is therefore bound by regulations emanating from more than one national jurisdiction.

The fact that the group contains many overseas subsidiaries means that their accounts are likely to be relied upon both at home and abroad, and so are transnational in nature.

(ii)   **Regulation and oversight of auditors differs from country to country**

In some countries audits are self-regulated, whereas in others a legislative approach is used. There is a risk that auditors of transnational groups may not be sufficiently aware of the requirements in all of the relevant countries.

Differences in auditing standards from country to country

Although International Standards on Auditing are now in operation in many countries, these standards are frequently modified by individual countries. Moreover, not all countries have adopted the standards.

There is a risk that auditors may not have the required understanding of the relevant auditing standards in each country.

Variability in audit quality in different countries

It may be the case that the quality of auditing required may differ between relevant countries. There is a risk either that the auditor does not perform an audit that is up to the required standard in some countries, or that the audits performed on some overseas subsidiaries are not up to the standard required to express an opinion on the group financial statements.

18 Pulp

Text references. Chapters 4 and 7.

Top tips. The examiner has stated that paper 'P7 will continue to test financial statement areas that are relatively hard to audit, and areas which are the subject of specific auditing standards, in this case ISA (UK & Ireland) 550 *Related Parties*'. You would have struggled with this question if you had not learnt and understood this standard.

In part (b) it is important to plan and structure your answer to make sure that all relevant points are included. Think about what headings to use and what needs to be included under each heading for part (b)(i).

Easy marks. Listing the disclosure requirements of IAS 24 *Related party disclosures* was straightforward. In addition you should have been able to gain some easy marks for making some suitable comments in part (c).

Examiner's comments. Despite the clue given in requirement (a), a surprising number of candidates did not mention that the transaction described in the scenario appeared to be a related party transaction. Those that did pick up on this fact failed to develop or explain the point fully, and although there were many comments along the lines of 'the transaction should be disclosed', hardly any answers provided an indication of what exactly should be disclosed and why.

On the whole the answers to (b)(i) were confused, resulting in inadequate answers to (b)(ii), where audit procedures should have been recommended. Very few candidates suggested that the auditor should try to understand the nature of the transaction in question ('normal' trade receivable or loan), with procedures usually restricted to vague comments like 'inspect invoice' – but what it is being inspected for, and would there even be an invoice? Answers to audit procedure questions must be much more specific.

Requirement (c) was often not attempted. Some candidates seemed to want to punish this year's audit senior for the deficiencies in the audit which happened in the previous year. Better answers discussed a need for the training of audit staff with respect to related parties, and the need for a thorough review of this relatively high risk section of the audit.

Marks

(a) **Problems in identifying related parties and transactions**

Generally 1–1½ marks per problem

Ideas list:

(i) Complex/subjective definition of related party
(ii) Reluctance of management to disclose
(iii) Hard to identify from accounting system
(iv) Deliberate concealment for fraud/window dressing
(v) Materiality relatively complex to apply

Maximum
5

(b) (i) **Matters to consider**

Generally 1–1½ mark for each matter identified

Ideas list:

– Immaterial by monetary amount – only award mark if calculation provided
– Material by nature
– Whether this is a one-off transaction
– IAS 24 – whether meets definition of related party
– IAS 24– matters to be disclosed ($^1/_2$ mark per specific disclosure point required)
– IAS 24– breach and impact on audit report – only give mark for specific reference to 'except for' modification
– Recoverability of balance
– Possible misclassification – could be a non-current asset investment

Maximum
5

(ii) **Audit procedures**

Generally $^1/_2$–1 mark for each comment
Ideas list:
– Specific written representations from Peter Sheffield ($^1/_2$ mark per specific point requested)
– Develop understanding of nature of transaction
– Review of Jarvis Ltd financial statements ($^1/_2$ mark per specific item looked for in the review)

Maximum
4

(c) **Quality control issues**

Generally 1 mark for each comment

Ideas list:
(i) Not identified as high risk area
(ii) Inexperienced member of team/poor training given
(iii) Inadequate review of working papers

Maximum
3

Total
17

(a) **Difficulties in identification**

Related parties

Related parties are defined by IAS 24 *Related party disclosures* and can be **complex, subjective** and **difficult to identify**. It is not always immediately obvious to management or the auditor whether a party is related. For example, IAS 24 states a party is related to an entity when the party 'controls, is controlled by, or is under common control with, the entity'. Control may not always be easy to identify within a complex multi-national group or if the controlling party is a trust, it may be difficult to prove who, if anyone, controls it.

There is frequently **little or no documentary evidence** of related parties and so the auditor often has to rely on management's **written representations** for their disclosure. If management wish to hide a related party, it may prove difficult for the auditor to identify it through normal audit procedures.

Related party transactions

Management systems are not designed to distinguish related parties or produce a summary of their transactions. Management will generally have to carry out additional work to identify and collate related party information. If this work is not completed, it may prove difficult for the auditor to detect all related party transactions.

Management may **conceal** a related party transaction in full or in part. This could be because they are motivated by more than ordinary business considerations, for example, to enhance the presentation of the financial statements (as part of a fraud or window dressing). If management conceal a related party transaction, it will be very difficult for the auditor to identify.

Related party transactions may be **material** in substance rather than size, so difficult to detect using ordinary audit procedures. It may also be difficult for the auditor to determine whether transactions are material to related parties who are individuals, such as directors and their families.

(b) (i) **Matters to consider**

Disclosure

The rules of IAS 24 state a party is related to an entity when the party 'controls, is controlled by, or is under common control with, the entity'. Since Jarvis Ltd is controlled by Peter Sheffield, it seems a related party relationship exists. Further audit procedures should be undertaken to confirm that this is the case. If so, the £25,000 receivable with Jarvis Ltd is part of a related party transaction.

IAS 24 requires the following to be disclosed for a related party transaction.

- Names of the transacting related parties
- A description of the relationship
- A description of the transaction and the amounts included
- The amounts due to or from the related party at the end of the year
- Any other element of the transaction necessary for an understanding of the financial statements

Pulp Ltd's financial statements should be amended so that the correct disclosure of the related party transaction with Jarvis Ltd is made. If Pulp Ltd do not make this change, the audit report should be modified to show a qualified opinion ('except for') as a result of a material misstatement paragraph.

Materiality

The receivable balance is 0.02% (£25,000/£12m) of total assets so would not be classified as material by its amount. However, as the transaction is with a related party it may be material in nature and so it should be considered whether it has been made on normal commercial terms.

Recoverability

The receivable has been in existence for over a year and so its recoverability needs to be taken into account. The representation from Pulp Ltd should be viewed with professional scepticism since the same representation was made in the previous year. If found to be a bad debt, then the balance should be written off, and the statement of profit or loss debited with the expense.

Misclassification

If Pulp Ltd are able to prove that the receivable is recoverable in the long term it may be reclassified as a non-current receivable. However, it could be argued that the balance is effectively a non-current asset investment, and if so, should be reclassified as such.

One-off transaction

The transaction between Pulp Ltd and Jarvis Ltd may not be a one-off and there could be further undisclosed related party transactions between the companies.

(ii) **Further audit procedures**

- Written representations should be obtained from Peter Sheffield which contain:

  - The exact nature of his control over Jarvis Ltd. For example, his percentage shareholding if he is a shareholder
  - Whether he believes the £25,000 receivable with Jarvis Ltd to be recoverable and a specific date by which the amount is be expected to be repaid
  - Confirmation there are no more transactions between Jarvis Ltd and Pulp Ltd or any further outstanding balances

- The terms of any written confirmation of the £25,000 receivable with Jarvis Ltd should be reviewed to see if Pulp Ltd is due interest for late payment. The terms of the confirmation should be analysed for details of any security offered.

- The purpose of the £25,000 receivable with Jarvis Ltd should be discussed with Peter Sheffield in order to ascertain whether the balance is a trade receivable or an investment.

- The board minutes should be inspected for evidence of the transaction with Jarvis Ltd and any discussion regarding its recoverability.

- The most recent audited financial statements of Jarvis Ltd should be reviewed as to:

  - Whether Peter Sheffield has been disclosed as the ultimate controlling party or key management personnel
  - Whether there is any disclosure of a £25,000 related party liability with Pulp Ltd
  - Whether Jarvis Ltd would be able to pay the £25,000 from liquid assets (perform a liquidity analysis)

(c) **Quality control issues**

There is evidence that this audit is poor from a quality control perspective.

The receivable with Jarvis Ltd was identified in the 20X7 audit together with the details about Peter Sheffield. Therefore, this should have been identified as a **high risk area** during the planning stage of the 20X8 audit. Suitable procedures should have been designed to confirm completeness, existence and valuation of related party transactions rather than just relying on management representations.

The audit work should have been carried out by a suitable member of staff and then reviewed by a more senior member of the team. As the related party transaction was not identified as a high risk area during the planning stage, it is likely that an **inexperienced** team member was assigned to carry out the work.

The review carried out by the audit senior and manager in the prior year was **inadequate** as it did not identify the weakness of written representations from management as a source of evidence for the transaction.

19 Aspersion

Text references. Chapters 7, 9 and 10

Top tips. When faced with a general requirement such as 'comment on matters you should consider' it is important to thoroughly record your thought processes and not to omit anything which you feel is obvious. For example, for each of the situations in this question, you need to write down your 'alarm bells', in other words, the problems you feel could exist in the situation. This will lead to you then explaining the implications of these problems for the financial statements, and therefore the things you will need to find out and confirm in discovering whether a true or fair view has been given. Remember that there are certain matters which an auditor should always consider, such as materiality. The examiner has clearly given you scope in the scenario to consider materiality, so not to do so will lose you marks.

Easy marks. Section (a) was probably the most straightforward here.

Examiner's comments. This question was answered relatively well apart from item (3) on deferred tax – candidates were very hazy about whether an adjustment would be appropriate and some completely failed to even attempt this section. However, it should have been answered much better.

Candidates need to be able to recognise the principle accounting issues involved in this type of question. These were:

(a) Related party transaction (IAS 24)

Relatively good marks were gained here. Candidates that did particularly well spent sufficient time identifying the audit evidence they would look for. Weaker candidates who insisted that the transaction 'must be on an arm's length basis' scored few marks.

(b) Impairment (IAS 36)

Most candidates missed the point and got bogged down with discussion on depreciation rates when the issue was impairment. A disappointing majority of candidates suggested (incorrectly) that the carriers should have been depreciated over three years. That some candidates believed that the two light aircraft should have been accounted for as a construction contract under IAS 11 was very worrying.

(c) Deferred tax (IAS 12)

The majority of candidates clearly felt so nervous about the accounting of deferred tax that they failed even to go 'back to basics' and consider whether the event after the reporting period was adjusting or non-adjusting. Advice to candidates who do not know a relevant Accounting Standard is to revert to principles (eg the change in rate does not give rise to a liability because it did not apply at the end of the reporting period). Nevertheless, some marks were gained for the audit evidence part where most candidates managed to suggest that they would need a copy of the calculation and would need to re-perform casts etc.

Although it was not in the marking scheme, those exceptionally perceptive candidates who pointed out that writing down the assets in (b) for impairment would have an impact on the deferred tax provision were awarded marks.

References to any documentation supporting 'payments of deferred tax' showed a staggering lack of understanding of the concept of deferred tax.

Marks

(i)   *Matters*

Generally 1 mark each comment

Maximum 5 marks any one issues × 3   Maximum   12

Ideas
- Materiality (assessed)
- Relevant IASs (eg 1, 10, 12, 24, 36)
- Risk (eg completeness assertion)
- Implications for auditor's report (eg explanatory para)

(ii)   *Audit evidence*

Generally 1 mark each item of audit evidence (source)

Maximum 5 marks any one issues × 3   Maximum   12

Ideas
- Oral vs written
- Internal vs external
- Auditor generated
- Procedures (relevant, reliable, sufficient)   Maximum   <u>20</u>

(a)   Maximum   7
(b)   Maximum   7
(c)   Maximum   <u>6</u>
Total
                                                                                     <u>20</u>

(a)   **Sale of cargo carrier to Abra**

(i)   **Matters to consider**

A cargo carrier has been sold to a party which is potentially related to Aspersion under the requirements of IAS 24. A loss has been made on that disposal of a non-current asset.

Materiality

The loss on disposal has reduced profit before tax by £400,000. This 14% reduction is material to profit.

Related party transaction?

Iain Jolteon, the finance director who approved the sale of the cargo carrier, has a substantial equity interest in Abra, the company to whom it was sold. As such, Abra appears to fall within the criteria of a related party under IAS 24.

This connection would appear stronger if Mr Jolteon owned shares in Aspersion or was a director in Abra, and if Abra was controlled by his close family members.

Implication

The transaction should be disclosed in the financial statements as a related party transaction. This disclosure should include:

- The names of the transacting related parties
- A description of the relationship between the parties
- A description of the transactions
- The amounts involved
- Any money outstanding due to the company/related party

Other related parties

The auditors should consider, and be alert for evidence of, other related parties and transactions.

Reasons for the sale

The fact that a large loss has been made on the sale raises other matters for the auditor to consider:

- Whether the sale has been made at an undervalue (this may have tax implications)

- Why the machine was sold:
  - Maintenance problem
  - Reduction in operations
  - Movement in technology rendering others obsolete

- Whether the depreciation policy was incorrect (over 20 years)

These questions will lead the auditor to review the remaining non-current assets to ensure that they are not impaired and that the depreciation policies are reasonable.

Disclosure of loss on sale

As this item is material it would be disclosed separately in accordance with IAS 1 *Presentation of financial statements*.

(ii) **Audit evidence**

The following evidence will be sought:

- A copy of the sales agreement

- A copy of any valuation report carried out on the asset

- Evidence of receipt of the proceeds through the bank

- The calculation of the loss (this should be checked for accuracy)

- Notes of discussions with management about procedures for the identification of related party transactions

- Results of reviews of board meetings, share registers and other statutory records

- Written management representations regarding the completeness of related party disclosures

- A copy of the disclosure note which is to be included in the financial statements

(b) **Light aircraft**

(i) **Matters to consider**

Aspersion owns two light aircraft which are used to service a contract which will not be renewed when it comes up in six month's time.

Materiality

The total cost of the aircraft was £900,000. They have been owned in the region of three years, and have been depreciated over 15 years. Therefore, their carrying value is in the region of £720,000. This represents 7% of total assets and is therefore material to the statement of financial position.

Impairment

The aircraft were purchased to service a contract which will not be renewed when it expires six months after the end of the reporting period. This significant change in the market in which the assets operate indicates impairment of the asset and requires management to carry out an impairment review under IAS 36. The auditors need to establish whether this has been carried out.

Management intentions

The auditors need to discover what management's future intentions for the assets are:

- Sale
- Alternative use

These intentions will impact on the impairment review.

Impairment loss

If an impairment loss has been identified, the auditors need to discover.

- Whether it is material ($\geq$ £100,000, say)
- Whether it has been properly disclosed in the financial statements

(ii) **Audit evidence**

- A copy of the service contract and any correspondence
- Results of inspection of the aircraft (to ascertain condition)
- Notes of enquiries of management to ascertain

  - Future intentions
  - Whenever an impairment review was carried out

- Evidence from the impairment review – for example, any draft sales agreements, cash flow projections relating to value in use, any contracts relating to new uses for the aircraft

(c) **Deferred tax**

(i) **Matters to consider**

Deferred tax has been provided for in respect of accelerated capital allowances in accordance with IAS 12.

Materiality

The tax provision amounts to 21% of profit before tax and is therefore material. The increase in the provision, of £76,000, is not material to profit before tax.

IAS 12 – rate of tax to use

IAS 12 requires that deferred tax is calculated at a rate of tax that is 'substantively enacted' and expected to apply to the period when the deferred tax is to be settled. Substantively enacted generally means that it has been made into law, not merely suggested or announced.

In this instance, therefore, the directors are proposing to amend the provision to apply a tax rate that is not substantively enacted, but has merely been announced.

Implication

If the directors do make the provision bigger, they will no longer be complying strictly with the requirements of IAS 12. The auditors should discuss the matter with the directors and dissuade them from making such an addition to the provision.

However, the additional provision is immaterial to the financial statements, so the auditors are unlikely to conclude that the deferred tax balance does not give a true and fair view.

(ii) **Audit evidence**

- A copy of all the calculations made in relation to the tax balances
- The client's schedules relating to the tax basis used
- Agreement of tax rate to tax legislation
- Schedules of non-current assets used in tax calculations agreed to non-current asset register/ general ledger
- Audit programme for non-current assets with evidence of verification of changes (eg additions)
- A reconciliation of the tax expense with the accounting profit
- Minutes of directors' meetings confirming details of any major additions etc in non-current assets

20 Mac

Marking scheme

		Marks
(a)	**Benefits of outsourcing internal audit**	
	Up to 1½ marks per point evaluated:	
	– Improved quality/experience	
	– Greater authority	
	– Bigger resource base	
	– Independent viewpoint	
	– Better ability to focus and prioritise issues	
	– Finance function benefits from staff reassigned	
	Maximum	6
(b)	**Impact of outsourcing on the external audit**	
	Generally 1 mark per point:	
	– Assess extent of reliance per ISA (UK & Ireland) 610/402	
	– Likely to place greater reliance than previously	
	– Impact on audit strategy – less substantive procedures	
	– More efficient audit/lower fees	
	– Need to document and evaluate changes to systems/controls	
	– Access to information and working papers	
	Maximum	4

(c) **Procedures regarding fraud**

Up to 1 mark per procedure:
- Review process for adding approved suppliers to list
- Review all payments authorised by the account manager
- Use CAATs to identify suppliers with same bank details
- Supplier statement review
- Select invoices and trace to supporting documentation
- Consider likelihood of insurance reimbursement
- Consider prosecution of account manager and recovery of funds

Maximum   4

(d) **Report to client on audit committees**

Professional marks to be awarded for format (heading, introduction, conclusion) – 1 mark, and clarity of explanation, use of language appropriate to client – 1 mark

Generally 1 mark for each comment from list below:

(i) **Responsibilities in relation to fraud:**
- ½ mark ref ISA (UK & Ireland) 240
- Management primary responsibility
- Management responsible for controls and culture of entity
- Auditor only responsible for detection of frauds with material financial statement impact
- Auditor not responsible for prevention but does make recommendations on controls
- Both review strength of systems and controls

(ii) **Benefits and drawbacks**
- Increase confidence/credibility
- Stronger control environment
- Bring external experience/expertise
- Provide impartial consultation
- Easier to raise finance/gain listed status
- Problems in recruitment
- Expense

Maximum – technical   8

Professional marks   4

Total   26

(a) **Staff**

Lindsay only qualified recently, and the two other internal auditors are still studying for their professional qualifications. There is therefore a question mark over whether the team as a whole is sufficiently technically competent and experienced to do the work required of it.

An external provider would have access to good quality staff. This would improve the quality of work done, and would release Mac Ltd from the burden of training unqualified staff.

Authority

It appears that Lindsay's recommendations lack sufficient authority for them to be taken seriously by managers, possibly because she is only recently qualified and was previously a junior manager. An external provider may command greater authority, so that its recommendations may be more likely to be followed.

Independence

At present the internal audit team reports to the finance director, and there is therefore a chance of it being reluctant to criticise the finance department overtly. An external provider would be under no such restrictions.

Resources

The internal audit department appears to be under-resourced, as it lacks the time to perform much testing of financial or operational controls. Outsourcing would give immediate access to a well-resourced internal audit function.

Focus

At present internal audit seems to lack focus, or a specific remit. Its work seems to be determined by the finance director's priorities. An external provider would be able to focus on the full range of internal audit work.

Staff to finance department

Moving Lindsay and her team into the finance department is likely to improve the control environment and the embedding of controls procedures within the organisation, as the team will bring with it the perspective they have gained from working in internal audit.

(b) ISA (UK & Ireland) 610 *Using the Work of Internal Auditors* and ISA (UK & Ireland) 402 *Audit Considerations Relating to an Entity Using a Service Organisation* should be considered here. In line with ISA (UK & Ireland) 610, the auditor will have to consider the scope and organisation of the internal audit department, and then evaluate the specific audit work they are interested in. ISA (UK & Ireland) 402 requires the auditor to consider the impact that outsourcing internal audit will have on Mac Ltd's accounting and control systems.

It is likely that Manhatten & Co will place more reliance on an outsourced internal audit function than on the present internal audit team, as such a function is likely to provide work of better quality. This may lead to a reduced audit fee, which will be helpful for Mac Ltd in view of its concerns over cash flow.

If new internal control procedures are implemented as a result of outsourcing internal audit, this may increase the amount of audit work required. Alternatively, the amount of audit work could decrease if new procedures are very significantly better than the old ones.

(c) Procedures to quantify loss include:

- Use of computer techniques to identify other payments made to the account manager's bank account, and consideration of whether these payments are legitimate

- Review of all suppliers to whom payments were approved by this manager, and comparison with the list of approved suppliers

- Testing a sample of payments to each supplier back to invoice, and then tracing the transaction through to existence in the form of delivery notes, etc

- Review terms of insurance cover taken out by Mac Ltd with a view to a possible claim

- Discussion with legal counsel over whether any reimbursement might be received from the manager in the event of charges being pressed

(d) **Report**

To: **D. & S. Hudson**
Re: **Auditor's responsibilities on fraud; audit committees**

Introduction

The objectives of this report are to explain the responsibilities of the external auditor and management regarding fraud, and to outline the benefits and drawbacks of Mac Ltd establishing an audit committee.

(i)   **Responsibilities on fraud**

According to the International Standard on Auditing (ISA) 240 *The Auditor's Responsibilities Relating to Fraud in an Audit of Financial Statements*, the primary responsibility for preventing and detecting fraud lies with those charged with governance and management of an entity. Management does this by establishing a system of operational and financial controls, along with an appropriate cultural environment for those controls, to reduce the risk of fraud taking place.

The auditor's responsibility is to obtain reasonable assurance that the financial statements are free from material misstatement, whether due to fraud or error. The auditor is only responsible for detecting fraud, therefore, insofar as it affects the accounts (by causing a material misstatement). For instance, the fraud recently perpetrated by an account manager in Mac Ltd may not have had a material impact on the financial statements, in which case the auditor would not have been responsible for detecting it.

There is some overlap between the responsibilities of management and the auditor on internal controls, in that both have to make an assessment of the effectiveness of controls. It is possible that the auditor may make a recommendation to management of ways for it to improve the effectiveness of controls. The key difference, however, is that it is the responsibility of management alone to implement a system of controls that prevent and detect fraud.

(ii)   **Audit committees**

The benefits to Mac Ltd of an audit committee include:

- Increased confidence in the credibility of financial reports. This may help Mac Ltd to raise external finance in the future if required.

- The committee would specialise in financial reporting problems and to some extent discharge the directors' responsibilities in that area. This would free the executive directors to devote their attention to management.

- In case of conflict between the executive directors (eg the finance director) and the employees (eg internal audit), the committee may provide an impartial body for the external auditor to consult.

- Establishing the committee should help improve the control environment, which would help to prevent future frauds, and may improve the efficiency and the cost of the external audit.

- An audit committee is a requirement of many corporate governance codes, and if in future Mac Ltd wishes to seek a listing, it would have to establish an audit committee anyway.

- Members of the audit committee would bring valuable business skills and knowledge into the company. They would be non-executive directors, who would provide impartial advice and guidance to the executive directors. This could be particularly valuable in a family-owned business such as Mac Ltd.

The drawbacks to Mac Ltd of an audit committee include:

- Cost. Members of the committee should ideally have a high level of experience and expertise, for which they would require a substantial fee.

- It can be difficult to recruit audit committee members with a level of experience sufficient for the committee to be really effective.

Conclusion

This report distinguishes between the responsibility of management, for preventing and detecting fraud and for establishing a system of internal controls to do this, and that of the auditor, which is for detecting material misstatements.

An audit committee would provide Mac Ltd with a number of benefits, particularly in view of what may be a relatively weak control environment at present. However, the costs and difficulties associated with establishing such a committee must be considered carefully.

BPP
LEARNING MEDIA

21 Falcon

Marking scheme

			Marks
(a)	**Prospective financial information**		
	Generally 1 mark per point	Maximum	5
	• Definition of prospective financial information		
	• Distinguishing between forecasts and projections		
	• Level of assurance provided		
(b)	**Matters to be considered**		
	Generally ½ mark each matter identified and 1 mark a point explaining its relevant	Maximum	14
	• PFI 'general' ideas		
	• Form and content		
	• Period covered		
	• Intended use		
	• Recipients of report		
	• Relevance and reliability of PFI		
	• Report required		
	• Timescale		
	• Confidentiality		
	• Purpose of engagement		
	• Other service opportunities		
	Ideas specific to Imperiol		
	• Who is Paulo Gandalf?		
	• Why has auditor not been engaged for assignment?		

(c)   **Procedures**

Generally 1 mark each point contributing to a description of procedures   Maximum   9
Ideas
- General (ie applicable to both profit forecast and forecast SOFP)
- Specific (ie relevant to profit forecast or SOFP)
- Arithmetic accuracy
- Assumptions, bases, etc
- Inter-relationship

Professional marks for format, style and clarity of answer   4
Total   32

Briefing notes

For: Jennifer Jones
By: Helen Heller
Date: December 20X9
Subject: Imperiol Ltd

Introduction

These notes discuss prospective financial information and the level of assurance that can be provided in engagements to report on it. They then explain the matters that should be considered by the professional accountant before accepting an engagement to report on Imperiol Ltd's prospective financial information. Finally, they describe the procedures to be undertaken in order to report on Imperial Ltd's forecasts for the year ended December 20Y0.

(a)   **Prospective financial information** is information based on assumptions about events that may occur in the future and possible actions by an entity.

Prospective financial information can be of two types (or a combination of both):

Forecasts are prospective financial information based on assumptions as to future events which management expects to take place and the actions management expects to take (best-estimate assumptions).

Projections are prospective financial information based on hypothetical assumptions about future events and management actions, or a mixture of best-estimate and hypothetical assumptions.

Prospective financial information is difficult to give assurance about because it is **highly subjective** and this makes it a difficult area to examine and report on. Hence the level of assurance provided is **negative**, as opposed to external audits, which examine historical financial information, and where the assurance provided is reasonable.

Guidance on reporting on it is given in ISAE 3400 *The examination of prospective financial information*. The ISAE suggests that the auditor express an opinion including:

(i)   A statement of **negative assurance** as to whether the **assumptions** provide a reasonable basis for the prospective financial information

(ii)   An opinion as to whether the prospective financial information is **properly prepared** on the basis of the assumptions and the relevant reporting framework

(iii)   Appropriate **caveats as to the achievability** of the forecasts

(b)   **Matters to be considered before acceptance**

The terms of the engagement

In particular Hal Falcon should clarify whether there will be any restrictions put in place in terms of access to information and personnel.

Status of Paulo Gandalf

There may be an issue of independence if Paulo both produces the PFI and appoints those who are responsible for reviewing it.

The nature of the business plan

This could be made up of a number of different elements including profit forecasts and cash flows. The content needs to be confirmed as the procedures which will be adopted will depend on the nature of the material covered.

The intended use of the information

In this case the information is to be used by the bank/venture capitalists as a basis for determining whether to finance the business restructuring. It is likely that this information will be a significant factor in the decision making process.

Specific requirements of the recipients

If a bank or venture capitalist has already been identified they may have specific requirements of the information in terms of content and presentation.

The nature of the assumptions

These may be best estimates or hypothetical assumptions. Ideally Hal Falcon would wish to be able to distinguish between the two.

Probable reliability of the information

This will depend on management expertise and integrity. As the business has already experienced a number of restructurings it should be possible to assess the management's ability to produce PFI by comparing forecasts and actual results based on an earlier restructuring.

The period covered by the information

The forecast information is produced to 31 December 20Y0. Assumptions normally become more speculative as the length of period covered increases. In this case, however, the period covered does not seem excessive. Consideration would need to be given to any specific time scale requirements set down by the bank/venture capitalist.

Form of opinion required

Normally this would be a statement of negative assurance.

Time available

Hal Falcon must ensure that they have sufficient time to perform the necessary procedures.

Experience of Hal Falcon staff

The firm should only accept the appointment if they have the necessary expertise to perform the engagement.

Knowledge of the business

Hal Falcon need to be confident that they will be able to obtain a sufficient level of knowledge of the business to be able to evaluate whether all significant assumptions required for the preparation of the prospective financial information have been identified.

Degree of secrecy required

This may go beyond the normal duty of confidentiality.

Communication with Discorpio

In particular Hal Falcon would wish to enquire if there was any reason as to why they should not accept this appointment. This may be an issue particularly as Discorpio have not been asked to perform this work.

Provision of other services

Hal Falcon may be able to offer external audit services and internal audit services as these are currently outsourced.

(c)   **Procedures**

Applicable to all PFI

(i)   Discuss with management the way in which the PFI is prepared.

(ii)   Compare the actual results of previous restructurings with forecasts to determine overall level of accuracy of PFI.

(iii)   Determine who specifically is responsible for the preparation of the PFI and assess their experience and expertise.

(iv)   Assess the role of internal audit and other control procedures over the preparation of PFI.

(v)   Check the accounting policies normally adopted by the company. These should have been consistently applied in the preparation of the PFI.

(vi)   Check the arithmetical accuracy of the PFI by making clerical checks such as recomputation. Internal consistency should also be assessed through the use of analytical procedures.

(vii)   Obtain written representations from management regarding the intended use of the prospective financial information, the completeness of significant management assumptions and management's acceptance of its responsibility for the prospective financial information.

Profit forecast

(i)   Discuss with management the means by which they have predicted expected revenues/profits. For example extrapolation of historical data may be inappropriate due to the restructuring.

(ii)   Check that any assumptions made are consistent with one another. For example if revenue is expected to grow certain costs would also be expected to increase (although not necessarily in direct correlation). Assess the assertion by the business that the restructuring will result in a lower cost base.

(iii)   Compare assumptions made for forecast purposes with other internal information produced by the business. For example expected sales growth can be compared to sales and marketing plans.

(iv)   Compare budgeted expenditure on R&D with budgets and final costings on completed products. (This is particularly important as the aim of increasing market share is dependent on innovative products. R&D is likely to be a major cost.)

(v)   Compare assumptions made with general industry data and trends particularly in respect of the building systems market.

(vi)   Compare predicted costs against actual costs incurred. Clarify the rationale behind any significant cost savings.

Forecast statement of financial position

(i)   Perform analytical review comparing key ratios including ROCE, current ratio and gearing, based on the forecast information with Dec 20X8/June 20X9 results.

(ii)   Determine the way in which the balance for intangible assets has been calculated. Development of new products would result in increases in intangibles. However assets related to discontinued operations would need to be written off.

(iii)   Agree proposed additions to tangible assets to capital expenditure budgets. Ensure assumptions regarding depreciation are consistent with the profit forecast. (This would also apply to intangibles.)

(iv)   Agree cash balance to other forecast information eg cash flow.

(v)   Determine the level of provisions made in respect of discontinued activities and assess whether they seem reasonable.

(vi)   Compare predicted movements in loans to cash flow.

(vii)   Analyse movement on reserves (ie is movement on reserves equal to forecast profit? If not what do the other movements represent?).

Conclusion

It is not possible to give a level of assurance in respect of prospective financial information that is comparable to that given on historical financial information. There are a number of matters that should be considered by a professional accountant even before accepting an engagement to report on prospective financial information, regarding in general the precise form of the report that is to be provided, and the overall context of the engagement. There are a variety of specific procedures that should be performed in order to provide such a report to Imperiol Ltd.

22 Juliet

Text references. Chapters 2, 7 and 18.

Top tips. The first part of this question was difficult, and doubtless many candidates would struggle to make up 8 marks here. It is important with discussion questions that you plan your answer before you write. If you don't plan, there is a danger that you will change your mind about what you want to say while you are already writing. This will only waste time and will be unlikely to score marks. You need to plan your answer, and divide your discussion into clearly structured paragraphs. Within each paragraph, you should aim to have an introduction, a point, and a conclusion.

It is also important that you didn't go over time on this part of the question – perhaps through struggling to write clearly – as there were some easier marks to be had in part (b).

Easy marks. Part (b)(ii) was probably the easiest part of the question, as most of the ethical implications should come out of the scenario.

Examiner's comments. Candidates were asked to discuss firstly whether auditors should accept some of the blame when a company on which they have expressed an unmodified opinion subsequently fails, and secondly whether auditors should do more to highlight going concern problems. Very few answers were worthy of more than a few marks, most answers simply listing the auditors responsibilities from ISA (UK & Ireland) 570 *Going Concern*, with no discussion at all of the statement provided in the question. Those who did refer to the statement provided tended to just state whether or not they agreed with it but provided no discussion at all. Answers were especially poor at discussing whether auditors should disclose more in relation to going concern, with most just describing the various ways that going concern issues may affect the audit opinion. It is inadequate that at this level of examination candidates seem simply unable to express an opinion of their own or base a reasoned discussion around a statement provided to them, especially around such a significant current issue facing the profession.

Candidates were firstly asked in requirement (b)(i), for six marks, to identify and explain the matters that should be considered, and the principal audit procedures that should be performed in respect of the funding being sought. The main problem with answers were that they did not focus as required on the additional funding being sought, but instead discussed more generally the plight of the company.

Requirement (b)(ii) was the best answered requirement of this question. Most candidates correctly identified and went on to explain the self-review, management and advocacy threats created by the situation, and many discussed the potential liability issue caused by attending the meeting.

Marking scheme

		Marks
(a)	**Discussion**	
	Up to 2 marks for comments discussed from ideas list	
	– Management responsibility for risk assessment	
	– Auditor should be aware of going concern issues	
	– Auditor must not take on management role	
	– Misunderstanding of roles of management and auditor	
	– Auditor may be to blame if overlooked a fraud/other matter	
	– Financial statements contain disclosure on risk assessment	
	– Users may not be financially literate	
	– Auditors could make problems more visible and understandable	
	Maximum	8

(b) (i) **Matters and procedures on funding**
Up to 1 mark each point:
Matters:
  – Area of critical importance to the audit
  – Bank reluctant to confirm arrangements
  – Assets impaired – little collateral to offer
  – Have alternative providers been discussed?
  – Potential impact on FS and audit report if significant doubt remains over going concern
Procedures:
  – Review assumptions used in forecasts and projections
  – Management representation on reasonableness of assumptions used
  – Review potential finance for adequacy
  – Consider if any previous defaults
  – Consider terms of finance – can the company meet repayment terms?
  – Written confirmation from bank
  – Discuss with bank
  – Discuss with management
Maximum   6

(ii) **Ethical and other implications**
Up to 1 mark each point explained:
  – Advice is a non-audit service
  – Self-review threat
  – Advocacy threat
  – Management threat
  – Safeguards should be used to reduce threats
  – Firm may decide that no safeguards can reduce threats to an acceptable level
  – Attending meeting could create legal proximity
Maximum   6

Total   20

(a) The concept of an expectations gap between auditors and the public is a key lens through which assertions such as this one can be viewed. The first part of the statement would appear to assert that the auditor is in some way responsible for the failure of a company. This is not the case: those charged with governance are responsible for risk assessment and risk management. It is not the role of the auditor to become involved with the entity's risk management processes – indeed, this could be deemed to constitute a management role, which would compromise the auditor's independence.

However, it is true that the auditor should gain an understanding of the client's business; this is a crucial requirement of ISAs. Amongst other things, it is necessary for an auditor to audit management's assessment of the appropriateness of the going concern assumption, for which a good understanding of the business risks faced by the client is necessary. The auditor must judge whether the going concern assumption used is appropriate. However, this is never a matter of cut-and-dried logic: it is a judgement, based on an assessment of risk. It is in the nature of risk for there to be uncertainties, and it is in the nature of judgement to contain elements of doubt.

It is therefore to be expected that there will be cases where the auditor has judged the going concern assumption to be appropriate, and yet the company fails within the year. The question is not whether the assumption was proved correct by subsequent events, but whether the auditor's assessment was reasonable and in line with auditing standards.

There is more scope for discussion on the question of whether auditors should do more to highlight problems. This may be the responsibility of management; it would be possible for regulators and setters of accounting standards to require increased disclosure on going concern. For example, financial statements could be required to provide more narrative detail regarding the risks faced by an entity.

At present, auditors should disclose the presence of material uncertainties over going concern by way of an emphasis of matter paragraph in the auditor's report, and if they deem the assumption to be inappropriate then the opinion would be modified. It may be possible for these disclosures to be made clearer than they are, or for auditors to use their report to draw users' attention to any parts of the financial statements that are significant to the assessment of going concern.

In conclusion, it is unfair to require auditors to accept the blame for company failures which are the proper responsibility of management, although it may be argued that more could be done by auditors to highlight going concern problems where they exist.

(b) (i) The central issue here is going concern; there are a number of indications that Juliet Ltd may not be a going concern. For instance: declining sales and profitability over two years; the loss of key customers; the impairment of assets; debts going bad. Most significant of all is the question of whether the loan will be obtained.

If Juliet Ltd does not obtain the loan, then the financial statements must contain disclosures regarding the material uncertainty over going concern. The auditor's report should contain an emphasis of matter paragraph discussing the uncertainty and referring to the note. If the financial statements do not contain these disclosures, then the auditor's opinion would need to be either qualified or adverse.

Procedures in respect of the loan include:

- Obtain and review the forecasts and projections prepared by management and consider if the assumptions used are in line with business understanding.

- Obtain a written representation confirming that the assumptions used in the forecasts and projections are considered achievable in light of the economic recession and state of the automotive industry.

- Obtain and review the terms of the loan that has been requested to see if Juliet Ltd can make the repayments required.

- Consider the sufficiency of the loan requested to cover the costs of the intended restructuring.

- Review the repayment history of any current loans and overdrafts with the bank, to form an opinion as to whether Juliet Ltd has any history of defaulting on payments. (Any previous defaults or breach of loan conditions makes it less likely that the new loan would be advanced).

- Discuss the loan request with the company's bankers and attempt to receive confirmation of their intention to provide the finance, and the terms of the finance.

- Discuss the situation with management and those charged with governance, to ascertain if any alternative providers of finance have been considered, and if not, if any alternative strategies for the company have been discussed.

- Obtain a written representation from management stating management's opinion as to whether the necessary finance is likely to be obtained.

(ii) **Ethical**

These forecasts are crucial for the assessment of whether the company is a going concern. There is a self-review threat if the auditor is both advising on the preparation of the forecasts, and auditing them as part of its work on going concern under ISA (UK & Ireland) 570 *Going Concern*.

The issue is given added weight by ISA (UK & Ireland) 570's insistence that where cash flow is important for the assessment of going concern, particular consideration should be given not only to what the forecasts say, but to their reliability. This exacerbates the potential impact of the self-review threat.

There is potentially an advocacy and management threat, as the auditor is advising on a matter significant to the company's operational existence, and promoting the company's position to the potential provider of finance.

The auditor must consider whether safeguards can be put in place to reduce these threats to an acceptable level. For instance, a separate team could review the forecasts, and management could be asked to provide representations to the effect that they alone are responsible for the forecasts.

If the firm decides that the threat is still not reduced to an acceptable level, then either, or both, of the services should not be provided.

Other

A further issue is that if the auditor does attend the meeting with the bank, it must be careful not to create the impression that it is responsible for the forecasts, or is in any way guaranteeing the future existence of the company. In legal terms, attending the meeting and promoting the interests of the client could create legal 'proximity', which increases the risk of legal action against the auditor in the event of Juliet Ltd defaulting on the loan.

23 Apricot

Study text reference. Chapter 13.

Top tips. Part (a) should have been straightforward, provided that you had prepared this area. A good approach might be just to go down the forecast thinking about what procedures you could do to test each row of figures. The additional information given at the bottom of the question is the examiner's attempt to give you some context for the forecast. What you need to do is use this information to think of procedures that use this information to test the forecast. It should be possible to think of a procedure relating to virtually every point of information given – just as you should be able to think of a point for virtually every line in the forecast itself.

Note that our answer to this part of the question gives more points that you could probably have written down in the exam, although it is by no means comprehensive. Your approach should be to make sure that you get enough **good points** down in the time available. You should concentrate on properly developing the points that you do make, rather than taking the familiar 'scatter-gun' approach that so often characterises weaker students. It is also a good idea to try to cover all of the areas of the question (ie of the forecast), as you will probably be able to make stronger points over a number areas (by saying the obvious things that there are to say about each) than you would if you get bogged down in just one area of the question. Make sure you stick to your time!

Part (b) saw the examiner returning to an area that she mentioned in her last examiner's report as being poorly understood by students. If you had been diligent and had read her report, you would have revised this area carefully if this was your real exam. It would be a good idea for you to do this! The actual content of the question was not difficult, again provided that you had revised it thoroughly.

This time, our answer does represent something that a student could achieve in an exam – see the examiner's answer for something more comprehensive. You will notice that as this is a standalone, knowledge-based requirement, the answer can be based closely on the content of the study text – although it must still of course be applied to the scenario.

Easy marks. Marks were available in part (a) just for saying 'agree the opening cash balance to the bank statement/reconciliation', and 'cast the forecast'. These are very obvious marks, and would be applicable to virtually any other question relating to the audit of cash flow forecasts. Ignore them at your peril!

There is also an easy ½ mark in part (b) for saying that the report should have a title and an addressee.

Examiner's comments. This was by far the least popular of the optional questions in Section B, but those that did attempt the question tended to perform well.

Requirement (a) asked candidates to recommend the procedures that should be performed on the cash flow projection. The majority of answers produced many specific procedures, based on the information provided. Candidates that approached the answer logically and worked through each item on the cash flow forecast to derive appropriate procedures performed very well. However, some answers were limited to enquiry with management, which restricted the marks that could be awarded.

Requirement (b) asked for an explanation of the main contents of the assurance report that would be provided. Most candidates could make an attempt at a list of contents, but very few answers provided sufficient explanation of the content identified, eg most could identify that a statement of negative assurance would be provided, but few explained what that meant. Some answers provided a contrast between an audit and an assurance report, which was not asked for. The main problem with answers to this requirement is that they were just too brief for the marks available.

Marks

(a) **Procedures on cash flow forecast**
Generally 1 mark per specific procedure from ideas list:
- Accuracy checks – recalculation
- Agree opening cash position
- Recalculate patterns of cash in and out for credit sales and purchases
- Agree patterns using aged receivables analysis/working capital ratios
- Agree discounts received and allowed to invoices/contracts/correspondences
- Agree derivation of figures from profit forecast
- Agree monthly salary expense to payroll
- Review content of overheads – check non-cash expenses not included
- Review for missing outflows eg tax and finance charges
- Agree premises costs eg to legal documents
- Discuss timing of fixtures cash flow
- General enquiries with the preparer of the forecast

Maximum   11

(b) **Content of an assurance report**
Up to 1 mark per point if explained:
- Title/addressee ($^1/_2$ mark)
- Identification of PFI
- Management responsibility
- Purpose of PFI
- Restricted use of PFI
- Negative assurance opinion re assumptions
- Opinion on presentation
- When may qualifications be necessary/explanation of errors found
- Reference to engagement letter ($^1/_2$ mark)
- Statement/reference to procedures carried out ($^1/_2$ mark)

Maximum   5
Total   16

(a) **General procedures**

(i) Check that the forecast casts.

(ii) Check that the opening cash balance agrees to bank reconciliations and statements.

(iii) Enquire as to who prepared the forecast, and verify that they are competent to do so (evidence eg by being a chartered certified accountant).

Operating cash receipts

(i) Enquire as to the basis for the forecast rise in both cash and credit sales receipts.

(ii) Perform analytical procedures on historical information to confirm reasonableness of forecast revenues, taking into account knowledge of the business.

(iii) Confirm split between cash and credit sales to past trends and to knowledge of the business.

(iv) Recalculate cash receipts from credit sales from revenue figures in profit forecast and ageing structure of receivables.

(v) Verify that the 10% discount for cash payment has been taken into account when calculating cash received from cash sales.

(vi) Enquire as to who Apricot's major customers are and confirm that they are to continue trading with Apricot, eg that none are going into administration.

Operating cash payments

(i)   Confirm that forecast is prepared on the assumption that all purchases are paid for within 30 days.

(ii)   Confirm that 12% supplier discount is received from suppliers' invoices, supplier statements, etc.

(iii)   Confirm that forecast is prepared on the assumption of receiving the 12% supplier discount.

(iv)   Verify the accuracy of the statement that suppliers are paid within 30 days by reviewing aged payables analyses for historical information.

(v)   Agree the salary payments to payroll information.

(vi)   Review the overheads to ensure that non-cash items such as depreciation are not included.

(vii)   Enquire as to the reason for no outflows for taxation (eg Corporation tax, VAT).

Other cash flows

(i)   Agree the cost of the licence to supporting information from the health and safety authority, and confirm the cost of £35,000.

(ii)   Enquire as to the likelihood of actually receiving the licence – whether the inspection will be passed. For example: if the inspection has already taken place, ask what the result was; if it has not taken place, consider the use of a health & safety expert.

(iii)   Agree the fixtures outflow of £60,000 to underlying information, eg to supplier quotations.

(iv)   Confirm that the fixtures outflow will take place during March – this seems unlikely given that the premises will only be bought on 30 March. This may cast doubt over the reliability of other information in the forecast.

(v)   Agree the £500,000 to be paid for the premises to documentation and verify that it is complete.

(b)   In accordance with the requirements of ISAE 3400, the report should contain the following:

(i)   Title and addressee

(ii)   Identification of the prospective financial information (PFI) being reported on

(iii)   A reference to the purpose of the PFI, which in this case is to provide assurance to Pik Choi's financial advisor regarding Apricot Ltd's cash flow forecast

(iv)   A statement of negative assurance as to whether the assumptions provide a reasonable basis for the prospective financial information

(v)   An opinion as to whether the prospective financial information is properly prepared on the basis of the assumptions and is presented in accordance with the relevant financial reporting framework

(vi)   Date of the report, auditor's address and signature

24 Poppy

Marking scheme

			Marks

(a) **Discuss whether recognition of fair values leads to increased audit risk**
Generally 1 mark per point
- (i) Introduction referring to widespread need to recognise fair values due to financial reporting standard requirements
- (ii) Example of item recognised at fair value (other than investment property)
- (iii) Discussion of inherent risk – subjectivity
- (iv) Discussion of inherent risk – deliberate manipulation
- (v) Discussion of inherent risk – complexity
- (vi) Discussion of control risk – non routine transactions
- (vii) BUT may lead to increased level of monitoring
- (viii) Discussion of detection risk
- (ix) Conclusion
Cap marks at 5 if no attempt is made to produce a rounded discussion
(ie should not assume that fair value automatically increases audit risk)
Maximum   **7**

(b) (i) **Enquiries regarding valuer**
Generally ½ mark per enquiry and 1 mark per point of explanation from ideas list:
- – Membership of professional body
- – Whether a licence is held
- – Reputation – references, etc
- – Experience with Poppy Ltd's type of property
- – Experience with preparing valuations under IAS 40
- – Financial interest
- – Personal interest

Up to 4 mark for assessment of reliability, up to 2 marks for assessment of objectivity
Maximum   **7**

(ii) Audit procedures
Generally 1 mark per procedure from ideas list:
- Review written instructions
- Evaluate assumptions
- Check consistent method used
- Check date of report close to year end
- Method to follow IAS 40 fair value framework
- Physical inspection
- Review of purchase documentation
- Subsequent events
- Management representation

Maximum

Total

6

20

(a) **Fair value and audit risk**

The measurement of an asset or liability at fair value can be due to a requirement of IFRS or a conscious choice by the entity. Examples of items measured at fair value include properties and financial instruments. IFRS 13 *Fair value measurement* contains extensive guidance in this area.

Items measured at fair value are often material balances in the statement of financial position and so will require the auditor to collect sufficient appropriate evidence to ensure they meet the requirements of the applicable accounting standard. Guidance for auditors can be found in ISA (UK & Ireland) 540 *Auditing accounting estimates, including fair value accounting estimates, and related disclosures*.

Through understanding the entity and its environment as required by ISA (UK & Ireland) 315, the auditor will gain knowledge of the balances which have been measured at fair value and then assess their impact on the audit strategy and risk.

Audit risk is a product of inherent risk, control risk and detection risk and the impact of material balances recognised at fair value on each of these is discussed here.

Inherent risk

Fair value measurements are inherently subjective in nature as they generally involve making estimates based on a number of assumptions. Management may not be sufficiently experienced or skilled to make these assumptions. Assumptions can also be manipulated by individuals to obtain the most favourable fair value in the financial statements, in other words window-dressing.

The calculation of fair value is complex for many balances, for example, actuarial calculations used to value a pension fund. This makes them inherently more difficult to audit as the likelihood of an error is higher in complex calculations.

However, not all fair value balances are so complex and subjective. For example, the valuation of assets which are regularly bought and sold on open markets. This type of balance will not increase audit risk as a fair market price can be readily ascertained.

Control risk

Fair value measurements are not routine transactions and are likely to only take place once a year. They are therefore more likely to fall outside the system of controls set up by the entity to deal with regular transactions. This increases the likelihood that controls are not as strong as in other more routine areas.

However, as the fair value balances are often material, management are more likely to closely monitor any fair value measurement which will reduce the control risk.

Detection risk

Detection risk will be minimised through proper planning of audit work. There is a risk that the audit team may lack the knowledge to make an assessment of the fair value measurement themselves and may rely too heavily on the work of an expert. This could result in an increased risk of errors not being detected.

Conclusion

A large number of material balances measured at fair value may increase audit risk in the financial statements, but this is not always the case. Not every balance will contain a material misstatement and the risk associated with each balance will need to be individually assessed.

(b) (i)

Enquiry	Reason
What is the professional certification of the valuer?	To determine the competence of the valuer so the reliability of the valuation can be assessed
Is the valuer a member of a recognised professional body/industry association, such as an institute of chartered surveyors, and how long has the valuer been a member for?	
Do any professional or other standards, and regulatory or legal requirements apply?	
What assumptions and methods are used by the management's expert, and are they generally accepted within that expert's field and appropriate for financial reporting purposes?	
The nature of internal and external data or information the expert uses	
Is there any relevant evidence regarding the reputation of the valuer of which the auditor should be aware? For example, professional references.	
Does the valuer hold a licence to carry out a valuation of investment properties (if applicable)?	To establish that the valuer is suitably experienced in valuing the type of investment property held by Poppy Co
What experience does the valuer hold in the valuation of investment properties and their recognition at fair value?	To ensure that fair values have been reached using methods permitted by IAS 40 *Investment property*
Is the valuer related to the entity in any way, for example, by being a close family member of a director at Poppy Co?	To determine the objectivity of the valuer so that the auditor can judge the independence of the valuation
Does the valuer have any financial interest in Poppy Co, such as shares?	To assess the method by which Poppy Co has appointed the valuer
Is the fee received by the valuer reasonable and at market price?	If the fee was not at market price (for example too high) the valuer's independence may have been threatened in order to provide the required result

(ii) **Procedures**

- Inspection of the written instructions given to the valuer by Poppy Ltd which should include the objectives and scope of the work, the intended use of the valuer's work and the extent of the valuer's access to records and files

- Consideration of the assumptions and methods used by the valuer to ensure they are reasonable based on other audit evidence and the auditor's previous knowledge of Poppy Ltd

- An evaluation of the method used to measure fair value to ensure consistency with IAS 40

- Examination of the valuation report to ensure each property has been valued consistently and that the date of valuation is reasonably close to Poppy Ltd's year end

- Physical inspection of the valuation properties to ensure their condition is in line with the valuation report

- Inspection of purchase documentation for the investment properties to ensure that any revaluations made in the year of purchase are reasonable and not significantly different from the purchase price

- A review of subsequent events for additional evidence on the valuation of the investment properties

- Obtain management representations concerning the reasonableness of any stated assumptions in determining fair value

- Evaluate the appropriateness of that expert's work as audit evidence for the relevant assertion

25 Magpie

Text references. Chapters 4, 6, 7 and 11.

Top tips. Part (a)(i) was a fair requirement, but one that may have left you struggling for ideas to make up eight marks. The requirement divides itself naturally into two parts, with four marks each for the individual company and the consolidated financial statements. Make sure you noticed what point we were at in the audit process: it is audit planning, after the engagement has been accepted but before the audit work as such has begun. Comments relating to specific procedures will get no marks here, and neither will comments relating to eg audit acceptance procedures.

Part (a)(ii) was the longest part of the question, and was a fairly typical test of applying your knowledge to the scenario. The question did require perhaps a bit more financial reporting knowledge than in some previous sittings of P7 – IFRS 3, IFRS 9 and IAS 20 came up – but you should not have struggled with any of it. Passing this part of the question is a matter of working steadily through the issues contained in the scenario. You can flag to your marker that you are answering the question by specifically stating for each issue something like 'the risk here is', and then using auditing terminology to pick out where there may be eg an understatement or an overstatement.

It should be possible to pass part (a)(iii) fairly easily, as there is one mark available per specific procedure. You therefore only need three good, specific procedures to get three/five marks. As with many questions asking for audit procedures in a specific area of financial reporting, a good approach is to think of each of the specific figures involved, and then think of what could go wrong with each of them and how you would test them. The question makes it easy for you here, as you have a goodwill calculation laid out for you. All you need to do is think of one or two good procedures for each figure in the calculation, and hey presto, you have passed the requirement!

Part (b) contained three tricky ethical scenarios. Even if you were not sure of the final answer in a given situation, you can try approaching questions like this by (1) working out what the issue is, perhaps using the general types of threats as a guide (self-interest, self-review, advocacy, familiarity and intimidation); then (2) trying to think of safeguards that might remove the issue; and then (3) if no safeguards would make the threat go away, recommending that the auditor doesn't do it.

Easy marks. There were plenty of easy marks in part (a)(iii) for thinking of procedures – provided you had not gone over time on the long part (ii) that preceded them.

ACCA examiner's answer. The ACCA examiner's answer to this question can be found at the end of this Practise & Revision Kit.

Marks

(a) (i) **Audit implications of Canary Ltd acquisition**

Up to 1½ marks for each implication explained (3 marks maximum for identification):
- Develop understanding of Canary Ltd business environment
- Document Canary Ltd accounting systems and controls
- Perform detailed analytical procedures on Canary Ltd
- Communicate with previous auditor
- Review prior year audit opinion for relevant matters
- Plan additional work on opening balances
- Determine that Canary Ltd is a significant component of the Group
- Plan for audit of intra-company transactions
- Issues on auditing the one month difference in financial year ends
- Impact of acquisition on analytical procedures at Group level
- Additional experienced staff may be needed, eg to audit complex goodwill

Maximum   **8**

(ii) **Risk of material misstatement**

Up to 1½ marks for each risk (unless a different maximum is indicated below):
- General risks – diversification, change to group structure
- Goodwill – contingent consideration – estimation uncertainty (probability of payment)
- Goodwill – contingent consideration – measurement uncertainty (discounting)
- Goodwill – fair value of net assets acquired
- Goodwill – impairment
- Identify that the issues in relation to cost of investment apply also in Crow Ltd's individual financial statements (1 mark)
- Loan stock – premium on redemption
- Loan stock – accrued interest
- Loan stock – inadequate disclosure
- Identify that the issues in relation to loan stock apply to cost of investment in Crow Ltd's individual financial statements (1 mark)
- Online sales and risk relating to revenue recognition (additional 1 mark if calculation provided of online sales materiality to the Group)
- No group accounting policy for online sales
- Canary Ltd management have no experience regarding consolidation
- Financial performance of Crow Ltd and Starling Ltd deteriorating (up to 3 marks with calculations)
- Possible misstatement of Canary Ltd revenue and profit
- Grant received – capital expenditure
- Grant received – amount not yet spent
- Prior period error – clearly trivial
- New IT system
- Starling Ltd – no finance director in place at year end

Maximum   **18**

(iii) **Goodwill**

Generally 1 mark per specific procedure (examples shown below):
- Confirm acquisition date to legal documentation
- Confirm consideration details to legal documentation
- Agree 100% ownership, eg using Companies House search/register of significant shareholdings
- Vouch consideration paid to bank statements/cash book
- Review board minutes for discussion/approval of acquisition
- Obtain due diligence report and agree net assets valuation
- Discuss probability of paying contingent consideration
- Obtain management representation regarding contingency
- Recalculate goodwill including contingency on a discounted basis

Maximum   5

(b) **Ethical matters**

Generally 1 mark per comment:
- Reasonable for partner to attend board meetings
- But must avoid perception of management involvement
- Partner must not be appointed to the board
- Seconded manager would cause management and self-review threat
- Safeguards could not reduce these threats to an acceptable level
- Some recruitment services may be provided – interviewing/CV selection
- But avoid making management decision and put safeguards in place

Maximum   6

Total   37

(a) (i) **Planning implications of Canary Ltd acquisition**

Individual financial statements

ISA 315 Identifying and Assessing the Risks of Material Misstatement through Understanding the Entity and Its Environment requires us to understand the entity and its environment, and internal control.

To understand Canary Ltd ('Canary') and its environment, we must consider any relevant regulatory factors, eg whether it uses the same financial reporting ('FR') framework as the group; the nature of the entity's operations, ownership and governance, and the kinds of transactions and balances that should be expected in the financial statements; and its selection and application of accounting policies, and whether they are in line with its business and the FR framework.

To understand Canary's internal controls, we must consider its accounting systems as well as any other controls relevant to the audit. Our understanding of these controls must be documented. This is particularly important with a new audit client because we have not had time to build up knowledge of the entity, and so need to place special emphasis on this area now.

IT is likely to form a significant part of Canary's systems (since 30% of sales are online), and these will be different from the rest of the group. We should consider if we need to use an auditor's expert in this area.

It will be necessary to perform detailed analytical procedures on Canary at the planning stage. This will be necessary to determine planning materiality, and to help identify any significant events or transactions in the period.

ISA 300 *Planning an Audit of Financial Statements* requires us to communicate with Canary's predecessor auditor, asking if there is anything we should be aware of that may influence our plan. We should also review the prior period audit opinion and report.

Finally, we will need to perform additional procedures on Canary's opening balances, as these were audited by a predecessor auditor.

Consolidated financial statements

The first thing to consider is whether Canary is a significant component according to ISA 600 *Special Considerations-Audits of Group Financial Statements (Including the Work of Component Auditors)*. Canary's forecast revenue is 11.9% (16/135) of group revenue, and profit is 23.5% (2/8.5), so it is definitely a significant component.

Although we are both the group auditors and Canary's individual auditors, we still need to (i) consider whether audit evidence obtained for the individual company is sufficient and appropriate for the group, and (ii) perform procedures on matters relevant to the consolidated accounts. This includes procedures to determine whether intra-group balances have been eliminated, and whether IFRS 3 has been applied correctly in relation to the acquisition itself.

A particular issue is that Canary's 30 June year end is different from the rest of the group. In practice this will usually be changed soon after the company is acquired, so we need to obtain evidence to determine whether or not this has happened. This matter is absolutely crucial to the audit. If the year end has not been changed, then additional procedures must be performed on Canary's financial information so that its financial statements as at 31 July 20X2 can be consolidated.

Care must be taken when performing analytical review on at a group level, as Canary's figures are only included since the acquisition date and will not be comparable with the whole-year figures of the rest of the group.

Finally, the new acquisition introduces new complexities into the audit, so we must ensure that these aspects of the audit are done by staff with appropriate levels of experience, eg the goodwill asset and the contingent consideration.

(ii) **General**

There are several factors which together mean that this is a high risk audit: there has been a significant acquisition, a move into a new line of business, and the introduction of new IT systems relating to financial reporting.

Goodwill

Goodwill is material to the financial statements, at 8.2% of total assets (45/550).

The contingent consideration is a significant audit risk. It is currently recognised in full as an asset, which is in line with the IFRS 3 *Business combinations* requirement to recognise it at its fair value at the acquisition date. However, this amount should be discounted to its present value, because in this the consideration is not payable until 1 February 2015. As this has not been done, goodwill appears to be overstated.

A further risk relates to the valuation of identifiable net assets. This has been done by a management's expert in the context of a due diligence review. ISA 500 *Audit evidence* requires the auditor to evaluate the expert's competence, capability and objectivity; to obtain an understanding of their work; and to evaluate the work's appropriateness as audit evidence. The auditor's evaluation of each of these issues should be documented.

IAS 36 *Impairment of assets* requires goodwill to be tested for impairment annually, and there is no mention of this having been done at the year end. There is therefore a risk that goodwill may be overstated.

Loan stock

The loan stock issued is material, at 18.2% of total assets (100/550).

The premium of £20m should be recognised as a finance cost over the period of the loan using the amortised cost method, in line with IFRS 9 *Financial instruments*. The risk is that this has not been done, and that finance costs are understated.

An interest cost of 5% is also payable in arrears, and there is a risk of further understatement of finance costs if this has not been accrued for.

These issues apply to both the group accounts and Crow Ltd's individual company financial statements.

Online sales

Canary's online sales represent 30% of its revenue, with approximately £4.8m (0.3 × 16) included in the group accounts – a figure that should be even higher in future, when a full year's revenue will be included in the group accounts.

There is a risk that IAS 18 *Revenue*'s requirements on when revenue should be recognised are not met. This will be heavily dependent on the reliability of the IT system involved, its appropriateness for financial reporting, and its integration with the accounting system.

E-commerce can also represent a business risk as it may expose Canary to eg lost sales or reputational damage if its website does not operate effectively. With online sales at 30% of revenue, any significant problems in this area could affect Canary's status as a going concern.

Canary's management

Canary's management have no prior experience of the consolidation process at the CS Group, so it is possible that the process will operate inefficiently and that errors will be made. It is likely that more audit work will need to be done on the consolidation of Canary's results than on the rest of the group.

Financial performance

At first sight, the group's results are encouraging – revenue is up 8% and profit before tax is up 1.2%. However, this is not comparing like with like: the prior year figures do not include any of Canary's results, whereas the current year figures include Canary for six months.

If we include only Crow Ltd and Starling Ltd's results and compare them with the prior year, then a different picture emerges:

	20X2 Crow + Starling forecast	20X1 Group actual	% change
Revenue	119	125	(4.8%)
Profit before tax	6.5	8.4	(22.6%)

Instead of profit and revenue both growing, the picture these figures paint is of profit and revenue shrinking. This may be for operational reasons, but it is also possible that there has been a misstatement, with either costs being overstated or revenue understated.

Government grant

The grant is material, at 6.4% of total assets (35 / 550).

There are two issues in relation to the grant. The first is that in line with IAS 20 *Accounting for Government Grants and Disclosure of Government Assistance*, this is a grant related to assets. This may either be deducted from the cost of the related assets (in this case, solar panels), or recognised as deferred income that is released systematically into profit or loss. At the year end only £25m of the £35m grant had been spent, so some of the grant should be deferred until the next year. There is a risk that this has not been done, and eg the £35m has simply been recognised in income during the year.

The second issue is that the grant is for capital expenditure on environmentally friendly assets, but Starling Ltd intends to spend the remaining £10m on upgrading its production and packing lines. This seems unlikely to meet the conditions of the grant, and it is possible that some of it will need to be repaid if it is spent in this way. The matter is likely to be material to the group, at 1.8% of total assets (10/550).

Prior period error not relevant

Deferred revenue in the prior period was overstated by £10,000. This is 0.014% of Crow Co's forecast revenue (= 100,000 / 69,000,000), and 0.29% of profit. It is clearly immaterial, and is not relevant to the audit planning.

New IT system

The new IT system, which is relevant to financial reporting, represents a risk of material misstatement per ISA 315. There are two main issues: firstly, errors may have been made in transferring the data from the old to the new system; and secondly, the new system is likely to take time to bed in, and it is possible for teething problems to lead to a loss of data.

New FD

The fact that Starling Ltd's FD has recently left increases the risk of errors as it deprives the company of accounting skills it may need when producing its financial statements, and for the consolidation process. It may also make the audit more difficult to conduct, as it may not be possible to obtain explanations that are needed if there is no FD.

Finally, the reasons for the FD leaving should be ascertained, as it is possible that there has been a disagreement over accounting policies, or even a fraud.

(iii)   **Audit procedures on goodwill**

- Obtain the legal purchase agreement and confirm the acquisition date

- Confirm (from the legal agreement) the consideration, and details of the contingent consideration

- Confirm that Canary is wholly owned by Crow Ltd through a review of its register of shareholders

- Agree cash payment of £125 million to cash book and bank statements

- Review board minutes for discussion regarding, and approval of, the purchase of Canary

- Obtain due diligence report on Canary and confirm estimate fair value of net assets

(b)   **Partner at board meetings**

It is acceptable for the audit engagement partner to attend board meetings. There are even some times when the partner should attend, eg to raise issues with management and/or those charged with governance.

The important thing is that the partner does not take on a management role, and that they are not involved in any discussions that are not relevant to the audit. If the partner served as a director of an audit client, then the self-review and self-interest threats created would be insurmountable.

Audit manager secondment

This is a temporary staff assignment, and is acceptable as long as it is for a short period of time, and no management responsibilities are taken on. In this case, the member of staff would probably be involved in making management decisions as they would be the finance director. They would not be under the control of the audit client.

It is therefore unlikely that any safeguards could reduce this threat to an acceptable level, so no member of staff should be seconded into this role.

Recruitment help

It is possible for help to be provided with recruitment, but only if the auditor does not make any management decisions. It would be possible to eg review a shortlist of candidates' CVs, but only against criteria set out by the CS Group itself.

If help is provided then the final decision about recruitment must be left to the client. Safeguards should also be put in place, such as obtaining written acknowledgement from the client that they are responsible for the recruitment decision.

26 Beech

Marking scheme

Marks

(a) **Fir Co**
Generally 1 mark per matter/evidence point explained:
Matters:
- Whether a present obligation exists
- Assumptions used in estimate are complex/subjective
- Investigate why provision fallen in value
- IAS 37 disclosure requirements not met
- IAS 1 disclosure requirements not met
- Potential misstatement due to insufficient disclosure

Evidence:
- Supporting documentation regarding existence of obligation
- Assess whether assumptions in line with business understanding/other evidence
- Discuss assumptions and estimation method with management
- Review supporting documentation (operating licence/government agreement)
- Assess controls in place
- Written representation

Maximum   8

(b) **Spruce Co**
Generally 1 mark for each procedure:
Share-based payment plan:
- Consider whether expert has followed auditor's written instructions
- Ensure expert's findings consistent with other evidence obtained
- Ensure expert's work considers events after the year end where necessary
- Compare expert's results with those determined by management
- Reperform calculations
- Consider suitability of models used in the expert's work
- Evaluate assumptions and ensure in line with auditor's understanding
- Verify source data
- Agree figures and terms to supporting documentation

Maximum   5

(c) **Pine Co**

Generally 1 mark per matter explained:
– Consider whether change in estimate is valid
– Incorrect accounting treatment used (up to 2 marks for detailed explanation)
– Insufficient notes to the financial statements
– Discuss with management and encourage amendments value
– Opinion to be qualified 'except for' due to material misstatement
– Description of reason for qualification to be provided in auditor's report

Maximum   5

Total   18

(a) **Fir Co**

Matters to consider

IAS 16 *Property, plant and equipment* requires that where there is an obligation to dismantle an asset, then the costs of doing so should be provided for, and included in the cost of the asset. The question here is whether an obligation exists in accordance with IAS 37 *Provisions, contingent assets and contingent liabilities*. It is not sufficient for Fir Ltd merely to 'intend' to incur the costs, rather; there must be a legal or constructive obligation as a result of a past event. If there is no such obligation, then no provision should be recognised.

The provision should be for the present value of the future outflow of economic benefits. Measuring a provision for costs to be incurred in 20 years' time is inherently risky. For example, the cost to be incurred may only be an estimate; the remaining useful life of the power stations is definitely just an estimate; the selection of a discount rate to calculate the present value involves judgement and is therefore not certain.

The provision has decreased in value since last year, which is unusual as provisions normally increase over time as the present value is built up. This could mean that circumstances have changed, or may signal new measurement assumptions being made. It may also be a sign of profit-smoothing, as earnings have effectively been shifted from last year's statement of profit or loss into this year's. The reasons for this need to be investigated.

The note to the financial statements does not conform to IAS 37's requirement to provide narrative information, including disclosure of the reasons for making the provision together with any uncertainties in relation to them. The notes should also analyse the movement in the year. Unless this is remedied then this is a material misstatement which may lead to a qualified audit opinion.

Audit evidence

• Review of evidence that there is an obligation to dismantle, eg from regulatory authorities

• Review of management's calculations used to measure the provision, considering their consistency with other audit evidence obtained (eg that the remaining life of the assets is 20 years)

• Review of documentation supporting management's assumptions (eg to support the estimated cost of decommissioning)

• Discussion with management about reasons for the fall in the provision, and evaluation of these reasons (eg regarding IFRS, knowledge of the entity)

(b) **Spruce Co**

The expert should have been provided with clear written instructions covering the objectives of the work and any specific issues to address. The first procedure would therefore be assessing whether the work done meets these objectives, and whether it has been performed in accordance with any standards specified, and that it is consistent with the applicable financial reporting framework.

The expert's work should be reviewed to confirm that the correct source data was used, and that it relates to the right financial instruments in the right period. Any assumptions made by the expert should be compared with eg similar assumptions used by management in preparing the financial statements.

Any evidence contained in the report should be reviewed for consistency with our understanding of the entity and with other audit evidence obtained.

Evidence used by the expert should be agreed to supporting documentation, and any calculations contained in the work should be reperformed, eg fair value movements.

The appropriateness of any models used by the expert should be evaluated.

(c) **Pine Co**

IAS 8 *Accounting policies, changes in accounting estimates and errors* requires a change in accounting estimate to be accounted for prospectively, not retrospectively as has been done here; retrospective accounting should only be used for a change in accounting policy.

There should be no change to opening assets or equity; these are therefore materially misstated here (overstatement). The extension of the properties' useful life would probably decrease the depreciation expense, resulting in an overstatement of profit. Also it is not clear why all of the properties' useful lives have been extended; IAS 16 requires that the useful life is the period over which an asset is expected to be used. There is a risk that the useful lives used are not appropriate, and that the financial statements are materially misstated.

IAS 8 requires disclosure of the nature and amount of the change in estimate; as this has not been done, there is a material misstatement in respect of IAS 8's disclosure requirements.

The matter should be discussed with management, who should be asked to amend the financial statements. If satisfactory amendments are not made then the auditor's report will contain a qualified opinion. This will be 'except for' a material misstatement, as the amount is material but not pervasive.

The opinion paragraph in the auditor's report is headed 'Qualified opinion'. Immediately before this is a paragraph headed 'Basis for qualified opinion', which describes the matter giving rise to the qualification and quantifies the effects of the misstatement.

27 Setter

Marking scheme

Marks

(a)   **Assets held for sale**

Generally 1 mark for each matter considered/evidence point explained:

Matters:
- Assets held for sale are material (calculation)
- Amount written off is not material (calculation)
- Conditions required to classify assets as held for sale (up to 2 marks)
- Re-measurement at classification appears correct
- Further impairment review may be needed at year end
- Depreciation should not be charged after reclassification
- Disclosure in notes to financial statements

Evidence:
- Board minute at which the disposal of the properties was agreed by management
- Details of the active programme in place to locate a buyer
- A copy of any minutes of meetings held with prospective purchasers of any of the properties

- Written representation from management that the assets will be sold before October 2013
- Subsequent events review
- Confirm depreciation ceased on reclassification
- Details of any impairment review conducted by management

Maximum   8

(b) **Sale and leaseback**

Generally 1 mark for each matter considered/evidence point explained:

Matters:
- Asset is material (calculation)
- On disposal the asset should be re-measured to fair value
- Apparent profit should be deferred and amortised
- Accounting treatment currently not correct
- Discuss materiality of adjustments needed
- Implication for auditor's opinion
- Treatment as a finance lease appears correct

Evidence:
- A copy of the lease to confirm that the arrangement is a finance lease
- Physical inspection of the property complex
- A copy of insurance documents
- Confirmation of the fair value of the property complex, possibly using an auditor's expert
- Agreement of the £37 million cash proceeds to bank statement and cash book
- A schedule showing the adjustment required in the financial statements
- Minutes of a discussion with management regarding the accounting treatment and including an

Maximum   7

(c) **Distribution licence**

Generally 1 mark for each matter considered/evidence point explained:

Matters:
- Materiality of the asset (calculation)
- Identify event as intangible asset that should be capitalised
- Identify that no amortisation has been charged
- The non-amortisation is not material

Evidence:
- A copy of the licence
- Agreement of cost to bank statement and cash book
- Discussion with management regarding the non-amortisation
- Sales records of the soft drink since 1 September 2012

Maximum   5

Total   20

(a) **Matters**

The assets held for sale are material to the financial statements at 8% of total assets (= £24m ÷ £300m).

The amount written off is not material, at less than 1% of revenue (= £2m ÷ £620m) and 4.2% of profit before tax (= £2m ÷ £47.5m).

Assets are classified as held for sale if they meet the following criteria (among others):

- Management is committed to a plan to sell
- The assets are available for immediate sale in their present condition
- An active programme exists to locate a buyer
- The sale is highly probable, within 12 months of reclassification

The accounting treatment appears to be correct, measuring the assets at the lower of carrying amount and fair value less costs to sell.

The classification took place mid-year, so an impairment review should be conducted as it is possible that the assets have become impaired by the year end.

Depreciation should have ceased from when the reclassification took place in October.

Evidence

- Copy of board minutes to show management's intention to sell assets
- Physical inspection of assets to confirm that they are saleable in present condition
- Evidence of programme to locate buyer, eg copies of advertisements, correspondence with estate agent
- Written representation for management's commitment to sell within 12 months
- Copy of management's impairment review
- Confirmation that £2m written off is recognised in profit or loss
- Confirmation that depreciation ceased on reclassification

(b) **Matters**

The carrying value of £27m is material at 9% of total assets (= £27m ÷ £300m).

The leaseback appears to be a finance lease because:

- The risks and rewards of ownership are with Setter Stores
- The lease term is for the remaining useful life of the asset

Therefore the initial accounting entry appears correct. However, further entries are needed. The sale proceeds of £37m should become the asset's cost, with the asset being derecognised (£27m) and then re-recognised at £37m.

This leaves a gain of £10m on signing the lease, which should be recognised over the useful life of the asset – at the year end it is deferred income. The following entries should therefore be made.

Dr	Property, plant and equipment	£37m
Cr	Property, plant and equipment	£27m
Cr	Deferred income	£10m

The deferred income should be amortised over the useful life of 20 years, resulting in other income recognised in the statement of profit or loss. However, the amount recognised in the current year is £nil because the transaction took place at the year end.

Depreciation should also be charged over 20 years. The amount recognised in this period, however, will be based on the old carrying value of £27m.

As the finance lease is for 20 years, the effect of discounting is likely to be material. The liability should be recognised at its present value, with the effect of discounting being recognised as a finance cost in future periods.

As they stand the financial statements appear to be misstated in respect of deferred income and non-current assets. The misstatement is material at 3.3% of total assets (= £10m ÷ £300m). If this is not corrected then the audit opinion must be qualified on the grounds of a material misstatement.

Evidence

- A copy of the signed lease should be on file, with confirmation of its major clauses affecting its classification as a finance lease
- Copy of insurance documents showing that Setter Stores is responsible for insurance
- Copy of board minutes of discussion of lease for indication of whether this is a finance lease or an operating lease
- Agreement of £37m cash received to bank statement
- Confirmation of fair value of £37m, possibly using an auditor's expert

(c) **Matters**

The licence is material at 5% of total assets (= £15m ÷ £300m).

The asset can be recognised if:

- It is probable that future economic benefits will flow to the entity
- The cost can be measured reliably

As the licence has been acquired separately, it should be treated as an intangible non-current asset.

Amortisation should be recognised based on the useful life of five years, but this does not appear to have been done. This gives an additional expense of £1.25m (= (£15m ÷ 5 years) × 5 months). This amount is not material at less than 1% of revenue (£1.25m ÷ £620m) and 2.6% of profit before tax (£1.25m ÷ £47.5m).

Evidence

- A copy of the licence, confirming five-year term and cost of £15m

- Agreement of £15m cash paid to bank statement

- Minutes of discussion with management of non-amortisation of the licence

- Sales information in relation to the soft drink to confirm the probability of receiving economic benefits

28 Lamont

Marking scheme

			Marks
(i)	**Matters**		
	Generally 1 mark each comment		
	Maximum 6 marks each issue × 3	Maximum	12
	Ideas		
	– Materiality (appropriately assessed)		
	– Relevant IFRSs (eg IAS 2, 16, 24, 36, 40)		
	– Fundamental concepts (capital vs revenue)		
	– Risks (eg valuation (obsolescence)/disclosure)		
(ii)	**Audit evidence**		
	Generally 1 mark each item of audit evidence (source)		
	Maximum 6 marks each issue × 3	Maximum	12
	Ideas (ISA (UK & Ireland) 500)		
	– Documented on WP file – current vs PY		
	– Internal (eg age analysis) vs external (eg monthly returns)		
	– Auditor generated (analytical procedure)		
	– Results of procedures by which obtained (eg physical inspection)		
		Maximum	20
(a)		Maximum	7
(b)		Maximum	7
(c)		Maximum	6
Total			20

(a) **Chemical leakage**

   (i) *Matters to consider*

- The clean-up costs of £0.3m should not have been capitalised as an asset but should have been written-off to the statement of profit or loss. This amount represents 0.6% of total assets and 2.5% of profit before tax so is not material but should be adjusted for in the financial statements.

- The modernisation costs of £0.6m represent 1.2% of total assets and 5% of profit before tax and are therefore material to the accounts. Their capitalisation would be correct in accordance with IAS 16 *Property, plant and equipment* if the expenditure restores the economic benefits of the refrigeration units.

- The fine of £30,000 incurred by Lamont is immaterial but has been correctly written-off to the statement of profit or loss.

   (ii) *Audit evidence*

- Invoices to support the clean-up costs and modernisation costs
- Correspondence from the regulatory agency to confirm the amount of the fine
- Bank statement and cash book extracts to show payment of the amounts involved
- Board minutes referring to the chemical leakage
- Physical inspection of the refrigeration units to confirm the modernisation costs incurred

(b) **Inventory held by Hogg Warehousing**

   (i) *Matters to consider*

- Inventory is material to the statement of financial position, comprising 21% of total assets, therefore the auditors need to obtain sufficient, appropriate audit evidence of its valuation as at the year end.

- Inventory has increased from the year before by 51% which is very high – the reason for this increase needs to be investigated further.

- A written representation from management on the value of inventory held at the year end is not sufficient audit evidence as there should be other more reliable audit evidence available to confirm the £10.1 million figure.

- If the inventory figure cannot be adequately verified, this may result in a limitation on the scope of the audit, and a modification of the auditor's opinion on the grounds of an inability to obtain sufficient appropriate audit evidence.

- Although the quantity of inventory held by Hogg Warehousing can be provided, this does not provide evidence of its valuation as at the year-end date. Given that inventory comprises fish, it may be that some of the inventory might be damaged and therefore its value would be less. Inventory may therefore be overstated in the financial statements.

   (ii) *Audit evidence*

- Written representation from management referring to the value of year-end inventory

- Correspondence between Lamont and Hogg Warehousing regarding the inventory held by Hogg Warehousing on behalf of Lamont

- Hogg's monthly returns of quantities held

- Correspondence relating to the health and safety issues preventing access to cold storage areas

- Analytical procedures on inventory, such as month by month comparisons to the previous year, to try to ascertain why the value of inventory has increased so much this year

(c) **Residential apartment**

   (i) *Matters to consider*

- The senior sales executive is a related party in accordance with IAS 24 *Related party disclosures* as he would be a member of key management.

- A related party transaction has therefore occurred by virtue of the senior sales executive using the residential apartment of the company even though no money has exchanged hands – IAS 24 defines a related party transaction as 'a transfer of resources, services or obligations between a reporting entity and a related party, regardless of whether a price is charged'.

- IAS 24 requires related party transactions to be disclosed in the financial statements as they are material by their nature. The standard details what is required for disclosure, but it includes the names of the related parties, the relationships, the amounts involved and a description of the transactions.

(ii) *Audit evidence*

- Rental agreement to confirm charge of £3,000 per month and identification of the other party

- Deeds to confirm ownership of the apartment by Lamont

- Physical inspection of the apartment to confirm its existence and that it is being occupied

- A written representation from the directors of Lamont to confirm all related party transactions and that there are no others that need to be disclosed

- A written representation from the senior sales executive stating that he is occupying the apartment rent-free

29 Papaya

Study text reference. Chapter 6.

Top tips. Part (a) may have seemed a little tricky, and you may have struggled to think of enough ideas to gain marks, although in reality it was not a difficult requirement. You needed to stay calm and think practically about what an auditor would gain from doing analytical procedures at the planning stage, and about the practical limitations of those procedures. If you did this, you should have been able to pass this part of the question.

Part (b) should have been straightforward, as the distinction is a relatively simple one to understand. The key here was to make sure that you explained each term in enough detail to gain the marks.

The answer to part (c) was in a way obvious because no financial information was included within the question. You could have generated ideas by just thinking of all the information you could use in an ideal world when auditing this kind of company – ie a large listed company with a number of different operating divisions. It is important then to make sure you apply your ideas to the scenario in the question – take heed of the examiner's warning in the requirement to use 'the specific information provided'.

A good way to approach answering an 'explain' requirement like this would be, for each point, first to identify the piece of information needed, and then to give a reason why this is needed.

Part (d) should have been straightforward, provided that you have heeded the examiner's advice (in a recent article) to keep up with your financial reporting knowledge for auditing. It was important to realise that only risks of material misstatement were being asked for – candidates have often been caught out in the past by not reading the question properly, and subsequently just writing down any risk they can think of in a kind of scatter-gun approach. Take care not to do this! The risks themselves should have been readily identifiable in the question. As usual, work through the scenario with a pen in hand, writing down risks of material misstatement as you see them. This is essentially a question of finding bits of accounting that might have been done incorrectly, then phrasing this in your answer in terms of a risk of material misstatement. It is always worth including sentences in your answer like 'The risk is that xxx', just to make it clear to the examiner that you're answering the question.

Easy marks. Make sure you get the professional marks in part (d). There are two marks available: one for using the right format (heading, introduction, conclusion), and two for 'clarity of explanation' – essentially this means that you should write clearly and avoid waffle, but making sure that you write in full sentences and that everything you say makes sense. You could think about having a standard form of words ready to use in an introduction or conclusion so that you don't have to use up timing thinking about what to write in the exam.

Examiner's comments. In a departure from previous sittings, question one was answered inadequately by a majority of candidates. Many candidates seemed to lack a basic understanding of the use of analytical procedures at the planning stage of the audit. On the risks of material misstatement, many answers were vague, and despite being lengthy, did not address the question requirement.

In the first part of requirement (a), most candidates could suggest that analytical procedures should help to identify risks, a point suggested in the question, but fewer identified that such procedures would help the auditor to develop business understanding. Most candidates used examples to illustrate their comments, as required, but on the whole the examples were weak and did not help to explain why the procedure was being carried out. The answers to the second part of the requirement were extremely disappointing. The vast majority of candidates seemed not to have read the last eight words of the requirement, so failing to discuss the limitations of analytical procedures at the planning stage of the audit.

Requirement (b) asked candidates to explain and differentiate the terms 'audit strategy' and 'audit plan'. Some candidates performed well here, but some candidates mixed up the two terms or failed to differentiate between them. Many also re-used wording from the question requirement, for example 'the audit strategy is the strategy for the audit, 'the audit plan is the plan for the audit'. Clearly such comments add no value and cannot be awarded credit.

Requirement (c) was based on the scenario, and candidates performed well if they applied their knowledge to the question scenario. However, the majority of candidates failed to do this, and instead produced a list of vague bullet points, referring to information that would be required for the planning of any audit. Most candidates listed prior year accounts, management accounts, a cash flow statement, and little else.

Some candidates wrote at great length in answering requirement (d), but unfortunately quantity does not equate to quality. It was at times frustrating to see pages of writing scoring few marks, because points made were either irrelevant, technically incorrect, or not actually explaining the risk to the auditor. Many candidates provided numerous examples of substantive procedures or audit impacts ('we must discuss the court case with lawyers', 'we must see who can audit the overseas division'), again not relevant to the requirement.

Marking scheme

			Marks

(a) (i) **Reasons for performing analytical procedures during risk assessment**
Up to 1 mark for each reason, and 1 mark for relevant example:
– Develop business understanding + example
– Identify risks + example
Maximum   3

(ii) **Limitations of analytical procedures at planning**
1 mark each point explained (limit to ½ mark if just identified):
– Does not cover whole period
– Year end procedures not yet carried out
– Weaker controls/different reporting framework
– Small entities may lack interim financial data
Maximum   3

(b) **Explain and differentiate between the terms 'audit plan' and 'overall audit strategy'**
– Up to 2 marks for each explanation
– 1 mark for each point of comparison or comment on timing
Maximum   4

(c) **Identify, with reasons, information needed for analytical procedures**
Generally ½ mark for identification, 1 further mark for reasons, from ideas list
– Disaggregation by business segment ie supermarkets v financial services
– Separate out the different brands of supermarket
– Separate out the foreign division
– Information regarding one-off items
– Information regarding new accounting policies/treatments
– Budget information
– Industry/competitor comparisons
Maximum   6

(d) **Risks of material misstatement**

Professional marks to be awarded for format (heading, introduction, conclusion) – 1 mark, and clarity of explanation – 1 mark

Generally ½ mark for identifying risks of material misstatement, up to further 2 marks for explanation.

- Lack of disclosure of contingent liability/understatement of provision (IAS 37)
- Incorrect recognition and measurement of separate components of convertible debenture (IAS 32)
- No recognition of financial asset or liability regarding derivative/incorrect measurement/lack of disclosure (IFRS 7)
- Impairment of land (IAS 36)
- Undervaluation of PPE if inspection cost not capitalised (IAS 16)
- Operating segments – risk of non-disclosure (IFRS 8)
- Risk of capitalisation of internally generated brand (IAS 38)

Maximum – technical	16
Professional marks	4
Total	**36**

(a) **(i)** **Understanding of business**

Performing analytical procedures at the planning stage of the audit can help an auditor to develop an understanding of the client's business. An auditor can glean a lot of information from analysis of prior period and draft accounts. He can find out, for example, which are the client's key revenue streams, or which are the main areas of capital expenditure required for it to operate in this area. This is particularly relevant for a new client, as the auditor will have a particularly acute need to find out even the first and most basic facts about a client's business. For example, calculating a client's profit margin would allow the auditor to compare it with others in the industry, and so gauge the client's performance.

Identify risks

Performing analytical procedures can also help identify key audit risks. For example, it might be that a highly material intangible asset has been capitalised in the draft statement of financial position, or that operating profits have increased by 20% in an industry where the trend is for a decline. Both of these circumstances would point to a need to carry out more audit work in those areas.

This means that an auditor can work out a strategy that is specifically tailored to the risks of this particular engagement. This will help to minimise detection risk, and by allowing the auditor to direct work to risky areas will reduce the chance of doing work that is unnecessary.

(ii) There are several key limitations. Firstly, the figures will likely only be in draft form. Any analytical procedures performed on these figures may be invalidated by adjustments that are usually only made at the period end, such as the calculation of a finance lease liability.

Secondly, the information will not cover the entire accounting period. It is not always straightforward to extrapolate figures from just a part of the year to cover a full year, particularly when seasonality has to be taken into account. Analytical procedures performed on this information may therefore be misleading.

Thirdly, the information might not be produced on the same basis as the previous year, particularly if internal management accounts are being used. Care should be taken when extracting figures from management accounts so that it can be used to make meaningful analytical comparisons.

Finally, if the client is a small entity then it might not have a formal reporting system in place during the year, so that no proper information is available before the year end accounts are produced.

(b) ISA (UK & Ireland) 300 *Planning an audit of financial statements* distinguishes between the overall audit strategy, which sets out in general terms how the audit is to be carried out, and the audit plan, which details the specific procedures that need to be carried out in order to implement the strategy and complete the audit.

Considerations in establishing the strategy include:

(i)   Characteristics of the engagement
(ii)   Reporting objectives, timing of the audit and nature of communications
(iii)   Significant factors, preliminary engagement activities and knowledge gained on other engagements
(iv)   Nature, timing and extent of resources

By contrast, the audit plan draws these general requirements together into a schedule of the work that is required to reduce audit risk to the level required to give reasonable assurance. It deals with the actual procedures, including risk-assessment procedures, that are required at the assertion level (in respect of specific areas of the financial statements) to gather audit evidence.

The strategy is conceptually prior to the plan, and in theory should be prepared before it. In reality, though, they are interrelated, as changes in one may result in changes in the other.

(c)   Financial information would be required including details of the nature and amounts of all the income and expense items, as well as all assets and liabilities, acquisitions and disposals.

This should be broken down into Papaya's four main business segments – the Papaya Mart supermarket chain, the overseas Papaya Marts in Farland, the Papaya Express chain and the new financial services division. This would allow each part of the business to be analysed separately. This is necessary because each will probably have different levels of revenue, profit margins and structures of assets and liabilities, so that analytical procedures performed on Papaya as a whole would be meaningless.

Separate information is needed for the financial services division as it operates in a completely separate line of business from the rest of the company. It is likely to have a very different profit structure from the rest of the business. In particular, it is likely to require much less capital than the other divisions, which would affect ratios such as asset turnover and return on capital employed.

Separate information would be needed for the different supermarket brands because they are likely to have different profit margins. Specifically, the convenience 'Express' stores are likely to a high turnover of lower-margin items when compared with the more upmarket 'Mart' stores. As they operate in different markets, any trends that affect one might not necessarily affect the other.

Separate information would be useful for the new foreign operation in Farland. As it is operating in a different market from the other stores, it is likely to be subject to different trends. Also as this is its first year, there are likely to have been costs associated with the start-up that should not be taken together with the rest of the group's results.

Analysis of the Farland operations could be hampered by the accounts being in a foreign currency, which could be helped by providing the accounts in their original denomination. Finally, as this is the first year of operations, it would be useful to compare actual results with budgeted results, as well as making a comparison with competitors' accounts.

This last point applies equally to the new financial services division, for which no comparatives will exist either, making comparison with budget and with the industry as a whole more important.

The auditor should request details of any one-off entries affecting the accounts for the period, including details of the advertising costs associated with the Farland start-up, which may need to be considered separately from the rest of the accounts.

Equally, the auditor should request details of any changes in the accounting policies used, or in estimation techniques. It will be necessary in particular to enquire whether the Farland division's accounts have been prepared in accordance with IFRSs or with some other accounting principles.

(d)   **Briefing Notes**

Author: A Student
Subject: Papaya risks of material misstatement
Date: December 20X9

Introduction

These notes assess the risks of material misstatement to be addressed when planning the 20X9 audit for Papaya Plc.

Business segments

Papaya is divided into divisions that would be operating segments under IFRS 8 *Operating segments.* There is a risk that the disclosures required by IFRS 8 have not been made. There should be a note to the financial statements disclosing information about the performance of each segment. The risk of non-disclosure is particularly acute in respect of the new financial services division, and the new overseas operations in Farland.

Internally generated brands

The supermarket chains operate under internally generated brand names, which per IAS 38 *Intangible Assets* cannot be capitalised unless they have a readily ascertainable market value. There should be no non-current asset in the financial statements in respect of brands.

In particular, there is a risk that some of the advertising expenditure made in relation to the Farland expansion has been recognised as an asset. This would be an overstatement of non-current assets.

Business risk

The recently established financial services division is a departure from Papaya's core business. Financial services is potentially a risky area to trade in, and there is a possibility that if the new division is not successful, significant losses could be made. This is particularly pertinent in view of the difficulties experienced by providers of financial services during the recent banking crisis. In view of the strain exerted on Papaya's cash resources by the recent Farland expansion, there is a risk of the financial statements being prepared on the going concern basis when this is inappropriate.

Collusion and price fixing

Significant financial penalties will be imposed on Papaya if it is found guilty of collusion and price fixing. The situation needs to be assessed with reference to IAS 37 *Provisions, contingent liabilities and contingent assets* and the *Framework* definition of a liability. There are four possible situations with respect to IAS 37: the liability could be certain, probable, possible or remote. In this case the liability is not remote. If the liability is certain or probable then a provision should be created, measured at the fair value of the future cash outflow. The risk in this case is that there is no provision, and that profit is therefore overstated and liabilities understated.

The liability could also be possible. In this case it should be disclosed in a note to the financial statements. The risk is that adequate disclosure is not made.

Debentures

In accordance with IAS 32 *Financial instruments: disclosure and presentation*, the convertible debentures issued during the year should be split in the statement of financial position between an equity and a debt element. IAS 32 requires Papaya to split the debentures into a debt component calculated as the present value of the debenture on maturity, and an equity component calculated as the balancing figure.

There is a risk that IAS 32 has not been followed, either by failing to use split accounting or by calculating the split incorrectly. This would lead to misstatements of debt and equity in the statement of financial position, and may affect the statement of profit or loss through miscalculation of the finance cost of the debt.

Forward contracts

The categorisation of the forward contracts as 'fair value through profit and loss' financial instruments is correct as per IAS 39 *Financial instruments: recognition and measurement* (the provisions IAS 39 in respect of hedge accounting are still applicable). According to IAS 39, the contracts should be recognised at their value, which can be either an asset or a liability. The risk here is twofold: the contracts might not have been recognised at all, or they might have been measured incorrectly. This would mean that both assets or liabilities in the statement of financial position, and profit in the statement of profit or loss, would be misstated.

IFRS 7 *Financial instruments: disclosures* must also be applied. There is a risk that adequate disclosures are not made in respect of the contracts.

Land

The significant losses made on the sale of some plots of land should be separately disclosed in the statement of profit or loss. There is a risk that this has not been done.

The losses made on land sold also suggest that the land currently recognised at cost in the statement of financial position may be impaired. IAS 36 *Impairment of assets* requires an impairment review to be carried out in this case, and that any impairment losses are recognised. There is a risk of this not happening, overstating both non-current assets and profit.

Warehouses

IAS 16 *Property, plant and equipment* requires that the cost of the health and safety inspections be capitalised and then depreciated over three years. This would spread the economic benefit of having had them over their useful life. There is a risk that the £25,000 has been recognised during the period as an expense in full, understating both profit and non-current assets.

Conclusion

The above risks of material misstatement should be discussed at the audit planning meeting, and a plan formulated to reduce the risk of material misstatement in relation to them to a level required in order to give reasonable assurance that the financial statements present a true and fair view.

30 Bill

Text reference. Chapter 9

Top tips. As this was a large question, it was vital that you worked methodically and kept to your timings throughout its sub-sections.

You should have noticed when reading the question that the second paragraph of the information gives figures for calculating materiality. Remember, whenever a question includes these figures, it is very likely that you will have to calculate materiality at some point in your answer. These are easy marks, so be sure to get them.

Part (a)(i) should have been relatively straightforward, provided that your financial reporting knowledge is up to scratch. This is relatively in-depth financial reporting for P7, and is a good example of the kind of knowledge you need to be able to demonstrate. Assuming that you are comfortable with the accounting, the question itself should have been within your grasp if you are systematic and address all parts of the requirement for each of the two accounting issues.

Part (a)(ii) tested of your knowledge of ISAs and your ability to apply them. Your examiner has stated that knowledge of ISAs is a common weakness amongst candidates. You should have scored well on this part of the question, and may have found yourself going over your allocated time of 20 minutes (11 marks × 1.8). Make sure you stick to your timings, or you will struggle later in the paper.

Part (b) was relatively difficult. Part (b)(i) required you to think on your feet, as it did not ask you to explain how something should be audited, but rather to reflect on the difficulties involved in doing so. You should be looking to score at least 2–3 marks here. It's important not to panic, and to make sure you don't go over your time trying to think of things to write – especially given that the next part of the question was a bit easier. Part (b)(ii) should have been simpler, and required you to recommend audit procedures. A good bullet pointed list should have been able to score 3–4 marks (one mark per good, specific point).

Easy marks. Calculating materiality in part (a). There is one mark just for drawing an overall conclusion to the notes in part (a), which you should get (make sure you include a subheading, 'conclusion').

Examiner's comments. In answers to requirement (a)(i), most candidates recognised the loss-making nature of the contract described in the scenario, and correctly calculated the loss, and the majority then went on to discuss the risk of material misstatement that profit would be overstated if the loss were not recognised in full. However, having gone this far, many candidates then went on to consider other potential accounting issues and different financial reporting standards, leading to confused answers and often contradictory advice. No conclusion was provided and the contradictory comments clearly detract from the overall quality of an answer. Some candidates simply could not decide which financial reporting standard was most relevant.

It was common to see answers of this type stretching over many pages, when all that was needed was a succinct discussion of the loss making contract in the context of IAS 11, which could be done in a few short paragraphs. This wasted time and meant answers were overly long and largely irrelevant.

On the whole answers to requirement (b)(i) were satisfactory. However, answers to (b)(ii) were often unsatisfactory, as many candidates ignored the question requirement and just provided a rote-learnt list of procedures to identify related party transactions in general, not focussing on the transactions in the scenario. Even those that did think about the scenario provided inadequate procedures eg 'check the lease is market rate' – but not explaining how the auditor should do this.

Marking scheme

Marks

(a)   (i)   **Loss-making contract**

Generally 1 mark per comment on matter/risk of material misstatement/evidence point:
- Identify loss-making status of contract (only ½ mark if no calculation of loss)
- Per IAS 11 the loss must be recognised in full
- Risk of MM is overstated profit if loss not recognised
- Penalties for late completion may exist
- Risk of MM is overstated profit/understated liabilities if not recognised
- Incentive for loss not to be recognised due to planned sale of company
- Consideration of materiality

Evidence:
- Obtain budget and recompute anticipated loss
- Agree fixed price to contract
- Review contract for late-completion penalty clauses
- Review internal architect's report
- Inspect quote or other supporting document for amount of additional costs
- Consider use of an expert regarding amount of additional costs
- Discuss estimate of additional costs and timeframe with contractors
- Review cash flow forecasts

Held for sale disposal group

Generally 1 mark per comment on matter/risk of material misstatement/evidence point:
- Identify 'Treasured Homes' as a disposal group per IFRS 5
- Explain why meets criteria for treatment as a disposal group
- Assets should be presented separately and tested for impairment
- Risk of material misstatement is overvalued assets and incorrect presentation
- Identify 'Treasured Homes' as a discontinued operation per IFRS 5
- Risk of material misstatement is incorrect presentation of its results in SOCI and SOCF
- Consideration of materiality

Evidence:
- Review board minutes to confirm management's commitment to the sale
- Inspect any documents relevant to the negotiation
- Inspect 20X2 budgets to confirm 'Treasured Homes' not included
- Obtain and review management's impairment test on the disposal group
- Confirm disclosures made according to IFRS 5 in draft financial statements

Maximum (max 8 marks each issue)   16

Marks

(ii) **Critical evaluation of planning**

Up to 2 marks for each point evaluated from ideas list, plus 1 mark for overall conclusion:
- Insufficient analytical review performed
- No systems work or controls evaluation carried out
- Inadequate assessment and documentation of business risk
- Inappropriate to plan to use client employee as auditor's expert
- Ethical threats raised by offer to use office space
- Conclusion (1 mark)

Maximum 11

Professional marks for the overall presentation of the briefing notes, and the clarity of the explanation and assessment provided 4

(b) (i) **Limitation on identification of related party relationships and transaction**

1 mark each point explained (to maximum 4 marks):
- Management not aware of relationship or transaction
- Subjectivity/complexity in deciding on who or what is a related party
- Deliberate concealment of relationship or transaction
- Accounting systems do not specifically identify related party transactions
- Transactions at nil value especially hard to detect

(ii) **Audit procedures**

1 mark each specific procedure (to maximum 4 marks):
- Review invoices/inspect cash book to confirm amount of cash paid
- Review payables ledger to confirm any amount outstanding
- Consider if transaction is arm's length by comparing value to non-related party transaction
- Discuss/obtain written representation on details of informal lease
- Review any written documentation that may exist regarding the lease
- Review disclosures on draft financial statements

Maximum 8

Total 39

(a) **Briefing notes**

To: **Audit partner**

From: **Audit manager**

Re: **Bill Ltd audit plan**

Introduction

The following notes explain the risks of material misstatement and matters to consider, in relation to Bill Ltd (Bill), and then recommend audit procedures to address these risks.

The notes then evaluate the planning done so far, including ethical matters, before recommending actions to perform.

(i) First issue (Bridgetown)

Matters to consider

Contract loss

This appears to be a loss-making contract. In accordance with IAS 11 *Construction contracts*, the loss should be recognised immediately when expected costs exceed revenue.

This is the case here as the additional expected costs of £350,000 turn the previously expected profit of £200,000 into a loss of £150,000.

At 6% of profit before tax, the loss is material to forecast profit before tax.

BPP LEARNING MEDIA

Possible penalties

The contract will be completed two months late. This may result in penalties being incurred by Bill for late completion. These should be provided for in accordance with IAS 37 *Provisions, Contingent Liabilities and Contingent Assets*.

Possible management bias

Alex and Ben plan to sell the company in the next two years, and therefore may seek to increase its value.

Risks of Material Misstatement

Contract loss

There is a risk that profit is overstated by up to £350,000 if the loss is not recognised in full in line with IAS 11. There is also a risk that the expected costs of £350,000 have not been recognised in the FSs at all.

Possible penalties

The risk is that if there are indeed penalties and no provision has been made, then liabilities are understated and profits are overstated by the amount of those penalties.

Possible bias

The risk is that a provision, or a loss on a contract, are not recognised in an effort to increase Bill's valuation.

Audit procedures

- Inspect basis of estimate for the £350,000 extra costs, eg architect's report.

- Discuss £350,000 estimate with employees to assess if it is reasonable.

- Discuss two-month additional timeframe with employees to assess if it is reasonable.

- Recalculate forecast profit of £200,000 (loss of £150,000 including extra costs).

- Inspect the signed contract to verify the price and to check if there are any penalties for late completion.

- Review FS for provisions in relation to penalties.

Consider using an auditor's expert to estimate the contract costs to completion.

Second issue (Operating lease)

Matters to consider

The lease may be an onerous contract under IAS 37 *Provisions, contingent assets and contingent liabilities*, which is a contract where the unavoidable costs exceed the expected inflow of economic benefits.

Bill is not using the site, so is deriving no benefit from it in this way. A significant penalty would be incurred if the lease were cancelled. If the lease were sub-let, then costs would still exceed rental revenue received. Since both of these options would result in costs exceeding income, the lease appears to be an onerous contract.

A provision should therefore be created in the statement of financial position for the full amount of the present obligation under the lease, along with a corresponding expense in the statement of profit or loss.

Risks of Material Misstatement

Provision

The risk is that the provision is either not recognised at all, or is not measured correctly.

IAS 37.68 requires that the provision be measured as the "least net cost of exiting from the contract", ie the lower of the penalty incurred, and the potential excess of payments over sub-letting revenue. There is a risk that this calculation is not done correctly, or that management fails to do make this calculation at all.

There is a further risk in relation to the assumptions that must be made in relation to future revenue receivable, which is inherently risky as it involves the exercise of judgement.

Finally, IAS 37 requires that the provision be measured at its present value. As this measurement requires the use of judgement in relation to discount rates, there is a risk that management will seek to understate the extent of any liability in order to maximise the company's valuation before sale.

Audit procedures

Inspect signed lease agreement, and verify that it is non-cancellable.

- Confirm the existence and amount of the cancellation penalty to the signed lease agreement.

- Inquire whether a tenant has been found, and the amount of any rent receivable. Verify that these amounts have been included in the assumptions used to calculate any provision.

- Review correspondence with lessor for indications of whether Bill Ltd has attempts to negotiate out of the contract.

- Recompute any provision, confirming that an appropriate discount rate has been used (nominally risk-free and pre-tax).

- Review management's measurement of any provision, and review any assumptions made for reasonableness.

(ii) **Critical evaluation of audit plan**

The notes provided indicate that the audit has not been planned in line with the requirements of ISAs.

Ethics – long association

The IESBA *Code of Ethics* states that a familiarity threat to independence may arise with long-standing audit clients. This appears to be the case here, as some analytical procedures have not been performed because of past experience with the client. It may be necessary to implement further safeguards to reduce this threat to an acceptable level.

Analytical procedures

The need for analytical procedures must be reviewed each year in line with the requirements of ISAs, including the need for procedures not done in previous years.

No procedures have been performed on the statement of financial position, on the basis that there did not appear to be any significant movements. This is not an adequate reason for not performing more detailed procedures, but is in fact just an inadequate procedure itself. It may be the case that, given other changes in the accounts, movement would be expected in assets and liabilities, so 'no movement' is not in itself a sign that nothing is wrong.

Forecast accounts

Forecast accounts have been placed on file, but it is not clear if any procedures have been performed using them, for example to assess the adequacy of the going concern basis. Discussions have been held with management, but it is not clear whether the forecasts have been assessed in the light of these discussions.

Controls testing

Management said there were no changes to internal controls in the year, but no walkthrough tests were performed to verify whether this is in fact the case. Walkthrough tests should have been performed to ascertain whether controls are operating as described.

The auditor is effectively relying on previous years' audit work which showed that the long-standing controls were adequate in the past. However, they may no longer be suitable. ISA 315 (UK and Ireland) Identifying and Assessing the Risks of Material Misstatement through Understanding the Entity and Its Environment requires that the auditor obtain an understanding of the entity's internal controls. This has not been done here.

Business risk

Business risk has been assessed as low on the basis that all divisions are 'operating normally'. However, ISA 315 requires that the auditor obtain evidence of the specific objectives and strategies of the entity, and of its performance in relation to these objectives. This does not appear to have been done.

ISA 315 states that business risks need to be identified in relation to financial reporting. Without assessing specific business risks, this cannot be done.

Moreover, past performance is not necessarily a guide to the future. No assessment appears to have been done of the business environment and of the risks it may pose to the entity.

Risk assessment (material misstatement)

ISA 315 requires that the risks of material misstatement be assessed both at the financial statement level and at the assertion level. No risk assessment appears to have been carried out at the assertion level.

Property valuation/stage of completion

It is right that an expert be engaged to provide evidence regarding property valuations. In previous years this was an auditor's expert, this year it is a management's expert.

ISA 500 (UK and Ireland) *Audit evidence* requires that the competence, capabilities and objectivity of the management's be assessed. This has not been done here.

The architect is newly qualified, which may cast doubt over whether she has sufficient experience and competence to do this work.

The architect is employed by the entity, which according to ISA 500 is an indication that she may be less objective than if she were engaged for a specific task. Furthermore, there is a risk that the business owners, who intend to sell the business, may seek to inflate the valuations in order to achieve a better price on the sale.

Therefore the architect's work cannot be relied upon for the purposes of the audit. An auditor's expert should be engaged to provide independent valuations.

Office space rent

The IESBA *Code of Ethics* states that gifts and hospitality may create a self-interest threat to independence. Suki & Co must assess the nature, value and intent of the offer. In the UK, FRC Ethical Standard 4 Fees, remuneration and evaluation policies, litigation, gifts and hospitality includes similar guidance; the audit firm should not accept the gift unless its value is clearly insignificant.

The fact that the rent is of a nominal amount means that the effective value of the gift is likely to be substantial.

The intent is not clear, but it could be considered a bribe, given in the hope of obtaining an unmodified audit opinion before the sale of the company.

The offer should therefore be declined.

Conclusion

The audit has been inadequately planned, and fails to meet the requirements of ISAs. There are also a number of ethical threats to Suki & Co's independence.

Actions include possible further training for Tara Lafayette, and a reconsideration of the firm's ethical safeguards in place regarding long association with audit clients.

(b) (i) Related party transactions (RPTs) are difficult to identify because management may not themselves be fully aware of what constitutes a RPT, and may not therefore disclose all RPTs to the auditor.

IAS 24 *Related party disclosures* requires a degree of subjective judgement in deciding who is a related party. This makes it less likely that management will be able to prepare adequate disclosures in line with IAS 24.

Management may deliberately attempt to conceal RPTs, for example because they are being used to manipulate the financial statements. This is particularly difficult for the auditor to address, as knowledge of related parties must come largely from representations made by management.

Finally, accounting systems are not set up to identify RPTs separately from transactions in the normal course of business.

(ii) Audit procedures include:

- Review invoices from Lantern Ltd to verify the amount of the expense. Confirm cash payments to the cash book

- Inspect Lantern Ltd's trade payables account to confirm any amount outstanding at the year end

- Compare the cost of refurbishment carried out by Lantern Ltd to the cost of refurbishment carried out by other suppliers, to determine if the transaction is at arm's length

- Discuss the informal lease with management, and obtain a written representation regarding the nature of the arrangement, and whether any amount is payable to Bill Co

- Confirm through enquiry with management the date the lease arrangement commenced, and the expected period of the lease

- Enquire if any written documentation exists regarding the lease arrangement, if so, review and place on file

Review disclosures made (if any) regarding these transactions in the draft financial statements.

31 Mulligan

Text references. Chapters 13 and 14.

Top tips. In part (a) it is important to take time to plan your answers. In this question you should have taken to time to think of the main matters that need to be discussed prior to accepting any type of assurance assignment, and these would work well as sub headings in your answer. You should also make sure that you use the scenario to make your answer practical. In part (b) you need to think about how the forecasts would have been put together in the first place, and what could have gone wrong in the process to help you generate some relevant enquiries. In part (c) it is important to notice that you are not merely being asked for a definition but you must also link this with the quotation given in the question.

Easy marks. There are not many easy marks to be found in this question – each requirement demands professional judgement and application of knowledge. The basic definition in part (c) and the broad issues underlying part (a) are probably the easiest elements.

Examiner's comments. In requirement (a), candidates were asked to explain the matters that would be discussed at a planning meeting with their client. Answers were often blighted by two common factors.

Firstly, many comments were vague, examples of common vague points being 'discuss terms with management', 'outline the scope of work' and 'agree a fee for the assignment'. These comments on their own do not answer the requirement which is to **explain** the matters to be discussed. Candidates need to be much clearer in exactly what they mean – what does 'discussing terms' actually entail? How do you 'outline the scope of work'? Answers that are not even full sentences will rarely score well.

The second common problem comes back to the issue that candidates lack commercial sense. The vast majority of answers to requirement (a) stated that at the meeting they would discuss 'whether we are competent to take on the work'. Surely this is not something you would raise at a meeting with your client having just agreed to do the work. Similarly many candidates wanted to 'ask the management if they are competent to produce the figures'. I think that most clients would be quite insulted to be interrogated as to their competence in drafting some basic budgeted figures.

Marks

(a) **Matters to be discussed at planning meeting**
Generally 1 mark per matter specific to the scenario
Ideas list:
- Exact contents of business plan
- Recipient of report
- Confirmation report for information only
- Deadlines
- Liability issues
- Evidence availability
- Fees
- Professional regulations
- Personnel
- Complaints procedure
Maximum 8

(b) **Enquires regarding adequacy of finance requested**
Generally 1 mark per specific enquiry stated
Ideas list:
- Who prepared?
- Availability of internal finance?
- Operating cycle?
- Raw materials required?
- WIP period?
- Documentation to support costs?
- Inflation effects?
- Training costs?
- Advertising costs?
- Finance costs?
Maximum 7

(c) **Forensic accounting**
Definition – 1 mark
1 mark for each comment relevant to scenario:
- Investigate whether theft has actually occurred
- Example of factor other then theft that could have caused discrepancy
- Evidence to prove financial consequence of theft
- Evidence to prove identity
Maximum 5
Total 20

(a) **Matters to discuss with Mulligan management**

    (i)   Content of report/extent of assurance

        The firm should ascertain exactly what the business report will include and explain exactly what the assurance will relate to. It will differ from an audit report which gives assurance that figures are true and fair as the opinion will be limited as to whether the requested finance is adequate for purpose, not whether all the information presented in the report is true and fair.

    (ii)   Form of assurance

        The firm should make clear what form their assurance report will take as it will be different from the audit report that Mulligan's directors are used to. The auditors should explain that the assurance given will be in the form of negative assurance and should ensure that this form of assurance will satisfy the bank.

    (iii) Distribution of assurance report

        The firm should ensure that the client only intends to publish the report to the bank and that they will be the sole authorised users of the assurance report and that use will be restricted to determining whether to advance this finance.

    (iv) Limitation of liability

        The auditors should negotiate the limits of their liability with regard to this engagement and particularly state that their report is for information only and will not give rise to a liability to the bank.

    (v)   Deadlines

        The firm should ascertain when the client want the report finished by and ensure that there is sufficient time to carry out thorough procedures and draw a conclusion, and also that it has appropriate staff available at the time required to meet the deadlines, otherwise the deadlines should be renegotiated.

    (vi) Procedures and evidence

        The audit firm should set out the types of procedures they will perform and the type of evidence they will seek. As they will not have legal audit privileges in respect of this assignment, they should ensure that the client intends to provide them with all the information and explanations they require to provide the requested assurance and that explanations will be confirmed in writing if required.

    (vii) Engagement letter

        The firm should set up an engagement letter for this engagement as it will not be covered by the engagement letter associated with the audit for this client.

    (viii) Administrative matters

        The exact dates the firm's staff will attend client premises should be agreed and the client should be told who the staff members likely to be attending will be. In addition, matters relating to the fee and billing procedure should be finalised before work is carried out.

(b) **Adequacy of finance**

There should be sufficient finance to cover the costs of the new factory, starting the new business unit and working capital requirements to start production.

Questions

    (i)   Will the new venture be financed entirely by the bank or is Mulligan also advancing some capital? This is to establish whether the business plan is complete.

    (ii)   Who prepared the forecasts? This is to establish whether they have been prepared by someone with experience of preparing such budgets as this will give assurance as to whether the budgets are reasonable.

    (iii) Are figures in the forecasts supported by evidence such as quotations for machinery or building work? This is to see the degree of estimation included in the plans.

    (iv) Has the cost of finance been included in the forecasts? The cost of obtaining the finance appears to be missing from the initial forecast and will be a significant cost that should be included within the business projections.

(v)   How long before the products can be sold and begin to fund themselves? The budget does not contain any contingency and it is important to discover how tight the production schedule is and whether it is realistic.

(vi)   Have all construction costs been included in the cost projection – for example, the costs of electricity or the cost of employees not being used in the their usual roles?

(vii)   What is the timescale for the construction? Does the projection take account of inflation if necessary?

(viii) Does the projection contain budgets for all raw materials required? Currently it only seems to include timber, but there may be other items needed to make the product.

(ix)   What are the advertising costs based on? These must be appropriate to the specific product, so if they are based on the costs associated with other products of the company, they may not be sufficient.

(x)   What is the commercial viability of the new product? The auditor should look at market research because ability to pay the loan back will be an important factor for the bank.

(c)   **Forensic accounting**

Forensic accounting is undertaking a financial investigation in response to a particular event, such as fraud, where the findings of the investigation may be used as evidence in court or otherwise to help resolve disputes. In addition, the forensic accountant will often give advice on improving systems to prevent the problems occurring again.

In this case, the investigation the internal auditor is suggesting would be a forensic accounting investigation, the purpose of which in this case would be likely to form the basis of an insurance claim by the company if it has been subject to a repeated theft of inventory. It is likely that a company such as Mulligan would turn to their trusted professional advisers in relation to such an investigation, that is, their external auditors.

In this case, two matters should be determined:

(i)   Whether theft has taken place
(ii)   The value of that theft

There could be other reasons for inventory disappearance if controls are not strong. For example, inventory could have been identified as obsolete and disposed of or sold in a special sale but the inventory records not updated for this fact, or items could have been moved to a different location and simply not counted during the inventory count.

If the auditors concluded that theft had taken place, procedures should be carried out to determine by whom the theft was carried out and the value of the inventory stolen. Evidence found could be used to initiate criminal proceedings against the wrongdoer and also as the basis of any insurance claim.

32 Parker

Text references. Chapters 2 and 6.

Top tips. In evaluating audit risks, you needed to stick to the material in the question. There are no marks available for pre-learned knowledge, so do not be tempted to recite information, eg on obtaining an understanding of the entity and its environment, or on the theory of audit risk.

Try to strike a balance between words and numbers. Marks for calculations tend to be capped, so if you spend almost all your time performing calculations then you are unlikely to pass the question. The BPP answer given here, for example, contains more calculations than would be needed to reach the cap.

Equally, it is important that you do not go to the other extreme and perform too few calculations, as these are some of the easiest marks on the whole paper. Note that marks are available for:

•   Trends, eg that revenue has decreased by 8.2%. This would normally get a half mark.

•   Ratios, eg that gross profit has fallen from 31.8% to 27.2%. You must calculate the ratio for both years (so that a comparison can be made), which normally gets a mark.

Any adjustments or additional calculations you can make will tend to look good to the marker and will score well, eg adjusting cost of sales for the effect of reclassifying the provision.

In terms of organising your answer, little advantage is to be gained from dividing your answer into the different components of audit risk. You are advised to stick to picking risks out of the information in the question and then evaluating them.

You should note that the audit engagement has already been accepted, so there are no marks available for matters in relation to client acceptance (eg contacting the previous auditors). Again, you are advised to stick to evaluating the audit risks that are present in the scenario.

Finally, there are plenty of marks available for explaining additional information that is needed. You can gain an easy mark on most of the audit risks by simply thinking of some relevant information that would be helpful. However, you must take care not to start recommending audit procedures here, as that is not what is asked for.

Regarding the ethical and professional issues, the main pitfall would be discussing ethical issues from throughout the scenario. What is being asked for here are issues of professional ethics for the auditor, ie relating to auditor independence. No marks are available for discussing whether Parker's management is ethical, or whether the human resources arrangements might give rise to the possibility of ethical failings or fraud.

Easy marks. Some of the four professional marks were easy to come by. To get them you must include a header, an introduction and a conclusion, and make sure that your answer is written clearly and concisely, without waffling!

Calculations are easy marks, as long as you perform them quickly and accurately.

Marking scheme

Marks

Audit risk

Audit risk evaluation, preliminary analytical review and additional information requests
In relation to the matters listed below:
Up to 2 marks for each audit risk/area from preliminary analytical review evaluated
1 mark for each ratio and comparative calculated (½ mark for a trend) to
a maximum of 6 marks
1 mark for each additional information request to a maximum of 5 marks
 – Profitability
 – Liquidity
 – Solvency
 – Going concern
 – Provisions
 – Finance costs
 – Tax expense
 – Development costs
 – Property revaluation
 – Overtime payments control risk
 – New client detection risk
 – Opening balances

Ethical matters

Generally 1 mark per comment:
 – Conflict of interest threat to objectivity
 – Evaluate significance of threat and potential safeguards
 – Contact both parties to request consent to act
 – Identify safeguards (1 mark each)
 – If consent not obtained cannot act for both parties
 – Explain why corporate finance service creates advocacy threat
 – Explain why corporate finance service creates self-review threat
 – Explain why corporate finance service creates management threat
 – Identify safeguards (1 mark each)
Maximum   31

Professional marks for the overall presentation, structure and logical flow of the
briefing notes, and for the clarity of the evaluation and explanations provided.

Maximum   4

Total   35

BRIEFING NOTES

To: Harry Shepherd

From: A Manager

Date: 3 June 20X3

Subject: Parker Ltd (Parker)

Introduction

The following briefing notes contain: the results of preliminary analytical procedures in relation to the Parker Ltd audit; an evaluation of the audit risks to be considered in planning the audit; and a discussion of ethical issues raised along with a recommendation of relevant actions for our firm.

Analytical procedures are contained in an Appendix at the end of these notes. All figures quoted are in £000.

Trading

Revenue declined by 8.2%, but cost of sales only declined by 2.1%. The two are not in line, as would be expected. This points to a possible overstatement of cost of sales.

Indeed, cost of sales does appear to have been overstated by the misclassification of a provision there, which should have been classified within operating expenses. Removing the provision from cost of sales gives a decline of 6.4% (= (5,680 – 250) / 5,800), which is closer to the 8.2% fall in revenue. This degree of discrepancy might be explained by eg not all costs of sales being fully variable.

This misclassification casts doubt over the efficacy of Parker's internal controls. This increase in control risk may mean that more substantive testing will be required.

The decline in revenue is dramatic, but if anything a steeper decline might be expected given Parker's price cutting and the economic conditions. Revenue may therefore be overstated.

It is possible that the price cuts may not have been properly reflected in reported revenue. Further information is needed here, such as a detailed breakdown of revenue by product line, including information about prices and volumes.

Profitability

Parker's profitability has dropped during the year, with the projected operating margin of 11.4% (20X2: 15.6%). This is worrying, but the projections do still show a profit. However, as indicated later in these notes, some adjustments may be required to the financial statements which would worsen the picture further. This gives rise to significant uncertainties over Parker's future profitability, and so also its going concern.

Fine provision

IAS 37 *Provisions, Contingent Liabilities and Contingent Assets* requires a provision to be recognised where:

- There is a present obligation as a result of a past event. The past event here was the inappropriate advertising

- An outflow of resources embodying economic benefits is at least probable

The fact that Parker has recognised a provision at all implies that it thinks an outflow of resources is probable. Therefore it is likely that an obligation exists.

Further information is required here on why management has only recognised 250. We would need to examine the notice from the regulatory authority.

As this is a one-off event, IAS 37 requires measurement at the most likely amount, which in this case is likely to be the full 450. The required adjustment of 200 is material to net profit.

Finance costs

Finance costs have risen by 24%, presumably as a result of the increase in debt finance during the year.

Some initial calculations suggest that this may be understated. Interest-bearing debt at the year end is 12,725, against which there is a finance cost of 155. This implies an interest rate of 1.2%, which is very low.

Further information needed would include:

- Bank loan agreement, with details of interest rates and any restrictive covenants imposed
- Bank overdraft agreement, with details of interest rat
- Finance lease agreements, with details of interest rate implied in the lease

Taxation

The tax charge has fallen by 76.7%, and looks low. Indeed, the implied tax rate in 20X3 is 9.5% (= 70 / 735), which is significantly lower than the 25% (= 300 / 1,197) in 20X2.

The charge in the statement of profit or loss (70) does not agree to the liability (50), so there must be some misstatement. It seems likely that the tax computation has not yet been performed for the projected figures, and that adjustments will need to be made once this is done. The amount is material to profit for the year.

Taken together with the misclassification of the provision to cost of sales, this is further evidence of poor internal controls over financial reporting at Parker.

Further information needed would be the ledger accounts for both tax figures, along with tax computations for the expense.

Revaluation

The revaluation of PPE has given rise to a revaluation reserve, but the statement of profit or loss and other comprehensive income does not include a revaluation gain, or indeed any other comprehensive income at all. This appears to be a material misstatement, which could be argued to be pervasive.

We will be able to place some reliance on the management's expert's valuation, in line with ISA 500 *Audit evidence*. Further information is needed on the expert's qualifications and independence, as well as a copy of the report itself.

Given Parker's imperfect internal controls, it is possible that the depreciation may not have been remeasured at the point of the revaluation, leading to an understatement of expenses. Parker may have revalued assets selectively, whereas it is required to revalue all assets within a class. Finally, extensive disclosures are required in the notes to the financial statements, and there is a risk that these have not been made.

The main risk with the revaluation is that assets are overstated. Given Parker's poor profitability and liquidity position (see below), management has an incentive to overstate assets. There is therefore a risk of management bias in the revaluation.

Development costs

Further information is required regarding the costs capitalised, as there is a risk that Parker is capitalising internally generated brands, which is prohibited by IAS 38 *Intangible assets*. This would be in line with the possible management bias discussed above.

IAS 38 requires only development costs to be capitalised, with research costs being expensed. Given that operating expenses fell by 10.7% during year – more than the fall in revenue – it appears unlikely that significant research costs have been treated as expenses. Therefore it is very likely that assets are overstated.

Costs can only be capitalised if they meet specific criteria, such as the probability of future economic benefits flowing to Parker, and that costs can be measured reliably. The first criterion here is problematic, since it depends on the claim that there is a market for the product, and that Parker has the financial resources to complete the development.

It is possible that Parker's new range will arrive on the market too late to compete effectively with the competitor's new range. Further information is required, such as details of market research conducted.

Parker is also currently in dire straits when it comes to liquidity (see below), which raises doubts over its ability to complete the development.

At 2,250, the amounts involved here are highly material. If only half of these were expensed, it would completely wipe out profit for the year, from a profit of 625 to a loss of 500.

Finance leases

New assets were acquired under finance leases. There is a risk that these are in fact operating leases, and that assets may therefore be overstated.

Liquidity

The bank balance of 900 at the end of 20X2 is projected to have become an overdraft of 1,000 by the end of 20X3. The current ratio has nearly halved, from 1.8 to 0.96, meaning that current assets do not cover current liabilities.

Receivables days have risen from 34 to 42. This could be down to poor credit control; we already know that Parker's internal controls may not be entirely reliable. Alternatively, it could indicate the presence of irrecoverable receivables not provided for, which would further reduce assets and profit were provision to be made for them.

Inventory days have risen from 136 to 167. This could be a sign of inventory obsolescence; this is particularly likely given the competition that Parker is facing. If net realisable value is lower than inventory cost then write-downs may be required, which would affect both assets and profit.

Payables days have risen from 63 to 86. This is a sign of cashflow difficulties, with Parker struggling to pay its suppliers (a feat made difficult by its slow debt collection from its customers). This could damage supplier relationships, leading to interest charges or lost discounts, or to the breakdown of relationships. This could make trading very difficult for Parker.

Parker is currently dependent on its overdraft for trading. If the overdraft were withdrawn, then it would be virtually impossible for it to continue as a going concern. Further information is needed here regarding the overdraft limit and the date of any reviews.

Solvency

Interest cover has fallen from 10.6 to 5.7. The fall is worrying, although 5.7 is not a terrible figure. That being said, given that finance costs may be understated, the figure could become worse once appropriate adjustments are made.

Gearing has risen from 0.8 to 1. This is high, and may make it harder to raise finance in future. Given Parker's liquidity problems, it appears unlikely that the bank would want to renew the bank loan again, which would again affect going concern. Further information is needed regarding the terms of the loan, and in particular the repayment date.

Further information is needed on Parker's preference shares, as these may be redeemable. If they were to be redeemed then Parker may not be able to make the required payment or issue new shares, which could hit going concern.

Any payables not paid within a certain amount of time may consider action against the company to recover their debts, and there is a risk that proceedings could be initiated to liquidate the company.

Going concern

Parker's plan to get itself out of its current difficulties appears to be twofold: increased sales from the new product in development, and synergies from the acquisition of Beauty Boost Ltd.

More information is needed regarding the projected sales from the new product. Cashflow forecasts in particular are crucial, as at present it appears that Parker is haemorrhaging cash and needs to start receiving substantial inflows very soon.

The proposed acquisition of Beauty Boost Ltd may indeed provide some synergies, but it appears unlikely that any savings would be significant enough to restore profitability. More likely, it would leave Parker with still more debt, which it would then have to find more cash to service.

In any event, in view of its solvency position it appears unlikely that Parker will be able to raise sufficient funds to make the acquisition.

There is a risk that Parker will not make sufficient disclosure of the doubts that exist over going concern. It is also possible that the financial statements will have to be prepared under an alternative assumption to going concern – eg the break-up basis – but this would only become clear once audit evidence has been obtained in this area.

Control risk

As discussed, several factors point to high control risk on this engagement. In addition, Parker's internal auditors found deficiencies in the controls over payroll, which may mean that more substantive testing will need to be performed. The change during the year from HR to the finance department represents a risk, as procedures may not have been followed properly during the handover. Moreover, there is a risk of a lack of segregation of duties now that payments are handled by the finance department alone.

New client

As Parker is a new client, detection risk is increased as we will lack cumulative understanding of the business and its environment. We must therefore focus particularly on developing this understanding at the planning stage.

Appendix

		20X3	20X2
Revenue decrease	8.2%		
Cost of sales decrease	2.1%		
Finance costs increase	24%		
Taxation decrease	76.7%		
Operating expenses decrease	10.7%		
Operating profit margin		11.4%	15.6%
Current ratio		0.96	1.8
Interest cover (operating profit/equity)		5.7	10.6
Gearing		1	0.8
Receivables days		42	34
Inventory days		167	136
Payables days		86	63

Ethical issues

Potential acquisition – conflict of interest

There is a potential conflict of interest here, as Hound & Co may effectively be advising both sides of a potential acquisition negotiation. The IESBA *Code of Ethics* requires safeguards to be applied here. Crucially, both parties should be informed of the potential conflict, and should be asked for their consent to the arrangement. If either party declines, then the engagement should not be accepted.

If both say yes, then safeguards could include:

- Separate engagement teams, separated by information barriers
- Confidentiality agreements signed by employees and partners of Hound & Co

Potential acquisition – self-review

There is also a self-review threat in relation to the due diligence, as we will be performing procedures on financial statements which we have already audited. Safeguards here would include:

- Separate engagement teams
- Pre-issuance review of the non-audit service report by an independent professional accountant

Financing – advocacy

Providing advice on financing raises an advocacy threat if Hound & Co is asked to represent Parker's interests, for example to any potential lenders. Such a role should therefore be avoided.

Financing – management role

There is a risk that we could be seen as playing (or could actually play) a management role, which is prohibited by ES 5 *Non-audit services provided to audited entities*. This would be the case if eg we recommended a particular form of finance to Parker. The threat can be mitigated by making it clear that any decisions rest with Parker's management, and that we are providing them with advice only.

Financing – self-review

There may be a self-review threat here if the financial statements come to include amounts in relation to any financing obtained using our advice. Possible safeguards include:

- Using a separate corporate finance team from the audit team
- Pre-issuance review of the corporate finance service, and of the relevant area of the financial statements, by an independent professional accountant

If safeguards would not reduce the threat to an acceptable level, the engagement should not be accepted.

Conclusion

From the above it can be concluded that the audit of Parker Ltd is of relatively high risk overall, with particular risks in relation to overstatement of assets, understatement of expenses, and the company's ongoing solvency and liquidity problems.

Several important ethical issues are raised by Parker's request, and these must be considered carefully before any engagements are accepted.

33 Lapwing

Top tips. In part (a)(i), you should obviously take heed of the warning not to discuss ethical threats. It is abundantly clear that ethics are not being tested here, both from the question itself (which states that 'a second partner review … will reduce any threat … to an acceptable level') and from the requirement.

Many of the matters to consider here involve simple clarification of exactly what is being done, ie exactly what form the report will take, exactly what information will be reported on, exactly who the report is for, and so on. You could try to generate ideas by simply thinking about what is practically involved in the engagement, and what needs to be considered from a practical and commercial point of view. Alternatively, you could use as a starting point ISAE 3400's list of matters to be agreed – but if you do this, make sure that you're applying your answer to the scenario.

In part (a)(ii) there is one mark available for each procedure. Remember that procedures need to be specific. In addition to just listing the procedures, you should state why you would perform it as well. For example, don't just write 're-perform calculations', but 're-perform calculations to check arithmetical accuracy'.

This part of the question should not have been **too** difficult, and could be approached by simply working through all the information given – both the text and the financial statements – and thinking of the procedures you could perform to audit it. If you are going to pass P7, you need to be scoring at least 7–8 on a question like this.

In part (b), it is absolutely crucial that you notice the requirement to write briefing notes, as this is worth up to four marks. Remember to write an introduction and a conclusion, as well as the usual 'briefing notes' headings.

Part (b)(i) should be straightforward. All you really need to know here is that net liabilities generally make a company insolvent. Its cash position (its liquidity) is usually only a short-term consequence of this. One possible mistake here would be to just include figures from the question line-by-line, which would have meant comparing total assets with total **equity** and liabilities (rather than just comparing total assets with total liabilities). If you did this then you would have been lucky in this question because the company still had greater equity and liabilities than assets – but you need to make sure you don't do this next time!

The discussion of liquidity in the answer to part (i) is not strictly asked for by the requirement, but the fact that there were four marks available here should have made you think that a little bit more than just the calculation was required.

Part (b)(ii) was a little harder, but you should have been fairly comfortable with all of this. You needed only a basic knowledge of liquidation and administration, which you then had to apply to the scenario.

Reading the scenario carefully, you might have noticed several hints about what the examiner wanted you to discuss in your answer. For example, when you read that long-term borrowings were 'secured with a fixed charge over property, plant and equipment', this should have made you think of (i) discussing the priority for allocating assets in a liquidation, and (ii) applying this priority to the scenario – in this case, saying that the chargeholder would be likely to receive payment first. Likewise, when you see 'employees wages of £300,000', you should try to think about what the examiner wants you to do with this information.

Most candidates should have spotted that 'Jay Plus' is profitable, and that administration may therefore be the best option. In order to score well here, though, you needed to go a little bit further than this and think practically about what might happen in this situation. If you are proposing that the company could continue as Jay Plus, then you need to think about whether this is really feasible, and whether Jay Plus really could cover all of the company's continuing costs.

Easy marks. A mark was available in part (a)(ii) for saying 'Re-perform calculations to confirm arithmetic accuracy of the financial statements'. The four presentation marks were easy marks, although you do have to earn them.

ACCA examiner's answer. The ACCA examiner's answer to this question can be found at the end of this Practise & Revision Kit.

Marking scheme

			Marks

(a) (i) **Matters to be considered in agreeing the terms of the engagement**
Up to 1½ marks for each matter identified and explained (2 marks maximum for identification):
- – Management's responsibilities
- – Intended use of the information and report
- – The contents of the business plan
- – The period covered by the forecasts
- – The nature of assumptions used in the forecasts
- – The format and planned content of the assurance report

Maximum   **6**

(ii) **Procedures on forecast financial information**
Up to 1 mark for each procedure (brief examples below):
- – General procedures examples:
  - ○ Re-perform calculations
  - ○ Consistency of accounting policies used
  - ○ Discuss how joint venture has been included
  - ○ General analytical procedures
- – Procedures on statement of profit or loss:
  - ○ Discuss trends – allow up to 3 marks for calculations performed and linked to procedures
  - ○ Review and compare breakdown of costs
  - ○ Recalculate profit on disposal, agreement of components to supporting documentation
- – Procedures on statement of financial position:
  - ○ Agree increase in property, plant and equipment to capital expenditure budget
  - ○ Discuss working capital trends – allow 2 marks for calculations performed and linked to procedures
  - ○ Agree movement in long-term borrowings to new loan documentation
  - ○ Obtain and review forecast statement of changes in equity and confirm validity of reconciling items

Maximum   **10**

(b) (i) **Examine financial position and determine whether the company is insolvent**

Generally 1 mark per comment:
- Calculation of net liabilities position of Jay Ltd
- Determination that Jay Ltd is insolvent
- Explanation of meaning of insolvency
- Discussion of different results of JS and JP business segments

Maximum   4

(ii) **Evaluate the options available to the directors**

Up to 1½ marks per comment:
- Explanation of meaning of liquidation
- Application of order of priority in allocating proceeds of liquidation
- Discussion of means of placing a company in liquidation
- Explanation of meaning of administration
- Discussion of means of appointing an administrator
- Benefits of administration over liquidation
- Identify that a definite decision depends on further information
- Overall recommendation

Maximum   9

Professional marks for the overall presentation of the notes, and the clarity of the explanation and assessment provided.

Maximum   4

Total   33

(a) (i) The terms of the engagement to report on the business plan should be agreed in an engagement letter for this assurance engagement. The following matters should be considered.

Intended use of the business plan

It should be confirmed that the report will be provided to the bank, as this may establish Lapwing & Co as potentially liable to the bank.

Distribution of report

Clarification should be sought over whether the report will be distributed to any other parties. It may be necessary for the report to include a liability disclaimer.

Elements of business plan covered

The engagement is to report on the business plan, but clarification is needed about whether this means the business plan as a whole, or merely the forecast financial statements included in it. This will affect the extent of Lapwing & Co's possible liability, and the extent of procedures required.

Nature of assumptions

It should be clarified whether the plan's assumptions are best estimates or hypothetical. If the assumptions are clearly unrealistic, then ISAE 3400 *The examination of prospective financial information* states that the auditor should not accept the engagement.

Period covered

The forecast financial statements are for 12 months. It should be clarified that this is the only period on which assurance is to be provided. Clarification is also needed over whether the other elements of the business plan refer to only this period.

Fees and practical matters

The level of fees should be confirmed, together with billing arrangements. Practical matters to confirm include the timing of the report, which will enable Lapwing & Co to ensure that it has adequate resources (eg staff) available to perform the engagement.

Form of report

The planned form of the report should be agreed in advance in order to avoid any misunderstandings. The report would use a negative form of words to provide limited assurance.

Respective responsibilities

It should be confirmed that management is responsible for preparing the business plan, and for providing the auditor with all relevant information.

(a)   (ii)   **General procedures**

- Re-perform calculations to check arithmetical accuracy.

- Agree unaudited figures for period to 20X2 to management accounts to assess their reliability.

- Confirm that accounting policies applied consistently between the periods and audited financial statements.

- Assess accuracy of past forecasts by comparison with actual figures.

- Consider reasonableness of trends in light of auditor's understanding of Hawk Ltd.

- Review correspondence with bank re. negotiated terms of the loan, and confirm major terms and interest rate directly with bank.

Statement of profit or loss and other comprehensive income

- Discuss 21.4% increase in revenue with management, and consider if reasonable.

- Operating margin rises from 30% to 33.8%. Ask for explanation from management and consider if reasonable.

- Discuss sale of Beak Retail, including likelihood of sale and any likely terms. Review board minutes for details about the sale.

- Recalculate profit on disposal, and agree proceeds to any draft legal documentation.

- Consider reasonableness of finance costs. New loan should add 1m ($30m \times 4\% \times 10 / 12$), but finance costs are up by only 960,000 – need to ascertain the reason for this.

Statement of financial position

- Non-current assets are up £37.15m, but the loan which financed this investment was only for £30m. Enquire about other possible sources of finance used for this increase.

- Review reconciliation of movement in non-current assets, confirming that Beak Retail assets are derecognised.

- Confirm that any assets relating to the joint venture with Kestrel are accounting for in line with IFRS 11 *Joint arrangements.*

- Discuss the planned £5m increase in equity (is this to help finance the increase in assets?). Discuss what form this will take (ie rights issue, or at full market price).

- Agree the increase in non-current assets to capital expenditure budgets.

- Agree cash figure at May 20X2 to bank reconciliation & statement.

- Receivables days are predicted to fall from 58 days ($3,300 / 20,600 \times 365$) to 53 days ($3,600 / 25,000 \times 365$), improving the company's cash position. The reasons for this should be discussed with management, and considered for reasonableness.

- Payables days are predicted to fall from 137 days ($5,400 / 14,420 \times 365$) to 124 days ($5,600 / 16,550 \times 365$), worsening the company's cash position. The reasons for this should be discussed with management, and considered for reasonableness.

- Agree the increase in long-term borrowings to documentation obtained for the new loan.

- Discuss the deferred tax provision, and establish why there has been no movement (which is unexpected, given the capital expenditure).

- Discuss the movement on retained earnings, which have risen only by £0.8m, in spite of a profit before tax of £10.52m. It may be that a dividend is planned.

(b) **Briefing Notes**

For: Bill Kingfisher

By: Audit manager

Date: June 20X2

Re: Jay Ltd – financial results

Introduction

These briefing notes examine Jay Ltd's financial position and solvency, and evaluate the options available to its directors.

(i) **Jay Ltd's solvency**

Jay Ltd is clearly illiquid, as can be seen from the following calculation:

Inventory	500
Trade receivables	400
Cash	–
Trade payables	(1,250)
Bank overdraft	(1,400)
Current liabilities	(1,750)

However, this does not necessarily make it insolvent. To determine this, we must also consider its non-current assets and liabilities:

Current liabilities (above)	(1,750)
PPE	12,800
Long-term borrowings	(12,000)
Net liabilities	(950)

Jay Ltd therefore appears to be insolvent, because it has net liabilities.

(ii) **Evaluation of options available to directors**

There are two basic options: administration or liquidation. Some action will need to be taken, because if the company continues to trade then the directors may be found to have fraudulently traded (a criminal offence), or wrongfully traded (a civil offence). In either case the directors would face personal consequences for their actions.

Liquidation?

Process

Liquidation is the process of winding up the company. A liquidator would be appointed and tasked with selling the company's assets and making a distribution to its creditors (and, possibly, shareholders). There is a strict priority for allocating proceeds to creditors.

The liquidator's costs are the first thing to be paid – we do not yet know what these might be.

Fixed charge holders are next. Jay Ltd's long-term borrowings are secured with a charge over the property, plant and equipment. As much as possible of the £12,000 liability would be paid from the proceeds from selling these assets.

Preferential creditors are next, which here means the wages of £300,000.

After that it is unsecured creditors – trade payables and the bank overdraft. These are unlikely to receive the full amount owed, and may receive only a proportion on it.

Finally, the shareholders are paid anything left over – but it is very unlikely that there will be anything left in this case.

Type of liquidation

Liquidation may be voluntary or compulsory. A members' voluntary liquidation is not possible here, as the company is insolvent. A creditors' voluntary liquidation, however, could be recommended by the directors: the creditors would appoint a liquidator, and a committee composed of creditors and shareholders would have input into the liquidation.

If no action is taken then the creditors could apply to the court to wind up the company in a compulsory liquidation.

Administration?

Administration insulates the company from its creditors while an insolvency practitioner (administrator) tries to save the company as a going concern.

Administration can be begun by either the directors or the shareholders, depending on the articles of association. Creditors can also apply for a court order to appoint an administrator.

In the case of Jay Ltd, there appears to be potential to save the company through restructuring its operations. Jay Sport has clearly been affected by the problem with its ingredients, with revenue of only £50,000 but operating costs of £800,000. The Jay Sport segment is responsible for much of the company's loss, whereas Jay Plus was profitable over the eight months to May 20X2.

However, things may be more complicated than this suggests. Even without Jay Sport, the company would have made a loss before tax because of its finance costs of £800,000 (which are greater than Jay Plus's profit of £250,000). It is not clear how much of these finance costs relate to the Jay Plus segment, or to what extent any of them can be avoided, eg through early repayment of the loan.

Likewise, there may be amounts included within Jay Sport's operating costs that could not be avoided, eg there may be non-cancellable operating leases. These could be too much for Jay Plus's profits to cover.

Conclusion and recommendation

Jay Ltd is insolvent, and must choose between a liquidation (most likely a creditors' voluntary liquidation) and administration. It is likely that administration will be the preferred choice, although this will depend on the extent to which overheads (such as finance costs), and Jay Sport's operating costs, can be avoided in future.

If the company could be saved, then this would probable be preferred by the company's shareholders, who would be unlikely to receive anything from a liquidation. It may also be preferred by the employees, some of whom would keep their jobs, and by creditors, who would be more likely to receive full payment of their debts.

34 Azure Airline

Marking scheme

		Marks
(a)	**Business risks**	9

Generally ½ mark for identification +
1 mark each point of explanation
Ideas

Environment risks
–   Competition
–   Weather
–   Emergency

Financial risks
–   Overhaul costs
–   Fuel prices
–   Lease obligations
–   Economy
–   Loss of revenue

Compliance risks
–   Rights to operate
–   Safety management

Operations risks
–   Age of aircraft
–   Poor service levels (eg catering, timely operation)
–   Passenger/crew safety
–   Over-bookings

		Marks

(b) **Risk management processes**

Generally 1 mark each point   **9**

Ideas

Accept the risk

- Low impact risks
- Benchmark (or could reduce risk)

Reduce the risk

- By implementing improved internal controls
- Staff training
- Hedge against it (eg fuel prices)

Avoid unacceptable risks

- Non-compliance

Transfer the risk

- By insurance (amount/type)
- Contractual risk sharing

(c) **Operational performance measures**

Generally ½ mark each measure (eg efficiency, capacity)   **Maximum**   **6**

½ – 1 mark each source of evidence

Ideas

Performance measures

- Types of performance measure (eg efficiency, capacity)
- Numbers/proportions/%s
  - o   Fights
  - o   Passengers
  - o   Cargo (tonnes)

Audit evidence

- Oral vs written
- Internal vs external
- Auditor generated
- Procedures (relevant, reliable, sufficient)

(d) **Level of assurance**

Up to 1 mark for each well-explained point   **Maximum**   **5**

- Choice of reasonable or limited assurance
- Explanation of reasonable assurance
- Positive form of words
- Explanation of limited assurance
- Negative form of words

(e) **Types of conclusion**

Up to 1 mark for explanation of each type of conclusion   **Maximum**   **6**

Total   **35**

(a) **Business risks**

(i) **Leasing of equipment and specialist staff**. As Azure leases its equipment and the most specialised of its staff from another airline, there is a risk that its equipment and/or pilots could be withdrawn leaving it unable to operate.

(ii) **Conditions of exclusive right**. The PAA requires Azure's aircraft engines be overhauled biannually. There is a risk that Azure will be unable to meet this condition, if the lessor company does not agree to regular overhaul or that it will be too expensive for Azure to meet this requirement and it could lose the right to operate, or its exclusivity, opening it up to competition. There may be other conditions which Azure has to meet, such as the two weekly flights being a minimum.

(iii) **Necessary service suspension**. As Azure is required to overhaul its engines every two years, there will be a significant period every two years where Azure will either have to incur the cost of leasing other planes (assuming this is possible) or will have to suspend services. The cost of leasing other planes might be prohibitively expensive or the disruption to service might mean that conditions relating to the right to operate might not be met. As Azure only has one plane, service would also be interrupted if there was an emergency relating to the plane, such as fire or a crash.

(iv) **Age of aircraft**. The aircraft being leased is old. This raises operational risks (it may not always be able to fly due to necessary maintenance), finance risks (it may require regular repair) and compliance risks (it may not meet environmental or safety standards, now or in the future).

(v) **High proportion of expensive seats**. The plane leased by Azure has a high proportion of unrequired expensive seats and therefore insufficient (overbooked) cheaper seats. Although Azure can appease customers by upgrading them, this means the airline is operating well below capacity.

(vi) **Cargo**. The flight route results in the airline carrying a large amount of horticultural produce. This raises various risks – that Azure might be liable to passengers if their cargo degrades in transit, that the airline might be liable for any breaches of law by its passengers (for example, if prohibited items are transferred into Pewta or Sepiana, many countries prohibit the importation of animals or meat products or plants).

(vii) **On-board services**. Customers are currently dissatisfied with the food provision on the flight and there is a risk that food prepared in Lyme may become less appealing and even dangerous when served on a Darke to Lyme flight (when it has been prepared a substantial time earlier, given a six hour flight, at least an hour's turn around time, and time for getting to the airline in the first place). If the food makes customers ill, Azure might be faced with compensation claims.

(viii) **Pricing**. There is a complex system of pricing and a large number of sales agents, and Azure is at risk of operating at a sales value less than required to cover costs (for example, if too many of the cheapest tickets are sold).

(ix) **Safety**. The airline industry has stringent safety conditions and Azure may face customer boycott or difficulty in recruiting staff if safety requirements are not met.

(x) **Fuel**. The aircraft cannot fly without fuel, which can be a scarce or high-cost resource. If fuel prices escalate due to world conditions, the company might not be able to meet the costs of operating.

(b) **Managing risks**

(i) **Lease**. Azure must ensure that the terms of the contract with the international airline ensure that aircraft and staff cannot be withdrawn without reasonable notice, and that in the event of withdrawal, substitutes will be given.

(ii) **Conditions**. Azure must ensure that all staff are aware of any conditions and the importance of meeting them. However, this risk must simply be accepted as there is little Azure can do about conditions imposed on them by the governing body of their industry.

(iii) **Service suspension**. Azure must have contingency plans for service suspension, such as ensuring their contract with the international airline ensures alternative aircraft will be made available to them in the event of maintenance or damage to the aircraft, or by making arrangements to lease from a different airline in the event of emergency. As a minimum, Azure must ensure that the airline they lease from would give them financial compensation in the event of aircraft or staff not being available so that Azure's customers could be compensated.

(iv) **Age of aircraft**. Azure should have plans in place to be able to lease/afford newer planes if required to by law. Again, this could be written into their contract with the airline. Azure should manage cash flow and borrowing facilities so as to be able to afford ongoing maintenance when required.

(v) **High proportion of expensive seats**. Azure should negotiate a reconfiguration of the plane with the lessor so that business and first class seating could be reduced and more economy seats made available. If this is not possible with the current lessor, Azure should investigate leasing differently configured planes from another company. If it is not feasible to adjust the plane seating, Azure should consider its pricing and on-board facilities policies to make business and first class seats more attractive to customers. As the seats are not being sold anyway, it is probable that a reduction in prices would increase overall revenue, although this might reduce potential profit.

(vi) **Cargo**. Azure should publish a cargo policy to ensure that customers are aware of their legal obligations. They should ensure that staff are sufficiently trained to discuss the contents of baggage with customers and are aware what items Azure should not carry. They should insure against lost and damaged cargo.

(vii) **On-board services**. Azure should consider entering into a contract with a company in Darke to provide food for the Darke to Lyme journey. Obviously they must not breach any existing contract with the Lyme company and so in the meantime should review the type of food provided. For example, it might be safer to only offer cold food, for example sandwiches and cake until a Darke contract can be set up. Even if a new contract is set up, it might still be best to offer cold food as there is less chance of health problems arising as a result of serving cold food rather than hot food.

(viii) **Pricing**. As discussed above, Azure should review the pricing policy. They should also establish limits on how many of certain types of tickets (non-refundable/single etc) can be issued for one flight and they should institute a centralised system to ensure that each agent is aware when limits have been reached. As the agents must be linked to a similar system already (to be aware of whether tickets are available for sale) this should not be too difficult to achieve.

(ix) **Safety**. The company should appoint a member of staff to be specifically responsible for safety operations (such as training, updating for legal requirements, educating passengers) and should ensure that staff are regularly appraised about safety issues.

(x) **Fuel**. The company could take out hedging contracts against the cost of fuel. Other than this, there is little they can do about this matter, and it is another risk that has to be accepted.

(c) **Measures of operational performance**

(i) **Passengers/flight**. The airline could have a target number of passengers per flight and must review actual numbers against target. Evidence of the number of passengers per flight will be easy to obtain as it will be a safety requirement that Azure maintains significant records concerning its passengers. Evidence: ticketing information, check-in records.

(ii) **Time of flight/check-in**. The airline must have target times for flight time and check-in time and review the percentage difference which occurs on a regular basis. The flight times can be obtained from the pilot's timesheet and the check-in times could be monitored by asking passengers how long they have been waiting as they check-in. Evidence: timesheets, airport records.

(iii) **Customer satisfaction**. The airline should record customer satisfaction and have a target level which it hopes to achieve and maintain. This could be measured by customers completing questionnaires which ask them to rate the service, according to pre-designed ratings (for example, poor, adequate, good, excellent). Evidence: completed questionnaires.

(iv) **Safety**. The airline should have targets for safety, for example, no accidents/number of days or staff achieving safety qualifications. Evidence: accident log books and staff certificates and training records.

(d) **Level of assurance**

The engagement in question would be an assurance engagement, and would be performed on information other than historical financial information. The relevant technical guidance is therefore contained within ISAE 3000 (Revised) *Assurance Engagements Other than Audits or Reviews of Historical Financial Information*.

Such an engagement could be either a reasonable assurance engagement or a limited assurance engagement. Management is therefore in a position to choose which is most appropriate to its needs, and to the needs of users.

If the engagement were performed as a reasonable assurance engagement, then this would be a higher level of assurance than a limited assurance engagement. It would mean that the practitioner has reduced engagement risk to an acceptably low level, and would contain a conclusion expressed in a positive form of words.

If the engagement were performed as a limited assurance engagement, then this would leave a level of risk that is acceptable in the circumstances but is higher than for a reasonable assurance engagement. The assurance provided would be limited but nevertheless meaningful, and would enhance users' confidence in the integrated report to a degree that is clearly more than inconsequential.

The conclusion of a limited assurance engagement would be expressed in a negative form of words, such as 'No matter(s) has come to the practitioner's attention to cause the practitioner to believe the subject matter information is materially misstated.'

(e)   **Types of conclusion**

Irrespective of whether the level of assurance being provided is reasonable or limited, the types of conclusion which the practitioner may express in line with ISAE 3000 are as follows. The meaning of each type of conclusion, however, depends on the level of assurance being provided.

	Reasonable assurance	Limited assurance
Unmodified	Subject matter is prepared, in all material respects, in line with criteria.	No matter(s) has come to the attention of the practitioner that causes the practitioner to believe that the subject matter information is not prepared, in all material respects, in line with criteria.
Unmodified but with Emphasis of Matter paragraph	Need to draw users' attention to a matter presented or disclosed in the subject matter that is fundamental to users' understanding	
Unmodified but with Other Matter paragraph	Need to communicate a matter other than those that are presented or disclosed in the subject matter information that is relevant to users' understanding of the engagement, the practitioner's responsibilities or the assurance report	
Qualified due to material misstatement	There is a material misstatement, but its effects are not pervasive.	
Qualified due to scope limitation	A scope limitation exists and the effect of the matter could be material but not pervasive.	
Adverse	A misstatement is both material and pervasive.	
Disclaimer of conclusion	A scope limitation exists and the effect of the matter could be pervasive.	

35 Island

Marking scheme

Marks

(a) **Principal audit risks/planning matters**
Generally ½ mark each risk/matter identified
Up to 1 further mark for significant issues explained:
- Revenue recognition
- Legal claim
- Going concern
- Valuation of inventories
- Warranty provision
- CEO incentive to manipulate figures and disclosures
- Disputed receivable
- Cancelled orders
- Overseas supplier
- Related party disclosure
- CEO influence on audit team

Up to ½ further mark for obvious matters explained:
- New client
- Tight deadline

Up to 4 marks for format of briefing notes and clarity of explanation
Maximum

15

(b)   **Audit procedures for warranty provision**
      Generally 1 mark per procedure
      –   Review contracts
      –   Review correspondence
      –   Recalculate (max ½ mark)
      –   Review board minutes
      –   Consider assumptions
      –   Compare actual current year expenditure to prior year provision
      –   Post year end expenditure
      Maximum   5

(c)   (i)   **Four QC procedures for individual audit assignment**
            2 marks per procedure described (½ mark max if only identified
            and not described):
            –   Client acceptance
            –   Engagement team
            –   Direction
            –   Supervision
            –   Review
            –   Consultation
            –   Ref ISQC 1/ISA (UK & Ireland) 200 – 1 mark max
            Maximum   8

      (i)   **Two QC problems in small firm**
            2 marks per problem = 1 mark for problem,
            1 mark for recommendation:
            Ideas list:
            –   Consultation
            –   Training/CPD
            –   Review procedures
            –   Specialist experience
            –   Working papers
            Maximum   <u>4</u>

Total   <u>32</u>

(a)   **Briefing Notes**

      To: Marcus Fish
      From: S Patel
      Date: 4 December 20X8
      Subject: Island Ltd audit

      Introduction

      These briefing notes contain an explanation of the principle risks in relation to the Island Ltd audit, a
      summary of the audit procedures required to obtain assurance over the warranty provision, and details of
      quality controls that could be implemented in relation to an individual engagement, and by a small firm
      generally.

      Principal audit risks

      Revenue recognition

      Risk: revenue is materially overstated.

      Island recognises its revenue in three stages, 50% on order confirmation, 25% on delivery and 25% on
      installation.

      It is important that Island meets the accounting requirements of IAS 18 *Revenue* in recognising this income.
      This standard states that entities should only recognise revenue when the significant risks and rewards of
      the ownership of the goods have been transferred to the purchaser.

It is certain that significant risks and rewards have not passed to the purchaser at order completion stage and arguable that only risks have transferred (not rewards) at delivery stage, therefore Island is recognising a significant amount of revenue before it is entitled to do so by IAS 18.

Bad debt

Risk: receivables and profit materially overstated.

The disputed debt with Jack Mines is 3% of total assets and 50% of profit and is therefore material. If the debt will not be paid, assets and profit will be overstated unless the debt is written off.

Possible liability

Risk: liabilities are understated.

The auditors need to investigate whether the claim by Sawyer is likely to result in a liability to Island, because, although the CEO of Island is not taking it seriously, it may have to be disclosed or even recognised in the financial statements. The fact that Sawyer are communicating through legal counsel suggests that they are taking the matter seriously. In addition, the fact that Island has a warranty provision, suggests that there is precedent for Island making payments in respect of faulty installations.

If the auditors conclude that it is probable that Island will have to pay damages to Sawyer then the liability should be recognised in the financial statements and if Island does not do so, they will be understating liabilities in the financial statements.

Valuation of work-in-progress

Risk: work-in-progress is under or overstated.

Work-in-progress is nearly 9% of total assets and is therefore material. Given the nature of the product, valuation is likely to be sensitive to degree of completeness. The calculations of work-in-progress valuation were carried out two weeks before the year-end. It is not clear why this was necessary.

The risk is that work-in-progress will be materially over or under valued and this risk is increased by the gap between the valuation and the yearend as additional calculations will have to be carried out between the valuation date and the year-end date.

It will be important for the auditors to assess that the calculations of completeness and the absorption of overheads and other costs such as labour have been carried out consistently with prior years and that the roll-forward has been carried out correctly. This will be made more difficult by the fact that it is the first time they have audited Island.

Warranty provision

Risk: warranty provision is understated.

The warranty provision is based on estimates made by the CEO which makes it inherently risky. This risk is increased by the CEO's incentive to have good results (see below). The risk is that the provision will be understated, and the fact that it has risen insignificantly from the prior year when revenue has increased more significantly suggests that the provision may well be understated. The auditors must ensure that the provision is calculated consistently with previous years. (Again, this is made more difficult by the fact that this is the first year they have audited Island.)

CEO incentive

Risk: CEO has incentive to present a better than realistic picture in financial statements.

As the CEO is going to be selling shares in Island, she has an incentive to manipulate the results to obtain the best price. This increases the inherent risk associated with the entire audit and the auditors must ensure that they have their professional scepticism intact and corroborate evidence solely emanating from her. This will be a particular problem where accounting matters are affected by her judgement, such as the warranty provision.

Overseas supplier

Risk: foreign currency translation may be incorrect.

The fact that Island now has an overseas supplier subjects them to foreign exchange risk and the risk in the financial statements is that the liability will be over or understated due to translation error. The liability is not itself material to the statement of financial position, and the translation error would have to be substantial to be material to the statement of profit or loss and other comprehensive income. The auditors should ensure that appropriate controls over foreign exchange translation have been set up in relation to this new supplier.

Related party transactions

Risk: related party disclosures may be incorrect or lacking.

The fact that Kate Shannon controls Island and Pacific makes these related entities. There are several risks in connection with related parties – first that the relevant disclosures in respect of these related parties and any transactions that they might have might be omitted from the financial statements and second that there might be other related parties/related party transactions omitted from the financial statements and third that the auditors have little chance of discovering other related parties unless they are told about them.

Other matters

Kate Shannon has imposed a tight reporting deadline of January 20X8 on the audit. This increases audit risk as it reduces audit evidence provided by the course of events (such as the legal case developing or a receivable paying a debt).

In addition, it means that the audit firm may have to use additional staff on the audit which will increase the cost of the audit and this should be discussed with Kate Shannon.

(b) **Audit procedures in respect of warranty provision**

The warranty provision is an accounting estimate. The audit of accounting estimates is governed by ISA (UK & Ireland) 540 *Auditing accounting estimates, including fair value accounting estimates, and related disclosures*. Auditors should adopt one or a combination of the following methods to audit accounting estimates.

(i)   Determine whether events occurring up to the date of the auditor's report provide audit evidence regarding the accounting estimate.

(ii) Test how management made the accounting estimate and the data on which it is based.

(iii) Test the operating effectiveness of the controls over how management made the accounting estimate, together with appropriate substantive procedures.

(iv) Develop a point estimate or a range to evaluate management's point estimate.

In the audit of Island, reviewing events up to the date the of the auditor's report may be of limited use due to the tight reporting schedule. The auditor's will therefore:

(i)   Obtain relevant data used to make calculations by Kate Shannon

(ii)   Consider whether it is accurate, complete and reliable

(iii) Recalculate to ensure calculation is correct

(iv)   Review contracts to gain understanding of legal requirements in relation to warranties

(v)   Carry out analytical procedures on warranty provisions year on year and budgets against actual payments and discuss any variations with Kate Shannon

(vi)   Compare previous estimates with actual warranties paid out to see if assumptions are reasonable

(vii) Review board minutes for discussions of warranties and to ensure that the provision has been authorised by the board

(viii) Check the calculation made matches the accounting policy disclosed in the financial statements

(ix)   Consider whether the assumptions are consistent with other audit evidence and management's stated intentions

(x)   Review any warranty payments made after the reporting period and conclude whether they are consistent with budgets and projections

(xi)   Agree cash spent in respect of warranty payments to bank details and supplier invoices or employee job sheets (if done by employees)

(xii)   Review post year-end client correspondence to see if any warranty issues are raised

(c)   **Quality control policies and procedures**

(i)   **Procedures relevant to an individual audit**

Acceptance/continuance

Audit firms are required to carry out acceptance procedures and then ensure annually that nothing has changed that would have affected acceptance in the first place. Procedures include:

–   Obtaining information on new clients from previous auditors and third parties such as bankers and other sources, such as Companies House

–   Assessing the integrity of the client

–   Ensuring firm is able to carry out the assignment

–   Ensuring there is no ethical barrier to carrying out the assignment

–   Carrying out money laundering procedures

Engagement team

The audit partner must select the appropriate staff to carry out audit work and bear in mind such factors as:

–   Qualification
–   Experience
–   Training requirements

Direction

The audit must be directed by the partner by carrying out the following procedures:

–   Holding a planning meeting to ensure that all members of staff associated with the audit understand their role with regard to it

–   Informing all members of staff of their responsibilities

–   Sharing information about the nature of the business and any significant issues for the year

–   Identifying and discussing the risks associated with the audit

–   Outlining the detailed approach towards the audit work

Supervision

Each member of the audit team is supervised by persons senior to them on the team. The level of supervision depends on the seniority. For example, an audit senior will attend an audit with an audit junior whereas a manager will supervise a senior by telephone and meeting. Supervision includes:

–   Tracking of audit progress by the audit manager
–   Addressing significant issues during the audit and modifying the audit approach accordingly

Review

Audit work will be routinely reviewed by a more senior member of staff, for example, an audit senior will audit an audit junior's work, and an audit manager reviews the audit file. Ultimately, the audit partner will review the file. Review includes:

–   Ensuring that the work has been carried out in accordance with the plan
–   Significant matters have been raised for further consideration
–   Work performed supports the conclusions reached and is appropriately documented
–   Evidence obtained is sufficient and appropriate
–   Objectives of audit work have been achieved

Consultation

The audit partner should arrange consultation on difficult or contentious matters.

(ii) Problems for small firms

The most obvious areas of problems for small firms are when multiples of people are required to carry out quality control procedures, therefore **review** and **consultation**. The firm may lack the human resources to carry out reviews and consultations, particularly at the experienced level. It may be necessary to come to agreements with other firms to provide a forum for such reviews and discussions.

In addition, there may be problems with initial and ongoing **training** or with particular **specialist knowledge** if the firm does not have a lot of staff. Again, entering into agreements with other firms to pool resources in such cases may help with these problems.

36 Meadow

Text references. Chapters 6 and 10.

Top tips. This is a demanding question looking at high level planning issues. Having said that if you go back to basics this will provide you with a sensible plan of attack and a sensible structure. For example when thinking about risks you can consider the elements of audit risk (inherent risk etc). When considering other planning matters remember that these normally include materiality, accounting treatments, evidence and other practical matters. Always make sure that you read the requirement carefully. In part (a) you are asked to **identify** and **explain** the risks. You also need to note that the question refers to this as being the **final** audit. Part (b) should be more straightforward although a good understanding of some accounting issues is required.

Easy marks. These are available for identifying risks, but you must explain the risks to score well. Make sure you get the professional marks available too,

Examiner's comments. Part (a) was poorly answered with some candidates regurgitating the risk model. Others failed to read the requirement carefully. For example, even though the question stated that the information provided should be used many still went on to speculate, particularly in respect of control issues.

Few candidates demonstrated a knowledge of the retail method of **inventory** valuation, however many did make reference to materiality as an 'other matter' which was pleasing. It should be noted that it is as important to recognise a matter as not material eg receivables as it is to recognise material issues.

Answers to part (b) were disappointing with few candidates demonstrating a sound knowledge of segmental reporting.

	Marks

(a) Principal audit risks/matters
Generally ½ mark each risk/matter identified and up to 1½ for a description   17
Ideas – 'general'
- Inherent risks
    - o Entity (eg multiple locations)
    - o A/c balances (eg non-current assets, inventory, provisions)
    - o Going concern
- Materiality (assessed/quantified)
- Final audit strategy ('conclusion')
    - o Audit (or business) risk model – justified
    - o Analytical procedures (illustrated)
- Documentation (amended)
- Logistics (multiple locations, store visits)

Ideas – 'specific'

(1) Financial extracts
- Reliability
- Non-current assets ↓ = depreciation?
- Impairment?
- Receivables (low risk)
  (i) Provision for discontinuance
  - Material
  - A discontinuance? (IFRS 5)
  - Recognition of restructuring provision (IAS 37)
  (ii) Inventory valuation
  - Permitted IAS 2
  - How applied

(2) Segment information
- IFRS 8/CA 2006

(3) International restructure
- South American sale (see also (i) above)
- IAS 8 & IAS 10

(b) Audit work
Generally 1 mark each point contributing to a description to a maximum 5 marks for each of (i) and (ii)

8

Ideas
- Procedures
- Sources of evidence
  o Internal and external
  o Oral and written
  o Auditor-generated
- Subsequent events

Professional marks for the format and clarity of answer

4

Total

29

(a) **Briefing notes**

For: Maxim Gorky

By: Minim Sladky

Re: Meadow audit

These briefing notes identify and explain the principal audit risks and other matters to be considered when planning the approach to the final audit of Meadow for the year ended 30 September 20X8.

Audit risks and other matters

Risks

(i) The business operates in the retail industry. Transactions tend to be **high volume, low value transactions** often carried out in **cash**. (Trade receivables are therefore likely to be immaterial and therefore low risk.)

(ii) There is a risk that it will be difficult to establish **completeness of income**. In addition there is the potential of **theft**.

(iii) The company operates under the Vazandt brand name. **Emphasis on a single brand** increases risk as any damage to the brand name in one area/business unit could affect the other areas/business units.

(iv) The retail industry has suffered from a **reduction in consumer spending**. This may have the following impact.

Inventory valuation will need to be considered particularly in respect of luxury items, for example home furnishings and expensive clothes. (Food is less likely to be affected.) **Inventory** will be overstated if cost exceeds net realisable value. This may be the case if there are material amounts of **slow-moving inventory**. Under the retail method the gross profit margin would need to take account of any price reductions.

Management may feel under pressure to overstate revenues and profits (and understate expenses) in order to present the results in the most favourable light. Ultimately the viability of the company could be affected although going concern does not seem to be a critical issue at this stage.

(v)   The company operates in Africa, South America and the Far East. Inherent risk may be increased by the **diverse nature of these geographical locations**.

(vi)   The business is entering a period of **reorganisation**. This increases the risk of asset impairment, particularly in respect of the African and South American businesses.

Materiality

Preliminary materiality will be in the region of £17.7 million. This is the mid-point based on the assessment of revenue, total assets and profit before tax (see below). If this figure represents a significant change to the initial assessment, testing levels may also need to be modified.

$1/_2$%–1% revenue = £12.9m–25.85m
1%–2% total assets = £16.4m–32.8m
5%–10% PBT = £6.2m–2.4m

Accounting treatments

(i)   *African operations*

> **Tutorial note.** There are essentially three issues here; the provision for the loss, the discontinuance of the African operations and the potential for a restructuring provision.

The provision for the loss at £83.8m is material to the accounts (67% of operating profit).

IAS 37 *Provisions, contingent liabilities and contingent assets* prohibits the recognition of provisions for future operating losses as there is no obligation to incur losses at the end of the reporting period.

The announcement on 29 September does not seem to be sufficient to give rise to a constructive obligation (which is needed if a restructuring provision is going to be included) as:

*   There is no formal plan being implemented as yet
*   The company has not raised a valid expectation that it will carry out the plan

If a restructuring provision is appropriate it should only include costs which are necessarily entailed by the restructuring and not associated with the ongoing activities.

In order for the results of the African operations to be disclosed as discontinued operations the IFRS 5 definition must also be applied. In this case they do seem to constitute a separate line of business or geographical area of operations and do seem to be part of a single coordinated plan. However, to be classified as 'assets held for sale' management must, amongst other things, be committed to a plan to sell the assets, and must be actively searching for a buyer. The decision has not yet been finalised as it is still subject to consultation. On this basis the condition may not be met.

(ii)   *Sale of South American business*

This is merely mentioned in a draft note and there does not seem to be any attempt to present the information re the South American business as a discontinued operation. As things stand this appears to be the correct treatment.

Assets should be reviewed for impairment as a consequence of the decision to sell.

(iii)   *Segmental information*

This needs to comply with IFRS 8 *Operating segments* and the Companies Act 20X6. Meadow has provided information based on geographical segments.

South America is a reportable segment on the basis that it constitutes 10% of total revenue.

Africa is a reportable segment on the basis that it constitutes more than 10% of the operating losses.

The Far East does not meet either of the above tests in 20X8 but it could be argued that it is significant in that it is the only international operation which is not being sold or closed.

(iv) *Inventory valuation*

The appropriateness of the retail method as a means of establishing cost should be considered. In this case as Meadow is a retail organisation this is not uncommon.

The way in which gross profit margins are established for deduction from selling price should be assessed (see earlier point on risk).

Additional write-downs may be required as a result of the termination of the African operations.

Audit evidence

Due to the number of locations (211 stores) the auditor will have taken a risk-based approach.

Substantive procedures will have placed heavy reliance on **analytical procedures** due to the following factors.

- Availability of disaggregated information (trend analysis by store, by business unit, by location)

- The nature of the retail business (uniform operations, multiple locations, constant relationship between gross profit and revenue)

- The nature of the transactions (high volume, low value) making analytical procedures the most efficient

The reliability of the results depends on the accuracy of the information. The reliability of the draft financial statements should therefore be taken into account.

Practical aspects

Robert Bracco is represented by affiliated offices. The work of these will need to be coordinated in particular in respect of the attendance at inventory counts.

Conclusion

There are a number of specific audit risks in relation to the audit of Meadow, and the audit strategy and plan will need to show how these risks will be reduced to an acceptable level.

(b) **Audit procedures**

(i) *Segmental information*

- Check that geographical segments have been determined on a basis which is consistent with the previous year.

- Agree the segment totals to the corresponding figure in the statement of profit or loss.

- Check the arithmetical accuracy of the information.

- Check that each reportable segment meets the definition in accordance with IFRS 8 and that the way in which management have identified the different segments appears reasonable.

- Determine the way in which management have allocated revenues and expenses to the various segments. Test check the accuracy of these.

- If common costs have been allocated determine whether the way in which this has been done with reference for example to management accounts.

(ii) *International restructuring*

- Review board minutes approving the decision to close the African operations and to dispose of the South American operations.

- If available, obtain the detailed plan regarding the closure of the African operation. In particular the date on which the plan will be implemented will be relevant.

- Obtain copies of any press announcements made.

- Perform a review of subsequent events up to the date of the audit report to determine any progress made, for example, actual closures of African stores.

37 Butler

Text references. Chapters 7, 9 and 13.

Top tips. Part (a)(i) required you to critically review a cash flow forecast and a statement of financial position for ten marks. This should have been relatively straightforward. Your approach should be to look over the main figures in each statement, and think about whether they have gone up or down, and what their movement (or non-movement) might indicate. Each of the notes provided by the examiner is there for a reason, and will probably give rise to something to write in your answer. The main problem with this part of the question would have been the time constraint (10 marks = 18 minutes), so you should make sure you don't waffle, and divide your time logically between the two statements being analysed.

Note that the marks available for just identification (rather than explanation) are capped at three marks out of ten. Instead of writing lots of superficial points, you should look to make fewer points but which are better-explained.

Part (a)(ii) should have been OK, as most of the points should arise naturally out of your work on the cash flow forecast in (a)(i). The mark scheme give one mark per 'specific procedure', and the examiner has commented in the past that candidates are often not specific enough in their answers to get the mark. Make sure that each point you make is specific enough to get ½ - 1 mark.

Part (b) was on insolvency. This was a new area of the syllabus, and how well you did would likely have depended on how much work you had done in this area. If you had revised it, then you should have been able to score well on this requirement. Part (b)(i) was really knowledge, which you should be able to recall from your earlier studies. Part (b)(ii) required you to apply yourself to the scenario, but the requirement itself was not complicated. As only three marks were available, you should not have spent much time in this area – it was not necessarily, for example, to perform any calculations.

Easy marks. The professional marks in part (a) should be easy to get. There are also a lot of relatively easy marks throughout part (a); the difficulty here is making enough of them within the time available.

Examiner's comments. The answers to this question were generally unsatisfactory. The majority of candidates seemed to ignore the instruction in requirement (a)(i), providing an answer that did little more than work down the statement of financial position, calculating the materiality of each balance, and discussing the accounting treatment of each item, saying nothing about going concern. Only when turning to the cash flow forecast did these answers say anything about going concern, and then the comments were usually restricted to the likelihood of the company receiving a loan and a subsidy.

For requirement (a)(ii), most candidates could provide at least a few well explained procedures – the most common focusing on the loan from the parent company and the government grant. Some procedures were not well explained eg 'check the price of the financial asset' without saying how this could be done. Most candidates identified the extreme optimism of the cash flow forecast and that the closing cash position was negative, but not many candidates could recommend sound procedures to verify the claims of management regarding cash receipts from customers, which was a key issue.

In part (b), most candidates had obviously studied this new topic and consequently scored well. There was sometimes confusion between compulsory and voluntary liquidation, and often the order of payment of assets in the event of liquidation was incorrect. However, most candidates made a satisfactory attempt at this requirement.

(a) **(i)** **Going concern matters**

Up to 1½ marks per matter identified and explained (maximum 3 marks for identification):
- Negative cash position
- Net liabilities position
- Recurring losses
- Possible adjustment to deferred tax and development intangible asset exacerbate net liabilities position (allow 3 marks max)
- Fixed charge over assets
- Significant short term liabilities
- Potential misclassified provisions
- Forecast to remain in negative cash position
- Assumptions re sales optimistic
- Receipt of loan and subsidy not guaranteed
- Assumption of sale value of financial assets could be optimistic

Maximum   10

(ii) **Procedures on cash flow forecast**

Generally 1 mark per specific procedure:
- Enquire regarding and consider validity of assumption re cash sales
- Inspect any supporting documentation re additional resources for credit control
- Seek written confirmation from Rubery Ltd re loan
- Review financial statements of Rubery Ltd re adequacy of resources
- Inspect subsidy application
- Seek third party confirmation that subsidy will be awarded
- Confirm cash outflows for operating expenses and interest appear reasonable
- Enquire about potentially missing cash outflows
- Agree date and amount of short term loan repayment to loan documentation
- Agree opening cash to cash book and bank statements

Maximum   8

Additional information

Generally ½ mark per specific piece of information

Maximum   3

Professional marks for presentation and clarity of explanations   4

(b) **(i)** **Procedures for compulsory liquidation**

Generally 1 mark each point explained:
- Creditors petition court for a winding-up order
- Grounds for the petition must be demonstrated – usually a unpaid statutory demand
- Court appoints an Official Receiver
- Official Receiver informs company directors and takes control of company
- Shareholders can apply for compulsory liquidation (rare)
- The Crown can apply for compulsory liquidation (very rare)

Maximum   4

(ii) **Consequences for stakeholders**
- Generally 1 mark each consequence explained:
- Payables (Creditors)
- Employees
- Shareholders

Maximum   3

Total   32

(a)   **Briefing notes**

To: Audit partner

From: Audit manager

Re: Butler Ltd going concern

Introduction

These briefing notes contain an assessment of Butler Ltd's status as a going concern, based on a review of the draft statement of financial position (SOFP) and the cash flow forecast for the first three months of the next year.

These notes also recommend principal audit procedures for the cash flow forecast.

(i)   **Draft SOFP**

Cash

Butler Ltd has a negative cash balance, with an overdraft of £25m. This will make it difficult for Butler to raise the working capital it will need to operate in the short term, unless this overdraft can be extended. However, this is unlikely to be able to continue indefinitely.

Loan repayment

Butler has a total of £775m in loans repayable during the coming year. It appears unlikely that Butler will have the cash available to make this repayment (especially given the cash outflow forecast for the three months to August 20X1), unless it is able to raise additional finance.

Net liabilities

Butler has negative equity and net liabilities of £225m. It has significant retained losses of £525m, and made a retained loss of £620m in the year ended 20X1.

These are both conditions specified by ISA (UK and Ireland) 570 *Going concern* as casting doubt over the going concern assumption.

Working capital

Butler is drawing heavily on its working capital to extend its cash operating cycle:

	Cashflow £m
Trade receivables (increase = £2,100 – £1,860)	(240)
Trade payables (increase = £2,500 – £1,800)	700
Total cash inflow	460

Butler has effectively raised £460m through taking more credit from its suppliers, and still has a negative cash balance.

Inventory

The value of inventory held at the year end increased by £500m (= £1,300 – £800). This represents an effective cash outflow, and may be a sign of weak revenue during the year. Some of this inventory may be obsolete and in need to writing down.

Fixed charge

Fixed charges exist over assets valued at £25 million. If Butler fails to make repayments to the creditor holding this charge, the assets could be seized, disrupting Butler's operations.

Development costs

Development costs of £120m have been capitalised. IAS 38 *Intangible assets* states that these costs can only be capitalised if the entity has the resources to complete the development. As this is arguably not the case here, the costs should be recognised as expenses.

Deferred tax asset

A deferred tax asset of £235m has been recognised. However, such an asset can only be recognised in accordance with IAS 12 *Income taxes* to the extent that the inflow of future economic benefits is probable. IAS 12 specifically states that the existence of unused tax losses, as here, is evidence that there will be no such inflow. The tax asset should not be recognised.

Provisions

Provisions of £185m have been classified as non-current liabilities. However, a portion of warranty payments are very likely to be due within the next year, so at least some of this amount should be within current liabilities.

Parent company

Butler is a subsidiary of a multi-national group, and it is possible that its parent company will support Butler even if it is not a going concern on its own. Were this the case, written representations would need to be obtained from the parent company, along with evidence that it is capable of supporting Butler.

However, the £150m loan expected to be received in July 20X1 is unlikely to be sufficient to ensure Butler's survival.

Cash flow forecast

Overall position

For the three months to August 20X1 Butler expects a cash outflow of £30m (= (£40m) + £65m + (£55m)). This means it is unlikely to be able to repay its short term borrowings in September. Had the forecast covered four months not three, it would probably have shown a significantly gloomier picture.

Cash from customers

The assumption that there will be an economic recovery and that this will lead to increased cash receipts is open to question. There may be little or no economic recovery, and cash receipts still may not improve in any case.

The commitment of extra resources to credit control is a wise move given the cash outflow in this area during 20X1, but any estimate of the improvement in cash receipts resulting from this is very uncertain.

Financial assets

£50m is expected to be received from selling financial assets, which is twice their carrying amount at the year end. This £50m is very optimistic, particularly if they have been measured at their fair value in the SOFP.

Loan from parent

The expected loan receipt of £150m is still being negotiated, and may not actually be agreed or received.

Government subsidy

The application for the government subsidy has not yet been approved, so there is significant doubt over whether this amount will be received.

Operating outflows

Operating cash outflows exceed inflows for all three months of the forecast. This is the underlying basis for the company's ability to continue as a going concern in the long term.

(ii)   Audit procedures for cash flow forecast

- Discuss with management the reasons for assuming that cash collection from customers will improve due to 'anticipated improvement in economic conditions'. Consider the validity of the reasons in light of business understanding.

- Enquire as to the nature of the additional resources to be devoted to the credit control function, eg details of extra staff recruited.

- For the loan receipt, inspect written documentation relating to the request for finance from Rubery Ltd. Request written confirmation from Rubery Ltd of the amount of finance and the date it will be received, as well as any terms and conditions.

- Obtain and review the financial statements of Rubery Ltd, to consider if it has sufficient resources to provide the amount of loan requested.

- For the subsidy, inspect the application made to the subsidy awarding body and confirm the amount of the subsidy.

- Read any correspondence between Butler Ltd and the subsidy awarding body, specifically looking for confirmation that the subsidy will be granted.

- Regarding operating expenses, verify using previous months' management accounts, that operating cash outflows are approximately £200 million per month.

- Enquire as to the reason for the increase in operating cash outflows in August 20X1.

- Verify, using previous months' management accounts, that interest payments of £40 million per month appear reasonable.

- Confirm, using the loan agreement, the amount of the loan being repaid in August 20X1.

- Enquire whether any tax payments are due in the three month period, such as sales tax.

- Agree the opening cash position to cash book and bank statement/bank reconciliation, and cast the cash flow forecast.

- Ensure that a cash flow forecast for the full financial year is received as three months' forecast is inadequate for the purposes of the audit.

Additional information needed

- Loan agreement from Rubery Ltd, showing the amount of the loan received, the date it will be received, the repayment schedule, and any terms and conditions

- Rubery Ltd's audited financial statements and auditor's report

- Copy of subsidy application made to awarding body

- Copy of confirmation that subsidy was awarded, including details of the amount receivable

- Management accounts for January to May 20X1

- Copies of tax returns and any correspondence with the tax authorities

- Accounting records, including cash books, bank statements and any reconciliations

Conclusion

Butler Ltd is experiencing significant difficulties generating the cash that it needs to continue as a going concern. Even if it does receive a loan from its parent company, significant doubts remain over whether the going concern assumption is appropriate in this case.

(b)　(i)　A company is placed in compulsory liquidation when a payable (creditor) petitions the court, and this petition is advertised in the *London Gazette*.

The petition can be made on various grounds, the most common of which is that the company is unable to pay its debts. In this case the payable (creditor) must show that s/he is owed more than £750, and that it has served a written demand for payment at the company's registered office. The petition is presented in court if the company fails to pay within 21 days, and does not dispute the debt.

The winding up order is granted when the court is satisfied that the debt is undisputed, attempts have been made to recover it, and the company has not paid it.

The court will appoint an Official Receiver, who must inform the company of the situation within a few days of the court granting the winding up order.

The Official Receiver takes control of the company and usually begins to close it down. The directors must prepare a Statement of Affairs detailing the reasons for the company's failure.

At the end of the winding down, a meeting is held with the payables (creditors), and a final return is filed with the court and the Registrar. At this point the company is dissolved.

(ii) **Payables (creditors)**

The company's realised net assets are distributed in an order prescribed by legislation. If a creditor's debt is secured, then they will be prioritised for payment out of the assets on which the debt is secured. Unsecured creditors are only paid once these payments have been made, and may not receive all of the amount owed to them.

Employees

Employees are dismissed automatically when the company is liquidated. A prescribed amount of unpaid wages, accrued holiday pay, and pension contributions will be paid as preferential debts, before unsecured creditors.

Shareholders

Any surplus remaining after unsecured creditors are paid will be distributed to shareholders. In many cases, the shareholders receive nothing.

38 Grohl

Chapter references. Chapters 2, 6, 9 and 10.

Top tips. This was a fairly standard P7 question on audit planning, and should have been within your capabilities. Part (a)(i) required you to evaluate business risks. Your approach here should be to read the scenario closely, noting the risks as they occur. There were plenty of risks there for your 12 marks.

Part (a)(ii) was on the risks of material misstatement. Four risks were needed for eight marks, so that's two marks per well-developed risk. One possible pitfall here might have been talking about risks to do with the auditors themselves (eg that the Board members leaving might make it difficult to obtain explanations), when these are **not** part of the 'risk of material misstatement'.

Part (a)(iii) covered ethics in the scenario. The parts of the scenario that were relevant here should have stood out, although you might have struggled to write eight marks' worth of material here. It is important, then, that you do not try to 'pad' your answer with irrelevant information, as this will not earn you marks. With a focused and systematic discussion, you should have been able to pass this part of the question.

Part (b) should not have been difficult. The issue was fairly clear-cut, and there were plenty of marks available for some relatively straightforward points. Most of the procedures are really common sense, and come straight from the scenario itself.

Easy marks. There were easy marks in part (b) for the matters to consider – the insurance claim was obviously implausible. Also in part (a) it is basic knowledge for ethics questions that a contingent fee is not appropriate for an audit engagement. Make sure you get some of the professional marks as well.

Marks

(a)   (i)   **Business risks**
Up to 2 marks for each business risk evaluated (up to a maximum of 3 marks in
total if risks identified but not evaluated):
–   Exchange rate risk
–   Imports – transportation costs and potential for disrupted supply
–   Reliance on one supplier
–   Quality control issues
–   High-tech/competitive industry
–   Reliance on key customer contracts
–   Regulatory issues
–   Liquidity/solvency issues
–   Poor profitability
–   Change in key management
Risk of material misstatement
Up to 2 marks for each risk of material misstatement identified and explained (up to
a maximum of 2 marks in total for identification only):
–   Initial translation of foreign exchange transactions
–   Retranslation and exchange gains and losses
–   Obsolete inventory
–   Refunds to customers
–   Capitalisation of borrowing costs to new production line
–   Impairment of old production line
–   Loan classification, measurement and disclosure
Maximum   20

(ii) **Ethical issues**
Generally 1 mark per comment:
–   Explain why familiarity threat arises
–   Explain why intimidation threat arises
–   Significant connections should be evaluated
–   If significant connections remain, firm should resign
–   If continue with audit, consider modifying audit approach and change audit team
–   Review any work recently performed on Grohl Ltd audit by Bob Halen
–   Consider firms policies and procedures
–   Contingent fee not acceptable
–   The basis for calculation of the audit fee must be agreed with client
Maximum   8
Professional marks:
Generally 1 mark for heading, 1 mark for introduction, 1 mark for use of headings
within the briefing notes, 1 mark for clarity of comments made
Maximum   4

(b)   **Insurance claim**
Generally 1 mark per matter/procedure:
Matters:
–   Accounting treatment for contingent asset
–   Claim may not be covered by insurance
–   Amount of the claim seems unreasonable
–   Materiality
–   Potential risk of material misstatement and impact on report
Procedures:
–   Inspect claim and supporting documentation
–   Inspect insurance terms and conditions

- Review correspondence
- Communicate with insurance provider
- Enquiry with lawyers

Maximum

Total

(a) **Briefing Notes**

For:	Mia Vai
By:	Audit manager
Date:	Dec 20X2
Subject:	Grohl Ltd audit planning

Introduction

These notes will: evaluate the business risks faced by Grohl Ltd; identify and explain four risks of material misstatement to be considered in audit planning; discuss relevant ethical issues and recommend actions to be taken by our firm.

(i) **Evaluation of business risks**

Overseas supplier

Copper wiring is a key production material, and is imported from overseas. There is therefore a risk of unstable supply as a result of it being transported over a long distance, across borders. Any of the following could pose problems:

- A rise in fuel prices could affect the cost of materials

- Political instability could lead to difficulties transporting across borders

- Goods may not be subject to the same regulatory standards as those in Grohl's own jurisdiction, and could be of poor quality

- Environmental disruption could affect eg shipping or aviation, and lead disruption of the supply of materials

If there were a stock-out of this key material then this would severely affect Grohl Ltd's production, and its ability to supply its customers. This could lead to a loss of revenue and of customer goodwill.

Exchange rate risk

Purchases are made in a foreign currency, and fluctuations are not hedged against. This leaves Grohl Ltd exposed to the risk of price rises, which could affect both its cash position and its short-term profitability. It may be advisable for the company to use forward contracts to help mitigate this risk.

Key supplier

Grohl Ltd is reliant on just one supplier for all its copper wiring. It is thus exposed to any risks resulting from problems with this supplier, eg price rises, problems with supply, quality control.

Grohl Ltd also moved all of its copper purchases to just one new supplier, before first using the supplier for a trial period. It was therefore highly exposed to any problems with the new supplier.

Competitive pressure

Grohl Ltd operates in a competitive industry and is subject to price competition from overseas. There is a risk that Grohl will be unable to keep its prices low enough to compete on this basis. It may need to consider alternative strategies.

The industry is dynamic and subject to rapid change, so in order to remain competitive Grohl Ltd must adapt quickly to any changes. It may not have sufficient resources to do this.

Quality control

Quality problems with the new copper supply have led to goods being returned by customers. This seems likely to be related to the use of a new, cheaper supplier. There is a risk of losing customers as a result of poor quality products, which may be particularly dangerous in this competitive market.

It may be necessary in future for Grohl Ltd to test the quality of copper purchased. This would incur costs, which would in turn put further pressure on Grohl Ltd's already tight operating margins.

New regulations

New regulations come into force after the year end. There is a risk that these may not be complied with, which could lead to significant penalties. These could be fines, or could result in suspending production.

New loan

The new £30m loan is significant at 1/6 (16.7%) of total assets. It is not known what proportion of net assets this constitutes. Annual interest on the loan is 4% × £30m = £1.2m, which is a significant amount in the context of a loss of £300,000 before tax and a cash balance of only £130,000.

The fact that Grohl Ltd has a £2.5m overdraft may be indicative of a cash shortage, a view that is borne out by low current and quick ratios. There is a risk that Grohl Ltd may not be a going concern for the next year.

Management change

The loss of several executive directors means that key business expertise has been lost, which might have been especially important given Grohl Ltd's current financial position.

Profitability

Draft revenue is down by £1.3m from 20X1, or 9.4%. Operating profit has fallen by £500,000, or 50%, and the operating margin has fallen from 7.2% to 4%, a fall of 46%.

Grohl Ltd has made a pre-tax loss of £300,000, although this does not appear to include the finance costs from the new loan (finance costs for 20X2 are the same as 20X1). If these were included, then the loss would be about £0.5m higher, at £0.8m. This is a large loss, and may again indicate going concern problems.

Risks of material misstatement

Foreign exchange

There is a risk of non-compliance with IAS 21 *The effects of changes in foreign exchange rates*. IAS 21 requires that non-monetary items are recognised at the historical rate, which is the rate at the date of the transaction. This would include income and expenses in the statement of profit or loss. There is a risk that non-monetary items are not recognised at the correct historical rate, leading to under- or over-statement of these items.

IAS 21 requires monetary items to be measured at the closing rate. Thus any foreign currency payables and receivables must be retranslated at the year end, with any exchange gain or loss being recognised in the statement of profit or loss. There is a risk that the wrong rate is used, or that items are translated using the wrong date. There is also a risk that on exchange gain or loss is recognised in relation to payables and receivables settled during the year.

Product recall

Grohl Ltd may be liable to customers in relation to faulty goods supplied. Although the issue appears to be resolved, it is possible that there may be further liabilities which should be recognised in line with IAS 37 *Provisions, contingent liabilities and contingent assets*. There is thus a risk that provisions are understated.

There is a risk that the accounting treatment of the product recall was incorrect. Any revenue recognised on recalled items should be cancelled against the corresponding receivables balance. The risk is therefore that revenue and receivables may be overstated.

New production line

The construction of the new production line is likely to result in new non-current assets which should be recognised in line with IAS 16 Property, plant and equipment. There is a risk that this has not been done correctly, leading to either under- or over-statement of assets.

The production line is likely to be a qualifying asset in line with IAS 23 Borrowing costs, so all directly attributable borrowing costs should be capitalised. It is not clear how much of the £0.5m finance cost from the new loan would be capitalised, as the loan appears to have been used only 'mainly' for the new production line.

Old production line – impairment

The new regulations coming into force after the year-end indicate that the existing production may be impaired. IAS 36 *Impairment of assets* requires management to conduct an impairment review. If this is not done adequately, then non-current assets and profit may be overstated.

(ii) **Ethical issues**

Audit manager joining client

An audit manager from Foo & Co may leave to become a financial controller at Grohl Ltd. According to the IESBA *Code of Ethics*, this could create familiarity and intimidation threats.

The audit team may be so familiar with Bob Halen that they lose independence, for example they may not challenge him if this is necessary. They may fail to exercise enough professional skepticism. Bob is also likely to be familiar with Foo & Co's audit methodology, so would be well placed to think of ways of hiding things from the audit team if he were so inclined.

The IESBA *Code* states that if a 'significant connection' remains between the firm and the individual who joined the client, then no safeguard could mitigate the threat and the firm should withdraw from the engagement. This would be the case if:

- Bob is entitled to benefits or payments from Foo & Co, unless in line with fixed pre-determined arrangements
- Bob is owed an amount by the firm that is material to the firm
- Bob continues to participate in the firm's business or professional activities

Alternatively, if there is no significant connection then safeguards may be necessary. The threat here is significant, as Bob was in charge of the Grohl Ltd audit only very recently, and would have maintained contact with Grohl Ltd's management.

Safeguards might include reviewing any work that Bob has done on the audit, although there is not likely to be much of this as planning is only just starting.

Contingent fee audit

The IESBA *Code* clearly states that an audit firm may not enter into a contingent fee arrangement, as the self-interest threat would be too great for safeguards to reduce the threat to an acceptable level.

Conclusion

Grohl Ltd is facing some significant business risks, which may affect the going concern assertion. There are a number of significant risks of material misstatement in relation to which the audit plan should design procedures to obtain sufficient appropriate audit evidence. The ethical issue with Bob Halen requires that safeguards be put in place, and it should be communicated to Grohl Ltd's Board that the audit cannot be performed on a contingent fee basis.

(b) **Matters to consider**

At £5m, the claim represents 40% of draft revenue, and would turn a loss of £0.3m into a profit of £4.7. It is therefore highly material.

This is a contingent asset. IAS 37 requires that contingent assets are not recognised, unless it is virtually certain that the inflow of economic benefits will take place.

At the moment, it is not certain that the claim will even be paid, even if is more likely to be paid than not. Whether or not it is paid will depend on the specific terms of the insurance policy, which would need to be considered in detail and light of any communications with the insurer and/or Grohl Ltd's legal counsel.

Regarding the value of the claim, production was halted for just one week so 40% of annual revenue is far too high. It is very unlikely that this amount will be received.

Procedures

- Obtain a copy of the insurance claim made and confirm that £5 million is claimed.

- Enquire into the basis of the £5 million claimed, and review any supporting documentation such as extracts of management accounts showing lost revenue for the period of halted production.

- Inspect the terms of the insurance policy, to determine whether production halted in these specific circumstances would be covered.

- Seek Grohl Ltd's permission to contact the insurer, to ask about the status of the claim, and request written confirmation of any payment that may be made.

- Review correspondence between Grohl Ltd and the insurance provider, looking for confirmation of any amounts to be paid.

39 Champers

Text references. Chapters 6, 9 and 10.

Top Tips. In part (a)(i), there is a ½ mark available for just mentioning ('identifying') each aspect that needs to be considered, so try to get lots of these (you only need to recall information from the study text) – but don't go overboard, as the number of marks available for identification alone is likely to be capped. Then try to explain as many of them as you can within the time allocated to this part of the question. In part (a)(ii), try to explain at least three procedures within the time available (although of course, if you do have more time, say more!).

Part (b) is a standard question on business risks, and you should be scoring well on this part. Remember that you need to say enough about each risk (without waffling) to get the marks – don't just produce a list. There are 13 marks available here, so you should be looking to get at least 8–10 of them on a requirement like this. Finally, be careful not to exceed the time allotted to this part of the question if you find you have lots to write. Part (c)(i) is for five marks, so you should seek to describe at least three **principle** audit procedures to pass the question. Part (c)(ii) is more difficult, so you should seek to get at least 2–3 marks on this part, making sure that your answer is properly focused on the requirement.

Easy marks. Make sure you get the four professional marks in part (a) for: use of format, having a clear introduction and conclusion, and using appropriate language for an audit junior.

Examiner's comments. Some candidates performed well overall, especially those who spent an appropriate amount of time on each of the question requirements. In part (a), few candidates recognised the need to understand the internal control environment, and fewer still mentioned the importance of understanding the relevant financial reporting framework and performance measures of the client. Candidates tended not to gain the professional mark available for the clarity of their answer, because explanations were often confused, repetitive, or non-existent. Candidates also need to bear in mind that professional marks are awarded partly for the quality of language used.

Common weaknesses is part (b) included: failure to use the financial information provided to identify risks; focussing on risks of material misstatement, which was **not** a requirement of the question; trying to link every risk identified to a going concern risk.

For part (c)(i), few candidates could suggest anything other than 'check the relevant invoices' or 'check the amount was approved'. Most candidates in part (c)(ii) failed to read the requirement, and the scenario, both of which stated that the advertising costs had been expensed. Most discussed the merits of recognising the amount as an intangible asset, which as well as being completely irrelevant is also technically incorrect.

Marks

(a) (i) **Identify and explain aspects of understanding business and environment**
Generally ½ mark for identification and 1 mark for explanation:
- External factors
- Entity and accounting policies
- Objectives, strategies and business risks
- Performance measures
- Internal control
Maximum 6

(ii) **Recommend procedures to gain understanding**
Generally 1 mark per procedure described:
- Inquiry
- Analytical procedure
- Observation
- Inspection
Maximum 4

(b) **Business risk**
Generally ½ mark for identification, 1 further mark for explanation, from ideas list.
1 mark to be given for each appropriate calculation eg trends, materiality
- Risk of damage to brand name/bad publicity re injury to child and closed restaurant
- Investment needed in play areas to prevent health and safety problems
- Damage to the Happy Monkeys brand name may cross to other brand names
- Compliance risk re health and safety regulations – food preparation
- Fall in revenue from Quick-bite business segment
- The above linked to reduced demand for fast food/more emphasis on healthy eating
- Advertising ban could reduce revenue
- Rapid expansion plans for City Sizzler chain – danger of overtrading
- Potential lack of cash for the capital expenditure and on-going refurbishment costs
- Potential lack of cash for continued advertising
- Green George chain – need to monitor supply chain
- PBT fallen 13% – poor cost control?
- Minimum wage legislation will increase operating costs significantly next year
- Cash position worsened during year
- Cash based business – risk of fraud
- Internal structure may need addressing
Maximum 13

(c) (i) **Audit procedures on amounts capitalised**
Generally 1 mark per specific audit procedure
Ideas list:
- Agree sample of costs to invoice/tender documents
- Review capex budget and discuss variances actual v budget
- Agree interest rate of finance cost to terms of finance
- Agree period of capitalisation correct by reference to date of completion of restaurants
- Review list of items capitalised to ensure all capital in nature
Maximum 5

(c)   (ii)   **Audit work for advertising expense**

Generally 1 mark per specific audit procedure

Ideas list:

-   Agree sample of costs to invoices/reports from consultants
-   Analytical review
-   Discuss with relevant personnel/review of business plan
-   Inspect budgets
-   Physically inspect the advertising
-   After-date invoice review
-   Assess date advertising conducted

Maximum   4

Note. Professional marks to be awarded for format, use of introduction and

conclusion, use of language that an audit junior could understand.   4

Total   **36**

(a)   ISA (UK & Ireland) 315 *Identifying and assessing the risks of material misstatement through understanding the entity and its environment* identifies the main aspects of a client's business that must be considered in gaining an understanding of the company and its environment. This process is crucial to an auditor's assessment of the audit risks which it then seeks to reduce to an appropriate level during the audit.

(i)   **Aspects to be considered**

- **Industry, regulatory and other external factors**. For instance, some industries require businesses to carry specific levels of capital (such as 'bonded' travel agents). An auditor would need to gain knowledge of these regulations to assess their impact on the audit. This could also affect audit planning. If a client operates in an industry with unusual accounting treatments (construction or insurance, for example), it would be wise to choose an audit team with experience of that industry.

- **Nature of the entity**. An auditor must understand the legal structure of the entity (company or group). Complex ownership structures might increase the risk of misstatement – for instance if subsidiaries' results are not consolidated correctly.

- **Selection, application and reasons for changes of accounting policies**. An auditor must understand the entity's accounting policies together with the reasons for them being selected. This would include consideration of whether or not they are in line with the applicable financial reporting framework.

- **Objectives, strategies and related business risks**. Business risks are the risks that the company may not achieve its objectives. The main way this affects audit risk is that if there is a high risk of the company failing to meet its objectives (or if it adopts a risky strategy to try to meet them), there is a risk that the company may not be a going concern. Any financial statements prepared on the going concern basis would then be likely to be misstated.

- **Measurement and review of the entity's financial performance**. The auditor should understand how the entity's performance is assessed, because management could seek to manipulate the results so that it looks like the company is doing better than it is. This might trigger bonus payments, for example.

- **Internal control**. This is an absolutely crucial area in assessing audit risk, as the auditor may seek to place reliance on the entity's internal controls. The assessment of control risk would have a direct effect on audit strategy. This would include assessing the entity's control environment.

(ii)   **Procedures recommended**

- **Inquiries of management**. This would usually be the first place to start – management should be the best people to give the auditor information on the aspects of the company and its environment referred to in ISA (UK & Ireland) 315. The auditor could also consult others, such as an internal audit department.

- **Analytical procedures**. It is crucial to perform analytical procedures to gain an understanding of the major areas of the financial statements, as well as the dominant trends and anomalies. This will allow the auditor to assess the areas where there is a higher risk of material misstatement.

- **Observation**. Observing internal control activities, for instance, could help to cement the auditor's understanding of how they operate.

- **Inspection**. Documents such as business plans or internal control manuals may contain valuable information on how the entity operates. Inspecting these would supplement the inquiries already made of management.

(b)   **Briefing notes**

To: Champers audit team
From: Geoff Forest
Subject: Champers Ltd business risks

Introduction

These notes evaluate the business risks currently faced by Champers Ltd.

Happy Monkeys children's crèches

A child was slightly injured during the year in an incident at one of the crèches. The media criticism that was received could lead to significant damage of the Happy Monkeys brand, particularly given that the family-friendly orientation of the restaurants appears to be an important selling point. Although revenues from this segment rose 21% compared with 20X8 ((800 – 660) / 660 = 21%), this negative publicity probably did result in some lost revenue.

It is possible that regulatory bodies could take action as a result of this incident, with the potentially disastrous consequence of the crèches or even the whole restaurants being shut down.

If it wants to protect the Happy Monkeys brand, Champers will probably need to spend money to improve the standard of child care offered in the crèches. It would be difficult for it to do this given its falling cash balance (£116m in 20X9; £350m in 20X8). It would therefore have to divert funds away from other projects, such as the expansion of the City Sizzler grills.

Revenue derived from Happy Monkeys restaurants makes up 53% of total revenue (= 800 / 1500), so any damage to this revenue stream could have a significant effect Champers as a whole.

Happy Monkeys – health and safety

One restaurant was actually closed during the year as a result of significant breaches in kitchen hygiene standards. Health and safety authorities often have significant powers, and it is crucial that Champers' restaurants comply with them. Moreover, this could cause significant damage to the Happy Monkeys brand, and even to the other brands that Champers owns by way of association with it. If this was to happen revenues could drop sharply, which would clearly affect Champers' ability to meet its objective of maximising market share.

The effect of damage to the Happy Monkeys brand on Champers as a whole could be very significant indeed, owing to the fact that it makes up 53% of Champers' total revenue in 20X9.

Quick-bite chain

Marketing campaign

A significant marketing campaign was launched to support the Quick-bite brand, costing £150m in 20X9. This represents 10% of Champers' total revenue for the year, and is a significant expense. Indeed, this

outlay may have been partly responsible for the decrease in cash during the year, and because of Champers' poor cash position this level of spending is unlikely to be sustainable in the future.

Falling revenue

Revenue from this segment fell by 6% in 20X9. The fact that this happened even though £150m was spent on advertising during the year is a worrying sign, and may be indicative of a significant reduction in demand. This is borne out by the pressure exerted by government for the restaurants to provide nutritional information in its menus, which the company rightly responded to. It is possible that this highly competitive industry is experiencing falling demand as a result of increased public awareness of the importance of eating healthily. This would appear to cast significant doubt over the wisdom of the company having spent such a large amount on advertising during the year.

New advertising regulations

50% of Quick-bite's revenue derives from 'chuckle boxes' sold to children. These sales are likely to be affected by the new advertising regulations coming into force from September 20X9. Champers will have to consider how it is going to tackle this problem going forward.

City Sizzler grills

Expansion plans

Champers is planning to double the number of City Sizzler grills from 250 to 500 by the end of the current financial year. Given that the restaurants operate in the higher quality end of the market, this is likely to require significant expenditure to acquire new prime locations and to refurbish the locations acquired.

It is possible that Champers may not be able to afford this level of investment in the next year, owing to its already declining cash balance. There is a risk that it will begin to expand the chain, but then run out of cash once it has started.

There is a possibility that Champers will have to raise new funds in order to finance the expansion. Given the scale of its plans, it may struggle to raise the necessary funds. If it takes on new debt, this would expose the company to increased liquidity risk if it cannot make the required repayments.

Refurbishment costs

Champers plans to refurbish each City Sizzler grill every two years. This is likely to represent a significant and ongoing drain on Champers' cash resources, and there is a risk that Champers will not be able to afford it. Champers should therefore consider whether it can reduce the outlay in some way, perhaps by extending the amount of time between refurbishments from two to three years.

Green George cafes

Champers plans to double the number of cafes within the next 12 months. This would probably be costly, and again there is a question mark over its affordability to Champers. The combination of the plans to expand the Green George cafes and the City Sizzler grills, as well as a potential fall in revenue from the Quick-bite outlets as a result of increased regulatory pressure, represents a significant risk to the future success of Champers as a whole.

This risk is exacerbated by the fact that Champers financed the expansion in the Green George cafes by taking on debt, which may pose a threat to the company's liquidity if Champers fails to keep up with the necessary repayments.

Falling cash balance

Champers' cash balance fell by £234m from £350m at 31 May 20X8 to £116m at 31 May 20X9, a fall of 69%. At this rate it will run out of money approximately 180 days into the year (116 / 234 × 365). It is vital to Champers' ongoing survival that this trend is stemmed.

Falling profits

Champers' profit after tax fell by 13% from £155m in 20X8 to £135m in 20X9. This may be a result of some one-off expenses, such as the £150m advertising expenses in respect of the Quick-bite chain, or any expenses related to the investment in the City Sizzler grills and the Green George cafes. However, it is crucial that Champers' management considers its cost-control procedures in the future. This is particularly pertinent in view of the impending 15% increase in the minimum wage, which will significantly increase Champers' costs, as it will affect a third of employees in the labour-intensive restaurant industry.

Conclusion

The business risks currently faced by Champers are not insignificant, and there is even a risk that it may not survive the next financial year if its inability to generate sufficient cash inflows is not countered.

(c)   (i)   **Agree costs to invoice**

The audit team should agree a sample of costs capitalised to supporting documents. Labour costs should be agreed to payroll records and timesheets. Materials costs should be agreed to supplier purchase invoices. Costs relating to site acquisitions should be agreed to legal papers, such as completion statements.

Agree finance costs to contracts

Interest rates should be agreed to original finance agreements, and the interest charge for the period should be recalculated. If the rates are derived from an underlying figure (such as a central bank base rate), the rates applied should be agreed.

Agree cut-off for finance costs

Per IAS 23 *Borrowing costs*, capitalisation must cease when the related asset is ready for use, so the date on which this was the case should be agreed to underlying operational documentation, eg surveyor's reports.

Agree classification between revenue and capital expenditure

A sample of costs capitalised should be agreed to underlying documentation (such as purchase invoices) and the classification agreed. There is a risk that eg staff training costs could have been capitalised.

Compare actual vs. budget

Compare actual with budgeted capital expenditure, and discuss any significant variances with the appropriate employee (eg the manager for that budget area). If necessary carry out substantive testing in order to verify the actual amounts where there are significant variances.

(ii)   **Analytical procedures**

Compare the current year expense with the prior year, discussing any significant variances with an appropriate employee (eg a marketing manager) and performing substantive procedures if necessary.

Compare actual expenditure with budgeted expenditure, discussing with an employee and performing further procedures if required.

Agree sample of costs to underlying documentation

Costs should be agreed to purchase invoices or other supporting documentation, and then to the actual advert itself, which may exist in archive form for eg newspaper adverts. If judged necessary, costs could be traced to purchase orders and then to budgets, making enquiries of management in relation to any costs not budgeted for.

Cut-off testing

Review after-date advertising invoices and ensure that those relating to the 20X9 financial year are accrued for.

Review the dates on which advertising actually took place and verify that adverts taking place after the year end are accounted for correctly as prepayments.

Understanding of the business

Discuss the nature of the advertising expenditure with an appropriate employee, in order to form an expectation of the expense likely to be incurred and to design specific testing procedures.

40 Grissom

Marks

(a) **Evaluation of audit risks and other matters to be considered**

½ mark for identification (to a maximum of 5 marks) and up to 1½ further marks for evaluation and ½ mark for correct reference to relevant IAS/IFRS (max 1 mark)
- Classification of non-controlling interests (IAS 28)
- Auditors lack knowledge of activities of non-controlling interests
- Bonus and potential earnings management
- Change of accounting estimates (IAS 8)
- Lack of group finance director
- Capitalisation of dismantling costs (IAS 16)
- Provision – discounting and finance charge (IAS 37)
- Deferral of grant income (IAS 20)
- Potential provision or contingent liability (IAS 37)
- Mid-year acquisition
- Goodwill on acquisition – subjective (IFRS 3)
- Retranslation of Brass Co financial statements (IAS 21)
- Retranslation of goodwill
- Adjustments necessary to bring in line with group accounting policies
- Intra-group transactions

Maximum   18

Professional marks for presentation of answer, clarity of explanations   4

(b) **Matters to be considered and procedures – reliance on component auditor**

1 mark per comment on matters/procedure
- Ethics
- Competence/qualifications
- Skills/resources
- Quality control
- Monitoring activities
- ½ mark for ref to ISA (UK & Ireland) 600

Maximum   8

(c) (i) **Principal audit procedures for non-controlling interests**

Generally 1 mark per procedure
- Confirm % shareholding acquired
- Confirm if Grissom Co appointed any board members
- Consider relationship with other shareholders
- Discussion of involvement
- Written representation re involvement

Maximum   4

(ii) **Principal audit procedures for condition attached to grant**

Generally 1 mark per procedure
- Confirm 25% to terms of grant
- Ascertain from grant document:
- The period required to demonstrate reduction
- The amount that would be repaid if condition breached
- Review results of monitoring performed

Maximum   4

Total   38

(a)   **Briefing notes**

To: Audit team
Re: Grissom Ltd audit risks June 20Y0

Introduction

These notes consider the principal audit risks to be considered in planning the audit of the Grissom Group financial statements for June 20Y0.

Grissom Ltd

Non-controlling interests

There is an inherent risk that these investments have been classified incorrectly as associates.
IAS 28 *Investments in associates and joint ventures* requires Grissom to have significant influence over the investee. If this is not the case, the investments should be treated as trade investments. Alternatively they may be joint arrangements if control is shared jointly with one or more other entities.

These two investments are in areas quite different from the group's core activity. There is thus a risk that the group's finance team may not have applied appropriate accounting policies – eg deferring revenue for the travel agent – resulting in misstatement of the group accounts.

Bonuses and accounting estimates

The existence of profit-based bonuses for directors represents an inherent risk of manipulation, with income and profit being overstated, and expenses being understated.

The fact that the group finance director left after a disagreement over accounting estimates may indicate that senior management have indeed attempted to manipulate the financial statements. It is crucial that professional scepticism is exercised in this area. There is a risk that IAS 8 *Accounting Policies, Changes in Accounting Estimates and Errors* has not been adhered to, for instance if change in accounting policy has been mistaken for a change in accounting estimate.

Group finance director resigned

There is a risk that the financial statements, and in particular the consolidation, have not been properly prepared in the absence of a finance director overseeing the preparation process.

Moreover, the audit team may find it difficult to obtain appropriate explanations from management if there is no finance director, or if a new one is appointed who is not responsible for the accounts being audited.

Willow Ltd

New factory

The relocation to a new, very large factory may represent an increase in Willow's operational gearing, which may create a business risk to going concern if cash flow problems result. These could be exacerbated by any teething problems resulting from the new factory.

Dismantling costs

IAS 16 *Property, Plant and Equipment* requires the dismantling costs to be capitalised as non-current assets, and a provision created against them. Account should be taken of the effect of discounting if this is material, and a finance charge included in the statement of profit or loss to represent the unwinding of the discount. The risk is that the provision has not been created, and that assets and liabilities are therefore understated, and that the depreciation expense is understated, which would result in profit being overstated. There is also a risk that the provision has not been measured correctly in accordance with IAS 37 *Provisions, Contingent Liabilities and Contingent Assets*, eg in respect of the effect of discounting.

Hodges Ltd

Government grant

IAS 20 *Accounting for Government Grants and Disclosure of Government Assistance* requires that the grant income is matched to the costs it is intended to compensate for. This will result in deferred revenue being held on the statement of financial position. There is a risk that this has not done, leading to liabilities being understated and profit being overstated.

IAS 20 also requires that a grant is recognised only when there is reasonable assurance that Hodges will meet the condition specified by the government. Where there is doubt over this, a provision should be recognised in line with IAS 37. The risk is that this has not been done, and that liabilities are understated and profits overstated.

Brass Co

Consolidation

The subsidiary was acquired mid-year, and there is a risk that its results have not been consolidated from the correct date. If they are included from too early a date and the company is profitable, then group profits may be overstated.

The acquisition should be accounted for in line with IFRS 3 *Business combinations*. There is a risk that goodwill has not been calculated correctly, and that the fair values of Brass Co's assets and liabilities have not be estimated reliably.

Accounting standards

Brass Co's accounts must be restated so that they are in line with the group's accounting policies, which should conform to IFRS. This is a risky process, particularly in the absence of a group finance director, and there is a risk that Brass Co's accounts may not be in line with IFRSs.

Intra-group trading

Brass Co supplies about half of Willow Ltd's ingredients. There are therefore a significant number of intra-group transactions which need to be eliminated from the group accounts. There may also be inventories containing unrealised profit, which needs to be provided for. The risk is that this has not been done, potentially overstating revenues, expenses, assets and liabilities.

Conclusion

There are a number of risks which must be addressed during the planning of the audit of the Grissom Group financial statements for June 20Y0.

(b) **Factors to consider**

Guidance is provided in ISA (UK & Ireland) 600 *Special Considerations – Audits of Group Financial Statements (Including the Work of Component Auditors)*. Brass Co is a significant component of the group, and Sidle & Co are component auditors. As group auditors we should obtain an understanding of the component auditor, focusing on:

- Whether Sidle & Co complies with ethical requirements
- Sidle & Co's professional competence
- Whether the group audit team will be able to be sufficiently involved in the component auditor's work
- Whether Sidle & Co works in a regulated environment

Ethics

Sidle & Co should, per ISA (UK & Ireland) 600, be subject to the same ethical requirements as the group auditor, irrespective of regulations applicable in Chocland. These are contained in the IESBA's *Code of Ethics for Professional Accountants*, the ACCA's *Code of Ethics and Conduct* and the FRC's *Ethical Standards*.

Professional competence

As group auditor, Vegas & Co should check that Sidle & Co:

- Understand ISAs. Chocland audit regulations are not based on ISAs, so Vegas & Co must ensure that the work performed by Sidle & Co conforms to the requirements of ISAs.

- Have sufficient resources and skills to perform the necessary work. Various complex accounting issues will be involved in preparing the group accounts, such as the measurement of fair values on consolidation. The group auditor must assess whether Sidle & Co has the resources and skills to do this.

- Understand IFRSs. Chocland has not adopted IFRSs, and there is a risk that Sidle & Co is not competent to audit Brass Co's accounts after they have been adjusted to comply with IFRSs.

Procedures to perform

- Obtaining and reviewing the ethical code adhered to by Sidle & Co, and comparing it to those followed by Vegas & Co

- Obtaining a statement from Sidle & Co that it has adhered to this code

- Establishing through discussion or questionnaire whether Sidle & Co is a member of an auditing regulatory body, and the professional qualifications issued by that body

- Obtaining confirmations from the professional body Sidle & Co belong to, or the authorities licensing it

- Determining through discussion whether Sidle & Co is a member of a network of audit firms

- Discussion of the audit methodology used by Sidle & Co in the audit of Brass Co, and compare it with those used under ISAs (eg how the risk of material misstatement is assessed)

- A questionnaire or checklist could be used to provide a summary of audit procedures used

- Ascertaining the quality control policies and procedures used by Sidle & Co, both firm-wide and those applied to individual audit engagements

- Requesting any results of monitoring or inspection visits conducted by the regulatory authority under which Sidle & Co operates

- Communicating to Sidle & Co an understanding of the assurances that our firm will expect to receive, to avoid any subsequent misunderstandings

(c) (i)
- Determine the percentage shareholding acquired, using purchase documentation.

- Confirm that the percentage shareholding is between 20 and 50% of equity shares.

- Obtain a list of directors (eg using published financial statements) for the companies to confirm whether Grissom Ltd has appointed director(s) to the boards.

- Discuss with the directors of Grissom Ltd their level of involvement in policy decisions made at the companies.

- Obtain a written representation detailing the nature of involvement and influence exerted over the companies (eg a letter from the investee's board of directors confirming the voting power of Grissom Ltd).

- Consider the identity of the other shareholders and the relationship between them and Grissom Ltd. This may reveal that the situation is in substance a joint venture and would need to be accounted for as such.

(ii)
- Obtain the grant document and review the terms to verify that 25% reduction is specified.

- Determine over what period the 25% reduction must be demonstrated.

- Review the terms to establish the financial repercussions of breaching the condition – would the grant be repayable in full or in part, and when would repayment be made.

- Obtain documentation from management showing the monitoring procedures that have been put in place regarding energy use.

- Review the results and adequacy of any monitoring that has taken place before the year end to see if the condition has been breached (eg compare electricity meter readings pre and post installation of the packing line, to confirm reduced levels of electricity are being used).

- Discuss energy efficiency of the packing lines with an appropriate employee to obtain their views on how well the assets are performing.

41 Jacob

Text references. Chapter 12.

Top tips. Part (a) was of around average difficulty. You should have been able to pass this part of the question by making sure that you only provide three benefits, and explaining each of them well.

Part (b) should have been simpler than part (a). It was important here that you didn't go over your time limit, but that you wrote enough (in terms of quality, not quantity!) to gain marks for each thing you say. The key to actually getting marks is to be specific about what information you are asking for, and making sure that everything you say is relevant to the scenario. It is a waste of time asking for information that is relevant to due diligence in general, but not to Locke Ltd in particular. Also, it is no good just stating what information you need, you have to make sure that you say why you need it.

Easy marks. There were plenty of easy marks in part (b), for example, saying that more information needs to be obtained regarding the court case against Locke Ltd.

Examiner's comments. This was the second most popular of the optional questions, and focussed on due diligence. Requirement (a), for six marks, required an explanation of three benefits of an externally provided due diligence review to the audit client. This was reasonably well answered, though many answers were not made very specific to the scenario and tended to discuss the benefits of any due diligence review rather than an externally provided one.

Requirement (b), for 12 marks asked for additional information to be made available for the firm's due diligence review. Answers were satisfactory, and the majority of candidates did not struggle to apply their knowledge to the scenario, usually providing some very focussed answers dealing well with the specifics of the question scenario.

Marking scheme

Marks

(a) **Benefits of due diligence**

Up to 2 marks for each benefit explained (only three benefits required):
- Identify and value assets and liabilities to be acquired
- Identify and allow planning for operational issues
- Provision by external experts – technically competent and time efficient
- Assessment of potential impact of court case
- Evaluation of the liquidity position of Locke Co
- Enhanced credibility provided by an independent review

Maximum   6

(b) **Information required**

Generally ½ mark for identification and up to 1 further mark for explanation
(maximum 3 marks for identification):

–   Service contracts of directors
–   Organisational structure
–   Lease/arrangement regarding head office
–   Details of land purchased
–   Planning permission for new head office
–   Prior year accounts and management accounts
–   Forecasts and budgets
–   Loan agreement
–   Overdraft facility details
–   Legal correspondence
–   Customer satisfaction surveys
–   Details of warranty agreements
–   Outsourcing agreement

Maximum   12

Total   18

(a)   One benefit of due diligence here is that it will help in assigning a valuation to Locke Ltd. The review would seek to identify all of Locke Ltd's potential assets and liabilities and provide a value for them. This valuation may include amounts not included within the financial statements, for example any contingent assets or liabilities that are not required to be recognised or disclosed by IAS 37. Armed with this valuation, management would be in a better position to negotiate a price for the business.

A second benefit is that the review should obtain further information about the company's operations. For example, it may be able to obtain further information about the extent of Locke Ltd's possible liability relating to its court case. It may also be able to provide an indication of the extent to which Locke Ltd's reputation may be tarnished by the court case.

A third benefit is that since the due diligence review is prepared externally, the directors' time is freed up to concentrate on operational matters. The review will be prepared time-efficiently, and the independence of the firm providing the review helps contribute to the good governance of Jacob Ltd.

Tutorial note. The answer above includes three benefits (as required). Credit will be awarded for explanation of any three benefits which are specific to the scenario.

(b)   Further information should include:

Employment contracts

Contracts for directors and other key personnel should be obtained. It may be that Jacob will seek to terminate the employment of directors after the acquisition. The contracts should be inspected for any amounts payable on termination.

Organisational structure

It may be that Jacob will want to keep hold of key personnel. In order to identify them, an organisational structure should be obtained.

Lease agreements re: building

Jacob may wish to relocate away from the building owned by the family estate, in which case the signed lease agreements should be inspected for any penalty clauses for early termination.

New head office – purchase documentation

Documents relating to the land purchase should be obtained to ascertain its value should Jacob wish to sell it, or to see whether it might be put to an alternative use. Alternatively, it may be possible for the land not to be included in the acquisition.

Details should be obtained of any other commitments made in relation to the new head office. For example, construction contracts may have been entered into; these should be obtained, along with details of any possible penalties for termination.

Audited financial statements

Audited financial statements should be obtained in order to verify that Locke has indeed grown rapidly in the last three years.

These will also provide information helpful for the valuation of assets, the existence of contingent liabilities, etc.

Finally, they will allow an assessment to be made of Locke's liquidity, which may be particularly important in view of its use of an overdraft facility during the winter months.

Management accounts and forecasts

These should be obtained for future periods in order to assess Locke's possible future profitability.

Asset valuations

Any significant non-current assets should be assessed for their market value, if they are held in the accounts at historical cost.

Signed bank loan agreement

This should be obtained in order to ascertain the repayment terms, the interest rate, as well as any charges security over the company and/or its assets.

The amount of the loan may be significant, as purchasing a company with high financial gearing may affect Jacob's own exposure to risk.

Overdraft details

Details such as the maximum facility available to Locke, the interest rate, and when it is due for renewal.

It is possible that Locke may be a significant drain on Jacob's cash resources during the winter months, so Jacob will need to assess its own ability to take on such a possible commitment.

Information from legal counsel

This should be obtained regarding the court case with the famous actor. This should ascertain the extent of Locke's probably liability, along with the timescale for the case.

Information on bad publicity

The bad publicity from the legal case may affect Locke's ability to generate revenue in future, so information about the extent of the possible brand damage should be sought.

Information on Locke's 'good reputation'

This claim should be substantiated as far as possible, for example by reference to industry journals, customer satisfaction surveys, levels of customer complaints, etc.

Contract with Austin Ltd

This should be examined in order to understand exactly what services Austin provides, and what the cost of these services is. Jacob may wish to bring some of these activities back in-house.

42 Cusiter

Marking scheme

			Marks
(a)	**PFI**		
	Generally 1 mark each point of explanation	Maximum	3
	Ideas		

- – Definition
- – Forecast *vs*
- – Projection

(b) **Matters to be considered**

Generally ½ mark each relevant matter identified + up to 1 mark for explanation   Maximum   7

Ideas

- – Purpose of PFI – external vs internal use
- – Report/level of assurance required – 'negative'
- – Nature of engagement = examination to obtain evidence
- – Examination = inquiry + analytical procedures
- – Period covered
- – Management's previous experience, if any, preparing PFI
- – Basis of preparation of forecast
- – Any standards/guidelines followed
- – Time and fee budget

		Marks

(c) **Examination procedures**

Generally 1 mark each point contributing to a description of procedures   Maximum   9

Ideas

- –   Procedure ideas
- –   General (to both forecast statement of financial position and statement of profit or loss)
- –   Specific (to forecast statement of financial position or statement of profit or loss)
- –   Arithmetic accuracy
- –   Tenders for new equipment
- –   Assumptions, bases, etc (eg useful lives)
- –   Analytical procedures (eg inventory turnover, average collection period)
- –   vouching to available historic financial information

(d) **Professional accountant's liability**

Generally 1 mark each point contributing to a discussion of liability/measure to reduce   Maximum   6

Ideas

- –   How liability arises
- –   To whom liable

Measures to reduce

- –   Disclose assumptions
- –   Caveats
- –   Warnings
- –   Disclaimers
- –   Reporting
- –   Wording
- –   Terms of engagement
- –   Liability cap
- –   Indemnity

Professional marks   4

Total   **29**

MEMORANDUM

To: Douglas Groan

From: Trevor Ennui

Re: Cusiter Ltd – prospective financial information

This memorandum explains the term 'prospective financial information' (PFI); explains the matters to consider when planning the review of Cusiter Ltd's PFI; describes the procedures that should be used to verify Cusiter Ltd's PFI; and discusses the professional accountant's liability for reporting on prospective financial information and the measures that the professional accountant might take to reduce that liability.

(a) **Prospective financial information**

Prospective financial information relates to information that is based on assumptions about events that may occur in the future and possible actions by an entity. It is therefore highly subjective. Prospective financial information can be of two types: forecasts and projections.

Forecasts consist of prospective financial information based on assumptions as to future events which management expects to take place and the actions management expects to take (best-estimate projections).

Projections are prospective financial information based on hypothetical assumptions about future events and management actions, or a mixture of best-estimate and hypothetical assumptions.

Prospective financial information can include financial statements or one or more elements of financial statements and may be prepared as an internal management tool, for example, to assist in evaluating a possible capital investment or for distribution to third parties, for example, in a prospectus (to provide potential investors with information about future expectations) or in an annual report (to provide information for shareholders) or in a document for the information of lenders which may include cash flow forecasts.

(b) **Matters to consider in planning nature and scope of examination of Cusiter's forecast statement of financial position and statement of profit or loss**

Basis of preparation

The firm must consider how the information has been produced – it may be based on historic financial information which has been adjusted appropriately or it may include new information and assumptions about future performance.

Use of the prospective financial information

The information has been produced in order to support a loan application to the bank and therefore is only for the use of the bank. It will not be published and available for other users.

Assurance provided

A review of prospective financial information will provide only negative assurance as the information is very subjective and based on assumptions about future performance. The opinion will be based on whether the information has been properly prepared on the basis of the assumptions and whether it has been presented in accordance with the relevant financial reporting framework.

Nature of the review

The nature of the review of the prospective financial information will involve the use of analytical procedures, inquiry and corroboration from management.

Preparation of the prospective financial information

The firm will need to consider who prepared the information and any prior experience in preparing prospective financial information.

Evidence

For the forecast for the year ended 31 December 20X8, the firm should be able to find actual evidence for the first three months as this forecast includes some historical financial information.

(c) **Examination procedures to verify the prospective financial information**

A review of prospective financial information uses inquiry, analytical review and corroboration from management. The following procedures should therefore be carried out as part of the review.

The information should be recast and all the sub-totals and totals agreed.

The accuracy of the comparative information should be agreed to the audited accounts for that year to confirm it is complete and accurate. Similarly the figures for the first three months of 20X7 should be agreed to the trial balance and ledger.

Analytical procedures should be performed on the prospective financial information by comparing it to the actual figures in the prior year. Any unusual variances should be investigated further by discussing with management. For example, revenue is forecast to grow by 18% from 20X7 to 20X8 and 19% from 20X8 to 20X9. Since the investment is taking place in 20X9, revenue growth should be greater in this year. Management should explain why this is not the case and when the investment can be expected to start earning revenue.

A reasonableness check between statement of financial position and statement of profit or loss items should be undertaken. For example, the inventory turnover period at each of the quarter dates presented is 66, 88, 66 and 65 days respectively. Management should be able to explain the reason for the increase in days in the quarter to 31 March 20X8 and show how they expect to be able to reduce this ratio to the forecast amounts.

The terms of borrowings should be examined to ensure that the forecast takes account of all repayments that are required.

Tender and quotation documents for new machinery should be examined to verify the additional cost within non-current assets for the year ended 31 December 20X9.

The reasonableness of assumptions used should be considered by discussing with management.

The review should consider whether the desired loan of £250,000 will be sufficient to match the costs forecast in the prospective financial information, given that the new plant and equipment is forecast to cost £280,000.

(d) **The accountant's liability for reporting on prospective financial information**

A report on prospective financial information can only provide negative assurance because of its subjective nature as it is based on assumptions of future results. Reviews of prospective financial information are generally done for the bank to obtain a loan or extend borrowing. So if the forecast results do not materialise, the bank may lose money and the firm who reviewed the information could find itself in court as a result.

To determine whether the firm is liable, the criteria generally applied are that the firm is liable to persons with whom there is proximity only or whose relationship approaches privity and to persons of a limited group for whose benefit the information was supplied or who knew that the recipient was going to receive the information and to persons who can reasonably be foreseen to rely on the information.

To reduce the liability, the accountant must ensure that the report contains sufficient caveats as to the achievability of the forecasts. The report should also refer to the fact that the engagement was undertaken in accordance with ISAE 3400 *The examination of prospective financial information* (or relevant national standards or practices applicable to the examination of prospective financial information).

The report should include a statement that it is the management who is responsible for the prospective financial information, including the assumptions on which it is based, not the assurance firm.

Another important point to include is that the information is for restricted use, so it should include who it has been prepared for and who is entitled to rely on it. Reference should also be made to the fact that the engagement to review the prospective financial information was undertaken in accordance with the terms of the engagement.

The terms of the engagement should include an appropriate liability cap. In some cases, it may be possible to obtain indemnity from the client in respect of claims from third parties.

Conclusion

An engagement to report on PFI can only provide a lower level of assurance than a statutory audit, and is likely to place reliance on analytical review. There are a number of steps that an accountant should take to restrict his liability in relation to such a report.

43 Oak

Text references. Chapter 6.

Top tips. In part (a)(i) you do not actually need to do that many calculations. If you were to do only calculations but with no discussion then your marks would be capped to just four, or 17% of this part of the question. You need to do much more than just crunch the numbers if you are to pass the question. The trends in the financial statements should be fairly evident from just comparing the current year's figure with the previous year's. Once you've identified the basic trends (here, falling revenues and falling cash, leading to doubts over going concern), you should be in a position to select a few key ratios – such as interest cover, and the liquidity ratios. As ever, you need to focus less on the calculations than on what the numbers tell you. The principal audit risks should just come out of your analytical review, and the notes to the draft financial statements – each note gives rise to an audit risk of some sort.

The appearance of IFRS 2 in this question was quite technical, and you may have struggled to remember the accounting requirements in this area. In this case there would still have been some general points to make, such as the inherent risk of not complying with a complex accounting standard, or the risk of understatement of expenses and equity.

In part (a)(ii), you should be able to generate ideas by recalling the requirements of IFRS 2 and IAS 17. You may have found IAS 17 easier, in which case you should not have gone over your allotted time on IFRS 2.

In part (b), there were plenty of easy marks to be had. There were three issues here, corresponding to two marks each. You should have been looking to get at least 4–5 for this part of the questions.

Easy marks. The four professional marks were easy to come by. To get them you must include a header, and introduction and a conclusion, and write clear, concise English that makes sense and is in the appropriate register.

Marking scheme

	Marks

(a) (i) Audit risks and preliminary analytical review
Up to 2 marks for each audit risk/area from preliminary analytical review assessed
(to include 1 mark for each ratio and comparative as long as explained, to a
maximum of 4 marks for calculations):
–   Profitability
–   Liquidity
–   Going concern
–   Management bias
–   Operating expenses
–   Share-based payment (up to 3 marks)
–   Lease
–   Revaluation
–   Intangible asset
–   Current assets
–   Long-term borrowings
–   Provision
Maximum   23

(ii) Principal audit procedures
Generally 1 mark per audit procedure:
(1)   Share-based payment plan:
–   Review and obtain understanding of the terms of the share-based
     payment plan
–   Confirm 10% increase in share price and continued service as
     conditions
–   Review assumptions used to determine fair value of share options
–   Consider appropriateness of the model used
–   Consider use of an auditor's expert for the valuation of share options
–   Review assumptions relating to expected staff turnover
–   Perform sensitivity analysis
(2)   Lease:
–   Obtain and review lessor signed copy of lease
–   Confirm length of lease and estimated life of property and compare
–   Ascertain responsibility for repairs and insurance
–   Review lease for indicators of substance of lease
–   Recalculate present value of minimum lease payments and compare to
     fair value
–   Agree payments made to cash book and bank statement
–   Recalculate finance charge
Maximum   8
Professional marks for the overall presentation of the notes, and the clarity of the
explanation and assessment provided. One mark is specifically awarded for the
presentation of the results of analytical procedures.
Maximum   4

(b) Practice management and quality control issues
     Generally 1 mark per comment from ideas list:
     –   Raising materiality level increases detection/audit risk
     –   Materiality judgemental and should be specifically determined for each client
     –   Should not fix materiality at planning stage – against ISA 320
     –   Training promotes a culture of high quality auditing
     –   Cutting training is contrary to the principles of ISQC 1
     –   Audit teams will not be up to date on current developments
     –   Quicker audits cannot be guaranteed
     –   Short-cuts will reduce audit quality and increase detection risk
     –   The manager's suggestions are inappropriate
     Maximum   6
Total   41

(a) **Notes re: Oak Ltd audit planning**

Introduction

These notes outline the principal audit risks in relation to Oak Ltd ('Oak'), and contain the results of the preliminary analytical review, on the basis of the draft financial statements to 30 Nov 20X1. Analytical review calculations are contained in an appendix to these notes.

(i) **Liquidity**

There are uncertainties about Oak's liquidity, as well as its ability to continue as a going concern. Cash has fallen from an asset of £2,350 in 20X0 to a net liability (overdraft) of £1,200 in 20X1. The current ratio has fallen from 2.5 in 20X0 to 1.4 in 20X1, and the quick ratio has dropped from 2.1 in 20X0 to 1 in 20X1. This is a worrying situation.

This has been accompanied by a lengthening of the cash operating cycle, with receivables days rising from 55 days in 20X0 to 64 days in 20X0; inventory being held for longer, from 36 days in 20X0 to 39 days in 20X1; and payables being paid more slowly, from 73 days in 20X0 to 76 days in 20X1. Oak is taking longer to pay its suppliers, is receiving payment more slowly from customers, and has more items left unsold in inventory.

Although individually these changes may not signal going concerns problems, taken as a whole they are contributing to a substantial worsening of Oak's liquidity position, resulting in it having to make use of an overdraft to continue trading. The audit plan must therefore focus on going concern as a key area of audit risk.

Profitability

Oak's worsening liquidity situation has been accompanied by falling profitability, which has not yet been remedied by the launch of its new website. Revenues have fallen, and although costs of sales have also dropped, they have not done so to the same extent, resulting in falling margins. The gross margin fell from 46% in 20X0 to 40% in 20X1, and the operating margin fell from 19% to 16% over the same period. The return on capital employed (ROCE) fell from 7% to 4.4%.

This is before taking into account a number of material accounting judgements affecting the figures for 20X1, which if not permissible would significantly worsen these figures, especially the ROCE which would be hit by falling capital and falling profits. (Adjustments discussed below.)

Oak has incurred significant finance costs each year, which are fixed in relation to profit. As a result, interest cover has fallen from 3.7 to 2.7. This is acceptable for this year, but is unlikely to be so in the future if profits continue to fall, and particularly if any refinancing of Oak's loans resulted in a higher finance cost.

Finance cost

Finance costs have remained static, which may be as expected for long-term loan if this loan requires fixed interest payments. However, the overdraft taken out during the year would be likely to result in charges, so the finance cost appears to be understated.

Management bias

The background of falling profits and a shortage of cash gives management a motive to manipulate the financial statements, especially in view of the fact that the loan is being renegotiated. Manipulation could be to increase profitability, or to present a better view of Oak's net assets than is in fact the case.

Share-based payment

This is an equity-settled share-based payment, to be accounted for in line with IFRS 2 *Share-based payment*. This is a complex area and is therefore inherently risky to audit.

No expense has been recognised in the draft accounts, so the risk is understatement of expenses and of equity. IFRS 2 distinguishes between the estimation of the fair value of the options, and of the number of options that will vest. In estimating the fair value of the options, the market price of the shares will be taken into account. But in estimating how many options will vest, market conditions are not taken into account. Instead, an expense should be recognised as though the condition will be satisfied.

Finance lease

£5m has been capitalised in respect of a finance lease. But the signs are that this is an operating lease per IAS 17 *Leases*: the lease term is only five years, which is unlikely to be a major part of the remaining useful life of a property suitable to be a head office.

The £5m capitalised is well below the property's fair value of £20m. This may be a sign that non-current assets are understated, if the lease is indeed a finance lease. It is not clear what the £5m cost refers to, ie whether it is a lease payment, or perhaps a deposit. If it is a payment, then the total minimum lease payments could be in excess of the asset's fair value, at £5m x 5 years = £25m. This would seem to indicate that the lease is indeed a finance lease.

These considerations are inconclusive; there is an audit risk that the leases are not accounted for in line with IAS 17, so audit work needs to be focused on this material area. If the lease is really a finance lease, then non-current assets are significantly understated. If it is an operating lease, then operating expenses may be understated by the difference between the lease payments and any depreciation expense on the capitalised asset; it is not clear whether depreciation has been charged in the draft accounts, so it is not certain what the effect of correcting the wrong treatment would be on operating expenses.

Revaluation

The revaluation is very material at £10m, which is 10.2% of total assets and represents almost the whole increase in total assets from 20X0 to 20X1, besides the retained earnings. This is an inherently risky area to audit.

The independent expert providing the revaluation is a management's expert per ISA 500 *Audit evidence*. ISA 500 requires the auditor to evaluate such an expert's competence, capabilities and objectivity; to obtain an understanding of their work; and to evaluate the appropriateness of their work for the revaluation. It is important to approach the audit of this area with professional scepticism.

IAS 16 *Property, plant and equipment* requires that the entire class of assets to which an asset belongs should be revalued. There is a risk that only some properties have been revalued, which would result in an overstatement of assets. IAS 16 also contains extensive disclosure requirements, which must have been adhered to.

There is a risk that depreciation has not been calculated using the revalued carrying amount. There is also a risk that the deferred tax consequences of the revaluation have not been taken into account and that liabilities are therefore understated.

Website asset

There is a risk costs have been capitalised but not in accordance with IAS 38 *Intangible assets*. Specifically, costs relating to planning the website must be expensed, as should be costs incurred once it is operational.

An asset should only be recognised if it meets the definition of an asset, ie that it will generate an inflow of future economic benefits. Given that the website has only generated minimal sales since its launch, it is possible that the asset is overstated and should be impaired.

Working capital

Inventory has been moving more slowly this year than last, so there is a risk of obsolete inventory not having been written off, leading to an understatement of expenses.

Receivables have taken longer to collect, so there is a risk that the allowance for irrecoverable receivables has not included some debts that may not be collected.

Loan

The loan payment of £12.5m is due on 30 September 20X2. Oak does not have sufficient cash to make this payment at present, so unless its cash position improves considerable over the coming year, it will be wholly dependent on finding alternative finance. If this is not forthcoming then Oak may not be able to continue trading.

The £12.5m is due within the next year and so should be shown as a current liability. If this change is not made, then the financial statements are materially misstated.

Provision

The amount of the provision has been reduced by 20%, which is a greater fall than the fall in revenue to which it should relate. There is therefore a risk that both the provision and the related expense are understated.

Overdraft

The overdraft of £1.3m is nearing the limit of £1.5m. Over the last 11 months Oak has lost cash at an average rate of £323,000 per month (= (£2,350 – £1,300 – £100) / 11). If this continues, it will hit its overdraft limit within a month. This could make it unable to pay its debts as they fall due.

(ii)   (1)   **Share-based payment**

- Obtain details of the plan to ascertain its the major terms, including:
  - Grant date and vesting date
  - Number of executives and senior managers awarded options
  - Number of share options awarded to each individual
  - Required conditions attached to the options
- Fair value of share options at grant date
- Examine the conditions attached to the options, to confirm the 10% increase in share, and continued service.
- Review the assumptions used, and inputs into, the option pricing model used to estimate the fair value of the share options.
- Consider the appropriateness of the model used to estimate this fair value.
- Consider using an auditor's expert, eg a chartered financial analyst, to examine the fair value of share options used in the calculations.

- Obtain and review a forecast of staffing levels or employee turnover rates relevant to executives and senior managers over the vesting period and consider whether assumptions used appear reasonable.

- Check the sensitivity of the calculations to a change in the assumptions used in the valuation.

(2) **Lease**

- Review the major clauses of the signed lease contract to ascertion whether risk and reward has transferred to Oak.

- Confirm the length of the lease and compare it to the estimated life of the property.

- Ascertain from the lease contract who is responsible for repairs and maintenance of the property. If this is the lessor, then it is an operating lease.

- Scrutinise the lease contract for indications that the lease is a finance lease, eg the existence of a bargain purchase option, legal title passing to Oak at the end of the lease.

- Recalculate the present value of minimum lease payments and compare them with the fair value of the leased property at the inception of the lease.

- Agree amounts paid to the lessor to the cash book and bank statement.

- Recalculate the finance charge expensed, and agree the rate of interest to the lease contract.

Conclusion

The audit of Oak Ltd poses significant engagement risks, particularly in relation to going concern. The audit team must be particularly alive to the possibility of management bias. The principal audit procedures in relation to the share-based payment and finance lease have been outlined.

Appendix: calculations

Ratio	20X1	20X0
Receivables days (12 months)	$4,928 / 28,036 \times 365 = 64$	$4,815 / 31,964 \times 365 = 55$
Inventory days (12 months)	$1,800 / 16,822 \times 365 = 39$	$1,715 / 17,345 \times 365 = 36$
Payables days (12 months)	$3,500 / 16,822 \times 365 = 76$	$3,485 / 17,345 \times 365 = 73$
Current ratio	$6,828 / 4,800 = 1.4$	$8,880 / 3,485 = 2.5$
Quick ratio	$5,028 / 4,800 = 1$	$7,165 / 3,485 = 2.1$
Gross margin	$10,280 / 25,700 = 40\%$	$13,400 / 29,300 = 45.7\%$
Operating margin	$4,080 / 25,700 = 15.9\%$	$5,650 / 29,300 = 19.3\%$
ROCE	$4,080 / 62,278 + 31,000 = 4.4\%$	$5,650 / 54,895 + 26,250 = 7\%$

(b) **Materiality**

ISA 320 *Materiality in planning and performing an audit* requires that materiality be considered at all stages of an audit, and revised as necessary. Therefore fixing materiality at the planning stage would mean that Maple & Co's audits do not comply with ISAs.

It is true that a higher materiality threshold would, all things being equal, result in smaller sample sizes and less audit work. However, materiality is a matter of judgement; the same materiality threshold cannot just be applied to all audits, since the circumstances of each engagement will be different. If inherent risk is higher, for instance, then it is likely that materiality will be set lower in order that audit quality remains consistent.

Moreover, materiality reflects the level of audit engagement risk being taken on. Raising the materiality threshold in general would mean taking on more risk, and therefore reducing audit quality.

Training

It is a requirement that qualified members are professionally competent to perform their work, which in an audit department means being up to date with the latest professional developments. Cutting CPD spending would make it harder to do this. Moreover, if staff are not up to date with the latest developments then it is likely that audit quality will be reduced, as they may not be fully aware of what is required of them.

Cutting spending on the training of junior staff is not in itself a problem, however; staff must be competent to perform the work asked of them, and if training is not provided then this may not be the case. Further, ISQC 1 requires a firm to institute an internal culture that emphasises quality; if training is not provided, then ISQC 1 may not be complied with.

Quicker audits

Guaranteeing quicker audits to clients is unprofessional, and may prejudice audit quality. It is not possible to determine in advance the work that needs to be done on an audit, and hence the length of time it will take to do it. Hence requiring that audits be completed more quickly may lead to a reduction in audit quality and increased risk being taken on.

In addition, a guarantee that an audit be done quicker than last year will be inappropriate where there is a change of circumstances at a client resulting in more audit work needing to be done.

44 Geno Vesa Farm

Text references. Chapters 6, 7 and 9

Top tips. Make sure that you read this question carefully, not least the requirement so that you are clear what type of risks you are trying to assess. Then work through the requirement again, highlighting or jotting down the risks highlighted in the question. Work through the risks you have identified, making sure that they are all audit risks, or, if they are business risks, assessing what the related audit risks would be, so that when you commit the risks to paper, you are sure that you are answering the question properly. Remember that for 14 marks, you should aim to identify about nine or ten risks – working on the assumption that the examiner usually allocates half a mark for identifying and one mark for explaining. In part (b), try and think in basic terms about what you are trying to prove about the assets and what evidence will therefore be relevant. Make sure you are relevant to the scenario as well. New kids will not have purchase invoices – they have been born into the business!

Easy marks. These are available are for identifying risks, but harder marks are awarded for explaining those risks.

Examiner's comments. Candidates who ignored the fact that this was an audit risk question struggled on this part. Candidates are reminded that when asked to 'identify', they should be brief. Some candidates seemed focused solely on going concern risks. There are only so many marks that can be awarded for reference to 'going concern'.

Better candidates differentiated themselves by simply recognising the impairment reversal, the sale and repurchase of maturing inventory, a current liability if the grant should be repayable. The weakest candidates who, for example, expressed concern that all the inventory was sold to one customer, clearly had no grasp of the scenario in which sales were made to retail outlets.

Part (b) consisted of three parts for 12 marks – only four points needed for each part to score 100%. Many answers did not answer the question set, most typically ignoring the reference to 'carrying amount', preferring to write an irrelevant answer point for each item on a rote-learned list of financial statement assertions.

Marking scheme

		Marks
(a)	**Principal audit risks**	14
	Generally ½ mark for identification + 1 mark each point of explanation	

Ideas

Industry
- 'Farming' (weather, etc)
- Bad press etc

Goat herd
- Goats – non-current tangible assets
- Kids – inventory/current assets

Rabida Red
- Cost ↑, supply problems ⇒ going concern
- Socio-environmental reporting

Bachas Blue
- Contingent liability/going concern?
- Impairment *reversal* (IAS 36)
- Value in use

Cheese
- Sale and repurchase/substance over form
- Expensing of finance costs (IAS 23)
- Non-compliance with legislation ⇒ provision
- Compliance with legislation ⇒ discontinued operations

Grant
- Reason for implementation being deferred
- Repayable? ⇒ impact on cash flow

(b) **Audit work on carrying amounts**

Generally 1 mark each point

Max 4 each statement of financial position item × 3

Ideas
- FS assertions (valuation = quantity × price)
- Qty exists?
- Price = cost? Depreciable amount? MV?
- *Procedures*
  - Analytical
  - Enquiry
  - Inspection
  - Observation
  - Computation

12

Total

26

(a) **Audit risks**

Nature of the business

The company is a farm which produces farmhouse cheese that is sold by mail order. Farming is inherently risky as it is affected by many conditions which are outside the direct control of management. These include adverse effects of the weather and possible disease. The product sold appears to be a luxury product so sales are likely to fluctuate due to economic and seasonal factors.

Compliance

Farming and food production are heavily controlled businesses where there is a vast amount of legislation which must be complied with. There is a risk that the business will fail to meet the required standards and may be fined as a result. Any adverse publicity eg if fines relate to animal welfare issues may affect sales.

Nature of the assets

One of the key assets of the business will be the goat herd. This asset may be valued incorrectly if a clear distinction is not made between those animals which are inventory and those which are selected for herd replacement (ie tangible non-current assets).

There is a risk that the statement of financial position value of the production animals and charges made to the statement of profit or loss (eg for depreciation and fair value adjustments) would be misstated if:

(1) The split of animals between non-current assets and inventory is not carried out accurately
(2) Useful lives are not assessed in a reasonable manner
(3) Residual values are not estimated correctly
(4) Impairment reviews are not undertaken
(5) Fair values cannot be estimated reliably

Completeness may be an issue as the kids are born into the herd and as such there is no documentary evidence as there would be for purchased assets. Accurate records of kids born will be required to ensure that all animals are valued. Revenue would also be understated if kids were deliberately not recorded and subsequently sold for cash.

For animals held as inventory there may be difficulties in assessing cost and net realisable value. It may prove difficult to sell animals held after they have reached their optimum size and weight so NRV may fall. The cost of goats is likely to be based on an estimate of the cost of raising the animal (as it will not have a purchase price as such).

Availability of Innittu

This is an essential ingredient of Rabida Red cheese. Recent increases in the price of this raw material may affect sales if passed on to the customer or will affect profitability if borne by the company. Future supplies of this product may be further restricted. Depending on the company's ability to diversify into alternative ranges this may raise going concern issues. Any associated bad publicity regarding the exploitation of workers and the threat to the rain forest could also impact on going concern.

Bachas Blue

This product has been connected with a skin condition. There is a risk that contingent liabilities will be understated if there is any litigation against the company.

Although the effect of the bad publicity has been short lived the product is unlikely to be able to recover a second time if further health problems are proved.

The impairment loss recognised in relation to the equipment used exclusively for the manufacture of Bachas Blue may now need to be reversed if there has been a change in the estimates used to determine the asset's recoverable amount since March 20X8. The recoverable amount will need to be recalculated and is likely to be based on value in use. If future cash flows are not estimated on a reasonable basis, the asset and credit to the statement of profit or loss will be misstated.

Sale and repurchase agreement

The sale and repurchase agreement with Abingdon is in substance a loan secured on the inventory. There is a risk that the cash received might be treated as sales revenue. GVF should continue to recognise the cheese as inventory and the proceeds recognised as a liability.

The 7% interest should be treated as borrowing costs, which may be recognised as they are incurred. Alternatively GVF may adopt a policy of capitalisation. In this instance the interest should be included as part of the cost of the inventory (as it is incurred in bringing the product to its present location and condition).

Health and safety legislation

The new legislation came into effect in 1 January 20X9 and it is unclear as to whether the company has complied. If it has not complied there is a risk of penalties and fines being incurred. Provision for these may be required in the financial statements.

If the legislation has been complied with this may have had a significant effect on the ability of the business to produce medium and strong cheese. This represents a significant part of production. If these products are no longer available the business may no longer be viable.

There is also a risk that plant and equipment is overstated. The carrying value of the old shelves would need to be written off (assuming that they have no further use) and equipment used specifically in the production of medium and strong cheese may have suffered impairment.

Grant

The decision by management to defer the plan to convert the barn may mean that the terms of the grant are no longer met. The grant may be repayable and if this is the case it should be presented as a liability in the statement of financial position.

(b)   **Audit work**

(i)   *Goat herd*

- Physical inspection of the herd to confirm the existence and condition of the animals. On a test basis check for evidence of ownership eg branding stamp

- Discuss with management the system by which they distinguish between production animals and those held as inventory. Perform tests of controls on the system.

- For production animals (tangible non-current assets):

    - Agree value attributed to a sample of animals to market prices
    - Compare depreciation policy with farming industry norms industry norms
    - Check depreciation policy has been applied and calculated for a sample of animals
    - Perform a 'proof in total' or reasonableness check on the depreciation charge for the herd.

- For inventory:

    - Observe inventory count and assess adequacy of procedures
    - Review management calculations for costs included in the carrying value of animals and assess whether they are appropriate in nature eg feed, vets bills, housing. (As the kids will have been born into the herd there will be no invoice cost.)
    - For a sample of animals compare carrying value at 31 March 20X9 with market values

(ii)   *Equipment*

- Check that brought forward balances for cost and accumulated depreciation agree to previous year's working papers and accounts.

- Agree the cost of any new equipment purchased for the production of Bachas Blue.

- Check that the depreciation policy applied to this category of asset has been consistently and appropriately applied.

- For the previously impaired asset:

    - Check the basis of the current calculation of value in use (This should be the present value of the estimated future cash flows – IAS 36)
    - Compare the future cash flows with budgeted cash flow figures taking into account any other knowledge of the business which might result in variations eg any information regarding other health scares associated with the product
    - Check that sales of Bachus Blue are returning to their former level by comparing current sales levels and budgeted sales for 20X9 with sales levels before the adverse publicity
    - Agree any assumptions made by discussion with management and review of board minutes
    - Check the period over which the cash flow projections have been made (normally a maximum of five years – IAS 36)
    - Determine the basis on which the discount rate has been calculated. Reperform the calculation and check that management have considered the current assessment of the time value of money and the risks specific to this asset.
    - Calculate the assets depreciated carrying value (ie its value if the asset had not been originally impaired) and compare with the current carrying value (The reversal impairment loss cannot result in the asset being valued at an amount which exceed its depreciated carrying value – IAS 36)

(iii)   *Cheese*

        WIP

- Attend the inventory count and determine the process by which the stage of maturity is assessed and therefore costs attributed.

- Obtain a schedule showing the breakdown of costs and check that the basis on which they have been recharged is reasonable. (For example, the milk used is produced by the herd. The cost of milk will therefore be an estimation of the cost of producing it rather than a purchase price.)
- Check the system by which the age of inventory is monitored. Confirm that cheese which is not available for sale for more than 12 months after the year end has been disclosed as a non-current asset.

Finished goods

- Review the terms of the sale and repurchase agreement with Abingdon to confirm that it is in substance a secured loan.
- At the inventory count ensure that all cheese including that 'owned' by Abingdon is included in the count total.
- Review costing records to confirm that the 7% interest is included for every six months which elapses after maturity. Perform tests of control on controls over ageing of mature inventory.
- Obtain confirmation from Abingdon of the outstanding liability at 31 March 20X9. This will be the difference between the value of cheese purchased by Abingdon and the amount repurchased by GVF.
- Discuss with management the need to write down the value of inventory. The net realisable value of cheeses held on the new stainless steel shelving may be less than cost
- Confirm the adequacy of disclosure. The carrying amount of inventory pledged as security should be disclosed.

45 Cedar

Text reference. Chapter 14.

Top tips. Part (a) was a typical ethics question, in the context of a forensic audit. You needed to run through the three steps given by the IESBA *Code*, applying them to this scenario.

Part (b) should also have been within your grasp provided you were up to speed with your knowledge of this area, although you may have struggled to get more than 3–4 marks here. You should still have passed this part of the question though.

Part (c) was a current issue. You needed to think on your feet here, but as with all requirements of this sort it is actually not difficult to score well. There are six marks available, so you need to look to make 2–3 strong points both for and against. Notice that the requirement is to **evaluate** the arguments; the easiest way to show that you're doing this is to draw some sort of conclusion at the end of your answer.

Easy marks. Part (a) contained some marks on identifying and evaluating threats that were almost pure knowledge.

Marks

(a)   **Ethical and professional issues**
       Generally 1 mark per issue assessed:
       –   Non-audit service creates self-review threat
       –   Non-audit service creates advocacy threat
       –   Significance of threat to be evaluated
       –   Significance depends on materiality and subjectivity
       –   Examples of safeguards (1 mark each)
       –   Competence to provide service
       –   Resources to provide service
       –   Confidentiality agreements
       Maximum   6

(b) **Matters to be discussed**

Generally 1 mark for each matter explained:
- – Purpose, nature and scope of investigation
- – Confirm objectives of investigation
- – Time-scale and deadline
- – Potential scale of the fraud
- – How fraud reported to finance director
- – Possible reasons for fraud not being detected by internal controls
- – Resources to be made available to investigation team
- – Whether matter reported to police

Maximum   6

(c) **Provision of non-audit services**

Generally 1 mark per comment discussed and 1 mark for conclusion:
- – Simple way to eliminate threats to objectivity
- – Examples of threats eg lucrative nature of non-audit services
- – Benefit to audit market of outright prohibition
- – Benefits to client of auditor providing non-audit services
- – Benefits to audit firm of providing non-audit services
- – Safeguards should be used to reduce threats arising
- – Principles-based approach versus prescriptive approach

Maximum   <u>6</u>

Total   <u>18</u>

(a) There are two main threats to Cedar & Co's independence in relation to this engagement: advocacy and self-review. The IESBA *Code of ethics* requires a firm to identify threats to independence, evaluate their significance, and then apply safeguards to reduce them to an acceptable level. If this is not possible then the engagement must be declined.

Threats

The advocacy threat arises because acting as an expert witness in court for the client may be construed as representing the client's interests.

The self-review threat arises if the work done to investigate the fraud, particularly work done to quantify the loss incurred and to evaluate the client's systems and controls, is relied upon in a future audit. This is particularly risky if the amount of the fraud is material to the financial statements. There may also be a self-review threat to the fraud investigation if knowledge acquired as part of the audit is relied upon there.

Evaluation of threats

The firm must consider the potential materiality of the issue, and the extent to which judgement must be exercised in quantifying it. If the fraud is material and the investigation would involve judgement, then safeguards could not reduce it to an acceptable level.

Safeguards

Safeguards could include:

- Separate engagement teams for the forensic investigation and the audit
- Having an independent professional accountant review the forensic investigation
- Subjecting the audit to a hot review by a second partner

The situation must be disclosed to those charged with governance of Chestnut Ltd.

ES 5 and UK Corporate Governance Code

The FRC's ES 5 *Non-audit services provided to audit clients* requires that the audit engagement partner themselves is responsible for assessing whether the proposed engagement is ethically acceptable, and for documenting this assessment.

The *UK Corporate Governance Code* requires that the situation be disclosed to those charged with governance, which in this case means discussion with Chestnut Ltd's audit committee, or if there is none then with the board of directors.

Ability to do work

The *Code of ethics* requires that a professional accountant only undertake assignments they are competent to do. Forensic investigations are often only undertaken by individuals with specialist training and experience, which Cedar & Co may not possess. If it does not, then the assignment should be declined.

(b)   First of all it is necessary to identify the precise objectives of the investigation. If the aim is to quantify the loss then this will involve less risk (and less work) than if the aim is to gather evidence to use in court or to support an insurance claim. The terms of the engagement should also be discussed, with a view to including them in an engagement letter.

The expected time scale for the engagement, along with the matter of costs and possible fees, should be discussed. From this the resources needed can be determined, and their allocation planned, eg staff may need to be diverted from other assignments.

The best approach to meet the objectives, within time and cost limits, should be discussed. This will involve discussion of how the fraud came to light, along with the likely scale of the fraud. A key question at this stage is how many sales representatives were involved, as this will help indicate the scale.

The reasons why the fraud was not detected or prevented should be discussed. The role of internal audit should be discussed, as it is possible that internal auditors could have been involved in covering up the fraud.

Whether the engagement includes making recommendations about systems and controls to help prevent future frauds should be discussed.

Enquire whether Chestnut Ltd's internal auditors are available to assist in the investigation, which may affect considerations of timing and cost.

It will be necessary to confirm that the team will have unrestricted access to any individuals and documents that they need to conduct their investigation.

(c)   **In favour of prohibition**

The key argument is that audit quality would be improved by eliminating at a stroke a whole range of threats to independence. It is very difficult to argue that this would not be the case, so the arguments against prohibition tend to involve claiming not that it would not work, but that it is either unnecessary or would involve foregoing various benefits to auditors providing non-audit services.

The main issue here is that, being profit-making entities, auditors have an incentive to take on fee-earning work to the detriment of their independence. The argument is that given profit-making auditors, there is an insoluble conflict between the need to increase income by providing sometimes-lucrative non-audit services, and keeping the self-interest threat to an acceptable level.

A more sophisticated argument for prohibition is that it does not matter whether or not auditors actually are compromised by selling non-audit services to audit clients; what matters is that they are perceived to be so compromised. This raises the spectre of the expectations gap, and it is argued that if the gap may never be fully overcome then it is best for auditors to do what is necessary for users to perceive them to be independent.

Against prohibition

The first common argument against prohibition is that it actually benefits the client to have the auditor provide non-audit services. There may be cost savings to the client if the auditor provides the non-audit services, as the auditor will already possess knowledge of the client acquired as part of the audit.

It is argued that audit quality may actually be improved, because the auditor may get to know the client better by providing the non-audit services.

Another major argument against prohibition is that it is simply not necessary. Ethical standards distinguish between engagements where threats cannot be reduced to an acceptable level, which should not be undertaken, and those where safeguards are sufficient. It is argued here that a blanket ban on all non-audit services simply fails to take account of this distinction.

Conclusion

There are powerful arguments on both sides here, and it is likely that this argument will continue in practice for some time to come.

46 Willow

Text references. Chapters 7 and 9.

Top tips. The question gave you situations. Make sure you read the requirement carefully here, as there were a number of things to consider – you might have missed, for example, the requirement to recommend any further procedures. The trick with each of these issues is to take on a sceptical frame of mind. The audit work on inventory, for instance, appears to be complete as long as a written representation is obtained. But even if you did not remember the detailed requirements of ISA 580, you should have been able to question whether such a representation would be reliable, and to point out that it needs to be backed up by evidence. The further procedures are then just ways of obtaining this evidence.

The four short issues for your attention were deceptively difficult to deal with. On the face of it there should be two easy marks for each of the four issues, but in reality the first issue in particular was not easy. You should, however, have been able to gather together enough marks to pass the question.

Easy marks. The professional marks should be easy to come by. There were also some relatively easy marks in part (b) in relation to the ethics of accepting gifts and hospitality.

Marking scheme

		Marks

(a) **Audit implications**
Generally up to 1½ marks for each implication assessed and 1 mark for each impact on the financial statements identified:
Inventory:
–   Comment on individual materiality
–   Value at lower of cost and NRV and impact on profit
–   Written representation not sufficient evidence
–   Recommend procedures (1 mark each)
Legal claim:
–   Immaterial individually but material to profit when combined with inventory adjustment
–   Financial statements materially misstated when two issues combined – implication for opinion
–   Suitability of verbal representation as source of evidence
–   Recommended procedures (1 mark each)
Current assets:
–   Material by nature but not material in monetary terms
–   Identification of related party transaction
–   Disclosure in notes to financial statements inadequate – implication for opinion
–   Interest should have been accrued
–   Recommended procedures (1 mark each)
Maximum   15

(b)   **Issues for attention of audit committee**

Generally up to 2 marks for each matter discussed:

- Property revaluations
- Delay in receiving non-current asset register affects audit efficiency
- Weak controls in procurement department
- Lack of approved supplier list on integrity of supply chain
- Threat to objectivity from financial controller's actions

Maximum   **8**

Professional marks for the overall presentation of the briefing notes, and the clarity of the explanation and assessment provided

Maximum   <u>**4**</u>

Total   <u>**27**</u>

Briefing notes

To: Jasmine Berry, Audit engagement partner

From: Audit manager

Re: Willow Ltd audit

Introduction

These notes assess the matters raised by the audit senior, and explain the issues to be raised with the client's audit committee. Some further audit evidence needs to be obtained, as outlined in the first part of these notes.

(a)   **Matters raised by senior**

    (i)   **Inventory**

This area is not material to net assets or to income and expenses, but could become so in combination with any other immaterial misstatements detected. Unless this is the case, there would be no effect on the audit report.

IAS 2 *Inventories* requires inventory to be measured at the lower of cost and net realisable value (NRV). If the NRV is zero, then an expense of £130,000 will be incurred, reducing both and assets by the same amount.

ISA 580 *Written representations* states that a written representation is not of itself sufficient appropriate audit evidence. Therefore further evidence must be obtained.

The assertion that must be tested here is that NRV is not less than £130,000. The finance director's claim that the inventory can be recycled would therefore need to be supported by evidence that the NRV of this recycled inventory would not be less than £130,000.

Further procedures include:

- Making enquiries from an operations director to ascertain whether or not the materials could be recycled

- Obtaining documentary evidence of the costs of recycling together with the potential selling price of recycled materials

- Reviewing invoices raised after the period end for evidence that the materials have in fact been recycled and sold on

    (ii)   **Provisions**

This area is not material to net assets or to income and expenses, but could become so in combination with any other immaterial misstatements detected.

IAS 37 *Provisions, contingent liabilities and contingent assets* requires that a provision be recognised where it is probable that there would be an outflow of resources embodying economic benefits, as is the case here. If this adjustment is not made then liabilities and expenses are both understated. There is also unlikely to be adequate disclosure of the circumstances surrounding the case.

When combined with the inventory misstatement, the result is a total misstatement of £255,000, which is material to income and expenses. If neither adjustment is made then the audit opinion is qualified.

The verbal confirmation that the case will probably be paid is not sufficient, and written confirmation from the lawyers is required. The finance director's refusal to provide this evidence may constitute a limitation on the scope of the audit if the evidence cannot be obtained elsewhere, and throws into question management's integrity. This should trigger a re-assessment of any written representations from management relied on elsewhere in the audit, for example in relation to inventory. The auditor's report is also likely to include a Companies Act 2006 disclosure that information and explanations required for the audit have not been obtained.

Further procedures include:

- Review correspondence with lawyers for evidence regarding the outcome of the legal claim
- Review board minutes for evidence about the claim

(iii) Current assets

A loan to a director is material by nature, irrespective of its monetary value. In line with IAS 24 *Related party disclosures* Cherry is key management personnel and thus a related party. The financial statements must therefore disclose the loan principal amount, the amount outstanding at the year end, together with the terms of the loan including details of any security offered.

As the loan is not disclosed in the financial statements, there is a material misstatement in respect of IAS 24. If no adjustment is made then the audit opinion is qualified. This is also a breach of the Companies Act 2006 requirements regarding disclosure of directors' loans.

It is possible that the interest payment has not been made or accrued for. If not, then interest of 4% x £6,000 = £40 should be accrued (the adjustment is immaterial).

Further procedures include:

- Review the written terms of the loan to confirm the interest rate and any other conditions
- Review list of accruals to see whether interest has been accrued

(b) Property

A move from recognising properties at cost to at fair value would be acceptable in line with IAS 16 *Property, plant and equipment*, as long as it is applied across an entire class of assets. The Committee should be aware of the benefits and drawbacks of such a change. Benefits include more relevant information on the values of properties, and quicker recognition of fair value gains in the financial statements. But the drawbacks include the need to remeasure fair value at each period end. It may also be necessary to employ an external expert to estimate fair values, which could be costly.

Asset register

The delay in receiving the non-current asset register would have impaired audit efficiency, and potentially resulted in greater audit costs and therefore fees.

The fact that the issue was discussed with the committee last year but then recurred, suggests some sort of controls failure; either the last year's discussion was not acted upon by the committee, or at some other point. In both cases the reason for this needs to be ascertained.

The fact the financial controller has been on holiday at the start of the audit for two years running is not just unhelpful, but may be indicative of something deeper awry, such as fraud.

Procurement

No explanation is actually given for why invoices are not matched to goods received notes; there is no reason why this cannot be done if suppliers are changed frequently, for example. Without this control, it is possible that invoices are paid without goods ever being received. There is also a risk of fraud if this is done intentionally, either delivering goods to another address or using dummy invoices. The committee should seek to improve controls in this area as a matter of some urgency.

Frequently switching suppliers is not itself a problem, but again this would not seem to totally preclude maintaining a list of approved suppliers – it only means that such a list would be a long one. If totally new suppliers really are being used so frequently, then there may be issues with quality rather than price.

Financial controller

There are a number of ethical issues here. First, the offer of three weeks' use of her holiday home needs to be considered in light of the IESBA's *Code of Ethics'* requirements on gifts and hospitality. In this case the value of the offer is likely to mean that no safeguards could prevent the auditors' independence being impaired, so the offer should be declined. If the team considers that Mia Fern intends to influence the outcome of the audit by making the offer, then this casts doubt on her integrity. The audit committee should be notified of this situation.

The FRC's Ethical Standard 4 *Fees, remuneration and evaluation policies, litigation, gifts and hospitality* requires the cumulative amount of gifts or hospitality to be considered; it is likely that a similar conclusion would be reached and that the offer would not be acceptable.

The gifts of lunches are unlikely to impair independence as they are likely to be of an insignificant monetary value. Provided that this is the case, they may be accepted.

Conclusion

Further audit evidence needs to be obtained on a number of issues, some of which may involve a material misstatement, and there are a number of matters to be brought to the attention of the audit committee.

47 Jovi

Chapter reference. Chapter 6.

Top tips. You may have found part (a)(i) difficult, and therefore struggled to write enough for four marks here. You would have score well if you knew ISA 320 *Materiality in planning and performing an audit* well, but if you did not then there was no need to panic. The basic issue here can be worked out using common sense; the auditor would change materiality if they become aware of something that affects materiality. The requirement here is to 'explain', so giving examples is always going to be helpful. If you could think of just one good example, then you could get 50% of the marks on this part of the question.

In part (a)(ii), you could have worked out that there were notes notes (audit findings) and 18 marks available, which equates to two marks per note. This was not an easy question. Your approach should be to work through each issue in turn, trying to think of what the problem might be, and not forgetting to think about whether the audit evidence was adequate. Note the importance of reading the question here (and remembering the requirement as you are writing), as candidates who recommended specific audit procedures would have wasted their time.

Part (b) should not have been too difficult. To score six marks you should have looked to make two to three points both for and against. To score well here you need to apply your knowledge to the scenario. Although joint audits are a current issue, you are not being asked for your opinion on the issue generally; you are being asked about a joint audit of the financial statements of May Co. You therefore need to think about the specific scenario. The examiner tends to like students who make points like 'the small local firm will probably offer a cheaper audit service than Sambora & Co', as this is something that can only really be said about this specific situation.

Easy marks. There were easy marks in part (b) for some of the pros and cons of the joint audit, but all in all this was a difficult question.

Marks

(a) (i) **Materiality**

Up to 1 mark for each comment:

- Recognise materiality is subjective
- Auditor's business understanding may change during the audit, making some balances and transactions material
- Client's circumstances may change during the audit, making some balances and transactions more material
- Adjustments to the accounts mean materiality has to be revised
- Recognise the high-risk status of the client

Maximum   4

(ii) **Audit completion issues**

Up to 2 marks for each audit completion issue assessed:

- Property disposal/sale and leaseback
- Property revaluation
- Actuarial loss
- Goodwill impairment
- Goodwill classification into assets held for sale
- Associate
- Presentation of assets held for sale (separate and not netted off)
- Measurement of assets held for sale
- Lack of disclosure of discontinued operation
- Non-controlling interest
- Finance cost and loan

Maximum   18

(b) **Joint audit**

Up to 1 mark for each advantage/disadvantage discussed:

- Retain local auditors' knowledge of May Co
- Retain local auditors' knowledge of local regulations
- Sambora & Co can provide additional skills and resources
- Cost effective – reduce travel expenses, local firm likely to be cheaper
- Enhanced audit quality
- But employing two audit firms could be more expensive
- Problems in allocating work – could increase audit risk

Maximum   6

Total   28

(a) (i) **Revising materiality**

Auditors must reassess materiality if they become aware of new information that would have resulted in a different materiality level being set at the planning stage.

Planning materiality is likely to have been based on draft financial statements, but during the course of the audit it could become clear that the final financial statements will be substantially different. For example, the carrying amount of assets held at fair value could be much lower than originally expected, which would affect the amounts in the statement of financial position. In that case, the auditor would need to set materiality again, on the basis of the actual results and position.

Alternatively, something could happen during the audit, eg the client could decide to dispose of a subsidiary. This could change the appropriate materiality level, as well as performance materiality. The auditor should take this into account and revise materiality.

(ii) **Statement of profit or loss and other comprehensive income**

Copeland revenue

Copeland's 25% drop in revenue indicates that goodwill relating to this subsidiary may be impaired. There is a risk that this goodwill was not impaired when it should have been.

Property disposal

At £2m, the property disposal is material.

The option to repurchase the property in five-years' time points to the possibility that this could not be a genuine sale, but a finance arrangement whose economic substance is that of a secured loan. In this case the audit evidence obtained is inadequate, and further evidence needs to be obtained to determine the substance of the transaction.

If this is indeed a secured loan (in substance) then the asset will be recognised in the statement of financial position, and the cash receipt will be recognised as a loan (liability). Finance costs will be accrued over the period of the loan – five years.

If this is the case, then profit has been materially overstated, and liabilities understated.

Property revaluation

The gain of £800,000 was just below initial materiality of £900,000, but above the current materiality level of £700,000. Audit procedures must now be performed in this area, as it is possible that there could be a material misstatement here.

Actuarial loss

The actuarial losses are material, at £1.1m, as is the defined benefit liability of £10.82m.

Axle Ltd is a service organisation, and ISA 402 *Audit considerations relating to an entity using a service organisation* requires the auditor to obtain an understanding of this organisation. This can be obtained:

- From the Group itself, we should gain an understanding of how Axle Ltd arrives at its valuation, its systems and its controls

- By obtaining a report from the auditor of Axle Ltd (the service organisation's auditor), which contains an opinion on the description of Axle Ltd's systems and controls

This has not been done, and we have no information about how the plan assets and liabilities were valued, or how reliable their valuation might be. The audit team must therefore obtain this information before the service organisation's representation can be relied upon.

Goodwill impairment

There is an indicator that goodwill relating to the Copeland subsidiary is impaired, but this does not appear to have been considered by the audit team. Audit procedures must be performed on the assumptions used by management in conducting this review. The reasons why the 25% fall in revenue has not resulted in impairment must be specifically addressed.

Associate

The statement of profit or loss includes £1.01m share of profit of associate. The figure in the statement of financial position should include (as a minimum) the amount brought forward, plus any profit attributable, less any dividends received. It is thus highly unlikely that this figure would not have changed since last year.

Trading division held for sale

The division held for sale is part of a subsidiary. Therefore, some of the goodwill relating to this subsidiary may need to be reclassified as part of the disposal group of assets held for sale. Although it is possible that no goodwill will need to be reclassified, evidence needs to be obtained that this is the case.

The statement of financial position contains one line within assets for 'assets classified as held for sale'. This disclosure is incorrect: the assets held for sale should be a separate section within 'assets'.

It appears that this £7.8m could be a net figure, which again is incorrect – there should also be a separate section within 'liabilities' showing the liabilities from the disposal group. Audit procedures should be performed to ascertain whether this in fact a net figure, in order to get the classification right.

Although there are assets held for sale from a trading division, the statement or profit or loss shows no discontinued operations. IFRS 5 *Non-current assets held for sale and discontinued operations* requires the post-tax profit or loss of discontinued operations to be shown as a single line. This appears to be a material misstatement, and audit procedures should be performed to determine whether it is or not – whether there are any discontinued operations.

Non-controlling interest

There is no disclosure in relation to the non-controlling interest in the statement of profit or loss and other comprehensive income. Both profit for the year and total comprehensive income attributable to the non-controlling interest should be disclosed.

New loan

Finance costs should be included of £8m × 2% × 9 / 12 = £120,000. However, finance costs have only risen by £40,000. No loans appear to have been paid off during the year, as long-term borrowings have increased by exactly the £8m received for the new loan. Therefore, finance costs appear to be understated.

The amount is not material of itself, but should be accumulated together with any other misstatements that are discovered as they could become material in aggregate.

(b)   **Advantages of joint audit**

In the case of May Co, Sambora & Co would not currently have much understanding of May Co's business. It would therefore make sense to continue to make use of Moore & Co's accumulated understanding of the client's business.

The fact that May Co is located in Farland means that it could be subject to accounting, legal and professional regulations that are different from those under which Sambora & Co are accustomed to operating. It makes sense to continue to use the local auditors' knowledge of this potentially very different regulatory framework.

There may be some cost savings in using Moore & Co, as a result of the fact that Sambora & Co would no longer need to send the whole audit team out of Farland to conduct the audit procedures. It is also possible that Moore & Co might charge lower fees than Sambora & Co, so using Moore & Co's staff to perform procedures could work out less expensive.

Audit quality should increase as a result of a joint audit. As new auditors, Sambora & Co will be approaching the audit with a fresh outlook, unprejudiced by previous events and may be able to spot new issues or offer different solutions from those previously identified by Moore & Co.

Disadvantages of joint audit

A key disadvantage is the uplift in costs that results from the unavoidable duplication of work between the two auditors.

Moore & Co may use a different audit approach and methodology from Sambora & Co, leading to disagreements throughout the audit about which is the correct way to proceed. This could result in a loss of efficiencies, as time is spent agreeing on the best audit approach rather than carrying out actual audit work. If either audit firm's approach is followed exclusively, some of the benefits of a joint audit will be lost.

48 Kobain

Marking scheme

		Marks

(a) **Revenue recognition**

Up to 1½ marks for each matter discussed:
- Revenue often a subjective area
- Revenue often a complex area
- Adequacy of internal controls
- Link to fraudulent financial reporting/earnings management
- Example of deliberate manipulation of revenue
- Cash-based business particularly high risk
- Small/simple entities not high risk

Maximum   6

(b) **Kobain Ltd**

Up to 1 mark for each matter/evidence:

Matters
- Risk and reward not transferred to external vendor
- Kobain Ltd retains managerial involvement
- Revenue recognised too early
- Materiality
- Implication for auditor's opinion
- Opening balances could be misstated

Evidence
- Confirm terms of arrangement by review of signed contract
- Consider whether terms of contract mean that revenue should be recognised
- Confirmation of inventories held by external vendors
- Determine amount of returns normally made under the contract
- Attendance at external vendors inventory count
- Supporting documentation on opening balances

Maximum   6

(c) **Investigative procedures on false revenue claims**

Generally 1 mark per procedure:
- Obtain all claims made by the sales representative
- Agree all sales to supporting documentation
- Conduct external confirmation of sales made
- Reconcile claims to sales ledger/control accounts
- Conduct analytical procedures

Maximum   4

Total   16

(a) Whether or not revenue recognition is a high risk area of the audit depends to a large extent on the particular audit in question. It is possible that a company's revenue recognition could be simple; a small company, for example, might have only one revenue stream that is straightforward to audit. In this case, revenue recognition might not be particularly high risk in comparison with other parts of the audit.

Alternatively, if a company makes a lot of cash sales then this would increase the risk of misstatement. There is a risk, for instance, of cash being stolen before it is recorded as revenue. There may also be a risk here in relation to money laundering.

An element of subjective judgement is often involved in applying IAS 18 *Revenue*, which can make this a risky area to audit, particularly with larger companies. For example, there may be difficulties determining the exact time at which revenue should be recognised, and in which reporting period. This can easily become a material issue. Where management is required to use its judgement there is a risk of material misstatement if they make inappropriate or wrong judgements.

Revenue recognition can also be highly complex. Transactions may involve several elements which might pertain to differing reporting periods. In a sale which includes a warranty, for example, the revenue relating to the warranty should not all be recognised when the sale takes place, but should be matched to the period of the warranty.

ISA 240 *The auditor's responsibilities relating to fraud in an audit of financial statements* states that there should be a presumption that there is a risk of fraud in relation to revenue recognition. There is a risk of fraudulent financial reporting in particular, as this area is susceptible to management bias and earnings manipulation.

There could be issues particular to the company, eg if management receives a bonus that is linked to revenue or earnings figures, then this may provide a motive to commit fraudulent financial reporting.

(b) **Matters to consider**

IAS 18 *Revenue* requires that revenue be recognised where the significant risks and rewards of ownership have been transferred, and the entity does not retain managerial involvement with the goods.

Kobain Ltd retains legal title to the goods while they are with the vendor, and when they are sold, this title passes straight to the customer. Thus Kobain Ltd still legally owns the jewellery when it is with the vendor.

Kobain Ltd retains the ability to change the selling price of the jewellery when it is with the vendor. This constitutes managerial involvement. Kobain Ltd is also exposed to the risk of inventory not being sold, as unsold inventory must be returned back to it after nine months. Hence in addition to retaining legal title, Kobain Ltd also retains the significant risks and rewards of ownership.

This would suggest that Kobain Ltd should only recognise revenue once the vendor has sold an item on to a customer. However, Kobain Ltd currently recognises revenue as soon as the item is delivered to the vendor. This appears to be incorrect.

The required adjustments would derecognise revenue of £4m, recognise inventory of £3m, and reduce retained earnings by £1m. Profit before tax would be reduced by £1m or 6.7%, which is material. The understatement of inventory by £3m is also material at 5.5% of total assets. If these adjustments are not made, then the audit opinion should be qualified 'except for' a material misstatement.

Audit evidence

- Copies of sales contracts with key vendors and confirmation of their terms

- Review of contract terms to determine if Kobain Ltd retains risks and rewards relating to, and managerial involvement with, the goods

- Enquiries into the proportion of goods usually returned from vendors, to form an understanding of potential levels of obsolete goods

- Results of auditor's test counts of inventory at a selection of vendors' premises to ensure the existence of goods held on consignment

(c) **Procedures**

- Obtain all claims submitted by the sales representative since January 20X2 and total the amount of these claims.

- Reconcile the sales per the sales commission claims to the sales ledger control account.

- Agree all sales per the sales commission claims to eg customer-signed orders, and to other supporting documentation confirming that window installation took place, eg customer-signed agreement of work carried out.

- Obtain external confirmations from customers of the amount they paid for work carried out.

49 Cuckoo Group

Text references. Chapters 9 and 11

Top tips. The audit of groups is a topic which is likely to require quite a sophisticated approach. In this question, it is combined with inventory valuation and disclosures. You must be comfortable with the issues discussed in part (a). Part (b) is good practice at considering accounting issues.

Easy marks. This is a difficult question, requiring a sound knowledge of group audits. Part (b) is probably the most straightforward if you follow a methodical approach. Be sure to get the professional marks too.

(a) **Briefing notes**

For: Audit partner

By: Audit manager

Re: Cuckoo Group audit

Introduction

These notes describe the matters to consider and the procedures to apply as part of the planning and evaluation of the auditors of Loopy; and discuss the acceptability of the group's accounting policies in relation to inventory.

(i) As principal auditors of the Cuckoo Group we have **sole responsibility** for our opinion on the group accounts even if part of the group has been audited by others. Therefore we would wish to ensure that we are confident in placing reliance on the work of the auditors of Loopy (the 'component' auditors) and that sufficient appropriate audit evidence has been gathered for us to express an opinion on the financial statements of the group as a whole.

Law gives us the right to **require** that the **component auditors** give us such information and explanations as we may reasonably require.

As a matter of courtesy we will inform the directors of Cuckoo Group of our intention to communicate with the auditors of Loopy.

We will first obtain an understanding of the component auditor. This would involve an assessment of:

- Whether the component auditor is **independent** and understands and will comply with the ethical requirements that are relevant to the group audit

- The component auditor's **professional competence**

- Whether the group engagement team will be **involved in the work of the component auditor** to the extent that it is necessary to obtain sufficient appropriate audit evidence

- Whether the component auditor operates in a **regulatory environment** that actively oversees auditors

This may be dealt with by **meeting the component auditors** (most appropriate in this first year), by **questionnaire** or a combination of both. If Loopy is significant to the group, we may wish to **review** the other auditors' **working papers** and will need to document this review. In an extreme situation, where we felt we could not rely on Loopy's auditors' work, we would need to **reperform** some or all of their **work**.

As the group auditor, we are responsible for setting the materiality level for the group financial statements as a whole, and for components which are individually significant such as Loopy. This would be set at a lower level than the materiality level of the group as a whole. The component auditor will then perform a full audit based on the component materiality level.

Depending on whether or not Loopy is significant to the financial statements of the group as a whole, we would then review the component auditor's overall audit strategy and audit plan, and perform risk assessment procedures to identify and assess risks of material misstatement at the component level.

We would then discuss with the component auditor the component's business activities that are significant to the group, and the susceptibility of the component to material misstatement of the financial information due to fraud or error. We would then review the component auditor's documentation of identified significant risks of material misstatements.

It would then be necessary to review a questionnaire completed by the component auditor highlighting key issues identified during the audit. The effect of any uncorrected misstatements should also be evaluated. On the basis of this review we would then determine whether any additional procedures are necessary, such as further procedures to gather audit evidence, participating in any meetings between the component auditors and management, or reviewing any other relevant parts of the component auditor's documentation.

(ii) **Cuckoo plc**

The valuation of the bullion and precious metals contravenes IAS 2 *Inventories*, which requires that it should be valued at the lower of cost and net realisable value. However, this method is recognised as an acceptable way of valuing commodities when the company trades in commodities on a liquid market, so that inventory can be realised at close to its valuation price. Departure from IAS 2 needs to be stated and justified in the financial statements as required by companies legislation.

Loopy plc

LIFO is **not** an **acceptable** method of valuing inventory under IAS 2. In addition the standard requires that cost or valuation is determined for **separate items** of inventory or of groups of similar items and not on a total basis.

The auditors of Loopy will need to determine whether adjustment is needed to ensure that the inventory valuation conforms to IAS 2. Audit qualifications in the company and group accounts (if no adjustment is made) will depend on materiality.

Snoopy plc

Base inventory valuation is **not acceptable** under IAS 2. In addition the **statement of financial position** and **statement of profit or loss** should **show** the **same value** for inventory.

However the immateriality of the adjustment in the group accounts may mean that it can be ignored. If it is material in the company's own accounts a **modified auditor's opinion** may be required if the directors of Snoopy wish the adjustment to stand.

Drake Retail plc

The methods used in allocating costs to inventory need to be selected with a view to providing the **fairest possible approximation** to the expenditure actually incurred in bringing the product to its present location and condition. The practice of retail outlets using selling price less normal gross profit margin is given as an example of an acceptable method of approximating to cost. **Records** must be kept of **mark-ups** and any subsequent mark-downs, to ensure that the calculation still gives an approximation to cost.

Conclusion

There are a number of problems with the accounting politics used across the Cuckoo Group in relation to inventory.

(b) (i) **Cooperation between auditors**

The group engagement team has the right to require from auditors of subsidiaries the information and explanations they require, and to require the group management to obtain the necessary information and explanations from subsidiaries. However, in practice, the degree of cooperation may be limited by factors such as the component auditor not being subject to the requirements of ISAs, but of different national practice or the group auditor not having any legal right to contact the auditors of a component of the company preparing group accounts. ISA (UK & Ireland) 600 states that the group auditor should not accept a group audit if there are restrictions on his communication with component auditors.

(ii) **Multi-location audits**

ISA (UK & Ireland) 600 applies when the financial information of any component is included in the financial statements audited by the group auditor. A component is defined as an entity or business activity for which group or component management prepares financial information that should be included in the group financial statements. Clearly any of these could be in a different location to the parent company, so ISA (UK & Ireland) 600 does apply to multi-location audits.

However, there is no specific guidance in ISA (UK & Ireland) 600 or other standards on how to deal with the particular problems caused by such multi-location situations. ISA (UK & Ireland) 315 recognises that multi-locations might give rise to a risk but does not suggest any solutions in a group context. This is an area where additional guidance is required.

(iii) **Joint audits**

ISA (UK & Ireland) 600 specifically does not deal with instances where two or more auditors are appointed as joint auditors.

Joint audits are rare because they are often costly, as both sets of auditors are responsible for the audit opinion and therefore work can be replicated. However, they are used in some countries, for example, France. In addition, in the wake of the Enron scandal joint audits have been proposed as a potential solution to such problems occurring again.

Given this, joint audits are an area which requires guidance to be produced by the IESBA and the IAASB.

50 Bluebell

Text references. Chapters 6, 10 and 15.

Top tips. This question may appear daunting at first because of the amount of numerical data presented. In part (a) make sure you take a methodical approach working through the information to structure your answer. Credit will only be given for risks of material misstatement so do not waste time describing other types of risk here. Part (b) asks for audit procedures on share-based payments and deferred tax assets. In the October 2008 edition of *Student Accountant*, the examiner hinted that more complex areas were likely to be examined in detail. If you had read this article then the topics examined here would not have come as a surprise.

Easy marks. Part (c) is probably the easiest part of this question as it does not require any knowledge of complex accounting topics. Make sure you present your answer as briefing notes to get the two professional marks.

Examiner's comments. Requirement (a) asked the candidate to 'identify and explain risks of material misstatement to be addressed when planning the final audit'. This requirement should not have been a surprise, as risk of material misstatement had appeared in the previous exam, and a recent examiner's article had discussed how financial reporting issues impacted on the auditor at the planning stage of the audit.

Requirement (b) asked candidates to describe principal audit procedures in respect of specific assertions relevant to the share-based payment expense, and deferred tax asset. Requirement (b)(i) focused on the measurement of the expense, (b)(ii) on the recoverability of the asset. Unfortunately, the majority of candidates ignored the assertions and instead provided procedures irrelevant to the requirement, for example, on the calculation of tax rather than the likelihood of it providing a future benefit to the company. The second problem was that many so-called procedures provided were not actually audit procedures at all, but a vague hint as to what the auditor might do. For example, there were many 'procedures' along the lines of 'check calculation of share-based payment expense' – yes, the auditor would need to do this, but how? The 'how' is the audit procedure.

Requirement (c) tended to be either extremely well answered, or extremely inadequately answered. Sound answers provided specific key performance indicators (KPI) relevant to a chain of hotels, and clear sources of evidence. While inadequate answers did usually attempt to recommend KPIs relevant to hotels, they would usually describe the policies that a company should have in place rather than the KPI that would measure the success of such a policy.

Candidates should remember that most of the marks awarded in the paper are for application skills.

Marking scheme

Marks

(a) **Risks of material misstatement**
Generally ½ mark each risk/matter defined
½ mark for reference to correct IFRS/IAS – maximum 2 marks
Maximum 2 marks for materiality calculations

Ideas list:
–   Revenue recognition (2 marks + 1 mark for providing calculation/trend) *IAS 18*
–   Share-based payment (3 marks) *IFRS 2*
–   Provision for repairs (2 marks) *IAS 37*
–   Insurance reimbursement (1 mark)
–   Understatement of operating expenses (2 marks)
–   Impairment of properties (1 mark) *IAS 36*
–   Property disposals (3½ marks)
–   Property revaluation (1½ marks) *IAS 16*
–   Deferred tax on property revaluation (1½ marks) *IAS 12*
–   Deferred tax asset (2 marks + 1 mark for recalculating profit for any suggested charges) *IAS 12*
–   Going concern (1 mark)
Maximum   14

(b) (i) **Audit procedures**

Generally 1 mark per procedure:
- Agree components of calculation to scheme documentation (½ mark per item agreed, Max 2)
- Recalculate + check vesting period
- Agreement of grant date, fair values, etc to specialist report
- Review of forecast staffing levels
- Written representation from management
- Discussion with HR assumptions used

Maximum

6

(ii) **Audit procedures**

Generally 1 mark per procedures
- Obtain client tax comp + deferred tax schedules, recalculate
- Form independent estimate of amount
- Profitability forecasts – assumptions
- Profitability forecast – time period for losses to be utilised
- Tax authority agreement of c/f of losses

Maximum

4

(c) **Social and environmental KPIs**

Up to 4 professional marks for format, logical structure and use of language appropriate to internal auditor ie free from jargon, all comments clearly explained Tabular format not

Tabular format not required

Generally ½ mark per KPI, ½ mark per evidence point. can increase to 1 mark (for either) if the point is very specific to a hotel business

Ideas list

Employees:
- Training spend
- Absenteeism rates
- Employee engagement index

Customers
- Customer satisfaction rate
- Number of complaints
- Number of accidents
- Repeat business rates

Community
- Charitable donations
- Free use of hotel facilities

Environment
- Waste recycling
- Energy efficient items purchased
- Carbon footprint

Maximum

12

Total

36

(a) **Risks of material misstatement**

Revenue recognition

Bluebell Ltd recognises income when a room is occupied in line with IAS 18 *Revenue*. A deposit of 20% is taken when the room is booked and this revenue should be deferred and shown as a liability on the statement of financial position. There is a risk of material misstatement that deposit revenue is recognised immediately leading to an overstatement of revenue and an understatement of liabilities. It is worth noting that revenue has increased by 24.8% at Bluebell Ltd. This is above the industry average of 20% and could be a result of deposit revenue being recognised in the incorrect period.

Share-based payment expense

The calculation of the share-based payment expense is complex and any inaccuracies or incorrect assumptions may cause it to be over or understated in the financial statements. In particular, the assumption of 0% staff turnover in three years sounds dubious and this needs to be investigated in order to judge the accuracy of the expense.

The model used to assess the fair value of the share options must comply with IFRS 2 *Share-based payment*. If a prohibited model is used, then the financial statements will not comply with accounting standards. Fair value must also be measured at the grant date in order to calculate the expense or the financial statements will be inaccurate.

Damaged property repair expenses

A provision of £100m has been made for flood damage to three hotels. However, since flood damage to hotels is already covered by insurance, it appears this provision was made in error. Hence there is a risk that operating expenses are overstated in the financial statements.

Additionally, under IAS 37 *Provisions, contingent liabilities and contingents assets*, a provision can only be recognised if an entity has a legal or constructive present obligation as a result of a past event. Bluebell Ltd may be intending to repair the damaged properties but it would be difficult to argue this is because of a legal or constructive obligation, rather than a desire to obtain future operating profits. Therefore, a risk exists that the financial statements do not fully comply with the requirements of IAS 37.

Other operating expenses

If the two new items included in operating expenses are excluded, other operating expenses have fallen from £690m in 20X7 to £597m in 20X8. This does not seem in line with the increase in revenue in the business. If sales of rooms have increased it would be expected that the associated costs would also increase, for example the costs of cleaning the rooms. This could highlight a possible understatement of other operating expenses in the statement of profit or loss. However, it may be that the decrease is reasonable and due to the hotels being able to increase their rates rather than increases in occupancy that would lead to increased costs.

Profit on property disposal

The statement of profit or loss includes £125m profit on the disposal of hotels where Bluebell Ltd is retaining a hotel management contract. Bluebell Ltd has an option to repurchase the hotels in fifteen years and this purchase seems likely. The transaction will need to be investigated in more detail during the audit. The substance of the transaction could be a sale and repurchase, rather than merely a sale, in which case the properties should remain on the statement of financial position. Thus, there is a risk that property and assets are understated and operating income is overstated.

If evidence proves the hotels should have remained on the statement of financial position, depreciation and operating expenses will also be understated. Bluebell Ltd will have stopped depreciating the hotels in March 20X8 when they were sold, eight months before the year-end.

Additionally, finance charges should be accrued for any sale and repurchase agreement and allocated over the period of the agreement. If the hotel sale and repurchase have not been correctly shown, then it is unlikely that finance charges have been included and are possibly understated.

Property revaluation

Property has been revalued during the year and a revaluation gain of £250m has been made. Since Bluebell Ltd are known to be seeking long-term funding to solve their liquidity problems, there is a risk that the properties have been overvalued in order to strengthen their statement of financial position and make the company a more attractive lending prospect. The basis of the valuation will need to be examined during the audit to ensure that any revaluations comply with IAS 16 *Property, plant and equipment*.

As per IAS 12 *Income taxes*, a deferred tax provision should be recognised on the revaluation of a property for which the debit is charged to equity. If any properties are found to have been overvalued, then the related deferred tax provision and equity charge will also be overstated.

Deferred tax asset

Under IAS 12, deferred tax assets can only be recognised where the recoverability of the asset can be demonstrated. Bluebell Ltd will therefore need to show that future profits will be generated for the unutilised tax losses to be offset against. If this is not possible, the deferred tax asset should be limited to the amount of profits that can be measured with reasonable certainty.

The statement of profit or loss currently shows a profit of £145m before tax, the first profit after several years of losses. However, this profit may need to be adjusted to take into account the items discussed previously and could turn out to be a loss. If so, it may be difficult for Bluebell Ltd to demonstrate a flow of future profits and the deferred tax asset is more likely to be overstated.

Going concern

Bluebell Ltd has suffered several years of losses, has poor liquidity and is trying to raise long-term finance to secure its future. The going concern of the company may be a problem and if so, will require disclosure in the financial statements. There is a risk of material misstatement that the incorrect disclosure requirements are made.

(b) **Procedures**

    (i) *Share-based payment expense*

- Review contractual documentation for the share-based payment scheme and agree the following to the management calculation of the £138m expense.

        – Number of employees and executives in scheme
        – Number of options per employee
        – Length of vesting period
        – Grant date of the share options
        – Any performance conditions attached to the options

- Re-perform the management calculation of the share-based payment expense, ensuring fair value is spread correctly over the vesting period.

- Agree the fair value of the options to a specialist report calculating their fair value.

- Assess whether the specialist report is reliable and objective evidence.

- Check that fair value is calculated at the grant date.

- Enquire of directors as to why the forecast staff turnover is 0% during the three year vesting period and evaluate the assumptions used in making this forecast.

- Perform sensitivity analysis to assess the effect on the expense for changes in the assumptions used, especially 0% staff turnover.

- Discuss the reasonableness of the 0% staff turnover assumption with human resources at Bluebell Co.

- Obtain written representations from management confirming that the assumptions used in measuring the expense are reasonable and there are no share-based payment schemes in existence that have not been disclosed to the auditors.

    (ii) *Recoverability of deferred tax asset*

- Check the arithmetical accuracy of Bluebell Ltd's deferred tax and corporation tax computations.

- Agree the figures used to any tax correspondence and the financial statements.

- Calculate an independent estimate of the deferred tax asset and compare this to management's estimate.

- Obtain profitability forecasts and ensure there are enough forecast taxable profits for the losses to be offset against.

- Evaluate the reasonableness of the assumptions used in the profitability forecast.

- Assess the length of time it will take to generate enough profits to offset the tax losses and judge whether recognition of the asset should be restricted.
- Check tax correspondence to ensure that Bluebell Ltd can carry the losses forward and offset these against taxable profits.

(c) **Key performance indicators**

Briefing notes for meeting with Daisy Rosepetal, internal auditor Bluebell Ltd

Guidance on social and environmental key performance indicators (KPIs)

Introduction

These notes detail social and environmental KPIs that could be used at Bluebell Ltd and the evidence that would be necessary for each.

KPIs

Social

KPI	Nature of evidence
Percentage female employees	Human resources permanent files
Number of customer accidents at a hotel	Hotel log of accidents which should include a description of incident and whether the emergency services needed to be called
Customer satisfaction scores – for example scores out of ten for cleanliness of room or efficiency of staff	Customer satisfaction surveys
Number of customer complaints	Hotel log of complaints Number of refunds issued via sales system

Environmental

KPI	Nature of evidence
Percentage of waste recycled at hotel	Amount invested in recycling facilities at hotel for both guests and staff
Amount spent on environmentally friendly products such as energy efficient light bulbs or rubbish bins with separate sections for recycling in all rooms	Preferred suppliers list will contain suppliers stocking these products Products visible throughout hotels
Percentage change in utilities usage since prior year	Supplier bills for gas, water and electricity to compare the cost and volume supplied versus the previous year Comparison of actual to budgeted use of utilities with explanations for unexpected variances
Percentage of sustainable or recycled materials used in building new hotels or when undertaking refurbishment	Project plans for new hotels or refurbishment details Invoices from suppliers detailing sustainable or recycled materials

Conclusion

The KPIs listed are just some of the possible measures which could be used at Bluebell Ltd. The company should ensure the environmental and social targets it sets are quantifiable and that evidence is available for each. The exact KPIs chosen will need to fit in with the overall priorities of the hotel chain.

51 Robster

Marking scheme

Marks

(a) (i) **Leases**
Generally 1 mark per matter/evidence point:
Matters:
- Correct calculation and assessment of materiality
- Classification of lease
- IAS 17 indicators of finance lease
- Finance charge
- Depreciation
- Disclosure

Evidence:
- Lease clauses re risk and reward
- Recalculate Present Value of Minimum Lease Payment v fair value
- Recalculate depreciation and finance charge
- Cash book for payments
- Review of disclosures
- Split payable < 1 year; > 1 year

Maximum marks   8

(ii) **Financial assets**
Generally 1 mark per matter/evidence point:
Matters:
- Correct calculation and assessment of materiality
- Classification as held for trading
- Assets shown at fair value – could be subjective
- Disclosure

Evidence
- Agree purchase price
- Agree fair value
- Recalculate gain
- Review of disclosures in notes
- Review of disclosure in OFR/other information published with financial statements

Maximum

(b) **Interim financial information**

Generally 1 mark per procedure:

- Comparisons with past data eg to preceding period, to corresponding interim last year, to last audited accounts
- Comparisons to anticipated results
- Comparisons of non financial data/ratios
- Comparisons to similar entities
- Disaggregation of data

Maximum

4

Total

17

(a) (i) Matters to consider

Materiality

Both the non-current assets recognised and the total finance lease payable are material at 8% and 7.1% of total assets respectively (breaching the 2–5% threshold).

Accounting treatment

- Whether the leases have been classified correctly as finance leases in line with IAS 17 *Leases*
- The assertion that the leases are finance leases means that they are in substance assets rather than expenses. This means that Robster Ltd must have the risks and rewards of ownership, including:
    - Responsibility for repairs and maintenance
    - Transfer of legal title at the end of the lease term
    - The lease is for most of the assets' useful life
    - The present value of the minimum lease payments is 90% or more of the assets' fair value
- The leases result in finance charges against profit and loss, calculated using the actuarial method.
- The finance lease payable of £3.2 million should be split between payables falling due within one year, and payables falling due after more than one year in the statement of financial position.

Audit evidence

- A copy of Robster Ltd's workings in relation to the finance leases
- Check the additions and calculations of the workings.
- To verify that the leases are classified correctly as finance leases, review the lease ontracts for indicators of transfer of the risks and rewards of ownership, such as:
    - That Robster is responsible for repairs and maintenance of the assets
    - That legal title is transferred to Robster at the end of the lease term
    - Confirmation that the leases are for the major part of the assets' useful lives
    - That the present value of the minimum lease payments is substantially all of the assets' fair value
- Recalculation of the finance charges charged against profit and loss
- Agreement of interest rates used in calculations to lease agreements
- Recalculation of depreciation charges applied to non-current assets
- Verify the split of the payable between the amounts due in less than one year and more than one year from the year end
- Recalculation of operating lease expenses, on a straight-line basis over the lease term

BPP
LEARNING MEDIA

(ii)   **Matters to consider**

Materiality

The financial assets of £1.26m are material at 2.8% of total assets. The gain of £350,000 is material at 10.9% of profit before tax.

Accounting treatment

- IFRS 9 *Financial instruments* sets out the categories that financial instruments must fall into, along with the appropriate accounting treatment for each. The initial classification of the financial assets as 'held for trading investments' is therefore a crucial area of judgement as it determines the accounting treatment – in this case, at fair value. This means measuring the fair value at the year end, and recognising any gains or losses directly in profit or loss.

- The assets should therefore have been purchased in order to sell them in the short term, and must be part of a whole portfolio of instruments that are managed together with a view to short-term profit.

Audit evidence

- A schedule showing all the investments held in this category and the fair values of each

- Agreement of the fair values to external evidence such as year end market price (current bid price)

- Recalculation of the total gain or loss as the overall movement in fair value over the course of the year

- Review of the internal controls and procedures followed by the trading department. Testing to confirm that details (quantities, dates, etc.) shown on the schedule can be relied upon

- Analytical procedures to confirm that there is a portfolio of investments that are traded frequently with a view to short-term profit. Corroboration by a review of events after the year end

(b)   According to ISRE 2410, the auditor's analytical procedures should include the following.

- Comparing the interim financial information (IFI) with forecasts and budgets, obtaining explanations from management for any discrepancies

- Comparing the IFI with prior periods, such as the same period in the last financial year

- Comparing the IFI with other entities in the same industry

- Analytical procedures designed to identify relationships and unusual items that may reflect a material misstatement

- Considering the nature of any corrected or uncorrected misstatements in last year's financial statements

- Considering any significant risks that were identified in the audit of the year end financial financial statements

52 Efex Engineering

Text references. Chapters 12 and 14

Top tips. This is another 34-mark compulsory Section A question so again, as for Question 1, it is key that you stick to time for both the question in total and each of the four parts.

You should be able to score well in part (a) which is knowledge-based on forensic auditing. Make sure you answer the question requirement fully – ie describe its applications as well as define what it means.

In part (b), use the clues in the scenario to help structure your answer. When you are asked for procedures, make sure these are specific and well explained – vague answers will not score well.

In parts (c) and (d), the questions are split into two requirements. Again when describing tests, make sure they are specific and well thought out. Use sub-headings to give more structure to your answers, as well as to improve presentation.

BPP LEARNING MEDIA

Easy marks. Easier marks on this question are available in part (a) which is knowledge-based. You should make sure you get the professional marks available in part (b). Using the information in the scenario should help you score marks in the other parts of this question.

			Marks
(a)	**'Forensic auditing'**		
	Generally 1 – ½ mark each point	Maximum	5
	Ideas		
	Definition		
	– Eg of Institut des Fraud Auditeurs de Fraude (IFA-IAF)		
	– Audit (examination) + forensic (legal)		
	Application to fraud investigation		
	– Irregular nature of fraud		
	– Objective(s)		
	– Reactive vs proactive (preventative)		
(b)	**Prior to commencing investigation**	Maximum	10
	Generally 1 mark each matter/ procedure		
	Ideas		
	Matters		
	– Terms of reference (obtaining is a procedure)		
	– Purpose/scope of investigation		
	o Possible understatement of inventory at 30/6		
	o High material consumption in quarter to 30/6		
	o To give credence to y/e amount (next quarter to 30/9)		
	– Scope of access to records relevant to the investigation (any restriction?)/Information to be supplied		
	– Staffing – level/experience/number/availability/other client commitments		
	– Degree of reliance to be placed on report		
	By whom? – insurer?		
	– Timeframe – before next (= annual) physical count		
	– Form of report required – Any caveats?		
	Procedures		
	– Discuss assignment with directors – responsibilities etc		
	– Obtain engagement letter (terms are a matter)		
	– Agree investigative fee		
	Note. Two professional marks are included		
	Professional marks – up to		4

Tutorial note. There is no maximum to be awarded for each of matters and procedures as answer points about matters may be constructed as procedures (and vice versa). Marks should be awarded for either/or (not both).

(c) **Inventory undervaluation**

Generally up to 1½ marks each matter explained 1 mark each test max 8   Maximum   8

Ideas

(i)   Matters
- Omission from count
- Cut-off
- Scrap/waste etc

(ii)   Tests
- Physical inspection
- Arithmetic checks
- Cut-off tests
- Analytical procedures
- Tests on production records/pricing

Tutorial note. Tests must address **under**statement of inventory at 30 June.

(d) **High materials consumption**

Generally up to 1½ marks each matter explained 1 mark each test   Maximum   7

Ideas

(i)   Matters
- Cut-off
- Losses
- Obsolescence etc
- Major contracts
- Change of supplier

(ii)   Tests
- Physical inspection
- Arithmetic checks
- Cut-off tests
- Tests of control

Tutorial note. Matters must address **over**statement of materials consumption in the quarter to 30 June.

Total   **34**

(a) **Forensic auditing**

Forensic auditing is the process of gathering, analysing and reporting on data, in a pre-defined context, for the purpose of finding facts and/or evidence in the context of financial or legal disputes or irregularities and giving preventative advice in this area.

Forensic auditing is a rapidly growing area and demand for this has arisen in part due to the increased expectation of corporate governance codes for company directors to take very seriously their responsibilities for the prevention and detection of fraud. Fraud investigations can involve:

(i)   Quantifying losses from theft of cash or goods

(ii)   Identifying payments or receipts of bribes

(iii) Identifying intentional misstatements in financial information, such as overstatement of revenue and earnings and understatement of costs and expenses

(iv)   Investigating intentional misrepresentations made to auditors

Forensic accountants may also be engaged to act in an advisory capacity to assist directors in developing more effective controls to reduce the risks from fraud.

(b)   **Briefing notes**

To:	CJ, Senior partner
From:	Reginald Perrin, Audit manager
Date:	July
Subject:	Efex Engineering Ltd

Introduction

These briefing notes contain an outline of the matters to consider and the procedures to perform in respect of the investigation of Efex Engineering Ltd.

Matters to consider in planning

- Whether our firm has the necessary resources and experience to carry out the investigation of Efex Engineering's losses

- What reliance is to be placed on the report that we produce as a result of the investigation and whether it will be relied upon by any third parties such as lenders

- What type of report it is to be and what level of assurance will be given

- Whether any potential independence issues exist with other clients that our firm has and therefore potential conflicts of interest

- What level of detail is required in terms of the work to be undertaken

Procedures to carry out

- Review staff availability and timings to assess whether sufficient resource for the investigation exists.

- Discuss with the management of Xzibit the scope of the investigation and its purpose (eg whether any third parties will be relying on it or whether it is an internal report only) and other issues such as expected timing, fees etc.

- Clarify the terms of reference of this engagement in writing from the management of Xzibit.

- Draft an engagement letter for this investigation and obtain agreement of terms in writing from the management of Xzibit.

(c)   (i)   **Matters to consider re. undervaluation of inventory**

- Inventory will be undervalued if cut-off has not been appropriately applied therefore particular focus needs to be on this area of the quarter-end count.

- Inventory will be undervalued if not all inventory items have been included in the count therefore the investigation should focus on the procedures in place for the quarterly counts.

- Inventory will be undervalued if the valuation methods are incorrect. Inventory is valued manually so the investigation should examine how items of inventory, such as scrap are valued.

(ii)   **Procedures to carry out**

- Obtain inventory counting instructions in place at Efex Engineering and review to make an assessment of their adequacy for the quarterly counts, together with discussion with appropriate staff at Efex Engineering.

- Perform analytical procedures using figures from the quarterly management accounts, such as comparisons between 30 June and 31 March.

- Discuss scrap and wastage policy with warehouse staff.

- Examine details of scrap and discuss figures with appropriate staff to establish whether there are any reasons for wastage being higher in this quarter.

- Test cut-off is correct by tracing the last goods delivery notes and despatch notes to the invoices.

- Recast additions on inventoriesheets to verify accuracy.

Reasons for high materials consumption in quarter ended 30 June 20X8

If closing inventory has been undervalued or undercounted, this could explain a high materials consumption in this quarter. It could also be due to excessive consumption or wastage of materials.

If recorded inventory has been stolen from production areas this could be another contributory factor to a high materials consumption in this quarter.

If cut-off was incorrectly applied, then this would affect the materials consumption, ie if goods delivered after the year end were incorrectly included as purchases in the quarter then this would give rise to a higher materials consumption. Also if revenue is understated due to incorrect cut-off, then materials consumption as a % of revenue will be overstated.

(ii) **Procedures to carry out**

- Test cut-off of purchases and sales has been done correctly by matching purchase invoices to goods received notes and matching despatch notes to invoices raised around the quarter-end date.

- Compare value of inventory identified as obsolete or damaged at the quarter-end to the previous quarter-end, discussing discrepancies with appropriate staff.

- Discuss levels of scrap and wastage with warehouse managers to ascertain normal levels and understand how it arises.

- Review a sample of credit notes received after the quarter-end to identify any returned materials.

- Inspect scrap materials to confirm it is not suitable for manufacture and therefore is not included in inventory.

53 Bateleur Zoo Gardens

Text references. Chapters 6 and 7.

Top tips. This question appears daunting because of the unusual context for the scenario. A zoo is an unusual context in which to think of internal controls, and the assets such as animals are also unusual. However, the question is actually reasonably straightforward. You could complete your answer to the requirement for factors to consider when planning substantive analytical procedures, which is essentially rote learning of ISA 520, before attempting the rest of part (a) if that seems tricky at first glance. However, even the rest of (a) should be manageable. Try to think of the practical business and financial statement implications of the zoo. Animals are assets in this context, which are impaired if people don't want to come and see them. Unrecorded donations are in effect unrecorded additions to non-current assets. The risks have been identified for you, you have to focus on how those risks might be controlled. Make sure you read the question properly and answer it. For example, in part (a), you are planning to use analytical procedures as substantive procedures for income. You will not gain marks talking about analytical procedures at the planning stage or at the review stage.

Easy marks. Some of the internal controls required in part (a) are more straightforward than others. Do not panic if the first applicable risk seems complicated. Read through the question completely and identify the more straightforward ones, for example, cash misappropriation, and you can gain easy marks listing controls and risks of material misstatement applicable in this area, which would not be out of place in the lower level auditing paper.

Examiner's comments. In part (a), candidates mostly sought to address internal controls selected from 'compare' or other mnemonics – failing to appreciate that these are only specific control procedures. Candidates needed to consider more pervasive controls and monitoring activities also … Regarding the next part of (a), few candidates recognised that failure to record reciprocal advertisement arrangements would result in an understatement of advertising expense (and sponsorship income). Most candidates did not read the requirement of analytical procedures and did not answer the question.

Marks

(a) **Internal controls**
Generally 1 mark each point, max 3 any one risk
Ideas
(i)   Control procedures/specific controls
(ii) Control environment/pervasive controls
(iii) Monitoring activities (including reconciliations)

Risk of material misstatement   6
Generally 1 mark each point
Ideas
Assets
(i)   Impairment (IAS 36)/overstatement (tangibles)
(ii) Useful lives
(iii) Existence assurance (tangibles, cash)
(iv) Completeness (tangibles, receivables)
Profit and loss account
(i)   Admission fees (understatement)
(ii) Sponsorship income/advertising expense understatement
Reserves – Existence/disclosure
Disclosure risk – Going concern (IAS 1)

Substantive analytical procedures
Generally ½ mark each factor + up to 1 mark a comment   7
Ideas (ISA 520)
(i)   Audit objectives
(ii)   Nature of entity
(iii)   Degree of disaggregation of information
(iv)   Availability of information
(v)   Reliability of information
(vi)   Relevance of information
(vii)   Source of information available
(viii) Comparability of information
(ix)   Expectation of relationships
(x)   Materiality
(xi)   Other audit procedures
(xii)   Accuracy of predictions
(xiii) Inherent and control risk assessments
(xiv)   Tests of controls

(b) Internal control effectiveness
Generally 1 mark each comment
(i)   Responsibilities of management and auditors
(ii) Sarbanes – Oxley Act
(iii) ISA 330   5
Professional marks for format, style and clarity of answer   4

Total   34

(a)   **Memorandum**

For: Charlotte Brain
By: Laura Liver
Date: December
Subject: BZG audit

Introduction

This memorandum sets out both the risks of material misstatement arising from the applicable risks identified by the management of BZG, and internal controls that could implement in order to manage those risks. It then comments on the factors to consider when planning analytical procedures in respect of BZG's income.

	Internal controls	Financial statements risks
(i) *Lack of investment in new exhibits*	• Regular review of admission fees/visitor numbers/lapsed memberships and sponsorships • Regular (monthly/quarterly/ annually) review of competitors' service/assets • Annual capital expenditure budget for animals/attractions and approval of it • Annual review of additions of animals/attractions in year against budget	Existing assets (animals and non-current assets such as enclosures) may be impaired if they are not generating income in use. Impairment tests in line with IAS 36 should be carried out. Ultimately, failure to invest in the assets of the zoo might lead to going concern problems. There may be disclosure risk if correct disclosures under IAS 1 are required and have not been made.
(ii) *Failure to invoice animal sponsorships*	• Regular reconciliation between sponsorships and sponsorship income • Pre-numbered sponsorship documentation • Sequence checking of sponsorship documentation by invoicing staff • Monitoring of instances of lack of data transfer • Investment in automatic computerised data transfer between sponsorship/invoicing departments	Income may not be recorded completely.

	Internal controls	Financial statements risks
(iii) *Rates for corporate sponsorship*	• Approved price list • Price list reviewed annually • Approved discount list • Key official to authorise discounts for new clients • Sharing of discount information with invoicing department • Review of sponsorship income vs budget to identify any shortfalls • Review of advertising cost vs budget to identify 'free' advertising (and associated sales)	Income and expenses may not be recorded completely if sponsorship is given in exchange for advertising. Ultimately, if sponsorship is recurrently undercharged, going concern might be affected.
(iv) *Cash misappropriation*	• CCTV in ticket booths to record cash sales • Electronic till records kept and reconciled to cash received by cashiers in accounts department • More than one officer at each gate • Reconciliation of ticket stubs with cash • Secondary gate to ensure that all visitors have been issued with a ticket/to collect ticket stubs	Income will be understated if cash is misappropriated at source (and by implication, the sale is not recorded).
(v) *Booking/ticket issuing system unavailable*	• Contingency plans (see below) required • Manual tickets kept in entrance gate ticket offices • Telephone booking system alternative to website if website unavailable • Maintenance/downtime of website at anti-social hours	Loss of sales in this manner could affect the going concern status of the company, but other than that there may be no impact on the financial statements of sales lost in this manner.
(vi) *Donations of animals not recorded*	• Animal register to be maintained • Regular reconciliations between animals in zoo and animals in register	Assets may be understated if new assets have not been valued and included in non current assets in accordance with IAS 16.

Analytical procedures (income)

The auditor should consider the expected effectiveness and efficiency of the available audit procedures, including:

(1) *The fact that substantive analytical procedures are based on an expectation that relationships among data exist.*

For example, the relationship between current year income and prior year income can be expected to exist unless there have been any major changes in the year (for example, new attractions) and it should be predictable even if there have been changes. For example, the impact of a new attraction should be predictable on the basis of prior new attractions. In addition, BZG's income will be seasonal, and there should be clear and predictable patterns of sales in high summer season and in school holidays.

(2) *The nature of the assertions and the auditor's assessment of risk*

The objectives will be to test the assertion around the completeness of sales income. The results are likely to be reliable, given the expected relationship between sales income each year as outlined above. However, the risks affecting sales income discussed above ((ii) and (iii)) would merit some other substantive work being carried out in this risk area. If comparing income last year to this year, it may be that there were significant new attractions in the prior year that will impact on the comparison with this year.

As sales is a material balance and could potentially contain single items (large sponsorship deals) that are individually material, some additional substantive procedures are likely to be necessary, for example on sponsorship. In addition, given the control problems in connection with income, control risk is higher and additional substantive tests may be required on income completeness.

(3) *The degree to which the information can be disaggregated*

The auditor should consider what records are available with regard to sales: monthly sales figures, daily sales figures, electronic till receipt records, prior year records in the same detail, sales budgets, in order to assess how detailed the level of analytical review he is going to be able to carry out. The types of sale (sponsorship, retail outlets, gate entry) are distinct and their records should be distinct which will allow greater detail of analysis on sales generally to be made.

(4) *The availability of the information*

The information outlined above should be easily available to the auditor if it exists. In addition, non-financial information, such as number of visitors, should be available, giving the auditor scope to assess whether actual income is consistent with income for that number of visitors etc.

(5) *The nature and relevance of the information*

For example, if the auditor is comparing budget to actual, he should ascertain whether the budget was realistic or a tough target. He should be able to verify this by reference to the budget setter, or to sales meeting minutes or prior year budgetary practice. Information from gates (ie number of visitors) will be more relevant if there is no other method of gaining access to the zoo.

(6) *The comparability of the information available*

For example, if the auditor intended to compare BZG's results with those of a competitor zoo, he should bear in mind whether the zoos have comparable attractions, target markets and opening times. However, as the zoo is fairly specialised, more meaningful comparisons are likely with prior period information from BZG itself.

(7) *Availability and reliability of the information needed*

This will depend upon the source of the information provided by management and the effectiveness of any controls over the preparation of the information.

Conclusion

Controls are suggested above that would appropriate to help manage the significant risks of material misstatement that arise from the applicable risks identified by management. There are a number of factors that must be considered when planning substantive analytical procedures in respect of BZG's income.

(b) **Effectiveness of internal financial controls**

Responsibilities

Management is responsible for ensuring that internal financial controls are effective. This is often a process that management employ an internal audit department to carry out.

In the UK, auditors of listed companies are required by the UK Corporate Governance Code to review the company's corporate governance statement which will include a review of the Board's review of the effectiveness of internal controls.

An auditor must test the effectiveness of internal controls if seeking to rely on them for audit evidence. The auditor is not required to report to management directly on their effectiveness, unless engaged specifically to do so in an engagement other than the audit.

Current guidance

Although auditors have always had the option of testing internal control effectiveness as part of their audit, ISA 330 *The auditor's responses to assessed risks* makes it more likely that they will do so than was previously the case. The standard states that the auditor shall design and perform tests of controls if:

(i)   The auditor's assessment of risks of material misstatement at the assertion level includes an expectation that the controls are operating effectively (that is, the auditor intends to rely on the operating effectiveness of controls in determining the nature, timing and extent of substantive procedures); or

(ii)   Substantive procedures alone cannot provide sufficient appropriate audit evidence at the assertion level.

This changes audit practice from testing controls if the auditor intends to rely on the effectiveness of controls as audit evidence, to testing controls if the auditor believes the controls to be effective. This will result in tests of controls being performed regularly because it is likely that auditors will expect a company's internal control system to be operating effectively more often than not.

In the US, the Sarbanes-Oxley Act requires CEOs and CFOs to certify that they are responsible for internal control and have reported on their effectiveness and that all major control weaknesses and management frauds have been reported to the auditors. Auditors in the US are required to report on management's report about internal control effectiveness.

In the UK, the UK Corporate Governance Code has recently been revised with more emphasis being put on non-executive directors paying attention to such matters as internal control effectiveness if they are members of the non-executive audit committee.

54 Sci-Tech

Text references. Chapters 9, 12, 15 and 16.

Top tips. Time management is critical in this question – there are six separate requirements so remember to work out how much time you can allocate to each part of the question and stick to this. If you miss out whole parts of questions you are at very high risk of failing.

In part (a) as well as showing that you understand outsourcing, you need to consider the outsourcing of payroll in this particular scenario. Knowledge of ISA (UK & Ireland) 402 will gain some marks but it is important to apply this to the specifics of this question. In part (b) your financial reporting knowledge will be vital as will your ability again to use the detail in the scenario. In part (c)(i) it is important to describe the procedures in some detail. Part (d) would appear difficult as there is no specific technical material on which to base an answer. What was needed here was a commonsense approach, thinking about factors that affect the levels of assurance, and the nature of information that would be likely to exist about the particular performance indicators given in the question.

Easy marks. Parts (a),(b) and (c) contain the easiest marks in this question, as in each of these parts there is an element of technical knowledge, either from ISAs or from your financial reporting knowledge that will give you a foundation for your answers. Also be sure to get some of the professional marks available.

Examiner's comments. Part (b) focussed on the audit of development costs which had been capitalised as an intangible asset. The answers were on the whole rather disappointing. Requirement (b)(i) required a discussion of matters to be considered in deciding on the appropriateness of capitalising the development costs. Most candidates could reel off the criteria for capitalisation under IAS 38 *Intangible Assets*, which is relevant, but few candidates then went on to apply the criteria to the scenario provided. It is very important that candidates appreciate that at this level of professional examination, few marks can be awarded for the rote-learning and regurgitating of facts, such as accounting standards criteria, without any application to the question.

In answering the final requirement, which invited candidates to suggest procedures used to verify the number of serious accidents reported, the marks awarded to scripts were polarised. Many candidates seemed to think that the auditor has access to absolutely any kind of evidence that they could wish for. Common sources of evidence referred to included the private medical records of employees, police reports on 'dangerous' incidents, hospital admissions data, interviews with ambulance drivers/paramedics/doctors and death certificates.

Candidates need to appreciate that although the auditor will have access to books and records held by their client, they will not be able to access external and possibly highly confidential information as a means to gather evidence. The above examples show of a lack of commercial, or even, common sense.

Marking scheme

	Marks

(a) Outsourcing – definition and matters to be considered
Definition – 1 mark
Matters to be considered – generally 1½ marks for each matter explained:
- Materiality
- Accessibility
- Control issues (extend to 2 marks for detailed answer)
- Independent records
- Compliance
- Transactions

Maximum   **9**

(b) Recognition of development costs
- Materiality – max 2 marks
- IAS 38 criteria – max 1 mark
- Application of criteria to scenario – max 3 marks

Maximum marks   **5**

Evidence on technical feasibility
Generally 1 mark per procedure
- Review documentary evidence of scientific test results
- Discuss test results
- Licences
- Analytical procedures
- Board minute review

Maximum   **3**

(c) Evidence on amortisation rate
Generally 1 mark per procedure
- Market research results
- Actual sales patterns
- Management assumptions
- Discussion of sales trends
- Correspondence with retail outlets
- Advertising budgets

Maximum   **5**

(d) (i) KPI assurance difficulties
- Discussion of problems in defining KPI terms
  (max 2 marks)
- Discussion of difficulty in gathering evidence
  (max 2 marks)

Maximum   **4**

    (ii)   **Procedures on number of accidents**

Generally 1 mark per procedure:

Ideas list:

- Review log book
- Discuss and clarify criteria
- HR/payroll records
- Employee correspondence
- Board minute review
- Legal letter review
- Discuss with employees

Maximum   4

Professional marks for format and clarity of answer.

Total   <u>**34**</u>

Memorandum

To:	Robert Nesbitt
From:	James Cotter
Subject:	Sci-Tech planning

Introduction

This memorandum explains the matters to be covered by the planning document for the Sci-Tech audit and the review assignment.

(a)   **Outsourcing/payroll expense**

Outsourcing is the process of purchasing key functions from an outside supplier (service organisation). In other words, it is contracting-out certain functions, for example, internal audit, or information technology, or, in this case, the payroll function.

Audit of salary expense – matters to consider

The audit firm must ensure it follows the guidelines of ISA (UK & Ireland) 402 *Audit considerations relating to an entity using a service organisation*. This requires them to consider an approach to parts of the audit affected by a service organisation.

Materiality

Salaries are 8.4% of revenue and are separately disclosed on the face of the statement of profit or loss and other comprehensive income. In addition, an element of salary cost for research and development staff will be included in research and development costs. Salary costs are therefore material for the audit.

Audit approach

The fact that salary costs have been audited by systems audit in the past implies that when the payroll was carried out in-house, there was a good control environment and effective controls.

As ProPay now control the payroll function, the auditors need to determine the audit approach they will take to salaries now.

In order to continue with a systems approach, they will need to be satisfied that a good system of control over payroll exists at ProPay. If they are not so convinced, they may need to take a substantive approach.

The fact that a company with good controls over its payroll is prepared to outsource to ProPay suggests that ProPay has good controls. However, the auditors must not rely on this assumption but determine this for themselves.

Accessibility

In order to make the determinations discussed above, the auditors really need access to ProPay's books and records. However, they have been engaged by Sci-Tech, not ProPay. It is not certain that they will be granted such access. The auditors should ask Sci-Tech to request that its auditors are allowed access to Pro-Pay's records. If the auditors were involved in the process of obtaining the contract with Pro-Pay it is likely that such access has been negotiated. If not, it may have been overlooked.

If such access is declined, the auditors will have to consider other means of gaining the assurance they require about ProPay's systems. They may be able to get this assurance from:

- Third-party reports about ProPay, such as the auditor's report of Pro-Pay or reports of any regulatory agency

- Other reports, such as ProPay's internal auditor's reports, if made available to clients

- Requested procedures by ProPay's external or internal auditors

If the auditors are unable to obtain the assurance they require about ProPay's systems or access to records to carry out proposed substantive tests, this would constitute an inability to obtain sufficient appropriate audit evidence which would result in the need for a qualification.

Compliance

The auditors need to ensure that Sci-Tech is still fulfilling its legal obligations in respect of maintaining financial records in respect of payroll, despite the administrational burden being carried by Pro-Pay.

Records

The auditors should determine whether Sci-Tech keep any payroll records or whether solely ProPay keep the records. If Sci-Tech kept some records, these would provide corroboration of the figures kept by ProPay.

(b)   (i)   **Matters to consider in determining whether capitalised development costs are correctly capitalised**

Materiality

The auditors will be concerned with whether the capitalised development costs are correctly capitalised only if there is a risk of material misstatement. In this case, net book value of development costs is 7% of total assets, so they are material.

Analytical review

Capitalised development costs have risen fairly significantly on the previous year and research costs have fallen. However, given the nature of the asset and the fact different projects will have different cost and feasibility structures, this is not necessarily indicative that research costs have been capitalised wrongly.

Accounting standard criteria

The key issue in determining whether development costs have been correctly capitalised is whether the costs meet the criteria in IAS 38 *Intangible assets*.

There are six criteria, all of which must be met to permit a development cost to be capitalised:

- There must be a separately identifiable project
- The expenditure must be separately identifiable
- It must be expected to be commercially viable
- It must be technically feasible
- An overall profit must be expected, and
- There must be adequate resources available to complete the project

There is a risk that all these criteria might not be met and therefore that the development costs are overstated. In particular, the auditors should consider:

- Whether the developed products meet government criteria for sale (for example, do they have a license) otherwise they may not be saleable

- Whether the existence of a competitor (specifically to the drug Flortex) means that the drug is no longer saleable

- Whether the funding that makes completion of the work technically feasible will continue (particularly since in 20X8 the company has broken one of its KPIs on which the funding is dependent)

(ii) **Evidence of technical feasibility**

- Establishing the existence of, and reviewing, scientific tests on the development such as safety testing

- Reviewing the adverse results of such tests and ensuring that corrective action has been taken and tested

- Enquiring whether appropriate licenses have been applied for/granted and reviewing correspondence in relation to such licenses

- Reviewing board minutes for discussion of technical feasibility and plans for products

(c) **Audit procedures on validity of amortisation rate re Plummet**

(i) Obtain copies of the market research carried out in respect of Plummet to determine whether it supports an expected life span of five years

(ii) Compare budget and forecast sales to date in Plummet's life to determine whether actual sales are in accordance with what market research suggested

(iii) Discuss sales trends with sales manager to ensure that actual performance continues in line with expectations

(iv) Consider contracts with retailers/order book to ensure that future sales are still in accordance with market research and budgets

(v) Obtain future budgets and ensure finance is still expected to be available to support Plummet's useful life expectation

(d) **Key performance indicators**

(i) *Level of assurance over meeting KPIs*

There are two main reasons why the level of assurance given in relation to the KPIs can not be a high level of assurance:

- Lack of precision in the description of the KPIs
- Likely lack of appropriate audit evidence

Lack of precision

The KPIs are defined imprecisely and are also subjective. For example:

- Donated product should be 1% of revenue, but what price will be free product be valued at – cost or retail price?

- Similarly, how will 'donations' to local charities be valued if these donations are more than just financial donations, such as the use of Sci-Tech's expert employees or products?

- 'Serious' accidents should be fewer than 5, but what constitutes 'serious'?

Audit evidence

Some of these matters may be well documented, such as cash donations or accidents, because of health and safety procedures, but others, such as time spent by employees at local charities, may not be so well documented.

(ii) *Evidence in relation to serious accidents*

- Obtain and review health and safety accident log-books for all Sci-Tech's premises and review the number of accidents.

- Discuss the definition of 'serious' with the directors and obtain written verification of this definition.

- Select a number of accidents designated serious and not-serious and review associated correspondence, payroll records and compensation payments to determine whether the accidents have been properly designated serious or not.

- Review correspondence with legal advisors to ascertain if any action has been taken in relation to accidents not designated serious by the directors.

- Review board minutes to obtain directors' opinions on the increase in serious accidents in 20X7.

- Review correspondence and reports from regulatory bodies to ensure that controls over health and safety reporting are considered to be strong.

- Discuss health and safety controls with health and safety officer to ensure that all accidents are reported.

55 Rosie

Text references. Chapters 11 and 12.

Top tips. As always, time management is key in this question – there are five separate requirements so work out how much time you can allocate to each part of the question and stick to this. If you miss out whole parts of questions you are at very high risk of failing to pass the question and ultimately the whole paper.

Group audits are a key current topic. Having a good understanding of the basics and keeping up to date with the articles in *Student Accountant* would have helped you here.

Easy marks. Parts (c) contained some easy marks for a simple definition and some sensible suggestions of advantages and disadvantages relevant to the scenario. Some easy professional marks were available if you set out your report correctly in part (a).

Examiner's comments Requirement (b)(i) asked for 'matters to consider' and 'evidence you would expect to find' regarding the cost of an investment made during the year. The wording of the requirement should be familiar, as this type of question has appeared regularly in advanced audit examinations. However, most candidates were completely unable to restrict their answer to the cost of investment as shown in the scenario, and most launched into a discussion of the accounting treatment of goodwill. This was **not** asked for.

Requirement (b)(ii) was also not well answered. The majority of candidates seemed not to know the contents of a consolidation schedule, or how to audit it. However, those candidates who had read the relevant article in *Student Accountant* tended to score well on this requirement.

Marking scheme

			Marks
(a)	(i)	**Purpose and benefits of due diligence**	
		Award up to 4 professional marks for good style of report with clear explanations and logical flow	4
		Generally 1 to 1½ marks for each point	
		– Introduction	
		– Fact finding	
		– Verify specific representations	
		– Identify and value assets, especially intangibles, and contingencies	
		– Tool to aid negotiation of consideration	
		– Operational issues identified – staff, suppliers, customers, contracts	
		– Consideration of commercial impact – synergies and drawbacks	
		– Benefit of external provision – free up management time, independent investigation	
		– Enhanced credibility	
		Maximum	10

(ii) **Due diligence scope – comparison with audit**
Generally ½ mark for identification and 1 mark for explanation
- Wider scope – more information sources
- No detailed testing of transactions/balances – unless specifically agreed
- No detailed evaluation of internal systems and controls
- Greater use of analytical procedures, reduced scope for substantive procedures
- Forward looking

Maximum   4

(b) (i) **Dylan Ltd**
Generally 1 mark per procedure and 1 mark per matter
No marks to be awarded for discussion of materiality as scenario states that all figures are material
No marks awarded for discussion of goodwill – this is not asked for
- Completeness – missing professional fees
- Agree consideration to legal documentation
- Agree cash consideration to bank statement
- Deferred consideration – discounted per IFRS 3
- Recalculate (1/2 mark only)
- Agree reasonable discount factor used
- Contingent consideration – only accrue if probable per IFRS 3
- Review forecasts and assumptions

Maximum   7

(ii) **Principle audit procedures**
Generally 1 mark per specific procedure
- Agree figures to individual co financial statements
- Cast and cross cast schedule
- Agree brought down figures
- Recalculate consolidation adjustments – award ½ mark for each adjustment clearly identified, max 2 marks
- Reconcile opening and closing reserves

Agree only post acquisition reserves consolidated for Dylan Ltd

Maximum   4

(c) **Joint audit**
Definition – 1 mark
Advantages and disadvantages – 1 mark each & max 3 marks each
Advantages
Knowledge sharing
- Increase resource availability
- Easier to meet tight deadline
- Improve audit quality
- New insight of new auditor
- Current issue – increase competition

Disadvantages
- Higher cost for client
- Bureaucracy
- Difference in audit approach
- Problems in working together
- Joint liability

Maximum   7

Total   36

(a) **Report to Leo Sabat**

To:	Leo Sabat
From:	Chien & Co
Subject:	Due Diligence
Date:	June 20X8

Introduction

The aim of this report is to set out the purposes and benefits of a due diligence investigation and to explain how the scope of such an investigation differs to that of an audit of financial statements. This report is solely for the use of the intended user and should not be relied upon by any third party.

Due diligence is a specific type of review assignment where an advisor is engaged by a company making an investment, typically an acquisition. The advisor will perform an assessment of the material risks associated with the transaction to ensure the company has all the necessary facts before making a judgment. Thus, due diligence minimises the risk of making the wrong investment decision.

(i) **Purpose and benefits of a due diligence investigation**

Information collecting

A due diligence investigation will gather information on a target company, such as Maxwell Ltd, regarding:

- Details of business operations
- Financial performance
- Financial position (for example any hidden covenants or contingent liabilities)
- Legal issues
- Tax situation

Armed with this information, Rosie Ltd can make an informed decision on whether to acquire Maxwell Ltd. Any potential problems should be uncovered before the company is acquired, and the risk of unpleasant surprises after the purchase is minimised.

Verification of specific management representations

Due diligence work should corroborate verbal representations made by the vendor to the potential acquirer. For example, management at Maxwell Ltd may have stated that the company has no legal claims against it. Due diligence work would be able to verify this kind of representation giving confidence to the potential acquirer.

Identification of assets and liabilities

A due diligence investigation will ensure that all assets and liabilities of the target company are identified. It is particularly important to identify any contingent liabilities and understand the potential cost to the acquirer if the liability crystallises. This work can be complex and so it may be advisable for Rosie Ltd to use the expertise of an external due diligence provider.

Operational risk

A due diligence investigation will identify operational risks in the target company which are not apparent from examining financial information alone. For example, the patent of a key engine part manufactured by Maxwell Ltd may be about to expire or a key customer may wish to renegotiate terms. The issues discovered could mean that Rosie Ltd decides the acquisition of Maxwell Ltd is too risky or alternatively may offer a useful bargaining tool in negotiating the consideration paid.

Acquisition planning

Post-acquisition strategy will also be assessed during a due diligence investigation. Potential economies of scale and operational synergies will be highlighted to the acquirer along with the costs of any necessary reorganisation. The due diligence report may be able to advise Rosie Ltd how best to integrate Maxwell Ltd into the existing group structure.

It is worth noting here that as Rosie Ltd has only just completed the acquisition of Dylan Ltd in January 20X8, the group may find it difficult to integrate Maxwell Ltd as it is already in a period of immense change. Additionally, it may be difficult to secure funding for the acquisition so soon after the payment for Dylan Ltd has been made and the group should examine its liquidity before deciding to proceed.

Management time

It is possible for due diligence to be performed by directors of the acquiring company. Although this can be cheaper for the acquirer it has several drawbacks, the main one being that due diligence can be incredibly time-consuming for the directors, leaving them little time to carry out their day to day activities. Additionally, the directors may lack the experience and expertise in acquisitions that a professional due diligence advisor can offer.

Credibility

A third party review will add to the credibility of the investment decision in Maxwell Ltd and give shareholders some comfort over the consideration paid.

(ii) **Scope**

The table below summarises the key differences in scope between a due diligence investigation and an audit of financial statements.

Due diligence	Audit
Draws on a wide range of information including cash flows, profit forecasts, business plans and management accounts	Concentrates on the most recent set of financial statements
Provides a reviewed set of information to the client	Provides assurance that data is free from material misstatement
No detailed audit procedures performed unless specifically requested or a cause for concern	Detailed audit procedures performed
Mainly uses analytical procedures where sets of data are compared, for example, to each other, benchmarks and competitors	In addition to analytical procedures, substantive procedures are used where samples of information are tested and agreed to supporting documentation
Forward looking – looks at forecasts and future expectations for a business	Backward looking – concentrate on the most recent set of financial statements and only looks at future events that are relevant to these
No testing of systems and controls unless specifically requested	Systems and controls will be evaluated and, if appropriate, tested

Conclusion

Due diligence provides management with the confidence to make investment decisions based on all the available facts. It can be carried out by management but it is often better to employ a specialised advisory firm.

(b) (i) **Dylan Ltd**

Matters to consider

- Whether the cost of investment provided by the client is complete. In particular legal and professional fees should not have been included which is a requirement of IFRS 3 *Business combinations.*
- Whether the cash consideration of £2.5m was paid before the year end and if not, that the liability has been correctly recognised on the statement of financial position
- Whether the £1.5m deferred consideration has been discounted to its present value at the date of the acquisition as required by IFRS 3 (unless immaterial to the financial statements). There is a risk that the liability and cost of investment is overstated if discounting has not taken place.
- Whether the revenue of Dylan Ltd is likely to grow by 5% per annum resulting in the payment of £1m contingent consideration. If so, has an accrual been made for the £1m?

Evidence

- Agreement of cost of investment in Dylan Ltd and payment dates of consideration per the client schedule to legal documentation signed by both Dylan Ltd and Rosie Ltd
- Agreement of £2.5 million cash consideration paid to Rosie Ltd's bank statement and cash book (if prior to year end)
- Inclusion of £2.5m cash consideration paid to Rosie Ltd as accrual within 'payables: falling due within one year' on the individual company and consolidated statement of financial position (if payment occurs after year end)
- Board minutes detailing approval of acquisition of Dylan Ltd
- Recomputation of discounting calculations performed on deferred and contingent consideration
- Agreement that pre-tax discount rate used which reflects the current market assessment of the time value of money (for example, by comparison to Rosie Ltd's weighted average cost of capital)
- Revenue and profit projections of Dylan Ltd are arithmetically correct
- An assessment of the assumptions used in the projections for Dylan Ltd and agreement they are comparable with the auditor's understanding of the business

(ii)   **Principle audit procedures**

- Compare the audited accounts of Timber, Ben and Dylan Ltd to the consolidation schedules to ensure figures have been transposed correctly.
- Verify the arithmetical accuracy of the consolidation schedule by checking it casts horizontally and vertically.
- Review consolidation adjustments to ensure they are appropriate and comparable to the prior year.
- Recalculate all consolidation adjustments, including goodwill, elimination of pre-acquisition reserves, cancellation of intercompany balances, fair value adjustments and accounting policy adjustments.
- Consider whether the previous treatment of Timber Ltd and Ben Ltd is still correct and that the brought forward figures agree to prior year audited financial statements and audit working papers.
- Ensure that Dylan Ltd has been appropriately treated as an acquisition, and that any post acquisition profits have been correctly included.
- Prepare a reconciliation of movements on group reserves.

(c)   **Joint audit**

A joint audit is one where two or more auditors are responsible for an audit engagement and jointly produce an auditor's report to the client.

Advantages

(i)   A joint audit of Maxwell Ltd will result in time savings as Chien & Co can use the knowledge accumulated by Lead & Co in previous audits (for example, on Maxwell's business, systems, controls and prior audit issues). This is important for Chien & Co as any risks inherent in Maxwell Ltd could affect their overall risk assessment of the group.

(ii)   Maxwell Ltd is expected to increase operating facilities by 40% and so will be a significant addition to the Rosie group. As sole auditors, Chien & Co may struggle to adequately resource the audit of Maxwell Ltd as this will be at the same time as the audit of other companies in the group. A joint audit will mean there is sufficient resource to be dedicated to all group companies.

(iii)   The audit of all subsidiaries in the Rosie group will need to be completed before the group audit starts. A joint audit will ensure that there is enough resource to meet the tight deadlines for the individual subsidiary audits.

(iv)   Audit quality of Maxwell Ltd should increase as a result of a joint audit. As new auditors, Chien & Co will be approaching the audit with a fresh outlook, unprejudiced by previous events and may be able to spot new issues or offer different solutions to those previously identified by Lead & Co.

Disadvantages

(i)   A joint audit will probably be more expensive for Maxwell Ltd. The client should receive an improved service to justify the increased fee but it could be argued that the cost is not necessary.

(ii)   Chien & Co may use a different audit approach and methodology to Lead & Co leading to disagreements throughout the audit about which is the correct way to proceed. This could result in a loss of efficiencies as time is spent agreeing on the best audit approach rather than carrying out actual audit work. If either audit firm's approach is solely followed, some of the benefits of a joint audit will be lost.

(iii)   Lead & Co may be uncooperative as they believe they will eventually be replaced by Chien & Co as sole auditor.

(iv)   Both audit firms are jointly liable and must both sign the auditor's report. This may make it more complicated if any litigation arises as it is harder to see where any fault lies.

56 Medix

Text references. Chapters 5 and 6.

Top tips. This question was especially time consuming, particularly in part (c). Always make sure that you plan your time at the start of a question and stick to it.

In parts (b)(ii) and (c) it is important to explain the risks and not just identify them. Make sure the risks are tailored to the scenario.

Easy marks. Part (b)(i) contains some easy marks for auditing concept definitions. Parts (a) and (c) are not difficult but are time-consuming. As ever, make sure you get some of the professional marks available.

Examiner's comment. On the whole, there were some strong answers to this question, with many excellent answers to part (c) in particular, with a significant minority of candidates achieving full marks in this part of the question. However, failure to read and understand the scenario or the question requirements meant that many answers were disappointing.

Common weaknesses in answers to (a) included:

- Failure to produce the answer in the required format – meaning that full professional marks could not be awarded

- Listing general acceptance considerations rather than making the comments specific to Medix

- Making comments that are wholly inappropriate to the scenario. An example of this is where many answers urged the audit partner to 'make contact with the previous auditor to find out matters we should be aware of'. This shows that many candidates simply failed to read the question carefully enough, as approximately one third of the information provided in the scenario comes from a discussion that has already taken place with the outgoing auditor in which his reasons for vacating office were outlined.

- Lack of prioritisation. At this level it is important to try to prioritise issues, which will then help to reach a logical conclusion

- Failure to reach a conclusion as to whether or not the appointment should go ahead – note that requirements containing the verb 'assess' should contain a conclusion. Failing to reach a conclusion restricts the professional marks that can be awarded.

One of the main problems noted with part (c) is that many candidates spent too long on this section, at the expense of time that would have been better spent on the optional questions. Candidates should be aware that failing to attempt four questions, as required, is unlikely to lead to success in this paper.

Part (b) produced the worst answers to Question 1. Most candidates attempted a definition of the two terms, but the discussion of the link between them was weak.

Marks

(a) **Note.** Comments must be derived from the information provided in order
to be awarded marks.
Ideas list:
- Poor reputation of Medix Ltd
- Potential advocacy threat from frequent litigation
- Public interest in the company
- Potential liability to lender
- Short timeframe to build business knowledge
- Aggressive management style
- Incentive to manipulate financial statements
- Poor systems and controls
- Extra work on opening balances (max 1 mark)
- Need expertise in this regulated industry
- Fee pressure
- Creditworthiness
- Possible management fraud
- Indicator of money laundering
- Question competence of previous auditors

Maximum   10

(b) (i) **Business and risk of material misstatement**
Generally ½ mark per definition and 1 mark per comment
- Business risk leads to specific risk of material misstatement
- Business risk leads to general risk of material misstatement
- Relationship regarding going concern

Maximum   4

(ii) **Risks of material misstatement – breach of planning regulations**
2 marks per risk explained (½ mark max if only identified and not
described):
- Overstatement of tangible non-current assets
- Overstatement of other assets (max 1 mark)
- Possible understatement of provision/non disclosure of
contingency
- Possible understatement of provision for demolition costs
- Going concern (max 1 mark)
- Reference to IAS 36, IAS 37 (1/2 mark each)

Maximum   6

(c) **Principal business risks**
- Generally ½ mark each risk identified
- Up to 1 further mark for significant issues explained:
- Declining demand for main product and revenue/cash flow implication
- R+D represents cash drain
- Lack of management focus on long term strategy
- Breach of planning – risk of facility being shut down and bad publicity
- Regulated industry and reliance on licence for commercial production
- Over reliance on scientist
- Reliance on agents
- Commission payments – high risk of fraud
- Overseas manufacturing plant – hard to control and maintain quality
- High and volatile costs of importing goods
- Capital expenditure likely in near future
- Future exposure to fluctuating interest rates
- Non compliance with tax regulations – fines and penalties

- Legal action – finance director and planning office
- Weak controls, risk of fraud
- Owner-managed business

Maximum   **12**

Up to 2 professional marks for clarity of discussion, style appropriate for audit partner

2 professional marks for format, introduction and conclusion provided

1–2 marks per issue discussed   **4**

Total   **36**

Briefing notes

To:	Charles Banks
From:	Gavin Jones
Date:	June 20X8
Subject:	Medix Ltd

Introduction

These notes consider the professional, ethical and other issues to be considered in deciding whether to proceed with the appointment as auditor of Medix Ltd. They also discuss the concepts of business risk and risk of material misstatement, and include a discussion of the business risks facing Medix Ltd.

(a) **Professional, ethical and other issues**

    (i) *Sign of fraud or money laundering*

    Mick Evans, the current audit partner has informed us that Jon Tate, the owner and managing director of Medix Ltd has kept two cash books. This requires further investigation but is a possible sign of fraud or money laundering. This offence alone is enough for Mitchell & Co to seriously consider rejecting the appointment.

    (ii) *Legal actions and investigations*

    Medix Ltd has recently been subject to two tax investigations, and legal action is presently being taken by both the former finance director and the local planning department. The local planning department has also successfully sued the company previously. The reputation of Mitchell & Co may be damaged by accepting a client who has been subject to so many legal actions and investigations. It is not entirely clear from the previous auditors whether the tax investigations have now been resolved and as a result, there is a risk we could be exposed to an advocacy independence threat.

    (iii) *Negative publicity*

    The local newspaper recently reported on the current and past legal action by the local authorities against Medix Ltd. This negative publicity is something we may not wish to be associated with.

    (iv) *Timeframe and resources*

    Given it is now June and Medix Ltd has a 30 June 20X8 year end, the time frame for planning the audit and gaining a thorough understanding of the business and its processes is tight. Mitchell & Co should ensure there are adequate staff available to complete the work with the necessary industry expertise before accepting this appointment. It should be noted that the previous audit partner has stated that Medix Ltd like a 'quick audit'. If accepted, we should ensure that our proposed approach causes the least disruption to the client whilst maintaining the necessary levels of documentation and testing required for a quality audit.

    (v) *Potential liability to bank*

    Medix Ltd are in the process of negotiating a bank loan, the terms of which will be finalised once the audited financial statements have been viewed by the bank. The bank will be using the audited financial statements as the basis of its decision and relying heavily on our audit opinion. It may be sensible to reject the audit engagement as it could expose Mitchell & Co to an unnecessarily high level of liability to the bank, especially given that this is a time-pressured first year audit. However, disclaimers may be sufficient to limit our liability.

(vi) *Management bias*

Medix Ltd will be aware that the bank is basing their financing decision on the audited financial statements. There is a risk that the company may deliberately misstate the financial statements in order to gain the bank's approval. Mitchell & Co will need to be aware of this risk before carrying out any audit work.

(vii) *Potentially aggressive management style*

The previous finance director is currently taking legal proceeding against Medix Ltd and the auditors prior to the current practice resigned due to a disagreement over fees. This indicates that management at the company are aggressive and so it may be difficult for Mitchell and Co to form a good working relationship with them. The problem is compounded by the fact that the company is owner-managed.

(viii) *Internal systems and controls*

The current auditors have said they have found internal controls at Medix Ltd weak. Mitchell and Co would therefore not be able to rely on internal controls or carry out a controls based audit. A fully substantive approach would be necessary and we should consider whether we have sufficient resource as this is always more time consuming approach than a controls based audit.

(ix) *Opening balances*

As per ISA (UK & Ireland) 510 *Initial engagements – opening balances and continuing engagements – opening balances,* opening balances need to be verified for all new audit clients. Detailed procedures will need to be carried out at Medix Ltd due to the weak internal control environment and the possible incompetence of the current auditor who ignored a potential money laundering indicator. It is worth noting that Medix Ltd is the only audit client of the current auditor.

(x) *Fees*

The current auditor has indicated that Medix Ltd may pressure us to keep the audit cost as low as possible. We should only accept the audit engagement if the company are willing to pay us a reasonable fee, especially given the extra work that will be required for such a high risk assignment.

There is a chance that Medix Ltd will be unable to pay their audit fees as the company appears to be experiencing cash flow difficulties. If such a self-interest threat to our independence arises we will be unable to continue as auditors.

(b) (i) **Business and risk of material misstatement**

Business risk is the risk inherent to the company in its operations and includes all risks facing the business.

Risk of material misstatement is the risk of material misstatement in the financial statements.

In response to business risk, management institute a system of **controls**. These will include controls to mitigate against the risk that the financial statements are materially misstated, which is an aspect of business risk.

Business risks and their associated controls could affect specific or more general parts of the financial statements. For example, the use of sales agents has been identified as a **specific** business risk at Medix Ltd. The associated risk of material misstatement is that sales are overstated. A more **general** business risk that will impact upon all areas of the financial statements is the weak control environment at Medix Ltd.

If a business risk materialises, the **going concern** basis of the financial statements could be affected, especially if the risk affects the continued existence of the business. For example, at Medix Ltd there is a business risk that licences may not be granted for the laser surgical instruments. If the licence was refused and the company carries on experiencing cash flow problems, there is a risk that the financial statements could be incorrectly prepared on a going concern basis.

(ii)   **Risks of material misstatement – breach of planning regulations**

Tangible non-current assets overstated. From the press cutting, it appears that the local authority aim to close the R&D building before year end. There is therefore a risk of material misstatement that the building is overvalued on the statement of financial position. Under IAS 36 *Impairment of assets*, the directors at Medix Ltd should carry out an **impairment** review if there is any indication assets are impaired. If the carrying amount exceeds the recoverable amount (the higher of fair value less costs to sell and value in use), the building should be impaired and the impairment loss recognised as an expense.

The recoverable amount of the building is likely to be lower than the carrying value if it cannot be used as intended. If the local authority is successful and the building is shut down, the recoverable amount is likely to be nil. This is because the building has no value in use, cannot be used for trading, and has no market value as it will probably be demolished.

Other assets overstated. Any tangible assets within the building (such as laboratory equipment) are likely to have a carrying value that exceeds their value in use and should also be tested for impairment. The risk of material misstatement is that their value is overstated on the statement of financial position.

Possible understatement of provision/non-disclosure of contingency. The press cutting indicates the local authority may once again take legal action against Medix Ltd and so this raises the question of whether a provision needs to be made. IAS 37 *Provisions, contingent liabilities and contingent assets* states that a provision should only be recognised if:

–   An entity has a **present obligation** as a result of a **past event**
–   It is probable that a **transfer of economic benefits** will be required to settle the obligation
–   A **reliable estimate** can be made of the obligation

If the local authority instigates legal action before year end, Medix Ltd will need to assess the probable outcome and whether a provision needs to be made. There is a risk of material misstatement that no provision will be made and liabilities and expenses understated.

If the local authority has not started legal proceedings before year end, then Medix Ltd should disclose a contingent liability in a note to the financial statements. The risk of material misstatement is that the correct disclosure is not made.

No provision for demolition costs. If the local authority rules that Medix Ltd must demolish the building before year end, a provision should be made for demolition costs. There is a risk of material misstatement that the company does not make the provision leaving liabilities and expenses understated.

Going concern assumption is incorrect. All the above, especially the closure of the research and development building, may impact the viable future of the company resulting in a risk of material misstatement that the going concern status is incorrect.

(c)   **Principal business risks**

(i)   **Demand for main revenue stream falling.** Revenue and profits at Medix Ltd have fallen as demand for metal surgical instruments has rapidly declined. Medix Ltd makes use of the bank overdraft facility most months and a falling revenue will only exacerbate any cash flow problems the company has.

(ii)   **Laser instrument R&D in early stage.** Although demand for metal surgical instruments has been falling for four years, research and development into the growing area of laser instruments has only just started. This suggests a short-term outlook and little investment in long-term strategy by the company.

(iii)   **Little cash for R&D.** Research and development is a significant cash outflow for any business. The monthly use of the bank overdraft indicates Medix Ltd are already having cash flow problems and may find it difficult to fund R&D into laser instruments. If the company cannot invest in this area and demand for metal surgical instruments continues to fall, there is a risk the business is no longer viable.

(iv) **Only one scientist working on R&D.** The future survival of Medix Ltd seems to depend on their ability to sell laser instruments, yet the company has just one sub-contracted scientist working in this area. Relying so heavily on one sub-contracted member of staff is a very risky strategy for a business. If this scientist were to leave the company, Medix Ltd would lose knowledge crucial for securing the continued existence of their business. Research and development would be on hold until a new scientist could be recruited which, given this is such a specialised role, could take some time.

(v) **R&D scientist is freelance.** There is nothing to suggest that Medix Ltd have taken out patents on designs from the subcontracted scientist. There is a risk that the scientist could be using the designs while freelancing for competitors of Medix Ltd unless patents are taken out.

(vi) **Licences.** The new laser products require licences before they can be produced commercially. If these are not granted, the future of the company could be at risk and cash invested in R&D will have been wasted.

(vii) **Use of sales agents.** The commission-based sales agents are not employed by Medix Ltd. It may be in an agent's best interest to promote a competitor's products resulting in reduced revenues for the company. Additionally, there is a risk that an unscrupulous agent could overstate sales in order to increase his or her commission. Since the control environment has been described as weak by the previous auditor, there is a high risk this fraud may go undetected.

(viii) **Overseas manufacturing plant.** Communication difficulties generally make it harder to control production overseas. There may be language barriers and different time zones mean it simply takes longer for important information to be relayed or discussed. It will also be harder for Medix Ltd monitor the quality of production in an overseas plant. Quality is important for a highly regulated industry such as surgical instruments and inferior products could have a significant impact on sales.

(ix) **Foreign currency fluctuations.** The overseas plant will need to make payments in the local currency of the country where it is based, exposing Medix Ltd to the risk of fluctuations in exchange rates.

(x) **Air transport.** Since Medix Ltd have chosen to import most of their products by air, they are exposed to fluctuations in the price of fuel.

(xi) **Tax investigations.** Two previous investigations by the taxation authorities indicate Medix Ltd may have broken tax regulations. Any further breaches could result in serious penalties or fines.

(xii) **Breach of planning regulations.** If the local planning authority are successful, the extension to the R&D facility will have to be demolished. This could result in a substantial delay to the crucial laser instrument R&D as it may take some time to find suitable new premises. The local planning office may also impose fines which could cause Medix Ltd further cash flow problems. The building may have to be impaired at year-end, and the reduced net asset position on the statement of financial position will make it harder to generate capital. Sales could fall as a consequence of the bad publicity.

(xiii) **Exposure to interest rates.** The company is currently negotiating a significant bank loan which will carry a variable interest rate. If interest rates rise, the company will need to make increased interest payments further aggravating the cash flow problems at Medix Ltd.

(xiv) **Legal action by prior finance director.** Medix Ltd could be subject to substantial costs and negative publicity if the legal case is lost.

(xv) **Capital expenditure.** The company's manufacturing plant is twelve years old and was built specifically for the production of metal surgical instruments. Provided the R&D is successful, the company is hoping to switch to production of laser instruments and a substantial capital outlay will be necessary to adapt the plant. This could prove difficult for Medix Ltd in light of their cash flow problems.

(xiv) **Weak control environment.** The previous auditors have commented that the control environment at Medix Ltd is poor. Jon Tate, the managing director, seems to have a dominant management style with frequent disagreements and violation of tax and local planning laws. This raises the chance of management disregard for, and override of, controls resulting in an increased opportunity for fraud or management decisions being made on inaccurate financial information.

Conclusion

There are several areas in which we should gather further information before making a final decision on whether to accept Medix Ltd as an audit client. The information gathered so far indicates that Medix Ltd would be a high risk client and we need to consider whether we are willing to accept the engagement given this knowledge.

57 Prosperitas

Text reference. Chapter 13.

Top tips. Notice that the email asks you to 'explain' the grounds. This means that you must say what they are, and then give as much further information as you can. For example, what does 'just and equitable' mean? How does a court decide that a company cannot pay its debts – how much does it have to owe?

It is important to be clear about what you are being asked. In the second part of the question, do not confuse members' and creditors' (payables') winding up on one hand, with compulsory and voluntary winding up on the other.

Easy marks. In questions like this which are very technical, marks are available for just stating the law and require little application. You should be able to pass the question by repeating book knowledge.

Briefing Notes

For: Sue Dixon
By: Khalid Huq
Subject: Prosperitas Ltd

These briefing notes identify and explain the main grounds for winding up a company; explain the distinguishing features of a creditors' voluntary winding up; and explain the immediate legal effect of a court order for compulsory winding up.

(a)   **Compulsory winding-up**

A compulsory winding-up is one ordered by the court under s.122 of the Insolvency Act 1986, on one or more of seven specified grounds. The most important of these grounds are:

- That the company is unable to pay its debts
- That it is just and equitable to wind up the company

Unable to pay its debts

Where a creditor is owed more than £750 and makes a written demand for payment and the company fails to pay the debt, or offer reasonable security for it, within three weeks, the company is deemed unable to pay its debts. The creditor may persuade the court of the company's inability to settle its debts in other ways, for example by proving that the company's assets are less than its liabilities.

Just and equitable ground

The just and equitable ground is usually relied on by a member who is dissatisfied with the directors' or controlling shareholders' management of the company, provided they can show that no other remedy is available and satisfactory.

A member who is dissatisfied with the directors or controlling shareholders over the management of the company may petition the court for a winding up on the basis that to do so is just and equitable. Such winding up orders have been made where the substratum (the only main object) of the company no longer exists (*Re German Date Coffee Co* 1882), where the company was formed for an illegal or fraudulent purpose, where there is a complete deadlock in the management of the company's affairs (*Re Yenidje Tobacco Co Ltd* 1916) and where the trust and confidence between both directors and shareholders in a small company have broken down (*Ebrahimi v Westbourne Galleries Ltd* 1973).

(b)   **Creditors' voluntary winding-up**

The winding up is instigated by a special resolution of the company in a general meeting, by which the company states that it cannot continue to trade because of its liabilities. Private companies may pass a written resolution with a three quarters majority.

Creditors' meeting

The company must call a meeting of creditors for a day not later than the 14th day after the day on which the special resolution was passed. The creditors must receive at least seven days notice of the meeting.

The notice must state either:

- The name and address of an insolvency practitioner who will furnish creditors free of charge with such information as they reasonably require, or

- A place in the locality where on the two business days before the meeting of creditors is held, a list of the names and addresses of the company's creditors will be available for inspection free of charge.

Notice of the creditors' meeting must be advertised in the Gazette and in at least two newspapers circulating in the locality in which the company's principal place of business was situated.

Liquidator

During the period before the creditors' meeting but after the resolution for winding-up the members' nominee will act as provisional liquidator. They will have restricted powers to act during this period, subject to application to the court. This restriction is necessitated by the practice of 'centrebinding', whereby the assets are fraudulently disposed of before the creditors' meeting.

At the creditors' meeting the creditors may appoint their own nominee to act as liquidator. The creditors' choice will prevail over the members' choice if there is a conflict; usually there is not.

Statement of affairs

The directors of the company must prepare and lay before the creditors' meeting a statement of affairs of the company but, importantly, they do not have to make a statutory declaration of solvency.

(c) **Compulsory winding-up**

The statutory provisions on **compulsory winding up** are in the Insolvency Act 1986, to which all section references in this question refer.

The two **general effects** of compulsory liquidation are:

- That the management of the company passes to a liquidator and the **directors' powers cease**
- **Dispositions** of the company's **property** or **shares**, and **actions** against the company, are **restrained**

There is **no** automatic cancellation of company contracts, but many commercial contracts provide for cancellation at the option of the other party if the company goes into liquidation.

Commencement

Compulsory winding up is deemed to commence from the date on which the petition was presented, unless the company was then already in voluntary liquidation. In effect the order for compulsory liquidation is retrospective.

Effects

The more **specific effects** of compulsory liquidation are as follows.

- The **Official Receiver** becomes **liquidator** from the making of the order, and they continue until some other liquidator, who must be an insolvency practitioner, is appointed: s 136.

- The **powers of the directors are terminated** and they are **dismissed**.

- Any **disposition of the company's property** from the commencement of the liquidation **is void** unless approved by the court.

The court may give approval with **retrospective effect** but it is safer to apply for it in advance, when the petition has been represented. The court will only give its approval if it considers that it is in the interests of the company and its creditors that the company should continue to carry on its business pending a decision on the petition.

- Any **transfer of the company's shares is void** unless approved by the court: s 127.
- **No creditor may commence or continue legal action** against the company except with the leave of the court: s 126.
- The **employment of the company's staff ceases** unless the liquidator retains them to carry on the business.
- **Floating charges crystallise**.

58 Peter

Notes on audit risks

IAS 1 requires financial statements to be prepared on a going concern basis, except where:

(a) An entity is being liquidated and has ceased trading
(b) The directors have no realistic alternative but to cease trading or liquidate the business

In the case of Sebastian Ltd and Simon Ltd, neither company has been liquidated or have ceased trading. But the second condition above needs to be assessed carefully. IAS 1 suggests that directors should review the history of the companies' profitability, their access to financial resources, and debt repayment schedules.

Both companies have significant retained losses and thus have a history of poor profitability. Both have significant debentures held by banks. There are therefore two key questions on going concern:

(i) What is the risk that the companies' creditors (payables) might seek to have the companies wound up?
(ii) Will the Peter group continue to support the companies for the foreseeable future?

Careful consideration needs to be given to both of these questions. It is likely that assurances would be required from the Peter group that it will continue to support the companies for the foreseeable future.

ISA (UK & Ireland) 570 *Going concern* requires consideration to be given to disclosure in the financial statements and in the audit report. If there is a material uncertainty over going concern, and the financial statements are prepared on the going concern basis with adequate disclosures, then the audit report should contain emphasis of matter paragraph. If the financial statements do **not** contain adequate disclosures about going concern, then the audit opinion should either be qualified or adverse, in line with ISA (UK & Ireland) 705. If the financial statements are prepared on the going concern basis but it is inappropriate to do so, the audit opinion should be adverse.

There is a chance that some of both companies' assets are impaired, as their net realisable values are below their carrying amounts. This is an IAS 36 indicator of impairment. Management should have conducted an impairment review, which needs to be audited to confirm that it is in line with IAS 36. If no impairment review has been conducted, then the audit report should be qualified as appropriate.

REPORT

To	Trevor McDouglas
From	A Senior
Date	24 July 20X0
Subject	Peter Plc, liquidation of Sebastian Ltd and Simon Ltd

Advice on liquidation

The best strategy from the perspective of the members (ie Peter plc) would seem to be to liquidate both Sebastian Ltd and Simon Ltd.

Sebastian Ltd

The net realisable values of the assets are:

Freehold land	3,800
Other non-current assets	600
Current assets	400
Total	4,800

Total liabilities are:

Debenture holders	1,600
Bank overdraft	2,900
Preferential creditors	100
Unsecured creditors	700
Liquidator's fees	250
Total	5,550

There is a shortfall of £750,000. This means that a loss will be made if Sebastian is liquidated.

However, this shortfall is smaller than the estimated £1m that would be lost if Sebastian were to continue to trade. On this basis, it would appear to be best for Peter Plc to liquidate Sebastian.

Furthermore, if Sebastian were to continue trading, the whole of its estimated £1m of trading losses would be suffered by its shareholders (Peter Plc), after which time it would probably then still find itself in a position of having to liquidate the loss-making company anyway.

But if the shareholders choose to liquidate now, it will be the creditors who will suffer the shortfall of £750,000 because the shareholders have limited liability. Liquidation would therefore be a way of moving the loss from equity to debt holders.

As Sebastian Ltd has significant retained losses and appears to be in a position of net liabilities, the effect of the liquidation on Peter's group accounts is likely to be positive.

As there is currently a shortfall of liabilities over assets, Sebastian Ltd could not make a declaration of solvency. Sebastian therefore could not be wound up by a members' voluntary liquidation. A creditors' voluntary liquidation would be possible here, although the disadvantage of this route is that the creditors, rather than the members, would usually appoint the liquidator.

Simon Ltd

For Simon Ltd the net realisable values of the assets are:

Freehold land	4,500
Other non-current assets	700
Current assets	800
Total	6,000

Total liabilities are:

Debenture holders	1,500
Bank overdraft	1,000
Preferential creditors	200
Unsecured creditors	700
Liquidator's fees	250
Total	3,650

This leaves a surplus of £6,000,000 − £3,650,000 = £2,350,000. As this is greater than the estimated net present value of £1m, it would actually be better to liquidate Simon Ltd, even though it would be able to continue to trade as a going concern.

The figure for net present value is an estimate, and as such there is a risk of it being wrong. The basic figure on its does not give any indication of the risk of a different outcome. In this case, there appears to be a chance that Simon Ltd might prove profitable, so that Peter Plc would be better off not liquidating it. It would therefore be wise to consider very carefully the basis of the net present value assigned to Simon Ltd. Peter Plc's decision over whether Simon Ltd should continue trading would depend both on this and on its attitude to risk.

A disadvantage of liquidating is that Simon Ltd does appear to have net assets of around £3,150,000, which would be removed from Peter's group accounts. However, this amount is likely to be quite small in the context of Peter group as a whole.

As Simon Ltd is currently solvent, its directors would be able to make a statutory declaration of solvency. It could therefore be liquidated through a members' voluntary liquidation, which would mean that the members (ie Peter Plc) had the right to appoint the liquidator.

Repayment of debts

Sebastian Ltd and Simon Ltd's creditors would paid in the following order.

	Sebastian Ltd	Simon Ltd
	£'000	£'000
Non-current asset – freehold land	3,800	4,500
Less costs (= liquidator's costs)	(250)	(250)
	3,550	4,250
Less fixed charge realisation (on freehold land)	(1,600)	(1,500)
	1,950	2,750
Other assets:		
Non-current assets	600	700
Current assets	400	800
Assets available to preferential creditors	2,950	4,250
Less preferential creditors	(100)	(200)
	2,850	4,050
Less prescribed part (W1)	(573)	(600)
Less floating charge realisation (bank)	(2,277)	(1,000)
	Nil	2,450
Less unsecured creditors	Nil	(100)
Surplus to shareholders	Nil	2,350

Workings

1   Sebastian's prescribed part is calculated as:

50% × £10,000	£5,000
20% × (£2,850,000 – £10,000)	£568,000
	£573,000

The liquidator's fees are paid first. Then the holders of the fixed charge over the land are paid from the funds realised from the land.

From the remaining assets are paid the preferential creditors, the prescribed part for the unsecured creditors, and the floating charge holders (the bank).

In the case of Sebastian Ltd, the bankers would receive £2,277,000 of their £2,900,000 debt. Unsecured creditors would only receive the 'prescribed part' of their debt, which is £573,000. They would therefore have received 82p for every £1 of debt, which is in fact a good outcome for unsecured creditors in situations such as this one.

In the case of Simon Ltd, all debts, including that debt owed to the bank, are repaid in full. The shareholder (Peter Plc) receive the surplus of £2,350,000.

59 Yew

Text references. Chapters 9 and 17.

Top tips. Part (a) was a typical question on audit reports, this time mixed in with IAS 38 and some issues around audit completion. You should have had plenty to say here; the main difficulty would have been staying within the time limit of 21 minutes for this part of the question.

Part (b) contained just two short situations for only three marks each. The situations were fairly straightforward, so how you did came down to your knowledge.

Easy marks. A lot of part (a) was easy – for example, stating that the treatment of the development costs was not in line with IAS 38.

Marks

(a) **Yew Co**

Generally up to 1½ marks for each matter discussed/recommended:
- Calculate and comment on materiality
- No probable economic benefit – IAS 38 recognition criteria not met
- Lack of finance – IAS 38 recognition criteria not met
- Consider whether sufficient appropriate evidence obtained
- Financial statements contain material misstatement and implication for auditor's report
- Could indicate fraudulent financial reporting
- Lack of cash may indicate going concern problems – extend audit procedures
- Audit work should be subject to 2nd partner review
- Consider asking for a delay in issuing financial statements if necessary for further evidence to be sought
- Discuss apparent inconsistency in chairman's statement wording
- Discuss accounting treatment, potential qualification and chairman's statement wording with those charged with governance
- Include *Other Matter* paragraph in report if material inconsistency remains

Maximum   12

(b) (i) **Signing of auditor's report**

Generally 1 mark per point:
- Date report when all necessary evidence received, including written representations
- Especially important with regard to subsequent events
- Contrary to ISA 700 to sign report prior to receiving written representations

Maximum   3

(ii) **Prior year auditor's opinion**

Generally 1 mark per point:
- Generally auditors do not refer to third parties in their report
- But optional to refer to predecessor auditor unless prohibited by law and regulations
- If reference made, should be in *Other Matter* paragraph
- Describe contents of reference made to predecessor auditor
- If prior year modified, explain this in *Other Matter* paragraph

Maximum   3

Total   18

(a) The intangible asset is material to profit (54% of profit before tax) and to the statement of financial position (6% of total assets).

IAS 38 *Intangible assets* states that for development costs to be capitalised, the existence of a market – or the entity's ability to use the asset itself – must be demonstrable. The audit team has obtained documentation and a written representation which confirms that this is not the case.

IAS 38 also requires the entity to have the financial resources to bring the asset to the market. As Yew Ltd is short of cash, this may not be the case.

As a result, the financial statements appear to be materially misstated, and that the £12.5m should be treated as expenses. The matter must be discussed with management, who should be asked to amend the financial statements.

The matter should also be discussed with the chairman, as it is possible that he has different information which could change our assessment of the situation. If this is not the case, and if the financial statements are not amended, then the audit opinion will be qualified 'except for' a material misstatement (but one which is not pervasive).

The fact that Yew Ltd is finding it difficult to raise finance casts doubt over going concern. Further work may need to be done in this area. If there is significant doubt then disclosures should be included in the financial statements, and an emphasis of matter paragraph in the auditor's report in respect of going concern.

If a modified opinion is expected to be expressed, then it may be necessary to consult externally on the effects of doing this, or at a minimum subjecting the audit work to review by another partner.

Consideration needs to be given to whether the misstatement is an indication of fraudulent financial reporting, and a possible lack of management integrity. The fact the company is struggling to raise finance provides a motive for it to inflate its results and statement of financial position. If this is the case, then any written representations relied upon elsewhere in the audit must be reconsidered.

If the development costs should not be capitalised and the financial statements are amended, then there will be an inconsistency with the directors' report. First, the chairman should be asked to amend his statement. If this is not done then ISA 720B *The auditor's statutory reporting responsibility in relation to directors' reports* comes into play. ISA 720B states that in these circumstances, the auditor's report should state that the directors' report is materially inconsistent with the financial statements, and describe the nature of this inconsistency.

(b) (i) ISA 700 *Forming an opinion and reporting on financial statements* requires that the audit report only be signed once sufficient appropriate audit evidence has been obtained on financial statements.

Written representations from management are audit evidence, so logically there is not sufficient appropriate audit evidence until these are received.

It is therefore not appropriate to sign the report and date it before these are received.

(ii) Cross-referencing allows for a shorter and more concise auditor's report which is more focused on the auditor's opinion and is more user-friendly.

The disadvantage of this is that the information that is left out may not be read by users, and that the expectations gap may be widened as a result.

Users may also experience practical problems accessing the FRC's website. This can be partially overcome by making the cross-reference as clear as possible, eg by providing an actual link to the FRC's side, which makes it hard for users to claim that it is difficult to find.

60 Snipe

Top tips. Part (a) was deceptively simple. This was a straightforward financial reporting-based requirement, and you should have been able to score well on it. You might have noticed that the question gave you quite a few numbers. When a question includes numbers like this then the examiner probably wants you to do something with them. In this case, you will almost certainly have to calculate the materiality of the issue. It is then obvious that you need to say whether the treatment given in the question is correct, and comment on its materiality.

Part (b) should have been straightforward, as long as you knew the formats for auditor's reports with modified opinions, per ISA 705. It is 'bread and butter' at this level to be able to criticise an auditor's report, and the report in this scenario had a number of errors that you should have noticed straight away – in particular the naming of the paragraphs, the order of the paragraphs, and the failure to quantify the misstatement.

Easy marks. There were plenty of easy marks in part (a) for applying IAS 23 to the scenario.

ACCA examiner's answer. The ACCA examiner's answer to this question can be found at the end of this Practise & Revision Kit.

Marks

(a) **New processing area**

Generally 1 mark for each matter/specific audit procedure:

Matters:
- Materiality calculation
- Borrowing costs are directly attributable to the asset
- Borrowing costs should be capitalised during period of construction
- Amounts are correctly capitalised
- Depreciate from September 20X1
- Additions to non-current assets should be disclosed in note

Evidence:
- Review of costs capitalised for eligibility
- Agreement of sample of costs to supporting documentation
- Copy of approved capital expenditure budget/discuss significant variances
- Agreement of loan details to loan documentation
- Recalculation of borrowing costs, depreciation, asset carrying value
- Confirmation of completeness of disclosure in notes to financial statements

Maximum   8

(b) **Audit report**

Generally 1 mark per comment:
- Inappropriate headings
- Paragraphs wrong way round
- Amounts not quantified
- Impact on financial statements not described
- Unclear from audit report if any accounting taken place for the pension plan
- No reference made to relevant accounting standard
- Use of word 'deliberate' not professional
- Materiality calculation
- Discuss whether adverse opinion appropriate (up to 2 marks)

Maximum   7

Total   15

(a) **Matters to consider**

At £5m, the total cost of the area is 2.9% of total assets (= 5 / 175) and is material to the statement of financial position. The borrowing costs are less than 1% of total assets and not material to the statement of financial position. However, they represent 10% of profit before tax and are therefore material to the statement of profit or loss.

IAS 23 *Borrowing costs* requires directly attributable costs to be capitalised as tangible non-current assets. This would include the borrowing costs, which are capitalised over the period of construction. This would be the six months from 1 March to 1 September. The date when the asset started being used is not relevant to this calculation.

The borrowing costs that should be capitalised over this period are stated correctly at £100,000 (= £4m × 5% × 6 / 12).

Depreciation should be charged on the asset from the time it is in the location and condition necessary for it to be operated, which in this case is also 1 September. Depreciation will be from 1 September to 31 January, which is five months, and will be calculated using a useful life of 15 years. Thus the statement of profit or loss should include a depreciation charge of £138,889 (= £5m (total cost of asset including borrowing costs) / 15 years × 5 / 12).

Evidence

- A breakdown of the components of the £4.9 million capitalised costs (excluding £100,000 borrowing costs) reviewed to ensure all items are eligible for capitalisation

- Agreement of a sample of the capitalised costs to supporting documentation (eg invoices for tangible items such as cement, payroll records for internal labour costs)

- A copy of the approved budget or capital expenditure plan for the extension

- An original copy of the loan agreement, confirming the amount borrowed, the date of the cash receipt, the interest rate and whether the loan is secured on any assets

- Documentation to verify that the extension was complete and ready for use on 1 September, such as a building completion certificate

- Recalculation of the borrowing cost, depreciation charge and carrying value of the extension at the year end, and agreement of all figures to the draft financial statements

- Confirmation that the additions to property, plant and equipment are disclosed in the required note to the financial statements

(b)   **Paragraph format**

ISA 705 Modifications to the opinion in the independent auditor's report states that for an adverse opinion, the report **should**:

- Explain the reasons for the adverse opinion in a paragraph entitled 'Basis for Adverse Opinion'. This paragraph is placed immediately before the opinion paragraph.

- Express an adverse opinion in a paragraph entitled 'Adverse Opinion'

The draft auditor's report for Snipe Ltd does not do this: both paragraphs are titled incorrectly, and are placed in the wrong order.

'Explanation' paragraph

The explanation of the basis for the adverse opinion is not sufficient. ISA 705 states that the matter must be quantified where this is practicable: the paragraph should state that the plan is in deficit by £10.5m.

The paragraph should describe the impact of this omission on the financial statements. In this case, it should state that if the deficit had been recognised then this would increase total liabilities, and reduce shareholders' equity, by £10.5m.

Reference should be made to the relevant accounting standard, in this case IAS 19 *Employee benefits*, as this would help improve users' understanding of the misstatement.

Wording

The explanation paragraph describes the omission as 'deliberate'. This is an unprofessional choice of words, but more importantly it is a matter of judgement whether or not the omission is deliberate. By making this assertion, the auditor leaves himself open to the risk of litigation if the client takes this to be defamatory.

Adverse opinion?

It is open to question whether this issue alone would result in an adverse opinion. At 6% of total assets (=10.5 / 175) the matter is definitely material, but may not be pervasive. An adverse opinion should only be expressed where the misstatement is both material and pervasive.

It may be that there are other matters (eg other misstatements) that have caused the firm to express an adverse opinion. In this case, ISA 705 requires the firm to describe all other identified matters that would have required a modification of the auditor's opinion.

61 Nassau Group

Text references. Chapters 11 and 17.

Top tips. Part (a) of this question was deceptively difficult. At first sight it may appear to be a standard question on group audits, but delve into it more deeply and you will find that it is actually relatively tricky. The key issue is making sense of what has already happened: the component auditor has sent you a draft report.

This report contains a qualified opinion which appears to be drafted correctly – you need to draw on your knowledge of ISA 705 *Modifications to the Opinion in the Independent Auditor's Report* to make this assessment. If you didn't know ISA 705 well enough to do this correctly, then you might have struggled with this question.

The auditor says in the report that a provision should have been made, but in Note 12 to the financial statements, management says that the probability of an outflow is only 20%, so no provision is necessary. The question for the group auditor (which is you!) is: who is right? In order to decide this, the auditor must review the audit evidence that the component auditor based its conclusion on. If the evidence is sufficient and appropriate, then the draft audit report is OK; if the evidence is not sufficient and appropriate, then either further evidence must be obtained, or the draft audit report is wrong.

You then have to think about the matter practically: what would happen from here? If Exuma is right, then the draft auditor's report is wrong. If the auditor is right, then Exuma may change the financial statements. If this does not happen, then the group accounts may or may not need changing, all of which will have an impact on the group auditor's report.

This is quite a lot of work for the ten marks on offer, and you should make sure that you do not go over time on this part of the question. The important thing is to be scoring marks with each point you make.

Part (b) should have made up for the difficulty of part (a). If you had revised the audit procedures on the consolidation the most of this was just knowledge.

Easy marks. Calculating materiality in part (a) was easy – but don't just do the figures, make sure you say what you are doing and conclude on whether or not the matter is material to the group, and on whether the component is significant or not.

Most of part (b) was easy, if you knew it. If not, then there is a very easy mark available for suggesting checking the 'arithmetical accuracy' of the consolidation schedule.

Examiner's comments. Requirement (a), for ten marks, asked candidates to identify and explain the matters that should be considered and the actions that should be taken by the group audit engagement team in forming an opinion on the consolidated financial statements. Most candidates gained marks by calculating the materiality of the provision to the group and to the individual financial statements of the subsidiary. However, few determined the materiality of the component itself to the group.

Candidates are usually happy to be critical of auditors in question scenarios, but in this case when it was actually appropriate to raise concerns over the evidence (or lack of it) obtained to support the qualified opinion, very few answers tackled this issue. However, some candidates did waste time criticising the extract audit report that had been provided – this was not asked for – and implied that candidates had not read the question requirement at all.

The UK and IRL requirement (b) was different, and concerned a subsidiary that had been disposed of during the year. The requirement was to comment on the matters that should be considered and the evidence that should be found in a review of audit working papers. Candidates responded well to this, and most earned marks by calculating materiality, discussing the appropriate accounting treatment in the consolidated financial statements, and could provide several examples of relevant evidence.

Marks

(a) **Matters/actions**

Up to 2 marks for each matter/action identified and explained
(max 3 marks for identification):

- Exuma Ltd is a significant component
- Matter is material to individual and group financial statements
- Accounting treatment/qualification for Exuma Ltd's financial statements
- Review of audit work performed
- Consideration of further audit work
- Discuss with group management and those charged with governance
- Request that Exuma Ltd's management adjust financial statements
- Adjustment could be made on consolidation
- Impact on group opinion if no adjustment made

Maximum   10

(b) **Matters/audit evidence**

Generally 1 mark per matter/specific piece of evidence:

Matters:

- Materiality to group profit
- Whether it should be treated as a discontinued operation
- Consideration of accuracy of inclusion of Andros Ltd's results up to date of sale
- Removal of assets, goodwill, liabilities from SOFP
- Consideration of parent company profit on disposal and accrual of tax due

Evidence:

- Agree proceeds to bank statement and recomputed group profit
- Confirm value of proceeds to sale documentation (to ensure completeness)
- Confirm date of sale to sale documentation
- Review all disclosures in draft financial statements
- Review any press release/statement on company website

Maximum   8

Total   18

(a) **Materiality to group**

ISA 600 (UK and Ireland) *Special Considerations – Audits of Group Financial Statements (Including the Work of Component Auditors)* states that a component is significant (material to a group) where a chosen benchmark is more than 15% of the same figure for the group as a whole.

Exuma Ltd's profit before tax is 20% of group profit before tax (PBT), and total assets is 23.5%. Exuma is therefore a significant component.

Materiality of issue

The £2m legal claim represents 50% of Exuma's PBT, and 10% of total assets.

The claim is also material to the group, at 10% of PBT and 2.4% of total assets.

Qualified opinion – Exuma

Jalousie & Co have expressed a qualified opinion on Exuma in relation to IAS 37 *Provisions, Contingent Liabilities and Contingent Assets*. Audit evidence was obtained that led the auditor to conclude that the Note 12 to the financial statements of Exuma material misstates the probability of the claim against the company being successful. Presumably Jalousie & Co must have obtained audit evidence that the claim's chance of success was not 20% as stated, but was 50% or more. This would mean that a liability should have been recognised in accordance with IAS 37.

This misstatement is material but is unlikely to be deemed pervasive, the qualified opinion is correct provided that the audit evidence obtained is sufficient and appropriate.

Audit evidence

Exuma Ltd is material to the group, as is this specific issue. The group auditor should therefore review Jalousie & Co's audit evidence in relation to it.

The key question is the assessment of the probability of the court-case being lost, and the consequent future outflow of £2m. The group auditor should discuss the matter with Jalousie & Co's audit engagement partner. Audit evidence should include copies of all legal correspondence, as well as written representations from Exuma's management regarding their accounting treatment of the matter.

Depending on the strength of this evidence, it may have been appropriate for Jalousie & Co to have used an auditor's expert to provide a separate legal opinion on the matter.

Further evidence

The group auditor may determine that further audit evidence needs to be obtained, such as the opinion of an auditor's expert is this has not been sought. This can be done either by collaboration with the component auditor, or by the group auditor alone.

It is possible that there is not sufficient appropriate evidence to qualify the opinion on this matter, and that Exuma Ltd's management is correct. In this case, Jalousie & Co would have to redraft its auditor's report to show an unmodified opinion.

Impact on group – discussion with group management

The matter should be discussed with group management in order to ascertain what the impact will be on the group financial statements and auditor's report. There are a number of possible outcomes, examined below.

Exuma's financial statements changed

The group auditor should request that Nassau Group's management ask Exuma to adjust its financial statements and recognise a provision. This would mean that Jalousie & Co's audit report, which has not yet been issued, could potentially be issued with an unmodified opinion if the adjusted financial statements are not materially misstated.

Only group accounts changed

If Exuma's financial statements are not adjusted, then the group financial statements themselves could still be adjusted to rectify the material misstatement. The auditor's opinion on Exuma would still be qualified, but the group auditor's report would not be modified in relation to this matter.

No adjustment made at all

If no adjustment is made to Exuma's or the Nassau Group's financial statements, then the group audit opinion is qualified ('except for') due to a material misstatement. The work of the component auditor would not be referred to in the group auditor's report.

(b)   **Matters**

The profit on disposal is material to the consolidated statement of profit or loss and other comprehensive income at 25% (= £5m / £20m) of PBT. This amount should be included in comprehensive income as it results from the loss of control over a subsidiary.

The parent company's financial statements must include a profit on disposal. There is a risk of this calculation being performed incorrectly, as it must be done on a different basis from the profit on disposal in the consolidated accounts.

The auditor must consider whether this is a discontinued operation in line with IFRS 5 *Non-current assets held for sale and discontinued operations*. If it does, then its results should be shown separately on the statement of profit or loss and other comprehensive income.

The auditor must consider whether the results of Andros Ltd have been included only up until the date of disposal, and not past this date. If this has not been done correctly then there is a risk of group profit being overstated.

Any tax due on the sale of the shares should be accrued for, and included within group liabilities and group tax expense. The risk is that this amount has been measured inaccurately or omitted from the financial statements.

Evidence

- Recompute group profit on disposal, and agree major amounts to supporting documents.

- Inspect legal documents to confirm value of disposal, and to ensure any other contract clauses (eg contingent consideration) are accounted for correctly.

- Agree the date of sale to legal documents, and confirm that disposal is accounted for correctly at this date.

- Consider whether the disposal is a discontinued operation in line with IFRS 5.

- Review consolidated financial statements to ensure that amounts relating to Adros Ltd have been derecognised.

62 Cinnabar Group

Text references. Chapters 8 and 17.

Top tips. Part (a) to this question is relatively straightforward asking for an explanation of the auditor's responsibility in respect of going concern. This part of your answer is one of the few opportunities to score marks for rote-learned knowledge. Part (b) is much more biased towards higher skills and is therefore more difficult. It is important that you score well in part (a) to compensate for lost marks in part (b). Make sure you distinguish between auditors' and directors' responsibilities. In part (a) it is the auditors' responsibilities which are relevant.

In part (b) you need to take the information at face value. It is quite clear that the company is not a going concern so don't hedge your bets! Make sure you discuss alternative forms of the auditor's report which are relevant, rather than every other form of auditor's report that you can think of.

Easy marks. These are available in part (a) of the question. You should be able to score well in this section as this part of the requirement is knowledge-based.

Examiner's comments. Surprisingly few came close to scoring full marks in part (a). Most correctly stated the key point which was that the auditors' responsibility was to assess the appropriateness of the going concern basis being used but few went further than this basic point. Answers to part (b) were weak and showed a clear lack of focus and planning. Many did not take in the key facts in the question. For example, it was clear that the company was **not** a going concern and the two notes provided **did** relate to the same issue.

Marking scheme

			Marks
(a)	**Explanation of auditor's responsibilities for going concern**		
	Generally 1 mark each comment	Maximum	5
	Ideas (ISA (UK & Ireland) 570)		
	– Consider ability to continue as going concern		
	– Assess management's procedures		
	– Gather evidence		
	– Document concerns		
	– Obtain written management representation		
	– Assess disclosure		
	– Modify auditor's report (as appropriate)		

(b) **Proposed auditor's report**

Generally 1 mark a comment   Maximum   10

Ideas

- – Meaning of unqualified/'T&F'
  - – Appropriate accounting policies (IAS 1)
  - – Adequate disclosure
  - – In accordance with legislation
- – Going concern – a pervasive concept
- – Basis of preparation (going concern or other)
- – Disclosure required (IAS 1/ISA (UK & Ireland) 570)
- – Sufficiency of evidence/limitation (**not** appropriate)
- – Vs material misstatement?
- – Materiality vs pervasive
- – Unmodified (**not** appropriate)
- – Adverse opinion (if going concern basis used)
- – Explanatory para (if additional disclosure made)
- – 'Except for'

Total $\underline{\underline{15}}$

(a) **Auditor's responsibilities**

These are as follows:

- To consider the appropriateness of management's use of the going concern assumption in the preparation of the financial statements

- To consider whether there are any material uncertainties about the entity's ability to continue as a going concern that need to be disclosed. The auditor should remain alert for these throughout the audit, and particularly as part of the risk assessment procedures.

- To consider the same period as that used by management in making its assessment. This should be at least twelve months from the date the financial statements are approved

- When events or conditions have been identified which cast significant doubt on the entity's ability to continue as a going concern, to:
  - – Review managements plans for future action
  - – Gather sufficient appropriate audit evidence to confirm or dispel whether or not a material uncertainty exists
  - – Seek written representations from management regarding its plans for future action

- Where the auditors consider that there is a significant level of concern about the ability of the company to continue but do not disagree with the preparation of the financial accounts on a going concern basis, to issue an unqualified opinion provided that disclosures are adequate. The auditor would also include an emphasis of matter paragraph.

- If the disclosures are inadequate, to issue a qualified or adverse opinion depending on the circumstances

- If the auditor disagrees with the basis of preparation, to issue an adverse opinion on the basis that the financial statements are seriously misleading

(b) **Suitability of the auditor's report**

Unmodified report

From the information in the disclosure notes it is apparent that the company is **not a going concern**. However it is not clear on which basis the financial statements have been prepared. They may have been prepared:

- On the going concern basis; or
- On an alternative basis.

An unmodified auditor's report means that:

- The accounts give a true and fair view
- They have been prepared in accordance with statute

If the accounts have been prepared on a going concern basis, an unmodified opinion would not be appropriate as this does not reflect the true position of the company. The results would be misleading as the readers would make assumptions about the company's ability to continue, which are clearly not the case. In addition to the inappropriate basis of preparation, disclosure is inadequate as the notes to the accounts do not highlight the significant problems the company is facing. In this respect they are not properly prepared.

However, even if the accounts have been prepared on an alternative basis, an unmodified opinion would still not be valid. This is due to the **inadequacy of disclosure**. The going concern assumption is a fundamental principle. **Readers of accounts assume the company is viable unless it is clearly stated otherwise**. In this case even though the basis of preparation is correct the lack of disclosure means that they are not properly prepared.

Alternative opinions

The 'except for' or disclaimer of opinion would not be appropriate, irrespective of the basis of preparation, as the issue is not one of uncertainty. The company has liquidated assets and we are told that the company has ceased to trade in October.

If the financial statements have been prepared on a going concern basis an **adverse opinion** should be expressed. This would be due to a material and pervasive misstatement in relation to the basis of preparation. For example assets and liabilities are likely to be misclassified as non current, when they should be classified as current. The opinion would be adverse as the misstatement is pervasive to the overall true and fair view.

If the accounts have been prepared on an alternative basis reflecting that the company is not a going concern, for example the break-up basis, provided that this has been applied correctly the auditor would agree with this treatment. However a qualified **'except for'** auditor's opinion should then be issued on the grounds of a material misstatement in respect of the adequacy of the disclosure regarding the basis of preparation.

63 Poodle

Text references. Chapters 7, 8 and 11.

Top tips. The part on Toy Ltd was quite a nice question part. You could perhaps have written lots here, in which case it would have been important to have stuck to your time allocation of 12 minutes. Make sure that you address each part of the requirement – including eg further procedures necessary.

The trade receivable issue was perhaps complicated by a possible confusion over whether Terrier was a subsidiary of Poodle. Its dog-related name may have suggested that it was, but the examiner's answer indicates that it was not. The fact that 'trade receivables' and 'trade payables' were referred to may be taken to indicate that the transactions were not group transactions.

The part on the chairman's statement was another nice question, provided of course that your technical knowledge was of a sufficient standard. It was right at the very end of this exam paper, which is testament to the importance of sticking to your timings – otherwise you may have missed out on easy marks here.

Easy marks. Calculating materiality where relevant. There are also easy marks for describing the 'Basis for Qualified Opinion' paragraph whenever the opinion is modified – many candidates miss out on these.

Marks

Audit completion and procedures

Audit completion, adjustments necessary, additional audit procedures, implications for auditor's report
Generally up to 1 mark for each point assessed/procedure recommended:

Toy Ltd
- Potential provision is material to Group accounts (calculation)
- Group accounting policy should be applied
- Adjustment needed to operating profit and current liabilities
- Recommend additional procedures (1 mark each)
- Material misstatement if not adjusted and qualified opinion
- Describe 'Basis for Qualified Opinion' paragraph

Trade receivable
- Potential impairment of receivables is material to Group accounts (calculation)
- Account for as an adjusting event
- Adjustment needed to operating profit and current assets
- Recommend additional procedures (1 mark each)
- Material misstatement if not adjusted and qualified opinion

Potential adjustments in aggregate
- In aggregate, the two matters almost wipe out profit before tax
- Could be considered to be pervasive to financial statements leading to adverse opinion
- Must be discussed with those charged with governance

Chairman's statement
- Auditor required to read other information which includes the draft chairman's statement
- Other information should be consistent with financial statements
- Inconsistencies undermine the audit opinion
- The draft chairman's statement contains a misstatement of fact regarding revenue
- Review audit work performed on revenue
- Request draft chairman's statement to be amended
- If inconsistency remains, the auditor's report to include an *Other Matter* paragraph
- Consider speaking at meeting of shareholders regarding the inconsistency

Total

20

(a) **Implications**

The value of the claim is material to the group financial statements, at 25% of group profit before tax (= £0.5m ÷ £2m).

The treatment in Toy Ltd's individual financial statements appears correct in line with the local financial reporting framework. However, these financial statements must be restated in accordance with IFRS for consolidation into the group accounts.

According to IFRS, a provision should be recognised. This is because there is a probable outflow of resources which can be measured reliably. The omission of the provision means that the financial statements are materially misstated.

Procedures

Verbal evidence is not sufficient for the group audit, and Toy Ltd's legal advisors should be asked to provide a written statement that, in their opinion, it is probable that damages will have to be paid.

As this is a material matter which could result in a qualified auditor's opinion, further evidence surrounding the claim should be obtained. The claim itself should therefore be reviewed, along with any board minutes discussing the claim.

Report

The Group should be asked to adjust the group financial statements for the claim, and it should be explained to them that if the adjustment is not made then a qualified opinion will be expressed.

The Group's reluctance to make changes, taken together with the impending deadline for releasing the financial statements, represents a significant intimidation threat to the auditor's independence. This may call into question the integrity of the management and the reliability of its written representations.

If the financial statements are not adjusted then the auditor will express a qualified 'except for' opinion on the grounds that the financial statements are materially misstated.

The misstatement is not pervasive as it appears to be confined to one specific area of the financial statements, so an adverse opinion is not necessary.

The auditor's report should include a paragraph headed 'Basis for Qualified Opinion' immediately before the Opinion paragraph, in which the reasons for the qualification are described.

(b)   **Implications**

The trade receivable is material to the group financial statements, at 2.8% of total assets and 80% of profit before tax.

ISA 560 *Subsequent events* requires the auditor to consider evidence obtained after the year end and before the issuance of the auditor's report. The notice constitutes evidence that the receivable is impaired at the year end; the insolvency of Terrier is therefore an adjusting event.

The receivable is impaired by £1.44m (= £1.6m × 90%), which should be recognised as follows.

Dr	Operating expenses	£1.44m
Cr	Trade receivables	£1.44m

Procedures

A copy of the notice from Terrier's administrators should be obtained to confirm that the company is insolvent and that 10% of the debt will be received.

Obtain written confirmation from the administrators regarding the expected timing of the payment.

Bank receipts post-year end should be reviewed for evidence of the payment being received. However, given when the notice was received and the tight deadline for the auditor's report, it is not likely that amount will have been received.

Report

If the financial statements are not adjusted, then the auditor's opinion will be qualified 'except for' in relation to this issue.

Aggregate effect on financial statements

The overall effect of the provision and the impaired receivable is to reduce net profit by £1.94m, which would reduce profit before tax to just £60,000.

It could reasonably be argued that this is a pervasive misstatement, as it affects multiple areas of the financial statements and is highly material to profit before tax.

In this case, an adverse auditor's opinion should be expressed.

The auditor's report should include a paragraph headed 'Basis for Adverse Opinion' immediately before the Opinion paragraph, in which the reasons for the adverse opinion are described.

(c)   **Implications**

The chairman's statement is other information, which ISAs require the auditor to read. The auditor is looking for material inconsistencies with the audited financial statements, which may undermine the credibility of the financial statements and the auditor's report.

The chairman's claim that revenue has risen by 20% is materially inconsistent with the financial statements, which indicate a rise of 5.9%.

Procedures

ISAs require the auditor first to determine which of the chairman's statement and the financial statements needs to be amended.

It will be necessary to review the audit evidence obtained on revenue to ensure that it is sufficient and appropriate.

Explanation should be obtained from the chairman of how his figure of 20% was arrived at, as it is possible that this will shed further light on the real figure for revenue. If no further information comes to light and the chairman's statement is incorrect, then he should be asked to amend it.

Report

If management refuses to amend the other information then the auditor's report must be modified to include an Other Matter paragraph. This would not affect the auditor's opinion, which would be unmodified in this respect (although it may be modified in other respects, as discussed in parts (a) and (b)).

This paragraph should be presented immediately after the opinion paragraph, and should describe the material inconsistency clearly.

The matter should be communicated to those charged with governance. It may be necessary for the auditor to speak at a shareholders' meeting in order to explain the reasons for including the Other Matter paragraph in the report.

64 Dexter

Text reference. Chapter 8.

Top tips. You would have required a good knowledge of going concern to score well in part (a) of this question. Part (b) required you to come up with some practical and commercial reasons why directors would be reluctant to include a note to the financial statements addressing the going concern issues the company was facing. Part (c) demanded a methodical approach, looking at all possible outcomes for the auditor's report. Reporting is a topic which is regularly is examined in this exam so make sure you know and understand the different auditor's reports.

Easy marks. This was a relatively straightforward question with a strong emphasis on technical knowledge in parts (a) and (c). Provided you knew and could apply the basic principles, these sections were not complicated.

Examiner's comments. Requirement (a) asked candidates to 'compare and contrast the responsibilities of management, and of auditors, in relation to the assessment of going concern'. The main deficiency in answers to this requirement was the lack of any kind of comparison of the responsibilities of management and auditors, despite the fact that the requirement began with 'compare and contrast'. The other problem was that many candidates did not restrict their answer, as requested, to the assessment of going concern, but digressed into issues such as corporate governance and maintaining shareholder value.

Requirement (b) asked candidates to consider why the directors may be reluctant to provide such a note. Many answers were provided here. However, some candidates failed to provide more than a couple of reasons, which is not enough for the mark allocation.

Requirement (c) was rarely well answered, and many candidates obviously do not understand the different types of modifications to auditor's reports at all, let alone the implication for the auditor's report of non-disclosure of going concern issues. There was a tendency in (c)(i) to go straight for an adverse opinion, without any discussion of the level of significance of the non-disclosure. There was also confusion over the use of an adverse opinion and a disclaimer of opinion. Some candidates put down all possible types of audit opinion as their answer in the hope that one of them would be correct. In (c)(ii) very few candidates suggested that the auditor should consider the adequacy of the note if the directors agree to provide one. In this advanced audit paper it is inexcusable that students do not know these basic facts about the auditor's report. Candidates should also remember that writing one or two sentences is unlikely to be sufficient to answer an eight mark question requirement.

Marking scheme

Marks

(a) **Compare and contrast management and auditor's responsibilities regarding going concern**

Management	Auditors
Focus is to follow IAS 1 requirements regarding disclosure of going concern problems or to prepare on break up basis	Focus is to form independent opinion on going concern status and to see if IAS 1 requirements adhered to
Range of indicators assessed	Range of indicators assessed
No requirement to perform specific procedures	ISA 570 requires specific procedures ISA 570 requires assessment period used by management
Should be part of on going management of the business	Going concern should be considered throughout the audit

Generally 1 mark per explained point
Maximum marks to be capped at 4 where no attempt made to explain similarities or differences
Maximum — 7

(b) Reluctance to disclose note
Generally 1 mark per comment:
– Directors fear they will be held accountable for problems
– Trigger further financial distress as necessary finance is withheld
– Trigger operational distress due to reactions of suppliers and customers
– Trigger operational problems if key members of staff leave
– Directors may genuinely feel that the financial and operating problems do not impact On going concern status
Maximum — 5

(c) (i) Auditor's report implication – note not provided
Generally 1 mark per comment:
– Breach of IAS 1 leading to material misstatement
– Opinion could be qualified or adverse
– Judgement needed
– Report to refer to material uncertainty
Maximum — 4

(ii) Auditor's report implication – note provided
Generally 1 mark per comment
- Review adequacy of disclosure
- If note is sufficient – no breach of financial reporting standards – unmodified Opinion
- Emphasis of matter paragraph to highlight uncertainties
- If note is inadequate – qualify 'except for' material misstatement

Maximum 4

Total 20

(a) **Responsibilities of management and auditors in relation to going concern**

IAS 1

ISA (UK & Ireland) 570 *Going concern* discusses the responsibilities of management and auditors in relation to the going concern assumption. It explains management's responsibilities with regards to going concern are detailed in IAS 1 *Presentation of financial statements.* This standard requires management to make an assessment of an entity's ability to continue as a going concern. If management becomes aware of material uncertainties casting significant doubt on the entity's ability to continue as a going concern, these must be disclosed. Management should also disclose if the financial statements are not prepared on a going concern basis and if so, the basis on which they are prepared and the reason the entity is not regarded as a going concern.

The auditor is responsible for obtaining sufficient, appropriate evidence about the appropriateness of management's use of the going concern assumption in the financial statements. Based on the evidence collected, the auditor must conclude whether there is a material uncertainty about the entity's ability to continue as a going concern and then determine the implications for the auditor's report.

Therefore, the main responsibility of management is to assess the entity's ability to continue as a going concern, use the correct basis of presentation and make the correct disclosures in the financial statements. The auditor is responsible for providing an opinion on whether management have fulfilled these obligations and collecting enough evidence to support this.

Indicators

Both management and auditors use a range of indicators in making an assessment of going concern. They will both look at financial indicators, such as adverse key financial ratios, and also operating indicators, for example the emergence of a highly successful competitor. Management use indicators as part of their day to day management of the business, while auditors do so in order to understand the business and carry out analytical procedures.

Procedures

Auditors are required to carry out additional procedures if events or conditions are identified that cast significant doubt on the entity's ability to continue as a going concern. Specifically, these procedures include:

- Analysing and discussing cash flow, profit and other relevant forecasts with management
- Analysing and discussing the entity's latest available interim financial statements
- Reading minutes of meetings of shareholders, those charged with governance and relevant committees for reference to financing difficulties
- Reviewing events after the end of the reporting period to identify those that either mitigate or otherwise affect the entity's ability to continue as a going concern

Management are not required to carry out any additional procedures if there is doubt the entity will continue as a going concern. However, they should look into and respond to any difficulties as part of good governance.

Timing

As per ISA (UK & Ireland) 570, the auditor shall remain alert throughout the audit for audit evidence of events or conditions that may cast significant doubt on the entity's ability to continue as a going concern. Similarly, management should consider going concern in their ongoing management of the business. The auditor covers the same period as management in the evaluation of management's assessment of going concern.

(b) **Reasons why directors are reluctant to provide a note to the financial statements**

Directors accountable

The directors at Dexter Ltd may not want to highlight the difficulties the company is experiencing as they will be held directly responsible by shareholders and other stakeholders. Even if the problems are a result of an external force, such as a new competitor, the directors could still be held accountable and will want to protect their own interests.

Trigger further financial distress

Dexter Ltd is currently trying to raise finance to cover its operating cash flows. The likelihood of being able to raise this finance is reduced by including the note in the financial statements as potential lenders will be concerned about non-repayment. Additionally, it could cause existing lenders to recall their funds early as they too are worried about the company's ability to pay in the future. The directors may therefore be concerned that the note may only exacerbate any financial difficulties Dexter Ltd is suffering.

Operational problems – customers and suppliers

The directors could be concerned that including the note in the financial statements would lead to operating problems, worsening the current situation. Suppliers may choose to withdraw business if they are concerned about Dexter Ltd's ability to pay. Customers may be worried that the company will close leaving them without supplies at short notice and so choose to go elsewhere.

Operational problems – loss of staff

Employees at Dexter Ltd may decide to find alternative employment rather than risk redundancy. The directors may fear that the inclusion of the note will cause valued employees to leave and have a negative impact on the business.

Directors do not think going concern is impacted

The directors could genuinely feel the going concern status of the company is not impacted by the problems it faces. The directors may believe that they are likely to secure the finance they require to cover their cash flow difficulties and so the future of the company is secure.

(c) **Implications for the auditor's report**

(i) *The directors refuse to disclose the note*

According to IAS 1, management must disclose any material uncertainties related to events or conditions that may cast significant doubt upon the entity's ability to continue as a going concern. Working papers from the audit of Dexter Ltd indicate there is material uncertainty over the going concern status of the company. If the directors refuse to include the note, then IAS 1 has not been adhered to.

The auditor will need to modify the auditor's report to express either a qualified or an adverse opinion, depending on how significant they believe the omission of the note to be. If they believe that the non-inclusion of the note is so material and pervasive that a qualification would not be adequate to disclose the misleading nature of the financial statements, then they should express an adverse opinion. If the auditor believes that the lack of note is not so material or pervasive that an adverse opinion is required, then a qualified 'except for' opinion will be adequate.

A statement that there is a material uncertainty which casts significant doubt on the entity's ability to continue as a going concern will also need to be included in the auditor's report.

(ii) *The directors agree to disclose the note*

If the directors include the note and the auditor believes that the use of the going concern assumption is appropriate but that a material uncertainty exists, then certain provisions of ISA (UK &

Ireland) 570 *Going concern* will apply. The auditor will need to review the note to ensure that it adequately describes the cash flow difficulties which have cast significant doubt on Dexter Ltd's ability to continue as a going concern and how management intends to deal with these. He will also need to ensure the note clearly discloses there is a material uncertainty casting significant doubt on Dexter Ltd's ability to continue as a going concern.

If the auditor finds that adequate disclosure is made in the note, then he should express an unmodified opinion and include an emphasis of matter paragraph in the auditor's report. This paragraph should highlight the cash flow difficulties Dexter Ltd is experiencing and that these cast significant doubt on the entity's ability to continue as a going concern. It should also draw the reader's attention to the disclosure note in the financial statements.

If the auditor finds that the note does not make adequate disclosure in line with IAS 1, then a qualified or adverse opinion should be expressed as in (i).

65 Johnston and Tiltman

Text references. Chapters 8 and 17.

Top tips. This question is straightforward if you are comfortable with ISA (UK & Ireland) 510 as part (a) is worth a third of the marks for explaining the auditor's responsibilities in initial engagements. Part (b) is trickier as you need to apply your accounting and auditing knowledge to the question. However, don't be put off by this part of the question; instead, take each issue in turn and consider materiality and accounting treatment and then the impact on the auditor's report. By taking a methodical approach, you should be able to score reasonably well.

Easy marks. These are available in part (a) of the question if you are familiar with ISA (UK & Ireland) 510 *Initial engagements – opening balances*.

Examiner's comments. In part (a) the requirement was to explain the auditor's reporting responsibilities specific to initial engagements. However many candidates did not read the question and produced an answer that related to new engagements and pre-acceptance procedures. Where answers were answered by considering ISA (UK & Ireland) 510, marks were not awarded for detailing audit work to verify the balances.

In part (b), candidates did not score marks for calculating inappropriate materiality figures. Other weaknesses included copying out information from the question, dealing with issues that had no bearing on the auditor's report, taking a scattergun approach and assuming that an emphasis of matter was a universal solution.

Marking scheme

		Marks
(a)	**Auditor's reporting responsibilities for initial engagements**	
	Generally 1 mark each point of explanation	Maximum 5

Ideas (ISA (UK & Ireland) 510)

Sufficient appropriate evidence
- Opening balances
- Prior period's closing balances
- Appropriate accounting policies

If insufficient ⇒ limitation on scope/inability to obtain evidence
- Qualified opinion ('except for')
- Disclaimer
- If permitted, qualified/disclaimed on results

(unqualified on financial position)

Material misstatement ⇒ qualified opinion/adverse
- Misstatement not properly accounted for
- Inconsistent accounting policies

Prior period modification
- Modify again if still relevant

Marks

(b) **Implications for auditor's reports**

Generally ½ mark each implication and 1 mark each comment   Maximum   10

Ideas
- Materiality of Tiltman to Johnston
  - (i) Inventory overvaluation
    - Non-compliance
    - Materiality to Tiltman
    - Prior year report unmodified ⇒ auditor concurred?
    - Prior period adjustment needed
  - (ii) Restructuring
    - Materiality to Tiltman
    - Constructive obligation?
    - Reverse unless employees validly expect
    - Disclose non-adjusting event
    - Risk of goodwill overstatement
    - Non-compliance
    - Not a contingent liability of Johnston

Overall
- Adjustments needed in Tiltman ⇒ unmodified Tiltman (also Johnston)
- Materiality (combined effect) to Johnston
- Adjust on consolidation ⇒ unmodified Johnston
- No adjustments ⇒ 'except for' (material misstatement)

Total $\overline{\overline{15}}$

(a) **Auditor's responsibilities for initial engagements**

The auditor must obtain sufficient, appropriate audit evidence that the opening balances do not contain misstatements that materially affect the current period's financial statements. The auditor must obtain evidence that the prior period's closing balances have been brought forward correctly to the current period or have been restated, if appropriate. The auditor should also obtain sufficient, appropriate audit evidence that appropriate accounting policies are consistently applied or changes in accounting policies have been properly accounted for and adequately disclosed.

If this evidence cannot be obtained, the auditor's report should include a qualified opinion (inability to obtain sufficient appropriate audit evidence) or a disclaimer of opinion or, in those jurisdictions where it is permitted, a qualified opinion or disclaimer of opinion regarding the results of operations and an unqualified opinion on the financial position.

If the opening balances contain misstatements that could materially affect the current period's financial statements, the auditor should inform the client's management and the predecessor auditor. If the effect of the misstatement is not properly accounted for and disclosed, a qualified or adverse opinion will be expressed.

If the current period's accounting policies have not been consistently applied to the opening balances and the change not accounted for properly and disclosed, a qualified or adverse opinion will be expressed.

If the prior period's auditor's report was modified, the auditor should consider the effect of this on the current period's accounts. If the modification remains relevant and material to the current period's accounts then the current period's auditor's report should also be modified.

(b) (i) Inventory should be valued at the lower of cost and net realisable value in accordance with with IAS 2 *Inventories*. The overvaluation of £2.7 million was identified in the year ended 30 September 20X7 and should have been written off then. It should not be written off over three years.

Inventory is therefore overvalued by £0.9 million in the year ended 30 September 20X8. This represents 5.6% of Tiltman's total assets and 129% of the profit before tax and is therefore clearly material. In the prior year, inventory would have been overvalued by £1.8 million, so the reported profit then should actually have been a loss.

The prior period's auditor's report was unqualified, implying that the previous auditor either agreed with the accounting treatment, or else issued an inappropriate opinion on the financial statements for the year ended 30 September 20X7. A prior period adjustment is required in accordance with IAS 8 *Accounting policies, changes in accounting estimates and errors*, so the comparative figures for the preceding period should be restated in the financial statements, and notes and an adjustment made to the opening balances of reserves for the cumulative effect, as well as being disclosed appropriately in the notes to the accounts.

(ii) A provision for £2.3 million has been made in Tiltman's accounts for the redundancies and non-cancellable lease payments that would result from the restructuring. This represents 14% of the total assets for the year and is very material.

According to IAS 37 *Provisions, contingent liabilities and contingent assets*, a provision should only be recognised if an entity has a present obligation (legal or constructive) as a result of a past event, it is probable that a transfer of economic benefits will be required to settle the obligation and a reliable estimate can be made of the amount of the obligation.

In this case, it is unlikely that there was a present obligation at the end of the reporting period, given that Tiltman was acquired sometime in September 20X8 and therefore very close to the end of the reporting period. Furthermore the provision for restructuring costs should only be recognised if a formal plan had been prepared and a public announcement made of the plan. If this had not happened, the provision should not have been recognised in the accounts for the year ended 30 September 20X8. The restructuring should, however, be disclosed in the accounts for the year ended 30 September 20X8 as a non-adjusting event after the reporting period in accordance with IAS 10 *Events after the reporting period*.

Effect on the auditor's report of Tiltman

If the adjustments required in respect of the two issues discussed above are made to the accounts, then the audit opinion for Tiltman should be unqualified. However if the amendments are not made, the audit opinion will be qualified on the grounds of a material misstatement. This would be an 'except for' qualification as the matters are not pervasive to the accounts.

Effect on the auditor's report of Johnston

If the adjustments required to the financial statements of Tiltman are made then the audit opinion on the financial statements of Johnston will also be unqualified. If the adjustments are not made, they could be made on consolidation of Tiltman to avoid a qualification of the opinion on the financial statements of Johnston. However, an 'except for' qualification would result on the financial position if these adjustments were not made upon consolidation, but the results of operations would be unqualified.

66 Lychee

Study text references. Chapters 8 and 17.

Top tips. Part (a) should have been straightforward, provided that you had a good grasp of the material. As usual, a good answer to this part would have a clear structure. It is often a good idea to start with a definition of the term, and then explain what that definition means by referring to specific circumstances – in this case, evens occurring up to the date of the audit report, facts discovered after the date of the report, and so on. The examiner is attuned to the fact that weaker students tend to only be able to make general statements, whereas stronger students make specific, accurate statements that are clear about what they are saying. Make sure that your comments are specific, and avoid rambling!

Part (b)(i) contained some easy marks for knowing the financial reporting implications of a proposed restructuring after the year end. The examiner has previously written an article in which she emphasised the importance of financial reporting knowledge for the P7 paper, so take note! Generally speaking, the financial reporting found in P7 is not going to be as intricate as in P2, but if you don't revise it then you are depriving yourself of the easy marks to be found in questions like this one.

Although the financial reporting marks here were easy, the audit marks here were not. Many students would have struggled to think of enough procedures to make it up to six marks here. What is important in this situation is making sure that the procedures you suggest are specific. Notice that the marking scheme only awards marks here 'per specific procedure provided'. The examiner frequently complains that most students are able to write things like 'look at the board minutes', but that to get the marks a student would need to be more specific, saying something like 'verify the approval both of the restructuring plan itself and of the announcement of the plan by reviewing board minutes'. Being specific in what you write can help you turn your general ideas of what the audit procedures might be into actual marks.

You should have been able to pass part (b)(ii) easily, as this is a major area of the syllabus and you should know it well. Whenever a question asks you to 'recommend action', the main thing an auditor can do is modify/qualify the auditor's report. Marks were therefore available just for identifying the type of modification/qualification, the effect on the opinion, and then the fact that the audit report should contain a description of the reason for the qualification.

Easy marks. If you know their names and numbers properly, the ½ mark for referring to the accounting and auditing standards are easy. The mark in part (b) for just defining subsequent events is easy.

Examiner's comments. Unfortunately, despite the majority of candidates attempting this question, performance was on the whole unsatisfactory. Requirement (a) was a fairly factual requirement, asking for an explanation of the auditor's responsibility in relation to subsequent events. It was obvious that some candidates had studied ISA (UK & Ireland) 560 *Subsequent Events*, and those that had done so performed well on this requirement. However, the majority of candidates clearly knew very little about ISA (UK & Ireland) 560 (making it therefore surprising that they would pick to attempt this question), leading to answers which almost exclusively focussed on the financial reporting requirements of IAS 10 *Events After the Reporting Period*, while other answers simply listed the various types of audit reports that could be issued in relation to a variety of subsequent events.

In requirement (b)(i), although some candidates wrote at length, few performed well on this requirement. The main problems were:

- Incorrect or absent materiality calculations

- Identifying the event as both adjusting and non-adjusting according to IAS 10, eg stating that the event is non-adjusting but that a provision should be recognised in the statement of financial position

- Failing to provide any audit procedures at all, other than 'discuss with management'

- Writing at length about going concern issues – though this may be a consideration, the question clearly states that the factory in question is being closed and relocated, so there is no hint that the company is insolvent or that operations are likely to cease

Requirement (b)(ii) asked candidates to recommend the actions to be taken by the auditor if the financial statements were not amended. The approach taken by many candidates here was to list every possible type of modification or qualification to the audit report, in the hope that one of them would be a correct answer. This displays a complete lack of understanding of the impact of non-amended financial statements, which is a crucial area of knowledge for this syllabus. It also indicates a lack of professional judgment skills. Marks are not awarded to candidates who attempt to 'hedge their bets' in this manner.

Marks

(a) **Auditor's responsibility in relation to subsequent events**
1 mark per comment explained:
- Definition of subsequent events
- Responsibility divided into three distinct periods
- Active duty up-to-date audit report issued
- Examples of procedures up-to-date of audit report
- Procedures to be as near to date of report as possible
- No active duty after date report issued
- Facts discovered before financial statements issued – discuss with management/reissue audit report if financial statements revised
- Facts discovered after financial statements issued – discuss with management/issue new audit report/need emphasis of matter/take legal advice

Maximum   6

(b) (i) **Audit procedures in respect of announcement of restructuring**
1 mark per specific procedure provided:
- Non-adjusting event after the reporting date
- 1 mark for calculation/consideration of materiality which can be awarded in either (b)(i) or (b)(ii)
- IAS 10 requires note to financial statements
- Obtain copy of announcement and review for details
- Confirm date of approval and announcement of restructuring
- Read minutes of board meetings where the restructuring was discussed
- Agree numerical disclosures to supporting documentation
- Consider completeness of the amount disclosed
- Discuss/review potential note to financial statements

Maximum   6

(ii) **Action to be taken if amendments not made**
1 mark for each comment:
- Material misstatement
- 'Except for' opinion
- Description of reason for qualification
- Report to those charged with governance
- Raise at AGM

Maximum   4

Total   16

(a) A subsequent event is any event occurring after the date of the financial statements being audited. The question for the auditor is whether these have been accounted for properly in accordance with IAS 10 *Events after the reporting date*.

ISA (UK & Ireland) 560 *Subsequent events* divides this into three periods.

Events occurring between the date of the financial statements and the date of the auditor's report

The auditor has an active duty to perform audit procedures to identify events all the way up to when the audit report is signed.

Procedures would include asking management whether any such events have occurred, or reviewing board minutes in order to identify events. Examples of enquiries that might be made of management are: has the entity made any new commitments, borrowings or guarantees? Have any equity or debt instruments been issued? Have any assets been destroyed? Have there been any events or developments regarding contingencies, estimates or provisions?

Facts discovered after the date of the auditor's report but before the financial statements are issued

The auditor has no active duty to perform procedures (or make enquiries) during this period. However, if it does discover any facts that require the financial statements to be amended, then it should enquire how management intends to address them in the financial statements that are issued.

If this happens and the financial statements are amended, then the auditor should perform extended procedures on the amendments, and issue a new audit report on the amended financial statements.

Facts discovered after the financial statements have been issued

Again, the auditor has no active duty to perform procedures during this period. As before, if something is discovered then it should discuss with management how this is going to be addressed. If management then amends the financial statements, a revised audit report should be issued including an Emphasis of Matter paragraph discussing the amendment. If management does not amend the financial statements but the auditor thinks that they should, then the auditor needs to take legal advice in the relevant national jurisdiction to prevent reliance on the audit opinion.

(b) (i) The restructuring does not relate to conditions at the reporting date, so under IAS 10 this is not an adjusting event. IAS 10 requires that this event be disclosed in the financial statements, usually by way of a note explaining the event and its financial effect.

Audit procedures would include:

- Verifying that management have included a note disclosing this event in the financial statements, and that it is drafted in line with IAS 10

- Agreeing the estimated cost of the closure to underlying calculations and supporting documentation, such as staff employment contracts

- Reviewing the announcement for details, and agree these details to the disclosures made in the financial statements

- Reviewing board minutes for details of the plan and to verify that it has been approved by the board

- Discussing the reasons for the plan with management and consider whether it is consistent with the auditor's knowledge of the business

(ii) If the financial statements are not amended then they are not in accordance with IAS 10. Considering the materiality of the cost of closure:

Based on revenue: $\dfrac{£250,000}{£15m} = 1.67\%$

Based on profit: $\dfrac{£250,000}{£3m} = 8.3\%$

Based on assets: $\dfrac{£250,000}{£80m} = {<}1\%$

The cost of closure is material to the profit and loss account, so non-disclosure of this event is a material misstatement. In line with ISA (UK & Ireland) 705 *Modifications to the Opinion in the Independent Auditor's Report*, the auditor should express a qualified 'except for' opinion, as the misstatement is material but not so pervasive as to render the profit and loss account meaningless.

The audit report should contain a paragraph discussing the reasons for the qualified opinion, in which the auditor would explain the nature of the costs not disclosed, state the financial effect of the costs and state that this is in breach of IAS 10. It would also be helpful for the auditor to state that this does not affect profit for the year, but is a disclosure only.

67 Grimes

Marking scheme

Marks

(a) (i) **Action to be taken**

Generally 1 mark each comment made:
Recommended actions
Revenue recognition:
- Discuss with management/TCWG non-application of stated accounting policy
- Discuss potential qualification of opinion re: material misstatement
- Discuss relevance of IAS 8 and why change in policy not allowed (½ mark ref IAS 8)
- Review audit files/consider other areas that could be subject to bias
- Second partner review of files recommended

Property development costs:
- Consider alternative sources of evidence are available
- Enquire about back up data/recovery of corrupted files
- Report control deficiency under ISA (UK & Ireland) 260 and ISA (UK & Ireland) 265 (½ mark ref either ISA (UK & Ireland) 260 or ISA (UK & Ireland) 265)
- Discuss potential qualification due to inability to obtain sufficient appropriate audit evidence

Maximum 6

(ii) **Impact on auditor's report**

Generally 1 mark each comment made:

Revenue recognition:

- Revenue recognition: Material misstatement on misapplication of accounting policies – must be explained and quantified
- Property costs: Material inability to obtain sufficient appropriate audit evidence – must be explained and quantified
- Basis of opinion paragraph to precede the audit opinion

Property development costs:

- Material inability to obtain sufficient appropriate audit evidence
- Companies Acts disclosure on inadequate records

Maximum   4

(b) (i) **Methods of reducing exposure**

Up to 1 mark for each method

- Client screening
- Engagement letter
- Adherence to ISAs and other regulation
- Quality control
- Disclaimer paragraphs

Maximum   4

(ii) **Implications of liability limitation agreements**

Up to 1½ marks each:

- Audit quality
- Less confidence in financial statements
- Pressure to reduce fees
- Distort audit market

Maximum   6

Total   20

(a) (i) **Revenue recognition**

The treatment of the revenue from these properties is not in line with Grimes Ltd's stated accounting policy. The engagement partner must discuss this matter with those charged with governance, and must inform them that if no changes are made to the financial statements, the auditor's opinion will be modified.

Two solutions to the problem are possible: either the treatment must be changed, or the accounting policy must be changed.

IAS 8 *Accounting policies, changes in accounting estimates and errors* stipulates that an accounting policy may be changed only if the change is required by an accounting standard, or results in more reliable and relevant information being provided. Neither of these appears to be the case here.

Indeed, it is possible that recognising revenue in this way may be an example of creative accounting, as it results in the overstatement of profit and revenue. This raises questions over the integrity of management, and the file should be reviewed carefully, looking particularly at any areas involving the use of judgement or management estimates.

It is likely that a 'hot' review of the file by a second partner may be required. It is important that this is done urgently, in spite of the pressure being exerted by management to issue the report by 25 June.

Development costs

The partner should consider whether evidence to verify the costs can be obtained from any other source. The accounting system should be able to provide some evidence.

In addition, the partner should enquire of management whether any back up data exists, or if the corrupted data might be recovered in any way.

This would appear to constitute a major deficiency of internal control. If the data cannot be recovered, the matter should be raised with those charged with governance, as required by ISA (UK & Ireland) 260 *Communication with those charged with governance* and ISA (UK & Ireland) 265 *Communicating deficiencies in internal control to those charged with governance and management*. The communication should describe the deficiency and its potential impact on the financial statements, and a recommendation for improvement should be given.

The situation could result in a qualification of the audit opinion due to limitation on scope, and management and those charged with governance should be made aware of the potential qualification.

(ii) **Revenue recognition**

If the financial statements are not amended, this constitutes a material misstatement. The auditor's opinion should be qualified in the form 'except for'.

ISA (UK & Ireland) 705 *Modifications to opinions in the independent auditor's report* requires a clear description of the reasons for the qualification to be provided in the report, and unless impracticable, a quantification of the potential effect on the financial statements.

The audit report should state the amount of revenue and profit that has not been recognised in accordance with the company's stated accounting policy. The effect on the statement of financial position should also be referred to, and the impact on total assets quantified.

This description should be provided in a paragraph entitled 'Basis for Qualified Opinion', which should be placed immediately before the opinion paragraph in the auditor's report.

Development costs

The lack of records gives rise to a limitation on the scope of the audit, which results in an inability to obtain sufficient appropriate audit evidence. A qualified opinion must be issued. As the limitation is material but not pervasive, an adverse opinion is not necessary.

The auditor's report should describe the reason for the qualification, in the 'Basis for Qualified Opinion' paragraph. In the case of Grimes Ltd there will be two separate qualifications which both should be described and quantified in this paragraph.

In addition, the Companies Act 2006 requires the auditor to report by exception on various matters, including if a company has not maintained adequate accounting records. If Grimes Ltd cannot corroborate the development costs due to a failure of its accounting records to capture these costs, then a report by exception should be made within the auditor's report.

This disclosure should be made in a separate paragraph, under the heading 'Matters on which we are required to report by exception'. In this paragraph the auditor should describe its reporting responsibilities, and incorporate a suitable conclusion on the matter discussed.

(b) (i) An audit firm's exposure to litigation claims can be reduced by a number of methods.

Client acceptance procedures

Firms should accept only those clients that carry a low enough risk of litigation for the firm to manage, given its resources. Screening procedures should be used to identify factors that create potential exposure, for instance, a new client with going concern problems is likely to carry more risk than one without such problems.

Performance of audit work

Firms should make sure that all audits are carried out with professional standards and best practice, adhering to the requirements of ISAs. It is crucial in particular that proper documentation is kept, as this will be useful in the event of litigation.

Quality control

Firms should implement quality control procedures in line with guidance contained within ISQC 1 *Quality Control for Firms that Perform Audits and Reviews of Financial Statements, and Other Assurance and Related Services Engagements* and ISA (UK & Ireland) 220 *Quality Control for an*

Audit of Financial Statements. This includes both firm-wide procedures and those related to individual assignments.

Issue of appropriate disclaimers

There is a risk of a legal duty of care arising to a third party even if the auditor is unaware of this duty. Disclaimers may be used in an attempt to restrict the auditor's duty of care to shareholders, but there is no guarantee that they will be effective in law.

(ii)   Liability limitation agreements carry several possible implications for the audit profession.

Audit quality

A key argument against these agreements is that auditors will not be as concerned with the quality of their work if they know that the consequences of failure are limited.

Value of audit opinion

If audit quality is reduced, then the auditor's opinion will be relied upon less by users, and will be less valuable.

Audit fees

If auditors are exposed to less financial risk, then they are likely to come under pressure to reduce the reward (in the form of fees) they get for doing so.

Competition

It is possible that bigger firms will be able to take on more risk than smaller firms, and thus set a higher liability cap, making them more competitive. This could increase the gap between the bigger and smaller firms, and thus reduce competition in the market.

68 Pluto

Text reference. Chapter 17.

Top Tips. Part (a) was straightforward, and you should have been looking to score close to maximum marks here. Note that you don't need to write as much as this model answer contains. Write your best points first, and make sure that you don't go over your time allocation – this is very easy to do on a requirement that you know well. Part (b) was a difficult but fair requirement. Owing to the limited space the examiner has for questions like this, they will not have included much information that is not relevant. You should therefore think carefully about everything in the auditor's report as there is likely to be at least one thing you can criticise about it. Go through it sentence by sentence and think about anything that might be wrong with it. It should go without saying here that you need to have a deep understanding of the different types of modified reports and the circumstances in which they apply. Part (c) would have required you to think on your feet a bit, but you should have been able to do enough to at least pass this part – provided that you had not gone over your time in the other parts of the question. The key thing here is to be specific in your matters to be considered, so for instance don't just say that the reviewer needs to be 'independent', but try to think about what the specific threats to their independence might be.

Easy marks. The knowledge marks available in part (a) for explaining 'fraudulent financial reporting' were easy. There were also some easy marks available in part (b), for example for pointing out that the opinion should not have been adverse.

Examiner's Comments. The final question of the paper focussed on auditor's reports, and fraudulent financial reporting, which had been discussed in a recent examiner's article. Requirement (a) asked for an explanation of the term 'fraudulent financial reporting', with some examples to illustrate the explanation. Answers on the whole were reasonable, and in terms of illustration, a range of examples were usually provided. Answers to part (b) were on the whole unsatisfactory. As noted in previous examiners' reports, candidates seem not to understand the concepts underpinning the qualification of an auditor's report, and have even less comprehension of the use of an emphasis of matter paragraph. Looking initially at the adverse opinion, most candidates correctly suggested that a material misstatement had indeed occurred, and that an adverse opinion may be too harsh, meaning that an except for qualification would be more suitable.

Most candidates did not appraise the wording of the extract, but there were easy marks to be gained here. The best answers rightly criticised the use of the word 'feel' in an auditor's report, as well as it being inappropriate to put forward the views of the directors in the report. Regarding the emphasis of matter paragraph, a significant proportion of candidates did not attempt this part of the requirement. Those that did gained credit for briefly explaining the correct use of such a paragraph, but fewer went on to say why its use in this situation was inappropriate.

Requirement (c) asked for an explanation of the matters to be considered in deciding who is eligible to perform an engagement quality control review for a listed client. Answers tended to be very brief, often in a bullet point format. The majority of answers mentioned that it should be a partner with experience who should perform the review. Though most candidates could suggest that the reviewer should be independent of both the audit team, and the audit client, few could suggest why.

Marking scheme

Marks

(a) **Fraudulent financial reporting**
Generally 1 mark per comment/example:
- Material misstatement in financial statements
- Deliberate/intentional
- Manipulation of underlying accounting records
- Misrepresentation/omission in financial statements
- Misapplication of IFRS
- Earnings management

Maximum   4

(b) **Critical appraisal of auditor's report**
Up to $1\frac{1}{2}$ marks per issue explained:
Adverse opinion:
- Inadequate explanation of material misstatement
- No financial impact given
- Clearer title needed
- Better to refer to IAS 37 in full
- Clearer reference to note needed
- Explanation of material misstatement should be in separate paragraph
- Should it be 'except for' rather than adverse?
- No reference to impact on statement of financial position

Emphasis of matter:
- Refers to a breach of financial reporting standards
- 'Except for' material misstatement
- EOM not used for this situation

Maximum   9

(c) **Eligibility to perform an engagement quality control review**
Generally 1 mark per comment:
- Technical expertise
- Experience
- Authority
- Independence from audit team

Maximum   4

Total   17

(a) There are two aspects to fraudulent financial reporting. Firstly, it involves misstatements in the financial statements, either by misstating the information they contain or by omitting information from them. Secondly, like all fraud it is not a result of error but of a fraudulent **intention**. It is the intentional creation of misstatements in the financial statements.

This falls into three general categories:

(i) Manipulation, falsification or alteration of accounting records/supporting documents. An example of this would be changing the date on a sales invoice so as to manipulate the year-end cut off for revenue.

(ii) Misrepresentation (or omission) of events, transactions or other significant information in the financial statements. An example of this might be failing to include a provision for a future liability.

(iii) Intentional misapplication of accounting principles. An example of this could be misapplying IAS 23 *Borrowing Costs* so as to include interest payments as an expense when they should be capitalised.

Such fraud may be carried out by overriding controls that would otherwise appear to be operating effectively, for example by recording fictitious journal entries or improperly adjusting assumptions or estimates used in financial reporting.

Aggressive earnings management is a topical issue and, at its most aggressive, may constitute fraudulent financial reporting.

(b) **Adverse opinion paragraph**

The auditor's report does not take the form recommended by ISA (UK & Ireland) 705 *Modifications to the opinion in the independent auditor's report*. The Pluto plc auditor's report contains one section that includes both the reasons for the audit opinion and the audit opinion itself. ISA (UK & Ireland) 705, however, requires that there be two paragraphs, the first entitled simply 'Basis for adverse opinion', and the second 'Adverse opinion'. The opinion paragraph should not state the reason for the opinion in its title. The presentation offered in the Pluto plc auditor's report could be confusing for readers.

There are also some difficulties with the paragraph itself. It is not appropriate for the auditors to give the argument offered by the directors for not recognising the provision. Details of the directors' view should be available in the note to the accounts referred to. The auditor's report should then be giving the auditor's opinion as to why this constitutes a material and pervasive misstatement.

This leads onto another problem. There is an insufficient amount of detail given regarding the misstatement itself. It is not enough simply to refer to a note to the accounts, as this note would give details of the director's judgement. The auditor's report should refer to a specific note in the accounts, and state why this is a misstatement. In this context, the word 'feel' is inappropriate to describe the auditor's judgement in an auditor's report, and may be indicative of a lack of rigour on the part of the auditor. A related point is that the full name of IAS 37 *Provisions, contingent liabilities and contingent assets* should be given, as omitting it could be confusing to readers.

The paragraph states that the profit for the year is overstated, but it does not say by how much, and does not discuss the effect on the statement of financial position, where liabilities are understated. An estimate should be given of the financial effect of omitting the required provision. After all, it is as a result of their view that such an estimate can indeed be made that the auditor disagrees with Pluto plc's treatment. The auditor's report should then also give further details, such as the timings of the probable cash outflow.

However, perhaps the most important point is that the adverse opinion given may not be correct. An adverse opinion should be given only when a misstatement is so pervasive that the financial statements are rendered meaningless by it, but this misstatement would appear to relate to the specific matter of the omission of a provision. It may be that a qualified opinion of the type 'except for' would have been more appropriate.

Emphasis of matter paragraph

Non-disclosure of the earnings per share figure is a material misstatement, as per IAS 33 *Earnings per share*, it is material by nature. As a listed company, Pluto plc must disclose both basic and diluted EPS irrespective of whether or not it feels it to be distorted by discontinuing operations. If it feels this to be the case, it should simply say so in its directors' report.

As this is a material misstatement, the auditor's report should be qualified in respect of it. An 'except for' qualification would appear to be the most appropriate, as the matter is material but not pervasive. A paragraph discussing this misstatement should be inserted, in which its financial effect would be quantified – which in this case would probably mean disclosing the EPS figures.

(c) There are four key matters to consider:

Technical knowledge

The reviewer must have a high level of technical knowledge if they are to help identify errors in auditing techniques used, and in the financial reporting in the accounts. They should also have knowledge of any relevant industry-specific regulations, such as stock-exchange listing requirements.

Experience

The review should have a substantial amount of audit experience, ideally in the same industry as the client being audited.

Independence

The reviewer should be independent of the engagement team. The key threat is to their objectivity, so care must be taken to ensure that they are fully independent, for example by limiting the extent to which the reviewer's perspective is influenced by any discussions with the audit engagement partner.

Authority

The review should have sufficient authority within the firm for their criticisms to carry weight, and for them not to be afraid of criticising work done by the engagement team. They would normally need to be at least a senior manager, but for listed clients a partner would be required.

69 Cleeves

Text references. Chapters 2 and 17.

Top tips. In this question, part (a) is knowledge-based and you should be able to score well if you are familiar with ISA (UK & Ireland) 250A *Consideration of laws and regulations in an audit of financial statements*. In part (b)(i), ensure you go through the auditor's report extract carefully as there are seven marks available here. Part (b)(ii) should be fairly straightforward for three marks so make sure your points are succinct to score well. Note that the requirement in part (b)(i) asks you to appraise the audit opinion for *both* years.

Easy marks. These should be available in part (a) of the question on ISA (UK & Ireland) 250A. Part (b)(ii) should also be straightforward for three marks on the impact on the auditor's report of the group financial statements.

Marking scheme

			Marks
(a)	**Auditor's reporting responsibilities for reporting non-compliance**		
	Generally **1 mark** each point of explanation	Maximum	5
	Ideas (ISA (UK & Ireland) 250A)		
	– Meaning of non-compliance		
	To management		
	– Communicate with those charged with corporate governance		
	– Timing		
	– Level of authority		
	To users of the auditor's report		
	– Material		
	– Not properly reflected ⇒ material misstatement 'except for'/adverse		
	– Insufficient evidence ⇒ limitation 'except for'/disclaimer		
	To enforcement authorities		
	– Normally precluded by confidentiality		
	– Duty may be overridden		
	– Take legal advice/consider public interest		

		Marks

(b) (i) Appropriateness of Parr & Co's audit opinion
Generally **1 mark** a comment   Maximum   7
Ideas
- Auditor's opinion heading
  - What is it? ('adverse')
  - Reason
- Reference to notes giving more detail is appropriate
- Non-compliance (IAS 36) – material misstatement
- 'Profit or loss' **vs** loss – inconsistency
- IAS 36 title should be in full
- Information is light on detail
  - Effects not quantified – but should be quantifiable (maximum being
    carrying amount of non-current assets identified as impaired)
  - Why unable to quantify? – limitation on scope
  - Non-current assets **vs** tangible and intangible (what intangible assets?)
- Why adverse? **vs** 'except for' – not pervasive

- Prior year
  - ISA (UK & Ireland) 710 *Comparative information – corresponding figures and comparative financial statements*
  - Not new (no 'as previously reported')

(ii) Implications for audit opinion on Cleeves
Generally **1 mark** an implication/comment thereon   Maximum   3
- Request adjustment in subsidiary's financial statements ⇒ unqualified
- Adjust on consolidation ⇒ unmodified
- No adjustment ⇒ 'except for'
- Disclosure name of other auditor

Total   15

(a) The auditor is not responsible for preventing non-compliance with laws and regulations. However, the auditor does have some responsibilities for reporting non-compliance to management, users of the accounts and to the regulatory and enforcement authorities.

The auditor should, as soon as practicable, either communicate with those charged with governance at the client or obtain audit evidence that they are appropriately informed regarding any cases of non-compliance. If the auditor believes the non-compliance to be intentional and material, he should communicate the findings as soon as possible. However, if the auditor suspects that senior management at the client, including the board of directors, are involved, he should report to the next higher level of authority, such as an audit committee or supervisory board. If this does not exist or the auditor believes his report will not be acted upon or is unsure who to report to, he should consider seeking legal advice. In the case of suspected money laundering, it might be more appropriate to report the matter directly to the relevant authority.

If the auditor concludes that the non-compliance gives rise to a material misstatement, he should issue a qualified or adverse opinion. If the auditor is prevented from obtaining sufficient audit evidence to assess whether non-compliance that might be material has occurred (or is likely to have occurred), he should express an modified or a disclaimer of opinion, on the basis of limitation on the scope of the audit, leading to an inability to obtain sufficient appropriate audit evidence. If the auditor is unable to determine whether non-compliance has occurred because of limitations imposed by circumstances rather than by the entity, he should consider the effect on his auditor's report.

If the auditor becomes aware of an actual or suspected non-compliance which gives rise to a statutory duty to report, he should make a report to the relevant authority without delay (subject to compliance with legislation relating to 'tipping off').

(b) (i) The title of the opinion section does not clarify whether the opinion is unqualified or qualified, and if qualified, on what basis (material misstatement or inability to obtain sufficient appropriate audit evidence).

The quantitative effects of the failure to recognise the impairment losses have not been set out in the report, but they should have been – the report simply states that they would increase the loss and reduce the value of non-current assets if they had been recognised.

The wording of the opinion indicates that it is an adverse opinion but it is unlikely that this would be the case – it is more likely to be a qualified opinion rather than an adverse opinion if the reason for it is that impairment losses on non-current assets have not been recognised. Without any quantifications of the amount involved it is not clear why the auditors consider the matter to be 'pervasive'.

The title of IAS 36 *Impairment of assets* should be given in full in the report.

It is not clear from the wording of the report whether the qualification is on the grounds of material misstatement or an inability to obtain sufficient appropriate audit evidence. The first sentence suggests a material misstatement but later in the report, it states that the directors have not been able to quantify the amounts and this seems to indicate an inability to obtain sufficient appropriate audit evidence.

The prior year opinion was qualified on the same basis so the current year report should also be qualified for the comparatives. This prior year qualification should be referred to in the current year auditor's report.

(ii) Howard Co is material to Cleeves. Therefore a modified audit opinion on the financial statements of Howard Co may also affect the consolidated financial statements of Cleeves if the adjustments required in Howard Co's accounts are material to the group accounts. If they were immaterial, there would be no impact on the group audit opinion.

If the adjustments required in Howard Co's accounts are made, then there would be no implication for the auditor's report on the consolidated financial statements. However, if the adjustments are not made, then it is likely that the audit opinion for the consolidated financial statements of Cleeves would be 'except for'.

70 Blod

Text references. Chapters 2 and 17.

Top tips. In part (a)(ii) make sure that you explain why the matters you have identified have been included. Only half a mark is available for each matter identified but a further two marks are available for an explanation.

Easy marks. Part (a)(i) was straightforward and should have gained you two easy marks.

Examiner's comments. Part (a) required candidates to identify the main purpose of including management letter points (often referred to as 'findings from the audit') in a report to those charged with governance, and provided a brief scenario, from which candidates needed to recommend matters that would be included in such a report. However, some candidates simply repeated facts from the scenario and provided very little comment of their own as to why the matters they identified should be included.

			Marks

(a) (i) **Purpose of including findings from the audit in a report to those charged with governance**

Generally 1 mark per comment:
- Formal communication of key audit matters
- Recommendations made to management

Maximum | 2

(ii) **Findings from the audit**

Generally ½ mark for identification and up to 2 marks for explanation
- Capital expenditure controls
  - Not material to financial statements
  - But indicates serious deficiency which could allow fraud to occur
  - Recommendations to help management reduce business risk
- Internally generated brand name
  - Financial statements materially misstated
  - Give technical detail to non-financial directors
  - Report to state opinion will be modified unless brand derecognized
  - Management have full facts and can decide whether to amend
- Paperwork delays
  - Audit inefficiencies and possible increased audit fee
  - Management to realise problems caused and react

Maximum | 7

(b) **Preparation of financial statements**

Generally 1 mark per comment
- Typing service not prohibited
- ES5 – But could be seen as part of preparation of financial statements
- For listed client risk is increased
- Safest option to refuse/service could be provided if significant safeguards in place

Maximum | 3

(c) **Liability disclaimer paragraph**

1 marks for each point
- Content of disclaimer
  - Report intended for use by company's members as a whole
  - No responsibility accepted to third parties
  - Commonly used but not required by standards
- Advantages
  - Potential to limit liability exposure
  - Clarifies extent of auditor's responsibility
  - Reduces expectation gap
  - Manages audit firm's risk exposure
- Disadvantages
  - Each legal case assessed individually no evidence that a disclaimer would offer protection in all cases
  - May lead to reduction in audit quality

Maximum | 5

Total | 17

(a) (i) **Purpose of including findings from the audit in a report to those charged with governance**

Guidance on 'findings from the audit' or management letter points can be found in ISA 260 *Communication with those charged with governance* and ISA (UK & Ireland) 265 *Communicating deficiencies in internal control to those charged with governance and management.*

The purpose of such communication is:

- To ensure key findings from the audit have been brought to the attention of those charged with governance and that this has been documented
- To provide recommendations to those charged with governance so they can take appropriate action and fulfil their responsibilities, for example in improving internal controls

(ii) **Findings from the audit**

Capital expenditure controls

Purchase of an asset costing £225,000 has not been authorised indicating a deficiency in the controls over tangible non-current assets.

Reason for inclusion

The asset is not material for the purpose of the audit (£225,000 / £78m = 0.3% of total assets). However, the breach in control should still be brought to the attention of those charged with governance as it represents a business risk to Blod Plc. The risk of fraudulent purchases is greater where there is a lack of controls over the purchase of non-current assets. This should be explained in the report to those charged with governance at Blod Plc along with recommendations of how the controls over capital expenditure could be improved.

Internally generated brand name

An internally generated brand name has been recognised on the statement of financial position. This is in contravention of the treatment permitted under IAS 38 *Intangible assets*. The asset is material as it represents 13% of total assets (£10m / £78m).

Reason for inclusion

There is a material misstatement in the financial statements which, if unchanged, would result in a qualified audit opinion. Under ISA (UK & Ireland) 260, the auditor should communicate any expected modifications to the auditor's report to those charged with governance. The report to those charged with governance should state that if the financial statements are not modified the auditor's report be qualified with an 'except for' opinion due to material misstatement. The report should clearly explain the permitted IAS 38 treatment and why Blod Plc is in breach of this, bearing in mind that the readers may not be from a financial background. Once the full facts have been given, Blod Plc should be given an opportunity to amend their financial statements and discuss the correct treatment of internally generated brands.

Paperwork delays

Documentation of inventory was not available for the auditors on a timely basis. This seems to have been a consequence of poor organisation.

Reasons for inclusion

Those charged with governance at Blod Plc should be made aware that the audit was delayed as a result of the late receipt of the inventory documentation. It may be necessary for the firm to bill for the extra time. In future, management should make an effort to ensure that documentation is, as far as possible, readily available to the auditor.

(b) **Preparation of financial statements**

Preparation of financial statements for clients is allowable however a **self-review threat** exists where an audit firm prepares financial statements and then audits them. There is also a risk that the audit firm may undertake or be perceived to undertake a **management role**. Safeguards should be in place to ensure the risk is reduced to an acceptable level in this situation. For example, staff members other than the audit team should be responsible for typing the financial statements.

ES5 *Non-audit services provided to audited entities* prohibits the preparation of accounts or financial statements for clients that are public interest entities, unless an emergency arises as the threats to objectivity and independence are too high. Unless Blod Plc are able to show an emergency situation has occurred, the audit firm should decline Uma Thorton's request to type the financial statements.

(c)   **Liability disclaimer paragraph**

Content

- The report is intended to be used only by the company's members as a body.
- The report is not to be relied upon by any third party.
- Not required by any auditing standards therefore no prescribed content

Advantages

- Reduces exposure of the audit firm to liability claims from anyone other than the company or the company's body of shareholders

- Could help to bridge the 'expectation gap' by clarifying the responsibility of the auditor

- Audit firms can manage their risk exposure in an increasingly litigious environment

Disadvantages

- Every legal case is unique, and although a disclaimer might protect the audit firm in one circumstance, it may not offer any protection in another

- Could encourage low quality audits as there should be no need for a disclaimer if the audit is of a high enough quality

71 Axis & Co

Text references. Chapters 8 and 17.

Top tips. This is a fairly straightforward question on auditor's reports, split into three mini scenarios. For each one, you need to comment on the suitability of the proposed auditor's report, and in any cases where you disagree, you need to state what qualification should apply instead. You should be very comfortable with the topic of auditor's reports, having studied it in-depth in your previous auditing studies.

The best way to approach this question is to look at each scenario in turn, pulling out the relevant points and commenting on them. Your answer should conclude with an assessment of the suitability of the proposed auditor's report and an alternative where you disagree. Use your financial reporting knowledge to help you where possible. The mark allocation for each part will assist you with how much time to spend on each scenario – generally about eight or nine minutes on each one.

Easy marks. Since auditor's reports should be very familiar to you now, you should be able to score well in this question, provided your answers are logical and well presented.

		Marks

Auditor's reports proposals

Generally 1 mark each comment on suitability and 1 mark each conclusion
(alternative, if any)

Ideas

(a)	Change in accounting policy – inadequate disclosure	Maximum	6
(b)	'Other information' (ISA (UK & Ireland) 720A + 720B)	Maximum	4
(c)	Subsequent event (ISA (UK & Ireland) 560)	Maximum	5

     –   Maximum Misstatement vs inability to obtain evidence
     –   Material vs pervasive
     –   Statutory/professional requirements
     –   Relevant IFRSs (IASs 1, 8, 36, IFRS 3)
     –   Disclosure (adequate?) => misstatement
     –   Evidence (sufficient?) => inability to obtain sufficient appropriate audit evidence
     –   Validity of senior's argument/justification
     –   Alternative proposal => Conclusion

Total   **15**

(a)   Lorenze Co

The company has changed its accounting policy for goodwill during the year and failed to disclose this in the financial statements. In accordance with IAS 8 *Accounting policies, changes in accounting estimates and errors*, the change in policy should be disclosed in the accounts.

An unmodified opinion on the financial statements with the inclusion of an emphasis of matter paragraph is therefore not suitable as the opinion should be modified on the grounds of a material misstatement regarding disclosure – depending on the materiality of the issue, the modification would either be qualified ('except for') (if material) or adverse (if pervasive).

(b)   **Abrupt Co**

Although the auditors are not required to provide an opinion on other information in documents containing financial statements, they are required to read the other information and consider its consistency with the accounts in accordance with ISA (UK & Ireland) 720A *The auditor's responsibilities relating to other information in documents containing audited financial statements* and ISA (UK & Ireland) 720B *The auditor's statutory reporting responsibility in relation to directors' reports*.

There is a material inconsistency between the financial statements and what is stated in the directors' report. It is the directors' report that contains the misstatement. If the directors refuse amend their report so that it is consistent with the accounts, then although an unmodified opinion on the financial statements can be issued, ISA 720 B requires the auditor's report to state that the directors' report is materially inconsistent, and to describe the inconsistency.

(c)   **Jingle Co**

A wholly-owned subsidiary of Jingle has commenced trading on 7 July 20X8, subsequent to Jingle's year end. It is not clear whether the company was incorporated prior to 30 June 20X8.

The auditors should obtain more information about Bell. It should be possible to obtain details about its registration from the companies' registry. If this information is unavailable, this would represent an inability to obtain sufficient appropriate audit evidence in respect of which auditors would have to qualify their audit opinion in respect of it.

If the company was incorporated after 30 June 20X8, it requires disclosure in the financial statements as a non-adjusting event after the reporting period. If these disclosures are not made, the auditors would have to qualify the audit opinion for 20X8 due to a misstatement regarding the disclosure. However, assuming the subsidiary was accounted for correctly in the 20X9 financial statements, the 20X9 auditor's report would be unaffected.

If the company was incorporated before 30 June 20X8 then the subsidiary needs to be consolidated in Jingle's financial statements and the relevant disclosures have to be made. If this is not the case, then the audit opinion for 20X8 would have to be qualified over a material misstatement in respect of the accounting treatment of the subsidiary Bell. This would also result in the 20X9 audit opinion having to be qualified over the same issue if it was not corrected, as the problem would affect the comparative financial information in the following year.

72 Dylan

Chapter references. Chapters 4 and 17.

Top tips. Part (a)(i) on auditor's reports was a fairly difficult question in this area. You should have known that either a qualified opinion or a disclaimer of opinion would be issued, but the difficulty comes from the fact that you cannot be entirely sure from the information given in the question.

Notice that there are marks available here for actions such as communicating with those charged with governance before issuing a report with a modified opinion. The examiner likes this kind of point because it shows that you are thinking practically about what would happen, rather than simply reciting your knowledge about the different kinds of audit opinions. There are also usually marks available for the format of any modified report, eg stating that there should be a 'basis for modification paragraph', what the paragraph should say, and that it should be immediately before the opinion paragraph.

Part (a)(ii) required you to have noticed that the company was listed, and that an engagement quality control reviewer was necessary. However, even if you had missed this, you still could have thought to yourself, 'What quality controls would be relevant to this engagement?' A review of the audit file before the audit report is issued should have been at the top of your list!

Part (b) was straightforward, as long as you were familiar with the reporting requirements for review engagements of this sort.

Easy marks. There were easy marks for calculating and applying materiality in part (b).

Marking scheme

			Marks
(a)	(i)	**Actions and implications in respect of the auditor's report on Dylan plc**	
		Up to 1½ marks for each action/implication	
		− Insufficient appropriate audit evidence so far obtained	
		− Possible to extend audit procedures on reconstructed figures/other procedures	
		− Majority of transactions during the year likely to have sufficient evidence	
		− If no further evidence available, consider modification to opinion	
		− Discuss whether material or pervasive	
		− Description of audit report contents if opinion modified	
		− Communicate with those charged with governance	
		− Report by exception on inadequate accounting records	
		Maximum	7
	(ii)	**Quality control procedure**s	
		Up to 1 mark for each comment:	
		− EQCR required as Dylan plc is listed	
		− EQCR to review sufficiency and appropriateness of evidence obtained	
		− EQCR to consider judgement used in forming audit opinion	
		− EQCR to ensure matters communicated to those charged with governance	
		Maximum	3

(b) **Interim financial statement review**

Up to 1½ marks for each matter to be considered in forming conclusion/implication for report:

− Interim financial information should use applicable financial reporting framework
− Identify and explain unrecognised provision
− Correct calculation of materiality (1 mark)
− Communicate necessary adjustment to management/those charged with governance
− If amount unadjusted, the conclusion will be qualified
− Reason for qualified conclusion to be explained in the report
− Consider withdrawing from engagement/resign from audit appointment

Maximum   6

Total   16

(a) (i) **Actions**

We have not performed audit procedures on payroll, revenue and receivables, and have not obtained sufficient appropriate audit evidence as yet.

Hendrix Ltd has reconstructed the figures 'as far as possible', which means that they could still be materially and pervasively misstated. In any event, their representation is not sufficient audit evidence.

It may be possible to perform procedures on the information that Hendrix Ltd has reconstructed. This could obtain evidence about revenue and payroll. Receivables could still be tested by a circularisation.

It is not clear, however, what records may still be in existence: Hendrix Ltd may have sent information to Dylan Plc during the year. As the virus attack only happened in August, Dylan Plc could have 10 or 11 months' information on which it might be possible to perform audit procedures.

As a listed company, Dylan Plc may have issued interim financial statements, which could provide accounting information for part of the year that could be audited.

Practically, it may be necessary to request an extension to any deadlines for completion of the audit.

Auditor's report

It is possible that additional procedures may obtain sufficient appropriate evidence, in which case an unmodified report could be issued.

If this evidence is not obtained, then either a qualified opinion will be expressed, or the auditor will disclaim an opinion.

A qualified opinion would be expressed if the auditor judges that the inability to obtain sufficient appropriate audit evidence is material but not pervasive. The auditor would then state that the financial statements give a true and fair view 'except for' the areas where there is insufficient evidence − payroll, revenue and/or receivables.

A disclaimer of opinion would be made if the problem is both material and pervasive.

Further actions

The details of any potential modification should be communicated in advance to those charged with governance, who should be given a chance to provide further explanations.

(ii) **Quality control procedures**

Dylan Plc is a listed company, so in line with ISA 220 *Quality control for an audit of financial statements* an engagement quality control reviewer must be appointed. The review must be completed before the auditor's report is issued.

The reviewer should review the financial statements and the proposed auditor's report, together with relevant audit documentation.

The issue of whether sufficient audit evidence has been obtained in relation to payroll, revenue and receivables should be paid very close attention, considering in particular whether it might be possible to obtain evidence about these balances by any other means. This is important, because if it is in fact possible to obtain this evidence, then the auditor must not express an opinion saying otherwise.

The review should ensure that there is adequate documentation supporting any judgements made in forming the opinion, and that adequate communications have been made where necessary to those charged with governance.

(b)   The review should be conducted in line with ISRE 2410 *Review of interim financial information performed by the independent auditor of the entity*. The key elements of the review are enquiry and analytical procedures, which do not lead to reasonable assurance.

The applicable financial reporting framework should be the same as for the annual financial statements, so IFRS applies.

In line with IAS 37 *Provisions, contingent liabilities and contingent assets*, a provision should be recognised for the warranty on the cars. Thus the treatment in the 20X2 annual financial statements appears correct.

Squire Plc has stopped offering warranties on cars sold from 1 July 20X2 onwards. However, it still has an obligation to honour warranties on cars already sold. Hence it should still provide for the cost of honouring those warranties. The interim financial statements therefore appear to understate liabilities and overstate profit.

If the same warranty provision needed to be recognised in the interim financial statements as at the year end, this would be £1.5m. This is 5% of total assets (= £1.5m / £30m), and is material.

The auditor should communicate this misstatement to management. If management does not respond appropriately, then the auditor must inform those charged with governance.

If appropriate adjustments are not made, then the report should contain a qualified or adverse conclusion. The report must include a 'Basis for qualified conclusion' paragraph immediately above the 'Qualified conclusion' paragraph.

73 Bertie & Co

Marking scheme

Marks

(a) (i) **Comment on auditor's report – Alpha Plc**
Generally 1 mark per comment:
- Discontinued operation criteria (IFRS 5)
- Disclosures necessary in financial statements
- Disagree with senior's proposal
- Material – except for
- Misstatement – reason must be explained in auditor's report
- Audit opinion does not cover other information

Maximum   6

(ii) **Comment on auditor's report – Deema Ltd**
Generally 1 mark per comment:
- Accounting treatment of contingency (extend to 2 marks for detailed discussion)
- Unmodified opinion appears correct
- Report does not need to be modified by emphasis of matter paragraph
- Explanation why emphasis of matter not needed

Maximum   4

(b) **Benefits to Hugh Ltd in choosing to have financial statement audit**

Generally 1 mark per comment

Note. Comments must be specific to Hugh Ltd

- Improves reliability of figures
- Improve quality of management accounts
- Detective and preventative control
- Increased assurance for external users
- Reduces accumulation of errors carried down
- Advice provided in letter to management
- May need audit in future years

Maximum   4

(c) **Objective of review engagement and assurance provided**

Definition/objective – 2 marks maximum

2 marks for each comment on level of assurance

(**Note.** Needs to be contrasted with audit)

- Limited procedures
- Negative assurance
- Only moderate level of assurance

Maximum   6

Total   20

(a) **Auditor's reports**

Alpha

The major matter to consider in respect of Alpha's financial statements is whether the discontinued operations meet the criteria to require separate classification in the statement of profit or loss and other comprehensive income per IFRS 5 *Non-current Assets Held for Sale and Discontinued Operations*. As the closures were finalised in the year, there may not be any assets held for sale at the year end, but if there are, these should also be accounted for correctly under IFRS 5. If these matters are not accounted for and disclosed correctly, the auditor would have to modify the audit opinion on the grounds of a material misstatement, as at 10% of revenue, the closures are material.

In order to be separately disclosed, the discontinued operations should be a component that is separately identifiable from the rest of the business. All the factories produced the same product. If that product is different from the products continuing to be made, then it is arguable that a component has been closed as part of a single co-ordinated plan to dispose of a separate major line of business. As such it should be disclosed separately.

If the item produced by the closed factories was the same as the item produced by the other factories which have not been closed, then the discontinued operations are not separately identifiable unless they are in the same geographic region and the closure represents a single co-ordinated plan to dispose of a separate geographical area.

If the discontinued operations are not separately identifiable either by product or geographical location, there is no need to make separate disclosure and the financial statements are fairly stated in respect of this matter, therefore the auditor's report is appropriate.

Deema

If the matter has been appropriately disclosed in the financial statements as suggested then the audit senior is right not to modify the audit opinion as there is no material misstatement in respect of accounting treatment and no inability to obtain sufficient appropriate audit evidence.

An emphasis of matter paragraph is used when an unmodified opinion is being given in respect of a particular issue but, in the auditor's judgment, the matter is of such importance that it is fundamental to users' understanding of the financial statements. For example, an emphasis of matter paragraph will be used where there is a fundamental uncertainty, such as over the going concern status of a company.

In this case, there is no fundamental uncertainty and an emphasis of matter is unnecessary. The item has been correctly disclosed in the financial statements and an unmodified audit opinion with no further information can be issued.

(b) **Potential benefits of audit to Hugh**

Hugh may find having a voluntary audit provides the following benefits.

(i) **Confidence for the entrepreneurs in their part-qualified accountant**. An audit would give the two owner-directors a degree of assurance that their accountant was on the right tracks and that the management and financial statements produced by him that they are legally responsible for are appropriate and reasonable. In addition, it would give them added confidence to make the types of operational and finance decisions they will have to make as they grow their business.

(ii) **Confidence given to banks/other investors**. The existence of an external audit gives confidence to banks and other investors when they are asked to provide finance, particularly to a new business, such as Hugh. As Hugh is expanding rapidly, it may find it needs new finance and quickly, in order to maintain operations. Many new companies are affected by overtrading, when they cannot finance their operations in order to meet the high sales demand for their product, and ultimately fail as a result.

(iii) **Secondary benefits of additional finance expertise**. Hugh might also benefit from having an audit in terms of the secondary benefits an audit gives, such as systems review. Although Hugh has a part-qualified accountant, having other finance professionals being involved with it from the start will benefit the company in terms of how its systems develop to cope with expanding operations and keep them on a good track. In addition, as the business expands, it will have to take on more staff and more complex controls and systems will be required to protect the entrepreneurs from error and fraud.

(iv) **Getting things right in the first place**. An extension of the above argument is that if Hugh's business is rapidly expanding, it will be required to have an audit soon enough and having auditors involved from the start will ensure there is not a shock down the line, when auditors do get involved and encourage changes when systems have started to settle and be established. In addition, when audits become mandatory there will be no risk of having to qualify due to lack of evidence about opening balances.

(v) **Acceptability for tax**. The company will be subject to income tax whether or not it has an audit, but the tax authorities may be more inclined to rely on audited accounts than not, and be less inclined to make inspections themselves, which a new business might prefer to avoid.

(c) **Objective of a review engagement**

A review engagement is an engagement designed to enable an auditor to state whether anything has come to his attention to believe that the financial statements are not prepared in accordance with an identified financial reporting framework. This is on the basis of fewer procedures than would be necessary for an audit.

In the case of Hugh therefore, this option would cost them less than an audit but the assurance given to them would be useful. The usefulness of a degree of assurance has been discussed above. In a review engagement, the type of assurance given would be negative. This means that the reviewer would state there was no reason to suppose that anything was wrong rather than I positively believe that nothing is wrong.

The reviewer would approach the engagement with professional scepticism, for example, as the accountant is part-qualified, the reviewer would believe that the risk that the financial statements were subject to error would be higher.

The types of procedures to be carried out would largely be enquiries of the directors and the accountant.

The cost benefit of a review might be good for the two directors, as they would gain a degree of assurance at a much lower cost. However, other parties seeking assurance, such as potential finance providers, might request the higher level of assurance that audit provides.

Mock exams

ACCA Professional Level

Paper P7

Advanced Audit and Assurance (United Kingdom)

Mock Examination 1

Question Paper	
Time allowed	
Reading and Planning Writing	**15 minutes** **3 hours**
SECTION A	TWO compulsory questions to be attempted
SECTION B	TWO questions ONLY to be attempted
During reading and planning time only the question paper may be annotated	

DO NOT OPEN THIS PAPER UNTIL YOU ARE READY TO START UNDER EXAMINATION CONDITIONS

SECTION A – BOTH questions are compulsory and MUST be attempted

Question 1

Your name is Thom Croft and you are a recently-promoted audit manager in Cup & Co, a firm of Chartered Certified Accountants. Richard Hill is a senior partner in the firm. You have just received the following email from him.

To: Thom Croft <t.croft@cupandco.com>
From: Richard Hill <rich@cupandco.com>
Subject: Matthew Manufacturing audit

Thom

As you know, we have only recently been appointed to the audit of Matthew Manufacturing (MM), a limited liability company. It is a glass business with 100 employees, manufacturing glasses, jugs and vases.

I would like you to prepare a memorandum for me setting out the business and audit risks relating to this client, and the kind of audit strategy you feel should be adopted in the audit, stating why you have chosen that strategy, and why you have not chosen other possible strategies.

MM sells glassware predominantly to a large high street retailer, but also sells directly to a number of local, cheaper retailers. The glassware sold to the high street store must be designed to their specification, and cannot be sold to any one else. In recent years MM has made a small but increasing number of sales from its website, which was set up but an external consultant but is now run internally.

The company has a small accounting function which consists of the chief accountant Mr Crow, who reports directly to the managing director and major shareholder, Mr Lofthouse, and an accounts clerk, Debbie. There is a small, PC based accounting system. Debbie enters invoices into the computer and maintains the manual cash book. Mr Crow is in charge of preparing management accounts on a monthly basis; the payroll, which is approved monthly by Mr Lofthouse; the tax affairs of the company; and the tax affairs of Mr Lofthouse. Mr Lofthouse controls purchasing and sales, although he has an assistant who produces the paperwork and liaises with Debbie in accounts.

The previous auditors did not offer themselves for re-election due to disputes with Mr Lofthouse, but have stated that they are aware of no ethical reason which bars your firm from acting. They have passed some relevant working papers over to your firm, and have met with you to give you some background information on the audit. One of the things which they mentioned about the audit was that they have always assessed internal control as poor.

I would also like you to include in your memorandum an explanation of the term 'professional scepticism', and a brief discussion of its role in the detection of fraud.

Please get to work on this for me straight away. I look forward to reading what you have to say.

Thanks,

Rich

Required

Respond to Richard Hill's email. The following marks are available.

(a)   Identify and explain, from the information given, the key

    (i)   Audit risks **(8 marks)**
    (ii)   Business risks **(7 marks)**

(b)   Discussion of the audit strategy which you feel should be adopted, and the reasons why you have chosen that strategy and not another. **(9 marks)**

(c)   Explanation of the term 'professional scepticism' and comment on its role in the detection of fraud.

(7 marks)

Professional marks will be available for the format and the clarity of the answer. **(4 marks)**

(Total = 35 marks)

Question 2

(a)   Define the following terms:

    (i)   Forensic Accounting

    (ii)   Forensic Investigation

    (iii)   Forensic Auditing   **(6 marks)**

You are a manager in the forensic investigation department of your audit firm. The directors of a local manufacturing company, Crocus Ltd, have contacted your department regarding a suspected fraud, which has recently been discovered operating in the company, and you have been asked to look into the matter further. You have held a preliminary discussion with Gita Thrales, the finance director of Crocus Ltd, the notes of this conversation are shown below.

Notes of discussion with Gita Thrales

Four months ago Crocus Ltd shut down one of its five factories, in response to deteriorating market conditions, with all staff employed at the factory made redundant on the date of closure.

While monitoring the monthly management accounts, Gita performs analytical procedures on salary expenses. She found that the monthly total payroll expense had reduced by 3% in the months following the factory closure – not as much as expected, given that 20% of the total staff of the company had been made redundant. Initial investigations performed last week by Gita revealed that many of the employees who had been made redundant had actually remained on the payroll records, and salary payments in respect of these individuals were still being made every month, with all payments going into the same bank account. As soon as she realised that there may be a fraud being conducted within the company, Gita stopped any further payments in respect of the redundant employees. She contacted our firm as she is unsure how to proceed, and would like our firm's specialist department to conduct an investigation.

Gita says that the senior accountant, Miles Rutland, has been absent from work since she conducted her initial investigation last week, and it has been impossible to contact him. Gita believes that he may have been involved with the suspected fraud.

Gita has asked whether your department would be able to provide a forensic investigation, but is unsure what this would involve. Crocus Ltd is not an audit client of your firm.

Required

(b)   Prepare a report to be sent to Gita Thrales (the finance director), in which you:

    (i)   Describe the objectives of a forensic investigation

    (ii)   Explain the steps involved in a forensic investigation into the payroll fraud, including examples of procedures that could be used to gather evidence   **(13 marks)**

(c)   Assess how the fundamental ethical principles of the IESBA's *Code of Ethics for Professional Accountants* should be applied to the provision of a forensic investigation service.   **(6 marks)**

                                                               (Total = 25 marks)

SECTION B – TWO questions ONLY to be attempted

Question 3

You are the manager responsible for the audit of Verdi, a long-established limited liability company. Verdi manufactures, distributes and installs heavy engineering machinery (eg turbines) for the oil and gas industry. The draft financial statements for the year ended 30 September 20X8 show revenue of £330 million (20X7 – £228 million), profit before taxation of £15.9 million (20X7 – £13.7 million) and total assets of £187 million (20X7 – £159 million).

The following issues arising during the final audit have been noted on a schedule of points for your attention.

(a)   During the year technological advancement of the manufacturing process resulted in an increase in production capacity in three of the company's factory buildings. The remaining factory building became surplus to Verdi's production requirements. On 29 September 20X8, Verdi contracted to sell this building for £11.5 million. The building had last been revalued in September 2005 and had a carrying amount of £9.2 million at the date of sale. The gain on disposal has been credited to revenue and the balance of the revaluation surplus relating to the building, £3.7 million, has been credited against other operating charges in the statement of profit or loss and other comprehensive income.   **(8 marks)**

(b)   £7 million was lent to Verdi on July 20X7 for five years at 5%, to finance investment in manufacturing equipment. The loan became repayable on demand on 1 July 20X8 when Verdi failed to pay the annual interest charge for the first year. On 17 October 20X8 the lender agreed to 'roll over' the overdue interest by adding it to the principal amount due. The draft financial statements classify the loan as a non-current financial liability and the first year's interest charge is accrued in 'trade and other payables'.   **(6 marks)**

(c)   Verdi's scale of charges for installing machinery was increased by 40% with effect from 1 January 20X8. This increase takes into account Verdi now giving a warranty to reinstall any item which fails to perform to specification, through an installation defect, for a period of up to three years. The notes to the financial statements disclose the following.

> 'The company guarantees all installations of equipment sold since 1 July 20X7. No provision has been recognised as the amount of the obligation cannot be measured with sufficient reliability.'

Installation fees for the year to 30 September 20X8 amounted to £5.2 million of which £1 million related to the three months to 31 December 20X7.   **(6 marks)**

Required

In undertaking your review of the audit working papers and financial statements of Verdi for the year ended 30 September 20X8, for each of the above issues:

(i)   Comment on the matters that you should consider
(ii)   State the audit evidence that you should expect to find

Note. The mark allocation is shown against each of the three issues. You should assume it is 11 December 20X8.

(Total = 20 marks)

Question 4

(a) Discuss the current auditing guidance for group auditors when requesting a component auditor to perform work on the financial statements of a component. **(8 marks)**

(b) You are an audit manager in Moltisant, a firm of Chartered Certified Accountants, and currently assigned to the audit of Capri Group. The consolidated financial statements of Capri Group are prepared in accordance with IFRS. The draft financial statements for the year ended 30 June 20X8 show profit before taxation of £6.2 million (20X7 – £5.5 million) and total assets £32.5 million (20X7 – £29.8 million).

One of the Group's principal subsidiaries, Capri (Overseas), is audited by another firm, Marcel. You have just received Marcel's draft auditor's report as follows.

Basis of audit opinion (extract)

'As set out in Notes 4 and 5, expenditure on finance leases has not been reflected in the statement of financial position but included in operating expenses and no provision has been made for deferred taxation. This is in accordance with local taxation regulations.

Opinion

'In our opinion the financial statements give a true and fair view of the financial position of the company as of 30 June 20X8 and of the results of its operations and its cash flows for the year then ended in accordance with ...'

'The draft financial statements of Capri (Overseas) for the year ended 30 June 20X8 show profit before taxation of £1.9 million (20X7 – £1.7 million) and total assets £6.5 million (20X7 – £6.6 million). The relevant notes (in full) are:

(4) **Leased assets**

During the year the company has incurred expenditure on leasing agreements that give rights approximating to ownership of non-current assets with a fair value of £790,000. All lease payments are charged against profit and loss as incurred.

(5) **Taxation**

This includes current taxes on profit and other taxes such as taxes on capital. No provision is required to be made for deferred taxation and it is impracticable to quantify the financial effect of unrecognised deferred tax liabilities.'

Required

Comment on the matters you should consider before expressing an opinion on the consolidated financial statements of the Capri Group. **(12 marks)**

Note. Assume it is 11 December 20X8. **(Total = 20 marks)**

Question 5

(a) Explain what the term 'lowballing' means and discuss current guidance in this area. **(5 marks)**

(b) You are an audit manager in Sepia, a firm of Chartered Certified Accountants. Your specific responsibilities include advising the senior audit partner on the acceptance of new assignments. The following matters have arisen in connection with three prospective client companies.

   (i) Your firm has been nominated to act as audit to Squid, a private limited company. You have been waiting for a response to your letter of 'professional enquiry' to Squid's auditor, Krill & Co, for several weeks. Your recent attempts to call the current engagement partner, Anton Fargues, in Krill & Co have been met with the response from Anton's personal assistant that 'Mr Fargues is not available'.

   (5 marks)

   (ii) Sepia has been approached by the management of Hatchet, a company listed on a recognised stock exchange, to advise on a take-over bid which they propose to make. The target company, Vitronella, is an audit client of your firm. However, Hatchet is not. **(5 marks)**

   (iii) A former colleague in Sepia, Edwin Stenuit, is now employed by another firm, Keratin. Sepia and Keratin and three other firms have recently tendered for the audit of Benthos, a limited liability company. Benthos is expected to announce the successful firm next week. Yesterday, at a social gathering, Edwin confided to you that Keratin 'lowballed' on their tender for the audit as they expect to be able to provide Benthos with lucrative other services. **(5 marks)**

Required

Comment on the professional issues raised by each of the above matters and the steps, if any, that Sepia should now take.

Note. The mark allocation is shown against each of the three issues.

(Total = 20 marks)

Answers

DO NOT TURN THIS PAGE UNTIL YOU HAVE
COMPLETED THE MOCK EXAM

A PLAN OF ATTACK

If this were the real Advanced Audit and Assurance exam and you had been told to turn over and begin, what would be going through your mind?

An important thing to say (while there is still time) is that it is vital to have a good breadth of knowledge of the syllabus because the question requirements for each question will relate to different areas of the P7 syllabus. However, don't panic. Below we provide guidance on how to approach the exam.

Approaching the answer

Use your 15 minutes of reading time usefully, to look through the questions, particularly Questions 1 and 2 in Section A which are compulsory, to get a feel for what is required and to become familiar with the question scenarios.

It is vital that you attempt all the questions in the paper to increase your chances of passing. The best way to do this is to make sure you stick to the time allocation for each question – both in total and for each of the question parts. The worst thing you can do is run over time in one question and then find that you don't have enough time for the remaining questions.

Section A is compulsory and consists of two long case-study style questions. These may contain detailed information such as extracts from financial statements and audit working papers. A range of requirements will be set for each question, covering areas from across the whole syllabus.

Question 1 is for 35 marks. The scenario is quite long so make sure you have used your reading time well to familiarise yourself with it and make some notes on key issues. The key to success in this question is to stay focussed, don't run over time and answer the questions set. In part (a), notice the requirement to distinguish between audit risks and business risks – you must explain the risks fully to score well in this part of the question. Your answer to part (b) should follow on from your answer to part (a) – make sure you explain fully your chosen audit strategy as there are nine marks available here. Part (c) is on professional scepticism and fraud so you should be able to pick up some marks here.

Question 2 is worth 25 marks, and was all on forensics, Part (a) was all knowledge recall, so should not be too difficult. Although you are only asked to 'define' each term, there are six marks available for this part, which comes to two marks for each term. You should therefore make sure that your answer is detailed enough to be worth two marks for each term. Part (b) was the heart of this question, and was a mixture of knowledge and application marks. You need to make sure that you stick to your timings here, and that your answer is focused and concise. Part (c) offered quite a lot of marks for this area, so you needed to be systematic and detailed in your approach.

Section B contains three questions, from which you must attempt two.

Question 3 is on audit evidence and matters to consider in the context of three mini scenarios. Note the mark allocation in each. Your answers must be focussed and coherent if you are going to score well and your financial reporting knowledge needs to be sound as you will have to apply it in this question.

Question 4 is on the audit report in a group company context. In part (a) you need to discuss current guidance and you will be able to score well if you also mention the revised ISA 600. In part (b) 12 marks are available so your answer needs to be relatively detailed if you are going to score good marks for this part of the question.

Question 5 is on ethical and professional issues. In part (a) you have to explain lowballing and the extent of current guidance in this area. Part (b) has three short scenarios on which you have to comment. Note that the requirement also asks you what steps the firm should now take – don't overlook this part of the question.

Forget about it!

And don't worry if you found the paper difficult. More than likely other candidates will too. If this were the real thing you would need to forget the exam the minute you left the exam hall and think about the next one. Or, if it is the last one, celebrate!

Question 1

Marking scheme

				Marks
(a)	(i)	**Audit risks**		
		1½ marks for each clearly explained point		
		Maximum		8
	(ii)	**Business risks**		
		1½ marks for each clearly explained point		
		Maximum		7
(b)		**Audit strategy**		
		2 marks for each strategy fully discussed, including the reasons why it should or should not be chosen		
		Maximum		9
(c)		**Professional scepticism**		
		Definition	1	
		Link to fraud	1	
		Management	1	
		Concealed nature	1	
		Not persuaded by past experience	1	
		Documents	1	
		If suspicions raised	1	
				7
	Professional marks for format and clarity of answer			4
Total				**35**

Memorandum

For: Richard Hill
By: Thom Croft
Subject: Audit of Matthew Manufacturing

Introduction

This memorandum sets out the audit and business risks relating to the client Matthew Manufacturing, the audit strategy to be adopted, and what the term 'professional scepticism' means and what its role is in detecting fraud.

(a) **Risks at Matthew Manufacturing**

(i) **Audit risks**

Inherent risk

- The business is **overly reliant** on **one major customer** who is significantly larger than Matthew Manufacturing and therefore is likely to have more bargaining power. This will affect receivables and sales, and could impact upon going concern.

- At a balance level, **inventory** may be risky because it is by its nature fragile and this could cause a degree of **obsolete inventory**. Much of it is **designed to specification** and may not be sold to others, so this could also cause a high level of obsolescence.

- The business is **controlled by one man**, which could have an impact on going concern, eg if anything were to happen to him.

Control risk

- The controls in the business have always been assessed previously as **poor**.

- There is likely to be **little segregation of duties**, although management have a 'hands on' authorisation style.

- There is a risk that sales made from the website are not incorporated correctly in the financial statements. This risk is heightened by the fact that the controls in MM as a whole are likely to be poor.

Detection risk

You have recently been appointed, so this is likely to be the **first audit**. This is an inherent risk because you are not going to have all the knowledge of the business which you would have on an established audit, and risk of not detecting material misstatements is therefore higher.

(ii) **Business risks**

Operational risks

- The issue noted above in inherent risk of the business supplying one customer who is significantly bigger than them. This means in effect that the **customer controls operations** and holds significantly more power over the company than would be good for the company.

- The website represents a security risk. Cyber criminals could gain access to the site and cause damage to MM's IT systems, or could steal customers' data. This could lead to legal problems and reputational damage.

Financial risks

- The company is dominated by one man (Mr Lofthouse) and **raising capital** if required might be restricted beyond him. He his likely to have to give personal guarantees to the bank for lending, there is no other obvious method of raising finance for the business.

- Lack of segregation of duties leads to higher opportunities for **fraud** and **misappropriation of cash.**

- The company deals in **portable, saleable items** at high risk of being thieved.

Compliance risks

- There are a **number of employees** so the risk arising from the need to comply with the **employment laws** is significant, as the company is unlikely to employ an expert in this area.

- **Glass** is a dangerous product to work with and this will have **health and safety implications**.

(b) **Audit strategy**

The first stage of the audit will be to understand the entity. This will include documenting and confirming the systems and internal control. However, it appears likely that the controls will be assessed as ineffective, or at best, strongly reliant on the control of the key manager. Therefore, it is extremely unlikely that a **systems and controls approach** will be taken to the audit. It is far more likely that a **substantive approach** will be taken.

Risk

Audit and business risks have been discussed above. Auditors often take a risk approach to an audit in connection with a substantive approach. This can either be a business risk approach or an audit risk approach. Usually it involves an assessment of both as the two issues are related. (ISA 315 requires the auditor to assess the risks faced by the business as a means of identifying risks of material misstatement in the financial statements.)

The **business risk approach** is often taken for large companies, who have strong controls who are accustomed to the concepts of risk management and awareness. In a smaller firm, such as Matthew Manufacturing, it is less likely that the auditor will be able to rely on the business's own ability to manage risk effectively. Concerns over the controls of the business indicate that a detailed substantive approach would be more appropriate.

There are clear audit risks in this client. It is therefore sensible to take an **audit risk approach** and focus the detailed audit tests in the areas of the business where problems are most likely to arise.

Substantive approach

The fact that a detailed substantive approach is required has been mentioned several times already. This would suggest that an **analytical approach** would not be appropriate. This is compounded by the fact that it is a first year audit and with a lack of knowledge of the business to apply to the financial information, an analytical approach would be less effective.

In terms of detailed testing then, two approaches could be taken. The audit could be conducted around the statement of financial position (the **balance sheet approach**) or the transactions (the transactions, or **cycles approach**). In my opinion, the cycles approach is the more sensible approach for the following reasons.

(i)   Controls are believed to be poor, so there is a substantial chance of transactions being misstated.

(ii) Last year's statement of financial position was not audited by our firm.

(iii) Testing the transactions will give us a significant insight into how the business operates and increase our knowledge of the business.

Conclusion

The appropriate approach is an audit risk approach, combined with a detailed substantive cycles approach.

(c) **Professional scepticism**

The IESBA's definition of professional scepticism is 'an attitude that includes a questioning mind and a critical assessment of evidence'.

ISA 240 *The auditor's responsibilities relating to fraud in an audit of financial statements* requires the auditor to '**maintain professional skepticism throughout the audit**'. The auditor should recognise that a material misstatement as a result of fraud could exist regardless of the auditor's previous experience of the client and its management and those charged with governance. This attitude is important when considering fraud, due to the concealed nature of fraud. It is possible that things might not be as they seem.

In other words, it is necessary to keep an open mind to the commercial reality of the possibility of fraud while carrying out an audit and to ensure that all audit evidence gathered is critically assessed. An auditor should not be persuaded by less-than-persuasive audit evidence as a result of the fact that in the past the management and staff of the company have appeared to be honest and trustworthy.

However, the auditor is entitled to take documents on face value unless he has reason to believe otherwise. In other words, auditors are not required routinely to check whether documents presented to them as audit evidence are authentic. If their suspicions are roused, then they would be required to make further enquiries, for example, they should attempt to obtain evidence from a third party.

Conclusion

The audit of Matthew Manufacturing presents a number of significant business and audit risks which need to be addressed. The appropriate audit approach is an audit risk approach, combined with detailed substantive testing. Professional skepticism will be necessary throughout the audit, but the auditor has no specific responsibilities in relation to fraud.

Question 2

Text reference. Chapter 14.

Top tips. This question looks at the topic of forensic audits. Many of the points were covered in the September 20X8 article by the examiner in *Student Accountant* and you would have scored well if you had read this article. It is vital that you keep up to date with relevant articles in *Student Accountant* to do well in this paper.

Easy marks. These are available in parts (a) and (c) of this question as they are both knowledge-based. Part (b) has three professional marks available.

Examiner's comments. This question provided the first opportunity for candidates to display their knowledge of forensic investigations, which was introduced to the syllabus from December 20X7. Requirement (a) asked for definitions of forensic accounting, forensic investigation, and forensic auditing. There were many sound displays of this factual knowledge, though some candidates who did not know the difference between the three tended to write the same thing for each one.

Requirement (b) was the core of the question. Encouragingly, the vast majority of candidates produced their answer in an appropriate format and included an introduction and conclusion, enabling at least some of the professional marks available to be awarded. However two common problems detracted from the quality of many answers for this requirement. Firstly, providing tactless and unnecessary comments regarding whether the assignment should be accepted. Such comments show that candidates had failed to read and understand the scenario. Secondly, the procedures suggested where often too vague, or not even procedures at all.

Requirement (c) was not often well answered. This requirement asked for the application of the fundamental ethical principles to the provision of a forensic investigation service. Many answers were just not applied in any way, making little or no reference to forensics.

Marking scheme

		Marks
(a)	**Definitions** – 2 marks per definition (general principle rather than exact wording, examples can be used to illustrate definition) Maximum	6
(b)	**Report on aims and method of conducting a forensic accounting investigation**	

Up to 1½ marks per comment:
(i) Introduction referring to reason behind the report and to clarify contents (1 mark)
(ii) Aim – clearly fraud taken place
(iii) Aim – discover the perpetrator(s)
(iv) Aim – prosecute the perpetrator(s)
(v) Aim – quantify losses
(vi) Method – consider type of fraud – ghost employee
(vii) Method – understand how it could have taken place – controls override
(viii) Method – collect evidence – sufficient and relevant – allow up to 2 extra marks here if examples given of procedures that could be performed
(ix) Method – interview suspect
(x) Method – produce reports
(xi) Expert witness
(xii) Advice and recommendations to prevent another fraud
Maximum 13

(c) **Professional ethics – application of fundamental principles**
Up to 1½ marks per comment:
(i) Integrity (max 1 mark)
(ii) Objectivity (max 3 marks)
(iii) Professional competence and due care
(iv) Confidentiality
(v) Professional behaviour
1 mark for recognition that principles apply to all professional engagement
Maximum

6

Total

25

(a) (i) **Forensic accounting** is the undertaking of a financial investigation in response to a particular event, where the findings of the investigation may be used as evidence in court or to otherwise help resolve disputes. The event being investigated is often fraud, but forensic accounting work can also involve business closures or matrimonial disputes.

(ii) A **forensic investigation** is carried out for civil or criminal cases. These can involve fraud or money laundering. The stages in a forensic investigation are similar to an audit of financial statements as they both involve planning, collection of evidence, review and the production of a final report.

(iii) **Forensic auditing** is the process of gathering, analysing and reporting on data, in a pre-defined context, for the purpose of finding facts and/or evidence in the context of financial or legal disputes and/or irregularities and giving preventative advice in this area. An example would be establishing the amount of loss suffered by the plaintiff in a negligence case.

(b) **Report to Gita Thrales**

Subject: forensic investigation into payroll fraud

Introduction

This report describes the objectives of a forensic investigation and explains how a forensic investigation into the alleged payroll fraud at Crocus Ltd would be conducted.

(i) **Objectives of a forensic investigation**

When investigating an alleged fraud, such as at Crocus Ltd, the first objective of a forensic investigation would be to **prove that deliberate fraudulent activity has actually occurred**. The employees may have been left on the payroll in error, rather than a deliberate attempt to misappropriate cash.

Once it has been established that a fraud has taken place, a forensic investigation would then aim to **identify the perpetrator** or perpetrators of the fraud. Evidence would be gathered for use in any potential court proceedings, for example, an interview with the suspected fraudster(s).

Finally, the forensic investigation will try to **quantify the financial loss** suffered as a result of the fraud. Legally, no crime has been committed unless Crocus Ltd has suffered a financial loss.

(ii) **Steps involved in a forensic investigation into the payroll fraud**

Establishing the type of fraud that has taken place

At Crocus Ltd, redundant employees have not been removed from the payroll. Payments to these fictitious employees (known as 'ghost employees') are now being made to the fraudster.

Determining how long the fraud has been operating

It is likely that the fraud started on the date of the factory closure, but this will need to be confirmed.

Identifying how the fraud operated and was concealed

The forensic investigation team will determine how the fraud was conducted at Crocus Ltd and how the perpetrator concealed their actions. It appears there was a problem with internal controls over amendments to payroll data. Somehow an employee has been able to make changes to the payroll data without being detected until after payments have taken place. A control should have been in place to ensure that all amendments to payroll data are approved by a more senior member of staff before any payments are made.

Gathering evidence

Evidence will be collected by the forensic investigation team and must be sufficient to prove the following.

- That a fraud has taken place
- Who has committed the fraud and how
- The amount of financial loss suffered by Crocus Ltd

The evidence must also be relevant to the alleged case. It is important to use a skilled team to collect the evidence and keep a clear trail of its custody so that it cannot be challenged in court.

At Crocus Ltd, evidence could be obtained by the following methods.

- Reviewing and testing the authorisation procedures for the monthly payroll

- Using computer assisted audit techniques (CAATs) to look for alteration of payroll details

- Using CAATs to search for employees with no contact details, employees who have not taken holiday or sick pay and bank account details which are the same for more than one employee

- Reconciling employees' details in the payroll database with human resources records

- Interviewing the suspect and ideally acquiring a confession. This interview is generally delayed until there is enough evidence to extract a confession and will form a key part of evidence to be presented in court.

Reporting

Once all the evidence has been collected, the forensic investigator will produce a report to the client. This report will summarise all evidence, detail the amount of financial loss suffered as a result of the fraud and identify the suspected fraudster. It is likely that this report is used as evidence in court.

The report may also include advice to the client to help prevent a reoccurrence of the fraud. Advice given is often in the form of suggested improvements to internal controls and systems.

Court proceedings

The forensic investigation team is likely to be called as an expert witness in any resulting court case. Team members will be asked questions about the investigation and to explain the evidence presented.

Conclusion

A forensic investigation will prove that a fraud has taken place, identify the perpetrator and quantify the financial loss suffered. The forensic investigation team will gather sufficient and relevant evidence on the type of fraud that has taken place, how the fraud occurred and for how long. This evidence can then be used in court proceedings against the fraudster.

(c) **Application of fundamental principles of IESBA's *Code of Ethics for Professional Accountants* to a forensic investigation**

The fundamental principles of the IESBA's *Code of Ethics* apply to all professional assignments.

Integrity

Forensic accountants are often, by definition, working in an environment dealing with individuals who are dishonest and lack integrity. If there is any risk that their own integrity will be compromised they should decline or withdraw from the assignment.

Objectivity

The report produced by the forensic investigator will be used as evidence in court and must apply an opinion which is independent . A useful test of independence is that the investigator would express the same opinion if given the same instructions by the opposing party. Investigators should not take it upon themselves to promote the point of view of the party instructing them or engage in the role of advocates. Any perceived threats to objectivity will undermine the credibility of the accountant's opinion.

A perceived threat to objectivity may occur when an audit firm asks its auditors to conduct a forensic investigation. In this case there would be three threats to the firm's objectivity:

(i)   **Advocacy.** The audit firm may feel compelled to promote the view of the client in court as they are concerned about losing an audit client and the resulting fees.

(ii)   **Management involvement.** The audit firm may be seen as making management decisions about the implication of the fraud.

(iii)   **Self-review.** A forensic investigation will require any loss suffered to be quantified. If this amount is material to the financial statements, the audit firm may end up auditing their own estimation.

The Code states that appropriate safeguards should be put in place to minimise these threats. If safeguards cannot reduce the threat to an acceptable level, then the firm cannot provide both services.

Professional competence and due care

Forensic investigations may require very specialised skills which require training. Examples of these skills would include:

- Evidence gathering that requires specific IT skills
- An understanding of the legal framework
- Knowledge of evidence gathering methods and the safe custody of evidence

A firm should consider very carefully whether they have adequate skills and resources before accepting the assignment. Evidence presented in court could be discredited if the team is thought to be incompetent.

Confidentiality

Forensic accountants will often be working for one party to a dispute, and have access to very sensitive information. Subject, of course, to legal rules of disclosures in court cases, it is clearly essential to maintain the strictest confidentiality.

Professional behaviour

Fraud cases and other situations such as takeover disputes can be very much in the public eye. Any lapse in the professionalism of, say, an expert witness could do serious damage to the reputation of the profession as a whole.

Question 3

Marks

(i) **Matters**
Generally 1 mark each comment maximum 6 marks each issue × 3   Maximum   12
Ideas
- Materiality (assessed)
- Relevant IASs (eg 1, 10, 16, 18, 37) & 'The Framework' (eg consistency)
- Risks (eg FS assertions – fair presentation and disclosure, completeness, appropriate valuation)

(ii) **Audit evidence**
Generally 1 mark each item of audit evidence (source) maximum 5 marks each issue × 3
Ideas   Maximum   12
- Oral vs written
- Internal vs external
- Auditor generated
- Procedures (analytical procedures, enquiry, inspection, observation, computation)

Total   **20**

(a) **Buildings**

(i) *Matters to consider*

- The profit on disposal (£2.3 million) is 14% of profit before tax (and 0.7% of the revenue it is included in) and is therefore material to the statement of comprehensive income.

- The profit should not be included in revenue but disclosed separately in the statement of comprehensive income as an exceptional item.

- The revaluation gain (also material at 23% of profit before tax) should not be credited against operating charges in the statement of comprehensive income but transferred to retained earnings.

- The total gain relating to the sale of the non-current asset represents 37% of profit before tax for the year and it relates to a transaction on nearly the last day of the year, so the auditor should exercise professional scepticism in relation to its timing.

- The sale should only be recognised in the year if the contract to sell is binding.

- If the contract is not binding before the year-end but is completed before the audit report is signed, it will be a non-adjusting event after the end of the reporting period requiring disclosure in the financial statements.

- If the contract is binding but not completed at the year-end, there will be a material receivable of £11.5 million (6% of total assets).

- As the sold asset is a revalued asset, all the assets in the same class will also be revalued as required by IAS 16.

- IAS 16 requires that revalued assets are revalued with sufficient regularity that the carrying amount does not differ materially from that which would be determined using fair value at the date of the statement of financial position. The valuation on the sold building appeared to be out of date, as it sold at 25% above the valuation, which is material, and therefore it will be necessary to ensure that the valuations on the other buildings are correct, particularly if the increase in capacity has increased their value.

- If management refuse to adjust the profit on disposal and revaluation gain, then these matters are material and will necessitate a qualified opinion.

(ii) *Audit evidence*

- Sale contract for the building – for details of whether the contract is binding, what its value is, when payment is due

- Receipt of sale proceeds in bank statement

- Details of carrying amount from prior year file and non-current asset register

- Valuer's certificate for other properties

(b) **Loan**

(i) *Matters to consider*

- £7 million is 3.7% of total assets and is therefore material.

- The interest for the first year of approximately £400,000 is not material to total assets or to profit before tax.

- The liability may have been misclassified if it was technically payable on demand at the year-end (30 September), although classifying it as non-current would be consistent with the prior year.

- In this instance the condition rendering it on demand has been waived but it was not waived at the end of the reporting period.

- The waiver of the condition on 17 October is a non-adjusting event after the end of the reporting period which should be disclosed in the financial statements.

- As the loan was technically on demand at the year end, it should all (the original loan and the outstanding interest) be included in current liabilities.

- As the loan is material to total assets, if management do not reclassify the loan, the audit report will have to be qualified on the grounds of disagreement.

(ii) *Audit evidence*

- Details of the loan (amount, interest rate, conditions) agreed to prior year working papers

- Confirmation of the amounts owed and details of the loan at 30 September from the lenders at the year end

- The correspondence to Verdi setting out the waiver of the conditions and the terms of agreement about the outstanding interest

- Proposed disclosures in the financial statements

(c) **Warranty provision**

(i) *Matters to consider*

- Installation fees in the period covered by the warranty are £4.2 million, and, at 1.2% of revenue, are material.

- As a result of its new warranty provision, Verdi has a present obligation (to reinstall) as a result of a past event (the original installation).

- Verdi's policy on warranties claims that no provision has been recognised as the amount of the obligation cannot be measured with sufficient reliability.

- However, IAS 37 requires that where there are a number of similar obligations (giving warranties as an example), the probability that a transfer will be required in settlement is determined by considering the class as a whole.

- Therefore, although there may only be small likelihood that each individual warranty might be taken up, there is a larger likelihood that a warranty out of all of them will be taken up.

- IAS 37 therefore determines that a provision for all the warranties should be made.

- The provision should be for the best estimate of making good all the items sold under warranty. It is unlikely that Verdi would not be able to make an estimate of these costs, particularly as they will have undertaken calculations to establish the 40% increase in the price of installations.

- Such a provision is likely to be material (the provision would have to be less than £800,000 (that is, 20% of original sales cost) to be less than 5% of profit before tax).

- Given that the provision is likely to be material, if a provision for warranties is not made in the financial statements, the auditors would have to qualify their report over this issue, on the grounds of disagreement in respect of non-compliance with IAS 37.

(ii) *Audit evidence*

- The terms of the warranty

- The costings of the warranty which will have been used to calculate the corresponding increase in price

- The schedule of installations undertaken in the nine months to 30 September 20X8, agreed on a sample basis to invoices

- Costs of any reinstallations already undertaken

- Average cost of an installation (taken from job cards)

Question 4

Text references. Chapters 11 and 17.

Top tips. This is a demanding question set in the context of a group audit which requires some thought and planning. The requirement for part (a) is reasonably straightforward but you need to ensure that you discuss current guidance in this area. Part (b) is more tricky and there is a danger that you can become bogged down in the detail of accounting treatments. Essentially it is an audit report question. If you can spot this from the outset you have a better chance of picking up the relevant points.

Easy marks. This is a tough question on group audits. No easy marks are available as such but a logical approach is the best for this question.

Examiner's comments. In part (b) many failed to spot that this was essentially an auditor's report question. Most candidates identified that the accounting treatments mentioned were incorrect but many did not make any reference to the audit report extract. Few identified the correct impact of the matters on the audit report ie 'except for'.

Tutorial note. The ideas are listed in roughly the order in which the information presented in the question might be extracted for synthesis. The suggested answer groups together some of these points under headings which give the analysis of the situation a possible structure.

			Marks
(a)	**Current guidance for auditing group accounts**		
	Generally 1-1½ marks each well-explained point to a maximum of		8
(b)	**Matters to be considered (before expressing an opinion)**		
	Generally 1 mark per comment	Maximum	12

Ideas
- Materiality of subsidiary
- Basis para – meaning?
- Non-compliance (IAS 12 and IAS 17)
- Marcel concurs?
- Emphasis of matter should be after opinion para
- Materiality of non-compliance(s)
- Adequacy of note disclosures
  - o (4) Finance vs operating
  - o (5) Reason for non-compliance?
- Prior year
  - o Accounting treatment(s), materiality
  - o Auditor's report
  - o How resolved
- Request adjustment in subsidiary's fs ⇒ unmodified
- Adjust on consolidation ⇒ unmodified
- No adjustment ⇒ 'except for'

Total   <u>20</u>

(a) Current guidance on the audit of groups is provided by ISA 600 *Special considerations – audits of group financial statements (including the work of component auditors)*. The guidance introduces the concept of a **component** as a 'An entity or business activity for which group or component management prepares financial information that should be included in the group financial statements'.

The stated objective of the ISA is to determine whether to act as the auditor of the group financial statements; and if acting as the auditor of the group financial statements:

(i) To communicate clearly with component auditors about the scope and timing of their work on financial information related to components and their findings

(ii) To obtain sufficient appropriate audit evidence regarding the financial information of the components and the consolidation process to express an opinion on whether the group financial statements are prepared, in all material respects, in accordance with the applicable financial reporting framework

The standard distinguishes between the group engagement team and the component auditors. The **group engagement partner** is responsible for reporting on the group accounts and has sole responsibility for the audit opinion. **Component auditors** are auditors who are responsible for reporting on the financial information of a component included within the financial statements audited by the group engagement team.

The ISA conforms to the requirements of other ISAs, for example, ISAs 220, 315 and 330, in respect of the procedures required to **accept** the group audit, obtaining knowledge about the group and assessing risk. The group engagement team should gain an understanding of the group as a whole, and assess risks for the group as a whole and for individually significant components. The group engagement team has to ensure component auditors are professionally qualified, meet quality control and ethical requirements and will allow the group engagement team access to working papers or components.

Procedures

If the group engagement team plans to request a component auditor to perform work on the financial information of a component, the group engagement team shall obtain an understanding of the following.

(i)   Whether the component auditor understands and will comply with the ethical requirements that are relevant to the group audit and, in particular, is independent.

(ii)   The component auditor's professional competence.

(iii) Whether the group engagement team will be able to be involved in the work of the component auditor to the extent necessary to obtain sufficient appropriate audit evidence.

(iv)   Whether the component auditor operates in a regulatory environment that actively oversees auditors. If a component auditor performs an audit of the financial information of a significant component, the group engagement team shall be involved in the component auditor's risk assessment to identify significant risks of material misstatement of the group financial statements. The nature, timing and extent of this involvement are affected by the group engagement team's understanding of the component auditor, but at a minimum shall include:

- Discussing with the component auditor or component management those of the component's business activities that are significant to the group
- Discussing with the component auditor the susceptibility of the component to material misstatement of the financial information due to fraud or error
- Reviewing the component auditor's documentation of identified significant risks of material misstatement of the group financial statements. Such documentation may take the form of a memorandum that reflects the component auditor's conclusion with regard to the identified significant risks.

Evaluating the component auditor's work

The group engagement team shall evaluate the component auditor's communication.

The group engagement team shall:

(i)   Discuss significant matters arising from that evaluation with the component auditor, component management or group management, as appropriate

(ii)   Determine whether it is necessary to review other relevant parts of the component auditor's audit documentation

If the group engagement team concludes that the work of the component auditor is insufficient, the group engagement team shall determine what additional procedures are to be performed, and whether they are to be performed by the component auditor or by the group engagement team.

(b)   **Matters**

Risk

Risk is increased by the fact that the work of the component auditor, Marcel, may prove to be unreliable. This is evidenced by the confusing nature of the draft auditor's report.

Materiality

Capri (Overseas) is material to the group as a whole. It constitutes 30.6% of the group's profit before tax and 20% of the group's total assets.

The accounting error in respect of leases is material to both the subsidiary's own accounts and the group accounts. The £790,000 of unrecognised assets constitute 12.2% of the total assets of Capri (Overseas) and 2.4% of the total assets of the group.

Accounting treatments

(i)   *Treatment of leased assets*

The treatment of leased assets appears to be incorrect. The disclosure note suggests that the lease agreements give rights approximating to ownership in which case they should be treated as finance leases. It is also unclear if the lease payments charged to the statement of profit or loss and other comprehensive income all relate to this type of lease or if some relate to operating leases (in which case the correct treatment has been adopted for these elements).

Treatment of deferred tax

The treatment of deferred tax also appears to be incorrect. It is unclear why no provision has been made or why it is impractical to quantify the financial effect.

(iii) *Adequacy of disclosures*

In addition to the confusing nature of the disclosures provided, key information is also omitted. This includes details of the relevant standards from which the subsidiary has departed and any reason for the non-compliance.

In respect of deferred tax there is a suggestion that the treatment adopted is to accord with local legislation. This is referred to in the draft audit report. This is an inappropriate use of the report. This information should be provided in the disclosure notes accompanying the financial statements.

Marcel's auditor's report

The first extract is entitled 'basis of audit opinion'. If the auditor agrees with the accounting treatments and the level of disclosure – as is indicated by the unmodified opinion – there is no need for this paragraph at all, as it does not appear to be a matter which needs to be brought to the attention of the shareholders.

This type of paragraph cannot be used instead of modifying the opinion. In any case it does not make it clear whether the auditor agrees with these treatments or which of the issues are in accordance with local tax regulations. If it is an emphasis of matter it should be presented after the opinion paragraph, and should be entitled as such. This is to avoid giving the impression that the audit opinion is modified.

Effect on group audit opinion.

The management of Capri Group could request that the accounts of Capri (Overseas) be redrafted in accordance with IAS 12 and IAS 17. (As a subsidiary Capri (Overseas) is controlled by Capri Group.) The audit opinions on the financial statements of both Capri (Overseas) and Capri Group would then both be unmodified.

Adjustments for compliance with IAS 12 and IAS 17 could be made on consolidation only. Again the group auditor's opinion would be unmodified.

If no adjustments are made in the subsidiary's accounts or those of the group the group audit report would be qualified ('except for') in relation to non-compliance with IAS 12 and IAS 17. The effect of non-compliance should be quantified and disclosed.

Question 5

Text references. Chapters 2 and 5.

Top tips. When trying to identify professional and ethical issues, think about general themes such as independence, integrity, objectivity and confidentiality. Try and relate relevant ethical and professional guidance that you are aware of to each situation and explain why it is relevant.

Easy marks. There are easy marks available in this question for knowledge brought forward from your earlier auditing studies, such as being able to give a definition of lowballing and knowing the etiquette with regard to professional clearance letters. Easy marks can also be obtained for coming up with simple steps to take in respect of each issue – for example, if no answer has been received in part (i), it seems logical to repeat the request.

Examiner's comments. The technical content of this question was not difficult.

In part (b)(i), many candidates made a big issue of the preliminary procedures of the professional etiquette already gone through and ended their answers with Sepia no closer to a resolution to the problem than when they started.

In part (b)(ii), nearly everyone identified a 'conflict of interest' but few stated that they would refuse the assignment. Many referred to 'Chinese walls' but did not consider how unacceptable to Vitronella the assignment would be. Those that proposed resigning the audit (of Vitronella) showed a lack of professionalism.

Part (b)(iii) was probably the worst answered part. Many candidates referred the matter to the partner for his/her decision. Weaker candidates proposed unsuitable 'solutions' (eg that Sepia withdraw their tender). Few candidates acknowledged that little could be done. Candidates who referred to 'insider dealing' clearly had no understanding of the term.

Marking scheme

		Marks
(a)	Lowballing	
	Generally 1 mark for each well-explained point	5
(b)	Generally 1 mark each comment	15
	Maximum 5 marks each of three matters	

Ideas

Professional issues raised
- Integrity (management and/or audit firm)
- Objectivity/independence
- Confidentiality
- Relevant ethical guidance – ie
  - (i) Changes in professional appointment
  - (ii) Corporate finance advice including take-overs
  - (iii) Fees
- Meaning of 'lowballing'
  Steps (ie **actions**)
- Obtain ... what? ... why?
- Ask/advise ... who? When?

Total   20

(a)   **Lowballing** is the practice of a firm quoting a significantly lower fee level for an assurance service than would have been charged by the predecessor firm. This creates a significant self-interest threat. If the firm's tender is successful, the firm must apply safeguards such as maintaining records such that the firm is able to demonstrate that appropriate staff and time are spent on the engagement and complying with all applicable assurance standards, guidelines and quality control procedures

Current guidance in the form of ACCA's *Code of ethics and conduct* and IESBA's *Code of ethics for professional accountants* states that members can quote whatever fee is deemed appropriate.

It is not considered unethical for one firm to offer a lower fee than another, however doing so may create threats to compliance with the fundamental principles. For example, a **self-interest threat** to professional competence and due care would arise if the fee quoted was so low that it would be difficult to perform the engagement in accordance with applicable technical and professional standards.

Safeguards to mitigate such threats could include making the client aware of the terms of the engagement and the basis on which fees are charged and what services are covered by the quoted fees, and also assigning appropriate time and staff to the engagements.

The International Ethics Standards Board for Accountants of IAASB recently issued an exposure draft proposing changes to enhance the independence and objectivity of accountants performing assurance engagements with a view to strengthening the independence requirements of IESBA's *Code of ethics for professional accountants*.

(b)   (i)   **Squid**

Professional issues

Sepia has requested a professional clearance letter from Krill & Co in respect of the audit of Squid. Krill & Co has not responded. Krill & Co has a professional duty of confidence to Squid, and therefore should have sought permission from Squid to respond to Sepia's request.

The fact that Krill & Co has not responded could indicate that Squid has refused permission for Krill & Co to respond to Sepia. However, this seems unlikely for two reasons: firstly, that Squid nominated Sepia to act as auditors and therefore should have no objection to Krill & Co responding to them and allowing them to take up that nomination, and secondly, that if Krill & Co had simply been refused permission to give that clearance, then as a professional courtesy they should have responded to Sepia informing them that they could not give them the information they requested and why.

Therefore it is possible that Anton Fargues, on behalf of Krill & Co, is not replying because he has a concern as to the integrity of the directors of Squid that he does not wish to share with Sepia due to concerns over confidentiality issues. However, if Squid has given them permission to respond, this should not be a problem. Therefore, it appears that Anton Fargues is acting unprofessionally in not responding to Sepia's request.

Steps

The manager at Sepia should ask Squid whether the company has given Krill & Co permission to respond to Sepia, and if they confirm that permission has been given, Sepia should get this confirmed in writing.

He should send a duplicate request for professional clearance by recorded delivery so that receipt has to be acknowledged by Krill & Co and gives legal evidence that it was received.

This should include a letter stating that lack of response to his letter will be taken to mean that there are no professional issues preventing Sepia accepting appointment and that if Krill & Co fails to respond, Sepia will report Anton Fargues to his professional body for unprofessional conduct.

If a reply is received, Sepia's actions will then be directed by the contents of the reply.

If there is still no reply within reasonable time, Sepia should accept the appointment and report Anton Fargues to his professional body so that his behaviour can be investigated.

(ii) Hatchet

Professional issues

Sepia has been approached by Hatchet to offer a non-audit service. Sepia does not provide audit services to Hatchet, so in relation to Hatchet itself, there is no independence bar to accepting appointment.

However, the service is advice in relation to a proposed take-over of Vitronella, an audit client of Sepia. This is likely to raise a conflict of interest such that it is necessary to refuse the appointment. This depends on several factors:

- Whether Hatchet or Vitronella object to Sepia offering the services
- What the services are in detail
- Whether Sepia would be Vitronella's primary advisor in the event of a takeover

(1) The fact that Sepia are Vitronella's auditors is public information reported in the financial statements. As such, it is likely that Hatchet are aware that Sepia are Vitronella's auditors and therefore do not mind. Vitronella, the target company, will be unaware at this point that their auditors have been asked to advise a company about a proposed takeover of themselves and might mind very much. Professional advice in respect of such conflicts of interest states that the firm (Sepia) should make both parties aware of the conflict so that they can decide whether they want Sepia to be advisors.

(2)/(3) The professional guidance states that one firm should not be principal advisor to both parties involved in a takeover. Therefore, if Hatchet wants Sepia to be its principal advisor, and Sepia anticipates that as auditor, it is likely to be Vitronella's principal advisor, the partners of Sepia will have to decide which side they want to advise. Being auditor does not automatically mean they would be Vitronella's principal advisors, but there is often an advantage to a company in having its auditor advise in such situations and, providing that the combined fees do not cause a problem, there should be no bar to independence in doing so. It is possible that Vitronella would expect Sepia to act as their principal advisors.

It would not be possible for Sepia to resign from the Vitronella audit in order to be able to be Hatchet's principal advisors as this would still pose a conflict of interest as far as Vitronella was concerned.

If Sepia was not principal advisor to both parties, and both parties agreed, it could advise Hatchet and do Vitronella's audit. The best way to ensure confidentiality was maintained in this instance would be to have entirely separate engagement teams and set up strict procedures for ensuring information was kept secret, for example, having teams in different areas of the office or from different offices of a national firm.

Steps

Sepia should determine whether Hatchet requires Sepia to be their principal advisors in relation to this takeover. The partners should inform Hatchet that before they accepted any engagement of this nature they would require permission from Vitronella.

Sepia should notify Vitronella that Hatchet has asked them to be principal advisor and gauge the reaction.

Ultimately it is likely that Sepia would refuse to advise Hatchet due to the conflict of interest being so great.

(iii) **Keratin**

Professional issues

Lowballing is the practice of tendering for audits at a lower price than the audit can actually be carried out for, often with the intention of obtaining other, more profitable, work from the audit client.

Lowballing is not forbidden by professional rules, because it is seen as a reasonable marketing tactic. However, it is important that the client is aware of the scope of the work that is going to be carried out and is aware that prices might rise in the future.

Professional guidance indicates also that auditors must ensure that they do not provide a service lower than is required by quality standards regardless of the price that it is being done for. Keratin must ensure that they do not fall into the trap of providing a poor audit service because they have tendered at an unreasonable price. They would be putting themselves at risk of being found to be negligent by a professional body or even in a court of law should problems arise.

Keratin would be within their rights to provide other services to an audit client as long as this did not affect the independence of the audit. However, given that the provision of other services to audit clients is increasingly frowned upon, for example, in the US, where audit firms are prohibited from providing other services to audit clients, Keratin should be careful of taking such an approach.

Edwin Stenuit may be in breach of a duty of confidentiality to his employer, discussing the firm's affairs in such a way at a social gathering.

Steps

Sepia can take no steps against Keratin in the matter of this tender as Benthos is entitled to choose whichever audit firm they like to do their audit.

If Keratin is successful, Sepia may have to review its own pricing policy if it is likely to be tendering against Keratin in the future.

Sepia could report Edwin Stenuit to ACCA for misconduct as a result of his breach of confidentiality to his employer, but it is unlikely that they would do so.

ACCA Professional Level

Paper P7

Advanced Audit and Assurance (United Kingdom)

Mock Examination 2

Question Paper		
Time allowed		
Reading and Planning Writing		**15 minutes** **3 hours**
SECTION A	TWO compulsory questions to be attempted	
SECTION B	TWO questions ONLY to be attempted	
During reading and planning time only the question paper may be annotated		

DO NOT OPEN THIS PAPER UNTIL YOU ARE READY TO START UNDER EXAMINATION CONDITIONS

SECTION A – BOTH questions are compulsory and MUST be attempted

Question 1

Jolie Ltd is a large company, operating in the retail industry, with a year ended 30 November 20Y0. You are a manager in Jen & Co, responsible for the audit of Jolie Ltd, and you have recently attended a planning meeting with Mo Pitt, the finance director of the company. Notes from your meeting are:

Jolie Ltd sells clothing, with a strategy of selling high fashion items under the JLC brand name. New ranges of clothes are introduced to stores every eight weeks. The company relies on a team of highly skilled designers to develop new fashion ranges. The designers must be able to anticipate and quickly respond to changes in consumer preferences. There is a high staff turnover in the design team.

Most sales are made in-store, but there is also a very popular catalogue, from which customers can place an order online, or over the phone. The company has recently upgraded the computer system and improved the website, at significant cost, in order to integrate the website sales directly into the nominal ledger, and to provide an easier interface for customers to use when ordering and entering their credit card details. The new on-line sales system has allowed overseas sales for the first time.

The system for phone ordering has recently been outsourced. The contract for outsourcing went out to tender and Jolie Ltd awarded the contract to the company offering the least cost. The company providing the service uses an overseas phone call centre where staff costs are very low.

Jolie Ltd has recently joined the Ethical Trading Initiative. This is a 'fair-trade' initiative, which means that any products bearing the JLC brand name must have been produced in a manner which is clean and safe for employees, and minimises the environmental impact of the manufacturing process. A significant advertising campaign promoting Jolie Ltd's involvement with this initiative has recently taken place. The JLC brand name was purchased a number of years ago and is recognised at cost as an intangible asset, which is not amortised. The brand represents 12% of the total assets recognised on the statement of financial position.

The company owns numerous distribution centres, some of which operate close to residential areas. A licence to operate the distribution centres is issued by each local government authority in which a centre is located. One of the conditions of the licence is that deliveries must only take place between 8 am and 6 pm. The authority also monitors the noise level of each centre, and can revoke the operating licence if a certain noise limit is breached. Two licences were revoked for a period of three months during the year.

You have just received the following e-mail from the audit engagement partner, Toni Pacino.

To: Audit manager
From: Toni Pacino
Regarding: Audit planning for Jolie Ltd

I would like you to begin the audit planning for our new audit client, Jolie Ltd. Mo Pitt has just sent to me extracts from Jolie Ltd's draft accounts and comparative figures, which should help you to prepare some briefing notes which will be used at the audit planning meeting. I understand you met recently with Mo, and I am sure you discussed a variety of issues relevant to the audit planning. In your briefing notes, you should evaluate the business risks facing Jolie Ltd. The notes will be used to brief the audit team members about the issues facing the client, and to help them gain some business understanding of Jolie Ltd.

Thanks,

Toni

Extract from draft statement of profit or loss

Year ending 30 November	20Y0 Draft £m	20X9 Actual £m
Revenue:		
Retail outlets	1,030	1,140
Phone and online sales	425	365
Total revenue	1,455	1,535
Operating profit	245	275
Finance costs	(25)	(22)
Profit before tax	220	253

Additional information:

Number of stores	210	208
Average revenue per store	£4.905m	£5.48m
Number of phone orders	680,000	790,000
Number of online orders	1,020,000	526,667
Average spend per order	£250	£300

Required

(a) Respond to the e-mail from the audit partner. **(16 marks)**

Professional marks will be awarded in part (a) for the format of the answer and the clarity of the evaluation.
(4 marks)

(b) Using the information provided, identify and explain **five** risks of material misstatement. **(10 marks)**

(c) Recommend the principal audit procedures to be performed in respect of the valuation of the JLC brand name.
(5 marks)

(Total = 35 marks)

Question 2

You are a manager in Newman & Co, a global firm of Chartered Certified Accountants. You are responsible for evaluating proposed engagements and for recommending to a team of partners whether or not an engagement should be accepted by your firm.

Eastwood Ltd is an existing audit client and is an international mail services operator, with a global network including 220 countries and 300,000 employees. The company offers mail and freight services to individual and corporate customers, as well as storage and logistical services.

Eastwood Ltd takes its corporate social responsibility seriously, and publishes social and environmental key performance indicators (KPIs) in a Sustainability Report, which is published with the financial statements in the annual report. Partly in response to requests from shareholders and pressure groups, Eastwood Ltd's management has decided that in the forthcoming annual report, the KPIs should be accompanied by an independent assurance report. An approach has been made to your firm to provide this report in addition to the audit.

To help in your evaluation of this potential engagement, you have been given an extract from the draft Sustainability Report, containing some of the KPIs published by Eastwood Ltd. In total, 25 environmental KPIs, and 50 social KPIs are disclosed.

Extract from Sustainability Report	Year ended 31 October 20Y0 DRAFT	Year ended 31 October 20X9 ACTUAL
CO2 emissions (million tonnes)	26.8	28.3
Energy use (million kilowatt hours)	4,895	5,250
Charitable donations (£ million)	10.5	8.2
Number of serious accidents in the workplace	60	68
Average annual spend on training per employee	£180	£175

You have also had a meeting with Ali Monroe, the manager responsible for the audit of Eastwood Co, and notes of the meeting are given below.

Notes from meeting with audit manager, Ali Monroe

Newman & Co has audited Eastwood Ltd for three years, and it is a major audit client of our firm, due to its global presence and recent listing on two major stock exchanges. The audit is managed from our office in Oldtown, which is also the location of the global headquarters of Eastwood Ltd.

We have not done any work on the KPIs, other than review them for consistency, as we would with any 'other information' issued with the financial statements. The KPIs are produced by Eastwood Ltd's Sustainability Department, located in Fartown. We have not visited Eastwood Ltd's offices in Fartown as it is in a remote location overseas, and the departments based there are not relevant to the audit.

We have performed audit procedures on the charitable donations, as this is disclosed in a note to the financial statements, and our evidence indicates that there have been donations of £9 million this year, which is the amount disclosed in the note. However, the draft KPI is a different figure – £10.5 million, and this is the figure highlighted in the draft Chairman's Statement as well as the draft Sustainability Report. £9 million is material to the financial statements.

The audit work is nearly complete, and the annual report is to be published in about four weeks, in time for the company meeting, scheduled for 31 January 20Y1.

Your firm has recently established a sustainability reporting assurance team based in Oldtown, and if the engagement to report on the Sustainability Report is accepted, it would be performed by members of that team, who would not be involved with the audit.

Required

(a)   Identify and explain the matters that should be considered in evaluating the invitation to perform an assurance engagement on the Sustainability Report of Eastwood Ltd.   **(11 marks)**

(b)   Recommend procedures that could be used to verify the following draft KPIs.

   (i)   The number of serious accidents in the workplace
   (ii)   The average annual spend on training per employee   **(6 marks)**

(c)   You have a trainee accountant assigned to you, who has read the notes taken at your meeting with Ali Monroe. She is unsure of the implications of the charitable donations being disclosed as a different figure in the financial statements compared with the other information published in the annual report.

Required

Prepare briefing notes to be used in a discussion with the trainee accountant, in which you:

   (i)   Explain the responsibility of the auditor in relation to other information published with the financial statements

   (ii)   Recommend the action to be taken by Newman & Co if the figure relating to charitable donations in the other information is not amended.   **(8 marks)**

(Total = 25 marks)

SECTION B – TWO questions ONLY to be attempted

Question 3

Clooney Ltd is one of the world's leading leisure travel providers, operating under several brand names to sell package holidays. The company catered for more than 10 million customers in the last 12 months. Draft figures for the year ended 30 September 20Y0 show revenue of £3,200 million, profit before tax of £150 million, and total assets of £4,100 million. Clooney Ltd's executives earn a bonus based on the profit before tax of the company.

You are the manager responsible for the audit of Clooney Ltd. The final audit is nearing completion, and the following points have been noted by the audit senior for your attention:

In July 20Y0, thousands of holiday-makers were left stranded abroad after the company operating the main airline chartered by Clooney Ltd went into liquidation. The holiday-makers were forced to wait an average of two weeks before they could be returned home using an alternative airline. They have formed a group which is claiming compensation for the time they were forced to spend abroad, with the total claim amounting to £20 million. The items which the group is claiming compensation for include accommodation and subsistence costs, lost income and distress caused by the situation. The claim has not been recognised or disclosed in the draft financial statements, as management argues that the full amount payable will be covered by Clooney Ltd's insurance.

One part of the company's activities, operating under the Shelly's Cruises brand, provides cruise holidays. Due to economic recession, the revenue of the Shelly's Cruises business segment has fallen by 25% this year, and profit before tax has fallen by 35%. Shelly's Cruises contributed £640 million to total revenue in the year to 30 September 20Y0, and has identifiable assets of £235 million, including several large cruise liners. The Shelly's Cruises brand is not recognised as an intangible asset, as it has been internally generated.

On 15 November 20Y0, Clooney Ltd acquired Craig Ltd, a company offering adventure holidays for independent travellers. Craig Ltd represents a significant acquisition, but this has not been referred to in the financial statements.

Required

Comment on the matters that you should consider, and state the audit evidence you should expect to find in your review of the audit working papers for the year ended September 20Y0 in respect of:

(a)   The compensation claim   **(8 marks)**
(b)   Shelly's Cruises   **(7 marks)**
(c)   The acquisition of Craig Ltd   **(5 marks)**

(Total = 20 marks)

Question 4

(a)   You are a manager in Neeson & Co, a firm of Chartered Certified Accountants, with three offices and 12 partners. About one third of the firm's clients are audit clients, the remainder are clients for whom Neeson & Co performs tax, accounting and business advisory services. The firm is considering how to generate more revenue, and you have been asked to evaluate two suggestions made by the firm's business development manager.

(i)   An advertisement could be placed in national newspapers to attract new clients. The draft advertisement has been given to you for review:

> Neeson & Co is the largest and most professional accountancy and audit provider in the country. We offer a range of services in addition to audit, which are guaranteed to improve your business efficiency and save you tax. If you are unhappy with your auditors, we can offer a second opinion on the report that has been given. Introductory offer: for all new clients we offer a 25% discount when both audit and tax services are provided. Our rates are approved by ACCA.

(8 marks)

(ii)   A new partner with experience in the banking sector has joined Neeson & Co. It has been suggested that the partner could specialise in offering a corporate finance service to clients. In particular, the partner could advise clients on raising debt finance, and would negotiate with the client's bank or other provider of finance on behalf of the client. The fee charged for this service would be contingent on the client obtaining the finance with a borrowing cost below market rate. **(5 marks)**

Required

Evaluate each of the suggestions made above, commenting on the ethical and professional issues raised.

Note. The mark allocation is shown against each of the issues.

(b)   You have set up an internal discussion board, on which current issues are debated by employees and partners of Neeson & Co. One posting to the board concerned the compulsory rotation of audit firms, whereby it has been suggested in the press that after a pre-determined period, an audit firm must resign from office, to be replaced by a new audit provider.

Required

(i)   Explain the ethical threats created by a long association with an audit client.   **(3 marks)**

(ii)   Evaluate the advantages and disadvantages of compulsory audit firm rotation.   **(4 marks)**

(Total = 20 marks)

Question 5

(a)   You are the manager responsible for the audit of Willis Ltd, a large client of your audit firm, operating in the pharmaceutical industry. The audit work for the year ended 30 August 20Y0 is nearly complete, and you are reviewing the draft audit report which has been prepared by the audit senior. You are aware that Willis Ltd is developing a new drug and has incurred significant research and development costs during the year, most of which have been capitalised as an intangible asset. The asset is recognised at a value of £4.4 million, the total assets recognised on the draft statement of financial position are £55 million, and Willis Ltd has a draft profit before tax of £3.1 million.

Having reviewed the audit working papers, you are also aware that management has not allowed the audit team access to the results of scientific tests and trials performed on the new drug being developed.

An extract from the draft audit report is shown below.

Basis of opinion (extract)

Evidence available to us in respect of the intangible asset capitalised was limited, because of restrictions imposed on our work by management. As a result of this we have been unable to verify the appropriateness of the amount capitalised, and we are worried that the asset may be overvalued. Because of the firm of the item, and the lack of integrity shown by management, we have been unable to form a view on the financial statements as a whole.

Opinion (extract): Disclaimer on view given by financial statements

Because of the lack of evidence that we could gain over the intangible asset, we are unable to form an opinion as to whether the financial statements are properly prepared in accordance with the relevant financial reporting framework.

Required

(i)   Critically appraise the draft audit report of Willis Ltd for the year ended 30 August 20Y0, prepared by the audit senior.

Note. You are **not** required to re-draft the extracts from the audit report.   **(10 marks)**

(ii)   Identify and explain any other matters to be considered, and the actions to be taken by the auditor, in respect of the management-imposed limitation on scope.   **(5 marks)**

(b)   You are also responsible for the audit of Moore Ltd, with a year ended 30 September 20Y0. The following notes have been left for your attention by the audit senior.

'Our audit testing performed so far on trade payables revealed some internal control deficiencies. Supplier statement reconciliations have not always been performed by the client, and invoices were often not approved before payment. We have found a few errors in the purchase ledger and the individual accounts of suppliers making up the trade payables balance, the total of which is material to the statement of financial position.'

Required

Recommend the further actions that should be taken by the auditor, and outline any reporting requirements in respect of the internal control deficiencies identified.   **(5 marks)**

(Total = 20 marks)

Answers

DO NOT TURN THIS PAGE UNTIL YOU HAVE
COMPLETED THE MOCK EXAM

A PLAN OF ATTACK

If this had been the real Advanced Audit and Assurance exam and you had been told to turn over and begin, what would have been going through your mind?

An important thing to say (while there is still time) is that it is vital to have a good breadth of knowledge of the syllabus because the question requirements for each question will relate to different areas of the P7 syllabus. However, don't panic. Below we provide guidance on how to approach the exam.

Approaching the answer

Use your 15 minutes of reading time usefully, to look through the questions, particularly Questions 1 and 2 in Section A which are compulsory, to get a feel for what is required and to become familiar with the question scenarios.

It is vital that you attempt all the questions in the paper to increase your chances of passing. The best way to do this is to make sure you stick to the time allocation for each question – both in total and for each of the question parts. The worst thing you can do is run over time in one question and then find that you don't have enough time for the remaining questions.

Section A is compulsory and consists of two long case-study style questions totalling 60 marks. These may contain detailed information such as extracts from financial statements and audit working papers. A range of requirements will be set for each question, covering areas from across the whole syllabus.

Question 1 is for 35 marks. The scenario is quite long so make sure you have used your reading time well to familiarise yourself with it and make some notes on key issues. The key to success in this question is to stay focussed, don't run over time and answer the questions set. In part (a) you are asked for business risks. This is a standard P7 question, that should almost be second nature to you by now. Part (b) asks for five risks of material misstatement. Make sure you actually give five risks here. Part (c) asked for procedures to test a valuation, which should have been relatively straightforward.

Question 2 is also worth 25 marks and relates to environmental and social reporting. Part (a) is based on the scenario, and requires you to be practical in your approach. In part (b) you needed to be precise and come up with specific procedures. Part (c) was almost a standalone requirement, and should have been within your reach.

Section B contains three questions, from which you must attempt two. This section will be worth 40 marks and will use short scenarios.

Question 3 is on audit evidence and matters to consider in the context of three issues. Note the mark allocation in each. Your answers must be focussed and coherent if you are going to score well and your financial reporting knowledge needs to be sound as you will have to apply it in this question.

Question 4 is on ethics and practice management, and deals with advertising, a suggestion on fees and a current issue. This was a well-balanced question that should have provided you with a good but fair test of your abilities.

Question 5 is on auditor's reports. Part (a) requires you to critically appraise an auditor's report, and to explain matters to consider in relation to a limitation on scope. Part (b) examines the impact of a specific area on the auditor's report. Throughout this question you were required to think not just about the technical contents of the auditor's report, but also the practical issues in the auditor's relationship with the client.

Forget about it!

And don't worry if you found the paper difficult. More than likely other candidates will too. If this were the real thing you would need to forget the exam the minute you left the exam hall and think about the next one. Or, if it is the last one, celebrate!

Question 1

Marks

(a) **Evaluate business risks**

½ mark for each risk identified (to max 4 marks) and up to 1½ further marks for explanation

Up to 2 marks for calculation of margins, trends, etc

- High fashion items/high staff turnover in design team
- Obsolete inventory and pressure on margins
- Widespread geographical business model hard to control
- Volume of e-commerce sales – ability of systems to cope
- Security of e-commerce operations
- Tax and regulatory issues on e-commerce
- Foreign exchange risk on new overseas transactions
- Outsourcing of phone operations – quality issues
- Outsourcing of phone operations – unpopular with customers
- Long-term sustainability of outsourced function
- Ethical Trading Initiative – supply chain issues
- Potential restrictions on operation of distribution centres
- Financial performance – general comments on revenue/profitability/margins   16

Professional marks: 2 for presentation, 2 for quality of evaluation   4

(b) **Risks of material misstatement**

½ mark for identification up to 1½ further marks for explanation, **five** matters only

- Inventory valuation (IAS 2)
- Inventory existence (IAS 2)
- Unrecorded revenue
- Capitalisation of IT/website costs
- Valuation of brand name (IAS 38)
- Valuation of properties (IAS 36)
- Recognition of provision/contingent liability (IAS 37)
- Opening balances and comparatives (1 mark only)   10

(c) **Audit procedures: brand name**

1 mark per specific procedure

- Agree cost to supporting documentation/prior year accounts
- Review assumptions used in management impairment review
- Perform independent impairment review
- Review planned level of expenditure to support the brand
- Review results of any marketing/customer satisfaction surveys
- Consider whether non-amortisation is GAAP for this industry
- Discuss reasons for non-amortisation with management   5

Total   35

(a)   **Briefing notes**

Subject: Business risks facing Jolie Ltd

Introduction

These briefing notes evaluate the business risks facing the new client Jolie Ltd, which has a financial year ending 30 November 20Y0.

Continuing quality of product

Jolie operates in a dynamic and volatile business environment, with new ranges being introduced every eight weeks. There is a constant need for talented designers to develop product ranges, and given the high staff turnover it may be difficult to retain talented staff. The risk is that if Jolie fails to recruit the right designers the quality of the product could be reduced, which could lead to a fall in revenue. Lower quality products could potentially tarnish the JLC brand, which is so crucial to Jolie's success.

Obsolete inventory

New ranges are introduced every eight weeks, so there is a risk of inventory becoming obsolete if it is not sold during this short period. Any older inventory may be marked down, which would affect margins. Margins fell from 17.9% in 20X9 to 16.8% in 20Y0, which could be related to this.

E-commerce – sales volume

Online sales now account for £255 million (£250 per order × 1,020,000 orders). In the previous year, online sales accounted for £158 million (£300 per order × 526,667 orders). This represents an increase of 61.4% (255 – 158 / 158 × 100%).

The risk is that the system may be overwhelmed by the increase in sales volume, which could lead to difficulties fulfilling orders and potential damage to the all-important JLC brand.

E-commerce – new systems

There is a risk of system failure associated with any new system, which could result in unfulfilled orders and hence brand damage.

E-commerce – security

There is a risk that customers' details held on the system are not kept sufficiently securely. There is a risk that data protection laws could be breached. If security were to be breached then the brand would be very likely to suffer.

E-commerce – overseas sales

Making sales overseas exposes Jolie to several new risks. If sales are made in foreign currencies then there is a risk that the computer system may not be able to handle these sales (eg it could miscalculate foreign currency prices).

Overseas sales expose Jolie to potential tax complications, eg extra VAT to be paid on exported goods, and additional documentation to comply with foreign regulations.

Jolie may also now be exposed to foreign exchange risks, and may find its profit margins affected by currency fluctuations.

Outsourced phone ordering

Jolie outsourced its phone ordering system to the cheapest provider. If the phone ordering system is not of a good quality then this may be incongruent with the differentiated, high-quality nature of Jolie's products. If many errors occur with orders then this may lead to customer dissatisfaction and damage to the brand.

The location of the call centre overseas, which presumably reflects the low cost, may be a source of frustration to customers, and may ultimately lead to a fall in revenue.

However, the risks associated with phone ordering may to some extent be mitigated by the expansion of e-commerce, which customers may prefer to use.

Ethical trading initiative

The fact that Jolie has spent a significant amount money advertising its fair trade credentials leads to a risk of bad publicity if these credentials were to be undermined. Any ethical failings in the supply chain may be subjected to public scrutiny, which would again damage the JLC brand.

Distribution centres

There is a real risk of local authorities revoking distribution centres' licences if conditions are breached (eg in relation to noise levels). This could pose Jolie significant operational difficulties if any of the centres are closed, as with its short inventory turnover period Jolie is especially reliant on its ability to deliver inventory on time.

Financial performance

Overall revenue has decreased by £80 million, or 5.2% (80 / 1,535 × 100). Operating profit has also fallen, by £30 million, or 10.9% (30 / 275 × 100). Average spend per order has fallen from £300 to £250.

This may give cause for concern, but operating expenses for 20Y0 are likely to include one-off items, eg the costs of the new sales system. The fall in spend per customer could be a symptom of general economic difficulties. The company has increased the volume of online transactions significantly.

On balance the overall reduction in profit and margins is unlikely to be a significant risk at this year end, though if the trend were to continue it may become a more pressing issue.

Jolie Ltd's finance costs have increased by £3 million, contributing to a fall in profit before tax of 13%. The company has sufficient interest cover to mean that this is not an immediate concern, but the company should ensure that finance costs do not escalate.

Conclusion

Perhaps the most significant risk for Jolie is that it fails to produce products of sufficient quality, which relates to its ability to make use of talented designers. The risk of inventory obsolescence is also significant. The downward trend in Jolie's financial performance needs to be monitored carefully in the future.

(b) **Inventory valuation**

IAS 2 *Inventories* states that inventory must be valued at the lower of cost and net realisable value (NRV). The high rate of inventory turnover leads to a risk of inventory becoming obsolete and to a fall in its NRV, and if NRV falls below cost then it will need to be written down. This may be the case with any inventory that is being sold at a reduced price, or which is slow-moving and may not be sold at all. Jolie's declining overall revenue may indicate falling NRVs and hence that inventory is impaired.

Inventory completeness & existence

It will be difficult to count inventory accurately across all of Jolie's 210 stores, and there may be a large number of goods in transit to keep track of. All of this means that the auditor will find it difficult to obtain sufficient evidence over the existence of inventory. There is a risk of fraudulent financial reporting in this area as it is difficult to verify the levels of inventory actually held.

New systems

The existence of a new sales system poses the risk of teething problems if the system did not function properly at first. As a result sales could be recorded incorrectly in the nominal ledger, either through as a result of the new system not providing correctly information, or because of problems with the integration of the system and the nominal ledger.

There may also be a different system in place for the newly-outsourced phone sales, and there is a risk of sales being misstated if the systems are not properly integrated.

Website costs

The expenditure on the new IT systems may have been capitalised in line with IAS 38 *Intangible Assets*, according to which only expenditure in the development phase may be capitalised, with costs before (eg planning) and after (eg operational) being expensed. The risk is the overstatement of intangible assets.

Brand name

An intangible asset has been recognised in respect of the JLC brand name, as this was purchased and not internally generated. This appears to be in line with IAS 38. At 12% of total assets this amount is likely to material to the financial statements.

IAS 38 requires an impairment review to be conducted at the end of each reporting period. If this is not conducted, the asset could be overvalued. The decline in revenue could be an indicator of impairment.

The significant advertising expenditure during the year should be expensed, and there is a risk of overstatement of assets and non-occurrence of expenses if this expenditure has been capitalised.

Property valuation

Jolie owns numerous distribution centres (rather than leasing them), and there is a risk of these assets being impaired if their licences are revoked. Additionally, there has been a fall in revenue per store, which is an indicator of impairment per IAS 36 *Impairment of assets*.

(c) **Audit procedures on JLC brand**

- Agree cost of brand to supporting documentation, eg purchase invoice (if still available).

- Agree cost of brand to prior year audited financial statements.

- Review monthly income streams generated by brand, for indication of any decline in sales.

- Review results of impairment reviews by management, establishing the validity of any assumptions used in the review (eg discount rate used to discount future cash flows; growth rates used to predict cash inflows).

- Perform independent impairment review on the brand, and compare with management's impairment review.

- Review level of planned expenditure on marketing and advertising to support the brand name, and consider its adequacy to maintain the image of the brand.

- Inquire as to the results of any customer satisfaction surveys, to gain an understanding of the public perception of JLC as a high fashion brand.

- Consider whether non-amortisation of brand names is a generally accepted accounting practice in the fashion retail industry by reviewing the published financial statements of competitors.

- Discuss with management the reasons why they feel that non-amortisation is a justifiable accounting treatment.

Tutorial note. As this is a first year audit, no marks will be awarded for procedures relating to prior year working papers of the audit firm.

Question 2

Text references. Chapter 15.

Top tips. This area has not been examined very frequently in recent years, but the fact that it was examined here is a warning against trying to question-spot. You must be ready to answer questions on any area of the syllabus.

Part (a) may have been intimidating if you had not revised this area thoroughly, but actually a lot of the points in the marking scheme are applicable to most kinds of engagement. You could have thought of general points, and then applied them to the situation given in the question. Note the examiner's comment about application below; P7 tutors never tire of telling students to apply their knowledge to the question.

Part (b) should have been straightforward, but just as in part (a) you need to make sure you applied yourself to the actual question, in part (b) you needed to be as specific as possible in coming up with realistic ways of verifying the KPIs.

Part (c) should also have been straightforward, provided you knew the answer! There is no substitute for knowledge here, especially as this is not a difficult area of the syllabus.

Easy marks. The first few marks in part (b)(i) & (ii) were easy, as you should have been able to think of at least a few procedures without much effort.

Examiner's comments. Candidates responded reasonably well to parts of this question, though many answers did not reach their full potential by not being applied to the question scenario.

Some answers to part (a) were much too brief for the 12 marks available, amounting to little more than a bullet point list of matters to be considered but with no application to the scenario. Without application it was not possible to pass this requirement.

A fair proportion of answers to requirement (b) were sound, with precise procedures recommended. But, many recommended procedures relied too much on observation and enquiry, and ignored the fact that the client was a global company with 300,000 employees which led to some bizarre and meaningless procedures being given, such as 'observe a serious accident', 'inspect the location of a serious accident', 'ask how much is spent on training', and 'look at the training room to see how many chairs are there'. None of these could verify the KPIs and are pointless.

Requirement (c) was inadequately attempted overall. Answers were usually extremely brief, and it was clear that most candidates did not know the requirements of ISA 720A. Most answers took a guess that the matter would need to be discussed with management, and that if unresolved there would be some kind of impact on the auditor's report (an 'except for' opinion was the usual recommendation). But few could say more than this about the issue. Some candidates assumed that some kind of money laundering was taking place, leading to irrelevant discussions of reporting the situation to outside authorities. Very few candidates recognised that if uncorrected, the issue should be included in an Other Matter paragraph, as required by ISA 720A. This could imply a lack of knowledge, or that some candidates are studying from out of date learning materials.

Marking scheme

Marks

(a) **Matters**

Identify and explain acceptance matters
½ mark for each matter identified (to max 4 marks) and up to 1½ further marks for
  explanation
  – Objectivity (up to 3 marks allowed)
  – Client's specific requirements
  – Competence
  – Large scale engagement
  – Fee level and profitability
  – Time pressure
  – Global engagement
  – Risk
  – Commercial considerations   11

(b) (i) **Procedures on number of serious accidents**
    1 mark per specific procedure
    – HR records review
    – Accident book review
    – Determine criteria for serious accident
    – Review legal correspondence
    – Review board minutes
    – Review documentation of health and safety inspections
    – Ascertain any convictions for breach of health and safety rules

(ii) Procedures on average training spend

1 mark per specific procedure
- Review approved training budget
- Review components of total spend for misclassified items
- Agree sample of invoices/contracts with training providers
- Agree sample to cash book/bank statement (½ only)
- Recalculate average

6

(c) (i) Auditor's responsibilities regarding other information

1 mark per comment, ½ mark ref to ISA 720
- Definition/examples of other information
- Implication if inconsistency in financial statements not resolved (qualification)
- Implication if inconsistency in other information (Other Matter paragraph)
- Material misstatements of fact

(ii) Action by Newman & Co

1 mark per comment
- Review audit work on charitable donations
- Discuss inconsistency with management/those charged with governance
- If refuse to change the figure, reconsider reliance on management representations
- Implication for audit report

8

Total

25

(a)   Matters to consider include the following

In accordance with both the IESBA *Code of Ethics for Professional Accountants* ('Code') and the FRC's Ethical Standard 5, *Non-audit services provided to audit clients*, a non-audit service must only be provided to an audit client after careful consideration of whether the firm's independence and objectivity in respect of the audit may be impaired, and of whether safeguards could be put in place to reduce this threat to an acceptable level or to eliminate it entirely. If such safeguards cannot be put in place, then the audit firm should not accept the non-audit engagement or should withdraw from it.

This assignment would appear to carry particular threats in relation to fee dependence and advocacy.

Fees

Eastwood is a 'major client' of Newman & Co, and there is a risk that the provision of further, non-audit, services to Eastwood could lead to a breach in the acceptable level of recurring fees receivable from one audit client. In the case of a public interest client such as Eastwood, the IESBA Code states that the public may perceive an auditor's independence to be impaired where recurring fees are 10% of total fees.

Advocacy

Newman & Co has been engaged by the client partly in response to the client receiving requests for a Sustainability Report from shareholders and pressure groups. This is a potentially risky context in which to provide such a report, as the report is likely to be scrutinised closely. Furthermore, Newman & Co may be perceived as management's advocate, which would be particularly damaging in the event of any dispute.

Newman & Co's independence would be strengthened by the fact that assurance work would be carried out by a separate team from the audit team.

Level of assurance

Assurance reports may be provided giving varying levels of assurance. It will be necessary to obtain clarification from Eastwood of the level of assurance that it requires, and whether it requires different levels of assurance for different KPIs. Clearly, the level of assurance required would affect the level of evidence required and hence the amount of work that needs to be done, which would in turn affect the fees charged. This should be clarified before accepting the engagement, and a form and wording for the proposed report should be agreed with Eastwood.

Competence

It is possible that Newman & Co may not have staff with the requisite technical competence to undertake this engagement. The fundamental principle of professional competence and due care requires that members of an engagement team both possess and apply sufficient skill and knowledge to be able to perform the assignment.

If Newman & Co does not have staff with this skill and experience then it could contract an expert to do some of the work, but this would be likely to increase the costs associated with the engagement.

Resources

A total of 75 KPIs would be reported on, which means that this is likely to be a relatively large engagement. A large number of staff would probably be required to work on the engagement.

It is promising that Newman & Co has a dedicated sustainability reporting assurance team, which should put it in a good position to undertake the work. However, the fact that the team is new means that careful consideration must be given to whether it is capable of doing the work required.

Time pressure

It would be very difficult to gather sufficient evidence to provide an assurance report within the four weeks left until the annual report is published. This may cause staff to be working under significant time pressure, which increases the risk of mistakes being made. Newman & Co must clarify when Eastwood intends for the assurance report to be published.

Profitability

This is a large assignment, probably requiring the team to travel from Oldtown to Fartown to perform the work. This would clearly involve incurring significant costs, and should be reflected in the level of fees charged.

The amount of work that would need to be done, and the short time frame in which to do it, mean that a high fee could be commanded here.

Travel

It is likely that members of the assurance department would need to travel to Fartown, and for the engagement to be accepted they must be willing to do so. It is not clear whether there are any language barriers to working in Fartown, and whether these might be overcome.

Risk

The context of the assignment indicates the presence of risks relating to the degree of scrutiny to which the assurance report would be likely to be subjected. In addition to the presence of interested pressure group and shareholders (q.v.), Eastwood is listed on two stock exchanges and is thus fairly high profile. This may increase the level of evidence that Newman & Co would seek to obtain, which would in turn affect the level of fee charged.

Moreover, the inconsistency that has already come to light in respect of the charitable donations figure may indicate management manipulation of the KPIs, which adds to the risk associated with the assignment.

(b) (i) • Review HR records of the number and type of accidents in the workplace.

   • Review accident log books from a sample of locations.

   • Discuss the definition of a 'serious' accident and establish the criteria applied to an accident to determine whether it is serious.

   • Review correspondence with legal advisors which may indicate any legal action being taken against Eastwood.

   • Review minutes of board meetings for discussions of serious accidents and repercussions for the company.

   • Discussion with management/legal advisors, of whether Eastwood has any convictions for health and safety offences during the year.

- Enquire whether the company has received any health and safety visits. Review documentation from any of these for evidence of serious accidents.

- Talk to employees to identify any accidents not recorded in the accident book.

(ii)
- Review Eastwood's training budget in comparison with previous years to ascertain the overall level of planned spending on training.

- Obtain breakdown of the total training spend and review for any items misclassified as training costs.

- Agree significant components of the total training spend to supporting documentation, eg contracts and invoices from training providers.

- Agree the total amount spent on significant training programmes to cash book and/or bank statements.

- Using data on total number of employees provided by the payroll department, recalculate the annual training spend per employee.

(c) **Briefing notes**

To: Trainee Accountant

Subject: Other information – auditor's responsibilities

(i) **Introduction**

These notes explain the responsibility of the auditor in relation to other information published with the financial statements, in the context of Eastwood plc's charitable donations.

Auditor's responsibility

ISA 720A (UK & Ireland) *The auditor's responsibilities relating to other information in documents containing audited financial statements* defines as financial and non-financial information included in a document containing audited financial statements and the auditor's report. This would include Eastwood's Sustainability Report.

ISA 720A requires the auditor to read the other information to identify material inconsistencies with the audited financial statements, which may raise doubts over the auditor's opinion. If a material inconsistency is discovered, the auditor must determine whether it is the financial statements or the other information that should be revised.

If the financial statements need to be revised but are not, and are therefore materially misstated, then the auditor's opinion should be modified.

If the other information needs to be revised and is not (but the financial statements are unaffected), then the auditor's report should include an Other Matter paragraph describing the inconsistency. The auditor should consider requesting those charged with governance to consult its legal counsel. In extreme situations, it may be necessary for the auditor to obtain legal advice itself and to withdraw from the assignment.

If the auditor discovers a material misstatement of fact in the other information, which is unrelated to the financial statements and thus to the auditor's report, then the auditor should communicate this fact to those charged with governance.

(ii) Eastwood's Sustainability Report contains a material inconsistency with the financial statements; charitable donations are stated as £10.5m in the Sustainability Report and £9m in the financial statements.

Audit evidence has been obtained which supports the £9m figure in the financial statements. This evidence should be reviewed to ensure that it is sufficient and appropriate.

The matter should be discussed with management, who should be asked to change the figure in the Sustainability Report. If management refuse to make this change then the auditor's report should include an Other Matter paragraph immediately after the opinion paragraph, which should describe the inconsistency. The matter should also be communicated to those charged with governance.

The directors' report should be reviewed for any reference to charitable donations, as UK auditors are required to report whether the information given in the directors' report is consistent with the information in the accounts. Any inconsistency would therefore be highlighted in the auditor's report.

Eastwood is listed on several stock exchanges, so Newman & Co should consider whether it has any other responsibilities in relation to any Listing Rules.

Finally, if management refuses to change the Sustainability Report then this may indicate a lack of integrity on its part. Any reliance placed on management representations should be reconsidered in this light.

Conclusion

Newman & Co needs to consider carefully how it will meet its responsibilities in relation to Eastwood's other information.

Question 3

Text references. Chapters 6 and 9.

Top tips. As you are reading through the information, jot down the accounting standards you believe are relevant and note down the matters to consider that arise from them. Think if any ISAs are relevant as well (this is particularly important as your examiner has recently commented that candidates tend to show too little knowledge of the requirements of ISAs). Always comment on the materiality of matters. Bear in mind the mark allocation as well. In this question, you should have more to say in parts (a) and (b) than in part (c).

Easy marks. Easy marks are available for assessing and stating the materiality of items raised.

Examiner's comments. For requirement (a), almost all candidates were able to generate marks by calculating the materiality of the amount, and describing the basic accounting treatment for provisions. Fewer went on to discuss the potential impact of the insurance cover, and some answers drifted into a discussion of going concern and other business risks. Audit procedures were often inadequately focused, with no regard to the scale of the issue. Although most suggested looking at legal documents, candidates rarely mentioned looking at the group claim document. Some candidates proposed lots of very detailed tests on the validity of individual claims, such as checking hotel bills and airline tickets.

Requirement (b) was not dealt with well. Very few candidates recognised that the business segment represented a cash generating unit that required an impairment test. Even those candidates that did pick up on the impairment issue could rarely provide evidence points other than 'check the value of the assets' (too vague) or 'inspect the assets' (irrelevant).

Many candidates successfully discussed the issue in requirement (c). Unfortunately, many candidates wanted to see the new subsidiary consolidated, even though it had clearly been purchased after the end of the reporting period. At the other end of the spectrum, some candidates suggested that as the event happened after the year end, the auditor need not perform any procedures at all.

Marks

(a) **Compensation claim**

1 mark per matter, 1 mark per specific procedure

Matters:
- Materiality
- Provision/contingent liability
- Recoverability under insurance
- Management reluctant to provide
- Ref IAS 37 (½ mark only)

Evidence:
- Copy of legal claim
- Legal correspondence
- Press releases/news stories to establish constructive obligation
- Booking conditions to verify legal obligation
- Advice given by the company at the time of the incident
- Copy of insurance contract
- Copy of claim made on insurance
- Written representation on outcome

8

(b) **Shelley's Cruises**

1 mark per matter, 1 mark per specific procedure

Matters:
- Materiality
- Impairment of assets (**not** brand)
- Cash generating unit
- Subjective elements in impairment calculations
- Ref IAS 36 (½ mark only)

Evidence:

- Review management impairment test (max 2 marks if detailed)
- Discuss future strategy re Shelly's Cruises
- Review post-year end performance/bookings in advance

7

(c) **Acquisition of Craig Co**

1 mark per matter, 1 mark per specific procedure

Matters:
- Non-adjusting event
- Ref IAS 10 (½ mark only)
- Note to disclose
- Implication for audit report if not disclosed

Evidence:
- Copy of press release announcing acquisition
- Copy of legal agreement or due diligence report on acquisition
- Review of financial statements to determine significance of acquisition
- Review of any note disclosed

5

Total

20

(a) **Matters to consider**

The claim is material to profit at 13.3% of profit before tax (20 / 150 × 100%). It is not material to the statement of financial position at only 0.49% of total assets (20 / 4,100 × 100%).

Management have an incentive to manipulate the financial statements through fraudulent financial reporting, as their bonus is based on profit before tax. There is a risk that profit may be overstated. They may not want to provide for the claim because this would reduce profit.

IAS 37 *Provisions, contingent liabilities and contingent assets* requires a provision to be recognised where, as a result of a past event, an outflow of economic benefits is probable, the amount of which can be estimated reliably. If such an outflow is only possible but not probable then it is a contingent liability, and should be disclosed in a note to the financial statements. Further evidence is required to determine whether the compensation claim should be provided for or not.

If Clooney can make a claim on its insurance policy in respect of the legal case, then per IAS 37 this is treated as a separate event, in accordance with IAS 37's requirements on contingent assets. For an asset to be recognised, IAS 37 states that it should be certain to be received. As in this case receipt of an insurance payment is only probable, no asset should be recognised. The insurance claim should be disclosed by way of a note.

In addition to the provision that must be created, it may be necessary for Clooney to provide for any legal costs associated with defending the claim, which would further reduce its profit for the year.

Evidence

- Copy of claim made by the group of holiday-makers, detailing the £20 million claimed and the basis of the claim

- Review of correspondence between 'claim group' and the company

- Correspondence from Clooney's legal counsel, showing their opinion on the likely outcome

- Copy of any press releases made by Clooney, which could help establish there is a constructive obligation

- Review of press coverage of the situation, to assess any comments made in public by company representatives regarding the claim

- Review of the standard terms and conditions that holiday-makers agree to on booking a holiday – this could help to establish any legal obligation, eg to cover the cost of accommodation before being returned home

- Details of any helpline or other means by which the stranded holiday-makers were given advice at the time of the incident (eg if the company advised them to book alternative accommodation this may imply that the company is liable for the cost)

- Copy of insurance contract detailing level of cover, if any, provided for this situation, and any amount that will not be covered (eg an excess on the policy)

- Correspondence between insurance company and Clooney to establish whether an insurance claim has been made

- Written management representation stating management's opinion on the outcome of the court case, and the likelihood of reimbursement from the insurance cover

- Review of invoices received pre- and post- year end in respect of legal costs, to ensure adequately included in expenses and accrued for if necessary

(b) **Matters to consider**

The Shelly's Cruises (SC) operation is material to the financial statements, contributing 20% to revenue (640 / 3,200 × 100%). The identifiable assets of the business segment represent 5.7% of total assets (235 / 4,100 × 100%), and are thus material to the statement of financial position.

The brand is (correctly) not recognised as an intangible asset in accordance with IAS 38 *Intangible assets*, so there is no intangible asset that may be impaired. However, in accordance with IAS 36 *Impairment of assets*, SC's assets represent a cash generating unit as they are independent of the assets of the rest of the entity. The question is whether these are impaired.

The drops in revenue and profit are indicators of impairment per IAS 36. Management must have conducted an impairment test, calculating the value-in-use of the cash generating unit, and also the fair value less cost to sell, to determine the recoverable amount of the SC assets collectively. Any impairment loss should be expensed. Management will want to avoid recognising an impairment loss as it will reduce their bonus payment.

The impairment test will involve a number of subjective elements, eg the discount rate used to determine the present value of cash flows. Management's assumptions here should be approach with professional scepticism.

Evidence

- Review management's impairment test, including:
    - Assessment that an appropriate discount rate has been used
    - Agreement that the assumptions to determine future cash flows are reasonable
    - Agreement that correct carrying value of assets has been used for comparison of recoverable amount
    - Agreement that all identifiable assets have been included in the cash generating unit
    - Recalculation of all figures

- Discussion with management of the expected future performance of SC

- Review of post-year end management accounts for the performance of Shelly's Cruises

- Review of the level of bookings made in advance for cruises to be taken in the future

(c) **Matters to consider**

In accordance with IAS 10 *Events After the Reporting Period*, this acquisition is a non-adjusting event because it does not relate to conditions in place at the end of the reporting period.

However, if it is judged to be sufficiently material then it should be disclosed in a note to the financial statements, along with an estimate of its financial effect. As this note has not been included, we should ask management to include such a note. If they do not do so, then the auditor's opinion must be modified, in this case to an 'except for' qualification in respect of a disclosure required by IAS 10.

Evidence

- Copy of press release announcing the acquisition, including the date of the announcement

- Copy of any legal agreement relating to the acquisition, including the date control passes to Clooney

- Review of any due diligence report received, detailing the value of assets purchased, and the consideration paid

- Review of the financial statements of Craig, to determine that it represents a significant acquisition for the group which requires a disclosure note

- Review of any note provided by management to be included in the financial statements

Question 4

Text references. Chapter 2.

Top tips. This question looks at the issue of ethics in the context of practice management. Part (a) should be relatively straightforward, provided that you are familiar with the technical content. But even if you were struggling technically you could have picked up quite a few marks just by working through the material given in the question.

Part (b)(i) offered three marks that were virtually all knowledge, and you should have got at least two of these. Part (b)(ii) was more difficult, and required you to think on your feet. Remember that everybody would have found this question difficult, and that the key is to just get a few clear arguments down on either side, and to draw a conclusion.

Easy marks. Part (b)(ii) contained the easiest marks in the question.

Examiner's comments. This was the most popular of the optional questions, and focussed on ethics and practice management. It was very pleasing to see many candidates achieve a clear pass on both (a) and (b). The few unsatisfactory answers to part (a)(i) tended to simply repeat extracts from the advertisement and say 'this is unprofessional'.

Requirement (a)(ii) was not well answered. While most candidates could state obvious issues, like whether one person would be enough to provide the service, unfortunately very few clearly distinguished between audit and non-audit clients, which was a key issue, as the scenario clearly stated that only one third of the audit firm's clients were audit clients. Few dealt with the issue of the contingent fee in enough detail, with answers usually saying that it was 'unprofessional' but not elaborating further.

Requirement (b) dealt with the ethical problems raised by long association of audit firms and their clients. For seven marks, candidates were asked to explain the ethical threats, and to evaluate the advantages and disadvantages of compulsory firm rotation. On the whole, this was well answered. Most candidates could identify and explain to some extent the various ethical threats posed by long association, with the familiarity threat being the most common to be discussed. The advantages and disadvantages were often dealt with reasonably well, though a lot of answers were just bullet point lists with no real evaluation provided at all. For many candidates this was the last requirement attempted, so the brevity of answers was probably linked to time management in the exam.

Marking scheme

			Marks
(a)	(i)	**Evaluation of advertisement**	

Generally 1 mark per comment
- Advertising not prohibited but must follow ACCA guidelines
- Cannot be misleading/exaggerated claims
- Exaggerated claim re size
- Unprofessional claim re 'most professional'
- Cannot guarantee improvements/tax saving
- Second opinions
- Introductory fee
- Audit and non-audit services
- Fees not approved by ACCA
- Improper reference to ACCA   8

    (ii) **Corporate finance**

Generally 1 mark per comment explained:
- Partner is competent
- Advocacy threat
- Self-review threat
- Identify contingent fee
- Contingent fee not appropriate for audit clients
- Contingent fee allowed for non-audit client with safeguards
- Safeguards should be in place (examples   5

(b) (i) **Long association threat**

Generally 1 mark per comment
- Familiarity threat (½ mark only)
- Threat more significant for senior personnel
- Level of threat depends on various factors
- Lose scepticism
- Code requires partner rotation for listed client   3

    (ii) **Compulsory firm rotation**

Generally 1 mark per comment
- Eliminates familiarity threat
- Fresh pair of eyes for audit client
- Loss of fee income
- Unwilling to invest – lower quality audit
- Loss of cumulative knowledge – lower quality audit
- Increase in cost and audit fee
- Disruption to client   4

Total   20

(a) (i) Neither the ACCA *Code of Ethics and Conduct* nor the IESBA *Code of Ethics for Professional Accountants* prohibit advertising. However, a professional accountant must not bring the profession into disrepute, and adverts must be both honest and truthful. There are a number of question marks over whether this is the case with the draft advert here.

The advert claims that Neeson & Co is the largest accountancy and audit firm in the country, yet the firm has only three offices and 12 partners. This is neither honest nor truthful. Moreover, the claim that the firm is the most professional cannot be proven, and could imply that other firms are not professional, bringing the profession into disrepute.

The advert claims that a range of services are guaranteed to improve efficiency, which is not something that can be guaranteed, particularly given that the advert does not specify which services would do this.

The advert guarantees that tax would be saved, but again this cannot be guaranteed as it depends on the application of tax law in the specific circumstances of each client. To guaranteeing savings in this way may create a self-interest threat to the objectivity of tax work done by the firm, as rules may not be properly applied in order to save tax.

There is a risk of future litigation from clients who do not see improved efficiency or tax savings as a result of Neeson & Co's work.

It is possible for an audit firm to give a second opinion on another firm's report, but this is unusual. The advert may imply that Neeson & Co's opinion would be superior to another firm's, which brings the profession into disrepute. Moreover, it may compromise the firm's independence in such case by creating an expectation that Neeson & Co would not modify its audit report if it were necessary to do so.

The 25% 'introductory offer' is effectively lowballing, which is prohibited. If fees are too low, there is a risk that fees are not sufficient to allow staff to be assigned to audits who have appropriate levels of skill and experience.

A reduction is offered where both audit and tax services are provided. Non-audit services should only be provided to an audit client where any threats to auditor objectivity can be reduced to an acceptable level. Offering such a reduction may create self-review and advocacy threats. Moreover in the UK, ES 4 (Revised) *Fees, remuneration and evaluation policies, litigation, gifts and hospitality* requires that audit fees are not influenced by the provision of other services, as this may compromise the objectivity of the auditor.

Finally, the advert claims that rates are approved by the ACCA. This is false, because the ACCA does not approve specific firms' rates, and in view of the ethical concerns raised above over fees is disingenuous and dishonest in its intention too.

(ii) The new partner has experience of the banking sector and therefore appears to be competent in this area. However, there are a number of problems with the proposed service.

Negotiating financing arrangements on behalf of an audit client creates an advocacy threat to audit objectivity, as the firm is representing the client's interests to a third party. There may be self-review threat if the partner has been in any way involved with the accounting treatment of these arrangements.

Safeguards should be applied to reduce these threats to an acceptable level. These would include ensuring that the partner and any other staff members involved in giving advice are not involved in the audit. If an auditor's expert is required in relation to financing arrangements then the partner should not be used in this capacity.

A contingent fee is proposed, which the IESBA *Code* prohibits outright for audit engagements. For non-audit services such as this, the contingent fee creates a self-interest threat to audit objectivity. Safeguards must be applied to reduce this threat to an acceptable level. Safeguards may include ensuring that the partner is not involved with the audit.

However, if the fee relates to a matter that is material to the financial statements, or is material to the firm, then the threat cannot be reduced to an acceptable level. In this case Neeson & Co must not take on, or withdraw from, either the audit or the non-audit service.

(b)   (i)   Long association with an audit client may create familiarity and self-interest threats. This depends on a number of factors:

- How long an individual has been involved with the audit
- How senior the individual is
- The structure of the firm
- Whether the client's management has changed
- Whether the type of accounting issues has changed

The self-interest threat may arise because the firm does not want to jeopardise a continuing source of fee income. The familiarity threat may arise if audit personnel lose their professional scepticism, perhaps as a result of a close relationship with client staff, or because there being few problems in the past might lead the auditor to expect there to be no problems in the future.

The *Code* requires that for public interest entities, the key audit partner should be rotated after seven years, and should not be involved with the audit for two years, including helping with quality control, or giving the audit team advice on technical or industry-specific issues.

In the UK, ES 3 is more stringent, requiring rotation after five years for a listed client. For unlisted clients, careful consideration must be given to whether objectivity is impaired after ten years.

(ii)   The key argument in favour of firm rotation is that the familiarity and self-interest threats are more thoroughly safeguarded against by changing the whole audit firm instead of eg the partner alone. This would mean that not only the personnel but the whole infrastructure of the firm would be different. This could improve audit quality by bringing a 'fresh pair of eyes' to the audit.

Those who argue against this claim that an acceptable level of independence can be maintained by applying safeguards within the firm to mitigate the familiarity and self-interest threats.

It may actually be the case that firm rotation would **reduce** audit quality. Audit quality is enhanced by the years of knowledge and experience built up by an auditor in understanding the client entity, and this would be lost.

There would also be likely to be an increase in the cost of conducting audits, and hence in the fees charged, as a result of work that an incoming auditor needs to do, eg to gain an understanding of the entity and its environment.

Furthermore, audit firms may be unwilling to invest in systems that might enhance audit quality and cost-effectiveness, such as bespoke audit software for a client, if they know that they will lose the audit in a few years' time.

In conclusion, auditor rotation would probably be costly both for clients and auditors, and may not increase audit quality, possibly actually having the opposite effect of **reducing** it.

Question 5

Text reference. Chapter 17.

Top tips. This question tests your knowledge of the auditor's report. In Part (a) make sure that you are very familiar with the contents of the auditor's report, both unmodified and modified. This area comes up in virtually every sitting, so you just have to be comfortable with it.

Part (b) should have been straightforward. Take note of the examiner's comment (below) about candidates not mentioning ISA 265; the examiner has stated recently that candidates often do not have adequate knowledge of ISAs, so this is an area in which you need to show you can apply your knowledge.

Easy marks. Part (a) contained some easy marks for picking apart the more obvious failings of the audit report given in the question.

Examiner's comments. This was by far the least popular of the optional questions. Regarding part (a)(i), some answers were sound, and worked through the audit report, explaining its deficiencies in a logical manner. Some answers appreciated that the disclaimer of opinion may be an over-reaction, and that a qualification may be more suitable.

Unsatisfactory answers, which were by far the majority, tended not to appraise the audit report at all, and instead provided lengthy explanations of the accounting treatment for research and development, but completely missed the point that the auditor was unable to verify if the correct accounting treatment had been applied. Some blamed the audit team, rather than the client, for the lack of evidence, and suggested that the whole audit be reperformed.

Coming to part (a)(ii), most candidates suggested that the limitation in scope and its potential impact on the audit report be taken to audit committee or those charged with governance for discussion, and many also raised management integrity as an issue. Some candidates tended to repeat what they had written for (a)(i) without further development.

Part (b) was reasonably well attempted, with most answers referring to management letter points, and making recommendations for improving controls to the client. However, there were very few references to ISA 265, and only a handful of answers discussed the importance of determining whether a deficiency is significant or not.

Marking scheme

	Marks

(a) (i) Critical appraisal of audit report
Up to 1½ marks per comment applied to the scenario
- ½ mark ref ISA 705
- No explanation of imposed limitation
- Development costs not specifically referred to
- No quantification of the asset
- No reference to potential impact on profit
- ½ mark calculation materiality
- Disclaimer or qualification more appropriate (2 marks max)
- Incorrect headings used
- Incorrect wording of opinion
- Unprofessional to refer to management integrity
- 'We are worried' not professional   10

(ii) Further consequences
Generally 1 mark per comment
- ½ mark ref ISA 260
- Communicate limitation imposed to those charged with governance
- Communicate proposed modification to those charged with governance
- Consider alternative procedures for development costs
- Consider integrity of management
- Consider withdrawal from audit/resignation
- Audit pre-condition (ISA 210)   5

(b) Actions/implications of control deficiency identified
Generally 1 mark per comment
- ½ mark ref ISA 265
- Determine if deficiency is a deficiency or significant deficiency– Extend audit testing
- If significant report in writing to those charged with governance
- Communication to include description and recommendation
- Communication on a timely basis
- Insignificant deficiency need not be reported – depends on auditor judgement   5

Total   20

(a)   (i)   **Opinion**

This matter is material to the financial statements; at £4.4m the asset represents 8% of total assets, and if it has been wrongly capitalised then the resulting adjustment would turn the profit of £3.1m into a loss of £1.3m.

Management has not allowed the audit team access to the results of tests which have a bearing on whether or not an asset should be recognised here, in accordance with IAS 38 *Intangible assets*. The senior is correct to identify this limitation on the audit evidence available, and to recognise that this affects the opinion that should be given.

The draft auditor's report contains a disclaimer of opinion. ISA 705 (UK & Ireland) *Modifications to opinions in the independent auditor's report* states that such an opinion should be given where the matter in question is both material and **pervasive**, so that the auditor cannot reach an opinion on the financial statements as a whole. This may be overly harsh on this occasion. The matter is certainly material to the statement of financial position. In this case it would be appropriate to qualify the auditor's opinion 'except for', on the basis of an inability to obtain sufficient appropriate audit evidence as a result of a limitation on the scope of the audit.

However, as recognising an expense of £4.4m would turn a profit of £3.1m into a loss of £1.3m, the matter is fundamental to users' understanding of the financial statements, there is an argument for issuing a disclaimer of opinion as the senior has done.

Contents of report

The 'basis of opinion' paragraph should be shown immediately above the 'opinion' paragraph, as appears to be the case from the extracts given. However, the paragraph headings are not worded correctly. ISA 705 requires them to be headed 'Basis for Disclaimer of Opinion' and 'Disclaimer of Opinion' respectively.

The 'basis of opinion' paragraph should be more precise. It should refer to the relevant accounting standard (IAS 38), and should explain that a limitation has been imposed by management in respect of development costs. It should explain that management did not allow access to the results of scientific testing relating to these costs, and that the auditor has therefore been unable to determine whether the accounting treatment of the costs is correct.

The paragraph should then quantify the effect on the financial statements, stating that the asset is recognised on the statement of financial position at £4.4m, and that if this were to be treated as an expense, this would turn the profit of £3.1m into a loss of £1.3m.

The paragraph also contains the unprofessional form of words 'we are worried that the asset may be overvalued', which is not appropriate to an auditor's report. A lack of management integrity is referred to, and although the auditor should have considered the possible effects of this, it is inappropriate to refer to this in the auditor's report.

The opinion paragraph itself should use the specific form of words set out in ISA 705, including the statement that the auditor has been unable to obtain sufficient appropriate audit evidence, and that it is therefore unable to express an opinion.

In the UK, it is a requirement of Companies Act 2006 that if the auditor fails to receive all of the information and explanations necessary, this should be stated in the auditor's report.

(ii)   **Communication with those charged with governance**

ISA 260 (UK & Ireland) *Communication with those charged with governance* requires that significant difficulties encountered during the audit should be communicated, of which this is an example. In addition, where the auditor expects to modify the opinion, the circumstances leading to this should be communicated along with the expected wording.

Alternative procedures

The firm should consider whether evidence can be obtained by any alternative procedures. This may be difficult in this case.

Management integrity

The fact that management have imposed a limitation on the scope of the audit casts doubt over their integrity. The auditor must reconsider any representations made by management in this light. It may be necessary for the audit to be subject to an engagement quality control review.

Withdrawing from engagement

The firm should consider withdrawing from this audit engagement in order to protect its integrity. ISA (UK & Ireland) 210 *Agreeing the terms of audit engagements* effectively requires the auditor not to take on next year's audit, as it is a precondition for an audit that management acknowledges and understands its responsibility to provide the auditor with access to all information relevant to the preparation of the financial statements.

CA 2006

In the UK, Companies Act 2006 requires a statement to be made by auditors in relation to ceasing to hold office. The audit firm may wish to take legal advice to protect its position.

(b) The errors that have been found are already material to the statement of financial position, but further testing on trade payables is required to see whether they are isolated or whether there are more errors.

ISA 265 (UK & Ireland) *Communicating deficiencies in internal control to those charged with governance and management* defines internal control deficiencies as misstatements have not been prevented, detected or correctly on a timely basis as a result either of the absence of a control or of the manner in which a control is designed, implemented or operated. Both the absence of some supplier statement reconciliations and the absence of invoice approval before payment meet this definition.

We must consider whether this constitutes just a deficiency or a significant deficiency. A significant deficiency must be communicated to those charged with governance and management on a timely basis during the audit, so that action may be taken by management. If the deficiency is not deemed significant then we must consider whether it is important enough to bring to management's attention.

The written communication of a significant deficiency should include a description of the deficiency, details of its possible effects, and recommendations of how management might seek to correct it.

ACCA Professional Level
Paper P7
Advanced Audit and Assurance (United Kingdom)
Mock Examination 3

December 2013 Real Exam

Question Paper		
Time allowed		
Reading and Planning Writing		**15 minutes** **3 hours**
SECTION A	TWO compulsory questions to be attempted	
SECTION B	TWO questions ONLY to be attempted	
During reading and planning time only the question paper may be annotated		

DO NOT OPEN THIS PAPER UNTIL YOU ARE READY TO START UNDER EXAMINATION CONDITIONS

SECTION A – BOTH questions are compulsory and MUST be attempted

Question 1

You are an audit manager in Compton & Co, responsible for the audit of the Stow Group (the Group), having recently taken over from the previous manager who has left the firm. You are planning the audit of the Group financial statements for the year ending 31 December 20X3. All components of the Group have the same year end.

The Group audit engagement partner, Chad Woodstock, has just sent you the following email.

To: Audit manager
From: Chad Woodstock, audit partner
Subject: The Stow Group – audit planning

Hello,

We need to start planning the audit of The Stow Group. As this is your first time working on this client, I have provided you with some background information to help with your audit planning.

Yesterday I met with the Group finance director, Marta Bidford, and we discussed some restructuring of the Group which has taken place this year. She also raised the issue of our firm using the work of internal audit and suggested that this would prevent any increase in the audit fee.

I have provided you with a summary of issues which I discussed with Marta, and using this information I would like you to prepare briefing notes for my use in which you explain the risks of material misstatement to be considered in planning the Group audit, commenting on their materiality to the Group financial statements. You should also identify any further information which may be needed to help with the audit planning. I would also like you to recommend the principal audit procedures to be performed in respect of the disposal of Broadway Ltd.

I would also like you to discuss how Marta's suggestion relating to the use of the internal audit team potentially impacts on the planning of the audit of Zennor Ltd and the Group's financial statements, and comment on any ethical issue raised by her suggestion.

Thank you.

Background information

The Group is a car manufacturer, focusing on the luxury car market. Its operations are divided between a number of subsidiaries, some of which focus on manufacturing and distributing the cars, while others deal mainly with marketing and retail. In the last few years, the Group has achieved an impressive increase in revenue and profitability, which was the result of expanding sales into emerging markets such as China and Brazil. The Group became listed in 2005.

Compton & Co has provided the audit service to the Group for several years. Given the size of the Group, it represents an important client to Compton & Co. Based on last year's figures, the income which our firm received from the Group amounted to 4.5% of our firm's total income.

Notes from Chad Woodstock's meeting with Marta Bidford

1. **Acquisition of Zennor Ltd**

    In order to expand overseas, the Group acquired 100% of the share capital of Zennor Ltd on 1 February 20X3. Zennor Ltd is located in Farland, where it owns a chain of car dealerships. Zennor Ltd's financial statements are prepared using International Financial Reporting Standards and are measured and presented using the local currency of Farland, the Dingu. At the present time, the exchange rate is 4 Dingu = £1. Zennor Ltd has the same year end as the Group, and its projected profit for the year ending 31 December 20X3 is 90 million Dingu, with projected assets at the same date of 800 million Dingu.

Zennor Ltd is supplied with cars from the Group's manufacturing plant. The cars are sent on cargo ships and take approximately six weeks to reach the main port in Farland, where they are stored until delivered to the dealerships. At today's date there are cars in transit to Zennor Ltd with a selling price of £58 million.

A local firm of auditors was engaged by the Group to perform a due diligence review on Zennor Ltd prior to its acquisition. The Group's statement of financial position recognises goodwill at acquisition of £60 million.

Compton & Co was appointed as auditor of Zennor Ltd on 1 March 20X3.

2.   **Disposal of Broadway Ltd**

On 1 September 20X3, the Group disposed of its wholly-owned subsidiary, Broadway Ltd, for proceeds of £180 million. Broadway Ltd operated a distribution centre in this country. The Group's statement of profit or loss includes a profit of £25 million in respect of the disposal.

Broadway Ltd was acquired by a retail organisation, the Cornwall Group, which wished to bring its distribution operations in house in order to save costs. Compton & Co resigned as auditor to Broadway Ltd on 15 September 20X3 to be replaced by the principal auditor of the Cornwall Group.

3.   **Zennor Ltd – internal audit team**

Marta said that Zennor Ltd has a well established internal audit team. She has suggested that we use the internal audit team as much as possible when performing our audit of Zennor Ltd as this will reduce the audit fee. The Group audit committee appreciates that with the audit of the new subsidiary there will be some increase in our costs, but has requested that the audit fee for the Group as a whole is not increased from last year's fee.

The internal audit team was established several years ago and is headed up by a qualified accountant, Jo Evesham, who has a lot of experience in designing systems and controls. Jo and her team monitor the effectiveness of operating and financial reporting controls, and report to the board of directors. Zennor Ltd does not have an audit committee as corporate governance rules in Farland do not require an internal audit function or an audit committee to be established.

During the year, the internal audit team performed several value for money exercises such as reviewing the terms negotiated with suppliers.

4.   **Projected results for the year**

The Group's projected profit before tax for the year is £200 million and projected total assets at 31 December are £2,500 million.

Required

Respond to the instructions in the partner's email.   **(31 marks)**

Professional marks will be awarded for the structure and presentation of the briefing notes and for the clarity of explanations.   **(4 marks)**

(Total = 35 marks)

Question 2

You are a manager in the business advisory department of Goleen & Co. Your firm has been approached to provide assurance to Baltimore Ltd, a company which is not an audit client of your firm, on a potential acquisition. You have just had a conversation with Mark Clear, Baltimore Ltd's managing director, who made the following comments:

'Baltimore Ltd is a book publisher specialising in publishing textbooks and academic journals. In the last few years the market has changed significantly, with the majority of customers purchasing books from online sellers. This has led to a reduction in profits, and we recognise that we need to diversify our product range in order to survive. As a result of this, we decided to offer a subscription-based website to customers, which would provide the customer with access to our full range of textbooks and journals online.

'On investigating how to set up this website, we found that we lack sufficient knowledge and resources to develop it ourselves and began to look for another company which has the necessary skills, with a view to acquiring the company. We have identified Mizzen Ltd as a potential acquisition, and we have approached the bank for a loan which will be used to finance the acquisition if it goes ahead.

'Baltimore Ltd has not previously acquired another company. We would like to engage your firm to provide guidance regarding the acquisition. I understand that a due diligence review would be advisable prior to deciding on whether to go ahead with the acquisition, but the other directors are not sure that this is required, and they don't understand what the review would involve. They are also unsure about the type of conclusion that would be issued and whether it would be similar to the opinion in an audit report.

'To help me brief the other directors and using the information I have provided, I would like you to:

(a) Discuss the benefits to Baltimore Ltd of a due diligence review being performed on Mizzen Ltd.

(b) Identify and explain the matters which you would focus on in your due diligence review and recommend the additional information which you will need to perform your work.

(c) Describe the type of conclusion which would be issued for a due diligence report and compare this to an audit report.'

Mark Clear has sent you the following information about Mizzen Ltd:

Company background

Mizzen Ltd was established four years ago by two university graduates, Vic Sandhu and Lou Lien, who secured funds from a venture capitalist company, BizGrow, to set up the company. Vic and Lou created a new type of website interface which has proven extremely popular, and which led to the company growing rapidly and building a good reputation. They continue to innovate and have won awards for website design. Vic and Lou have a minority shareholding in Mizzen Ltd.

Mizzen Ltd employs 50 people and operates from premises owned by BizGrow, for which a nominal rent of £1,000 is paid annually. The company uses few assets other than computer equipment and fixtures and fittings. The biggest expense is wages and salaries and due to increased demand for website development, freelance specialists have been used in the last six months. According to the most recent audited financial statements, Mizzen Ltd has a bank balance of £500,000.

The company has three revenue streams:

(1) Developing and maintaining websites for corporate customers. Mizzen Ltd charges a one-off fee to its customers for the initial development of a website and for maintaining the website for two years. The amount of this fee depends on the size and complexity of the website and averages at £10,000 per website. The customer can then choose to pay another one-off fee, averaging £2,000, for Mizzen Ltd to provide maintenance for a further five years.

(2) Mizzen Ltd has also developed a subscription-based website on which it provides access to technical material for computer specialists. Customers pay an annual fee of £250 which gives them unlimited access to the website. This accounts for approximately 30% of Mizzen Ltd's total revenue.

(3) The company has built up several customer databases which are made available, for a fee, to other companies for marketing purposes. This is the smallest revenue stream, accounting for approximately 20% of Mizzen Ltd's total revenue.

Extracts from audited financial statements

Statement of profit or loss and other comprehensive income

	Year ended 30 September 20X3 £'000	Year ended 30 September 20X2 £'000	Year ended 30 September 20X1 £'000	Year ended 30 September 20X0 £'000
Revenue	4,268	3,450	2,150	500
Operating expenses	(2,118)	(2,010)	(1,290)	(1,000)
Operating profit/(loss)	2,150	1,440	860	(500)
Finance costs	(250)	(250)	(250)	–
Profit/(loss) before tax	1,900	1,190	610	(500)
Tax expense	(475)	(300)	(140)	–
Profit/(loss) for the year	1,425	890	470	(500)

There were no items of other comprehensive income recognised in any year.

Required

Respond to the request from Mark Clear. **(25 marks)**

SECTION B – TWO questions ONLY to be attempted

Question 3

Dasset Ltd operates in the coal mining industry. The company owns ten mines across the country from which coal is extracted before being sold onto customers who are energy providers. Coal mining companies operate under licence from the National Coal Mining Authority, an organisation which monitors the environmental impact of coal mining operations, and requires coal mines to be operated in compliance with strict health and safety regulations.

You are an audit manager in Burton & Co, responsible for the audit of Dasset Ltd and you are reviewing the audit working papers for the year ended 31 August 20X3. The draft financial statements recognise profit before tax of £18 million and total assets of £175 million. The audit senior has left a note for your attention:

Accident at the Ledge Hill Mine

On 15 August 20X3, there was an accident at the Ledge Hill Mine, where several of the tunnels in the mine collapsed, causing other tunnels to become flooded. This has resulted in one-third of the mine becoming inaccessible and for safety reasons, the tunnels will be permanently closed. However, Dasset Ltd's management thinks that the rest of the mine can remain operational, as long as improvements are made to ensure that the mine meets health and safety regulations.

Luckily no one was injured in the accident. However, the collapse caused subsidence which has damaged several residential properties in a village located above the mine. A surveyor has been commissioned to report on whether the properties need to be demolished or whether they can be safely repaired. A group of 20 residents has been relocated to rental properties in the local area and Dasset Ltd is meeting all expenses in relation to this. The Ledge Hill Mine was acquired several years ago and is recognised in the draft statement of financial position at £10 million. As no employees were injured in the accident, Dasset Ltd's management has decided not to report the accident to the National Coal Mining Authority.

Required

In respect of the accident at the Ledge Hill Mine:

(a)   (i)   Comment on the matters which you should consider, and
        (ii)   Describe the audit evidence which you should expect to find,

in undertaking your review of the audit working papers and financial statements of Dasset Ltd.

Note. The total marks will be split equally between each part.   **(14 marks)**

(b)   In relation to management's decision not to report the accident to the National Coal Mining Authority, discuss Burton & Co's responsibilities and recommend the actions which should be taken by the firm.

(6 marks)

(Total = 20 marks)

Question 4

You are an audit manager in Chester & Co, and you are reviewing three situations which have recently arisen with respect to potential and existing audit clients of your firm.

Tetbury Ltd's managing director, Juan Stanton, has approached Chester & Co to invite the firm to tender for its audit. Tetbury Ltd is a small, owner-managed company providing financial services such as arranging mortgages and advising on pension plans. The company's previous auditors recently resigned. Juan Stanton states that this was due to 'a disagreement on the accounting treatment of commission earned, and because they thought our controls were not very good.' You are aware that Tetbury Ltd has been investigated by the financial services authority for alleged non-compliance with its regulations. As well as performing the audit, Juan would like Chester & Co to give business development advice.

The audit of Stratford Ltd's financial statements for the year ended 30 November 20X3 will commence shortly. You are aware that the company is in financial difficulties. Stratford Ltd's managing director, Colin Charlecote, has requested that the audit engagement partner accompanies him to a meeting with the bank where a new loan will be discussed, and the draft financial statements reviewed. Colin has hinted that if the partner does not accompany him to the meeting, he will put the audit out to tender. In addition, an invoice relating to interim audit work performed in August 20X3 has not yet been paid.

Banbury Ltd is a listed entity, and its audit committee has asked Chester & Co to perform an actuarial valuation on the company's defined benefit pension plan. One of the audit partners is a qualified actuary and has the necessary skills and expertise to perform the service. Banbury Ltd has a year ending 28 February 20X4, and the audit planning is due to commence next week. Its financial statements for the year ended 28 February 20X3, in respect of which the audit report was unmodified, included total assets of £35 million and a pension liability of £105,000.

Required

Identify and discuss the ethical and other professional issues raised, and recommend any actions that should be taken in respect of:

(a)	Tetbury Ltd	**(8 marks)**
(b)	Stratford Ltd	**(6 marks)**
(c)	Banbury Ltd	**(6 marks)**

(Total = 20 marks)

Question 5

(a) You are the manager responsible for the audit of Burford Ltd, a company which designs and manufactures engine parts. The audit of the financial statements for the year ended 31 July 20X3 is nearing completion and you are reviewing the working papers of the going concern section of the audit file. The draft financial statements recognise a loss of £500,000 (2012 – profit of £760,000), and total assets of £13.8 million (2012 – £14.4 million).

The audit senior has left the following note for your attention.

'I have performed analytical review on Burford Ltd's year-end financial statements. The current ratio is 0.8 (2012 – 1.2), the quick ratio is 0.5 (2012 – 1.6). The latest management accounts show that ratios have deteriorated further since the year end, and the company now has a cash balance of only £25,000. Burford Ltd has a long-term loan outstanding of £80,000 with a covenant attached, which states that if the current ratio falls below 0.75, the loan can be immediately recalled by the lender.'

You are also aware that one of Burford Ltd's best-selling products, the QuickFire, has become technically obsolete during 20X3 as customers now prefer more environmentally friendly engine parts. Historically, the QuickFire has generated 45% of the company's revenue. In response to customers' preference, £1.3 million has been spent on designing a new product, the GreenFire, due for launch in February 20X4, which will be marketed as an environmentally friendly product.

A cash flow forecast has been prepared for the year to 31 July 20X4, indicating that based on certain assumptions, the company's cash balance is predicted to increase to £220,000 by the end of the forecast period.

Assumptions include:

(1) The successful launch of the GreenFire product

(2) The sale of plant and machinery which was used to manufacture the QuickFire, generating cash proceeds of £50,000, forecast to take place in January 20X4

(3) A reduction in payroll costs of 15%, caused by redundancies in the QuickFire manufacturing plant

(4) The receipt of a grant of £30,000 from a government department which encourages innovation in environmentally friendly products, scheduled to be received in February 20X4.

Required

Explain the matters which cast doubt on the going concern status of Burford Ltd and explain the audit evidence you should expect to find in your file review in respect of the cash flow forecast. **(14 marks)**

(b) Having completed the file review, you have concluded that the use of the going concern assumption is appropriate, but that there is significant doubt over Burford Ltd's ability to continue as a going concern. You have advised the company's audit committee that a note is required in the financial statements to describe the significant doubt over going concern. The audit committee is reluctant to include a detailed note to the financial statements due to fears that the note will highlight the company's problems and cause further financial difficulties, but have agreed that a brief note will be included.

Required

In respect of the note on going concern to be included in Burford Ltd's financial statements, discuss the implications for the audit report and outline any further actions to be taken by the auditor. **(6 marks)**

(Total = 20 marks)

Answers

DO NOT TURN THIS PAGE UNTIL YOU HAVE
COMPLETED THE MOCK EXAM

A PLAN OF ATTACK

If this had been the real Advanced Audit and Assurance exam and you had been told to turn over and begin, what would have been going through your mind?

An important thing to say (while there is still time) is that it is vital to have a good breadth of knowledge of the syllabus because the question requirements for each question will relate to different areas of the P7 syllabus. However, don't panic. Below we provide guidance on how to approach the exam.

Approaching the answer

Use your reading time well, to look through the questions, particularly Questions 1 and 2 in Section A which are compulsory, to get a feel for what is required and to become familiar with the question scenarios.

It is vital that you attempt all the required questions in the paper to increase your chances of passing. The best way to do this is to make sure you stick to the time allocation for each question – both in total and for each of the question parts. The worst thing you can do is run over time in one question and then find that you don't have enough time for the remaining questions.

Section A is compulsory and consists of two long case-study style questions. These may contain detailed information such as extracts from financial statements. A range of requirements will be set.

Question 1 is for 35 marks. As ever, the key to success in this question is to stay focused, don't run over time in each part, and answer the requirements set. In part (a)(i) you need to keep your answer concise and practical. There were plenty of things to say here from the scenario, so it is important that you are disciplined and make the best use you possibly can of the time you have. In part (a)(ii), the first thing is to make sure that you actually answer the requirement. There are usually lots of marks available for further information. Say what is needed and why. Part (b) on procedures should be approached methodically, thinking about how you would test the accounting treatment. Part (c) should have been OK, provided you had not run out of time for this part of the question. It was important here to comment on the ethical issue as well as just the issue of using internal audit's work.

Question 2 is worth 25 marks. Note that the professional marks were in Question 1, so there is no need to use a report format for your answer here. Part (a) was a mix of knowledge and application. If you think about the needs of the company in the question then that should help you to make relevant points. Crucially, do not explain more than three advantages, as any more probably won't be marked. Part (b) was the guts of this question. As ever, stick to the issues in the scenario and try to think about why Baltimore wants to acquire Mizzen. General points about matters to consider in due diligence are unlikely to score well. Part (c) was straight knowledge and should have been easy. You may have wanted to do part (c) before part (b) to make sure you got at least 1½– 2 marks here.

Section B contains three questions, from which you must attempt two. Choose wisely!

Question 3 is on audit matters and evidence in relation to an accident and some regulations. You should have scored well on part (a), which focused on the practical issues arising from the scenario. Part (b) was more difficult, but if well prepared you should have been able to do enough to pass this part.

Question 4 was a typical P7 ethics question. Notice that Part (a) is for eight marks but (b) and (c) are for only 6 marks each, so your answer to (a) should have been longer. As ever, try to pick up on practical issues involved. State the threat that is present and explain why it is present. Commercial considerations can be a good way to get marks here, wherever the question asks for 'professional issues'. There are also marks in part (a) for contacting the predecessor auditor, which is a professional issue.

Question 5 is on going concern and reporting. Part (a)(i) should have been straightforward as there was a lot in the scenario that gave rise to easy points. Don't blow your time on this part! Part (a)(ii) should have been OK, as the question practically gives you your starting point in the form of the 'assumptions' listed. Part (b) is a very commonly examined area and should not have posed significant difficulties by this stage in your studies.

Forget about it!

Don't worry if you found the paper difficult. More than likely other candidates will have too. If this were the real thing you would need to forget the exam the minute you left the exam hall and think about the next one. Or, if it is the last one, celebrate!

Question 1

Text reference. Chapter 6.

Top Tips. Be sure to get the **professional marks** here, for which you needed to: write out the heading for 'briefing notes'; write an introduction; set out your answer clearly using sub-headings; and write a conclusion. Your introduction and conclusion do not need to be too long – make sure you write the heading, and try to write a brief paragraph of about three or four lines. Make sure you get the marks, but don't spend too much time on it!

The first part of the question was on the risks of material misstatement, and therefore **excludes detection risks** – there are no marks available for risks that arise from difficulties in auditing the group such as the need to obtain an understanding of the newly-acquired subsidiary.

As ever you are advised not to spend time making **general points** about group audits, as many candidates in the real exam will have done. Almost everything you say needs to be based on the scenario, and if it isn't then you're in danger of spending time writing something which will get no marks.

It is often the case in P7 that it's relatively easy to score marks for specifying **further information**. Be specific – state what information you need, and why you need it (you can think of it as a ½ mark for each). It is also important to bear in mind here that the requirement is **not** asking for audit procedures, so there are no marks for information that would be needed to perform **procedures**. What you need to think of are pieces of information that would be useful at the **planning** stage of the audit – things like last year's audited financial statements for Zennor, which we wouldn't have because we didn't audit them. Information on, for example, exchange rate fluctuations would only be useful for conducting procedures on the foreign subsidiary, and would not be useful at the planning stage.

It is important that you calculate **materiality**, as you are asked to do so. It is best to do this separately with each item (eg 'goodwill is 2.4% of total assets and is therefore material'), rather than calculating the general materiality thresholds at the start of the question. There are no marks for just saying that something is material without performing a calculation (so if you put thresholds at the start of the question, you would still have to calculate the materiality of each item in order to get the marks). It's also important that you use the **appropriate benchmark** – total assets for statement of financial position items, and profit for items affecting the statement of profit or loss. Materiality for inventory should be calculated using total assets, with the materiality of any impairment being calculated using profit before tax. Likewise goodwill.

Take care not to spend time writing about business risks, eg the risk to the group of exposure to foreign exchange rate fluctuations. Unless you develop this into an audit risk (and this may be difficult to do) you won't get any marks for it at all.

A general point of exam technique that is relevant to this question is to read the question carefully. A careful reading shows that 'we' (ie Compton & Co) are auditing both the group and its components. This means that you can recite pre-learned knowledge about group and component auditors from ISA 600.

The second part of the question on procedures for the Broadway disposal should not have been too problematic. This is another area where you can score well (like 'further information'), as long as you state the **procedure**, and then state **why** you are performing it.

In the final part of the question, some candidates may have been tempted to write a lot about internal audit and the steps to take before deciding whether or not to rely on internal audit work. While this is valid and relevant, it is important not to go over your time allocation on this part. Finally, note that whenever an 'ethical issue' is raised in P7, this is almost always referring to the **auditor**'s ethics – whether Marta or the internal auditors are acting ethically is not really the issue.

Easy marks. The marks for further information are simple marks, as are those for audit procedures on the disposal of the subsidiary. Not to mention the professional marks.

ACCA examiner's answers. The ACCA examiner's answers to this question can be found at the end of this Practice and Revision Kit.

Marks

Risks of material misstatement, materiality and further information requests

Generally up to 1½ marks for each risk identified and explained (to a maximum of 4 marks for identification only):

Zennor Ltd
–   Retranslation of Zennor Ltd's financial statements using incorrect exchange rate
–   Treatment of exchange gains and losses arising on retranslation
–   Goodwill not measured correctly at initial recognition
–   Goodwill not tested for impairment before the year end
–   Time apportionment of Zennor Ltd's income and expenses not correct
–   Incomplete or inadequate disclosure
–   Cancellation of intercompany balances
–   Disclosure of related party transactions
–   Completeness of inventory

Broadway Ltd
–   Derecognition of assets, liabilities and goodwill
–   Time apportionment of profit up to date of disposal
–   Calculation of profit on disposal
–   Classification and presentation regarding the disposal
–   Treatment in parent company financial statements
–   Accrual for tax payable

Generally 1 mark for each of the following calculations/comments on materiality:
–   Appropriate retranslation of Zennor Ltd figures into £
–   Calculate materiality of Zennor Ltd to the Group
–   Determine if Zennor Ltd is a significant component of the Group
–   Calculate materiality of goodwill arising on acquisition
–   Calculate materiality of inventory in transit to the Group

1 mark for each piece of additional information identified:
–   Prior years' financial statements and auditor's reports
–   Minutes of meetings where the acquisition was discussed
–   Business background, eg from the company's website or trade journals
–   Copies of systems documentation from the internal audit team
–   Confirmation from Zennor Ltd's previous auditor of any matters that should be brought to our attention
–   Projected financial statements for the year to 31 December 2013
–   A copy of the due diligence report
–   Copies of prior year tax computations

Audit procedures

Generally 1 mark for each well described audit procedure:
–   Confirm the value of assets and liabilities which have been derecognised from the Group
–   Confirm goodwill that exists is derecognised from the Group
–   Confirm that the Stow Group is no longer listed as a shareholder of the company
–   Obtain legal documentation in relation to the disposal to confirm the date of the disposal and confirm that Broadway Ltd's profit has been consolidated up to this date only
–   Agree or reconcile the profit recognised in the Group financial statements to Broadway Ltd's individual accounts as at 1 September 2013
–   Analytical procedures to gain assurance that the amount of profit consolidated from 1 January to 1 September 2013 appears reasonable
–   Re-perform management's calculation of profit on disposal in the Group financial statements
–   Agree proceeds received to legal documentation/cash book/bank statements
–   Confirm that no deferred or contingent consideration is receivable in the future
–   Confirm that the profit on disposal is correctly disclosed as part of profit for the year

Marks

- Confirm that all necessary notes are given in the Group financial statements
- Obtain the parent company's statement of financial position to confirm that the cost of investment is derecognised
- Re-perform the calculation of profit on disposal in the individual financial statements
- Reconcile the profit on disposal recognised in the parent company's financial statements to the profit recognised in the Group financial statements
- Obtain management's estimate of the tax due on disposal, reperform the calculation and confirm the amount is properly accrued at parent company and at Group level
- Review any correspondence with tax authorities regarding the tax due
- If the tax is paid in the subsequent events period, agree to cash book and bank statement

Reliance on internal audit

Generally 1 mark for each discussion point:
- Impact on audit strategy, eg reliance on controls
- Impact on audit planning, eg systems documentation/business understanding
- Specific work can be performed, eg inventory counts
- Could lead to significant reduction in audit costs, eg travel costs can be avoided
- Need to evaluate how much reliance can be placed (objectivity, competence, quality control, etc) – up to 3 marks
- Reliance will impact on Group audit as well as on individual audit
- Pressure on fee is an intimidation threat
- Fee unlikely to be maintained given the change in Group structure
- Increased fee may cause total fee to cross 5% threshold
- Safeguards may need to be considered and situation disclosed

Maximum   31
Professional marks to be awarded for:
- Use of headings
- Introduction
- Logical flow/presentation
- Conclusion

Maximum   4
Total   35

Briefing notes

To: Audit Partner
From: Audit Manager
Subject: Stow Group planning, year end 31/12/X3

Introduction

Please find below an assessment of the risks of material misstatement in the Stow Group ('Stow') audit, indicating any further information needed, the principal audit procedures for the disposal of Broadway Ltd ('Broadway') and a discussion of Martha's suggestion and its effect on our audit.

Risks of material misstatement – Zennor

Zennor's profit translates to £22.5m, which is 11.3% of Group profit and is thus material. Zennor's total assets translate to £200m, which is 8% of Group total assets and is also material. Zennor may therefore be adjudged a significant component of the Stow audit as it is financially significant to it.

As these are projected figures, materiality will be recalculated at the year end on the basis of Zennor's actual figures and the closing exchange rate at that date.

Foreign exchange

IAS 21 *The Effects of Changes in Foreign Exchange Rates* requires Zennor's assets and liabilities to be translated at the closing rate on 31/12/X3, and income and expenses to be translated at the actual rates on the dates of the transactions. There is a risk that the wrong rates are used, which could over- or under-state total assets and profit.

IAS 21 also requires any exchange gain or loss to be recognised within profit or loss ('P/L'). Calculations here can be complex, so there is a risk of profit being misstated if this is not done correctly. Exchange gains or losses on translating a subsidiary's balances are recognised in other comprehensive income (OCI), so there is a risk of this not being done and thus of misclassification of these sums between P/L and OCI.

Goodwill on acquisition must also be retranslated at the year end, and there is a risk of this not being done.

Inventory

Inventory in transit is likely to be in the region of £58m at the year end. This is 2.3% of total assets and is material.

The group's controls need to be robust here in order to mitigate the risk of inventory being recorded incorrectly. Given that Zennor is newly acquired, there is a risk that this may not be the case. The risk may, however, be lessened by the presence of an internal audit department in Zennor.

Revenue and inventory

It is important that the group is clear about who owns the inventory at each point. There are many possible types of error here, which could lead to misstatements in both the group financial statements and those of the individual companies. For instance, Stow might consider the inventory as sold and thus recognise revenue that would need to be eliminated on consolidation. In its individual accounts, this would be considered consignment inventory and should not be recognised in revenue. If Zennor did not yet recognise the inventory, then it would be entirely missing from the group accounts, understating inventory and overstating revenue.

Alternatively, both Stow and Zennor could recognise the cars in inventory, leading to an overstatement of group inventory if this double-counting were not eliminated on consolidation.

Unrealised profit

If the inventory was recognised as sold to Zennor at a mark-up, then a provision for unrealised profit must be included. The risk is that it is omitted, which would overstate both inventory and profit.

Related parties

The intra-group transactions fall within the scope of IAS 24 *Related Party Disclosures*, and must be disclosed in the individual financial statements of the group companies. There is a risk that if disclosure is inadequate, this will be a material misstatement.

Goodwill

Goodwill of £60m is 2.4% of total assets and is material.

There are several risks here. First, calculating goodwill requires estimating the fair values of Zennor's assets and liabilities. This may involve judgement and can be complex, particularly when dealing with assets that are hard to value.

Second, it is possible that some assets and liabilities may have been missed, leading to overstatement of goodwill.

Third, the fair value of the consideration transferred could include contingent consideration, which may be complex to calculate. Improper measurement here could under- or overstate goodwill.

Fourth, goodwill must be reviewed annually for impairment whether or not there are indicators of impairment. If this has not been done then goodwill could be impaired, overstating assets and profit.

It is possible that Stow's management has valued Zennor's net assets on the basis of the due diligence review. There is a risk that the work of this management's expert is not suitable for this purpose, leading to misstatements in both net assets and goodwill.

Mid-year acquisition

Zennor was acquired on 1 February 20X3, one month into the year. There is a risk that Zennor's 20X2 year-end reserves are mistaken for its pre-acquisition reserves in the group accounts, which would misstate group reserves.

There is also a risk of the full year of Zennor's statement of profit or loss being consolidated, rather than 11 months. Assuming profits accrue evenly, this would result in a misstatement of £22.5m × 1 / 12 = £1.875m in the group accounts. At 0.9% of group profit, this would be immaterial.

Disclosure

IFRS 3 *Business Combinations* requires extensive disclosures, eg in relation to goodwill. There is a risk that these are not included in the group financial statements.

Opening balances

Zennor's prior year financial statements may not have been audited, or were audited by another auditor. There may therefore be misstatements in this year's opening balances which could materially misstate both this year's financial statements (eg the statement of financial position) and the corresponding figures.

Risks of material misstatement - Broadway

Profit on disposal

The profit on disposal of £25m is 12.5% of group profit and is material.

There is a risk that this has not been calculated correctly. For example, if a contingent consideration is involved then its miscalculation could affect the figure for profit on disposal.

Net assets

Broadway's net assets were £155m (£180m proceeds less £25m profit), which is material at 6.2% of assets.

There is a risk that not all of these balances were derecognised from the group accounts. This could misstate profit on disposal, or just the group financial statements.

Mid-year disposal

Broadway was disposed of on 1 September 20X3, meaning that for the first eight months of the year it was in the Stow group. Its results should therefore be consolidated for this period. The risk is that this has not been done correctly, overstating group profit.

Presentation of financial statements

There is a risk that the profit on disposal of £25m is not presented separately on face of the statement of profit or loss, as is required by IAS 1 *Presentation of Financial Statements*.

It is possible that Broadway is a disposal group of assets and a discontinued operation in line with IFRS 5 *Non-current Assets Held for Sale and Discontinued Operations*. In this case its net assets and liabilities should have be measured at fair value before disposal. If this was not done, then profit on disposal may be misstated.

Further, IFRS 5 requires Broadway's profit or loss after tax to be disclosed on the face of the statement of profit or loss as a discontinued operation, together with detailed disclosures in the notes. There is a risk of material misstatement if this is not done.

Further information

- Zennor's prior year financial statements and the auditor's report thereon, to determine approach to opening balances

- A copy of the local auditor's due diligence report on Zennor

- Confirmation from Zennor's previous auditor of any matters which should be brought to our attention

- Background on Zennor's business, eg from trade journals or company's website, to gain understanding of the entity

Procedures on Broadway disposal

- Recalculate profit on disposal.

- Obtain legal documentation of sale and confirm proceeds of £180m.

- Agree proceeds of £180m to bank statement.

- Inspect legal documentation for evidence of contingent or deferred consideration.

- Review register of shareholders to confirm that Stow is no longer a shareholder of the company.

- Review group statement of profit or loss and confirm separate disclosure of profit on disposal.

- Review group statement of profit or loss and confirm disclosure of discontinued operation is in line with IFRS 5.

- Review group asset register to confirm that Broadway's assets are not included.

- Confirm that Broadway's results for first eight months of the year are consolidated by reconciling consolidated profits to Broadway's individual financial records.

- Perform substantive analytical procedures to confirm that profit consolidated for Broadway is in line with expectations based on prior periods.

Internal audit

The immediate impact on planning is that we may be able to rely on the work of the internal auditors. This may improve the efficiency of our audit, allowing us to rely on Zennor's controls and so reduce the level of our substantive procedures. This would indeed work to reduce our audit fee by comparison with the situation in which Zennor did not have an internal audit function.

The prospective reduction in audit costs is increased still further by the fact that Zennor is located overseas. By using the work of internal audit, we would avoid the substantial travel costs which would otherwise be incurred.

It may be possible to rely directly on the work of internal audit, eg on tests of control they have performed. Moreover, we may be able to deepen our knowledge of Zennor's systems and controls, as well as its business in general, through contact with the internal audit team.

The decision about relying on internal audit should be based upon our assessment of its objectivity, competence and the systematic nature of its approach.

Internal audit would appear to be competent on the grounds of it being led by a qualified accountant. We do not have information about the team as a whole, however, and this would be required before reliance could be placed on their work. Further information would also be needed on the level of supervision, review and documentation of the work performed.

Internal audit's standing within the organisation appears to be enhanced by the fact that it reports to the board of directors. However, this is in reality something which may militate against its objectivity, since it may thereby be subject to the management's potentially baleful influence. The presence of an audit committee would have helped improve internal audit's independence from management, and might have given its work weight with those charged with governance.

It should be noted that there is a definite limit on the extent to which the work of internal auditors may be used: in the UK, ISA 610 specifically prohibits the use of internal auditors to provide direct assistance to the audit team.

Ethical issue

Marta's statement that we should rely on the work of internal audit is inappropriate, as this is rightfully the decision of the external auditor alone.

The group audit committee's request that the audit fee remain unchanged is inappropriate. Although its argument is not entirely specious, it overlooks the additional work that is required to audit a new subsidiary, for instance obtaining an understanding of it at the planning stage. Work would also still be required on the disposed subsidiary's statement of profit or loss, the majority of which will be consolidated this year.

It is instructive to observe that the audit fee must be charged based on the work done, rather than on the grounds of a purely commercial bargain between the client and the audit firm. There is a risk that charging too low a fee may induce the auditor to reduce inappropriately the extent of work performed. The request therefore amounts to an intimidation threat to the principle of professional competence and due care.

There is a further ethical issue here in the form of possible fee dependence on Stow. As a listed entity, the Stow is close to the threshold of 5%. If fees are 5% or more then ES 4 *Fees, remuneration and evaluation policies, litigation, gifts and hospitality* requires Compton & Co to consider the need for safeguards, and requires disclosure of the matter to the Ethics Partner and to those charged with the governance of Stow. If fees are higher this year then there is a risk that fees may breach this threshold.

Conclusion

There audit of the Stow Group contains a high overall risk of material misstatements as a result of the substantial group restructuring that took place during the year. Audit procedures must now be designed to detect any misstatements arising. These may involve relying on the work of Zennor's internal auditors, but it is important that the audit fee is substantial enough to allow sufficient audit procedures to be performed.

Question 2

Marking scheme

Marks

(a) **Benefit of due diligence**
Up to 2 marks for each benefit discussed:
- Identification of assets and liabilities
- Valuation of assets and liabilities
- Review of operational issues
- Examination of financial position and performance
- Added credibility and expertise
- Added value for negotiation of purchase price
- Other advice can be given, eg on obtaining finance

(b) **Areas to focus on and additional information**
Generally up to 1½ marks for each explanation of area to focus on:
- Equity owners of Mizzen Ltd and involvement of BizGrow
- Key skills and expertise
- Internally generated intangible assets
- Premises
- Other intangible assets
- Accounting policy on revenue recognition
- Sustainability and relevance of revenue streams
- Operating expenses
- Finance charges
- Cash management
1 mark for each specific additional information recommended:
- Contract or legal documentation dealing with BizGrow's investment in Mizzen Ltd
- A register of shareholders showing all shareholders of Mizzen Ltd
- An organisational structure
- A list of employees and their role within the company, obligations and compensation

- A list of freelance web designers used by Mizzen Ltd, and a description of the work they perform
- The key terms of contracts or agreements with freelance web designers
- A list of all IT innovations which have been created and developed by Mizzen Ltd, and details of any patent or copyright agreements relating to them
- Agreements with employees regarding assignment of intellectual property and confidentiality
- Copies of the customer databases
- A list of companies which have contracts with Mizzen Ltd for website development and maintenance
- A copy of all contracts with customers for review of the period for maintenance
- A breakdown of the revenue that has been generated from making each database available to other companies, and the dates when they were made available
- A summary of the controls which are in place to ensure that the database details are regularly updated
- A copy of the premises rental agreement with BizGrow
- Non-current asset register showing descriptions and values of all assets used in the business
- Copies of any lease agreements
- Details of any capital expenditure budgets for previous accounting periods, and any planned capital expenditure in the future
- Mizzen Ltd's stated accounting policy on revenue recognition
- Systems and controls documentation over the processing of revenue receipts
- Analysis of expenses included in operating expenses for each year and copies of documentation relating to ongoing expenses such as salaries and other overheads
- Copies of management accounts to agree expenses in the audited accounts are in line and to perform more detailed analytical review
- The full set of financial statements and auditor's reports
- Any agreements with banks or other external providers of finance

(c) **Conclusion on due diligence**
Generally 1 mark for each discussion point:
- Due diligence report to express conclusion using a negative form of words
- Limited assurance due to nature of work performed
- Audit opinion is a positive opinion of reasonable assurance
- Description of the general form and content of the report (up to 1 mark for each relevant point)

Total　　　　　　　　　　　　　　　　　　　　　　　　　　　　　　　　25

(a) **Identifying assets**

The review would aim to identify and value the assets and liabilities of the target company. This would include items not recognised on Mizzen Ltd (Mizzen)'s financial statements. For example, it is possible that Mizzen may have intangible assets that are not recognised separately, but which may be valued. These could become part of any goodwill acquired on acquisition.

The review would also seek to discover previously hidden liabilities, such as contingent liabilities, which could potentially be very significant to Baltimore Ltd.

Operational issues

The review would focus on operational issues. This might include, for example, an examination of Mizzen's different revenue streams with a view to assessing how Baltimore might seek to benefit from them after the acquisition. The review may also focus on the strategic fit between Baltimore and Mizzen, attempting to determine the extent to which Mizzen meets Baltimore's needs.

This could involve a review of Mizzen's financial position and performance, focusing in particular on its potential for future growth or profitability.

Credibility

Obtaining an external due diligence review would allow Baltimore's management to focus on its own operational matters and yet still receive a timely review. Such a review would be conducted by an independent expert, with experience and knowledge in this area which Baltimore's management lacks, since it has not previously acquired another company. The review would give the benefit of a sharp, fresh pair of eyes which might spot things that Baltimore's management may have missed.

It is for this reason that an externally-provided review would be more credible than an internal one, something which may help persuade Baltimore's bank to lend it the money which it believes itself to need.

(b) **Equity owners**

It is crucial to determine the identity of Mizzen's majority shareholder. It appears likely that this is Bizgrow, but further information is needed.

This is important because if Bizgrow does own the shares then it is with Bizgrow that Baltimore would need to negotiate the purchase of Mizzen. If Bizgrow does not want to sell its shares then Mizzen cannot be bought. However, it is unclear how Baltimore came to identify Mizzen as an acquisition target in the first place, and it is possible that Bizgrow may have had something to do with this.

Funding

It is noted that Vic and Lou secured funds from Bizgrow. The nature of any agreement that was made needs to be ascertained, as it is possible that Mizzen may owe Bizgrow a substantial amount of money. This would be material to any decision Baltimore might make about the acquisition.

The precise nature of the ongoing relationship between Mizzen and Bizgrow is unclear. It is possible that Bizgrow is involved with Mizzen at an operational level. Any agreements between the two parties should be obtained and scrutinised.

Examination of the statement of profit or loss reveals a finance cost of £250,000 which appears to be fixed. It is unlikely that this is interest on a loan because loan interest would change as the balance is repaid. It is therefore possible that this is a management charge from Bizgrow, which would be indicative of ongoing involvement. We would need to understand the nature of any liabilities Mizzen may have in relation to this charge.

Reputation

Mizzen's good reputation, and its having won awards for website design, is key evidence for its expertise in this area. This should be verified to external evidence. Customer satisfaction could be gauged by obtaining the results of any customer satisfaction surveys that may have been conducted.

Vic and Lou

Vic and Lou appear to be crucial to the success of Mizzen, so Baltimore would want them to be involved in future. It is not certain, however, that they would want to be involved with Baltimore and its website, and they may wish to concentrate on their own more innovative work. The acquisition would be much less attractive to Baltimore were they to leave.

Vic and Lou's intentions post-acquisition should be determined. It may be possible to structure any future deal in such a way that Vic and Lou would be required to continue working at Mizzen for a set period after the acquisition.

Staff

Mizzen is a business with few tangible assets, which relies heavily on the expertise of its staff, who may leave after any acquisition – particularly if Vic and Lou were to leave. It would make little sense to acquire Mizzen for its staff only to find that they leave on acquisition.

An organisational structure should be obtained in order to identify management and key personnel within Mizzen.

It is also possible that Baltimore may wish to restructure Mizzen after acquisition. In this case it is likely that redundancy payments would need to be made to staff members losing their jobs. The amount of any possible liability in this eventuality should be estimated as part of the review.

Freelancers

Mizzen has been using freelancers recently, which may result in a drop in the quality of work done by comparison with established staff. This should be investigated as it may affect Mizzen's ostensibly impeccable reputation.

Intangible assets

Mizzen has few assets, but is likely to have important intangible assets which would form part of any goodwill paid on acquisition. Vic and Lou have developed new website interfaces, and it should be determined whether any resulting intellectual property belongs to them personally or to Mizzen. Valuing these assets is likely to be difficult.

Customer databases should also be valued, which again is likely to be difficult owing to the absence of any active market for assets of this kind.

Premises

It is apparent that the £1,000 nominal rent paid to Bizgrow would increase after the acquisition, so it should be determined what an equivalent market rent might be for the premises. Alternatively, the premises may no longer be available, in which case the rent should be ascertained for premises meeting Mizzen's needs. It may be possible for Mizzen to operate from Baltimore's premises, in which case any opportunity costs should be considered.

Tangible assets

Mizzen's tangible assets need to be valued, and it should be determined whether they are owned or held under lease, as it is possible that Mizzen may be liable for any future lease payments.

Revenue recognition

The first revenue stream should be split into two components, with the revenue relating to maintenance being recognised as deferred income and spread over the contract period. There is a risk that revenue is recognised too early, inflating Mizzen's profit in the short term.

Relevance of revenue

Baltimore needs Mizzen to develop a website for it, and it should be asked whether Baltimore might be better off simply paying Mizzen £10,000 to develop a website rather than acquiring the whole company.

It is clear that Mizzen would have the expertise to do this because it operates its own subscription-based website. It should therefore be able to create something of a similar nature for Baltimore.

The third revenue stream in particular does not appear relevant to Baltimore, and it should be considered how this revenue stream would be managed after the acquisition.

Revenue increase

Revenue rose 23.7% from 20X2 to 20X3, which is an impressive increase although it is lower than the 60.4% increase from 20X1 to 20X2. The question is whether such a growth rate might feasibly be achieved in the future. It will therefore be necessary to scrutinise Mizzen's forecasts and plans for future growth.

Operating expenses

Operating expenses in 20X2 were 58.3% of revenue, but only 49.6% in 20X3. This is unusual, and may be indicative of efficiencies being achieved as Mizzen grows. It does not, however, tally with the fact that freelancers have been used this year, which would be expected to increase operating expenses in relation to revenue.

A detailed review needs to be performed on operating expenses to ensure that expenses are complete and are recorded accurately.

Cash

Mizzen's cash position should be confirmed to its bank statement. Although the company is not lacking cash, from its statements of profit or loss one would expect it to be in a better cash position than it is in. It is possible that cash has been paid out in dividends to shareholders.

Further information

- Copy of Mizzen's register of shareholders, to determine the identity of the majority shareholder

- Copy of any agreement between Bizgrow and Vic and Lou, to help understand their ongoing relationship as well as Bizgrow's planned exit route

- Agreements of any loans received by Mizzen

- Full audited financial statements of Mizzen

- Details of awards won for website design, including press reports, trade journals, for evidence of Mizzen's good reputation

- Details of any customer satisfaction surveys conducted by Mizzen

- Copies of contracts with Vic and Lou

- Copy of organisational structure

- Copies of contracts with key employees containing details of any redundancy payments that might be due in the future, along with other employee benefits and entitlements that are due to them

- List of freelance designers used by Mizzen, together with copies of contracts

- Details of any copyrights or patents owned by Vic and Lou or Mizzen

- Copy of rental agreement with Bizgrow, to be scrutinised for details of possible rental payments after acquisition

- Details of tangible non-current assets owned or operated by Mizzen

- Copies of any lease agreements for non-current assets such as computers or fixtures and fittings

- Copies of projected financial information for the next year

- Detailed management accounts, including breakdown of operating expenses to ascertain reasons for rising operating margin

- Details of any dividend payments made over the last three years

(c) Due diligence is a review report, and as such gives only limited assurance. By contrast an auditor's report gives reasonable assurance, which is a higher level of assurance. This is because a review engagement involves obtaining less evidence than is required for an auditor's report, and conducting procedures which are less thorough.

The conclusion of a review report is expressed negatively, and would begin with the wording, 'Based on our review, nothing has come to our attention...'

The conclusion of an auditor's report is phrased positively, and may state that the financial statements do in fact 'present fairly', or 'give a true and fair view of', the entity's financial position, performance and cash flows.

Question 3

Marking scheme

			Marks

(a) (i) **Benefit of due diligence**
Generally 1 mark for each point made:
- Materiality of the mine to total assets
- Impairment review should have been performed
- Materiality of the potential write-off to profit
- No impairment write-off means overstated assets and profit
- Potentially all of the mine may be closed down and therefore impaired
- Equipment which cannot be recovered also needs to be written off
- Improvements to health and safety should be capitalised
- Costs of abandoning/sealing up collapsed tunnels should be expensed
- Separate presentation of material impairment costs in financial statements
- Provision to be recognised for damaged properties/relocation costs of local residents
- Further claims may be made leading to provisions or contingent liabilities
- The authority may impose fine/penalty – provision or contingent liability
- Going concern disclosure if accident creates significant doubt
- Break-up basis if authority withdraw company's operating licence

(ii) **Evidence**
- Operating licence, reviewed for conditions relating to health and safety and for potential fines and penalties
- A written representation from management on their intention (or not) to bring the non-compliance to the attention of the National Coal Mining Authority
- A copy of board minutes where the accident has been discussed to identify the rationale behind the non-disclosure
- A copy of reports issued by engineers or other mining specialists confirming the extent of the damage caused to the mine by the accident
- Any quotes obtained for work to be performed to make the mine safe and for blocking off entrances to abandoned tunnels
- Confirmation, possibly by physical inspection, that the undamaged portion of the mine is operational
- A copy of the surveyor's report on the residential properties, reviewed for the expert's opinion as to whether they should be demolished

- A review of correspondence entered into with the local residents who have been relocated, to confirm the obligation the company has committed to in respect of their relocation
- Copies of legal correspondence, reviewed for any further claims made by local residents
- A review of the Ledge Hill Mine accident book, for confirmation that no one was injured in the accident
- A copy of management's impairment review, if any, evaluated to ensure that assumptions are reasonable and in line with auditor's understanding of the situation
- Confirmation that impairment losses have been recognised as an operating expense
- A review of draft disclosure notes to the financial statements where provisions and contingent liabilities have been discussed
- A review of cash flow and profit forecasts, forming a view on the overall going concern status of the company

Maximum   14

(b) **Responsibilities, actions and reporting**

Generally 1 mark for each point discussed:
- Management responsible for compliance with laws and regulations
- Auditor responsible for understanding applicable laws and regulations
- There is suspected non-compliance with laws and regulations and further procedures are necessary
- Matter should be discussed with those charged with governance
- Need to understand reason for non-disclosure/encourage management to disclose
- The need for external reporting should be evaluated
- Legal advice may be sought
- Confidentiality may be overridden in some circumstances
- Possibility of a statutory reporting requirement
- Consider disclosure in the public interest

Maximum   6

Total   20

(a) (i) The mine is recognised at £10m, which is 5.7% of total assets and is therefore material.

Impairment

The closure of a third of the mine is an indicator that the asset may be impaired. Management should therefore already have conducted an impairment review in line with IAS 36 *Impairment of Assets*.

At a minimum it would appear that no future economic benefit can be derived from one third of the mine. At £3.3m, this is approximately 18.5% of Dasset's profit before tax and is highly material.

It is possible, however, that the situation is far worse than this. If the whole mine were unusable, then an impairment loss of £10m would need to be recognised, which at 56% of profit before tax is very material indeed.

IAS 1 *Presentation of Financial Statements* requires separate disclosure of individual items of income or expense, so it is possible that such an impairment loss should be disclosed in this way. Inadequate disclosure would be a material misstatement.

Withdrawal of licence

It is possible that the National Coal Mining Authority ('NCMA') may withdraw Dasset's licence in relation to the Ledge Hill mine. This would result in a £10m impairment loss.

Fines could also be imposed in relation both to the accident and to Dasset's failure to report it. These would need to be either provided for or disclosed in line with IAS 37 *Provisions, Contingent Liabilities and Contingent Assets*. This would further reduce profit before tax, and failure to make the required provisions or disclosures would constitute a material misstatement.

Expenditure on mine

If the mine were to stay open then the monies spent improving the mine should be treated as capital expenditure. Clearly the amounts should be expensed if the mine cannot stay open. Any sums spent restoring the mine to its previous working condition should be treated as expenses, as should any expenditure required to make safe the unusable tunnels (which will not provide future economic benefits).

Provisions

IAS 37 requires provisions to be recognised for liabilities where there is a present obligation as a result of a past event. These criteria appear to have been met in the case of the residential properties because the accident took place before the year end, and the fact that the company is meeting the residents' expenses implies that it acknowledges its liability to them.

Provision should therefore be made for:

- Aany future costs of rental properties for which Dasset may be liable

- Costs relating to repairs or rebuilding of properties in the village for which Dasset may be liable

- Other future outflows, such as claims for compensation by affected residents. This may be more difficult to measure and may be less probable to be paid, so consideration should be given to whether these costs meet the IAS 37 criteria.

The surveyor, a management's expert, should be able to provide a reliable estimate for the first two categories of cost above.

Management integrity

Management's decision not to report the accident to the authorities casts doubt over its integrity, in which case any written representations received from management should be reviewed and treated with professional scepticism.

There does not appear to be any liability to Dasset's employees because nobody was injured in the accident, but given the doubts over management's integrity this claim should be questioned. Procedures need to be performed to determine whether liabilities and disclosures in the financial statements are complete.

Going concern

In addition to withdrawing the licence for the Ledge Hill mine, the NCMA could withdraw the license for the totality of Dasset's operations. This is unlikely, but not impossible, and its effects would be devastating for Dasset. The financial statements would then need to be prepared on the break-up basis.

A further risk to going concern arises from the effect of any bad publicity about the accident on Dasset's future sales.

(ii)   **Evidence**

- Copy of operating licence, reviewed for health and safety conditions and for potential penalties for non-compliance

- Written representation on management's intention (or not) to inform NCMA of non-compliance

- Board minutes discussing the accident, to identify the rationale behind non-disclosure

- Engineer's reports confirming extent of the damage caused to the mine

- Quotes obtained for work to be performed to make the mine safe

- Confirmation that the undamaged portion of the mine is operational, eg from reviewing engineer's report

- Surveyor's report on the residential properties, reviewed for opinion on whether they should be demolished

- Correspondence with relocated local residents, to confirm the obligation the company has committed to in respect of their relocation

- Copies of legal correspondence, reviewed for any further claims made by local residents

- Review of the Ledge Hill Mine accident book, for confirmation that no one was injured in the accident

- Copy of management's impairment review, if any, evaluated to ensure reasonableness of assumptions

- Confirmation that impairment losses have been recognised as expenses

- Review of draft disclosure re. provisions and contingent liabilities

- Review of cash flow and profit forecasts with respect to going concern

(b)   In line with ISA 250 A (UK & Ireland) *Consideration of Laws and Regulations in an Audit of Financial Statements* Dasset's management is responsible for ensuring that its operations comply with relevant law and regulations, in respect of which the auditor has no responsibility as such. The auditor must obtain a general understanding of the legal and regulatory framework and the entity's compliance with it.

Dasset's management appears in this case not to have complied with NCMA regulations, and has not informed the NCMA of this. The decision not to inform the authority may be a legitimate one, or it could signal a belief on the part of management that it needs to hide the accident from the NCMA.

Burton & Co must first obtain an understanding of the nature of the non-compliance and the surrounding circumstances, evaluating the possible effect on the financial statements and conducting further audit procedures where necessary.

Burton & Co should discuss the non-compliance with those charged with governance, and should obtain a written representation regarding the reason for the non-disclosure. The auditor should suggest that management report the incident to the NCMA.

ISA 250 A requires the auditor to consider whether there is a need to report a matter to a relevant authority in the public interest, even where there is no specific legal duty to report it. If, after obtaining legal advice, Burton & Co considers that the matter should be reported in the public interest then it must do so, having first notified those charged with governance of its view and given them the opportunity to report the matter themselves.

Burton & Co owes Dasset a duty of confidentiality and should therefore not disclose the accident without Dasset's prior consent. This duty may, however, be overridden where disclosure is in the public interest or is required by legislation. The auditor should consult with legal counsel to determine whether it has any legal duty to disclose, and whether disclosure on the grounds of the public interest would have any legal consequences.

Question 4

Marking scheme

Marks

Generally 1 mark for each point identified and discussed:

(a) **Tetbury Ltd**
- Customer due diligence/know your client procedures to be performed
- Audit firm's competence to audit a financial services client
- Acceptance decision should also include consideration of ethical threats
- Management integrity threatened by past investigation by financial services authority
- Integrity also threatened by possible inappropriate financial reporting
- Management may have intimidated the previous auditor
- Contact previous auditor for further information
- Controls appear weak leading to high audit risk
- Responses to high risk should be considered, eg use of experienced audit team
- Confirm client's intention to improve controls
- Threats to objectivity arise from giving business advice – perceived as assuming management responsibility
- Self-review and self-interest threats created
- Management threat created by giving business advice
- Safeguards to be put in place, eg management acknowledge responsibility for business decisions

Maximum   8

(b) **Stratford Ltd**
- Advocacy threat created by attending meeting
- Management threat exists
- Legal proximity may be created by attending meeting
- Intimidation threat from threat of removal from office
- Consider appropriate safeguards
- Integrity of the managing director questionable
- Overdue fees may represent self-interest threat

- But amount may be insignificant and not long overdue
- Audit engagement partner should discuss matter with ethics partner
- Advocacy threat created by attending meeting

Maximum   6

(c) **Banbury Ltd**
- Provision of valuation service creates self-review and self-interest threats to objectivity
- Management threat also created
- Service cannot be provided if the pension deficit is material
- Calculate and comment on materiality in 2013 financial statements
- Other matters to consider including level of subjectivity, lack of informed management (1 mark each)
- Safeguards may be used to reduce threat to acceptable level (1 mark each)

Maximum   6

Total   20

(a) **Tetbury Ltd**

Professional competence

Tetbury operates in the highly-regulated, complex environment of financial services. There is therefore a threat to Chester & Co's ability to conduct an audit in this area in line with the principle of professional competence and due care. This is a self-interest threat as a result of the prospective audit fee.

Customer due diligence

Given the complex and therefore risky nature of Tetbury's business environment, it is of paramount importance that Chester & Co conducts customer due diligence procedures before accepting such a client. The risk of Tetbury being involved in laundering money should be weighed carefully.

Previous auditors

The fact that the previous auditors resigned suggests that Tetbury's management may lack integrity. There is a risk that the problems which led to the previous auditors resigning may persist during the tenure of Chester & Co.

Chester & Co should ask Tetbury for permission to contact the previous auditors regarding the reasons for their resignation. They should be asked whether there are any matters of which Chester & Co should be made aware of in deciding whether to take on the audit. This is a self-interest threat to professional competence and due care, because Chester & Co may fail to exercise due care in order to secure the audit fee.

If Tetbury refuses permission to contact the previous auditors, then Chester & Co should withdraw from the tender process.

Controls

The fact that the reason given for the previous auditors' resignation points to a poor control environment at Tetbury. This is particularly worrisome given that it is an owner-managed business, in which the risk of management override of controls is perennially present. Bearing in mind also the increased need for robust internal controls in as highly-regulated an area as financial services, the Tetbury audit would surely be considered high-risk.

As a high-risk audit, Chester & Co would likely need to perform more audit procedures in order to reduce audit risk to an appropriate level. This would be costly, and would need to be reflected in a high audit fee. The threat to Chester & Co's professional competence is in this light particularly acute. Chester & Co would need to consider carefully whether the Tetbury audit would be worth such a high risk.

Financial services authority investigation

The investigation suggests either a lack of integrity or a poor control environment, or both. In any event Chester & Co ought to find out more about this, for example by contacting the authority for further details.

Business development advice

There is a self-interest threat here in relation to the fee. There is a self-review threat as it is possible that the advice may need to be audited, for example as part of the assessment of the going concern assumption.

The self-review threat can be mitigated by using separate engagement teams, separated by information barriers, or by an independent review of the audit work by a professional accountant.

It is important that Chester & Co avoids taking on a management responsibilities, because were they to do so the tender must be declined as a result of what ES 5 *Non-audit services provided to audited entities* describes as a management threat. Chester & Co must consider whether management is capable of making independent judgements and decisions on the basis of information provided. The threat can be avoided by obtaining written confirmation from Tetbury that it acknowledges responsibility for any decisions taken.

(b)   **Stratford Ltd**

Meeting

The request to attend the meeting with the bank suggests an advocacy threat, as the audit partner may be put in the position of supporting the view that the client will continue as a going concern, and that the bank should therefore offer it a loan.

There is also a management threat (ES 5) if Chester & Co finds itself making judgements and decisions which are really management's responsibility.

Legally, there is a risk of creating proximity between Chester & Co and Stratford which could result in the bank taking legal action against the auditor in the even of Stratford defaulting on its loan.

In addition, the financial statements being presented at the meeting are only draft versions and have not been audited. It is crucial that Chester & Co does not allow Stratford to give the bank the impression that these financial statements come with any assurance.

It would probably not be possible to mitigate the advocacy threat with the audit engagement partner attending the meeting. It may be possible for another partner to attend, however, if it was made clear that they were not the audit partner and that no assurance was provided in respect of the draft financial statements.

Threat

The managing director's threat to put the audit out to tender is an intimidation threat, since if the audit partner were to attend the meeting, this may give the bank the false impression that assurance has been provided on the draft financial statements.

This places a question mark over the managing director's integrity. Chester & Co should communicate with those charged with governance on this matter, for example with any other board members or with the audit committee. Chester & Co should consider resigning from the audit if the threat does not abate.

Fees

Overdue fees represent a self-interest threat per the IESBA *Code of Ethics* and ES 4 *Fees, remuneration and evaluation policies, litigation, gifts and hospitality*, as Chester & Co may not obtain sufficient appropriate evidence in relation to the audit opinion it expresses in order to receive the fees owing. There is also a risk that this may be perceived to be a loan made to Stratford.

In this case the fee relates to a debt that is only four months old, which reduces the seriousness of the problem. The severity of the threat would depend on the significance of the amount outstanding.

There is a risk that Stratford may not be able to pay the fees as a result of its problems with going concern. ES 4 notes that the engagement partner should consider whether the resulting self-interest threat is outweighed by the benefit to the public of continuing to act as auditor to a firm which might find it difficult to find a successor auditor were it to resign.

Chester & Co should request that the audit fee be paid, and should communicate the matter to those charged with governance. It may also wish to review the efficacy of its own system for credit control.

(c) **Banbury Ltd**

Threats

There is a self-interest threat here in respect of the fee for the non-assurance service.

A self-review threat is present because the partner's actuarial valuation may need to be audited, in which case Chester & Co would be reviewing its own work. It is not clear whether the audit partner in question is an audit engagement partner for the Banbury audit. If this is the case then the service cannot be performed unless the engagement partner is changed.

Assuming that the partner involved is not the engagement partner, and subject to the further considerations below, relevant safeguards here could include:

- Using separate teams to work on the actuarial valuation and on the audit, separated by information barriers
- Independent review of the audit and/or the valuation by an independent professional

Valuation

In assessing the significance of the self-review threat, a number of factors must be considered. Chief among these are:

- The materiality of the valuation to the audited financial statements
- The degree of subjectivity involved in the valuation
- The extent to which the client is involved in making any judgements necessary to the valuation

If, for instance, the valuation involves a high degree of subjectivity, and cannot be performed according to an established methodology then the self-review threat might be considered severe.

Materiality

Banbury is a listed – and therefore public interest – entity, so its auditor must not provide valuation services which materially affect the financial statements.

The pension liability was 0.3% of total assets last year and was thus immaterial. If the figures this year are similar, then materiality would not be a barrier to providing the service.

Question 5

Marking scheme

Marks

(a)   **Going concern indicators**

Up to 1½ marks for each going concern indicator discussed, for example:
– Declining profitability and implication
– Poor liquidity – inability to pay suppliers/employees/overheads
– Poor liquidity – breach of loan covenant and implication
– Development of new product is a further drain on cash
– Success of new product is not guaranteed

Procedures on cash flow forecast

Generally 1 mark for each well-described procedure:
– Agreement of the opening cash position to the audited financial statements and general ledger or bank reconciliation
– Confirmation that casting of the cash flow forecast has been reperformed
– Review of the results of any market research which has been conducted on the GreenFire product
– Discussion of the progress made on GreenFire's development with a technical expert or engineer
– Review of correspondence with existing customers to gauge the level of interest in GreenFire and confirm if any orders have yet been placed
– A review of any sales documentation relating to the planned sale of plant and equipment
– Physical inspection of the plant and equipment to be sold, to gauge its condition and the likelihood of sale
– Review of any announcement made regarding the redundancies
– Sample testing of a selection of those being made redundant, agreeing the amount they are to be paid to HR records
– Correspondence from the government department of the £30,000 grant to be received
– If the grant of £30,000 has been received, agree to cash book and bank statement
– Agreement that the cash flow forecast is consistent with profit and other financial forecasts which have been prepared by management
– Confirmation that any other assumptions used in the cash flow forecast are consistent with auditor's knowledge of the business and with management's intentions regarding the future of the company

- Comparison of the cash flow forecast for the period August–November 2013 with management accounts for the same period
- Analytical review of the items included in the cash flow forecast, for example, categories of expenses, to look for items which may have been omitted

Maximum   14

(b) **Implications for auditor's report and audit completion**

Generally up to 1½ marks for each point discussed:
- Review adequacy of note
- Evaluate its compliance with applicable financial reporting requirements

If note is adequate:
- No modification of auditor's opinion
- Emphasis of Matter paragraph to be included (up to 3 marks for discussion of its contents and positioning)
- Discuss use of EOM with those charged with governance

If note is not adequate:
- Non-compliance with financial reporting requirements therefore material misstatement
- Auditor's judgement as to whether misstatement is material or pervasive
- Content of Basis of Opinion paragraph
- Discuss modification of opinion with those charged with governance

Maximum   6

Total   20

(a) (i) **Performance**

Burford's decline from a healthy profit to a £0.5m loss is a veritable fall from grace. This appears to result from the obsolescence of its QuickFire product and the corresponding disappearance of as much as 45% of its revenue.

Profitability looks set to tumble still further in the coming year as the effect of the QuickFire's absence is felt for the full year.

Although Burford does have a replacement lined up in the form of the GreenFire, any new product will take time to gain market share and it is unlikely that such a product will reverse the declining trend in the immediate future.

Liquidity

Burford's worsening current and quick ratios paint a bleak portrait of declining liquidity. With current liabilities greater than current assets the company may be unable to pay its debts as they fall due, and may therefore be illiquid. If suppliers are not paid then they may restrict supply or refuse to extend credit to Burford, which could make trading impossible.

Moreover, if there are any items of the QuickFire still in inventory then impairment losses may have to be recognised in respect of them, in which case these ratios will decline even further.

The outlook of declining revenue and increasing costs (for example, marketing costs to help establish the new GreenFire) threatens to heap solvency problems on top of the liquidity problems.

Cash position

Burford's cash balance of £25,000 is very low, at only 0.2% of total assets. It is unlikely that Burford could survive for long with such little cash. It is not known whether Burford has any overdraft facility available to it which might help it survive at least a little longer.

Loan covenant

Given that the current and quick ratios have declined still further since the year end, it is possible that the covenant has been breached already. If the loan is recalled (as seems likely), the cash balance of £25,000 will be insufficient to repay it.

Burford may have to sell assets in order to repay the loan, which could put its future operations in jeopardy.

GreenFire launch

Burford's lack of working capital may make it impossible for it to fund the development and launch of the new product, which would surely be a fatal blow to its going concern.

    (ii)   **Evidence**

- Agreement of opening cash position to audited financial statements to ensure accuracy of extracted figures

- Re-cast of forecast to check arithmetical accuracy

- A review of results of market research on GreenFire, to ensure the assumption regarding its successful launch is appropriate

- Discussion of progress made on GreenFire's development with a technical expert, to gauge the likelihood of a successful launch

- A review of correspondence with customers to gauge interest in GreenFire and confirm if any orders have been placed

- A review of sales documentation relating to the sale of plant and equipment to confirm that £50,000 is achievable

- Physical inspection of plant and equipment to be sold, to gauge its condition and the likelihood of sale

- A review of any announcement made regarding the redundancies, to confirm the number of employees affected and the timing

- Sample testing of a selection of those being made redundant, agreeing the amount to be paid to HR records, to ensure accuracy of figures in the forecast

- A review of the application made to the government to confirm the amount of the grant. Confirmation to correspondence from government department of the £30,000 to be received

- Agreement that the cash flow forecast is consistent with profit and other financial forecasts prepared by management

- Confirmation that any other assumptions used in the cash flow forecast are consistent with auditor's knowledge of the business and with management's intentions

- Comparison of the cash flow forecast for the period August–November 20X3 with management accounts for the same period, to ensure accuracy of the forecast

- Analytical review of the items included in the cash flow forecast, for example, categories of expenses, to look for items which may have been omitted

(b)   IAS 1 *Presentation of Financial Statements* requires detailed disclosures to be made in the situations where there is significant doubt over going concern. A brief note is unlikely to suffice, since the note must describe the reasons for the doubt together with management's plans for dealing with them.

The key issue is whether or not the disclosure is adequate.

Adequate disclosure

In this case IAS 1 has been complied with, so the financial statements are not materially misstated. In this case the auditor is nevertheless required to include an Emphasis of Matter paragraph in the auditor's report.

This would draw users' attention to the disclosure note in the financial statements, and would itself contain a description of the uncertain conditions around going concern. The paragraph should be placed immediately after the Opinion paragraph, and should state that the auditor's opinion is not qualified.

The auditor should communicate with those charged with governance of Burford regarding the modification of the auditor's report.

Inadequate disclosure

In this case there is a material misstatement in respect of IAS 1. The question for the auditor is whether the misstatement is simply material, or both material and pervasive. In the former case, a Qualified Opinion would be expressed, and in the latter case an Adverse Opinion would be expressed.

In both cases the Basis for Qualified/Adverse Opinion paragraph would state the reasons for the modified opinion, and would clearly describe the material uncertainties giving rise to significant doubts about going concern. This paragraph would be placed immediately before the Opinion paragraph itself.

The auditor should discuss the situation with those charged with governance, giving them an opportunity to amend the financial statements in respect of the inadequate disclosure.

ACCA examiner's answers:
June and December 2013 papers

Note. The ACCA examiner's answers are correct at the time of going to press but may be subject to some amendments before the final versions are published

The June 2013 questions are located in the kit as follows:

June question number	Kit question reference
1	32
2	5
3	27
4	15
5	63

The December 2013 questions form Mock Exam 3 in this kit. Please note that the December 2013 answers (ME3) and the ACCA examiner's answers have not been updated for any technical changes coming into effect for exams in 2014 and 2015.

1   **Briefing notes**

   To: Audit Partner
   From: Audit Manager
   Regarding: Audit planning issues in relation to Parker Ltd

   Introduction

   These briefing notes include the results of a preliminary analytical review and evaluate the audit risks to be considered in planning the audit of Parker Ltd for the year ending 30 June 2013, and identify additional information required. In addition, ethical issues will be discussed and appropriate actions recommended.

   Results of audit risk evaluation

   The appendix to the briefing notes contains the detailed results of the analytical review performed, which are evaluated in the following section.

   Profitability

   Parker Ltd's profitability has declined, with gross profit falling by 21.5% and operating profit by 32.7%. The company's revenue has fallen by 8.2%.

   Ratio analysis shows that both gross and operating margins have fallen, the projected gross profit margin at the year end is 27.2% (2012 – 31.8%) and the projected operating margin is 11.4% (2012 – 15.6%). The return on capital employed also shows significant decline, falling from 6.2% to 3.8%. The declines can be explained by a price cutting strategy, difficult economic conditions, and the costs of the legal claim of the company amplify the fall in profitability.

   The trends in profitability cause going concern issues. If the company's results do not improve next year, for example, if the new organic range of goods is not successful, the company may become loss-making, especially if margins are squeezed by further price cuts.

   Some further information would be helpful to make a more detailed assessment of profitability, for example, an analysis of revenue and profit by product range, which would allow margins to be calculated for individual product ranges to identify those that are particularly underperforming. In addition, the results of any market research that has been performed on the new organic product range to evaluate the potential of the development to generate future profit.

   Further adjustments may be necessary to the financial statements, which may reduce the current year's profit further. These adjustments relate to possible incorrect accounting treatments applied to the provision, development costs, finance costs and tax expense, which are discussed later in the briefing notes.

   Liquidity

   The company's cash position has deteriorated dramatically during the year, moving from a positive cash balance of £1 million, to a projected overdraft of £900,000 at the year end. Analytical review shows that the current and quick ratios have both deteriorated, and it is projected that current assets will not cover current liabilities, as the current ratio projected at the year end is 0.96 (2012 – 1.8). Parker Ltd will therefore find it difficult to pay liabilities as they fall due, increasing the going concern risk.

   Payables days have increased from 63 days to 86 days; this indicates that the company is experiencing difficulties making payments to suppliers as they fall due. This could result in supplier relationships deteriorating and they may stop supplying Parker Ltd if they see them as a 'risky' customer. Suppliers may also restrict the credit terms offered to Parker Ltd, causing further working capital problems.

   Receivables days have increased from 34 to 42; this could be as a result of poor credit control. A significant control deficiency could affect our overall risk assessment of the client. Alternatively, the increased receivables balance could be the result of irrecoverable debts that require a provision to be made against them; this could further affect profit levels if such a provision is required.

   The current and quick ratios will deteriorate further if an adjustment is necessary in respect of the provision, which has been recognised for a potential penalty payment (discussed further below).

Working capital also seems to be a problem, with inventory holding period, receivables collection period and trade payables period all increasing. The inventory holding period is perhaps the most significant, increasing from 136 days to 167 days. This shows that a large amount of working capital is tied up in inventory, and it is likely that some of these goods are obsolete (for example, ranges of cosmetics that are out of fashion) and will never generate a cash flow.

This creates a further audit risk that the inventory is overstated and needs to be written off to net realisable value. Any write off necessary will put further pressure on the gross profit margin.

Solvency

Parker Ltd's gearing ratio is projected to increase from 0·8 to 1. This indicates a high level of gearing, and the company may, as a result, find it difficult to raise further finance if required, again increasing the going concern risk. The company extended its bank loan during the year and now also has a significant overdraft. It seems very reliant on finance from its bank, and it may be that the bank will be reluctant to offer any further finance, especially in the current economic climate.

It will be important to obtain the details of the bank loan and overdraft, as this will impact on the going concern assessment. In particular, additional information is needed on the overdraft limit to determine how close the current and projected overdraft is to the limit.

The interest cover has fallen from 10.6 to 5.7. Based on these figures, there still appears to be plenty of profit to cover the finance charges, but of course there is a lack of cash in the company, meaning that payments of interest and capital may be difficult.

Any payables who are not paid within a certain amount of time may consider action against the company to recover their debts, for example, a compulsory liquidation petition could be filed in court against the company.

Going concern issues – summary

Parker Ltd is not technically insolvent, as it is still in a position of net assets. However, clearly there are significant issues with working capital management and longer term solvency, which mean that if next year's cash flows continue to worsen, it may not be long before the company is facing insolvency.

To help the risk assessment in relation to cash management, a statement of cash flows projected to the year end would be useful. This is important in order to analyse the main cash generating activities and, more importantly, where cash has been used during the year. A cash flow forecast for at least the next 12 months would also help with going concern assessment.

It seems appropriate to prioritise going concern issues as a significant audit risk. As discussed above, Parker Ltd's lack of cash, working capital problems and reliance on the overdraft all give rise to a cause for concern over the long-term future of the company. Though it is not particularly relevant to this year's audit, the decision to take out a finance lease in respect of future capital expenditure indicates that management is concerned about the lack of cash being generated by the business.

Finance charge

The finance charge expensed in the statement of profit or loss and other comprehensive income appears very low when compared to the company's level of interest bearing debt and its overdraft. To illustrate, the year-end interest bearing debt and overdraft is £12.725 million (£11.825 million non-current liabilities + £900,000 overdraft), which when compared to the finance charge for the year of £155,000 implies an overall interest rate on all interest bearing debt of only 1.2%. This seems very low, especially when the preference shares have an interest rate of 2%.

This rough calculation indicates that finance charges may be understated. This may also be the case for the comparative figures and creates significant audit risk. If the finance cost needs to be increased, this will further reduce profit before tax and could cause either or both years to become loss-making.

There is a risk that the dividend paid to preference shareholders has been incorrectly accounted for as a distribution from retained earnings, but the correct treatment would be to include the dividend within finance charges, in accordance with IAS 32 *Financial Instruments: Presentation*.

Further information is needed, such as the dates that new finance leases were taken out, the interest rates applicable to each interest-bearing balance and the annual payment due to preference shareholders. This will help to assess whether the finance charge is at risk of understatement.

Tax expense

The effective tax rate based on the projected figures for 2013 is 9.5% (70 / 735), compared to 25% (300 / 1,197) in 2012. The tax expense for 2013 seems low and it is possible that a proper estimate has not yet been made of tax payable. The statement of financial position shows a tax payable figure of £50,000 whereas the tax expense is £70,000. This also indicates that the tax figures are not correct and will need to be adjusted.

Provision

A provision in relation to a fine against the company has been recognised in cost of sales. There are two audit risks in relation to this item. First, the provision may not be measured correctly. £450,000 is the amount of the potential amount payable, but only £250,000 has been provided. According to IAS 37 *Provisions, Contingent Liabilities and Contingent Assets*, a provision should be recognised where there is a present obligation as a result of a past event, a probable outflow of economic benefit and a reliable estimate can be made. Assuming that these criteria have been met, it would be reasonable to expect the full amount of the fine against the company to be provided. Therefore, there is a risk that profit is overstated and current liabilities are understated by £200,000. Additional information is needed from management to understand the rationale behind the amount that has been provided.

Furthermore, the provision has been charged to cost of sales. This is not the normal classification of items of this type, which would usually be classified as an operating expense. A presentation risk therefore arises, which affects the gross and operating profit figures. If the full amount of the provision were recognised in operating expenses, the operating margin for 2013 would only be 8·9%.

Development cost

A significant amount, £2.25 million, has been capitalised during the year in relation to costs arising on development of the new organic product range. This represents 8.3% of total assets. There is a risk that this has been inappropriately capitalised, as IAS 38 *Intangible Assets* only permits the capitalisation of development costs as an internally generated intangible asset when certain criteria have been met. There is therefore a risk that non-current assets and operating profit are overstated by £2.25 million if the criteria have not been met, for example, if market research does not demonstrate that the new product will generate a future economic benefit. There is also a risk that inappropriate expenses, such as revenue expenses or costs of developing a brand name for the organic range of products, have been capitalised incorrectly.

This is a significant risk, as if an adjustment were necessary to write off the intangible asset, the profit for the year of £665,000 would become a loss for the year of £1·585 million, and retained earnings would become retained losses of £975,000. Retained losses add to the risk of insolvency, and, overall, if the new product is not successful in generating profits from its launch date, this would add significant pressure to cash flow management and increases the risk of payables bringing insolvency proceedings against the company.

Revaluation of properties

A revaluation during the year has led to an increase in the revaluation reserve of £500,000, representing 1.8% of total assets. Despite the valuations being performed by an independent expert, we should be alert to the risk that non-current assets could be overstated in value. This is especially the case given that Parker Ltd faces solvency problems resulting in potential management bias to improve the financial position of the company. Information is needed on the expert to ensure the valuation is objective, thereby reducing the audit risk.

There is also a risk that depreciation was not re-measured at the point of the revaluation, leading to understated expenses.

The revaluation should also have a deferred tax consequence according to IAS 12 *Income Taxes*, as the revaluation gives rise to a taxable temporary difference. If a deferred tax liability is not recognised, the statement of financial position is at risk of misstatement through understated liabilities. Currently there is no

deferred tax liability recognised, indicating that liabilities are understated. The same is true for the comparative figures, so an adjustment may be needed in the opening balances.

Finally, a further audit risk is incorrect or inadequate disclosure in the notes to the financial statements. IAS 16 *Property, Plant and Equipment* requires extensive disclosure of matters such as the methods and significant assumptions used to estimate fair values, the effective date of the revaluation and whether an independent valuer was used, as well as numerical disclosures. The revaluation gain should also be disclosed as Other Comprehensive Income and there is a risk that this disclosure is not made. The financial statements provided by Ruth Collie do not contain any items of Other Comprehensive Income and the risk is that the financial statements have not been prepared in accordance with IAS 1 *Presentation of Financial Statements.*

Payroll

Parker Ltd's internal audit team found control deficiencies when auditing the processing of overtime payments. Additional information is needed on the nature of the deficiencies in order to determine the significance of them, and to plan our approach to the audit of overtime payments. The fact that the processing is no longer carried out by human resources could indicate that the problems were significant. We also need to know the monetary value of the overtime payments to determine its materiality to the financial statements.

The fact that the finance function is now performing the processing will affect our assessment of control risk. On one hand, finance department members should be familiar with the operation of internal controls and understand their importance, which would reduce control risk. However, as all of the processing is now done by one department there is less segregation of duty, which could lead to higher control risk.

New client

Parker Ltd is a new client, and therefore our firm lacks cumulative knowledge and experience of the business. This increases our detection risk somewhat, but this will be mitigated by thorough planning, including developing an understanding of the business including the internal control environment.

There may also be risks attached to the comparative information and opening balances, especially as the audit risk evaluation has highlighted some potential areas of concern.

Appendix: Results of preliminary analytical review

	2013	2012
Profitability:		
Gross profit margin:		
Gross profit/revenue	2,120 / 7,800 = 27.2%	2,700 / 8,500 = 31.8%
Operating profit margin:		
Operating profit/revenue	890 / 7,800 = 11.4%	1,322 / 8,500 = 15.6%
Operating profit margin for 2013 adjusted to include full amount of provision	890 – 200 / 7,800 = 8.9%	
Return on capital employed:		
Operating profit/capital employed	890 / 11,775 + 11,825 = 3.8%	1,322 / 11,455 + 9,725 = 6.2%
Return on capital employed adjusted to include full amount of provision	890 – 200 / 11,775 + 11,825 = 2.9%	
Liquidity:		
Current ratio:		
Current assets/current liabilities	3,500 / 3,650 = 0.96	3,965 / 2,185 = 1.8
Quick ratio:		
Current assets – inventory/current liabilities	3,500 – 2,600 / 3,650 = 0.25	3,965 – 2,165 / 2,185 = 0.82
Inventory holding period:		
Inventory/cost of sales × 365	2,600 / 5,680 × 365 = 167 days	2,165 / 5,800 × 365 = 136 days
Receivables collection period:		
Receivables/revenue × 365	900 / 7,800 × 365 = 42 days	800 / 8,500 × 365 = 34 days
Trade payables payment period:		
Trade payables/cost of sales × 365	1,340 / 5,680 × 365 = 86 days	1,000 / 5,800 × 365 = 63 days

	2013	2012
Gearing:		
Gearing ratio:		
Long-term liabilities/equity	11,825 / 11,775 = 1	9,725 / 11,455 = 0.8
Interest cover:		
Operating profit/finance costs	890 / 155 = 5.7	1,322 / 125 = 10.6

Tutorial note. Credit will be awarded for calculation of ratios on alternative bases and using different assumptions, as long as stated. Credit will also be awarded for relevant trend analysis.

Ethical matters

Parker Ltd is intending to acquire Beauty Boost Ltd, which is an audit client of our firm. This raises an ethical issue, as the auditor could be involved with advising both the acquirer and the intended target company in relation to the acquisition, which could create a conflict of interest. IESBA's (IFAC) *Code of Ethics for Professional Accountants* states that in relation to the fundamental principle of objectivity, an auditor should not allow bias, conflict of interest or undue influence of others to override professional or business judgements.

IESBA's Code requires that, when faced with a potential conflict of interest, an auditor shall evaluate the significance of any threats and apply safeguards when necessary to eliminate the threats or reduce them to an acceptable level.

An important safeguard is that both parties should be notified of the potential conflict of interest in relation to the planned acquisition. The notification should outline that a conflict of interest may exist and consent should be obtained from both Parker Ltd and Beauty Boost Ltd for our firm, Hound & Co, to act for both in relation to the acquisition. If the requested consent is not obtained, the auditor should not continue to act for one of the parties in relation to this matter.

The auditor shall also determine whether to apply one or more of the following additional safeguards.

- The use of separate engagement teams

- Procedures to prevent access to information (for example, strict physical separation of such teams, confidential and secure data filing)

- Clear guidelines for members of the engagement team on issues of security and confidentiality

- The use of confidentiality agreements signed by employees and partners of the firm

- Regular review of the application of safeguards by a senior individual not involved with relevant client engagements

If the conflict of interest creates a threat to objectivity or confidentiality that cannot be eliminated or reduced to an acceptable level through the application of safeguards, Hound & Co should not advise Parker Ltd regarding the acquisition.

Parker Ltd has specifically requested advice on financing the acquisition. IESBA's Code has specific guidance on such activities, which are corporate finance activities. Guidance is also given in Ethical Standard 5 (Revised) *Non-audit services provided to audited entities*.

The provision of such services can create self-review, management and advocacy threats to objectivity. The advocacy threat arises as the audit firm could be put in a position of promoting the audit client's interests, for example, when negotiating financial arrangements. The self-review threat arises because the financing arrangements will directly affect amounts that will be reported in the financial statements on which the firm will provide an opinion. There is also a risk that the audit firm will take on a management role, unless the firm is working with informed management.

The significance of any threat must be evaluated and safeguards applied when necessary to eliminate the threat or reduce it to an acceptable level. Examples of such safeguards given in ES 5 include ensuring that:

- The corporate finance advice is provided by partners and staff who have no involvement with the audit of the financial statements

- Any advice provided is reviewed by an independent corporate finance partner within the audit firm

- External independent advice on the corporate finance work is obtained

- An audit partner, who is not involved with the audit engagement, reviews the audit work performed in relation to the subject matter of the corporate finance services provided to ensure that such audit work has been properly and effectively reviewed and assessed in the context of the audit of the financial statements

The extent of the self-review threat should be evaluated, for example, by considering the materiality of the potential financing transactions to the financial statements, and the degree of subjectivity involved in determining the amounts to be recognised.

All of these matters must be assessed before agreeing to provide the corporate finance service to Parker Ltd and should be discussed with Parker Ltd's audit committee or those charged with governance. Where no safeguards could reduce the threat to an acceptable level, the corporate finance advice should not be provided.

Conclusion

These briefing notes have evaluated the audit risks to be considered in planning the audit of Parker Ltd, and going concern has been highlighted as a particular area of concern. Preliminary analytical review determined that Parker Ltd is facing problems with profitability, cash flow and long-term solvency. Our audit approach should focus on this issue. In addition, some specific areas of risk in relation to provisions, finance charges, tax and non-current assets have been identified. Further information as specified in the briefing notes should be requested from the client in order to complete our audit planning.

Our firm should also consider the ethical issues raised by acting for Parker Ltd and for its potential target acquisition. Furthermore, the provision of a specific corporate finance service to Parker Ltd must be evaluated as safeguards will be needed to reduce threats to an acceptable level.

2 Quality control, ethical and professional matters

There are many concerns raised regarding quality control. Audits should be conducted with adherence to ISA 220 (UK and Ireland) *Quality control for an audit of financial statements* and it seems that this has not happened in relation to the audit of the Retriever Group, which is especially concerning, given the Group obtaining a listing during the year. It would seem that the level of staffing on this assignment is insufficient, and that tasks have been delegated inappropriately to junior members of staff.

Time pressure

The junior's first comment is that the audit was time pressured. All audits should be planned to ensure that adequate time can be spent to obtain sufficient appropriate audit evidence to support the audit opinion. It seems that the audit is being rushed and the juniors instructed not to perform work properly, and that review procedures are not being conducted appropriately. All of this increases the detection risk of the audit and, ultimately, could lead to an inappropriate opinion being given.

Procedures not performed

The juniors have been told not to carry out some planned procedures on allegedly low risk areas of the audit because of time pressure. It is not acceptable to cut corners by leaving out audit procedures. Even if the balances are considered to be low risk, they could still contain misstatements. Directors' emoluments are related party transactions and are material by their nature and so should not be ignored. Also, a misstatement in relation to director's emoluments could breach the Companies Act disclosure requirements. Any modifications to the planned audit procedures should be discussed with, and approved by, senior members of the audit team and should only occur for genuine reasons.

Method of selecting sample

ISA 530 (UK and Ireland) *Audit sampling* requires that the auditor shall select items for the sample in such a way that each sampling unit in the population has a chance of selection. The audit manager favours non-statistical sampling as a quick way to select a sample, instead of the firm's usual statistical sampling method. There is a risk that changing the way that items are selected for testing will not provide sufficient, reliable audit evidence as the sample selected may no longer be representative of the population as a whole. Or that an insufficient number of items may be selected for testing. The juniors may not understand how to

pick a sample without the use of the audit firm's statistical selection method, and there is a risk that the sample may be biased towards items that appear 'easy to audit'. Again, this instruction from the audit manager is a departure from planned audit procedures, made worse by deviating from the audit firm's standard auditing methods, and likely to increase detection risk.

Audit of going concern

Going concern can be a difficult area to audit, and given the Group's listed status and the fact that losses appear to have been made this year in one of the subsidiaries, it seems unwise to delegate such an important area of the audit to an audit junior. The audit of going concern involves many subjective areas, such as evaluating assumptions made by management, analysing profit and cash flow forecasts and forming an overall opinion on the viability of the business. Therefore the going concern audit programme should be performed by a more senior and more experienced member of the audit team. This issue shows that the audit has not been well planned as appropriate delegation of work is a key part of direction and supervision, essential elements of good quality control.

Review of work

The juniors have been asked to review each other's work which is unacceptable. ISA 220 (UK and Ireland) requires that the engagement partner shall take responsibility for reviews being performed in accordance with the firm's review policies and procedures. Ideally, work should be reviewed by a person more senior and/or experienced than the person who conducted the work. Audit juniors reviewing each other's work are unlikely to spot mistakes, errors of judgement and inappropriate conclusions on work performed. The audit manager should be reviewing all of the work of the juniors, with the audit partner taking overall responsibility that all work has been appropriately reviewed.

Deferred tax

It is concerning that the client's financial controller is not able to calculate the deferred tax figure. This could indicate a lack of competence in the preparation of the financial statements, and the audit firm should consider if this impacts the overall assessment of audit risk.

The main issue is that the junior prepared the calculation for the client. IESBA's (IFAC) *Code of Ethics for Professional Accountants* states that providing an audit client with accounting and bookkeeping services, such as preparing accounting records or financial statements, creates a self-review threat when the firm subsequently audits the financial statements. The significance of the threat depends on the materiality of the balance and its level of subjectivity. In addition, Ethical Standard 5 *Non-audit services provided to audited entities* states that the provision of accounting services to an audit client creates a potential management threat, especially where the firm is not working with informed management at the audit client.

Clients often request technical assistance from the external auditor, and such services do not, generally, create threats to independence provided the firm does not assume a management responsibility for the client. However, the audit junior has gone beyond providing assistance and has calculated a figure to be included in the financial statements. The deferred tax asset that has been calculated is material to the financial statement, representing 11% of total assets. It is unclear why the junior was discussing the Group's tax position with the financial controller, as this is not the type of task that should normally be given to an audit junior.

ES 5 states that the audit firm shall not undertake an engagement to provide accounting services to an audited entity that is a listed company, except in emergency situations, or any audited entity where the accounting services involve the audit firm undertaking part of the role of management.

ES 5 also specifically states that where an audited entity is a listed entity, the audit firm shall not prepare current or deferred tax calculations that are reasonably expected to be material to the financial statements (except in emergency situations).

This would not appear to be an emergency situation (an example given in ES 5 of an emergency situation is where there is a need for the audit firm to provide accounting services arising from external and unforeseeable events and where the refusal of the audit firm to provide the service could affect the going concern status of the client).

Therefore the junior should not have calculated the deferred tax balance, and the calculations should be carefully reviewed and/or reperformed by management.

Tax planning

The audit junior should not be advising the client on tax planning matters. This is an example of a non-audit service, which can create self-review, management and advocacy threats to independence, with similar ethical threats arising as in the discussion above in relation to the provision of accounting services.

ES 5 states that the audit firm shall not provide tax services to an audited entity where the engagement would involve the audit firm undertaking a management role.

The junior's work on tax indicates that the audit has not been properly supervised, and that the junior does not seem to understand the ethical implications created. As part of a good quality control system, all members of the audit team should understand the objectives of the work they have been allocated and the limit to their responsibilities.

Planning a forensic investigation

Planning the investigation will involve consideration of similar matters to those involved in planning an audit.

The planning should commence with a meeting with the client at which the investigation is discussed. In particular, the investigation team should develop an understanding of the events surrounding the theft and the actions taken by the client since it occurred. Matters that should be clarified with the client include:

- The objective of the investigation – to quantify the amount to be claimed under the insurance cover

- Whether the client has informed the police and the actions taken by the police so far

- Whether the thieves have been captured and any stolen goods recovered

- Whether the thieves are suspected to be employees of the Group

- Any planned deadline by which time the insurance claim needs to be submitted

- Whether the client has contacted the insurance company and discussed the events leading to the potential claim

The insurance policy should be scrutinised to clarify the exact terms of the insurance, to ensure that both the finished goods and stolen lorry will be included in the claim. The period of the insurance cover should be checked, to ensure that the date of the theft is covered, and the client should confirm that payments to the insurance company are up to date, to ensure the cover has not lapsed.

The audit firm should also consider the resources that will be needed to conduct the work. Kennel & Co has a forensic accounting department, so will have staff with relevant skills, but the firm should consider if staff with specific experience of insurance claims work are available.

The client should confirm that the investigation team will have full access to information required, and are able to discuss the matter with the police and the insurance company without fear of breaching confidentiality.

The output of the investigation should be confirmed, which is likely to be a report addressed to the insurance company. It should be clarified that the report is not to be distributed to any other parties. Kennel & Co should also confirm whether they would be required to act as expert witness in the event of the thieves being caught and prosecuted.

Tutorial note. Credit will also be awarded for explanations of acceptance issues such as the need for a separate engagement letter drawn up to cover the forensic investigation, outlining the responsibilities of the investigation team and of the client. Fees should also be discussed and agreed.

Recommended procedures

- Watch the CCTV to form an impression of the quantity of goods stolen, for example, how many boxes were loaded onto the lorry.

- If possible, from the CCTV, determine if the boxes contain either mobile phones or laptop computers.

- Inspect the boxes of goods remaining in the warehouse to determine how many items of finished goods are in each box.

- Agree the cost of an individual mobile phone and laptop computer to accounting records, such as cost cards.

- Perform an inventory count on the boxes of goods remaining in the warehouse and reconcile to the latest inventory movement records.

- Discuss the case with the police to establish if any of the goods have been recovered and if, in the opinion of the police, this is likely to happen.

- Obtain details of the stolen lorry, for example the licence plate, and agree the lorry back to the non-current asset register where its net book value should be shown.

3 (a) Matters

The properties classified as assets held for sale are material to the financial statements as the year-end carrying value of £24 million represent 8% of total assets. The amount written off the assets' value at the date of classification as held for sale of £2 million represents less than 1% of revenue and 4.2% of profit before tax, which on both measures is immaterial to the statement of profit or loss and other comprehensive income.

Assets can only be classified as held for sale if the conditions referred to in IFRS 5 *Non-current Assets Held for Sale and Discontinued Operations* are met. The conditions include the following.

- Management is committed to a plan to sell.

- The assets are available for immediate sale.

- An active programme to locate a buyer is initiated.

- The sale is highly probable, within 12 months of classification as held for sale (subject to limited exceptions).

- The asset is being actively marketed for sale at a sales price reasonable in relation to its fair value.

- Actions required to complete the plan indicate that it is unlikely that the plan will be significantly changed or withdrawn.

There is a risk that the assets have been inappropriately classified if the above conditions have not been met.

IFRS 5 requires that at classification as held for sale, assets are measured at the lower of carrying value and fair value less costs to sell. This appears to have been correctly accounted for when classification occurred in October 2012. Though not specifically required by IFRS 5, an impairment review should take place at 31 January 2013, to ensure that there is no further impairment of the properties to be recognised at the year end. If an impairment review has not taken place, the assets may be misstated in value.

The assets should not be depreciated after being classified as held for sale, therefore audit procedures should confirm that depreciation has ceased from October 2012.

Disclosure is needed in the notes to the financial statements to include a description of the non-current assets classified as held for sale, a description of the facts and circumstances of the sale and its expected timing, and a quantification of the impairment loss and where in the statement of profit or loss and other comprehensive income it is recognised.

Evidence

- A copy of the board minute at which the disposal of the properties was agreed by management

- Details of the active programme in place to locate a buyer, for example, instructions given to a real estate agency, marketing literature

- A copy of any minutes of meetings held with prospective purchasers of any of the properties, or copies of correspondence with them

- Written representation from management on the opinion that the assets will be sold before October 2013

- Subsequent events review, including a review of post year-end board minutes and a review of significant cash transactions, to confirm if any properties are sold in the period after the year end

- Details of any impairment review conducted by management on the properties at 31 January 2013

- A copy of the client's depreciation calculations, to confirm that depreciation was charged up to October 2012 but not subsequent to the reclassification of the assets as held for sale

(b) **Matters**

The sale and leaseback arrangement relates to an asset with a carrying value of £27 million, which represents 9% of total assets and is material to the statement of financial position. The fair value of the asset (cash proceeds) is also material at 12.3% of total assets.

It appears appropriate to classify the leaseback as a finance lease, as Setter Stores Ltd retains the risk exposure of the asset and the economic benefit of using the asset for the remainder of its useful life.

The accounting treatment for a sale and leaseback transaction should follow the requirements of IAS 17 *Leases*. Where the leaseback is a finance lease, the substance of the transaction is a financing arrangement in which the lessee, in this case Setter Stores Ltd, never disposes of the risks and rewards of the asset, and so should not recognise a profit or loss on the disposal and should continue to recognise the asset in the statement of financial position. Any apparent profit, being the difference between the fair value of the asset and its carrying value, should be deferred and amortised over the lease term. The asset should be re-measured to fair value.

Setter Stores Ltd appears to have incorrectly accounted for the transaction. The following entry should have been made on the disposal and leaseback of the property complex.

Dr	Cash	£37 million
Cr	Property, plant and equipment	£27 million
Cr	Deferred income	£10 million

And the asset and finance lease liability should be recognised at fair value:

| Dr | Property, plant and equipment | £37 million |
| Cr | Obligations under finance lease | £37 million |

Therefore property, plant and equipment is understated by £10 million and deferred income also understated by £10 million.

£10 million represents 3.3% of total assets and is material. An adjustment should be made and, if not, the audit firm should consider the implication for the auditor's opinion, which may be qualified on the grounds of material misstatement.

In forthcoming accounting periods, depreciation should be calculated based on the £37 million carrying value of the asset allocated over the remaining life of the property of 20 years, and the deferred income should be amortised over the same period.

Evidence

- A copy of the lease, signed by the lessor, and a review of its major clauses to confirm that risk and reward remains with

- Setter Stores Ltd, and that the arrangement is a finance leaseback

- A copy of insurance documents stating that Setter Stores Ltd is responsible for insuring the asset

- Physical inspection of the property complex to confirm it is being used by Setter Stores Ltd

- Confirmation of the fair value of the property complex, possibly using an auditor's expert

- Agreement of the £37 million cash proceeds to bank statement and cash book

- A schedule showing the adjustment required in the financial statements

- Minutes of a discussion with management regarding the accounting treatment and including an auditor's request to amend the financial statements

(c) **Matters**

The amount capitalised as an intangible asset is material to the statement of financial position, representing 5% of total assets.

According to IAS 38 Intangible Assets, an intangible asset is recognised in the financial statements if it meets the definition of an intangible asset, if it is probable that future economic benefits will flow to the reporting entity, and if its cost can be reliably measured. It would seem appropriate that the licence is recognised as an intangible asset as it has been purchased as a separable asset without physical substance and has a reliable cost. Management should be able to demonstrate the economic benefit that has been, or is expected to be, derived from the licence.

As the licence has a fixed term of five years, it should be amortised over that period. However, it appears that amortisation has not been charged, as the amount recognised at the year end is the original cost of the licence. Amortisation of £1.25 million (15 million / 5 years × 5 / 12) should have been charged from 1 September to the year end. This amount represents less than 1% of revenue and only 2.6% of profit before tax, and is not considered material to profit.

Evidence

- A copy of the distribution licence, confirming the five-year period of the licence, and the cost of £15 million

- Agreement of the cash paid to the bank statement and the cash book

- Minutes of a discussion with management regarding the apparent non-amortisation of the licence, including any reasons given for the non-amortisation

- Sales records in relation to the soft drink and also forecast sales, to determine the future economic benefit to be derived from the licence

4 (a) **Spaniel Ltd**

It is not the auditor's primary responsibility to detect fraud. According to ISA 240 (UK and Ireland) *The auditor's responsibilities relating to fraud in an audit of financial statements*, management is primarily responsible for preventing and detecting fraud. The auditor is required to obtain reasonable assurance that the financial statements are free from material misstatement whether caused by fraud or error.

The total amount estimated to have been stolen in the payroll fraud represents 5.6% of Spaniel Ltd's assets. If the amount has been stolen consistently over a 12-month period, then £3 million (8 / 12 × 4.5 million) had been stolen prior to the year end of 31 December 2012. £3 million is material, representing 3.8% of total assets at the year end. Therefore the fraud was material and it could be reasonably expected that it should have been discovered.

However, material misstatements arising due to fraud can be difficult for the auditor to detect. This is because fraud is deliberately hidden by the perpetrators using sophisticated accounting techniques established to conceal the fraudulent activity. False statements may be made to the auditors and documents may have been forged. This means that material frauds could go undetected, even if appropriate procedures have been carried out.

ISA 240 requires that an audit is performed with an attitude of professional skepticism. This may not have been the case. Spaniel Ltd is a long-standing client, and the audit team may have lost their skeptical attitude. Necessary tests of control on payroll were not carried out because in previous years it had been possible to rely on the client's controls.

It seems that ISAs (UK and Ireland) may not have been adhered to during the audit of Spaniel Ltd. ISA 330 (UK and Ireland) *The auditor's responses to assessed risks* requires that the auditor shall design and perform tests of controls to obtain sufficient appropriate audit evidence as to the operating effectiveness of relevant controls if the auditor's assessment of risks of material misstatement at the assertion level includes an expectation that the controls are operating effectively. It can be acceptable for the auditor to use audit evidence from a previous audit about the operating effectiveness of specific controls but only if the auditor confirms that no changes have taken place. The audit partner should explain whether this was the case.

Substantive procedures have not been performed on payroll either. This effectively means that payroll has not been audited.

This leads to a conclusion that the audit firm may have been negligent in conducting the audit. Negligence is a common law concept in which an injured party must prove three things in order to prove that negligence has occurred:

- That the auditor owes a duty of care

- That the duty of care has been breached

- That financial loss has been caused by the negligence

Looking at these points in turn, Groom & Co owes a duty of care to Spaniel Ltd, because a contract exists between the two parties. The company represents all the shareholders as a body, and there is an automatic duty of care owed to the shareholders as a body by the auditor.

A breach of duty of care must be proved for a negligence claim against the audit firm to be successful. Duty of care generally means that the audit firm must perform the audit work to a good standard and that relevant legal and professional requirements and principles have been followed. For an audit firm, it is important to be able to demonstrate that ISAs (UK and Ireland) have been adhered to. Unfortunately, it seems that ISAs (UK and Ireland) have been breached and so the audit firm is likely to have been negligent in the audit of payroll.

Tutorial note. Credit will be awarded for references to legal cases as examples of situations where audit firms have been found to have been negligent in performing an audit, such as *Re Kingston Cotton Mill*.

Finally, a financial loss has been suffered by the audit client, being the amount stolen while the fraud was operating.

In conclusion, Spaniel Ltd is likely to be able to successfully prove that the audit firm has been negligent in the audit of payroll, and that Groom & Co is liable for some or all of the financial loss suffered.

(b) **The audit of financial instruments**

There are many reasons why financial instruments are challenging to audit. The instruments themselves, the transactions to which they relate, and the associated risk exposures can be difficult for both management and auditors to understand. If the auditor does not fully understand the financial instrument and its impact on the financial statements, it will be difficult to assess the risk of material misstatement and to detect errors in the accounting treatment and associated disclosures. Even relatively simple financial instruments can be complex to account for.

The specialist nature of many financial instruments means that the auditor may need to rely on an auditor's expert as a source of evidence. In using an expert, the auditor must ensure the objectivity and competence of that expert, and then must evaluate the adequacy of the expert's work, which can be very difficult to do where the focus of the work is so specialist and difficult to understand.

The auditor may also find that there is a lack of evidence in relation to financial instruments, or that evidence tends to come from management. For example, many of the financial reporting requirements in relation to the valuation of financial instruments are based on fair values. Fair values are often based on models which depend on management judgement. Valuations are therefore often subjective and derived from management assumptions which increase the risk of material misstatement.

It is imperative that the auditor retains professional skepticism in the audit of financial instruments, but this may be difficult to do when faced with a complex and subjective transaction or balance for which there is little evidence other than management's judgement.

There may also be control issues relating to financial instruments. Often financial instruments are dealt with by a specialist department and it may be a few individuals who exert significant influence over the financial instruments that are entered into. This specialist department may not be fully integrated into the finance function, leading to the accounting treatment being dealt with outside the normal accounting system. Internal controls may be deficient and there may not be the opportunity for much segregation of duty. However, some companies will have established strong internal controls around financial instruments, leading to a lower risk of material misstatement.

In planning the audit of Bulldog Ltd's financial instruments, the auditor must first gain an understanding of the relevant accounting and disclosure requirements. For example, the applicable financial reporting standards should be clarified, which are likely to be IFRS 9 *Financial Instruments* and IFRS 7 *Financial Instruments: Disclosures*. These standards can be complex to apply, and the auditor should develop a thorough understanding of how they relate to Bulldog Ltd's financial instruments.

The auditor must also obtain an understanding of the instruments in which Bulldog Ltd has invested or to which it is exposed, including the characteristics of the instruments, and gain an understanding of Bulldog Ltd's reasons for entering into the financial instruments and its policy towards them.

It is important that the resources needed to audit the financial instruments are carefully considered. The competence of members of the audit firm to audit these transactions should be assessed, and it may be that an auditor's expert needs to be engaged. If so, this should be explained to the client. Instructions will have to be drawn up and given to the expert to ensure that the work performed is in line with audit objectives and follows the relevant financial reporting requirements, for example, in relation to valuing the financial instruments.

The audit planning should include obtaining an understanding of the internal control relevant to Bulldog Ltd's financial instruments, including the involvement, if any, of internal audit. An understanding of how financial instruments are monitored and controlled assists the auditor in determining the nature, timing and extent of audit procedures, for example, whether to perform tests on controls.

Specific consideration should be given to understanding management's method for valuing financial instruments for recognition in the year-end financial statements. The valuation is likely to involve some form of estimate, and ISA 540 (UK and Ireland) *Auditing accounting estimates, including fair value accounting estimates and related disclosures* requires the auditor to obtain an understanding of how management makes accounting estimates and the data on which accounting estimates are based.

Finally, the materiality of the financial instruments should be determined and the significance of the risk exposure associated with them should be assessed.

5   **Toy Ltd**

The amount claimed against Toy Ltd is material to consolidated profit, representing 25% of consolidated profit before tax. The amount is not material to consolidated total assets, representing less than 1% of that amount.

The same accounting policies should be applied across the Group in the consolidated financial statements. Therefore in accordance with IAS 37 *Provisions, Contingent Liabilities and Contingent Assets*, a provision should be recognised in the consolidated financial statements if the amount is probable to be paid.

The adjustment needed is:

Dr	Operating expenses	£500,000
Cr	Current liabilities – provisions	£500,000

The audit evidence obtained by the component auditors is insufficient. Verbal evidence is not a reliable source of evidence. Further audit procedures should be performed, including:

- Obtain written evidence from Toy Ltd's legal advisors including a statement that in their opinion the damages are probable to be paid, and the basis of that opinion

- Review the claim itself to confirm that £500,000 is the amount claimed by the ex-employee

- Inspect the board minutes of Toy Ltd for evidence of discussion of the claim, to obtain an understanding as to the reason for the claim and whether it has been disputed by Toy Ltd

These further audit procedures may be performed by the component auditor, or by the Group audit team.

If, having obtained evidence to confirm that the damages are probable to be paid, the consolidated financial statements are not adjusted to include the provision, the consolidated statement of profit or loss and other comprehensive income will be materially misstated. This would result in a qualified 'except for' opinion due to the material, but not pervasive, nature of the material misstatement. In accordance with ISA 705 (UK and Ireland) *Modifications to the opinion in the independent auditor's report*, the report should contain a paragraph entitled 'Basis for Qualified Opinion' describing the matter giving rise to the qualification. A quantification of the financial effect of the misstatement should also be given.

Tutorial note. Credit will be awarded for answers referring to, and using the terminology from, APB Bulletin 2010/2 (Revised) Compendium of illustrative reports on United Kingdom private sector financial statements for periods ended on or after 15 December 2010.

The auditor should discuss the need for the adjustment with the client (including those charged with governance), and explain that a qualified opinion will result from the material misstatement.

Trade receivable

The trade receivable is material to the consolidated financial statements, representing 2·8% of total assets and 80% of profit before tax. The amount that is potentially irrecoverable is 90% of the total balance outstanding, ie £1.44 million. This amount is also material, representing 2.5% of total assets and 72% of profit before tax.

IFRS 9 *Financial Instruments* requires that impaired trade receivables are recognised at fair value, which is the present value of estimated cash inflows. According to the information provided by Terrier Ltd's administrators, it is likely that 10% of the amount outstanding will be paid and the remaining 90% should be written off. The adjustment needed is:

Dr	Operating expenses (irrecoverable debts expense)	£1,440,000
Cr	Trade receivables	£1,440,000

The amount should be adjusted in the financial statements for the year ended 31 March 2013, even though notice was not received until May 2013. This is because according to IAS 10 *Events After the Reporting Period*, an adjusting event is one that provides additional information about conditions existing at the year end.

If the financial statements are not adjusted for the impaired receivable, current assets will be overstated and profits overstated by £1.44 million. This is a very significant matter as the adjustment to profit is highly material.

Tutorial note. Credit will be awarded for comments relating to whether separate disclosure on the face of the statement of profit or loss and other comprehensive income is appropriate, due to the material and unusual nature of the item.

The auditor should perform additional procedures as follows.

- Obtain the notice from Terrier Ltd's administrators confirming that the company is insolvent and that only 10% of amounts outstanding is likely to be paid;

- Obtain a written confirmation from the administrators stating the expected timing of the payment;

- Check post year-end cash receipts to see if any of the amount outstanding has been received from Terrier Ltd;

- Recalculate the impairment losses and trace the posting of the impairment into the general ledger and the financial statements.

If the consolidated financial statements are not adjusted for the irrecoverable amount, both the statement of financial position and the statement of profit or loss and other comprehensive income will be materially misstated. This would result in a qualified 'except for' opinion due to the material, but not pervasive, nature of the material misstatement.

Aggregate impact on the financial statements

The materiality and overall significance of the two matters discussed above should be considered in aggregate. When combined, the adjustment needed to net assets and to operating expenses is £1.94 million. This adjustment would reduce the draft consolidated profit before tax to only £60,000.

The combined misstatement could be considered both material and pervasive to the financial statements as the profit figure is so impacted by the adjustments necessary. In this case, the auditor should express an adverse opinion, stating that the financial statements do not show a true and fair view. A paragraph should be included above the opinion, entitled 'Basis for Adverse Opinion', which describes the reason for the adverse opinion and provides quantification.

The auditor should discuss the need for the adjustment with the client (including those charged with governance), and explain that a qualified or adverse opinion will result from the material misstatements. This communication is required by ISA 705.

Chairman's statement

ISA 720A (UK and Ireland) *The auditor's responsibilities relating to other information in documents containing audited financial statements* requires the auditor to read other information, defined as financial and non-financial information, included in a document containing audited financial statements and the auditor's report.

The purpose of reading the other information is to identify material inconsistencies with the audited financial statements. A material inconsistency arises where the other information contradicts information in the audited financial statements, and may possibly raise doubt about the audit opinion. A material inconsistency undermines the credibility of the audit opinion.

ISA 720A requires that in the event of a material inconsistency being discovered, the auditor shall determine whether the financial statements or the other information needs to be revised, so that the inconsistency is removed. If the inconsistency is not resolved, the auditor's responsibilities depend on whether it is the other information, or the financial statements that have not been corrected.

In the Group's case, the chairman's statement contains an inconsistency, as according to the consolidated financial statements, revenue has increased by 5.9%, but the chairman states that revenue has increased by 20%.

The audit work performed on revenue should be reviewed to ensure that sufficient and appropriate evidence has been gained to support the figures in the financial statements.

The matter should be discussed with management, who should be asked to amend the disclosure in the chairman's statement. Management should be presented with the results of the audit work, to justify, if necessary, that the amendment needs to be made. The inclusion of the incorrect figure in the draft chairman's statement could be a genuine mistake, in which case management should be happy to make the change.

If management refuse to change the disclosure in the other information, then the audit report should contain an Other Matter paragraph. This should be presented immediately after the opinion paragraph and should describe the inconsistency clearly. The matter should also be communicated to those charged with governance.

ISA 720A states that if the auditor is unable to resolve identified inconsistencies through discussion with those charged with governance, the auditor should consider requesting those charged with governance to consult with a qualified third party, such as the entity's legal counsel, and to consider the advice received.

If the inconsistency remains, the audit firm may wish to speak at a meeting of shareholders of the Poodle Group to explain the additional paragraph that has been included in the audit report.

1   **Briefing notes**

To: Audit Partner
From: Audit Manager
Subject: Planning issues for the Stow Group, year ending 31 December 2013

Introduction

These briefing notes contain an explanation of the risks of material misstatement to be considered in planning the audit of the Stow Group. The risks which have been explained focus on a restructuring of the Group which has taken place during the year. Materiality has been considered where information permits, and further information which would be useful in planning the audit has also been identified. The briefing notes also contain recommended audit procedures to be performed in respect of the disposal of Broadway Ltd. In addition, the Group finance director's suggestion that our firm makes use of the new subsidiary's internal audit team when performing our audit has been discussed, along with the ethical implication of the suggestion.

Zennor Ltd

Materiality of Zennor Ltd

To evaluate the materiality of Zennor Ltd to the Group, its profit and assets need to be retranslated into £. At the stated exchange rate of 4 Dingu = £1, its projected profit for the year is £22.5 million (90 million Dingu / 4) and its projected total assets are £200 million (800 million Dingu / 4).

Zennor Ltd's profit represents 113% of Group projected profit for the year (22.5 / 200), and its assets represent 8% of Group total assets (200 / 2,500). Zennor Ltd is therefore material to the Group and is a significant component of it. A significant component is one which is identified by the auditor as being of individual financial significance to the group.

The goodwill arising on the acquisition of Zennor Ltd amounts to 2.4% (60 / 2,500) of Group assets and is material.

Because the balances above, including goodwill, are based on a foreign currency, they will need to be retranslated at the year end using the closing exchange rate to determine and conclude on materiality as at the year end.

Materiality needs to be assessed based on the new, enlarged group structure. Materiality for the group financial statements as a whole will be determined when establishing the overall group audit strategy. The addition of Zennor Ltd to the group during the year is likely to cause materiality to be different from previous years, possibly affecting audit strategy and the extent of testing in some areas.

Risks of material misstatement

Retranslation of Zennor Ltd's financial statements

According to IAS 21 *The Effects of Changes in Foreign Exchange Rates*, the assets and liabilities of Zennor Ltd should be retranslated using the closing exchange rate. Its income and expenses should be retranslated at the exchange rates at the dates of the transactions.

The risk is that incorrect exchange rates are used for the retranslations. This could result in over/understatement of the assets, liabilities, income and expenses that are consolidated, including goodwill. It would also mean that the exchange gains and losses arising on retranslation and to be included in Group other comprehensive income are incorrectly determined.

Measurement and recognition of exchange gains and losses

The calculation of exchange gains and losses can be complex, and there is a risk that it is not calculated correctly, or that some elements are omitted, for example, the exchange gain or loss on goodwill may be missed out of the calculation.

IAS 21 states that exchange gains and losses arising as a result of the restranslation of the subsidiary's balances are recognised in other comprehensive income. The risk is incorrect classification, for example, the gain or loss could be recognised incorrectly as part of profit for the year

Initial measurement of goodwill

In order for goodwill to be calculated, the assets and liabilities of Zennor Ltd must have been identified and measured at fair value at the date of acquisition. Risks of material misstatement arise because the various components of goodwill each have specific risks attached, for example:

- Not all assets and liabilities may have been identified, for example, contingent liabilities and contingent assets may be omitted

- Fair value is subjective and based on assumptions which may not be valid

There is also a risk that the cost of investment is not stated correctly, for example, that any contingent consideration has not been included in the calculation.

Subsequent measurement of goodwill

According to IFRS 3 *Business Combinations*, goodwill should be subject to an impairment review on an annual basis. The risk is that a review has not taken place, and so goodwill is overstated and Group operating expenses understated if impairment losses have not been recognised.

Consolidation of income and expenses

Zennor Ltd was acquired on 1 February 2013 and its income and expenses should have been consolidated from that date. There is a risk that the full year's income and expenses have been consolidated, leading to a risk of overstated Group profit.

Disclosure

Extensive disclosures are required by IFRS 3 to be included in the notes to the Group financial statements, for example, to include the acquisition date, reason for the acquisition and a description of the factors which make up the goodwill acquired. The risk is that disclosures are incomplete or not understandable.

Intra-group transactions

There will be a significant volume of intra-group transactions as the Group is supplying Zennor Ltd with inventory. There is a risk that intra-group sales, purchases, payables and receivables are not eliminated, leading to overstated revenue, cost of sales, payables and receivables in the Group financial statements.

There is also a risk that intercompany transactions are not identified in either/both companies' accounting systems.

The intra-group transactions are by definition related party transactions according to IAS 24 *Related Party Disclosures*, because Zennor Ltd is under the control of the Group. No disclosure of the transactions is required in the Group financial statements in respect of intra-group transactions because they are eliminated on consolidation. However, both the individual financial statements of the Group company supplying Zennor Ltd and the financial statements of Zennor Ltd must contain notes disclosing details of the intra-group transactions. There is a risk that this disclosure is not provided.

In addition, the cars may be supplied including a profit margin or mark up, in which case a provision for unrealised profit should be recognised in the Group financial statements. If this is not accounted for, Group inventory will be overstated, and operating profit will be overstated.

Completeness of inventory

There is a risk that cars which are in transit to Zennor Ltd at the year end may be omitted from inventory. The cars spend a significant amount of time in transit and awaiting delivery to Zennor Ltd, and without a good system of controls in place, it is likely that items of inventory will be missing from the Group's current assets as they may have been recorded as despatched from the seller but not yet as received by Zennor Ltd.

The inventory in transit to Zennor Ltd represents 2.3% of Group total assets (58 / 2,500) and is therefore material to the consolidated financial statements.

Tutorial note. Credit will also be awarded where answers discuss the issue of whether the arrangement is a consignment inventory arrangement, and the relevant risks of material misstatement.

Further information in relation to Zennor Ltd:

- Prior years' financial statements and auditor's reports

- Minutes of meetings where the acquisition was discussed

- Business background, eg from the company's website or trade journals

- Copies of systems documentation from the internal audit team

- Confirmation from Zennor Ltd's previous auditors of any matters which they wish to bring to our attention

- Projected financial statements for the year to 31 December 2013

- A copy of the due diligence report

- Copies of prior year tax computations

Tutorial note. Credit will also be awarded for discussions of risks of material misstatement and relevant audit procedures relating to the initial audit of Zennor Ltd by Compton & Co, eg increased risk of misstatement of opening balances and comparatives.

Broadway Ltd

Materiality

The profit made on the disposal of Broadway Ltd represents 12.5% of Group profit for the year (25 / 200) and the transaction is therefore material to the Group financial statements.

Given that the subsidiary was sold for £180 million and that a profit on disposal of £25 million was recognised, the Group's financial statements must have derecognised net assets of £155 million on the disposal. This amounts to 6.2% of the Group's assets and is material. This is assuming that the profit on disposal has been correctly calculated, which is a risk factor discussed below.

Risk of material misstatement

Derecognition of assets and liabilities

On the disposal of Broadway Ltd, all of its assets and liabilities which had been recognised in the Group financial statements should have been derecognised at their carrying value, including any goodwill in respect of the company. There is therefore a risk that not all assets, liabilities and goodwill have been derecognised leading to overstatement of those balances and an incorrect profit on disposal being calculated and included in Group profit for the year.

Profit consolidated prior to disposal

There is a risk that Broadway Ltd's income for the year has been incorrectly consolidated. It should have been included in Group profit up to the date that control passed and any profit included after that point would mean overstatement of Group profit for the year.

Calculation of profit on disposal

There is a risk that the profit on disposal has not been accurately calculated, eg that the proceeds received have not been measured at fair value as required by IFRS 10 Consolidated Financial Statements, or that elements of the calculation are missing.

Classification and disclosure of profit on disposal

IAS 1 *Presentation of Financial Statements* requires separate disclosure on the face of the financial statements of material items to enhance the understanding of performance during the year. The profit of £25 million is material, so separate disclosure is necessary. The risk is that the profit is not separately disclosed, eg is netted from operating expenses, leading to material misstatement.

Extensive disclosure requirements exist in relation to subsidiaries disposed of, eg IAS 7 *Statement of Cash Flows* requires a note which analyses the assets and liabilities of the subsidiary at the date of disposal. There is a risk that not all necessary notes to the financial statements are provided.

Tutorial note. It is possible that Broadway Ltd represents a disposal group and a discontinued operation, and credit will be awarded for discussion of relevant risks of material misstatement and audit procedures in respect of these issues.

Treatment of the disposal in parent company individual financial statements

The parent company's financial statements should derecognise the original cost of investment and recognise a profit on disposal based on the difference between the proceeds of £180 million and the cost of investment. Risk arises if the investment has not been derecognised or the profit has been incorrectly calculated.

Tax on disposal

There should be an accrual in both the parent company and the Group financial statements for the tax due on the disposal. This should be calculated based on the profit recognised in the parent company. There is a risk that the tax is not accrued for, leading to overstated profit and understated liabilities. There is also a risk that the tax calculation is not accurate.

Tutorial note. As Compton & Co is no longer the auditor of Broadway Ltd, there is no need for any further information in relation to audit planning, other than that needed to perform the audit procedures listed below.

Procedures to be performed on the disposal of Broadway Ltd

- Obtain the statement of financial position of Broadway Ltd as at 1 September 2013 to confirm the value of assets and liabilities which have been derecognised from the Group.

- Review prior year Group financial statements and audit working papers to confirm the amount of goodwill that exists in respect of Broadway Ltd and trace to confirm it is derecognised from the Group on disposal.

- Confirm that the Stow Group is no longer listed as a shareholder of the company.

- Obtain legal documentation in relation to the disposal to confirm the date of the disposal and confirm that Broadway Ltd's profit has been consolidated up to this date only.

- Agree or reconcile the profit recognised in the Group financial statements to Broadway Ltd's individual accounts as at 1 September 2013.

- Perform substantive analytical procedures to gain assurance that the amount of profit consolidated from 1 January to 1 September 2013 appears reasonable and in line with expectations based on prior year profit.

- Re-perform management's calculation of profit on disposal in the Group financial statements.

- Agree the proceeds received of £180 million to legal documentation, and to cash book/bank statements.

- Confirm that £180 million is the fair value of proceeds on disposal and that no deferred or contingent consideration is receivable in the future.

- Review the Group statement of profit or loss and other comprehensive income to confirm that the profit on disposal is correctly disclosed as part of profit for the year (not in other comprehensive income) on a separate line.

- Using a disclosure checklist, confirm that all necessary information has been provided in the notes to the Group financial statements.

- Obtain the parent company's statement of financial position to confirm that the cost of investment is derecognised.

- Using prior year financial statements and audit working papers, agree the cost of investment derecognised to prior year's figure.

- Re-perform the calculation of profit on disposal in the parent company's financial statements.

- Reconcile the profit on disposal recognised in the parent company's financial statements to the profit recognised in the Group financial statements.

- Obtain management's estimate of the tax due on disposal, re-perform the calculation and confirm the amount is properly accrued at parent company and at Group level.

- Review any correspondence with tax authorities regarding the tax due.

- Possibly the tax will be paid in the subsequent events period, in which case the payment can be agreed to cash book and bank statement.

Internal audit team and ethical issue

It is not improper for Marta to suggest that Compton & Co use the work of Zennor Ltd's internal audit team. ISA 610 (UK and Ireland) *Using the work of internal auditors* gives guidance on when it is appropriate to do so, and the considerations which the external auditor should apply when planning an audit involving the work of internal auditors.

It would be beneficial for Compton & Co to use the internal audit team as it may result in a more efficient audit strategy, for example, the internal audit team's monitoring of controls should have resulted in a strong control environment, so a less substantive approach can be used on the audit.

In addition, the internal audit team should be able to provide Compton & Co with systems documentation and information on control activities which have been implemented. This will help the audit firm to build its knowledge and understanding of the new audit client.

Compton & Co may also decide to rely on audit work performed by the internal audit team, for example, they may be asked to attend inventory counts of cars held at the port and awaiting delivery to Zennor Ltd.

All of the benefits described above are particularly significant given Zennor Ltd's overseas location, as reliance on the internal audit team would reduce travel time and costs which would be incurred if the external auditor had to perform the work themselves. However, there will be a limit to the amount of work that can be delegated to the internal audit team.

Before deciding how much reliance to place on the internal audit team, ISA 610 requires the external auditor to evaluate various matters, including the technical competence of the internal audit team, the objectives of their work, whether the work has been carried out with due professional care, and whether there is likely to be effective communication between the internal and external auditors. To perform these evaluations the external auditor may wish, for example, to discuss the work of the team with Jo Evesham including a consideration of the level of supervision, review and documentation of work performed, and also review the qualifications held by members of the team.

The fact that the internal audit team does not report to an independent audit committee may reduce the reliance that can be placed on their work as it affects the objectivity of work performed.

If Compton & Co chooses to use the work of the internal audit team, this will be relevant to the audit of both Zennor Ltd's individual financial statements, and the Group financial statements and will affect the audit strategy of both.

Tutorial note. Credit will be given for answer points based on the current FRC Consultation Paper on proposed revisions to ISA 610.

Marta states that reliance on the internal audit team will reduce the external audit fee, and the Group audit committee has requested that the Group audit fee remains the same as last year. This implies an intimidation threat to objectivity. IESBA's *Code of Ethics for Professional Accountants* states that an audit firm being pressured to reduce inappropriately the extent of work performed in order to reduce fees is an example of an intimidation threat. It should be brought to Marta's attention that the audit fee will not necessarily be reduced by reliance on internal audit, especially as this is the first year that Compton & Co have audited Zennor Ltd, so there will be a lot of work to be performed in developing knowledge and understanding of the client whether or not the firm chooses to rely on the work of the internal audit team.

Given that the Group audit fee last year amounted to 4.5% of our firm's income, there is a risk of fee dependence if the Group audit fee increases. According to ES 4 *Fees, remuneration and evaluation policies, litigation, gifts and hospitality*, for a listed audited entity and its subsidiaries amounts to 5% or more of the annual income of the audit firm, the need for safeguards should be considered, and the matter disclosed to the firm's Ethics Partner and to those charged with governance of the audit client. In this case the additional work to be performed on the new subsidiary, and on the disposal of Broadway Ltd, could push the audit fee over the 5% threshold.

Conclusion

The Stow Group's financial statements contain a high risk of material misstatement this year end, due to the restructuring which has taken place. The audit plan will contain numerous audit procedures to reduce the identified risks to an acceptable level. Compton & Co may choose to place reliance on Zennor Ltd's internal audit team, but only after careful consideration of their competence and objectivity, and communication between the external and internal audit teams must be carefully planned for.

2   (i)   **Benefits of due diligence to Baltimore Ltd**

One of the objectives of a due diligence review is for the assets and liabilities of the target company to be identified and valued. Therefore a benefit of due diligence to Baltimore Ltd is to gain an understanding of the nature of assets and liabilities which are being acquired, as not all assets and liabilities of Mizzen Ltd are recognised in its financial statements. For example, Mizzen Ltd has built up several customer databases, which, being internally generated, will not be recognised as assets in its statement of financial position, but these could be valuable assets to Baltimore Ltd.

A second benefit is that the due diligence review should uncover more information about operational issues, which may then help Baltimore Ltd's management to decide whether to go ahead with the acquisition. For example, only one of Mizzen Ltd's revenue streams appears to be directly relevant to Baltimore Ltd's expansion plans, so more information is needed about the other operations of Mizzen Ltd to determine how they may be of benefit to Baltimore Ltd. The due diligence review should cover a wide range of issues, such as reviews of the company's legal and tax positions, which may uncover significant matters.

An externally provided due diligence review, as opposed to a review conducted by management of Baltimore Ltd, is likely to provide information in a time-efficient, impartial manner. Baltimore Ltd's management has not previously dealt with an acquisition, whereas the audit firm has the financial and business understanding and expertise to provide a quality due diligence review. A review report issued by Goleen & Co will add credibility to the planned acquisition, which may help secure the bank loan which is needed to fund the acquisition.

The due diligence review will enable a fair price to be negotiated once Baltimore Ltd has full knowledge of the assets and liabilities it will be acquiring, and the operational issues which will need to be addressed if the acquisition were to go ahead.

In addition to performing the due diligence review, Goleen & Co may also provide other advice relevant to the acquisition, helping the acquisition go as smoothly as possible. For example, the firm could provide advice on financing arrangements, and could consult on an appropriate business strategy for Baltimore Ltd going forward.

Tutorial note. Credit will be awarded for other relevant benefits which are discussed.

(ii)   **Matters to focus on in the due diligence review**

Equity owners of Mizzen Ltd and involvement of BizGrow

The nature of the involvement of the venture capitalist company, BizGrow, is a crucial issue which must be the starting point of the due diligence review. Venture capitalists provide equity when a company is incorporated, and typically look for an exit route within three to seven years. Mizzen Ltd was incorporated four years ago, so it will be important to determine whether BizGrow retains its original equity holding in Mizzen Ltd, and if so, whether the acquisition of BizGrow's shares by Baltimore Ltd would be compatible with the planned exit route.

Key skills and expertise

It appears that the original founders of Mizzen Ltd, Vic Sandhu and Lou Lien, are crucial to the success of Mizzen Ltd and it would be in Baltimore Ltd's interests to keep them involved with the business. However, Vic and Lou may wish to focus on further work involving IT innovation rather than Baltimore Ltd's planned website and without Vic and Lou's expertise the acquisition may be much less worthwhile. However, there could be other employed personnel with the necessary skills and experience to meet Baltimore Ltd's needs, or much of the skill and expertise could be provided from freelancers, who will not be part of the acquisition.

Internally generated intangible assets

Mizzen Ltd is likely to have several important internally generated intangible assets, which will not be recognised in its individual accounts but must be identified and measured as part of the due diligence review. First, Vic and Lou have innovated and developed new website interfaces, and the review must determine the nature of this intellectual property (IP), and whether it belongs to Vic and Lou or to Mizzen Ltd. The measurement of this asset will be very difficult, and it is likely to form an important part of the acquisition deal if Baltimore Ltd want to acquire the IP to use in its new website.

There are also several customer databases which need to be measured and included in the list of assets acquired, which again may be difficult to measure in value. It is important for the due diligence review to confirm the relevance of the databases to Baltimore Ltd's operations, and that the databases contain up-to-date information.

Premises

Mizzen Ltd currently operates from premises owned by BizGrow and pays a nominal rent for this. Presumably if the acquisition were to go ahead, this arrangement would cease. The due diligence review should consider the need for new premises to be found for Mizzen Ltd and the associated costs. Possibly there is room for Mizzen Ltd to operate from Baltimore Ltd's premises as the operations do not appear to need a large space. The rental agreement may be fixed for a period of time and cancellation may incur a penalty.

Other tangible assets

Mizzen Ltd appears to own only items such as computer equipment and fixtures and fittings. It needs to be clarified whether these assets are owned or held under lease, and also whether any other tangible assets, such as vehicles, are used in the business. Any commitments for future purchases of tangible assets should be reviewed.

Accounting policy on revenue recognition

Mizzen Ltd has some fairly complex revenue streams, and the due diligence review should establish that the accounting policies in place are reasonable and in line with IAS 18 *Revenue*. The revenue generated from website development and maintenance should be split into two components, with the revenue for website development recognised once the website has been provided to the customer, but the revenue for maintenance spread over the contract period. There is a risk that revenue is recognised too early, inflating Mizzen Ltd's profit.

The revenue recognition policy for annual subscriptions should also be scrutinised, with revenue relating to future periods being deferred.

Sustainability and relevance of revenue streams

The financial statements indicate that revenue has increased each year, and that in the last year it has increased by 23.7%. This is an impressive growth rate and work must be done to analyse the likelihood of revenue streams being maintained and further growth being achieved. For example, the proportion of website development and two year maintenance contracts which are renewed should be investigated. Not all of Mizzen Ltd's revenue streams seem very relevant to Baltimore Ltd's operations, so how these may be managed post-acquisition should be considered.

Operating expenses

The financial extracts indicate a potentially unusual trend in relation to operating expenses. In 2011 and 2012, operating expenses represented 60% and 58.3% of revenue respectively. In 2013, this had reduced to 49.6%. This may be due to economies of scale being achieved as the company grows, or possibly expenses are understated or revenue overstated in 2013. As freelance web designers have been used in 2013, operating expenses may have been expected to have increased in proportion to revenue. The due diligence review should perform detailed analysis on the operating costs incurred by the company to gain assurance that expenses are complete and accurately recorded.

With the exception of 2010, the finance cost has remained static at £250,000 per annum. The due diligence review must uncover what this finance cost relates to, and whether it will continue post-acquisition. It may be a bank loan or it could be a payment made to BizGrow, as venture capitalist companies often impose a management charge on companies which they have invested in. Baltimore Ltd will need to understand the nature of any liability in relation to this finance charge.

Cash position and cash management

Mizzen Ltd's cash position should be confirmed. Given that the company appears to have limited need for capital expenditure and working capital, and given the level of profits which has been made in the last three years, it could be expected that the company would be cash-rich. The due diligence review should confirm how the cash generated by the company since incorporation has been used, for example, in dividend payments to BizGrow and to Vic and Lou.

Additional information required

- Contract or legal documentation describing the nature of the investment which BizGrow made when Mizzen Ltd was incorporated, and detailing the planned exit route

- A register of shareholders showing all shareholders of Mizzen Ltd

- An organisational structure, in order to identify the members of management and key personnel and their roles within Mizzen Ltd

- A list of employees and their roles within the company, and their related obligations including salary, holiday entitlements, retirement plans, health insurance and other benefits provided by Mizzen Ltd, and details of compensation to be paid in the case of redundancy

- A list of freelance web designers used by Mizzen Ltd, and a description of the work they perform

- The key terms of contracts or agreements with freelance web designers

- A list of all IT innovations which have been created and developed by Mizzen Ltd, and details of any patent or copyright agreements relating to them

- Agreements with employees regarding assignment of intellectual property and confidentiality

- Copies of the customer databases showing contact details of all people or companies included on the list

- A list of companies which have contracts with Mizzen Ltd for website development and maintenance

- A copy of all contracts with customers for review of the period for which maintenance is to be provided

- A breakdown of the revenue which has been generated from making each database available to other companies, and the dates when they were made available

- A summary of the controls which are in place to ensure that the database details are regularly updated

- A copy of the rental agreement with BizGrow, to determine whether any penalty is payable on cancellation

- Non-current asset register showing descriptions and values of all assets used in the business

- Copies of any lease agreements, for example, leases of computer equipment, photocopiers, etc.

- Details of any capital expenditure budgets for previous accounting periods, and any planned capital expenditure in the future

- Mizzen Ltd's stated accounting policy on revenue recognition

- Systems and controls documentation over the processing of revenue receipts

- An analysis of expenses included in operating expenses for each year and copies of documentation relating to ongoing expenses, such as salaries and other overheads

- Copies of management accounts to agree expenses in the audited accounts are in line and to perform more detailed analytical review

  - The full set of financial statements and auditor's reports for each year since the company's incorporation, to:

  - Confirm the assets and liabilities recognised

  - Agree the level of dividends paid each year

  - Review all of the accounting policies used in preparing the financial statements

  - Find the details of any related party transactions that have occurred

  - Review the statement of cash flows for each year

- Any agreements with banks or other external providers of finance, including finance advanced and relevant finance charges, or confirmation that no such finance has been provided to Mizzen Ltd

Tutorial note: Credit will be awarded for other relevant information which would be required as part of the due diligence review.

(iii) **Due diligence conclusion**

Due diligence is a specific example of a direct reporting assurance engagement.

The main difference between a review report and an audit report is the level of assurance that is given. In a review report a conclusion is expressed in a negative form. The conclusion would start with the wording 'based on our review, nothing has come to our attention...'

This type of conclusion is used because the nature of a due diligence review is that only limited assurance has been obtained over the subject matter. The procedures used in a review engagement are mainly enquiry and analytical review which can only provide limited assurance.

In comparison, in an audit of historical information, the auditor will use a wide variety of procedures to obtain evidence to give reasonable assurance that the financial statements are free from material misstatement. This means that an opinion expressed in a positive form can be given.

3 (a) (i) **Matters which should be considered**

Impairment of assets

The mine is recognised at £10 million, representing 5.7% of Dasset Ltd's total assets, and therefore material to the statement of financial position.

The accident has caused part of the mine to be unusable, which indicates that it has become impaired. IAS 36 *Impairment of Assets* requires that an impairment review should be conducted when there is an indicator of potential impairment, and therefore management should have performed a review to determine the recoverable amount of the mine.

If an impairment review has not been performed, and no adjustment made to the carrying value of the mine, then assets will be overstated and profit overstated. One-third of the mine has become unusable, so presumably no future economic benefit can be derived. Therefore one-third of the mine's carrying value may need to be written off. This amounts to £3.33

million, which represents 18.5% of profit for the year. The impairment write off is therefore potentially material to Dasset Ltd's profit.

A worst case scenario is that more than one-third of the mine is unusable. It could be that all of the mine is unsafe and should be shut down, or possibly the National Coal Mining Authority may withdraw its licence to operate the Ledge Hill mine completely. In either case, the impairment loss would then be extended to the full value of the mine, increasing the materiality of the matter in the financial statements.

Another consideration is there is likely to be some equipment which is contained in the tunnels which can no longer be used. It is possible that some of the equipment may be recovered, but it is likely that a large proportion of it will have to be abandoned and written off, increasing the impairment loss to be recognised.

IAS 1 *Presentation of Financial Statements* requires that an individual item of income or expense which is material should be disclosed separately, and gives impairment of assets as an example of a circumstance which may warrant separate disclosure.

The costs which have been incurred and are yet to be incurred to ensure the safety of the mine in the future should be treated as capital expenditure at the time when the costs are incurred. There may also be costs to be incurred in making the unusable tunnels safe, for example, entrances may need to be blocked up. These costs should be expensed as they do not relate to future economic benefit and so do not meet the definition of an asset. There is a risk that capital and revenue expenses have not been appropriately classified.

Provisions and liabilities

There has also been damage caused to some properties situated above the mine. Dasset Ltd may need to recognise a provision in relation to any costs it will suffer in relation to repairing or demolishing the properties. According to IAS 37 *Provisions, Contingent Liabilities and Contingent Assets*, a provision should be recognised if there is a present obligation as a result of a past event, a probable outflow of economic benefits, and a reliable estimate can be made.

It seems that the criteria have been met, as the accident happened before the year end and gives rise to an obligating event. Dasset Ltd is meeting all expenses of the residents who have been relocated, so the company appears to be acknowledging responsibility for the accident and its impact on the residential properties. The damage to the properties will result in a cash outflow for the company whether they have to be demolished or repaired, and the expert should be able to provide a reliable estimate of the amount. Therefore a provision should be recognised.

The company may suffer further cash outflows as a result of the accident, and consideration needs to be made as to whether a provision or a contingent liability should be recognised in respect of them. The residents may claim further damages against the company, for example, for stress caused by the accident, and compensation for expenses such as damaged fixtures in the properties.

There may also be a clause in the National Coal Mining Authority's operating licence that imposes a fine on Dasset Ltd in the event of any non-compliance with health and safety regulations. Any such fines may need to be recognised as provisions or contingent liabilities.

There is a risk that provisions have not been appropriately recognised, leading to overstated profit and understated liabilities, or that contingent liabilities have not been disclosed accurately and completely.

Going concern

Finally, there may be going concern implications as a result of the accident. Given the relatively small size of the Ledge Hill mine in relation to the company's total operations, it is unlikely that the closure of part, or even all, of the mine alone would create a risk to going concern. However, bad publicity may create difficult trading conditions, and a claim for high compensation from the group of local residents could place the company's cash flow under

strain. If these factors cast significant doubt on going concern, then disclosures should be made in the note to the financial statements.

The very worst case scenario is that the National Coal Mining Authority could withdraw the company's operating licence completely, which would cause it to cease operational existence. This may be very unlikely; however, it would mean that the financial statements should be prepared on the break up basis.

(ii) **Evidence**

- A copy of the operating licence, reviewed for conditions relating to health and safety and for potential fines and penalties which may be imposed in the event of non-compliance

- A written representation from management on their intention (or not) to bring the non-compliance to the attention of the National Coal Mining Authority

- A copy of board minutes where the accident has been discussed to identify the rationale behind the non-disclosure

- A copy of reports issued by engineers or other mining specialists confirming the extent of the damage caused to the mine by the accident

- Any quotes obtained for work to be performed to make the mine safe and for blocking off entrances to abandoned tunnels

- Confirmation that the undamaged portion of the mine is operational, eg from reviewing a specialist's report

- A copy of the surveyor 's report on the residential properties, reviewed for the expert's opinion as to whether they should be demolished

- A review of correspondence entered into with the local residents who have been relocated, to confirm the obligation the company has committed to in respect of their relocation

- Copies of legal correspondence, reviewed for any further claims made by local residents

- A review of the Ledge Hill Mine accident book, for confirmation that no one was injured in the accident

- A copy of management's impairment review, if any, evaluated to ensure that assumptions are reasonable and in line with auditor's understanding of the situation

- Confirmation that impairment losses have been recognised as an operating expense

- A review of draft disclosure notes to the financial statements where provisions and contingent liabilities have been discussed

- A review of cash flow and profit forecasts, forming a view on the overall going concern status of the company

(b) **Responsibilities to report the accident to the National Coal Mining Authority**

Dasset Ltd operates in a highly regulated industry, and Burton & Co must consider the requirements of ISA 250 A (UK and Ireland) *Consideration of laws and regulations in an audit of financial statements*. ISA 250 A states that it is management's responsibility to ensure that operations are conducted in accordance with relevant law and regulations. The auditor is expected to obtain a general understanding of the applicable legal and regulatory framework and how the entity is complying with that framework.

In this case, there is a suspected non-compliance with the National Coal Mining Authority's health and safety requirements. The accident may have been caused by using unsafe equipment or mining methods which failed to meet the authority's strict requirements. Management has not informed the authority, which may be for a genuine belief that there is no need to make a report concerning the accident, or it could be because management has something to hide and does not wish to come under the scrutiny of the authority.

ISA 250 A states that if the auditor becomes aware of information concerning an instance of non-compliance or suspected non-compliance with laws and regulations, the auditor shall obtain an understanding of the nature of the act and the circumstances in which it has occurred; and further information to evaluate the possible effect on the financial statements. Further audit procedures will therefore be necessary.

The matter should be discussed with those charged with governance, as required by ISA 250 A. Management should be asked to confirm the reason why the authority has not been notified of the accident, and a written representation should be obtained. Burton & Co may wish to encourage management to disclose the accident to the authority.

ISA 250 A also requires that auditor shall determine whether the auditor has a responsibility to report the identified or suspected non-compliance to parties outside the entity. Burton & Co needs to carefully evaluate their legal responsibility to report suspected non-compliance to the National Coal Mining Authority, and legal advice should be obtained to determine the appropriate course of action. There may be a statutory requirement for the accident to be disclosed to the authority, in which case according to ISA 250 A, the auditor ordinarily makes a report to the appropriate authority as soon as practicable.

ISA 250 A states that where the auditor becomes aware of a suspected or actual instance of non-compliance with law or regulations which does not give rise to a statutory duty to report to an appropriate authority, the auditor considers whether the matter may be one that ought to be reported to a proper authority in the public interest. If, having considered any views expressed on behalf of the entity and in the light of any legal advice obtained, the auditor concludes that the matter ought to be reported to an appropriate authority in the public interest, the auditor notifies those charged with governance in writing of the view and, if the entity does not voluntarily do so itself or is unable to provide evidence that the matter has been reported, the auditor reports it.

Confidentiality is an issue, as usually auditors cannot disclose information obtained during the audit to external parties without the prior consent of the client. Again, legal advice would be helpful here, to determine whether confidentiality can or should be breached and a report made to the National Coal Mining Authority if management fail to do so.

4   (a)   **Tetbury Ltd**

Chester & Co needs to conduct customer due diligence (know your client) procedures to ensure that anti-money laundering requirements are adhered to. This is especially important given the highly regulated nature of Tetbury Ltd's business. Background checks will need to be made on Juan Stanton and other members of management, and the nature of the business including the sources of income must be fully understood before deciding on accepting the audit appointment.

The competence of the audit firm in relation to the audit of a financial services firm should be evaluated, as it is a relatively specialised area. This is an ethical matter, with IESBA's (IFAC) *Code of Ethics for Professional Accountants* Code stating that a self-interest threat to professional competence and due care is created if the engagement team does not possess, or cannot acquire, the competencies necessary to properly carry out the engagement.

Chester & Co should consider whether it is appropriate to be appointed as auditor to Tetbury Ltd from an ethical point of view. The IESBA Code states that before accepting a new client relationship, a professional accountant in public practice shall determine whether acceptance would create any threats to compliance with the fundamental principles. Threats to integrity may arise from questionable activities by management of the company or from inappropriate financial reporting.

It appears that Tetbury Ltd's management may lack integrity due to its past investigation by the financial services authority. Chester & Co should find out more about this matter, for example, reading press reports or contacting the financial services authority for more information.

In addition, the resignation of the previous auditors over a disagreement indicates a possible problem with management's integrity. There may also be ethical issues, for example, management may have intimidated the previous auditors over the financial reporting issue which prompted their resignation.

Chester & Co should request permission to contact the previous audit firm to obtain further information on the reasons behind the resignation, and if there are any other matters which should be considered in deciding whether to take on the audit appointment. It is important that all relevant facts are known before an acceptance decision is made. A threat to professional competence and due care arises where the appointment is accepted without full knowledge of relevant information.

Juan's comment about deficient controls is also a cause for concern, as it indicates that the audit would be high risk. While this alone does not mean that the audit should not be taken on, Chester & Co should consider whether the audit risk can be reduced to an acceptable level, for example, by using an experienced audit team and a substantive audit approach. As part of its client acceptance decision, Chester & Co should consider whether the fee for the audit outweighs the risk involved.

The audit firm could apply a safeguard such as securing Juan's commitment to improve the company's control environment before accepting the client.

Tetbury Ltd is owner-managed. This means that management comes to rely on the auditor for advice and recommendations and the audit firm could be perceived to be taking on the responsibilities of management. This is especially relevant to Juan's suggestion that the audit firm can provide business advice.

According to the IESBA Code, this situation gives rise to potential self-review and self-interest threats to objectivity. If the audit firm were to assume management responsibilities, then no safeguards can reduce the threat to an acceptable level. However, providing advice and recommendations to assist management in discharging its responsibilities is not assuming a management responsibility.

Ethical Standard 5 *Non-audit services provided to audited entities* also identifies a management threat as existing when an audit firm undertakes work which involves making judgements and taking decisions which are properly the responsibility of management. In deciding whether a management threat exists, the auditor should consider factors such as whether a member of management has the capability to make independent management judgements and decisions on the basis of the information provided.

If the audit appointment is accepted, Chester & Co may wish to obtain written confirmation from management that it acknowledges responsibility for business decisions taken. Ethical Standard *Provisions available for small entities* provides guidance in relation to this safeguard, and recommends its use for auditors providing non-audit services to audit clients.

(b)   **Stratford Ltd**

The request to attend a meeting with the company's bank can give rise to an advocacy threat to objectivity. IESBA's Code defines an advocacy threat as the threat that a professional accountant will promote a client's or employer's position to the point that the professional accountant's objectivity is compromised. In this case, the managing director may want the audit engagement partner to support a view that Stratford Ltd will be able to continue as a going concern and that the loan ultimately will be repaid. This means that the audit partner is promoting the client which leads to the creation of an advocacy threat.

As discussed above in relation to Tetbury Ltd, ES 5 is also relevant here with respect to a management threat existing when an audit firm undertakes work which involves making judgements and taking decisions which are properly the responsibility of management. The significance of the threat and availability of safeguards should be considered.

In addition, from a legal perspective, the audit firm must be careful not to create the impression that they are in any way guaranteeing the future existence of the company or providing assurance on the draft financial statements. In legal terms, attending the meeting and promoting the interests of the client could create legal 'proximity', which increases the risk of legal action against the auditor in the event of Stratford Ltd defaulting on any loan provided by the bank.

It may be possible for a partner other than the audit engagement partner to attend the meeting with the bank, which would be a form of safeguard against the ethical threat. Chester & Co's partner responsible for ethics should consider the severity of the threat and whether this, or another safeguard, could reduce the threat to an acceptable level.

There is also an intimidation threat to objectivity caused by the managing director's hint at putting the audit out to tender. IESBA's Code states that an audit firm being threatened with dismissal from a client engagement represents an intimidation threat. The managing director's actions should also lead to questions over his integrity, and the audit firm may wish to consider resigning from the audit if the threat becomes too severe.

Overdue audit fees are a self-interest threat, according to IESBA's Code, which states that a self-interest threat may be created if fees due from an audit client remain unpaid for a long time, especially if a significant part is not paid before the issue of the audit report for the following year. The audit firm should determine the amount of fee that is unpaid, and whether it could be perceived to be a loan made to the client.

Ethical Standard 4 Fees, remuneration and evaluation policies, litigation, gifts and hospitality contains similar guidance for auditors, stating that where fees due from an audited entity, whether for audit or for non-audit services, remain unpaid for a long time – and, in particular, where a significant part is not paid before the auditor's report on the financial statements for the following year is due to be issued – a self-interest threat to the auditor's objectivity and independence is created because the issue of an unqualified audit report may enhance the audit firm's prospects of securing payment of such overdue fees.

ES 4 goes on to say that where the outstanding fees are unpaid because of exceptional circumstances (including financial distress), the audit engagement partner considers whether the audited entity will be able to resolve its difficulties. In deciding what action to take, the audit engagement partner weighs the threats to the auditor's objectivity and independence, if the audit firm were to remain in office, against the difficulties the audited entity would be likely to face in finding a successor, and therefore the public interest considerations, if the audit firm were to resign.

The audit engagement partner should discuss the overdue fees with Chester & Co's ethics partner to evaluate the significance of the threat. It may not be considered too severe a threat as the interim work was only performed four months ago, and the amount invoiced may not be significant. The matter should also be discussed with the client, with a view to securing payment as soon as possible.

(c)   **Banbury Ltd**

Providing an actuarial valuation service is an example of providing a non-assurance service. According to IESBA's Code, the provision of such services can create threats to objectivity of self-review and self-interest. The self-review threat arises because the defined benefit pension plan on which Chester & Co has been asked to provide a valuation service is included in the statement of financial position, and the audit firm would need to audit the figure which has been generated by a member of the firm. The self-interest threat arises from the fee which would be paid to the firm.

ES 5 also discusses the issue of valuation services, stating that the main threats to the auditor's objectivity and independence arising from the provision of valuation services are the self-review threat and the management threat. In all cases, the self-review threat is considered too high to allow the provision of valuation services which involve the valuation of amounts with a significant degree of subjectivity and have a material effect on the financial statements.

Chester & Co needs to evaluate the significance of the threats and whether safeguards could be used to reduce the threats to an acceptable level. In assessing the self-review threat the following factors should be considered:

- Whether the valuation will have a material effect on the financial statements

- The extent of the client's involvement in determining and approving the valuation methodology and other significant matters of judgement

- The availability of established methodologies and professional guidelines

- For valuations involving standard or established methodologies, the degree of subjectivity inherent in the item

- The reliability and extent of the underlying data

- The degree of dependence on future events of a nature that could create significant volatility inherent in the amounts involved

- The extent and clarity of the disclosures in the financial statements

A key matter to be considered is the materiality of the pension plan to Banbury Ltd's financial statements. Banbury Ltd is a listed company, and therefore a public interest entity. The Code states that an audit firm shall not provide valuation services to an audit client which is a public interest entity if the valuations would have a material effect, separately or in the aggregate, on the financial statements on which the firm will express an opinion.

Based on the 2012 financial statements, the pension liability at the year end represented only 0.3% of total assets and was immaterial. Chester & Co should consider whether there are any indications that the pension deficit may have become more significant during the year, which may have caused the balance to become material. In which case the audit firm should not provide the valuation service to Banbury Ltd.

An actuarial valuation involves significant subjectivity, for example, in determining the appropriate discount rate, and in estimating key variables to be used in the calculations. It is also unlikely that Banbury Ltd's management will possess sufficient knowledge and experience to have much involvement, if any, in the valuation. However, it may be possible to use safeguards to reduce the threats to an acceptable level.

Examples of such safeguards include:

- Having a professional who was not involved in providing the valuation service review the audit or valuation work performed; or

- Making arrangements so that personnel providing such services do not participate in the audit engagement.

5   (a)   **Going concern**

The information available in respect of Burford Ltd indicates many events or conditions which individually or collectively may cast doubt on the use of the going concern assumption in its financial statements.

Profitability – Burford Ltd's performance has deteriorated dramatically in the year, and despite being profitable in the previous year, it is reporting a loss of £500,000 for the year to 31 July 2013. It is likely that profitability will suffer even more in the next financial year due to the obsolescence of the QuickFire product which accounted for 45% of revenue. Substantial operating losses are an indicator of going concern problems.

Current and quick ratios show that Burford Ltd's current liabilities exceed its current assets, meaning that the company is unlikely to be able to pay debts as they fall due. If suppliers go unpaid they may restrict supply, causing further working capital problems. There may be insufficient cash to pay wages or other overheads, or to pay finance charges.

In addition, the company's cash inflows are likely to be very much reduced by the obsolescence of its major product, the QuickFire. The development of the replacement GreenFire product will have put severe strain on cash resources and given the company's cash position, there may be insufficient funds to complete the development. Hopefully there is enough cash to complete the development of GreenFire, and to keep the company afloat prior to its launch next year. Even then, it will take time for the new product to generate a cash inflow.

Loan covenant – given the further deterioration in the company's liquidity since the year end, it is likely that the current ratio now breaches the terms of the loan covenant. If this is the case, the loan provider may recall the loan, which Burford Ltd does not seem to be in a position to repay. It may be forced to sell assets in order to raise cash for the loan repayment, which may not raise the amount required, and would put operations in jeopardy.

Audit evidence

- Agreement of the opening cash position to the audited financial statements and general ledger or bank reconciliation, to ensure accuracy of extracted figures

- Confirmation that casting of the cash flow forecast has been reperformed to check arithmetical accuracy

- A review of the results of any market research which has been conducted on the GreenFire product, to ensure the assumption regarding its successful launch is appropriate

- Discussion of the progress made on GreenFire's development with a technical expert or engineer, to gauge the likelihood of a successful launch in February 2014

- A review of any correspondence with existing customers to gauge the level of interest in GreenFire and confirm if any orders have yet been placed

- A review of any sales documentation relating to the planned sale of plant and equipment to confirm that £50,000 is achievable

- Physical inspection of the plant and equipment to be sold, to gauge its condition and the likelihood of sale

- A review of any announcement made regarding the redundancies, to confirm the number of employees affected and the timing of the planned redundancies

- Sample testing of a selection of those being made redundant, agreeing the amount they are to be paid to human resource department records, to ensure accuracy of figures in the forecast

- A review of the application made to the government to confirm the amount of the grant applied for

- Confirmation to correspondence from the government department of the £30,000 grant to be received

- Depending on the timing of audit procedures, the £30,000 may be received prior to completion of the audit, in which case it should be agreed to cash book and bank statement

- Agreement that the cash flow forecast is consistent with profit and other financial forecasts which have been prepared by management

- Confirmation that any other assumptions used in the cash flow forecast are consistent with auditor's knowledge of the business and with management's intentions regarding the future of the company

- Comparison of the cash flow forecast for the period August–November 2013 with management accounts for the same period, to ensure accuracy of the forecast

- Analytical review of the items included in the cash flow forecast, for example, categories of expenses, to look for items which may have been omitted

(b) **Going concern impact on audit report**

The note on going concern should be reviewed by the auditors to ensure that the disclosure regarding going concern is sufficiently detailed, and that it includes all relevant matters and is understandable.

In evaluating the adequacy of the disclosure in the note, the auditor should consider whether the disclosure explicitly draws the reader's attention to the possibility that the entity may not be able to continue as a going concern in the foreseeable future. The note should include a description of conditions giving rise to the significant doubt, and the directors' plans to deal with the conditions. This is a requirement of IAS 1 *Presentation of Financial Statements*.

Note adequately describes going concern issues

If the note contains adequate information on going concern issues, then there is no breach of financial reporting standards, and therefore no material misstatement has occurred. The audit opinion should not be modified and should state that the financial statements show a true and fair view, or are fairly presented.

However, in accordance with ISA 570 (UK and Ireland) *Going concern*, the auditors should modify the auditor's report by adding an Emphasis of Matter paragraph to highlight the existence of the material uncertainties over Burford Ltd's going concern status, and to draw users' attention to the note to the financial statements where the uncertainties are disclosed. The Emphasis of Matter paragraph should contain a brief description of the uncertainties, and also refer explicitly to the note to the financial statements where the situation has been fully described.

ISA 706 (UK and Ireland) *Emphasis of matter paragraphs and other matter paragraphs in the independent auditor's report* states that the Emphasis of Matter paragraph should be placed immediately below the auditor's opinion, and it should re-iterate that the audit opinion is not qualified.

ISA 570 requires that going concern matters, including the adequacy of related notes to the financial statements, should be discussed with those charged with governance. ISA 706 also requires that those charged with governance should be informed by the auditor of the expected inclusion of an Emphasis of Matter paragraph in the auditor's report, and the proposed wording of the paragraph.

Note does not contain adequate information on going concern

It could be the case that a note has been given in the financial statements, but that the details are inadequate and do not fully explain the significant uncertainties affecting the going concern status of the company. In this situation the auditors should express a qualified opinion, as the disclosure requirements of IAS 1 have not been followed, leading to material misstatement. The auditor would need to use judgement to decide whether a qualified or an adverse opinion should be given.

ISA 570 requires that in this case the auditor shall state in the auditor's report that there is a material uncertainty which may cast significant doubt about the entity's ability to continue as a going concern.

ISA 705 (UK and Ireland) *Modifications to the opinion in the independent auditor's report* provides guidance on the presentation of the audit report in the case of a modification of the audit opinion. The audit report should include a paragraph entitled 'Basis for Qualified Opinion' or 'Basis for Adverse Opinion', which contains specific reference to the matter giving rise to material or pervasive misstatement. The paragraph should include a clear description of the uncertainties and should be presented immediately before the opinion paragraph.

The situation must be discussed with those charged with governance, who should be given opportunity to amend the financial statements by amending the note. ISA 705 states that when the auditor expects to modify the opinion in the auditor's report, the auditor shall communicate with those charged with governance the circumstances which led to the expected modification and the proposed wording of the modification

Review Form – Paper P7 Advanced Audit and Assurance (06/14)

Name: _____   Address: _____

_____

_____

How have you used this Kit?
(Tick one box only)

☐ Home study (book only)

☐ On a course: college _____

☐ With 'correspondence' package

☐ Other _____

Why did you decide to purchase this Kit?
(Tick one box only)

☐ Have used the complementary Study text

☐ Have used other BPP products in the past

☐ Recommendation by friend/colleague

☐ Recommendation by a lecturer at college

☐ Saw advertising

☐ Other _____

During the past six months do you recall seeing/receiving any of the following?
(Tick as many boxes as are relevant)

☐ Our advertisement in *Student Accountant*

☐ Our advertisement in *Pass*

☐ Our advertisement in *PQ*

☐ Our brochure with a letter through the post

☐ Our website www.bpp.com

Which (if any) aspects of our advertising do you find useful?
(Tick as many boxes as are relevant)

☐ Prices and publication dates of new editions

☐ Information on product content

☐ Facility to order books off-the-page

☐ None of the above

Which BPP products have you used?

Text	☐	Home Study Package	☐
Kit	☑	i-Pass	☐
Passcards	☐		

Your ratings, comments and suggestions would be appreciated on the following areas.

	Very useful	Useful	Not useful
Passing P7			
Questions			
Top Tips etc in answers			
Content and structure of answers			
Mock exam answers			

Overall opinion of this Kit	Excellent ☐		Good ☐		Adequate ☐		Poor ☐

Do you intend to continue using BPP products?   Yes ☐   No ☐

On the reverse of this page is space for you to write your comments about our Practice and Revision Kit. We welcome your feedback.

The BPP author of this edition can be e-mailed at: benjaminsmith@bpp.com

Please return this form to: Pippa Riley, ACCA Publishing Manager (Professional papers), BPP Learning Media, FREEPOST, London, W12 8AA

Review Form (continued)

TELL US WHAT YOU THINK

Please note any further comments and suggestions/errors below.